# INTRODUCTION TO
# MASS
# COMMUNICATIONS

# INTRODUCTION TO
# MASS
# COMMUNICATIONS

**WARREN K. AGEE**
*University of Georgia*

**PHILLIP H. AULT**
*South Bend Tribune*

**EDWIN EMERY**
*University of Minnesota*

*Twelfth Edition*

 **LONGMAN**

An imprint of Addison Wesley Longman, Inc.

New York • Reading, Massachusetts • Menlo Park, California • Harlow, England
Don Mills, Ontario • Sydney • Mexico City • Madrid • Amsterdam

*Senior Acquisitions Editor:* Deirdre Cavanaugh
*Development Editor:* Leslie Taggart
*Editorial Assistant:* Kwon Chong
*Project Coordination and Text Design:* York Production Services
*Cover Design:* Kay Petronio
*Art Coordination:* York Production Services
*Photo Researcher:* Roberta Knauf
*Electronic Production Manager:* Valerie Zaborski
*Manufacturing Manager:* Helene G. Landers
*Senior Marketing Manager:* Peter Glovin
*Electronic Page Makeup:* York Production Services
*Printer and Binder:* R. R. Donnelley & Sons Company
*Cover Printer:* The Lehigh Press

For permission to use copyrighted material, grateful acknowledgment is made to the copyright holders on p. 562, which is hereby made part of this copyright page.

**Library of Congress Cataloging-in-Publication Data**

Agee, Warren Kendall.
    Introduction to mass communications/Warren K. Agee, Phillip H. Ault,
Edwin Emery.—12th ed.
      p.  cm.
    Includes bibliographical references and index.
    ISBN 0-673-98082-0
    1. Mass media.  I. Ault, Phillip H., 1914– .  II. Emery, Edwin.  III. Title.
P90.A35   1996
302.23—dc20                               96–11530
                                                             CIP

ISBN 0-673-98082-0

12345678910—DOC—99989796

# BRIEF CONTENTS

# DETAILED CONTENTS

# PREFACE

This twelfth edition of *Introduction to Mass Communications* accomplishes two goals essential for a mass communications textbook on the threshold of the twenty-first century. It plunges into the stimulating, still uncertain electronic realm of the "information superhighway." At the same time, it examines the traditional mass media with the depth and perception that have made this textbook a leader for nearly 40 years. In the language of advertising, the text is user-friendly, a sprightly classic.

Students and instructors will find the textbook jammed with up-to-the-minute insights into contemporary mass communications practice. In a scholarly manner, it also describes the historical evolution that has brought today's methods and ethical principles into being.

## Close to Events

Among the topics covered are:

- The powerful effects of the 1996 Telecommunications Reform Act
- The role of the Internet, its uses and problems
- Tips on how to use online services for research
- The media's role in the O. J. Simpson murder case
- Controversy about sex and violence in the media
- The link between television and popular culture

- Consolidation of media ownership into the hands of a relatively few corporations
- Swift expansion of worldwide communication

This sampling illustrates how this twelfth edition is poised on the cutting edge of the mass communications revolution in progress.

The new "parallel universe" of cyberspace has become so ubiquitous that the perplexing legal, ethical, and other problems it has brought are now treated in a number of chapters previously devoted solely to traditional journalism and mass communications.

The unresolved questions concern libel, privacy, censorship, and copyright, among other matters. Lawmakers and Internet users struggle to devise ways to protect children from computer pornography without damaging free speech and the continued "open" development of the Internet.

At the same time print, broadcast, advertising, and public relations firms joined thousands of other companies and individuals, as well as the government, in learning the extent to which the Internet can be incorporated into their enterprises.

Two new features run through the entire text to give it additional cohesion: Media Questions to Think About challenges students to relate personally to the material covered. The Roles of the Media, opening each of the six parts, defines those roles in simple terms and supports the definitions with quotations from experts.

## Historical Perspective

One of the most important elements of *Introduction to Mass Communications* is the historical perspective it brings to the mass media. The text describes the evolution of each form of mass communication, to provide students with a better understanding of contemporary media practices.

Of particular importance is the chapter titled "Historic Press Freedoms." This traces the emergence of the press freedoms we take for granted today from the autocratic controls once imposed on the media. As an example of the chapter's value, the director of the U.S. Information Agency informed the authors and Longman publishers that, in an effort to counteract dictatorial tendencies in the country of Cameroon, a local newspaper had published in serial fashion much of the French translation of the chapter.

In this edition, "Historic Press Freedoms" has been updated to include problems of politically correct speech and largely unrestrained talk radio in relation to free speech principles.

## Features

In Part One, "The Media's Crucial Role," a new chapter follows Chapter 1, "Global Reach of the Media." Titled "The Media's Social Impact,"

Chapter 2 explores aspects of the controversial role that the media play in society.

Part Two, "The Print Media," reviews the development of and problems affecting newspapers, magazines, book publishing, and news services and syndicates, the latter condensed and incorporated into the newspaper chapter.

Part Three, newly titled, "Radio and Popular Music," discusses radio and recording. In Part Four, "The Visual Electronic and Film Media," chapters cover television, cable television, video, photographic and graphic communications, and film.

Part Five, "The Persuasive Professions," explores the development and current trends and problems affecting advertising and public relations.

Part Six, "Communications Worldwide," completes the examination of international mass communications begun in Chapter 1, including the "international scene" boxes in Chapters 5–7, along with international aspects integrated into other chapters.

The five Issues interspersed among the chapters are introduced with questions designed to pique the interest of students and help them identify specific topics. The employment of women and minorities is discussed in the industry chapters and the appendix, "Job Opportunities in the Media."

The radical shortening of the text that occurred with the tenth edition has been continued with the deletion of additional dated and peripheral material. Issue 4, "Credibility," in particular has been shortened.

Professor Barry Hollander of the University of Georgia provides a fully revised Instructor's Manual and Test Bank to accompany the text. This program readily enables instructors to replace questions or to intersperse their own as they design examination materials. In addition to more than 700 questions, the manual contains study materials and projects, lesson plans, and an audiovisual list. A number of successful approaches to the study of mass communications have been provided in the manual by instructors who have taught with the text during the past three decades and whose adoption of this pioneering book has made it one of the most widely used texts in the field. For sample copies, please contact your Addison Wesley Longman representative or write: Communications Editor, Longman College Publishers, 4th Floor, 10 East 53rd Street, New York, NY 10022-5299.

For supplementary use in this course and others, the authors have produced a reader, *Maincurrents in Mass Communications*, also published by Longman. It contains articles, surveys, speeches, and commentaries by prominent people designed to clarify further much of what is happening in mass communications. Essays by the editors introduce the six parts, "The Media's Role in Society," "Ethical and Legal Challenges," "The Technology Revolution," "The Communicators," "Media Trends and Techniques," and "Living in the Information Society."

## Acknowledgments

This edition of *Introduction to Mass Communications* represents a pooling of the professional media experience and scholarly interests of its authors, who wish to thank the more than 150 professors and media practitioners whose suggestions and criticisms, many elicited by questionnaire and others expressed personally to the authors, have helped shape these editions. In particular, we thank the following instructors, who gave us detailed feedback on the eleventh edition: Nona Bowes, Kent State University; Merritt Christensen, University of Wisconsin, Eau Claire; Bill Dean, Texas Tech University; Juliet Dee, University of Delaware; Sandra Ehrlich, Meramac Community College; Gail Hogan, Cuyahoga Community College; Kate Matichek, Normandale Community College; Arlan Ropp, Brevard Community College; Joseph Russomanno, Arizona State University; Judith Sylvester, Louisiana State University; Steve Troxel, Liberty University; and Carolyn Weber, Saint Mary's College.

We wish to thank the Freedom Forum Media Studies Center, one of the sources for our Part quotations. Thanks also are extended to the U.S. Information Agency, which has placed successive editions of the book in reading libraries throughout the world and for which translations have been published in Malaysian, Arabic, Korean, French, Spanish, and Portuguese, joining editions published in India, the Republic of China on Taiwan, and the Philippines.

*Warren K. Agee*
*Phillip H. Ault*

# FASCINATING POSSIBILITIES

Women and men starting their careers in mass communications as one century turns into another enjoy opportunities no earlier generation has experienced. They use extremely high-speed electronic tools their grandfathers knew only in the imaginings of science fiction authors and the hopes of laboratory experimenters. They have growing audiences of complex ethnic diversity ready to be served with new approaches to news and entertainment content and distribution.

As the possibilities of two-way television and digital transmission expand, and the scope of the global transmission grid enlarges, so will career possibilities. Innovation and ingenuity in applying these electronic methods will yield still-unforeseen results.

Preparation for this intriguing new day in mass communication is essential. Adam C. Powell III, the Freedom Forum director of technology studies and programs, states the situation bluntly: "Journalists must know how to navigate and use the grid, to become tour guides, as it were, for their readers and viewers, if they are to survive in the future information industries."

The traditional print, electronic, and film media are controlled by professional editors, who select the material and apply standards of accuracy, ethics, and social acceptability before releasing it to the public. These media are essentially one-way communication of information and entertainment, creator to consumer.

Added to these methods of communication recently, and growing swiftly, is the less recognized but potent channel of computer networks. Participants exchange information and gossip, hold debates, distribute news and rumors, call up government documents, obtain answers to questions from online databases, and send and receive electronic letters. These networks, of which there are hundreds large and small, are largely unregulated. In most instances, no editor exercises control over their content. This is two-way communication. Enthusiasts call this worldwide spider web of interlocking systems "digital democracy."

Largest and best known of the systems is the Internet, a loose confederation of networks that reaches around the globe. An estimated 30 million computer users have access to it—a potential audience larger than that for a television network comedy such as "Seinfeld" and powerful because it contains a high percentage of opinion leaders who influence others.

These networks are part of the global grid that, Powell insists, new entrants into mass communication must master.

This textbook introduces students to all forms of mass communication, the traditional and those on the electronic cutting-edge. It examines their history, methods, and impact on society as well as the fundamental values of accuracy, reliability, and ethical conduct that underlie them.

Entrancing as the new forms of electronic communication are, students—and professionals, too—must remember that they are only delivery tools, not an end in themselves.

Long ago, in 1849, Americans were excited about the construction of a telegraph line between Maine and Texas. Operators could click out dot-and-dash dispatches in Morse code at the speed of 30 words a minute, at a time when letters took weeks en route. The philosopher Henry David Thoreau wrote, "We are in a great haste to construct a magnetic telegraph from Maine to Texas, but Maine and Texas, it may be, have nothing important to communicate."

Thoreau's point is equally valid today, 150 years later, when digital transmission by satellite can carry the text of Tolstoy's massive novel *War and Peace* from one point to another in a few seconds. The quality of the information and entertainment transmitted is the ultimate test of success.

# PART ONE
## The Media's Crucial Role

## ROLES OF THE MEDIA—MESSENGER

Since the first printed pages appeared more than 500 years ago, the media have delivered information and entertainment, at first to limited audiences and now to every corner of the world.

*"Journalists endure hardships, danger, give their lives . . . so that free people may know the truth as best we can find it. We owe them so much."*

—*Louis D. Boccardi, Associated Press*

*"If editors and journalists insist on accuracy, professionalism, and sensitivity in reporting, the public will likely support a free press in the broadest sense."*

—*Bruce W. Sanford, media attorney*

*"An electronic information highway that's jammed with the likes of Jimmy Swaggart, Madonna, and Ice-T can easily be a road to nowhere."*

—*Leo Bogart, media columnist*

# CHAPTER ONE
## Global Reach of the Media

## Where Is Cyberspace?

The hot word in mass communications is *cyberspace*. Writers and speakers use it glibly but don't say where it is. The other side of Shangri-La, perhaps? Or in the heavens near the Big Dipper?

In reality, cyberspace is more a state of mind than a physical location. In William Gibson's *Cyberspace* it is defined as "a new universe, a parallel universe created and sustained by the world's computers and communication lines."

The explosion in electronic communications has brought new words into the English language and altered the use of others. Explorers who enter cyberspace need a new vocabulary.

Cyberspace communicators live in a universe of bytes and broadbands, surfing and encrypting, coaxial cable, and digitalization. They use e-mail, chat forums, uplinks, and fiber optics. We unload trucks in the physical world, but we download information in cyberspace. We enter a room, but we access a computer.

Definitions of mass communication terms, new and old, appear in page margins throughout this textbook.

Some terms are complex, some almost flippant. The grandiose "information superhighway," discussed in this chapter, has been deflated by the brash headline writers of *Variety,* the show business periodical. To them it is merely the "infopike."

The mass media are the messengers, distributors of news, and entertainers for the world. The printed page, the television screen, voices on radio, motion pictures, and intriguing new uses of the computer deliver information, stimulate our emotions, and give us pleasure.

Without the mass media, contemporary society could not function. The messages they deliver influence the course of government, pass freely over national frontiers, affect our behavior and attitudes, and popularize trends in our culture.

Early in the twentieth century, the printed word was the principal form of mass communication, supplemented by silent movies and early-day radio broadcasts. Today this has changed radically. We have become a visual society—and an electronic one as well.

This opening chapter explains the basic organization of the media and the tremendous recent changes in mass communications. It explains the highly publicized information superhighway and looks at how individuals are affected by the onrushing media revolution.

## The Global Impact

The planet Earth is enmeshed in an electronic net extending 22,300 miles into space. Through this invisible web pulses an unending barrage of messages—blunt and subtle, essential and trivial—that shape the decisions and values of every person. The almost unbelievably swift expansion of worldwide electronic communication makes the theory of the world as a global village, while still far from reality, a valid concept. Ownership and editorial direction of the mass media steadily become more international.

Transmission by satellite, discussed later in this chapter, brings remote corners of the world into touch with people everywhere. Giant corporations maintain almost instantaneous verbal and visual communication with their offices around the world. Facsimile messages sent by international telephone from one continent can be delivered within minutes to another continent. American motion pictures pirated electronically appear on screens in Asia within days of their release in the United States.

**Information overload**
Mass of information in general circulation from which individuals must select material that helps or pleases them

Once people hungered for information. Today the problem has become *information overload*. We are so inundated with information and entertainment that individuals face a vexing problem of selectivity and evaluation.

Columnist William Raspberry, who describes himself as a bicyclist on the information superhighway, is among those who worry that the flood of data available almost benumbs computer users in search of specific information.

Computers help enormously with that sort of thing, and we misled ourselves into believing that access to ever-increasing amounts of data would make us ever-smarter observers of the human condition. That unfortunately requires something that computers aren't (yet) very good at: helping you to sort things out, helping you to *think*,

These days we are not so much hungry for data as overwhelmed by it.

Neil Postman, chairman of the Department of Culture and Communications at New York University, expressed a similar view at an *Utne Reader* conference:

> . . . we created a new problem never experienced before: information glut, information incoherence, information meaninglessness . . . we have transformed information into a form of garbage and ourselves into garbage collectors. . . .
>
> Like the sorcerer's apprentice, we are awash in information without even a broom to get rid of it. Information comes indiscriminately, directed at no one in particular, in enormous volumes at high speed, severed from import and meaning.

Face-to-face conversation between individuals is the simplest, most effective means of communication. When messages must be delivered to large numbers of people, however, such personal intercourse is obviously impossible. Transmission of ideas and information must be achieved by use of mass communication techniques.

Researchers have proven that the total audience—global, national, and local—consists of multiple segments known as *target audiences*. Each of these has special interests, needs, and characteristics. Shrewd mass communicators try to identify the aspects of each target audience and shape messages to please it. As mass communication becomes increasingly global, tailoring messages is even more challenging.

**Target audience** A group of persons sharing demographic and/or psychographic characteristics

As a simple example, American motion picture producers have learned that action adventure films sell better to foreign audiences than love stories and "message" pictures because chases, shootings, and explosions are easily understood by viewers who cannot speak English. For the American audience, producers craft films to attract different age groups; for example, *Snow White and the Seven Dwarfs* for children, *Pulp Fiction* for the 18-to-24-year-old customers, and *Schindler's List* for older adults.

## The Messages: A Sample

Using the impressionistic technique seen so often in television commercials, let us catch a kaleidoscopic glimpse of mass communications in action.

- Television viewers in Singapore and Europe watch a CBS telecast of an American golf tournament with commentary by golf experts in England, where the program is also being seen.

- Quechua Indians in a remote Andean village get their first glimpse of the outside world when a satellite receiving dish made from corrugated iron roofing by an American priest brings in a Mickey Mouse cartoon in Spanish from Argentina. Soon they are watching "Miami Vice" on their small TV set.

- Sitting in their homes, Americans can send messages to the White House by computer, reacting to the President's announcements and offering him advice.

- An American professor on a Fulbright grant in Botswana sends copy for a college textbook to his coauthor in Arizona by facsimile—delivered within minutes.

- An American soldier stationed in Haiti marries her boyfriend in New York by satellite teleconference, in a service conducted by an Army chaplain at the bride's side.

- A football fan in Chicago watches a Sunday professional game beamed directly from a satellite to a home receiving dish only 18 inches in diameter. This method bypasses the cable television system.

- Using the Internet, a student at an international school in Hungary obtains the full text of entries in the *Encyclopedia Britannica* she needs for her studies.

- A television network anchor in New York questions a field reporter in the Bosnian war zone, with live pictures of both persons on the viewer's screen.

- A newspaper reporter covering an airplane crash writes her story on a portable computer at the scene. She calls her office and transmits the story directly into her newsroom computer by cellular telephone.

## Types of Media

The mass media fall broadly into two categories with certain attributes in common but with unlike physical characteristics. These groups are:

*Print:* Newspapers, magazines, newsletters, and books. Their words create images in the mind as well as transmit information.

*Electronics and Film:* Radio, recordings, television, still and motion pictures, and video. These media deliver their messages through visual and audio impact on the senses, sometimes with great emotional intensity.

In order to understand how the media deliver information and entertainment and how they deal with issues and problems, we must understand how they are organized and how they operate. Thoughtful consideration must also be given to the ethical dilemmas that challenge those who work in the mass communications field.

The Alfred P. Murrah Federal Building in Oklahoma City falls in a cloud of dust as it is demolished by implosion a month after it was shattered by a huge car-bomb explosion that made news worldwide. After the debris was removed, the site became a memorial to the 168 people killed by the terrorist attack in April 1995. (AP Photo/ George Wilson)

## Essential Tools

All the mass media just listed use at least one of three essential electronic tools that have come into general use during the past quarter-century. New uses for these tools, singly and in combination, are being developed constantly. They are:

- Satellites
- Computers
- Videotape

Another electronic tool, less basic than these but in abundant use worldwide, is facsimile (or fax) transmission.

## The Information Superhighway

The most far-reaching, visionary application of these electronic methods is popularly called the *information superhighway*. Its goal is to create a two-way visual, audio, and written communication system that ultimately will connect virtually all homes and offices in the United States, just as the telephone system does for voice alone.

Until recently, three forms of electrically powered communication entered our homes and offices as entirely separate entities—telephone, television, and computer. Using swiftly expanding electronic techniques, communication entrepreneurs are working to combine these three familiar methods into a two-way interactive system carrying spoken words, printed text, graphics, television, personal messages, motion pictures, and still photographs. Users of the consolidated system may order the various services as they desire them, delivered at the times they request,

Television cameramen and reporters jam around Robert Shapiro, a defense attorney in the O. J. Simpson murder trial, as he enters the courthouse in Los Angeles. Global coverage of the year-long trial was intense and at times controversial. (AP Photo/Kevork)

by sending electronic instructions back over the system to suppliers. Ordering movies on-demand is a typical application.

While scientists and engineers scramble to solve the remaining problems that impede completion of the ultimate system, communication corporations engage in high-stakes financial maneuvers to obtain profitable positions in the emerging plan. Billions of dollars are at stake. Still uncertain about exactly what will evolve, the corporations fight to obtain federal regulations favorable to them and invade each other's traditional territory. Cable television companies plan to deliver telephone services. Telephone companies seek to deliver cable TV programs. Two broadcast television networks, ABC and NBC, tried to protect their positions by owning cable networks. (See Issue 3 for a discussion of media ownership.)

In the following pages we will examine the principal elements constituting the superhighway concept, explain how they fit together, and give examples of how mass communicators can use the system.

## Satellites

Use of satellites as relay stations has truly revolutionized the transmission of messages and pictures around the world.

Instead of being sent from one point to another along the surface of the earth in the old way, information and entertainment are beamed up to satellites. The messages are bounced off transponder pods back to receiving dishes on the ground. The "parking lot" for satellites at the height of 22,300 miles, known as the geostationary belt, is used because at this point a satellite has an orbital period of 24 hours. It thus remains stationary above a fixed place on the earth's surface, always available for relaying news, entertainment, and other transmissions back to the ground.

Transmission by satellite is cheaper, faster, and more reliable than by ground lines. One computer can "talk" to another computer thousands of miles away via satellite about 160 times faster than can be done over land lines. As *National Geographic* magazine has pointed out, such computer-to-computer communication via satellite is fast enough to transmit Tolstoy's massive novel *War and Peace* from one point to another within a few seconds.

Use of satellite transmission grows constantly as the media and commercial, government, and private interests find new and ingenious applications for it. In later chapters we shall discuss teleconferencing, worldwide distribution of newspapers, and other satellite techniques.

## Computers

Development of personal computers has brought an immense increase in the flow of information to the news media and has created an essential element for the information superhighway. These and the large mainframe computers are *digital*—that is, they use zeros and ones to represent letters, a far faster method than the *analog* system that uses electrical impulses. (See marginal definition, Chapter 13.)

At first computers lacked the ability to communicate with each other except at close range. In the late 1960s, scientists supported by federal funds developed a method for one computer to "talk" to others over long distances. This ability led to the creation of computer networks, which are so commonplace today. These networks deliver *electronic mail (e-mail)*—messages sent by one computer user to another—and *electronic bulletin boards* on which a computer operator can post a message intended for all participants on the network. Soon lively discussion groups developed, in which computer operators typed out their opinions, a significant new way of crystalizing public opinion on social and political issues.

Next to emerge were the commercial *online* computer databases, electronic storehouses containing huge amounts of reference material,

**Electronic mail**
The delivery of correspondence including graphics by electronic means, usually the interconnection of computers, word processors, or facsimile equipment. Also known as *e-mail*

**Electronic bulletin board**
Internet site on which a message may be posted. Also called a *home page*

Arizona State University students work at computers in the university's Computer Commons. Indicative of the role computers play in higher education, ASU has more than 37,000 individual computer accounts for students, faculty, and administrators. (Phoenix Newspapers, Inc. photo)

**Online**
Active connection to a computer network, permitting interactive exchange of data, commands, and information

**Modem**
Device that connects a computer with the telephone system

documents, newspaper and magazine files, news, and sports reports. A computer user whose machine is suitably equipped can reach one of these *online* databases, select the desired material from on-screen "menus," and display it on the computer screen. The computer must have a *modem* (modulator–demodulator) that allows messages to flow between the computer's digital system and the telephone system. Databases are a rich factual resource for newspaper reporters, magazine writers, and broadcasters developing investigative and background stories. The cost of using databases varies, but generally it consists of a monthly base charge plus additional fees for heavy use.

### The Internet

The most intriguing of all the computer systems is the worldwide *Internet*. The Internet is not a commercial service such as, say, America Online. It is an electronic spider web of signals from regional networks around the world, flashing through cyberspace, that can be received by anyone who obtains access with a properly equipped computer. This may be done by paying a monthly fee to one of a myriad of providers such as Delphi or buying software such as Netscape, which can link any computer to the Internet and the World Wide Web. The Internet itself charges nothing; in fact, it is so loosely organized that it has no formal headquarters.

The Internet was created in the late 1960s by the U.S. government, defense contractors, and universities as a way for scientists, engineers, and academic specialists to exchange information and ideas. During the

## HOW WRITERS USE COMPUTER RESEARCH

Computer research provides an abundance of resources for writers and editors to use in creating and checking their print and broadcast reports. The facilities may be used to:

- Obtain the texts of Supreme Court decisions, White House news releases, and other government documents.
- Request comments on an electronic bulletin board from specialists in the field a reporter is writing about, for inclusion in the story.
- Check directories such as *Who's Who in America* and the *Encyclopedia of Associations* to obtain or verify information about prominent individuals or nonprofit organizations.

- Read the computer bulletin boards for story ideas.
- Read the files of prominent newspapers such as the New York *Times* and Washington *Post*, available on online databases.
- Recapture virtually all public words of a prominent politician or other public figure to check for contradictions and unkept promises.

CAUTION: Information appearing in an online database is not automatically accurate. Crosscheck it if possible.

*Source:* Extracted from *Computer Assisted Research* by Nora Paul. St. Petersburg, Fla., The Poynter Institute, 1994.

early 1990s access was made available to a general audience, and by the mid-'90s a rush was on by individuals and commercial firms to join the Internet. Because the Internet has no central controlling force, figures on the number of users are approximate. By mid-decade an estimated 50 million users had access to more than 15,000 Usenet discussion groups and thousands of websites on the World Wide Web, while the Internet had links to about 150 countries.

The Internet has been aptly described as a labyrinth. It has several major segments in addition to global e-mail. For example, a participant can join an online service that offers a wide-ranging menu of information, and browse the World Wide Web, the rapidly expanding text-and-graphics service that offers informational and commercial messages. Individuals as well as organizations can create their own *home pages* to appear on the Web. Numerous computer fans are doing so; they find the effort and expense worthwhile because of the sense of identity and belonging the page creates. Users can purchase numerous guidebooks to lead them through the Internet maze.

### Criticisms of the Internet

The Internet has grown so spectacularly that inevitably aspects of it concern and irritate some users.

Internet message from a chemist in Russia to his American collaborator at the University of Cincinnati. The scientists worked together on an international research project, the type of use for which the Internet was created. Note the elaborate addressing and encoding required to deliver the message. (Courtesy of Bruce Ault)

```
                          9-NOV-1994 09:49:26.33
From:         IN%"sen@hp.nnov.su"  "Peter G. Sennikov"
To:           IN%"ault@UCBEH.SAN.UC.EDU"
CC:
Subj:         sennikov

Return-path: <@ns.nnov.su,@hp.uucp:sen@hp.nnov.su>
Delivery-receipt-to: sen@hp.nnov.su
Received: from ns.nnov.su (inforis.nnov.su)
 by UCBEH.SAN.UC.EDU (PMDF V4.3-11 #4918)
 id <01HJ9RUTO4LCHV4B65@UCBEH.SAN.UC.EDU>; Wed, 09 Nov 1994 09:48:41 -0500 (EST)
Received: from hp.UUCP by ns.nnov.su with UUCP id AA12176
 (5.65.kiae-1  for ault@ucbeh.san.uc.edu); Wed, 9 Nov 1994 17:46:23 -0300
Received: by hp.nnov.su (UUPC/@ v5.09gamma, 14Mar93); Wed,
 9 Nov 1994 17:29:27 +0300
Date: Wed, 09 Nov 1994 17:29:18 +0300
From: "Peter G. Sennikov" <sen@hp.nnov.su>
Subject: sennikov
To: ault@UCBEH.SAN.UC.EDU
Message-id: <AA-oDmkOz5@hp.nnov.su>

Organization: Institute of Chemistry of High Purity Substances (Rus.Ac.Sci)
X-Mailer: BML [MS/DOS Beauty Mail v.1.36]
Content-transfer-encoding: 7BIT
Lines: 49


              Dear Bruce,

     I am preparing now the paper describing our experiments
on Ga (CH3)3 + AsH3 system. I read again carefully your
papers devoted to the matrix experiment on the same system
and can not understand one point - You write e.g. in your
paper in J.Phys.Chem., 1992, v.96,   on the p.1092 : "
(CH3)3 Ga has effective D3h symmetry, while each of the given
Va parent compounds has C3v symmetry. As a consequence, the
antisymmetric modes are doubly degenerated of E symmetry. If
the C3 rotation axis is lost upon complex formation, then
splitting of the degenerate vibrations is anticipated. This,
however, was not observed and points to C3v symmetry....".

But on the figure 1 of this paper the band at ~ 570 cm-1 is
splitted whereas the same Ga-C antisymmetric band is not
splitted in the pure TMG in matrix (see Fig. 1 in your paper
in J.Amer.Chem.Soc., 1989, 111, 8978 and Table 1 in paper of
S.Kvisle and E.Rytter in Spectrochem.Acta, 1984, 40A 1939).
What is the origin of splitting??
     Another question: how can you explain the high-frequency
```

Columnist Russell Baker, for one, deplores the level of discourse among some chat participants.

"Good manners are breaking down on the Internet," he wrote. "Rudeness, even savage insults, filling the e-mail. Assorted species of porn flourishing. The good fellowship of the nerds poisoned, souring into the bad fellowship of the electronic jungle." (See Issue 1.)

Most news groups on the Internet do use some type of self-policing action, such as posting an FAQ (Frequently Asked Questions) advisory for newcomers to read before joining the group. Some violations universally frowned upon by the Internet community include "overquoting" when responding to posts and creating excessively long signature lines. "Netiquette" violators will find themselves the object of "flames" (heaped-upon scorn) from other posters when they break an FAQ rule.

Baker contends that technology increases personal isolation and fosters lack of responsibility. "A human alone with his machine talking to machines activated by other humans alone," he observed. "Easy to hide in that maze."

Worries about the violated privacy of messages exchanged by e-mail also are expressed by some users. Instances have come to light in which a person's e-mail identification has been stolen, then improperly signed to

This menu screen of the America Online computer service lists categories of information available to subscribers, including access to the worldwide Internet.

hate messages the victim didn't write. Thefts of credit card numbers and fraudulent sales pitches that have obtained money from innocent victims have come to light.

Still another concern is the gullibility of many individuals: the old problem of believing everything one reads, in a new form.

Stephen Hansen, Stanford University's computer security officer, pointed out the risks: "Unfortunately, with the explosion of the number of new and less-than-computer-literate people on the network, a lot of people take what comes across as the gospel, and it wouldn't ever occur to them that it's not legitimate."

As this brief discussion suggests, the Internet is being put to some unlikely uses, and searchers may stumble on unexpected information. A midwestern university chemist, trying to obtain research material, was surprised to find the weather forecast for a South Pacific island on his screen. Internet users are able to order pizza, obtain U.S. income tax forms, watch hard-core pornography, and "chat" with movie stars promoting their new films.

## Television

The second fundamental portion of the projected information super-highway involves an enormous increase in the number of cable television

# ONLINE TOOLS FOR RESEARCHERS

Online computer services provide a rich lode of material for researchers. Some also provide gateways to the seemingly unlimited resources of the Internet.

The three largest general online services are America Online, CompuServe, and Prodigy. Here is a sample of what can be found on them and on several more specialized services.

*America Online.* Bulletin board services and interactive publications. Includes such materials as *Consumer Reports* and *Compton's Encyclopedia.*

*CompuServe.* Chat forums, full text of books, transcripts, public records. Includes *TRW Business Credit Reports* and *Peterson's College Database.*

*Prodigy.* Special emphasis on on-line shopping and public message areas. Includes *Academic American Encyclopedia* and *Magill's Survey of Cinema.*

Numerous newspapers are available on these three services.

*Delphi.* Forums, books, directories. Includes *Grolier's Encyclopedia* and *Hollywood Hotline.*

*Burrelle's Broadcast Database.* Transcripts of public affairs programs on ABC, CBS, and NBC networks dated back to 1989. Also material from such programs as "All Things Considered" on National Public Radio.

*Dow Jones.* Business and investment services, including *Wall Street Journal, Barron's,* and Dow Jones news wires.

*Media Data General.* Four subject areas: Legal (LEXIS), medical (MEDIS), government (LEGIS), news and business (NEXIS).

*Sources: Consumer Assisted Research* by Nora Paul. St. Petersburg, Fla., The Poynter Institute, 1994 and *Arizona Republic*, Phoenix, December 12, 1994.

channels. The most frequently heard projection calls for 500 channels. John Malone, president and chief executive officer of Tele-Communications Inc., the largest American cable TV company, thinks in even bigger terms. In an interview with *Broadcasting and Cable* in late 1994, he stated that 720 channels are technically possible if anyone desires that many.

Indeed, why would any viewer want 500 channels? Supplying programs for that many would be virtually impossible, and the mere act of channel sampling—*surfing* as it is called—would devour a viewer's time.

The answer is simple. Only a minority of the 500 channels, perhaps 25 percent, would be used to deliver entertainment and information shows to the home. The remaining channels would be assigned for two main purposes: (1) to handle responses from viewers to cable system operators and perform such personal business as ordering movies on-demand, using the video telephone, banking, shopping, and purchasing show tickets; and (2) to deliver to the home screen the movies viewers have ordered.

**Surfing**
Sampling television programs or information provided at various Internet sites

One suggested plan is for a cable system to offer its subscribers a choice of ten hit movies with starting times at 15-minute intervals.

While the so-called computer lane on the superhighway already is substantially in operation, the television "explosion" still lies in the future because of construction and financial problems, as well as technical questions.

Such an array of cable TV channels can be achieved only by digital compression; that is, compressing the channel signals into digital form so that many more can be transmitted in the available space. These compressed channels must then be decompressed by an electrical box on the viewer's set before they can be shown. Manufacture of suitable set-top boxes has been a delaying factor.

The standard coaxial cable used in current cable TV delivery cannot carry the load created by all these channels. *Fiber optics* cable must be used instead. This creates a massive construction problem.

## Fiber Optics Cable

An amazingly compact form of along-the-ground and underseas transmission, a fiber optics cable consists of glass strands finer than human hairs. Pulses of light representing zeros and ones flash through the strands so swiftly that a single fiber optics cable can carry 40,000 telephone calls at one time.

Glass fiber cables beneath the Atlantic and Pacific Oceans were opened in 1989. Technical experts believe that satellite transmission and fiber optics complement each other, with each having advantages under certain circumstances.

The cost of laying fiber optics cable in every community and through rural areas of the United States has been estimated as high as $100 billion. Although thousands of miles of the cable have been laid, many more years will be required to complete the job. John Malone, whose company is a leader in the project, expressed the belief that the ultimate system will consist of a fiber optics cable from a cable system site to a distribution point called a node, from which the lighter local load is carried by coaxial cable to 500 to 1000 homes and offices. With the cable and telephone companies fighting a legal and technical battle for admission to homes with telephone, video, and other services, control of these transmission lines still is uncertain as the end of the century nears. There were indications that the rivals would join forces, at least to some degree, in order to make the terrestrial delivery portion of the information superhighway more economically feasible.

Eager to obtain a position in the cable expansion, many companies have created new cable networks, even though space for them on many cable systems is limited. Most are "niche" networks aimed at target audiences. Typical are the Golf Channel, Classic Arts Showcase, and the Game Show Network.

**Fiber optics** Transmission of signals through highly transparent strands of extremely thin glass, instead of by wire

Fiber optics, consisting of glass strands finer than a human hair, makes possible transmission of a multitude of messages simultaneously at almost unbelievable speed. (AT&T Bell Laboratories)

## Videotape

The third essential tool, *videotape*, has multiplied our ability to capture, preserve, and display moving visual images.

Videotape can be erased and reused, an important economic factor. Small portable video cameras enable television news crews to record events and put the material on TV viewers' home screens quickly. Photographers have found scores of uses of videotape for news, entertainment, training, and record-keeping purposes.

The tape has brought into being an entirely new type of mass communication, *video*. More than 70 percent of families in the United States have *videotape recorders* (VCRs) on which they can play motion pictures and informational tapes, as well as record TV programs for later replay. The machines are also popular in other countries.

Selling videotapes of motion pictures has become a major source of income for the film industry. For technical reasons, however, major motion pictures and certain other materials still are photographed on film rather than videotape.

**Videotape recorder (VCR)** Instrument attached to a TV set that can play prerecorded videotapes on the screen, as well as record and replay television programs

Much of the material received in homes and offices through various elements of the emerging information superhighway, as well as traditional broadcast television, has been created or recorded on videotape.

# Other Forms of Communication

## Facsimile Transmission

Textual messages and graphics can be sent swiftly in exact form from one facsimile machine to another over telephone lines, locally or around the world.

Use of *fax* machines grew spectacularly in the late 1980s, reaching into many new fields. Businesses transmit memos and charts, doctors send prescriptions to pharmacies, public relations firms send news releases. A few newspapers dispatch one-page next-day news summaries to subscribers willing to pay a high price for an advance look at the news. Others offer information by facsimile in various forms, as their owners seek effective uses of electronic transmission to supplement the traditional newsprint form.

While facsimile provides a splendid service, uncontrolled use of it has created problems. Many owners of fax machines complain that they receive unwanted communications, including sales messages; these messages tie up their machines and consume fax paper for which the recipients must pay. This has created agitation for laws that, while not violating the First Amendment, would protect recipients against these abuses.

Facsimile machines also can be used to circulate rumors, falsehoods, and hate messages—another problem requiring examination.

**Fax**
Slang usage for facsimile transmission of written and graphic messages over telephone lines

## Direct Broadcast Satellite (DBS)

This service delivers TV programs to the home through an 18-inch satellite receiving dish, rather than through a cable system landline.

Available in the United States since 1994, DBS delivery has a longer history in Great Britain and Japan. Digitalized pictures are sent aloft, bounced off a satellite transponder, and returned directly to the subscriber's home. If the system gains wide popularity, it could become a threat to regular cable TV delivery. The equipment is expensive, however, and in addition to monthly subscription fees, the DBS customer pays extra for such attractions as National Football League games.

Early users of the service complained about poor picture quality under some conditions, but that problem has been reduced. The older, much larger 10-foot dishes can receive a wider range of pictures. A service using a 36-inch screen also is in operation.

**Direct broadcast satellite (DBS)**
Satellite that transmits television programs direct to small receiving dishes, bypassing cable

## The CD-ROM

The CD-ROM (Compact Disc-Read Only Memory), the multimedia version of the familiar compact disc that plays music, has come on the market. It can display up to 300,000 text pages of information, and can show full-color pictures, graphics, and even videos—all with the same high-quality CD sound. It becomes a multimedia performer when formated with special attachments for a personal computer or a TV set.

As the early high prices have fallen and an increased number of releases have reached the market, the popularity of CD-ROMs has grown. Some news organizations produce CD-ROMs as supplements to their news coverage. Cable News Network (CNN), for example, marketed "CNN Time Capsule 1994," reviewing the year with video, photos, and sound. Before testimony began in the O. J. Simpson murder trial, CNN issued a CD-ROM about the case. Viewers saw pictures of the crime scene, heard a "911" emergency call by Simpson's murdered wife Nicole, and watched O. J. run for a touchdown during his college days.

### Cellular Telephones

Because *cellular telephones* are so common today, many people fail to realize that these walk-around cordless telephones have only recently been added to the tools of mass communication.

A cellular system has interlocking low-power transmitters; as a motorist moves from one zone to another, calls from the car are switched by computer into the next zone, permitting continuous nonfading communication. For newsgatherers on the move during an assignment, the phones provide a swift method of delivering story material to the home office and for editors to keep in touch with field reporters.

Use of cellular telephones multiplied at a spectacular rate after the Federal Communications Commission (FCC) decided in late 1993 to license as many as seven new wireless systems in every U.S. city.

## Problems and Doubts with Advanced Technology

While the new era of electronic communication has many obvious benefits and promises to draw the peoples of the world closer together, it has created both physical and ethical uncertainties.

1. *Cost.* Installation of fiber optics lines and elaborate equipment involves billions of dollars. Only huge corporations can finance such ventures, putting control of much of the communications structure into relatively few hands. (See Issue 3 for further discussion.) Construction of all the proposed projects will run well into the twenty-first century, and some may eventually be cut back as economically unfeasible.

Individual customers face substantial investments for equipment and find their monthly charges rising as they adopt additional services. Some will refuse to spend money on services that, while fascinating, have little real value for them.

2. *Invasion of privacy.* Electronic services such as e-mail and databases theoretically protect the privacy of messages transmitted. As discussed earlier, however, hackers have intercepted messages and invaded the sup-

posedly secure storage of medical and other personal records. Fear that the government might monitor messages on the Internet, including electronic "chat" forums, has been expressed by some people. The Federal Bureau of Investigation, however, has stated officially that it has no interest in doing so. Yet the technical capability exists.

3. *Degree of editorial control.* This issue has conflicting sides, each with valid arguments. Only in rare instances do any of the databases and bulletin boards attempt to exercise editorial control over what is sent and received by their customers. The Internet has no controls at all. Lack of editorial control is hailed as basic freedom of speech under the First Amendment. Americans can say anything they desire without having an editor kill or amend their messages and decide what material should be transmitted.

In the print and broadcast media, editors acting as gatekeepers approve everything transmitted to the public in order to prevent invasion of privacy, and violations of the laws of libel, copyright, and trademark protection. They also delete racial slurs and similar hate messages, as well as pornographic material, following as best they can the decisions of the U.S. Supreme Court.

Lacking such control in most instances, the so-called digital democracy of cyberspace sometimes results in violations of these traditional legal and ethical standards. For those computer users who have the software, hard-core pornography is available on the Internet and some bulletin boards. Lawsuits have been filed by companies that believe their property rights have been violated by computer senders who misuse proprietory material and trademarks. Until a body of law has been developed concerning these issues, uncertainty will remain.

Indicative of the complexity of legal problems involved, a San Francisco couple who operated an "adult" computer service was arrested by federal agents, then charged, tried, and convicted in a Tennessee federal court of distributing pornographic material. The trial was held in a "Bible Belt" state with very conservative community standards because a viewer in that state had seen the material the couple transmitted, rather than in far more liberal San Francisco, from which it had been transmitted. The couple might have been acquitted there. Legal specialists argued whether the couple should have been tried in the receiver's state, the sender's state, or not at all. (See Issue 5.)

Another perceived danger of uncontrolled communication is the spread of falsehood and rumor. For example, a ridiculous joke in dubious taste circulated for a week on the Internet, claiming that the Microsoft Corporation was buying the Roman Catholic Church in exchange for Microsoft stock. Those who started the false tale pretended that it had been distributed by the Associated Press. The news service denied doing so.

Microsoft, a leading producer of computer software, received so many calls from people who believed the story or were offended by it that the company issued a news release disclaiming any connection with the affair.

4. *Ignorance of electronic devices.* Manufacturers often promote their products as being "user-friendly," but many people are baffled by anything more complicated than a videocassette recorder (VCR). They hesitate, even refuse, to try using equipment that involves inserting code words, striking multiple keys, or obeying commands appearing on a computer screen. This uneasiness may prevent them from adopting the new systems for home use.

## Summary

The burst of high-tech electronic development has largely conquered time and space, the principal barriers to mass communication. Words and pictures are transmitted around the world in seconds by satellite, surmounting political frontiers and cultural barriers.

Facsimile messages and electronic mail speed from one country to another. Masses of information stored in online computers are available with a few strokes on a keyboard. The Internet enables computer users around the world to exchange ideas, information, and social attitudes unfettered by censorship.

In the United States, an information superhighway, partly visionary and partly reality at present, eventually may tie homes and offices everywhere into a multimedia communication network.

Humanity's challenge is how to use these spectacular communication tools in the most imaginative, effective, and socially responsible manner.

## Points to Remember

1. Define a target audience and give an example of one.
2. What are the two basic categories of mass media? Name at least two media in each category.
3. Can you describe what the information superhighway will be when completed?
4. What is meant by a "parking lot" for satellites?
5. When two individuals send messages to each other through their computers, what are those messages called?
6. Who created the Internet? When?
7. Columnist Russell Baker made a complaint against the Internet. What was it?
8. Explain how obtaining the reception of 500 television channels can be achieved.

9. What advantage does direct broadcast satellite service (DBS) have for the customer over traditional cable television service?

10. Explain what is meant by the term "digital democracy of cyber-space."

## Media Questions to Think About

1. After weighing the opposing views, do you favor at least partial editorial control over the Internet?

2. If the goal of receiving 500 television channels is achieved, will it improve your life? If so, in what way?

3. What examples, if any, can you cite from your own experience to support Russell Baker's contention that the use of technology creates personal isolation?

# CHAPTER TWO
## The Media's Social Impact

## MTV: Intellectual Breakthrough?

Creation of the MTV music video channel is a line of demarcation between a new electronic literacy and the old printed form. At least one professor of English believes so.

Gregory Ulmer of the University of Florida describes MTV as a way to present several stories simultaneously with images and sound. "Our society is changing the technology we use to think with," he said.

Older people often are irritated or baffled by MTV's outpouring of quick-flashing images and throbbing sounds, but to Ulmer the channel is an intellectual breakthrough. He compares it to the ancient Greeks' development of a written alphabet 2700 years ago and Plato's concept of the logic of the written word.

"Music TV, advertising, etcetera is now teaching Americans and the whole world," he wrote. "If we say America is the Greece of the electronic moment, from this epicenter is spreading out all over the world this new apparatus."

The key to the breakthrough, as Ulmer sees it, is the viewer's ability to absorb multiple stories from the same video. "To be into MTV is like being able to play three games of racquetball and chess simultaneously."

The media are part of the social fabric just as are schools, governments, and churches and synagogues. They significantly influence other segments of society and in turn are influenced and restricted by them.

Probably the media are the most controversial portion of the social structure, because they have daily impact on people in so many ways. The television programs we watch, the magazines and newspapers we read, the radio talk shows we hear, the movies and videos we view—all deliver ideas and information that please, disturb, even anger the recipients. These messages often create conflict, lead to changes in government plans, or promote socially beneficial actions.

The media are messengers in a more complex sense than being the physical bearers of information. Their editors review and select the messages and therefore carry responsibility for what they tell the public.

This chapter examines the impact of the media on individuals and groups, public attitudes toward the media, and changing news values in the evolving electronic age.

## Media Influence and Restrictions

Clearly the mass media strongly influence our thinking and conduct. This is evident in obvious, simple ways: a teenage boy wears his cap backward in a TV situation comedy, and soon boys nationwide imitate the style. News stories describe a new toy, the Mighty Morphin Power Rangers, and the Fox television network builds a series around it. At Christmas parents jam stores, trying to find the Power Rangers for their children. Actors playing the characters perform for Congress in the House Office Building on the day in 1995 when the Republicans took command of the House and Senate.

The cultural, social, and political impact of the media, of course, runs far deeper than these surface manifestations. The media create public opinion to bring about significant changes. The national campaign to forbid smoking in public places, so strong in the mid-1990s, developed from a spate of news stories about the health dangers created by second-hand smoke. This led to a ban against smoking on airlines, creation of smoke-free areas in restaurants, and in some cities a total ban against smoking in restaurants and public buildings. Sensing public support, President Clinton took the issue into the national political arena in 1995 by authorizing a federal regulatory campaign to decrease smoking by teenagers. Similarly, national awareness of the outbreak of the acquired immune deficiency syndrome (AIDS) and the promotion of safe sex practices to avoid exposure to the fatal disease came about primarily through the mass media.

These are instances in which the media have crystalized public opinion for action. Sometimes the media merely reflect an existing attitude. Motion picture and television producers who make pictures filled with violence claim, for example, that they are merely giving the public what it desires. In support of this position they cite the high boxoffice sales and ratings for such products.

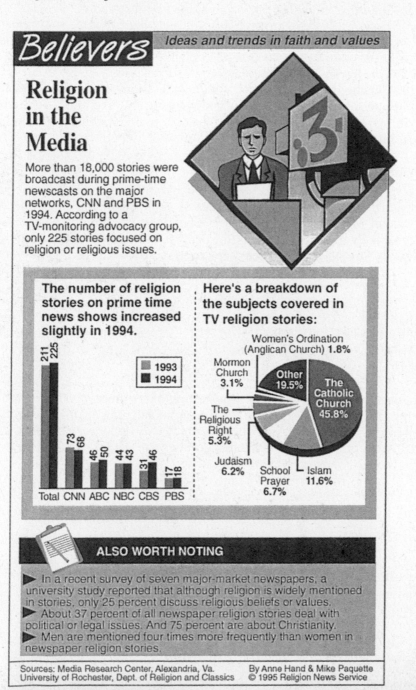

## Believers
### Ideas and trends in faith and values

## Religion in the Media

More than 18,000 stories were broadcast during prime-time newscasts on the major networks, CNN and PBS in 1994. According to a TV-monitoring advocacy group, only 225 stories focused on religion or religious issues.

### The number of religion stories on prime time news shows increased slightly in 1994.

1993
1994

211
225

73
68

46
50

44
43

31
46

17
18

Total  CNN  ABC  NBC  CBS  PBS

### Here's a breakdown of the subjects covered in TV religion stories:

Women's Ordination (Anglican Church) 1.8%
Mormon Church 3.1%
Other 19.5%
The Catholic Church 45.8%
The Religious Right 5.3%
Judaism 6.2%
School Prayer 6.7%
Islam 11.6%

### ALSO WORTH NOTING

► In a recent survey of seven major-market newspapers, a university study reported that although religion is widely mentioned in stories, only 25 percent discuss religious beliefs or values.
► About 37 percent of all newspaper religion stories deal with political or legal issues. And 75 percent are about Christianity.
► Men are mentioned four times more frequently than women in newspaper religion stories.

Sources: Media Research Center, Alexandria, Va.
University of Rochester, Dept. of Religion and Classics

By Anne Hand & Mike Paquette
© 1995 Religion News Service

Despite the significant role religion plays in the lives of many Americans, surveys show that relatively few news stories about religion are published or broadcast. A graph released by the Religious News Service shows the subjects covered by religious stories in television broadcasts. (Copyright ©1995 Religious News Service, Washington, D.C.)

Some researchers within the media believe, however, that decision makers in their industries have failed to learn what the public really desires. Jean Gaddy Wilson, director of the New Directions for News project, found this to be true during a national research tour.

She identified three major shifts—in ecology, culture, and information. "These three things spin us forward in a time leap that's going to make the last 15 years, we assume, look like it was a slow roller coaster," she wrote in the *Nieman Reports* summer 1994 issue.

"Outside this room exists a world, actually a country, that is creating itself outside the line of vision of the rest of us. . . . We found on the road that the people expect the media to be able to understand, to give understanding to the world people live in."

## Restrictions on the Media

Powerful as they are in social and cultural influence, the mass media in turn are restricted in numerous ways by other segments of society. Editors and producers are limited in what they present to the public by laws concerning libel, invasion of privacy, copyright, and pornography. Equally strong, and in some ways more restrictive, are pressures from special interest groups and difficulty in meeting loosely defined standards of good taste.

Using threats of boycotts to harm the supposedly offending media financially, activists for causes demand that editors delete story material and phraseology they dislike. They also demand publication of stories favorable to them, crying "biased reporting" if the editors reject their demands.

Among the strongest pressures on the media are those from the "religious right," from minority groups, and, on a different level, from some advertisers. Conservative religious groups campaign against motion pictures and television shows whose content fails to conform to their strict standards of behavior and language. (See Issue 1, Sex and Violence: Are the Media Weakening Public Morality?)

Various minority groups detect what they regard as racial slurs in public utterances and news coverage. Some newspapers have been pressured into apologizing publicly for editorial cartoons regarded as racist by activist organizations.

Commercial retaliation by advertisers displeased by stories they consider harmful to their businesses, while relatively rare, sometimes results in cancellation of advertising contracts as punishment. Public officials and local booster groups also seek revenge for unfavorable coverage by urging citizens to cancel subscriptions or refuse to watch a certain television show.

In sum, then, the mass media strongly influence public opinion and behavior, but public opinion in turn exercises substantial, if not always obvious, restraint on the media.

# FOUR VIEWS OF MEDIA INFLUENCE

These quotations from prominent observers of the American media represent aspects of the debate about the social impact and conduct of the media.

*Everette Dennis, executive director of the Freedom Forum Media Studies Center*

Today the near loss of fair trial rights in celebrated cases is due more than anything to frantic media competition wherein TV tabloid news shows and other print tabloid fare are actually driving the news media. The attitude of many in the media is that "if they do it, so must we," and there is the typical chuckling about the people's right to know, which ironically is not itself a stated constitutional right.

*Daniel J. Boorstin, historian and former Librarian of Congress*

We have suffered, too, from the consequences of our freedom. Totalitarian societies exaggerate their virtues. But free societies like ours somehow seize the temptation to exaggerate our vices. The negativism of our press and television reporting are, of course, the best evidence of our freedom to scrutinize ourselves. Far better this than the chauvinism of self-righteousness which has been the death of totalitarian empires in our time.

*Tom Shales, Washington* Post *columnist and Pulitzer Prize winner*

We have become so obsessed with the idea that television is the all-controlling influence on American life. It's a dominant influence in American life, but I don't think we're a helpless race of lemmings who are just led around by this tube all the time.

*Robert M. Steele, director of the journalism ethics program at the Poynter Institute for Media Studies*

I share the concerns that have been raised about the downsides of the press, and I think we are sensationalistic and lousy at times. But I also worry that our fault at times is that we're too timid in journalism.

Often our problem is not that we are too aggressive, but that we don't go after the powerful with the best of intentions and the best in journalism in the way we should, and we don't give voice to the voiceless in the way that our papers and our electronic journalism should in covering the important issues of our times.

## Messengers of Popular Culture

Scholars studying the phenomenon of American popular culture credit the mass media with being a compelling force in its growth, both in the United States and abroad.

When more than 2,000 educators examined pop culture at a meeting in Philadelphia in 1994, many correlated its post–World War II growth with the explosive emergence of television during the 1950s. The exuberance of rock and roll, the sexual revolution of the 1960s, the drug culture, protest marches against the Vietnam war, fascination with "celebrities": television delivered all of these into the nation's homes with visual punch. Seeing them was far more stimulating than reading or hearing about them. Radio contributed by blasting out rock songs; motion pictures had themes of drug usage and of youthful anger at traditional institutions.

Researchers into the growth of popular culture vary in their interpretations of its social value but agree about the hold it has on American life and the role of the media in promoting it.

Ray Browne of Bowling Green State University, a pioneer in the academic study of the trend, told the Philadelphia convention, "Popular culture is the driving machine of all that we are. It is what has developed democracy through the ages. It is the culture of the unenfranchised." In contrast, Joel Wooler of Carnegie Mellon University, citing fascination with objects such as sports shoes, concluded, "In many ways we're lost as a nation, and we need to know how we got to this point."

## 15 Minutes of Fame

Pop artist Andy Warhol's quip that every person will have 15 minutes of fame has a certain ring of reality. At least, people do get their 15 minutes in the limelight, whether they earn it or not. Persons unknown to the public become involved in a news situation, often inadvertently, and suddenly find themselves starring in the highly competitive media. An example is Brian "Kato" Kaelin, an aspiring actor who lived in O. J. Simpson's guest house the night Simpson's ex-wife and a friend were murdered. Kaelin testified in the trial and suddenly was a national figure. He tried later with only modest success to cash in on his short-lived fame. In the same trial, Judge Lance Ito noted caustically that jurors he had dismissed for cause were riding around Los Angeles in stretch limousines, which were taking them from one television interview to another.

At the other end of the financial spectrum, Donald Trump made newspaper front pages and network TV shows, not merely for his financial deals but for his battles with his ex-wife. His publicity agent planted stories with the media about his romantic affairs. Soon he became the object of jokes, but the media continued to carry stories about him.

What, indeed, is celebrity? Some entertainers and social figures are celebrities only because their press releases say they are. Mention in *People Weekly* and similar publications provides a certain distinction. Football players often become celebrities because they are promoted excessively by the media. As their salaries soar into the multimillion-dollar range, they cross a mysterious line and are called superstars. The hero worship seems to be directed nearly as much to their salaries as to their performances.

The motion picture critics team of Gene Siskel of the Chicago *Tribune* and Roger Ebert of the Chicago *Sun-Times* have achieved such national impact with their "two thumbs up (or down)" decisions that Chicago officially named a city block "Honorary Siskel & Ebert Way." (Copyright © 1995 Bill Stamets. Courtesy of Siskel & Ebert)

Some media promote these personal buildups by publicizing so-called nonevents staged primarily to provide a setting in which the celebrities appear and to sell TV commercials.

Psychologists contend that a principal reason for today's excessive emphasis on celebrity stems from the humdrum lives many individuals live. They seek vicarious self-esteem by mentally attaching themselves to sports stars and appropriating the deeds of their heroes as their own, a painless form of *personality transfer*. Life has always needed its heroes, and the media deliver today's crop ready-made.

Musing in her column about the weird aspects of celebrity, Erma Bombeck drew a provocative distinction: "Fame is Madonna, success is Helen Keller." This comparison between the raucous, publicity-hungry singer and the blind, deaf woman of an earlier generation who won deep admiration made a point too often overlooked by the media.

## Stereotypes in the Media

Because of their enormous impact, the media need constant awareness to avoid portraying racial and gender *stereotypes*. Accusations against them in this regard are made from time to time, but, after a long period of offenses, their record today is generally good.

The mass media did not create most of the social stereotypes imbedded in the American culture, although newspapers, books, and periodicals of the nineteenth and early twentieth centuries did enhance them. Primarily the stereotypes grew out of the societal circumstances and pressures of the time—for example, slavery and the Victorian tradition of masculine supremacy.

The media did perpetuate the stereotypes, however, until World War II and for many years afterward in some instances. They were slow to recognize the deep social ferment stirred by that conflict.

**The Role of Women.**    The fundamental change in the role of women is a case in point. Before World War II well-educated women who worked outside the home were primarily teachers, nurses, and librarians. Other young women tended to be stenographers, "stenos" in the jargon of the day (and, earlier, "typewriters"). Or they were sales clerks, a role recalled by a hit song of the 1930s, "I Found a Million-Dollar Baby in a 5-and-10-Cent Store."

When millions of men were sent overseas during the war, a grave manpower shortage developed. Housewives who went to work in war production factories were called by the slightly patronizing nickname "Rosie the Riveter." At newspapers, teenage girls appeared in the newsrooms as office "boys." A few women moved from writing about club meetings and weddings in the society section (known as "sock") to become general reporters.

Treatment of women in a secondary role by the media was more a habit of decades in a white male world and failure to recognize a basic social trend than a calculated putdown.

A female novelist who grew up on a Western ranch half a century ago cited her personal experience to illustrate the point. "I blame the media," she said. "They were out of touch."

As a young girl she saw her mother doing the same ranch chores as the men, in addition to running the home and feeding the cowboys. "Yet when I watched those cowboy TV shows starring Hopalong Cassidy, Gene Autry, and Roy Rogers, about the only woman ever shown was when Dale Evans turned up to sing with Rogers. I realized then that something was wrong. Those shows weren't reality."

During the following decades the media gradually recognized their error. Stories appeared about new job opportunities for women, the accomplishments of individual females, and the ways mothers combined their jobs and families. These became a driving force in the expansion of women's role in the world outside the home. Today visual and print coverage of sexual harassment in the workplace is an important educational factor in efforts to control that problem.

**Racial Stereotypes.**    Much the same pattern developed in handling racial stereotypes. For decades, blacks appeared only in menial roles in motion pictures. Stereotyped comedians such as Step'n'Fetchit, a shuffling, drawling lazybones who said such things as "Yowsa, mastah," and Rochester, Jack Benny's wisecracking chauffeur, were featured. Gradually, but significantly, the motion picture and television industries recognized that a pool of black artistic talent was waiting for opportunities and had something valuable to say. Many newsrooms, too, were slow to recognize the fundamental fact that in a democratic society all racial groups should be treated equally. Crime stories frequently identified suspects as black or Mexican but never as white. One midwestern newspaper owned by a sincere, generally open-minded family published a column headed "In Colored Circles" until the late 1950s.

Today, when racial hatreds boil up, the mass media as a whole are sensitive to the problems involved and seek to cover controversial racial situations even-handedly—not an easy task. This sensibility has developed in part from pressure by activist groups and in part from realization by media managements that fair, perceptive coverage can help to counteract the destructive strain of racism running through American society.

## Too Much "Right Now"

Criticisms of the media's role in the social changes of the past four decades include:

- Overemphasis on surface manifestations
- Failure to provide perspective
- Excessive emphasis on conflict, because confrontation makes more exciting news than cooperation
- Failure to provide moral leadership

News stories about social problems often appear in headlines and newscasts for a day or so, then disappear without being resolved. The fact that the story might be part of an historical pattern, and needs to be examined in that light, often is disregarded.

This emphasis on "right now" draws the ire of Haynes Johnson, Washington author and television commentator. He observes in his book *Divided We Fall*:

Through the constant media focus on today—not yesterday, not tomorrow—every issue was magnified and simplified. Politicians were under constant media pressure to respond immediately on short-term problems. And woe to them if they didn't; failure to react brought a chorus of media criticism.

Those who charge that the media fail to provide moral leadership contend that broadcasters, reporters, editors, and filmmakers have a social responsibility to avoid the "anything goes" approach to news coverage and entertainment so prevalent today, especially in tabloid TV shows and publications. (See Issue 1.) The problem, of course, is who decides what is moral leadership and what is unreasonable restraint on freedom on expression.

Typical front page of *Star,* one of the sensational weekly tabloids whose glaring headlines and titillating coverage of entertainers and other public figures sometimes is picked up by the mainstream press, which once ignored them.

## Changes in Media Usage

A substantial shift has taken place in homes concerning the media families use and the manner in which they use them. In some instances, it is difficult to determine which changes result from social evolution and which can be attributed to performance by the media themselves.

For example, before so many women held jobs, the standard pattern in many families was for the stay-at-home wife to read the afternoon paper when it was delivered about 4 P.M. Then she prepared dinner for the family. The husband read the paper before they ate or afterward. In 1960, 19 percent of women with children under 6 held jobs outside the home.

Newspaper reading time has greatly diminished. Today approximately 60 percent of women in the same category are employed. They get home from work, often picking up the children at a day-care center en route. They hurry to prepare dinner, unless fortunate enough to have husbands who do so. During or immediately after dinner families turn on the television set. Newspaper reading time has almost vanished.

Statistics show what has happened to newspapers as a result. In 1960, the 1459 evening newspapers had a total circulation of 34,852,958. By 1994 the number of evening newspapers had fallen to 947 and their circulation to 16,198,430. But during the same period the number of U.S. households grew from 52,799,000 to 96,391,000.

A look at television statistics shows the other side of the picture. According to A.C. Nielsen reports, the average American family in the early 1950s had its television set turned on three hours a day. By 1994, daily watching time had risen to 7 hours 42 minutes. More than four hours a day had been added to the family's time commitment to television. The TV set was turned on nearly one-third of every 24 hours.

Much of the time, however, the TV set isn't watched closely. A 1995 survey by Statistical Research, Inc., published in *TV Guide*, found that, two-thirds of the time family members are doing something else while the TV set plays. They may be cooking, cleaning house, talking on the telephone; 25 percent of the respondents said they fall asleep in front of the TV set at least three times a week.

Dr. Maura Clancey of the research firm told the magazine, "Now TV is more background to our lives, and 42 percent of us don't necessarily watch but keep TV on merely as noise."

## The Computer's Social Impact

Acquiring a computer upsets time allotments even further. In some homes the computer goes unused for extended periods. In others, computer enthusiasts spend hours daily working on projects or "surfing" the Net to see what they can find.

Sociologists are concerned that the computer user at the keyboard hour after hour loses important face-to-face contact with other humans. Persons who work at home, communicating with an office by computer, abandon the social interplay of office life—chit-chat during coffee breaks, discussion of work problems, group lunches.

Herbert Gans, professor of sociology at Columbia University, feels strongly about this lack of personal contact. He also cites the stay-at-home aspects of online shopping and other interactive computer services. Writing in *Media Studies Journal*, Gans said:

Obviously the promoters of the superhighway seek to make their customers more dependent on their phones, computers, and television sets than ever before. . . . However, that dependence has what sociologists call a latent function, an unintended and apparently unrecognized effect. It could turn the electronic travelers into virtual electronic shut-ins."

Gans equates them with shut-ins from illness and disability.

Pity for shut-ins reflects the fact that we are social animals, requiring a good deal of social contact of various degrees of intensity and closeness in order to function properly.

### Rich and Poor: Unequal Opportunity

Another problem inherent in a computer-dominated mass communications system involves access to the computers that carry news and information. Computers are expensive, and users are constantly being coaxed to purchase new ones, along with software. Affluent people can pay the price and enjoy as many services as they desire.

Similarly with television: as more TV services develop through digitalization, cable costs almost inevitably will rise. Yet more and more of the best TV programming is being carried by cable. Sports provide an example. A growing number of games are shifted from free over-the-air broadcasting to cable channels for which the would-be viewer must pay monthly fees.

Some critics foresee the time when the well-to-do, who can afford electronic services, will be better informed and entertained than the poor, who cannot. This is a problem for which no answers have been offered.

## Changing News Values

### What Is News?

A recurring tale in the newspaper business describes the crusty old editor who, when asked by a young reporter to define news, barked, "News is what I say it is!"

Many less ego-centered definitions of news have been advanced, but none can be taken as absolute. News is mercurial and is seen differently by various groups of people. News essential to one person may bore another. For general guidance, *news* may be defined as:

The report of recent events and happenings, especially those that are unusual or notable.

Rapidly shifting social and cultural values in the United States, partially brought about by growing diversity of the population, have led to changing interpretations of this definition. The New York *Times* uses the slogan, "All the news that's fit to print." But what guidelines do editors use when they decide what is fit to print? Today's standards of fitness and news values vary among the media and differ considerably from those of earlier decades.

Even the cloistered halls of monasteries have entered the computer age. At the Monastery of the Holy Cross in Chicago, Brother Patrick Creeden, front, works along with Sister Francesca-Marie Riddick and Brother Thomas Baxter entering data on their computers. (AP Photo/Beth Keiser)

As online databases and other stored-up masses of facts pour material onto computer screens, it is important to differentiate between raw information and news. Information is the basic ingredient of a news story, but the story must have another fundamental element. Bill Kovach, curator of the Nieman Foundation, defines this element as "the value of the systematic effort by journalists to gather, verify, organize, and present reliable and timely information in a meaningful context."

It is the lack of this extra value in the deluge of information flowing through most computer networks, unverified, that concerns many students of communication trends.

The concept of news developed over two centuries in newspapers, which during most of that period were dominated by white male editors. Most news they published was "hard" in nature. It concerned politics, crime, natural disasters, accidents, and meetings of public bodies such as city councils. Radio news and early television news broadcasts largely followed that format. More recently, TV news has paid more attention to social and cultural issues.

As television with its dramatic visual impact became the favorite news source for millions of Americans, newspaper editors undertook a self-study in an effort to stem the loss of newspaper circulation. They talked with nonsubscribers and found that the contemporary public has a wider range of interests than the editors had been serving. Research showed their papers failing to serve significant segments of the population.

After intensive study, New Directions for News, underwritten by the newspaper industry, identified what it called the Invisible Cities—that is, groups within the total urban population whose interests newspaper served inadequately. These are:

Women—who comprise 51.4 percent of the total population

Young adults—ages 18 to 34: 30 percent

Racial, ethnic, immigrant groups—25 percent

Plus 50s—21 percent

Kids/teens—ages 5 to 17: 15 percent

Each of these groups has a special interest in such issues as health, recreation, family relationships, education, neighborhood life, dress, and entertainment. For them, stories about such matters are as newsworthy, or more so, as coverage of business deals, zoning board meetings, society parties, and routine crime.

With the help of computer research, today's newspapers publish many valuable stories on topics appealing to these newly identified groups. A few examples: for women, stories about breast cancer research; for young adults, advice from personnel officers on finding jobs and handling employment interviews: for the Plus 50 group, articles on preparing for retirement.

## Lowered Professional Standards

Although the breadth of news reporting has improved substantially, many media critics believe a decline has occurred in accuracy, sense of fairness, reliability, respect for individual privacy, and exercise of good taste. They cite unverified stories containing damaging allegations against individuals, along with careless factual inaccuracies. Some editors of newspapers and magazines, along with producers of some television programs, seem obsessed with scandal. Their efforts to "get" something on somebody are known as "gotcha journalism."

As the number of news merchandisers multiplies, especially in cable television, competition to obtain viewer and reader attention has multiplied. Public restraint in matters of sex, crime, and privacy has diminished emphatically during the past half century. For example, when Nazi leaders convicted at the Nuremberg war crimes trials after World War II were executed, publication in some newspapers of newsphotos showing their bodies drew sharp public criticism. In contrast, a popular national TV show recently sought to televise an execution live but was refused official permission. A TV station did show live pictures of a public official as he committed suicide. While protests were heard, neither episode jarred the public consciousness very heavily.

This public apathy and seeming craving for personal scandal has led to the popularity of tabloid television programs such as "Hard Copy" and "A Current Affair." Their print equivalents, grocery checkout counter tabloids such as *The Star* and *National Enquirer*, thrive on the same appeal.

Newspaper and television news editors had to make a delicate decision on good taste when Pennsylvania state treasurer R. Budd Dwyer unexpectedly committed suicide before the cameras during a news conference. Although some editors used a picture of him pulling the trigger with the gun in his mouth, most chose this less graphic one taken a few seconds earlier. (AP/Wide World)

Television programs purporting to present "reality" use actors to reenact crimes. The tabloid sells copies with violent, exaggerated headlines. *Caution:* A newspaper printed in tabloid size, half the size of a standard newspaper page, is not automatically a scandal sheet. Many well regarded newspapers appear in that convenient format.

Mainstream newspapers and television news programs formerly ignored the newsstand and TV tabloids. Editors called their content trash. Then, worried about competition, respected newspapers began to pick up and pursue scandal stories from the tabloids. Nationally syndicated television talk shows, fighting each other for ratings, exploited sensational but trivial topics. The sleaze factor in the media multiplied, while ethical standards in newsgathering often were ignored. (See Issue 1.)

## "Checkbook Journalism"

Another recent practice with a chilling effect on traditional media standards is payment to news sources for their information. The cut-throat competition among TV tabloid shows in particular leads them to pay individuals with titillating tales thousands of dollars for exclusive rights. The veracity of many such stories is questionable; the more exciting the story, the more profitable it is to the teller.

*Checkbook journalism* presents a danger to the judicial system. Testimony given in court may be tainted because a witness may already have sold it to a tabloid. In the O. J. Simpson murder case, discussed in the accompanying case study, prosecutors decided not to call as a witness a woman who said she had seen Simpson driving near the murder scene. They believed that her credibility would be challenged because she already had sold her story to "Hard Copy" for $5000 and to *The Star* for $2000. Two witnesses at the Simpson preliminary hearing admitted they had sold their stories to the *National Enquirer* for $12,000.

**Checkbook journalism**
The practice of purchasing information customarily provided free to journalists

## The O. J. Simpson Trial: A Case Study

The murder trial of O. J. Simpson, football star, television commercial spokesperson, and sports commentator, provided revealing insights into the relationship between the media and the public.

The case fascinated people, because it involved the apparent downfall of a sports hero along with sensitive social issues including sexual harassment, wealth and privilege, racism and interracial marriage, drugs, and Hollywood glamor.

Prosecution and defense attorneys in the O. J. Simpson murder trial used visual aids frequently in their presentations to the jury. Barry Scheck of the defense points to a layout of the Simpson home while prosecutor Marcia Clark watches. (Sam Mircovich/Reuters)

Television, radio, and the print media indulged in overwhelming coverage during Simpson's arrest, the months of pretrial litigation, and the trial itself. The media's excesses provoked extensive criticism from the public, yet at the same time the public clamored for more details.

The trial became a national obsession and drew ardent foreign interest as well. Television coverage from the courtroom, provided by a pool camera of the Court TV channel, was beamed around the world. (See Issue 5.) It replaced soap operas and talk shows for millions of daytime TV watchers. Many people who ordinarily ignored daytime television also became Simpson "junkies" as, hour after hour, they watched the testimony and the legal maneuvering.

Analyzing this phenomenon, Neal Gabler in *TV Guide* concluded, ". . . this whole O. J. Simpson miniseries has been fabulously, deliriously, dizzyingly *entertaining*."

In fact, many watchers tended to judge the trial in the television drama terms to which they were accustomed. They expected it to come in neatly scripted episodes, not in loosely structured legal proceedings. The seemingly endless "sidebars," during which Judge Lance Ito and the rival attorneys conferred outside the hearing of the jurors and TV watchers, irritated them.

As the trial dragged through much of 1995, and technical experts on blood, hair, and fabric were cross-examined exhaustively, the television audience dwindled.

Unquestionably the attorneys played to the television camera, delaying progress of the trial. Debate arose among the public, and within the media as well, as to whether justice would have been better served and swifter if the trial had not been televised.

Especially during the early stages, the circus-like conduct by the media outside the courtroom created heavy criticism. Reporters and camera crews jostled, shoved, and shouted around the attorneys and other court figures, seeking comment. On the opening day of the trial, seven media helicopters hovered above Simpson as he was transported from the county jail to the courthouse. Many critics felt that in their competitive frenzy, the media had lost sight of the sordid fact that a woman and a man had been murdered and were more affected by the fame of the defendant.

Compounding the furor, many people tried to cash in on the trial. Souvenirs from T-shirts to Simpson Halloween masks, many in bad taste, were peddled. Quickie books about Simpson and the trial appeared. Simpson himself with a ghostwriter produced a self-serving book while in jail. Television and stage comedians told jokes about the judge, the attorneys, and other trial figures. Photographers made much about prosecutor Marcia Clark's new hair-dos. As one commentator remarked, Clark's wardrobe received more attention than her formidable legal skills. When several members of the sequestered jury were dismissed for various reasons, their comments about relationships within the jury were widely quoted.

Underlying all this confusion lurked the sensitive racial issue. A popular black man was on trial for murdering his white ex-wife and a young white man. Lacking any other suspect to whom they could divert attention, Simpson's attorneys tried to convince the jury that the Los Angeles police department had "framed" Simpson because its officers were racists. Racism exploded into the dominant issue late in the trial. Detective Mark Fuhrman, a key prosecution witness, was exposed as a virulent racist by his own words and was shown to have lied on the witness stand when he denied using insulting anti-black language.

The defense sought with considerable success to turn attention away from the murder charges to a denunciation of Fuhrman and the police department. In his closing argument defense attorney Johnnie Cochran likened Fuhrman to Adolf Hitler and urged the predominantly black jury to acquit Simpson as a protest against police racism.

After being sequestered during the eight months of testimony, the jury reached a verdict after less than four hours of deliberation: Simpson was found not guilty on all charges. Crowds of blacks cheered the news; white groups expressed dismay and anger. Announcement of the verdict attracted a huge worldwide television audience. For days afterward, television, radio, and newspaper commentators dissected the trial from every angle. Radio talk shows were flooded with heated calls.

In a sense the Simpson trial was a microcosm of American society in the 1990s—the gaping chasm between black and white populations, fringe of get-rich-quick schemers, admiration for wealth and fame, hunger for scandal, and a legal system that bogs down in technicalities and can be manipulated by clever lawyers.

## Points to Remember

1. Name three ways in which the mass media are restricted from publishing or broadcasting whatever they might desire.
2. Which of the mass media was especially important in spreading popular culture in the post–World War II period?
3. What two personalities did columnist Erma Bombeck compare in her discussion of celebrity?
4. In what way did World War II affect the traditional role of women in American society?
5. What habit of the news media does Haynes Johnson find objectionable?
6. Identify and discuss one reason why the circulation of American evening newspapers has fallen so sharply.
7. How much did the average American family's daily television viewing increase between the 1950s and the 1990s?

8. Why do sociologists see a danger that, increasingly, rich people will become better informed than poor people?

9. Explain the difference between information and news.

10. Define checkbook journalism and give an example of who uses it.

## Media Questions to Think About

1. Can you name three people who in your judgment deserve to be called celebrities, based on significant accomplishment? Explain why you selected them.

2. As you watch television shows, do you see any characters who represent racial or gender stereotypes? What are they doing to deserve such characterization?

3. As a newspaper editor, what six "do" or "do not" guidelines would you give your staff for publishing the news in a socially responsible manner?

# CHAPTER THREE
## Historic Press Freedoms

## A Centuries-Long Struggle

Americans love to criticize their government and its leaders, and do so vehemently and constantly.

Talk show hosts and their callers denounce the government as oppressive and domineering. Men and women argue on the air about abortion, taxes, racial disputes, and gay rights. Readers send letters to the editor calling members of Congress greedy tools of the lobbyists. Leaders of militia movements claim there is a government conspiracy to destroy their freedom. Television programs document cases of multimillion-dollar bureaucratic waste.

All speak their minds without hesitation because they take their freedom of speech for granted. They can't imagine a situation in which they would be forbidden to do so.

Too few realize that their freedom of speech, guaranteed by the First Amendment to the Constitution, resulted from a 300-year battle in which skirmishes still are being fought to preserve the gains of those centuries.

An odd mixture of individuals emerged among leaders of the fight—a German immigrant printer, John Peter Zenger; Thomas Jefferson and James Madison, both of whom became president of the United States; Jay M. Near, a small-time publisher described by his biographer as an unprincipled bigot, extortionist, and rumor-monger; and Robert McCormick, thundering conservative publisher of the Chicago *Tribune*, who helped save Near's newspaper although he despised much of what Near wrote.

It is a compelling story that every American should know.

This chapter traces the press and free speech battle from its roots in the controlled society of Renaissance Europe. A small ruling class that dominated life in each country determined what others should read, hear, and know.

Gradually pressure for wider dissemination of information grew during the Reformation of the 1500s. This was stimulated by the development of printing with movable type by Johann Gutenberg about 1440. The pressure expanded along with the democratic concept in the Western world but was rejected vehemently by dictatorial regimes in Russia, China, and elsewhere.

Gradually the role of the press changed. At first it was an instrument that spoke for the governors. It required a license from them in order to publish. Finally it became a free marketplace of ideas and information to be used by the governed.

The overthrow of communism in the Soviet Union and the breakup of that vast area into numerous independent states, including freedom for the former Soviet satellite countries, brought a somewhat unevenly applied freedom of speech to Eastern Europe in the 1990s. This freedom still is repressed or sharply curtailed in numerous countries.

We describe the step-by-step achievement of the basic elements that constitute freedom of speech and point out the persistent attempts being made to restrict these hard-won liberties.

## Society's Crucial Freedoms

Democratic society is built on four basic freedoms:

- Freedom of speech
- Freedom of the press
- Freedom of assembly
- Freedom of petition

Upon these freedoms rest freedom of religious expression, of political choice, and of communication of information and ideas. The history of journalism and the mass media begins with the story of the long struggle of people for these freedoms. In a society without them, the magic of print and electronic technology means little because these tools are not used to improve the fundamental conditions on which a life of personal liberty depends.

A society possessing and using these freedoms will advance and change. Very naturally, then, the freedoms will come under attack from those opposed to any change that might diminish their power or position in society. The closed mind sees the press as a dangerous weapon. Conditions in North Korea provide a good example. The government enforces rigid control and severely restricts contacts by its citizens with the noncommunist world. The country's economy is stagnating; its intellectual growth is stifled.

From the moment Gutenberg introduced movable type to the Western world in Germany, the printing press began to revolutionize people's ability to communicate information and ideas. Simultaneously, however, those in power erected barriers against its use to influence public opinion. In the English-speaking world, printers and writers struggled until 1700 to win the mere *right to print*. They fought for another century to protect that liberty and to win a second basic right: the *right to criticize*. Addition of a third right—the *right to report*—has come equally slowly and with less success.

As today's journalists and broadcasters know, these rights are never safe from official and sometimes judicial attack.

How fragile the free press concept is became apparent during the 1970s when, for the first time in the history of the American republic, the government imposed a temporary *prior restraint* on publication of a news story—once in the influential New York *Times* and again in the obscure *Progressive* magazine. Both stories were eventually published, but the future of press freedom was left undetermined, as it always has been in the duel between the people's press and the people's governors. (See Issue 4.)

**Prior restraint**
Action by government to prevent publication, as by licensing or censorship

## Two Press Theories

The social and political environments of the past five centuries have produced two contrary theories of the press—the *authoritarian* theory and the *libertarian* theory.

### Authoritarian Theory.
The controlled society of the Renaissance era, into which the printing press was introduced, functioned from the top down; a small and presumably wise ruling class decided what all of society should know and believe. This authoritarian concept of the relationship between citizens and the state could brook no challenge from those who thought the rulers were reflecting error, not truth. A license to publish was given only to selected printers who supported the rulers and the existing social and political structure. The authoritarian press theory still exists today in some parts of the world where similar controlled societies are dominated by small ruling classes.

**Authoritarian theory**
Assumption that a ruling class should determine what others read, hear, and know

### Libertarian Theory.
This second basic theory developed as the Western world advanced into the democratic modern era. Its roots extend back into the seventeenth century, but it did not become dominant in the English-speaking world until the nineteenth century. In libertarian theory the press does not speak for an elite ruling class. The mass of people are presumed able to discern between truth and falsehood themselves, and, having been exposed to a free press, will themselves help determine public policy. It is essential that minorities as well as majorities, the politically weak as well as the politically strong, have free access to public expression in the press of a libertarian society.

**Libertarian theory**
Free access by all segments of society to a free marketplace of ideas

In the battle against authoritarianism, the printer gradually became an ally of thinkers and writers who struggled for religious, political, and intellectual freedom and of the rising commercially based middle class that demanded economic freedom and political power in its contest with feudalism. Slowly the journalist developed dual functions: the opinion function and the news function. The journalist's media were the printed broadside and the pamphlet before the development of regularly issued newspapers in an established format. Such newspapers appeared on the European continent after 1609, in England after 1622, and in the American colonies after 1704. Their influence can be measured by the amount of effort expended by those in authority to erect barriers against them.

## Eloquent Explanations

The libertarian arguments for freedom of expression are stated eloquently in the writings of John Milton in 1644 and those of Thomas Jefferson more than a century later.

In his *Areopagitica* Milton argued against repression of freedom of expression by advocating reliance on truth: "Let her and Falsehood grapple: who ever knew Truth put to the worse in a free and open encounter?" Those who are afraid of truth will of course seek to prevent its entrance into the free marketplace of thought, but those who believe in the public's liberty should realize that its existence depends on freedom of the press.

Jefferson in 1787 put it well in a letter to his friend Carrington:

I am persuaded that the good sense of the people will always be found to be the best army. They may be led astray for a moment, but will soon correct themselves. The people are the only censors of their governors; and even their errors will tend to keep these to the true principles of their institution. To punish these errors too severely would be to suppress the only safeguard of the public liberty. The way to prevent these irregular interpositions of the people, is to give them full information of their affairs through the channel of the public papers, and to contrive that those papers should penetrate the whole mass of the people. The basis of our government being the opinion of the people, the very first object should be to keep that right; and were it left to me to decide whether we should have a government without newspapers, or newspapers without a government, I should not hesitate a moment to prefer the latter.

Jefferson qualified his final statement, however, by adding: "But I should mean that every man should receive those papers, and be capable of reading them." Jefferson used the word "reading" because the problem of literacy still was a major one in his day; he also meant "understanding" in the sense of intellectual literacy. In these words of Milton and Jefferson are found the libertarian arguments for freedom of printing and other forms of communication, for freedom to criticize, and for freedom to report.

There is both a public and journalistic responsibility to support the libertarian theory that everyone should be able to be freely heard in the press, through a variant concept called the *social responsibility theory* of the press. Today it is no longer economically feasible for most people to start printing or airing their views. Concentration of much of the mass media in the hands of a relatively few owners imposes an obligation on them to be socially responsible, to see that all sides of social and political issues are fairly and fully presented so that the public may decide. The social responsibility theory contends that should the mass media fail in this respect, it may be necessary for some other agency of the public to enforce the marketplace of ideas concept.

## The Right to Print

**Prior Restraint in England.**   William Caxton set up the first press in England in 1476. It was more than two centuries later, in 1694, before the freedom to print without prior restraint became a recognized liberty of the English people and their printer-journalists.

With prior restraint unauthorized printing in itself becomes a crime. Under our modern concept anyone is free to have his or her say, although subject to punishment if what is printed offends society (obscenity, sedition) or harms another individual (libel). Authoritarian government does not grant this much freedom: it wishes to control communication from the start and to select the communicators.

Caxton printed the first books in the English language and otherwise aided in bringing the culture of the Continent to England. He enjoyed royal support and needed subsidizing by the ruling class since his market was limited by illiteracy. He and his successors improved the quality and volume of printing during the next half-century, which saw the rise of the Tudor dynasty. Henry VIII, in his efforts to grasp absolute power, issued a proclamation in 1534 requiring printers to have royal permission before setting up their shops. This was a licensing measure, imposing prior restraint. Except for short periods, the theory of prior restraint remained in effect until 1694. Henry took other measures to control the press, but neither he nor Queen Elizabeth I was able to frighten all the printers and writers into compliance. After 1557 the Stationers Company, an organization of the licensed publishers and dealers, was given power to regulate printing and to search out bootleg jobs that had not been registered with it.

James I and succeeding Stuart kings found that Puritan opposition was increasingly difficult to contain, and the journalists more alert to their opportunities. While opposing the licentiousness of the royal court, the Puritans became increasingly extreme in the other direction. When they eventually took power, they banned dancing, the theater, and music with the exception of hymns. They even outlawed Christmas because they thought it was a pagan celebration. Public interest in the

The shop of William Caxton, who set up the first printing press in England in 1476. Caxton learned printing on the Continent, where it had been a craft since the middle of the fifteenth century. The press was established "at the Sign of the Red Pale" in the abbey of Westminster. Nearly two centuries elapsed, however, before England had a genuine newspaper. (Culver Pictures)

Thirty Years' War in Europe and in other political and economic affairs inevitably brought increased publication. Nathaniel Butter, Thomas Archer, and Nicholas Bourne produced the first regularly issued weekly news book in 1621, containing translated news from European news sheets. Reports of domestic events soon followed.

The 1600s were a century of slow progress toward freedom to print, interrupted by severe reverses. The struggle between the commercial and ruling classes, resulting in the revolution of 1640, gave printers some temporary freedom. But by 1644, John Milton was protesting against new licensing. During his rigid Commonwealth regime following the execution of Charles I in 1649, Oliver Cromwell permitted only a few administration publications. Their censor was none other than Milton. Milton's switch in attitude apparently came at least in part from his strong dislike of the heavy-handed rule of Charles I. During the 1640s Milton was a liberal, even writing a tract in favor of divorce. Shortly after the beheading of Charles, he published a tract defending the right of the people to execute a tyrant. This pleased Cromwell, whom Milton joined as Secretary of Foreign Tongues. That post involved his censorship duties. Today we would call his work pro-government propaganda. Writing in both English and Latin, he denounced Charles I, whose execution had shocked many Englishmen. Restoration of the monarchy under Charles II merely switched the power to license and censor to the royal officials.

When the Stuart royal line was overthrown in the revolution of 1688, the new monarchs William and Mary restored freedom to printers. The forced abdication of pro-Catholic James II and the importation from the Netherlands of William, a Protestant, to be king reduced religious tensions in England. Relaxation of restrictive laws soon followed.

The licensing law finally died permanently in 1694. The theory of prior restraint was dead. The first of the daily newspapers that appeared by the score was the *Daily Courant* in 1702. Among the new publications were the popular "essay" papers edited by Daniel Defoe, Richard Steele and Joseph Addison, and Samuel Johnson, which drew much discussion with their comments on political, literary, and social topics.

Licensing and the theory of prior restraint did not die immediately in the American colonies. The Puritans imported the first press to New England in 1638 to print materials for their schools and Harvard College. Commercial presses followed, and some news broadsides and pamphlets appeared. In 1690 a refugee editor from London, Benjamin Harris, issued the first number of a Boston newspaper, *Publick Occurrences.* His reporting was too frank for the colonial governor because it made the English army look bad. Harris wrote that the army had been forced to postpone an attack on the French because its Indian allies—"miserable savages," he called them—had failed to provide "canoos" for transportation. The Indians said they were too weak from smallpox to do so. The governor and his council ordered that the paper be suppressed and that henceforth nothing could be printed without a license from the governor.

When postmaster John Campbell brought out the first regular weekly paper, the Boston *News-Letter,* in 1704, he voluntarily trotted to the authorities for advance censorship and put "Published by Authority" at the top of his columns. It was not until 1721, when James Franklin began publishing his famed *New-England Courant,* that a colonial editor printed in defiance of authority.

## The First Amendment

Freedom to print became an accepted principle in America. Even before the Constitutional Convention met in Philadelphia in 1787, nine colonies had already provided such constitutional protection. When the convention adopted the U.S. Constitution, it did not include the contents of what later became the Bill of Rights—the first ten amendments—because a majority of the delegates believed that this was essentially an issue for the states.

Today, when some Americans want to restrict the free speech rights of people they disagree with, failing to realize that they would undermine their own freedom by doing so, it is important to understand how the First Amendment was created.

When the Constitution was sent to the 13 colonies for ratification, loud protests arose because it failed to include a list of guaranteed rights. Eight of the 11 new states that initially ratified the Constitution did so with the understanding that Congress would act quickly to create a list of citizens' fundamental rights as a set of amendments.

James Madison led the campaign to bring the Bill of Rights to fruition, and that document reflects his proposals. He believed strongly that a safeguard for press freedom should be included.

# THE
# New-England Courant.

[ Nº 58

From MONDAY September 3. to MONDAY September 10. 1722.

*Quod eſt in corde ſobrii, eſt in ore ebrii.*

*To the Author of the* New-England Courant.

SIR,        [ Nº XII.

IT is no unprofitable tho' unpleaſant Purſuit, diligently to inſpect and conſider the Manners & Converſation of Men, who, inſenſible of the greateſt Enjoyments of humane Life, abandon themſelves to Vice from a falſe Notion of *Pleaſure* and *good Fellowſhip.* A true and natural Repreſentation of any Enormity, is often the beſt Argument againſt it and Means of removing it, when the moſt ſevere Reprehenſions alone, are found ineffectual.

I WOULD in this Letter improve the little Obſervation I have made on the Vice of *Drunkenneſs,* the better to reclaim the *good Fellows* who uſually pay the Devotions of the Evening to *Bacchus.*

I DOUBT not but *moderate Drinking* has been improv'd for the Diffuſion of Knowledge among the ingenious Part of Mankind, who want the Talent of a ready Utterance, in order to diſcover the Conceptions of their Minds in an entertaining and intelligible Manner. 'Tis true, drinking does not *improve* our Faculties, but it enables us to *uſe* them ; and therefore I conclude, that much Study and Experience, and a little Liquor, are of abſolute Neceſſity for ſome Tempers, in order to make them accompliſh'd Orators. *Dic. Ponder* diſcovers an excellent Judgment when he is inſpir'd with a Glaſs or two of *Claret,* but he paſſes for a Fool among thoſe of ſmall Obſervation, who never ſaw him the better for Drink. And here it will not be improper to obſerve, That the moderate Uſe of Liquor, and a well plac'd and well regulated Anger, often produce this ſame Effect ; and ſome who cannot ordinarily talk but in broken Sentences and falſe Grammar, do in the Heat of Paſſion expreſs themſelves with as much Eloquence as Warmth. Hence it it is that my own Sex are generally the moſt eloquent, becauſe the moſt paſſionate. " It has been ſaid in the Praiſe of ſome Men, " ( ſays an ingenious Author, ) that they could talk " whole Hours together upon any thing ; but it " muſt be owned to the Honour of the other Sex, " that there are many among them who can talk " whole Hours together upon Nothing. I have " known a Woman branch out into a long extempo- " re Diſſertation on the Edging of a Petticoat, and " cenſure her Servant for breaking a China Cup, in all " the Figures of Rhetorick. "

BUT after all it muſt be conſider'd, that no Pleaſure can give Satisfaction or prove advantageous to a *reaſonable Mind,* which is not attended with the *Reſtraints of Reaſon.* Enjoyment is not to be found by Exceſs in any ſenſual Gratification ; but on the contrary, the immoderate Cravings of the Voluptuary, are always ſucceeded with Loathing and a palled Appetite. What Pleaſure can the Drunkard have in the Reflection, that, while in his Cups, he retain'd only the Shape of a Man, and acted the Part of a Beaſt ; or that from reaſonable Diſcourſe a few Minutes before, he deſcended to Impertinence and Nonſenſe ?

I CANNOT pretend to account for the different Effects of Liquor on Perſons of different Diſpoſitions, who are guilty of Exceſs in the Uſe of it. 'Tis ſtrange to ſee Men of a regular Converſation become rakiſh and profane when intoxicated with Drink, and yet more ſurprizing to obſerve, that ſome who appear to be the moſt profligate Wretches when ſober, become mighty religious in their Cups, and will then, and at no other Time addreſs their Maker, but when they are deſtitute of Reaſon, and actually affronting him. Some ſhrink in the Wetting, and others ſwell to ſuch an unuſual Bulk in their Imaginations, that they can in an Inſtant underſtand all Arts and Sciences, by the liberal Education of a little vivifying *Punch,* or a ſufficient Quantity of other exhilerating Liquor.

AND as the Effects of Liquor are various, ſo are the Characters given to its Devourers. It argues ſome Shame in the Drunkards themſelves, in that they have invented numberleſs Words and Phraſes to cover their Folly, whoſe proper Sgnifications are harmleſs, or have no Signification at all. They are ſeldom known to be *drunk,* tho they are very often *boozey, cogey, tipſey, fox'd, merry, mellow, fuddl'd, groatable, Confoundedly cut, See two Moons,* are *Among the Philiſtines, In a very good Humour, See the Sun,* or, *The Sun has ſhone upon them ;* they *Clip the King's Engliſh,* are *Almoſt froze, Feavouriſh, In their Altitudes, Pretty well enter'd,* &c. In ſhort, every Day produces ſome new Word or Phraſe which might be added to the Vocabulary of the *Tiplers :* But I have choſe to mention theſe few, becauſe if at any Time a Man of Sobriety and Temperance happens to *cut himſelf confoundedly,* or is *almoſt froze, or feavouriſh,* or accidentally *ſees the Sun,* &c. he may eſcape the Imputation of being *drunk,* when his Misfortune comes to be related.

I am SIR,
*Your Humble Servant,*

SILENCE DOGOOD.

## FOREIGN AFFAIRS.

*Berlin, May 8.* Twelve Pruſſian Batallions are ſent to Mecklenburg, but for what Reaſon is not known. 'Tis ſaid, the Emperor, ſuſpecting the Deſigns of the Czar, will ſecure all the Domains of the Duke of Mecklenburg. His Pruſſian Majeſty, to promote the intended Union of the Reformed and Lutherans in his Dominions, has charged the Miniſters of thoſe two Communions, the leaſt mention in the Pulpits of the religious Differences about ſome abſtruſer Points, particularly the Doctrine of Predeſtination, and to forbear all contumelious Expreſſions againſt one another.

*Hamburg, May 8.* The Imperial Court has order'd the Circles of Lower Saxony, to keep in Rea-

For weeks during 1789 the House of Representatives, and then the Senate, wrestled with the wording of the Bill of Rights. Some of Madison's proposed language was regarded as verbose. After various drafts were debated, the tightly drawn First Amendment of 43 words was approved by Congress. It states:

> Congress shall make no law respecting an establishment of religion, or prohibiting the free exercise thereof, abridging the freedom of speech, or of the press; or the right of the people peaceably to assemble, and to petition the Government for redress of grievances.

The Bill of Rights formally became the first ten amendments to the Constitution on December 15, 1791, after ratification by the required two-thirds of the states.

Under British common law and American judicial interpretation, prior restraint violates press freedom. Suppression of publications in anticipation of wrongful printing, or licensing measures to control those who would publish, cannot be authorized by Congress. In two landmark cases, *Gitlow* v. *People of the State of New York* (1925) and *Near* v. *Minnesota* (1931), the Supreme Court applied the press guarantees of the First Amendment to the states through the due process clause of the Fourteenth Amendment. The written decision in *Near* v. *Minnesota* became bedrock doctrine for all future cases involving prior restraint.

In 1925, the Minnesota legislature passed a public nuisance bill aimed originally at a transitory Duluth scandal sheet. The law allowed a newspaper to be put out of business if a single judge declared it to be "malicious, scandalous or defamatory."

Jay M. Near and Howard Guilford were running the *Saturday Press* in Minneapolis in unprincipled fashion, but they were also crusading against a corrupt mayor and police chief, thereby spoiling the game of bribery played by many citizens. Why not apply the new "gag law" to the obnoxious *Saturday Press*, which author Fred Friendly described as the "Minnesota rag"?

When a judge permanently banned the sheet, nearly everyone applauded, including the city's leading newspapers. They failed to realize that the gag law could also be used to silence them. Chicago *Tribune* publisher Robert R. McCormick saw the danger and took Near's case to the U.S. Supreme Court.

Chief Justice Charles Evans Hughes, reading a five-to-four decision June 1, 1931, to a packed Supreme Court chamber, declared, "It is no longer open to doubt that the liberty of the press and of speech is within the liberty safeguarded by the due process clause of the 14th Amendment from invasion by state action."

The Post Office, with its power to exclude publications from the mails under certain conditions, has given publishers many censorship troubles. Matters came to a head in 1946 after it sought to withdraw use of the second-class mailing rate from *Esquire* magazine on the grounds that the rate was a privilege intended only for those making a "special contribution to the public welfare." *Esquire*, faced with an additional half-million dollars a year in postal bills, appealed to the Supreme Court, which ruled in its favor. The court commented: "But to withdraw the second-class rate from this publication today because its content seemed to one official not good for the public would sanction withdrawal of the second-class rate tomorrow from another periodical whose social or economic views seemed harmful to another official."

**Motion Picture Self-Censorship.**   The motion picture industry instituted its own regulatory code in 1922, as a form of self-censorship, through the Motion Picture Association of America. Even before that date, state and city censorship boards were exercising precensorship functions by viewing and ordering the clipping of films in advance of movie showings, or banning them. Extralegal pressures have been brought by such unofficial groups as the former Legion of Decency. The same informal pressures have affected book publication and book purchases by public libraries and school systems. In addition, book publishers run the risk of having specific volumes barred from the mails as obscene.

Radio and television, like the printed media, are not subject to precensorship. But charges of censorship are often raised against media self-censorship or control of content in anticipation of adverse reaction. The broadcast media are more sensitive on this score because their managers realize that violations of what is considered to be "good taste" might cause difficulties for an individual station with the Federal Communications Commission under broadcasting licensing provisions.

**Licensing of Broadcasting Stations.**   If history has proved licensing to be a dangerous practice inimical to press freedom, why did the American public agree to licensing of radio and television stations? The answer is that by common consent we have recognized that broadcast channels are in the public domain. Congress in 1912 first legislated that the Department of Commerce should issue licenses to private broadcasters and assign them wavelengths so that they would not interfere with government wavelengths. After World War I, the numbers of stations increased rapidly and chaos developed on the airwaves. The radio industry, the National Association of Broadcasters, the Newspaper Association of America, and other groups petitioned the government for relief.

Congress passed the Radio Act of 1927, which established a five-member commission to regulate all forms of radio communication. The government retained control of all channels, granting three-year licenses to broadcasters "in the public interest, convenience, or necessity" to provide "fair, efficient, and equitable service" throughout the country. The Radio Act also banned "obscene, indecent, or profane" language on the air. In a 1995 monograph titled "The Origins of the Ban on 'Obscene, Indecent, or Profane' Language of the Radio Act of 1927," Milagros Rivera-Sanchez states that the act's prohibition "survived the act itself

Under the self-censorship code of the Motion Picture Association of America before World War II, moviemakers were forbidden to show a husband and wife occupying the same bed. This scene from the 1940 film *I Was an Adventuress,* a 20th Century Fox production, shows the permissible sleeping arrangement. (Culver Pictures)

and has evolved into a criminal statute that is currently used to penalize broadcasters that air indecent material."

Federal authority was broadened in 1934 with the establishment of the seven-member Federal Communications Commission to exercise jurisdiction over all telecommunications. The commission could refuse renewal of a license in cases of flagrant disregard of broadcasting responsibility, but the FCC rarely used this power. The law forbade any attempt at censorship by the commission—no station could be directed to put a particular program on or off the air. Government rules for cable TV differ from those for broadcast television. (See Chapter 11.)

American radio and television have widely broadcast the opinion programs of individual commentators. But they were long reluctant to broadcast opinion as that of the station itself. The FCC in 1941 issued a ruling that "the broadcaster cannot be advocate"; then in 1949 the commission decided that stations could "editorialize with fairness" and urged them to do so. Many broadcasters felt they did not have the trained staffs to do effective editorializing or did not wish to identify the station management as an advocate in controversial situations. Today numerous stations, especially in metropolitan areas, broadcast editorial opinions.

## The Right to Criticize

**Seditious Libel.** Winning the liberty to print without prior restraint did not free the press from the heavy hand of government. In eighteenth-century England, and in the American colonies, the laws of seditious libel ran counter to the philosophical theory that the press should act as

## THE PROBLEM OF POLITICAL CORRECTNESS

In today's contentious, hypersensitive society, "political correctness" has created a form of pressure that inhibits freedom of expression. This pressure is cultural, not legal. It seeks to make everyone conform to the views of the protesting groups, no matter how flimsy the issue.

Some protests against printed and broadcast statements have a valid goal—to point out and eliminate stereotypes about individuals and groups imbedded in the public's perception. At times, however, the protesters become extreme. Some people react angrily to trivial incidents, misinterpret innocently intended statements as insults, and denounce valid criticism as unfair and demeaning.

The mass media are frequently subjected to condemnation by those who perceive racial, religious, sexist, anti-gay, and anti-elderly bias in news stories, columns, editorials, and cartoons. The abundance of complaints from many sources sometimes causes newspapers and broadcasters to avoid discussing certain topics or to apologize publicly for an item that draws complaints.

The late New York *Newsday*, for example, apologized in print for a cartoon by Doug Marlette about the Pope's opposition to female priests, after many complaints from Catholics. In a response to his newspaper's apology, Marlette wrote, "It is always bad news when a newspaper apologizes for expressing an opinion—bad news for the First Amendment, bad news for journalism and bad news for readers."

The best editors try diligently to delete biased material from their publications and broadcasts, make careful judgments between the valid and the insignificant, and stand by their decisions.

"censor of the government." To the authoritarian mind, the mere act of criticism of officials was in itself a crime, and "the greater the truth, the greater the libel" was an established tenet. This meant that publishing a story about a corrupt official was all the more seditious if the official indeed was corrupt.

When charged with sedition or criminal libel, the journalist's problem was to win acceptance of truth as a defense. The mere fact of publication, then, would not be sufficient to determine guilt, and the accused printer or editor would be able to present the case in open court, preferably before a jury. Once the principle of truth as a defense could be won, governments would be less likely to press sedition charges, and laws defining what constitutes sedition could be revised.

**The Zenger Case.** The landmark case in what is now the United States was that of John Peter Zenger, who was tried in New York colony in 1735 for seditious libel. Zenger was an immigrant printer who lent the columns of his weekly paper, the *Journal*, to the cause of a political faction opposed to the royal governor. Some of the leading citizens of the colony were aligned with Zenger in the struggle against the governor, whom they accused of various arbitrary actions in the *Journal*'s columns. Zenger was jailed and brought to trial in a hostile court. At this juncture a remarkable 80-year-old lawyer from Philadelphia, Andrew Hamilton, entered the case as Zenger's attorney.

The crown prosecutor reviewed the laws of seditious libel and argued that since Zenger had admitted publishing the newspaper issues in question, the trial was as good as over. His aged opponent skillfully jousted with the presiding justice and the prosecutor and insisted that truth should be permitted to be offered as a defense, with the jury to decide on the truth of Zenger's publications. These arguments were denied by the court, but Hamilton ignored the ruling and delivered a stirring oration to the jury. He ended with a plea for the jury to take matters into its own hands: "The question before the court . . . is not just the cause of the poor printer. . . . No! It may in its consequence affect every freeman . . . on the main of America. It is the best cause; it is the cause of Liberty . . . the liberty both of exposing and opposing arbitrary power . . . by speaking and writing Truth."

Zenger was acquitted, and the court did not challenge the jury's verdict, even though it ignored existing law. A similar court victory on the issue of admission of truth as evidence was not won in England itself until the 1770s. The threat of trials for seditious libel remained until the end of the century, although in the colonies no further court trials of editors were held. Some editors were harassed by governors and their privy councils, but in general the colonial press was free to criticize the English authorities and to promote the cause of American independence (the reverse was not true, however, and Tory editors were suppressed by colonial radicals). In the early 1770s, such papers as the Boston *Gazette* fanned the fires of revolution.

**Jefferson and Hamilton.**   After the revolution, sharp differences arose along political and economic lines in the new nation. The newspapers continued to take pronounced partisan stands. Two political factions, the Federalists headed by Alexander Hamilton and the Republicans headed by Thomas Jefferson, split on many issues. Most of the weeklies and the few dailies that had started after 1783, published in seaboard towns for the commercial classes, tended to be Federalist in sympathy. Hamilton sponsored the New York *Evening Post*, and William Cobbett in the *Porcubine Gazette* was an especially vehement partisan critic.

Jefferson countered with Philip Freneau's *National Gazette;* Jefferson's other republican supporters included William Duane and the vituperative Benjamin Franklin Bache, grandson of Benjamin Franklin, at the *Aurora*. When war with France seemed imminent in 1798, the Federalists cracked down on their tormentors.

The Alien and Sedition Acts they passed in 1798 were aimed at deportation of undesirable aliens and at curbing criticism of the government. Undesirable aliens in Federalist eyes were those who supported Vice-President Jefferson; some were deported and others were harassed. Jefferson opposed war with France, favored as little government as possible, and was more sympathetic to refugees from autocratic regimes in Europe than the Federalists were. The Sedition Act by its terms restricted prosecutions to those who "write, utter, or publish . . . false, scandalous and malicious writing" against the federal government, its officials and legislators, or its laws (including the Sedition Act itself). It provided for admission of truth as a defense. In theory, only false criticism was to be punished; but in practice, Federalist politicians and judges set out to punish anti-Federalist editors. One, for example, was jailed and fined for printing a letter to the editor that accused President John Adams of "ridiculous pomp, foolish adulation, and selfish avarice."

Concerned about his personal safety in such an inflamed, retaliatory political atmosphere, Jefferson withdrew to his Monticello estate. Soon, however, federal excesses in administering the Alien and Sedition Acts contributed to a popular revulsion and to Jefferson's election as president in 1800. The dangerous Alien and Sedition Acts expired the same year. Jefferson insisted that his administration permit partisan journalism "to demonstrate the falsehood of the pretext that freedom of the press is incompatible with orderly government." He urged that individuals protect themselves against journalistic excesses by filing civil suits for libel. The calm course Jefferson took was vindicated when his party retained control of the government for a generation. Soon after 1800, the libertarian theory of the press had eclipsed the authoritarian theory by common consent.

**Wartime Restrictions.**   During wartime, national safety requirements and public emotion bring some restriction of criticism. The Civil War saw suppression of a few newspapers in the North, but considering the violence of many editors' criticisms, retaliation by Lincoln and his generals was almost negligible. During World War I, the Espionage Act of 1917 widened the authority of the Post Office to bar periodicals from the mails, and the Sedition Act of 1918 made it a crime to write or publish "any disloyal, profane, scurrilous or abusive language" about the federal government. The axe fell heavily on German-language newspapers—in many cases unfairly. It also fell on socialist and pacifist publications because they opposed the war. Max Eastman's brilliant magazine, *The Masses*, was barred from the mails, as were two leading socialist dailies, the New York *Call* and the Milwaukee *Leader*. Socialist party leader Eugene Debs went to prison for criticizing America's allies as "out for plunder." Clearly the theory of liberty to criticize was disregarded in these violations of minority opinion rights. During World War II, only pro-Nazi and Fascist publications were banned—and they had few friends to plead their cause. But the black press was harassed by J. Edgar Hoover's FBI for complaining about racial discrimination in the armed forces.

Out of prosecutions for political expression arose what became known as the "clear-and-present-danger" theory to determine protection of freedom of speech and press. It was advanced by Justices Oliver Wendell Holmes and Louis Brandeis in four landmark case decisions made between 1919 and 1927. In *Schenck* v. *U.S.*, the court upheld the conviction of Socialist party members who distributed antiwar leaflets urging repeal of the draft law. Holmes wrote: "The question in every case is whether the words used, are used in such circumstances and are of such a nature as to create a clear and present danger that they will bring about the substantive evils that Congress has a right to prevent. It is a question of proximity and degree."

In *Abrams* v. *U.S.*, the court's conservative majority applied this clear-and-present-danger rule to uphold the conviction of five New York radicals whose pamphlets condemned American troop intervention in Russia's revolution and urged a general strike. Holmes and Brandeis dissented, Holmes using the phrase "immediately dangerous" in an effort to prevent such use of his theory as a two-edged sword. In the cases of Benjamin Gitlow, convicted of criminal anarchy under New York law for issuing socialist manifestos, and of Anita Whitney, convicted under a California law outlawing the Communist party, the two liberal justices forcefully restated the clear-and-present-danger theory. Its negative use to curtail free speech and expression prevailed again during the anticommunist tensions of the McCarthy era in the 1951 case of Eugene Dennis, convicted under the Smith Act banning the Communist party. But in many other cases the clear-and-present-danger theory fended off conspiracy and criminal sedition charges involving free speech and press for minority political beliefs.

## The Right to Report

**Developing a Philosophical Concept.**   The right to report is not nearly as much a right safeguarded by law and legal precedent as the right to print and the right to criticize. Rather, it is based on a philosophical argument. What would be gained through the right to print and to criticize if no news were forthcoming? What good would a free press be for the reader if editors and reporters had no way to find out what government was doing? Denial of the right of access to news is a denial of the people's right to know, the journalist maintains.

Yet, no person can be compelled to talk to a reporter; no government official need grant an interview or hold a press conference; courts and legislatures admit the press through historical tradition and have the power to eject the press (unless specific statutes have been passed requiring open legislative sessions). There is another side to the coin: No

Expressions of opinion in print frequently draw complaints from offended groups. This cartoon in the St. Petersburg *Times* supported a measure requiring stricter building standards for mobile homes, opposed by the building industry. Dozens of elderly mobile home residents cancelled their subscriptions because they thought cartoonist Clay Bennett was calling them pigs. (Clay Bennett/St. Petersburg *Times*)

newspaper can be compelled to print any material it does not wish to use, including paid advertising.

When the laws of seditious libel were in vogue, no right to report was recognized. The mere reporting of a government official's action, or of a debate in Parliament, was likely to be construed as seditious (unfavorable) by some person in authority. William Bradford in Pennsylvania, James Franklin in Massachusetts, and other colonial editors were hauled before authorities for reporting a disputed action of government. In England reporting of the proceedings of Parliament was banned until 1771, when the satirical writings of Dr. Samuel Johnson and the open defiance of newspaper publisher John Wilkes crumpled the opposition.

The House of Representatives of the American Congress opened its doors to reporters in 1789, two days after it was organized as a legislative body. The Senate, however, excluded reporters until 1795. Congress came to depend on journalists, particularly the editors of the Jeffersonian party organ, the *National Intelligencer*, to publish a record of debates and proceedings. Not until 1834 did the government publish its own records.

**Today's Restrictions.**    Today there is little likelihood that Washington correspondents will be denied access to the congressional press galleries, except when the legislators are meeting in emergency executive session (a rare event). But reporters are admitted to sessions of legislative committees only with the consent of the committee chairperson and members. Some 40 percent of congressional committee sessions are closed to the press. The situation in state capitals is similar. Television and radio reporters and photographers have won access to legislative sessions only by persistent effort, and their ability to use all their equipment is often circumscribed.

Reporters similarly are admitted to court sessions only by the agreement of the presiding judge. They may be excluded with other members of the public, if the court deems it necessary. Juvenile courts, for example, operate without reportorial coverage in most cases. Ordinarily reporters are free to attend court sessions, since public trials are the rule, but they have no automatic right of attendance. Photographers and television-radio reporters have had only limited success in covering trials with cameras or microphones, due to restrictions applied to them by Section 35 of the Canons of Judicial Ethics of the American Bar Association (ABA). A long campaign by news organizations to persuade the bar association to revise its Canon 35 failed when that group reaffirmed its stand in 1963. In 1972 the association replaced Canon 35 with Canon 3A7, equally as restrictive, and the impasse continued until 1982, when the ABA relented.

Forty-seven states permit cameras in their courtrooms under controlled conditions. The Court TV cable network airs long portions of significant trials in progress. During the O. J. Simpson murder trial, a single Court TV camera served as a pool camera, delivering a continuous live picture of trial proceedings to all networks and stations requesting it. The camera was aimed carefully to avoid showing the identity of the jurors. Cameras still are forbidden in federal courts. (See Issue 5.)

**Qualified Privilege.**    An important doctrine that has emerged is that of *qualified privilege*. This doctrine protects a news medium from the threat of libel suits when reporting the actions of a legislative body or a court, provided its report is accurate and fair. This doctrine carries with it the implication that the media have an obligation to report legislative and judicial sessions so that the public may know what government and courts are doing. Defamatory statements made in legislative sessions and courts may therefore be reported without fear of damage suits.

The right to report is denied more often at the grassroots level of government than at the national level, insofar as legislative bodies are concerned. Boards of education, water commissions, city councils,

**Qualified privilege**
Legal protection that enables journalists to report fairly and accurately court, legislative, and other public proceedings without incurring risk of a libel suit

county boards, and other similar groups often seek to meet in private and conduct the public's business in virtual secrecy. Passage of "open meeting" laws somewhat improved the access to news at the local level. These laws provide that actions taken in closed sessions are invalid; they do not force a reluctant legislative group to open the doors wide. By 1975, virtually all states had some form of open meeting law as well as laws guaranteeing the opening of public records to reporters needing access to them.

Perhaps the most publicized denial of access to news has been in the national executive departments. This trend—stemming from the necessity for secrecy in limited areas of the national defense establishment and atomic energy research—has alarmed responsible journalists. The American Society of Newspaper Editors and the Society of Professional Journalists have well-organized campaigns demanding free access to news so that people may know the facts necessary to make intelligent decisions.

**Freedom of Information Act.**   A House committee headed by Representative John Moss of California, appointed in 1965 to study governmental information policies, focused attention on numerous abuses and brought some relief from excessive secrecy. Its efforts at reform led to passage of the Freedom of Information Act in 1966. The act was strengthened in 1974.

Under this law, reporters and ordinary citizens may submit requests for specific information. The FOI access can be slow and strewn with obstacles, but many significant news stories revealing government blunders, social trends, and personal misconduct have resulted from its use. (See Issue 5.)

The self-protective instinct of all bureaucracies remains an obstacle to reporting, even when their leaders promise greater access to information. The Reporters Committee for Freedom of the Press, a watchdog organization in Washington, heavily criticized the secrecy enforced by the Reagan and Bush administrations. It found improvement in the early portion of the Clinton administration but still reported numerous incidents of secrecy it deemed unwarranted.

## Points to Remember

1. What are the four basic freedoms of a democracy?
2. What are the two basic theories of the press?
3. How did the practice of prior restraint affect publication of news in England and the American colonies?
4. Why does the U.S. government license radio and television stations, when newspapers are not licensed?
5. What important legal principle was upheld by the acquittal of John Peter Zenger?
6. How does the doctrine of qualified privilege help the media cover the news?

## Media Questions to Think About

1. In a famous opinion, U.S. Supreme Court Justice Oliver Wendell Holmes, Jr. wrote: "The most stringent protection of free speech would not protect a man in falsely shouting fire in a crowded theater and causing panic." How do you relate this statement to the guarantee of free speech in the First Amendment?

2. How would your life be different if you obtained all your news from a single government source?

3. What recent news stories do you think might have been concealed from you if our government had the right of prior restraint?

# CHAPTER FOUR
## Audience Research:
## Concepts and Applications

## Swimsuits for Miss America?

Americans probably are more surveyed and polled than any other society. They are questioned about everything from their belief that flying saucers probably exist (47 percent said yes in one poll) to whether Miss America contestants should continue to appear in swimsuits (78 percent said yes).

Some polls are self-serving, with questions worded to draw answers favorable to their sponsors. Others are frivolous. Most polls and surveys, however, concern serious political or social issues and are taken objectively by professional polling organizations. Their purpose is to identify public attitudes and clarify public policy options.

A typical poll published by *U.S. News and World Report,* July 10, 1995, sought to learn how many Americans were alienated from their government and institutions.

The questions were designed to identify the percentages of voters who said that the following groups and the work they do conflicted with their own goals and those of their families. The findings: News media, 50 percent; prime-time TV entertainment, 49; welfare recipients, 49; lawyers, 45; talk-show hosts, 41; large corporations, 40; National Rifle Association, 38; elected officials, 36; and gun owners, 36.

**A**s has been made clear earlier in this book, media managers and researchers recognize that the mass public really consists of a collection of small audiences, each with special characteristics and interests. These are called *target audiences*.

How to identify and reach these audiences in order to inform, entertain, and persuade them requires intensive research. No target audience is an island unto itself. It shares some characteristics with other audiences. In certain circumstances, such as interest in a huge natural disaster, virtually all these segmented audiences share an equal interest, a common human concern that overrides the specialized concerns of each group.

Media research can be divided roughly into two kinds: *theory*, which seeks to identify the concepts underlying the communication process, and *application*, the methods used to make such everyday decisions as how to design a television program or how to select special-interest sections for inclusion in a Sunday newspaper.

We look first at communication concepts, then at ways they are used in daily practice.

## What Communication Means

Each of us communicates with another person by directing a message to one or more of the person's senses—sight, sound, touch, taste, or smell. This is known as *interpersonal communication*, in contrast to *intrapersonal communication*, in which one "talks to oneself." When we smile, we communicate a desire for friendliness; the tone in which we say "good morning" can indicate feelings all the way from surliness to warm pleasure; and the words we choose in speaking or writing convey a message we want to "put across" to the other person. The more effectively we select and deliver these words, the better the communication.

In today's complex society, one-to-one communication frequently is inadequate. To be effective, our important messages must reach numerous people at one time. The next step is *group communication*, such as when a homeowner couple invite their neighbors for coffee in order to propose a neighborhood improvement plan. If the sponsoring couple convinces a local television news program to air a story about the project, thousands of people learn about it. This is *mass communication*.

The success of the message, in all phases of communication, depends on the *frame of reference*—that is, the life experience and mind-set of both the sender and receiver of the message. The more these frames of reference overlap, the more likely there will be understanding and possible acceptance of the message. One-to-one communication has heavy overlap when people are close friends or agree wholeheartedly on the subject of interpersonal discussion. As the size of the receiving audience grows, these attributes decline. So does the degree of interpersonal success.

For example, a news story about plans by Congress to increase unemployment benefits raises hope in the mind of a person who fears being

**Communication**
Act of transmitting information, ideas, and attitudes from one person to another

**Interpersonal communication**
Transmission of information, ideas, and attitudes to one or more of an individual's senses of sight, sound, touch, taste, or smell

**Intrapersonal communication**
Communication process that takes place within an individual

**Mass communication**
Process of delivering information, ideas, and attitudes to a sizeable, diversified audience through use of media designed for that purpose

**Frame of reference**
A person's knowledge, based on his or her own life experience

laid off a job; the same dispatch may disturb a struggling entrepreneur who sees in it the possibility of higher taxes.

Similarly, when a presidential candidate appears on a national TV talk show he reaches millions of voters, vastly more than he could through handshaking tours. His use of mass communication may be a comparative failure, however, if he is unable to project over the air the same feeling of sincerity and ability that he displays through a handshake and a smile in personal contacts.

The art of mass communication, then, is much more difficult than that of face-to-face discussion. The communicator who is addressing thousands of different personalities simultaneously cannot adjust an appeal to meet their individual reactions. An approach that convinces one part of the audience may alienate another part. The successful mass communicator is one who finds the right method of expression to establish empathy with the largest possible number of individuals in the audience. Psychological research and knowledge of communication theory help the speaker to "push the right buttons."

## The Language of Research

Researchers identify four basic elements in the communication process. To be precise in their findings, they use specialized terms to describe them. These elements are:

The *communicator*, called the *encoder*.

The *message*. The words, pictures, or sounds comprising the message are called *codes* or *symbols*.

The *channel*. In mass communication, this is one of the media, such as newspapers, magazines, radio, or television.

The *audience*. A person in the audience is known as a *decoder*.

The communicator understands the characteristics of the channel to be used and studies the varying comprehension levels of the groups of people comprising the total audience. The message is molded to the requirements of each channel—pictures on television against only words on radio, for example—and to the characteristics of the audience being sought.

Figure 4.1 presents the widely used HUB model of mass communication, visualizing the process as a circular, ongoing progression. Its set of concentric circles forms a pool into which the familiar pebble (communication content) is dropped, sending ripples outward as the message progresses toward the audience.

Before a message enters our mass communication system, it must be approved by someone of authority within the medium. These men and women, known to researchers as *gatekeepers*, include the responsible editor on a newspaper or magazine staff, the news editor of a radio or television station, and an advertising director or the equivalent for commercial

**Figure 4.1**

The HUB model of mass communication. (*Source:* From *Mass Media IV* by Ray Eldon Hiebert, Donald F. Ungurall, and Thomas W. Bohn, p. 25. Copyright © by Longman Inc.)

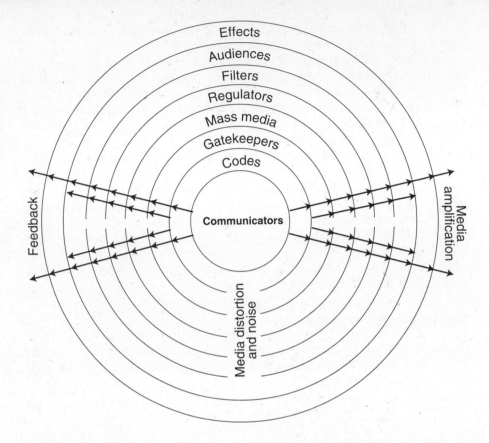

messages. These people judge the messages for public interest, effectiveness, taste, and legality. Since more candidates for publication exist than limited newspaper space and air time can absorb, news stories and entertainment offerings must be weighed against others in the same category—certainly not an exact science. The lack of such gatekeepers in most computer communication services, such as online databases and the Internet, differentiates them from traditional mass media.

Exerting pressure on the gatekeepers, in attempts to influence their decisions as to what will or won't be published, are organizations and individuals known to researchers as *regulators*. These include public pressure groups, government agencies, advertisers, consumers, courts, and legislatures. Such pressures, sometimes applied publicly and sometimes behind the scenes, do affect media content and performance.

## Disruptive Forces

Ideally, the communicator's message reaches the recipient's mind in the exact form the sender intended. Several physical and mental barriers, however, may distort the process. Researchers call them *filters*. The major ones include:

1. *Stored experience.* This consists in part of personal, ego-related beliefs and values and in part of those held by groups to which the individual belongs. A message that challenges those beliefs and values may be rejected, distorted, or misinterpreted. Conversely, an individual whose beliefs on a given subject are under pressure, such as traditional loyalty to a political party during an election, may strain unduly to find messages giving reassurance.

2. *Dissonance.* This occurs when the recipient takes an action that is inconsistent with what he or she knows or has previously believed. The person becomes uncomfortable and seeks messages that provide reassurance and reduce the dissonance. An example is the manner in which a person who has switched from longtime ownership of one automobile brand to another keeps reading advertisements for the newly adopted brand after completing the purchase.

3. *Channel noise.* Literally, this is anything that interferes with the fidelity of the physical transmission of a message, such as radio static or very small type. More broadly, the term is used for all distractions between source and audience (Figure 4.2). One way to counteract such distractions is the use of *redundancy;* that is, repetition of a key portion of the message, the way a radio announcer repeats a telephone number several times during a commercial.

A person's accent, for example, can cause channel noise. Chi Chi Rodriguez, the jovial Puerto Rican professional golfer, told an audience, "I told the caddy I wanted a sand wedge, and he brought me a ham on rye."

4. *Semantic noise.* Researchers use this term to describe situations in which a message is misunderstood even though it is received exactly as transmitted (Figure 4.3). A communicator may use words the recipient does not understand, or words that have one meaning to the communicator and another to the recipient.

**Stored experience**
Knowledge based on what one has observed, encountered, or undergone

**Dissonance**
Discomfort experienced by a message recipient because it conflicts with that person's experience or attitudes

## Feedback

Knowing how recipients respond to a message and what actions they take as a result is vital to successful communication (Figure 4.4). Media managers diligently seek feedback, because they know that their publications or broadcasts will be successful and survive only if they develop a sense of satisfaction among a substantial segment of the public.

Feedback is much more discernible in face-to-face communication than in mass communication, of course, but the mass communicator who

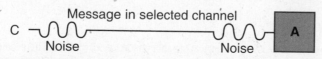

**Figure 4.2**

The communication process: Communicator (C) places message in selected channel to reach audience (A) but is subject to "noise" interferences.

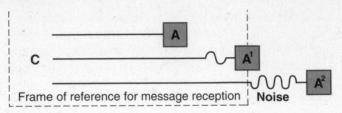

**Figure 4.3**

Communicator and audience member A have the same frame of reference; $A^1$ is only partially receptive; $A^2$ is unable to understand.

**Feedback effects**
Responses of recipient that shape and alter subsequent messages

seeks feedback reactions can learn much about the effectiveness of the message and ways to shape future messages.

Feedback from an audience is obtained in two basic ways: submitted voluntarily by audience members, or solicited in some manner by the message originator. Among the voluntary methods are letters and fax messages to the editor—messages either intended for publication or sent privately to influence the editor in the future; personal calls to an executive of the publishing source; and complaints or praise uttered in a public meeting being covered by the media. Broadcasters obtain voluntary feedback in the same manner. Newspapers providing audiotex service get valuable feedback on audience interests by checking the types of information the telephone callers request (see Chapter 5).

Numerous forms of inquiry are used to solicit feedback. Broadcasters depend heavily on reports from the audience rating services. Print publishers, as well as broadcasters, use polls and questionnaires conducted by telephone, mail, or in person; invited discussion groups (focus groups); coupons and write-in contests; and copy-testing. These methods are described later in this chapter.

Some methods are as simple as bluntly asking, "How are we doing?" Others are phrased with considerable subtlety. Media managements

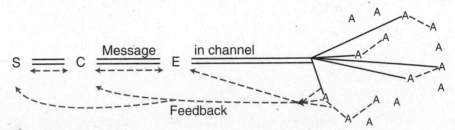

**Figure 4.4**

Mass communication for a given message at one moment in time is illustrated here: Source (S) has the message reported by communicator (C) in channel controlled by editor (E); some audience members (A) receive the message directly, but some are inattentive; feedback interactions may occur along the communication route.

need to weigh feedback carefully before reacting to it, considering its source, force, and volume. Ten vehement complaint letters about a controversial newspaper editorial from a circulation of 100,000 should not cause a newspaper editor to retreat from a position.

## Communication: How Much Effect?

For more than half a century, researchers and social scientists have sought to determine how public opinion is formed and how much influence the mass media have in that process. To what degree can the media change audience attitudes and move people to action? The answers to such questions are equally significant to political leaders advocating government programs; manufacturers promoting new products; and social agencies working to improve public well-being.

While presenting differing theories, researchers as a group agree that the mass media do affect public attitudes and behavior, minimally in some circumstances and strongly in others. A well-known episode demonstrates the potential power of media influence over public behavior.

On the night of October 30, 1938, actor Orson Welles and the CBS radio theater group broadcast a terrifying and realistic report of an invasion from Mars taking place near Princeton, New Jersey. Conventional radio news bulletin devices convinced thousands of citizens that giant mechanized monsters were roaming the countryside, and people fled in panic without waiting to hear that the report was only an adaptation of H. G. Wells's novel *War of the Worlds*.

Wilbur Schramm, a distinguished communication research scholar, cites the Orson Welles hoax as an obvious communication effect, saying that many people were emotionally aroused and that some of them abruptly changed their behavior in a way that could never have been predicted before the broadcast. It should be pointed out that this unintentional result was achieved only with words and sound effects, because television had not yet entered American homes.

## "Pictures in Our Heads"

In 1921 Walter Lippmann, eminent political columnist and author in the mid-twentieth century, wrote a brief book, *Public Opinion*. The opening chapter was called "The World Outside and Pictures in Our Heads." This phrase, still frequently quoted, catches the essence of public opinion formation.

"The world we have to deal with politically is out of reach, out of sight, out of mind," Lippmann wrote. "It has to be explored, reported, and imagined." He added that each person gradually makes for "himself a trustworthy picture inside his head of the world beyond his reach." The pictures in the minds of citizens collectively, he said, constitute public opinion. Fragmented, distorted, and subject to preconceptions and prejudices, these mental pictures often mislead people in their dealings with the

Front page of the New York *Daily News* reports the fear created nationwide in 1938 when Orson Welles presented a dramatized adaptation of the H. G. Wells novel *War of the Worlds* in a network radio broadcast. (New York *Daily News* photo)

# FAKE RADIO 'WAR' STIRS TERROR THROUGH U.S.

Story on Page 2

**"War" Victim**
Caroline Cantlon, WPA actress, listening to this radio in West 19th St., heard announcement of "smoke in Times Square." Running to street, she fell, broke her arm.

**"I Didn't Know"** Orson Welles, after broadcast expresses amazement at public reaction. He adapted H. G. Wells' "War of the Worlds" for radio and played principal role. Left: a machine conceived for another H. G. Wells story. Dramatic description of landing of weird "machine from Mars" started last night's panic.        —Story on page 2.

outside world. Lippmann wrote about the "trickle of messages from the outside" that reaches each individual's mind. Today, of course, that trickle has grown into a heavy stream since the arrival of television, satellite transmission, and other mass media technologies. Yet the messages are every bit as subject to distortion as they were when he wrote his landmark book.

Another distinguished leader in communication research study, Harold D. Lasswell of Yale University, focused the work of many scholars and students when he posed the provocative query, "Who says what, in which channel, to whom, with what effect?" As they study the operation and influence of the mass media today, students can learn much by using that question as a basis for analysis.

## Agenda-Setting

As stated earlier, the gatekeepers of the media have great power over what their audiences learn—more power, perhaps, than many of them realize. In the editorial offices of newspapers, magazines, and broadcasting stations, men and women who fill this role make many decisions every day, often under severe time pressure with limited print space and air time available, and at times without having all the facts at their disposal. Sometimes, critics contend, they release to their audiences a version of events that is either too narrow, or overblown and unbalanced.

These gatekeepers are engaged in what research scholars call *agenda-setting*. That is, the information and entertainment they distribute become the basis for public discussion, decisions, and attitudes. If the gatekeepers release abnormally large amounts of material on one subject, that subject tends to dominate public discussion. Bernard C. Cohen, a political scientist, in his book *The Press and Foreign Policy*, makes the significant point that "the press may not be successful much of the time in telling the public what to think, but it is stunningly successful in telling its readers what to think *about*." After a detailed study, two media scholars, Maxwell E. McCombs and Donald L. Shaw, concluded that media emphasis on an event influences the audience to view that event as important.

Further agenda-setting studies have developed evidence that the press selects certain issues to play up at times when these issues are not significant in the public mind; the issues then become part of the accepted agenda. For example, when the mainstream press focused heavily during the 1992 presidential campaign on an unsubstantiated supermarket tabloid story alleging sexual misconduct by Bill Clinton, the future president was forced for days to concentrate his campaign appearances on denying the charge. Temporarily he almost had to abandon discussion of major national issues.

## Application

Audience research also involves a second phase, beyond basic knowledge of communication theory—application of that knowledge to the daily life of the media. Operators of all media outlets desire to know the size and characteristics of their audiences, so they can serve them better and enlarge them. Good research can be reflected directly in larger profits.

Determining the total size of many media audiences is relatively easy. Newspaper, magazine, and book publishers know how many copies they

**Gatekeepers**
Editors and reporters who decide which material from the mass of information they control will be distributed to readers, listeners, and viewers

**Agenda-setting**
Ability of the media to influence the salience of events in the public mind, shaping awareness and action

Television network news editors prepare a broadcast. Selection of stories to be used in a newscast or publication is known as "gatekeeping." (Taylor/Sygma)

sell. Motion picture producers have a detailed accounting of tickets sold. For television and radio proprietors, however, the task is more difficult.

Broadcasting stations project their programs into the air, or in the case of cable television by wire into the homes, and do not have a precise check on how many people are watching or listening at any given moment. They obtain their information by subscribing to a rating service.

Researchers who seek to determine the characteristics of an audience and the breakdown of groups within its study its *demographics*. This involves obtaining information about the age, sex, income, racial heritage, household composition, and educational level of people in the audience.

**Demographics** Characteristics of a human population such as size, density, growth, distribution, and vital statistics

Obtaining such demographic information may seem a perplexing task, but experienced researchers can achieve remarkably good results. The 1990 U.S. Census is a treasure trove of such information. The annual *Statistical Abstract of the United States* contains facts on everything from a profile of racial groups to an analysis of the Scholastic Aptitude Test (SAT) scores. Many commercial publications provide valuable information drawn from the 1990 census report and other material produced by the Bureau of the Census.

Here is a simple example of how editors can use demographic information to build readership or viewership. The Census Bureau reports

# TARGET AUDIENCES IDENTIFIED BY THE VALS 2 SYSTEM

The Values and Lifestyles Program 2 divides people into eight groups, determined by their psychological makeup and what SRI International, developer of the program, calls their "resources." These include everything from income and education to intelligence, energy level, health, and eagerness to buy.

*Actualizers*—successful, sophisticated people with abundant resources; concerned with social issues and open to change.

*Fulfilleds*—mature, satisfied, reflective, and comfortable, but willing to consider new ideas and change.

*Achievers*—career-oriented people who value structure and predictability over risk, intimacy, and self-discovery.

*Experiencers*—young, enthusiastic and impulsive, savoring the new, the offbeat, and the risky; avid consumers.

*Believers*—people with a strong sense of principles; conservative consumers, favoring proven brands.

*Strivers*—similar to Achievers, but with fewer resources; deeply concerned about the opinions and approval of others.

*Makers*—action-oriented, like Experiencers, but devoted to self-sufficiency; often found building their own houses, canning vegetables, or working on the car.

*Strugglers*—almost entirely concerned with meeting the urgent needs of the moment.

---

that 26 percent of Hispanic households move every year—much higher than the national average of 18 percent—because they are more likely to rent. Logically, then, Hispanic readers or listeners should be especially interested in stories about trends in rental rates and availability, relations between landlords and tenants, rent controls, and the like.

In the 1970s, SRI International, a research firm based in Menlo Park, California, offered a *psychographic* approach to flesh out the demographic information. Under this Values and Lifestyles Program (VALS), people were divided into two basic categories: *inner-directed*, who take their cues from their own beliefs and values, and *outerdirected*, who look to society to guide their choices. Subgroups such as Belongers and Achievers were identified.

In the late 1980s, a VALS 2 system was developed to include an evaluation of whether consumers can afford the things their psyches motivate them to want. The categories are identified in the box shown on this page.

**Psychographics**
Psychological characteristics, such as lifestyle, of a given group

## Use of Television Ratings

The television rating system (explained in Chapter 10) provides only an approximation of the exact audience size and composition. Rating statistics do not show whether people in a room with a turned-on television

# "E.R." OR "NEW YORK UNDERCOVER"?

Researchers into audience behavior have found that the racial background of viewers makes a striking difference in the television programs they watch.

A study by the BBDO advertising agency during the 1995–1996 season compared prime-time programs selected by the total national TV audience, as reported by the Nielsen rating service, with choices made by the African-American and white segments of that audience. Choices by the African-American segment varied drastically from those by the whites.

Only two of the top 20 shows watched by African-American viewers also rated among the top 20 on the whites' list—"E.R." on NBC and "Monday Night Football" on ABC. "E.R." was first among whites, 20th among African Americans.

The No. 1 choice by African Americans was "New York Undercover," which ranked 122nd in white households. Second choice by African Americans was "Living Single"; third was "The Crew." These two shows tied for 124th among white viewers.

"Seinfeld," the NBC comedy, was the second most popular show among whites and among the total audience, which also included Hispanics, Asian Americans, and Native Americans. Among African Americans it rated 89th.

set are actually watching it. How many viewers logged in on a late night show have fallen asleep? How many husbands and wives are having fiery arguments while a situation comedy drones on unwatched? The advertisers who buy commercial spots in those programs would like to know but cannot.

Despite recognized flaws in the Nielsen and Arbitron rating systems, such as substantial turnover among the small number of viewers whose TV-watching habits are projected to represent the entire TV audience, these ratings are treated as virtual absolutes by the television industry. Efforts are being made to strengthen the rating systems.

Broadcasters are heavily influenced by the ratings as they select programs, because the ratings dictate the potential advertising revenue of a program.

Advertisers buy commercial time in a TV program based on the size and characteristics of its audience. They select programs whose viewers are most likely to purchase the products they advertise. Thus total audience size may be less significant to them than the makeup of the audience. Advertisers for an acne remedy will choose an MTV music channel, not one whose demographics show an audience predominantly above age 50.

The most sought-after age group by general advertisers is the 18-to-49-year category. These viewers are frequent purchasers of goods because many of them have young families and, with financial resources rising as their careers advance, are potential customers for automobiles and other big-ticket items. Some predominantly 18-to-49-age shows have more female viewers, others more male viewers; the advertiser chooses between them according to his or her marketing targets.

The Nielsen service publishes weekly ratings for the ABC, CBS, NBC, Fox, UPN, and WB prime-time programs, showing the ratings and audience shares achieved by each. In a typical week, ratings ranged from a high of 23.4 for "E.R.," a medical emergency show, down to 1.5 for "Pinky & The Brain." Most shows score in the 9-to-13 range.

Each week the Nielsen service publishes its ratings for the ABC, CBS, NBC, and Fox network prime-time programs, showing the rating and audience share achieved by each. In a typical recent week, ratings ranged from a high of 23.9 for "E.R.," a medical emergency show, down to 4.4 for "Get Smart." Most shows score in the 9-to-13 range.

Decreases in a show's rating send shivers up the spines of its producers, because in the extremely intense competition of commercial television only a small percentage drop may cause a show to be cancelled. Television programmers form a good audience for stress and ulcer medicine commercials.

**Rating**
Percentage of all households having television sets that viewed a particular program

**Share**
Percentage of households with television sets having their sets tuned to a given station at a given time

## Other Types of Research

In addition to research aimed directly at identifying audiences and defining their interests and desires, other forms of research contribute substantially to shaping the impact the mass media have on their local, national, and global audiences. Four such areas of investigation are now examined.

### Communicator Research

One way to improve communication is to find out what kinds of people are best suited for the role of communicator and what factors affect communicator performance. We need to know the essential characteristics of good reporters, editors, and advertising people, among others, so that the proper training may be offered to future professionals. Even the most professional communicator, however, may be unaware of some of the factors affecting performance. In one study it was found that stories resulting from assignments by editors were more accurate than those originated by the reporter or stemming from coverage of general meetings. Another study disclosed that news personnel with "supportive images" (more establishment-oriented than others) reported so-called good news more accurately than bad news, whereas those with critical images of society did a more accurate job on bad news. Communicators increasingly are using sophisticated tools such as the computer to analyze complex problems. How will journalists adjust to the new demands placed on

Voters mark their ballots in the privacy of individual cubicles. Researchers debate how much influence the media have in the decisions voters make. (Price, The Picture Cube)

them in the era of cable? How are reporters performing with the new technologies? These are questions for communicator research studies.

## Message Research

The effects of different forms of the same message may be compared through variations in style, length, degree of difficulty, and the like, with attention paid to comprehensibility, interest, and attention value. We often vary our personal conversations as to complexity and word usage in terms of some determination of the sophistication of the intended receiver. With scientific *content analysis* we can easily determine the relative degree of difficulty of any message, and we can make inferences about the intent of the communicator as well.

## Graphics Research

Typography, layout, and page makeup fall within the area called graphics by the print media. By experimenting with different methods of presentation, the researcher can tell the editor what the most effective means of presentation of a given item is. A book publisher or magazine or newspaper editor may choose to test audience preference for one kind of typeface as compared with another; the use of one large illustration instead of several smaller pictures; or the effectiveness of a news item published in an area two columns wide and 5 inches deep, as contrasted to the same item set in one column 10 inches deep. Much research has been done on the legibility of typefaces and aesthetic preferences for them.

Advertising people, too, are strongly interested in graphics research. Which ad gets across the most information—an ad with a big picture and a little text, or a little picture and a lot of text? Such research may be accomplished by split runs in the publication, with the alternatives presented to two different samples of readers whose reactions can be compared through a readership survey, or by experimenting with a relatively small group of persons before publication of the ad.

Graphics research has its parallel in the broadcasting media. Research can tell whether three minutes of commercial time are most effective at the beginning of a program, at the end, or spread through it. Or it can tell whether, on a radio newscast, a summary of headlines at the start of the program will increase interest in the news items that follow.

## Advertising Research

The various media and almost all advertising agencies conduct advertising research to help them in their job of persuading people to buy. *Market* research has been carried on since the start of the century and was the forerunner of other public opinion research. It includes consumer surveys on potential markets for new products, dealer studies, customer attitude surveys, and studies of effectiveness of brand names and package designs. Media use by advertisers is determined in part by market research results, and various media seek to point out their usefulness by undertaking market research studies for particular advertisers' products. *Copy* research includes analysis of advertisement readership studies, pretesting of advertisements, evaluation of printed advertisement campaign effectiveness, and graphics. In broadcasting, commercials and programs may be tried out on small samples of listeners by means of response-recording devices. Similarly, films may be tried out on small audiences whose responses are recorded.

**Market research**
Determining product appeal by using techniques later applied to all opinion research

## The Tools of Research

To accomplish their goals, researchers use an extensive array of investigative methods. Part of their job is digging through statistics available in computer databases or in printed form. Development of governmental and commercial databases has enormously broadened the amount of information to be found.

On a personal basis, asking people questions is a fundamental method of research. This is accomplished in diverse forms, including:

**Survey research**
Gathering demographic information or sociological facts, as well as opinions and attitudes, through a scientific sample

1. *Questionnaires*. Sets of questions distributed by mail disclose attitudes toward a publication or station and demographic information as well. Newspapers send questionnaires to subscribers who have cancelled, seeking their reasons for quitting. Content, cost, editorial policy, poor delivery? All are important. Return postage should be included, possibly with the offer of a small gift to stimulate response.

2. *Telephone surveys*. Questions are asked by telephone researchers, calling either at random or from selected lists, depending on the type of information sought.

3. *Polls*. Solicitations of opinion are made by telephone or in person. Polls are commonplace and, unless their questions are phrased very carefully, can be misused for propaganda purposes. Professional pollsters use controlled sampling to draw responses from balanced cross sections of the public. Voluntary poll calls to free 800 numbers or paid calls to 900 numbers are of scant value, because no controls exist over repeat calls and demographic balance.

4. *Focus groups*. A media proprietor invites small cross sections of individuals to sit down over coffee and talk frankly about their opinions of the newspaper or broadcast operation. A skilled discussion leader can elicit valuable and sometimes unexpected information.

### Devices to Draw Response

Dangling a reward in front of people is another approach to obtaining information. Often they don't realize that in responding to offers they actually are participating in audience research. Coupons and contests are the most common forms of this approach.

1. *Coupons*. When shoppers clip and mail in 50-cents-off coupons from a newspaper, they give the sponsoring company valuable geographical information about its audience as well as about the pulling power of the product involved. By plotting on a map the addresses received from the coupons, the company determines the areas in which its audience is large or small. It also obtains "live" names for a future mailing list.

2. *Contests*. These take various forms, usually designed to obtain names and addresses of listeners or readers in order to demonstrate to advertisers the media outlet's circulation distribution. A radio station may offer free tickets for a cruise, to be awarded by a drawing from entry

postcards submitted by listeners. Or a station may offer 100 tickets to a popular rock concert to the first 100 listeners who call in.

3. Somewhat related is *copy-testing* by advertisers, who seek the responses of a limited group to proposed advertisements before beginning a full-scale campaign. The company tests the pulling power of the proposed advertisements by running them in a single city, or perhaps different versions in separate cities. Or two versions of the same advertising message may be run in different portions of a single newspaper or magazine issue, to discover which draws better. This is called *split-run advertising*.

Many people are generous in giving information about themselves and their attitudes. If the material received by these methods is screened carefully to filter out obviously invalid responses, the media can learn much about the audiences they serve or seek to serve.

## Points to Remember

1. How is the term "frame of reference" used in audience research?
2. Name the four basic elements in the communication process.
3. What is the role of "gatekeepers" in mass communication and why are they so important?
4. Explain the difference between channel noise and semantic noise.
5. Would the invasion from Mars broadcast by Orson Welles a half-century ago have the same impact on the American public if it were broadcast today? Why or why not?
6. What is agenda-setting?
7. Explain the value of demographics and psychographics to the mass media.
8. What age group in the television audience are advertisers most anxious to reach?

## Media Questions to Think About

1. Can you recall an incident in your life when a failure of communication caused by channel noise or semantic noise created an awkward or embarrassing situation?
2. How do you classify yourself under the Values and Lifestyles Program 2?
3. Have you ever participated in a radio contest for free tickets or similar prizes? Did you win? Do you know anyone who has won?

# ISSUE ONE

# Sex and Violence

## Are the Media Weakening Public Morality?

Are depictions of violence and sex on television harmful to society? This is one of a number of controversial topics explored in this Issue. Read the discussion and draw your own conclusions. For example, how would you answer the following questions?

1. Why do television shows and movies contain so much violence?

2. Is our nation, as one observer put it, "a far more violent country than anyone wants to admit"?

3. Have the networks and cable systems taken sufficient action to lessen the amount of TV violence entering the home by adopting a system that warns viewers of such programs?

4. What do "trash TV" programs tell us about popular taste and network and cable industry standards?

5. Do depictions of violence on television and in the movies incite some people, especially children and teenagers, to commit acts of violence?

6. What constitutes obscenity?

7. What is the difference between softcore pornography and hardcore pornography?

8. Do you agree with the recommendations of the most recent Commission on Pornography?

9. Should "dial-a-porn" telephone messages be prohibited?

10. What problems are involved in restricting the transmission of pornographic materials on the Internet?

11. Have standards of good taste in sexual activity and language been relaxed too far on TV shows and in movies?

12. Why isn't cable regulated as closely as over-the-air television?

13. Do boycotts of companies that place commercials on objectionable television programs constitute censorship?

14. Is all that profanity on TV and in the movies necessary?

15. What types of language should be barred on radio?

16. Is there reason for concern about some of the lyrics and actions on rock music videos and recordings?

## Violence

### Television

Violence on television, a national concern for four decades, escalated in the 1990s as the networks, cable, and individual stations competed for audiences and revenue. In the wake of financial cutbacks and the deregulation of the television industry under the Reagan administration, ABC, CBS, and NBC reduced or eliminated their standards and practices departments. The growth of cable television, giving more than half of the nation's households access to almost-anything-goes programming, together with heavy VCR use, accelerated depictions of violence and sex.

Cable TV led the way, but the networks were close behind. A survey by the National Coalition on Television Violence showed that 37 percent of all programming on American cable and network television featured themes high in violence, and that the vast majority of the violence was glamorized and used to excite the audience. The six most violent channels were found on cable: HBO, USA Network, WTBS, WGN, Showtime, and Cinemax. Least violent: the Discovery Channel, PBS, Disney Channel, and Black Entertainment Television.

Facing dwindling audiences, the networks offered their own quota of violent series, including "Crime Story," "Miami Vice," "Spenser for

Scene from *Terminator 2* starring Arnold Schwarzenegger is typical of the violent action films, full of gunfire and dramatic visual effects, with which Hollywood studios attract large crowds to the boxoffice. (S.S., Shooting Star)

## NETWORKS, CRITICS DIFFER ON VIOLENCE

Can watching violence on television harm children? The American Psychological Association says yes. So do the U.S. attorney general, the National Institute of Mental Health, the Department of Justice, the American Academy of Pediatrics, and the National Parent–Teachers Association.

"TV violence can cause aggressive behavior and can cultivate values favoring the use of aggression to resolve conflicts," a psychological association task force concluded in 1992. Its report pointed out that the average child witnesses 800 murders and sees more than 100,000 other acts of violence by the time he or she has finished elementary school.

Contrast this with comments by the networks.

ABC asserted in its *A Research Perspective on Television and Violence* that "after more than 30 years of scientific investigation the issue of television violence remains open to debate."

The CBS director of research told congressional investigators that "there still is no convincing evidence." He challenged the methodology of the task force report.

NBC reported a study of 2300 children and adolescents in Fort Worth and Minneapolis which, it stated, found no evidence that watching television led to aggression.

Hire," "Hunter," and "The Equalizer." Hollywood studios produced violent movies for cable, video, and the networks. Some states took action to keep the most violent videos out of the hands of minors.

**"Trash TV."**     Television programs fell still lower in quality during the late 1980s and the 1990s with the popularity of "trash TV." Network programs and syndication shows alike tried to shock audiences with bloody reconstructions of lurid crimes, emphasis on sexual deviations, and confrontations on racial, sexual, and family problems.

**Trash TV**
Pejorative term for sensationalized television shows

Many of these programs were presented in news and feature formats that emphasized such "news" as exposés of sexual misconduct by doctors, detailed depictions of grisly murders, and friendly interviews with prostitutes. News directors expressed anger, contending that the format debased their own legitimate work.

The prime example of sensationalized TV was Geraldo Rivera, who hit perhaps his lowest level with a show on satanism on NBC in which dismembered corpses and ritualistic child abuse were displayed.

To the dismay of many television officials and critics, this program was the highest-rated two-hour documentary ever shown on network television. Indeed, putting this show in the same category with such true documentary classics as CBS's "The Selling of the Pentagon" was a gross misnomer.

In the 1990s, some signs emerged that the orgy of sleaze was diminishing as advertisers began to shun the more extreme programs under pressure from viewers' groups and Congressional inquiries. Sleaze persisted, however, in such shows as "Cops" and its spinoff series including "Top Cops" and "Real-Life Cops" as well as "Studs," "The Love Connection," "Married . . . with Children," "X-Files," and "Tales from the Crypt."

Violence predominated in many other shows not considered among the sleaze genre. The National Coalition on Television Violence attacked two extremely violent series, "Freddy's Nightmare" and "Friday the 13th." The former featured intense torture, rape, the meathouse slaughter of women, cannibalism, and the killing of parents. Equally violent themes, including the serial killing of prostitutes, slow-motion murders, and satanic human sacrifice, characterized the "Friday the 13th" series. Late-evening horror movies replaced the two series in the mid-1990s.

These are only examples of a broad range of shows with violent themes that led Congress in 1989 to approve a measure that would waive the Sherman Antitrust Act to permit television networks, cable channel operators, and other program producers to draw up voluntary standards to curb violence on television. Network leaders countered at first that their own standards on violent content were adequate and that such action might lead to a further loss of viewers.

In 1996, after a year-long $1.5 million study, researchers at four universities concluded that "psychologically harmful" violence is pervasive on broadcast and cable TV programs. Among the findings:

- Perpetrators of violent acts go unpunished 73 percent of the time.
- Most violent portrayals fail to show the consequences of violent acts.
- About 25 percent of violent incidents involve the use of handguns, which can "trigger aggressive thoughts and behaviors."
- Few programs containing violence (4 percent) emphasize nonviolent alternatives.

The researchers were led by a team from the University of California at Santa Barbara.

Tabloid TV.  A new genre in television, the news-information-tabloid magazine program, gained increasing popularity. Akin to "sleaze TV" and called "reality" shows, tabloid TV increased in popularity during the 1990s, specializing in sometimes lurid reports on crime, sex, and scandal. Termed "the granddaddy of tabloid television," 20th Century Fox Television's "A Current Affair" spawned three other syndicated magazine programs: "Inside Edition," produced by King World, "Hard Copy," offered by Paramount Television, and "Now It Can Be Told," produced by Geraldo Rivera and Tribune Entertainment.

These programs pushed mainstream TV and newspapers to offer more details about sex, violence, and other subjects that once were treated gingerly. According to some sociologists, media critics, and journalists, the result speaks poorly of American society. "Only a small fraction of people who use the media are interested in what we would call significant vital issues," said Alvin Baskoff, an Emory University sociology professor. The tabloid TV shows, he said, "are just continuing a process that's been going on for several generations. They're not harmless. People can't distinguish between the trivial and the important on television and in newspapers."

**Television Talk Shows.**    A spate of sleazy TV talk shows during the 1990s focused on such topics as women who confront unfaithful lovers and teenagers who love "one-night stands." Hosts included Jenny Jones, Montel Williams, Ricki Lake, Charles Perez, and Jerry Springer. Techniques were developed to rile guests without, according to critics, offering enough after-show counseling. (See Chapter 10.)

During a 1995 "Jenny Jones" episode dealing with secret admirers, Scott Amedure, 32, embarrassed John Schmitz, 24, by revealing he was a "secret admirer" of Schmitz. Soon thereafter Amedure was shot to death, and Schmitz was charged with first-degree murder. The action prompted show producers to review their procedures.

**Effects of TV Violence.**    Violence is a major characteristic of humankind's history and literature, including religious writings and children's fairy tales. In the United States, violence was an inevitable part of the expanding frontiers, with law and order coming slowly but leaving a heritage of violent behavior as a principal means of settling arguments. The approximately 25,000 murders in the United States each year, most of them by people using handguns, far exceed those of any other country. As Harry Henderson pointed out in an article in *The Press*, "This is a far more violent country than anyone wants to admit."

Because television is central in our lives, a debate has raged for many years over the effects that viewing acts of violence on TV have on the American public—particularly on children, other young people, and the emotionally disturbed. In about 3000 studies conducted over three decades, researchers have determined that a steady diet of violent entertainment does contribute to antisocial and aggressive activity when added to other factors such as violence in the home and neighborhood.

Public concern over televised violence had earlier intensified with news reports that a young woman was fatally set on fire with kerosene in a lonely Boston neighborhood soon after a similar scene had been depicted on television. Concern turned into outrage when three adolescents (two girls and a boy) raped a 9-year-old girl with a bottle in San

**Tabloid TV**
Television shows based on real-life happenings

Gruesome scenes of death and destruction caused by terrorist bombs create difficult problems for television editors, who must try to present the news stories visually without offending the sensibilities of viewers. (Pavolovsky/Sygma)

Francisco only three days after, the attackers admitted to police, they had seen the made-for-television movie *Born Innocent*.

Charging that television had become "a school of violence and a college for crime," the California Medical Association filed a friend-of-the-court brief urging that NBC and the station be held accountable for the assault. The brief also pointed out that several months previously, "based on the overwhelming scientific and medical evidence," the American Medical Association had declared television violence to be "an environmental health risk." After viewing the film and hearing arguments, Superior Court Judge John A. Ertola threw the case out of court. He ruled that the First Amendment gives broadcasters absolute immunity from civil liability for personal injuries arising out of their programming.

Annual "violence profiles" made by Professor George Gerbner of the Annenberg School of Communications at the University of Pennsylvania have shown a continual increase in network TV violence. In 1992, a *TV Guide* study found televised violence at an all-time high. Researchers recorded 1846 acts of violence during a single day of broadcasting. Cable programming clocked in more gunplay, punching, dragging, pushing, slapping, and menacing than broadcast network fare. Most violent acts occurred on children's cartoons, followed by TV show promotions, movies, toy commercials, music videos, commercials for theatrical movies, TV dramas, news, "reality" shows, sitcoms, and soap operas.

**Violence profile** Annual record, compiled by George Gerbner and associates, of the incidences of violence on network television shows

The Rev. Donald Wildmon, director of the American Family Association, Tupelo, Mississippi, in 1994 issued his 16th rating of sex and violence on the broadcast networks. He counted an average of 47.38 acts of sex, violence, and profanity during each network hour. Fox led the other networks

## "A TERRIBLE DILEMMA"

Publishers of the Washington *Post* and the New York *Times* faced a wrenching dilemma during the summer of 1995.

A terrorist who had killed three people and wounded 22 during 17 years of random bombing wanted to make a deal. He would not plant bombs to kill more people if one of the newspapers would publish his 37,000-word condemnation of modern technology and industrial society, along with three annual follow-up messages.

Publishing would set a dangerous precedent. Not doing so might result in loss of lives.

"We will act responsibly and not rashly, knowing that lives might be at risk," said *Times* publisher Arthur O. Sulzberger, Jr.

The anonymous terrorist, known as the Unabomber because many of his target sites have been universities and airlines,

gave the newspaper executives three months to agree to the demand.

"I think they are going through journalistic hell," said Marvin Kalb, media analyst and former broadcaster. Everette Dennis, executive director of the Freedom Forum Media Studies Center, agreed. "It's a terrible dilemma."

Shortly before the September deadline, at the request of Attorney General Janet Reno and the FBI, the *Post* published the unaltered manifesto. The *Times* shared printing costs.

Ironically, the publication led to the arrest of a suspect, Theodore J. Kaczynski, living in a Montana cabin, when his brother compared the ideas and style with writings found in their Chicago area home.

What would YOU have done?

---

in all categories except sex outside of marriage, in which it slightly trailed NBC. In all other categories, Wildmon noted, Fox was profane and indecent at almost twice the rate of the next highest-rated network.

A 10-week study of news programming on the five major local TV channels in Chicago in 1994 showed that, when weather, sports, and commercials were excluded, more than 50 percent of the news was devoted to violence. In general, the study found that local TV news portrays "an urban America seemingly out of control: night after night the news overflows with victims and perpetrators of violence."

The study also included the Chicago *Tribune* and Chicago *Sun-Times*. Said Professor Robert Entman of Northwestern University, who conducted the study: "The findings of the *Tribune* suggest that profit-oriented media can cover violence without arousing audiences' fears to the same extent TV apparently does."

Across the country, many TV news directors moved to reduce the volume of stories involving violence.

*Anti-Violence TV Chip.* The Telecommunications Reform Act of 1996 required that manufacturers of television sets equip new sets with a computer chip (called a V-chip) so parents could electronically block out material rated offensively violent or sexual.

Heavily armed Woody Harrelson and Juliette Lewis rampage through a store while customers cringe in Oliver Stone's contro-versial motion picture on violence, *Natural Born Killers*. (Copyright © Warner Bros.)

The bill gave the television industry one year to set up its own system for rating violence; if not, the government would create a commission of people from industry and education to organize such a system. Confronted with that threat and overwhelming public pressure, the networks agreed to adopt a ratings system that would enable viewers to screen out objectionable material. The cable industry also approved such a plan.

## Violence in Movies

A 15-year-old youth, charged with the shotgun slayings of his parents in Coweta County, Georgia, in 1995, wrote friends that he would like to live the story of the movie *Natural Born Killers*, suggesting that they launch a cross-country killing spree.

Letters and notes exchanged by the suspect and several of his friends referred to Mickey and Mallory, the couple in the Oliver Stone movie who killed 52 people in three weeks.

Although boasting to an interviewer months earlier that, "I shoot good violence, I mean, I know I do," Stone said he believed the movie was ultimately anti-violent because the maniacal killers escape their demons in the end.

*Natural Born Killers* and another movie, *True Romance*, were cited by Senate Majority Leader Bob Dole as too violent in an attack on the Hollywood movie industry while campaigning for the Republican nomination for the presidency in 1995. Dole criticized the movies as "films that revel in mindless violence and loveless sex."

In a virtual replay of scenes from a just-released movie, *Money Train*, two men in November 1995 squeezed a flammable liquid into a New York City, subway token booth and ignited it, blowing it up and fatally burning the clerk, Hollywood again was the subject of criticism from Dole and others.

Dole charged that Hollywood unduly promoted violence, rape, and casual sex in music and movies and said that for the good of American children "the mainstreaming of deviancy must come to an end." He also cited Time Warner and three recording groups, Cannibal Corpse, Geto Boys, and 2 Live Crew as promoting antisocial behavior.

Producers replied that the rating system for films and parental advisory labels for recordings should protect children from unsavory material and that artistic freedom should not be curtailed.

## Violence in Newspapers

Because of the nature of the medium, the reporting of violent crimes in American newspapers has drawn less criticism than its display in television and films. However, through the years many readers have objected to sensationalistic treatment of murders, rapes, and other such crimes often in the form of detailed front-page stories and photographs published under large headlines. Some people have felt that newspapers glorified violent activities, in effect making heroes of criminals. Objections have also been expressed against mayhem in the comic strips (although comic books were more severely criticized on this account) and against the reporting in some papers of almost every minor crime that occurs in the community. Newspaper accounts of violent actions, however, have a minimal impact compared with that which is televised and shown in movie houses.

Newspapers that formerly depended on sensationalism for their circulation have, for the most part, been replaced by those such as the Washington *Post* and the Louisville *Courier-Journal*, which subordinate crime news of this sort to stories treating criminal activities in a sociological manner. One reason is that, since the advent of radio and television, single-copy street sales constitute only a minor part of most newspapers' circulation; most copies are delivered to homes. For such sales, so-called screaming headlines and breathtaking accounts of crime are no longer necessary. Another reason is that most readers today, more educated than in the past, want their news in a different form. And the better newspapers are inquiring into the causes of conflict and violence, presenting in-depth background stories to throw more light on social problems.

During much of the 1980s, however, the New York *Post*, with Rupert Murdoch as publisher, assumed an increasingly sensationalist tone. The typographic menu included such bannerline entrees as HEADLESS BODY IN TOPLESS BAR, UNCLE TORTURES TOT WITH HOT FORK, and LEPER RAPES VIRGIN, GIVES BIRTH TO MONSTER BABY. Such stories were designed for the huge street sales necessary to keep the paper alive as major retail stores placed most of

When the Florida woman who accused William Kennedy Smith of rape at the Kennedy family compound testified against him, her face was covered on the television screen to conceal her identity. Some newspapers published her name, however, causing a sharp debate about the right of privacy. (AP/Wide World)

their advertising in competing newspapers. After its purchase in 1988 by Peter S. Kalikow, a New York real estate developer, the *Post* toned down its sensationalism, and some major retail advertisers returned to its pages. Murdoch resumed control of the *Post* in 1993, and sensationalism persisted.

## Obscenity

Pornography in books, magazines, films, and cable television became big business during the 1960s and 1970s as sexual mores changed and a new permissiveness in regard to individual conduct permeated American society. At the same time, serious works of art increasingly dealt with so-called adult themes and explicit sexual acts of every nature. The right to read and view what one desired conflicted with the opinions of those who felt that society had the innate right to proscribe such activities.

Obscenity, although a legal concept, is discussed here instead of in Issue 5 because of the difficulty in differentiating it from forms of pornography of broad social concern that are not considered obscene.

Obscenity usually is defined in terms of whether the materials are lewd, lascivious, prurient, licentious, or indecent. After more than four decades, however, the U.S. Supreme Court has been unable to draw firm legal lines as to what is obscene and what is not. Each of the nine justices has had his or her own definition ("I know it when I see it," declared Justice Potter Stewart). Yet the Court maintained that certain materials are

**Obscenity**
Depiction of materials of a lewd, lascivious, prurient, or licentious nature

**ASIAN SEX SLAVES IN N.Y.**

Crackdown bares massage parlor scandal: Page ?

# DAILY ● NEWS

40¢     NEW YORK'S HOMETOWN NEWSPAPER     Monday, May 17, 19

## Dr. Death helps #16 die – this time he may pay

# JACK THE REAPER

Dr. Jack Kevorkian was arrested yesterday in Michigan on charges of helping a lung cancer patient commit suicide by carbon monoxide poisoning.

**STORY ON PAGE 3**

The circulation war between New York's tabloid newspapers is stimulated by garish front page headlines stressing violence and sex. This New York *Daily News* front page is typical.

not protected by the First Amendment and that the government may suppress those materials. Recognizing the importance of safeguarding constitutional freedom, the Court in each decision has attempted to limit severely the kinds of materials that can be suppressed as obscene. The problem has remained, however, that fundamental First Amendment values have been encroached upon, and are in constant jeopardy, because all the Court definitions are, as three justices wrote in 1973, "so elusive that they fail to distinguish clearly between protected and unprotected speech."

For more than 70 years the so-called Hicklin rule, stemming from a landmark obscenity decision in England, was applied by courts in America. Under this rule published matter was regarded as obscene if isolated passages might be construed as depraving and corrupting even the most feebleminded reader. In a 1933 case involving the book *Ulysses*, a U.S. judge said a better test would be the dominant effect of the entire book on the average reader, and the Supreme Court agreed.

With *Roth* v. *United States* in 1957, the Supreme Court, relaxing this rigid rule, based its definition of obscenity on community standards. Then in *Memoirs* v. *Massachusetts* involving the celebrated eighteenth-century novel *Fanny Hill* the Court set forth a new definition of "obscene" wherein three elements must coalesce: "(1) that the dominant theme of the material taken as a whole appeals to a prurient interest in sex; (2) the material is patently offensive because it affronts contemporary standards relating to the description or representation of sexual matters; (3) the material is utterly without redeeming social value." The Court stressed that material must be "utterly"—that is, unqualifiedly—worthless.

### The Present Standard.

In *Miller* v. *California* (1973), however, the Court, in a five-to-four vote, revised its definition to "(1) whether the average person, applying contemporary community standards, would find that the work taken as a whole appeals to the prurient interest; (2) whether the work depicts or describes in a patently offensive way, sexual conduct specifically defined by the applicable state law; (3) whether the work taken as a whole lacks serious literary, artistic, political, or scientific value."

The *Miller* decision differed from the previous *Memoirs* test in three significant areas: First, community standards, as opposed to national standards, are to be used. The Court did not, however, specify what area it meant as "community." Second, the "utterly without redeeming social value" test became "lacks serious literary, artistic, political, or scientific value." This omits religious, entertainment, and educational genres and leaves more materials open to attack. Third, each state must specifically define the types of sexual conduct prohibited. Chief Justice Burger gave as an example: "(a) patently offensive representations or descriptions of masturbation, excretory functions, and lewd exhibition of the genitals; (b) patently offensive representations or descriptions of ultimate sexual acts, normal or perverted, actual or simulated."

In *Jenkins* v. *Georgia* (1974) the Court, ruling that the film *Carnal Knowledge* was not obscene, declared that "community standards" may be those of the state but do not necessarily have to be representative of any specific geographical boundary; they may be the jury's "understanding of the community from which they come as to contemporary community standards." On the other hand, the Court declared that juries do not have "unbridled discretion in determining what is 'patently offensive'" and may therefore be overruled on appeal (as here the decisions of the local and supreme courts of Georgia were reversed). The Court said that nudity alone is not obscene, and prohibitions apply only to "public portrayal of hardcore sexual conduct for its own sake."

In 1987, in *Pope* v. *Illinois*, the Court largely reaffirmed the *Miller* ruling but voted, five to four, that judges and juries must assess the social value of the material from the standpoint of a "reasonable person," rather than apply community standards.

## Pornography Commissions

As a result of the *Jenkins* ruling and another decision in 1974, the legislatures of almost every state set about revising their own obscenity laws. They did so in the light of the sexual revolution of the previous 20 years or so and the controversial report in 1970 of the Commission on Obscenity and Pornography, established by Congress. Concerning the effects of pornography, the commission declared:

> The conclusion is that, for America, the relationship between the availability of erotica and changes in sex-crime rates neither proves nor disproves the possibility that availability of erotica leads to crime, but the massive overall increases in sex crimes that have been alleged do not seem to have occurred. . . . In sum, empirical research designed to clarify the question has found no evidence to date that exposure to explicit sexual materials is a factor in the causation of sex crime or sex delinquency.

In contrast to its recommendations affecting adults, the commission did recommend "legislative regulations upon the sale of sexual materials to young persons who do not have the consent of their parents." The commission was of the opinion, however, that only pictorial material should be legally withheld from children.

In 1986, a second such commission submitted an advisory report through the office of Attorney General Edwin Meese. It called for a national assault on pornography through a combination of more vigorous law enforcement and increased vigilance by citizens' groups.

In sharp contrast with the earlier report, the 11-member Commission on Pornography concluded that exposure to most pornography "bears some causal relationship to the level of sexual violence, sexual coercion or unwanted sexual aggression." Critics, including two commission members, contended that this conclusion was not based on firm scientific evidence, pointing out that social scientists are divided on whether most pornography is harmful.

In its 1960-page Meese report the commission listed the titles of 2325 magazines, 725 books, and 1270 films found in "adults only" stores that it visited and provided detailed, explicit descriptions of the activities depicted in some of those publications and films.

**Hardcore pornography** Materials designed to arouse a person sexually by graphically depicting *actual* intercourse

The commission urged concerned citizens to band together into "watch groups" to file complaints, put pressure on local prosecutors, monitor judges, and, if necessary, boycott merchants selling pornographic material. As reported in Chapter 6, a commission letter sent earlier to chain drug and convenience stores, suggesting that the owners might be cited in the report for distributing pornography, resulted in the removal of such magazines as *Playboy*, *Penthouse*, and *Forum* from hundreds of these establishments.

The commission rejected proposals to seek broadening of the legal definition of obscenity, which embraces some but not all pornographic material. Instead, it said, current laws should be strengthened and enforced. In its report the commission used the word "pornography" to mean material that is "sexually explicit and intended primarily for the purpose of sexual arousal."

**Softcore pornography** Materials designed to arouse a person sexually but graphically depicting only simulated (not actual) sexual activity

Numerous changes in federal and state laws were among the 92 recommendations, including curbs on the production, transmission, and possession of child pornography and sexually explicit material portraying violent abuse of women by men.

The report was widely praised as helpful in eliminating "the plague of pornographic pollution that has ravaged our society," as one group spokesperson put it. It was condemned by civil libertarian and other organizations and individuals as encouraging moral vigilantes—inviting inroads into First Amendment rights guaranteeing freedom of speech and the press. Attorney General Meese said it would not be used as a basis for censorship.

Meese's successors continued the assault on pornography on several fronts. By 1990 Project PostPorn, a joint operation of the Justice Department and the U.S. Postal Inspection Service, had forced four nationwide adult-oriented companies out of business, mainly by hitting them with the expense of defending obscenity charges in several states at once. Convictions were obtained in 15 states, with fines totaling more than $3 million and six resulting in prison terms. The Justice Department mainly pursued videotape producers and distributors in conservative jurisdictions, typically avoided by the industry, because indictments were more likely there.

Applying the obscenity forfeiture provisions of the Racketeer Influenced and Corrupt Organizations Act (RICO), prosecutors seized the entire businesses of some book publishers and video operators. Some federal appeals courts upheld the seizures, but others ruled that such broad efforts violated the First Amendment.

The Supreme Court, in *Alexander* v. *United States*, ruled in a 5-to-4 vote in 1993 that the First Amendment does not prohibit prosecutors from seizing an entire chain of adult bookstores and movie houses and then destroying thousands of books and other materials after finding several obscene books for sale. The Court, however, returned the case to a lower court to devise its own rules about when seizure of property is constitutionally excessive under the Eighth Amendment.

In 1994, the Supreme Court, in *U.S.* v. *X-Citement Video*, upheld the federal law against child pornography, rejecting arguments that it violates the First Amendment. But in order to save the law from being found unconstitutional, the Court ruled that prosecutors must prove that defendants knew that an underage person was involved. The defendant, Rubin Gottesman, had been convicted of selling tapes starring Traci Lords, who was 15 when some of her 150 films were made.

In 1995, the Court, in *American Library Assoc.* v. *Reno*, again rejected a challenge to the law.

**FCC Ruling.**  Complying with a congressional mandate, the Federal Communications Commission in 1989 banned sexually explicit material from radio and television. The new rule applied only to over-the-air broadcasts and did not cover cable TV. Previously the FCC had ruled, under its interpretation of existing law, that broadcasts aired after midnight and before 6 A.M. would be safe from action by the agency. In enforcing the policy, the FCC had fined KZKC-TV, a Kansas City, Missouri, station, $2000 for broadcasting a movie titled *Private Lessons* at 8 P.M. on May 26, 1987.

In 1991, a federal appeals court declared the 24-hour ban unconstitutional. The court ordered the commission to establish so-called "safe harbor" periods, during which the number of children in the audience is small and broadcasters may air indecent programming with impunity. In 1995, an appeals court ruled that indecent material could be broadcast only from 10 P.M. to 6 A.M. The Supreme Court in early 1996 rejected a constitutional challenge to the action.

**"Dial-a-Porn" Messages.**  In 1989, the Supreme Court refused to shut down the billion-dollar "dial-a-porn" industry. The unanimous decision nullified a 1988 law passed by Congress prohibiting the telephone message services largely because of their availability to children. Only obscene messages, and not messages that are merely "indecent," may be outlawed, the Court ruled. It said a blanket ban would violate free speech rights. "The case before us today does not require us to decide what is obscene or what is indecent," said Justice Byron R. White, writing for the Court.

A telephone conversation, like an explicit movie or centerfold in an adult magazine, may or may not be obscene, a designation that must be decided by local juries on a case-by-case basis. Acknowledging that Congress has a legitimate interest in preventing children from being exposed to indecent messages, Justice White said the law "has the invalid effect of limiting the content of adult telephone conversations to that which is suitable for children to hear. It is another case of burning up the house to roast the pig."

The total ban had never been imposed because a federal court in Los Angeles, in a case involving Sable Communications of California, struck

**"Dial-a-porn"**
Dialing a "900" number to hear a message or hold a conversation of a sexual nature

down the law on the ground that it was "over-broad and unconstitutional." But the court upheld the ban on obscene messages on the ground that the First Amendment does not protect obscenity.

### "Indecent" Material on the Internet

The Computer Decency Act, a provision of the Telecommunications Reform Act of 1996, made it a crime to transmit or allow indecent material to be transmitted over public computer networks to which minors have access. The bill authorized the government to restrict online speech and conduct, imposing fines up to $250,000 and jail sentences of as long as five years for anyone who makes indecent material available to children in a public online forum.

The bill defines indecency as "any comment, request, suggestion, proposal, image, or other communication that, in context, depicts or describes in terms patently offensive as measured by contemporary community standards, sexual or excretory activities or organs."

Civil liberties groups and computer users immediately protested in cyberspace and in the courts that the bill violates free speech. The American Civil Liberties Union, the Planned Parenthood Federation of America, the Electronic Frontier Foundation, and other Internet users obtaineda restraining order against the provision. The court later temporarily blocked the law. Calling the Internet "a never-ending worldwide conversation," Judge Stewart Dalzell said Internet users are entitled to the strongest protection possible.

The controversy reflected a disagreement in Congress in which the Senate had voted 17–16 to impose the restrictions and the House of Representatives sought to prohibit such regulation and encourage parents to use electronic devices to protect children from explicit material, obscenity, and other adult traffic.

The Supreme Court had not yet ruled on whether the Internet is a print medium such as a newspaper, protected from government censorship, or a broadcast medium such as TV, whose content is closely regulated by the Federal Communications Commission.

Among other actions involving sexual material on the Internet:

- In 1992, police in Santa Clara County, California, seized computers and electronic images, mostly of teenage girls and men engaged in sex acts, which were being transmitted over telephone lines. "The same laws apply to pornography on a computer as apply to magazines," said Julius Finkelstein, assistant district attorney. "The difficulty is in finding the networks and then locating the resources and time to prosecute them."

- In 1994, a California couple was convicted of sending obscene pictures over telephone lines in Memphis, Tenn., where authorities downloaded images from the couple's computer bulletin board. They appealed their conviction on grounds that the U.S. Supreme Court in 1973 had defined obscenity by local community standards, whereas in cyberspace there are no boundaries.

- In 1995, a University of Michigan student was charged with interstate transmission of a threat after he posted stories he had written about raping and murdering a classmate to a widely read newsgroup on the Internet, and then discussed by e-mail how to carry out such a crime. A court cleared him of the charges, and he threatened to sue the university, which had expelled him over the action.

- A study by a Carnegie Mellon University undergraduate student purporting to show that pornographic images were available on public networks of the Internet gained credibility when it was published by the *Georgetown Law Journal* and was the subject of a *Time* magazine cover story. The findings were embraced by anti-pornography activists while critics criticized its methodology and said it recklessly extended its conclusions from the analysis of adult bulletin boards to suggest that extreme pornography is pervasive on public networks as well.

- In late 1995, CompuServe, under pressure from prosecutors in Germany, blocked its 4 million subscribers worldwide from reaching 200 sexually oriented forums on the Usenet section of the Internet. Providing parental control capability, CompuServe soon reopened most of the newsgroups.

**Download** Transferring information from a network or host computer to a personal computer

## Sex and Good Taste

### Television

Standards of good taste in depictions of sex, as well as of violence, were relaxed considerably on primetime network programming during the latter part of the 1980s. The use of profanity increased as well.

For many years the networks and individual stations had followed, on a voluntary basis and with mixed success, the tenets of the Television Code of Good Practice. The department of broadcast standards of each network sought to ensure that nothing was broadcast that exceeded generally accepted standards of public taste as represented by their huge national audiences. During a typical season, editors of each network made judgments on more than 2000 program outlines and scripts, as well as commercials. They looked at a variety of potential problems, including sex, violence, language, treatment of crime, use of narcotics, religious sensitivities, attitudes toward gambling and drunkenness, depiction of physical handicaps, the image of minorities, treatment of animals, and television adaptation of theatrical motion pictures.

The censors' problems increased when television producers, in an effort to retain mass audiences while presumably downplaying violence, began in the late 1970s to load situation comedies with scripts of an increasingly salacious nature, using themes such as pornography and sadomasochism, as well as suggestive dialogue. In so doing, the producers seemed to be following the radically changed lifestyles of young people and many older persons as revealed by nationwide surveys of people's sexual habits and viewing preferences.

When parts of the television code were held to violate antitrust laws in 1982, the National Association of Broadcasters suspended all its broadcasting code activities. As the government relaxed its regulation of the media, monitoring by the networks also was relaxed.

The federal courts have made distinctions that give cable wide latitude in program content. On grounds of vagueness or being too broad, the courts have struck down local ordinances for cable that sought to prosecute purveyors of indecency and profanity. There is a difference, said the courts, between cable, which subscribers buy and put into their homes at their choice and cost, and broadcast television, which is so pervasive and unrestricted in its entry into the home that it must be held accountable to a higher standard of review. The Supreme Court in 1987 struck down a Utah law that restricted cable telecasts of nudity and sex acts that the state deemed indecent but that did not meet the Court's definition of obscenity.

Asserting that its complaints had been virtually ignored by network executives, a coalition known as Christian Leaders for Responsible Television, or CLEAR-TV, both threatened and carried out boycotts against advertisers on shows featuring sex and violence as well as on those considered "anti-Christian." The coalition included more than 1600 top officials from 70 mainline and conservative Protestant denominations and more than 100 Roman Catholic bishops. The group relied on the monitoring system of the American Family Association, cited previously in this Issue.

The coalition's first attempt at boycotting advertisers in 1987 resulted in two companies' dropping out of its "top 10 list" of advertisers. Another such list was developed after the group monitored programs during the "sweeps" month of May 1989, one of the periods when ratings determine rates for advertisers.

In 1989, four other companies decided not to advertise on Fox Broadcasting Corporation's "Married . . . with Children" series after a much-publicized letter-writing campaign led by Terry Rakolta, who protested sexual innuendo on the program. The suburban Detroit woman established Americans for Responsible Television (ART), which urged the networks to return to observance of family viewing time (8–9 P.M.).

The complaints caused many advertisers and their agencies to monitor programs more closely, a difficult task because of the hundreds shown. A model guideline provided by a company to its agency specifies avoidance of shows that contain "graphic and unnecessary violence, explicit sexual situations, excessive use of vulgarity or profanity, scenes glamorizing drug or alcohol use, and sensationalism involving delicate and controversial social situations." Most advertising agencies rely on a screening service, most often Advertising Information Services, which is owned by 21 large agencies and employs 20 people to watch tapes of shows.

The Planned Parenthood Federation of America has long complained that network television programs promote sexual activity among teenagers without portraying the consequences. Expressing a similar concern, the National Research Council asked the networks to include mention of contraceptives in dramatic scenes in which sexual innuendos are made or when actors are seen in bed before or after sexual activity. Many persons, however, are strongly opposed to any mention of contraceptives. In 1991, Fox became the first TV network to accept condom advertising.

Surveys have shown that sexual subject matter is acceptable to most viewers when it is presented with good taste and at times when children ordinarily are not watching. One survey found that people worry most about sexual themes that seem to impinge on the welfare of their children or their own concepts of normal family life. Some of the most strongly held opinions concerned child exploitation and homosexuality. Four out of five respondents, however, wanted to retain sex-related material on TV, but at times when children were not watching, and with parents assuming responsibility. Few favored censorship.

With only a few exceptions, such as an edited version of the movie *Midnight Cowboy*, commercial television has never shown X-rated movies. However, the popularity of hardcore films such as *Deep Throat* and softcore films such as the *Emmanuelle* series increased substantially with the advent of videocassettes, which could be shown in the privacy of one's home. Even so, with its puritanical heritage, the United States has never witnessed such programming as is viewed in some other countries; for example, more than 150 private stations in Italy have presented hundreds of X-rated movies, striptease shows, nude exercise and sex-advice programs, and nude ballets.

Given the fact that television in the United States is constantly trying to please most of the people much of the time, without giving them more than they want, the medium has shown remarkable growth in intellectual freedom in recent years. Much of the maturation has gone virtually unnoticed because television has endeavored to keep pace with the reality of the nation's social growth.

"Those of us in network television particularly do not wish to see a slowdown in the legitimate expansion of programming boundaries," said Herminio Traviesas, former vice-president in charge of broadcast standards for NBC-TV. "For while we do hear from our more conservative viewers, we also hear from the more liberal elements of our audience and, lest we forget, from the progressive people in the creative community. In a sense we are like Indians with our ears to the tube instead of to the ground. We are among the first to hear and witness new calls for greater freedom of expression. At the same time we are hearing complaints that television is going too far, too fast."

## Radio

Profanity, obscenity, smut, and vulgarity are forbidden under the codes of conduct promulgated by the radio industry. Indeed, the Federal Communications Commission maintains a file of complaints against any such utterances and calls station managements to account at license renewal time if matters of sex and good taste have been violated.

When controversial "call-in" shows multiplied during the 1970s, a few stations encouraged late-night listeners openly to discuss their sex lives. This became known as "topless radio." Society's new permissive attitudes caused many listeners to accept such programs with equanimity; others were shocked. The industry in general and the FCC in particular, however, criticized instances of extreme verbal candor to such an extent that the practice has been abandoned except in such popular radio and cable television call-in shows as those of psychologist Dr. Ruth Westheimer, and in isolated instances of so-called "raunch radio." One station, WGLD-FM, Oak Park, Illinois, was fined $2000 for broadcasting a call-in show on oral sex. The use of a device that delays the broadcast of telephoned observations for seven seconds, giving station personnel time to delete offending remarks made by callers, has been a major help with call-in shows.

Station WBAI-FM, New York, was reprimanded by the FCC in 1978 for broadcasting George Carlin's "seven dirty words" comedy routine. The Supreme Court ruled that broadcasters do not have a constitutional right to air obscene words that apply to sex and excretion.

After receiving more than 20,000 protest letters, the FCC announced in 1987 that it would apply new rules to future decisions about "decency" on radio and television. The commission cited suggestive language used by so-called "shock radio" personality Howard Stern on WYSP-FM in Philadelphia, whose show was simulcast elsewhere. In 1992, the FCC fined Infinity Broadcasting Company, Stern's employer, $600,000 for indecency and also levied a $105,000 fine against KLSX-FM, a Los Angeles station airing Stern's show. Many station executives expressed apprehension at the increased involvement of the FCC in program content.

## Video and Recordings

Critics express concern about the effect of music videos, with their emphasis on sex and violence, on the predominantly teenage audience that watches them. A study by five researchers—Richard L. Baxter, Cynthia De Riemer, Ann Landini, Larry Leslie, and Michael W. Singletary—analyzed 62 MTV music videos with this concern in mind. Their findings, published in the *Journal of Broadcasting & Electronic Media*, included these observations:

> Music video sexual content was understated, relying on innuendo through clothing, suggestiveness, and light physical contact rather than more overt behaviors. . . .
>
> The study's results indicate, however, that sexually oriented, suggestive behavior is portrayed frequently in music videos. Questions regarding the impact of this portrayal on adolescent socialization, peer relationships, and modeling are raised.
>
> The frequency of instances of violence and crime content also merits further attention. . . . The most frequently coded content elements were physical aggression, not the use of weapons, murder, or sexual violence. Violent action in music videos often stopped short of the fruition of the violent act.

Clearly, the addition of a provocative visual element accentuates the sexual and violent aspects already present in numerous rock music recordings. Such an incident occurred when superstar Michael Jackson grabbed his crotch during his 11-minute "Black or White" music video in 1991. And ABC's "Nightline" program won its highest rating in 1990 when it broadcast an uncut version of Madonna's "Justify My Love" music video, which MTV wouldn't run.

Rock music lyrics came under heavy attack in the mid-1980s from the Parents' Music Resource Center and the Parent-Teachers Association. In a hearing before a Senate committee, the groups urged that a label of "R" (or even "X") be placed on records and tapes with lyrics that included explicit sexual language, profanity, or references to violence or the occult. The groups also wanted the lyrics of labeled music, as well as industry-wide guidelines, available to consumers before purchase. At issue were such albums as Bruce Springsteen's "Born in the U.S.A.," which includes the songs, "I'm on Fire" and "I'm Going Down."

In response, half of the 44 member companies of the Recording Industry Association of America, representing 80 percent of records released in the United States, agreed to urge the display of possibly objectionable lyrics on album covers or label the records, "Explicit Lyrics–Parental Advisory." For cassette tapes, which represent the majority of rock music sales, record companies may print, "See LP for Lyrics," on the tape box because there is often no space for lyrics on a cassette. No ratings would be made. In 1990, as public outcries mounted, six major companies agreed to devise an industrywide labeling sticker for albums. Record censorship bills were pending in more than a dozen states.

Law enforcement organizations in several states called for a boycott of Time Warner after the company distributed rapper Ice-T's song, "Cop Killer." Among lyrics on the "Body Count" album that enraged police: "I got my 12-gauge sawed off. I got my headlights turned off. I'm 'bout to

Emergence of rap music, whose swiftly delivered messages in street language frequently voice anger over society's ills, has brought prominence to several stars. The performer Ice-T, shown here with his wife Darlene, stirred national argument with a recording urging "kill the cops." (Aloma, Shooting Star)

bust some shots off. I'm 'bout to bust some cops off. Die, die, die, pig, die." The song's chorus specifically addressed the Los Angeles Police Department and the Rodney G. King beating case. Defending the album, Ice-T said the song was intended to condemn racism and police brutality. Ronald Hampton, executive director of the National Black Police Association, said, "This song is not a call for murder; it's a rap of protest. Ice-T isn't just making this up. He's expressing his concerns about police misconduct." At the request of Ice-T (Tracey Morrow), following months of protests, Time Warner deleted the song from the album.

After a federal judge ruled in 1990 that the 2 Live Crew album, "As Nasty as They Want to Be," was obscene, a Fort Lauderdale retailer was convicted on obscenity charges for selling it. In 1992, two Omaha, Nebraska, stores were prosecuted in separate sting operations for allegedly selling copies of 2 Live Crew albums to minors. Washington legislators passed a law making record store owners subject to criminal charges if they sell to minors recordings with sexually explicit lyrics. The governor called the law "a subtle warning shot" to the music industry, which has pledged to impose self-censorship.

Under pressure from groups protesting rap music lyrics, Time-Warner Chairman Gerald Levin in 1995 directed the company's top music executives to develop "standards" for handling controversial music.

## PUSHING THE LIMITS?

Examples of "shock radio" on the Howard Stern talk show, according to the Atlanta *Constitution*:

- Interviews conducted by Stuttering John, a man with a speech impediment who quizzes celebrities on the street.
- "Lesbian Dial-a-Date," seeking to pair up gay women.
- "Bestiality Dial-a-Date," which allegedly got Stern fired from the NBC Radio network.

- Discussions of penis size—his or any guy's. Female callers are urged to reveal their breast sizes.
- The "Out-of-the-Closet Show," in which callers are invited to expose prominent gays.
- Questions such as, "How can Jeffrey Dahmer [the Milwaukee murderer] get a fair trial unless there are more guys on the jury who want to have sex with dead men?"

He said it is necessary to balance creative expression with corporate responsibility. Soon thereafter, the company severed all ties with Interscope Records, the Los Angeles-based firm whose gangsta rap performers had plunged the firm into the controversy.

The Federal Communications Commission, although it has no jurisdiction over the recording industry, has warned broadcasting stations that they would be held accountable for knowing the content of songs played on the air. Monitoring the records, however, has been no easy task.

# PART TWO
## The Print Media

## ROLES OF THE MEDIA—SOCIAL INTERPRETER

The mass media report, stimulate, and interpret the social changes occurring around the world, including the impact of American popular culture abroad.

*"The role of the press is to inform society about problems, not to solve them."*

—Reuven Frank, news executive

*"Freedom is the right to tell people what they do not want to hear."*

—George Orwell, British novelist

*"One of the things the press is not covering well is the general boredom of the public."*

—Henry Graff, historian

# CHAPTER FIVE
## Newspapers

## 100 Years-Plus of Comic Strips

He was a bald-headed, jug-eared street urchin who walked along Hogan's Alley and said sassy things. He wore a loose, tent-like garment that turned bright yellow on Sundays.

He was "the Yellow Kid," chief character in the world's first comic strip. The strip, drawn by R. F. Outcault, first appeared in the New York *World* on February 17, 1895. In the Sunday comic sections, the Kid's outlandish costume was printed in yellow.

In the century since then, newspaper comic strips have become a lively part of the American culture. American "funnies" also are published around the world with the dialogue in various languages. Often the names of the characters are changed.

Every generation has had its favorites. Among them: "Gasoline Alley," whose orphan character Skeezix married Nina Clock . . . "Li'l Abner," the bashful hillbilly whose pursuit by his girl friend created Sadie Hawkins Day . . . "Popeye," who got his strength from eating spinach and admired a woman named Olive Oyl . . . "Nancy," eating ice cream cones with her pal Sluggo . . . "Dick Tracy," the jut-jawed detective with his wrist watch radio.

Today's most popular comic strips worldwide, according to *Editor & Publisher*, and the approximate number of publications carrying each, are: "Peanuts," 2400; "Garfield," 2400; "Blondie," 2000; and "Hagar the Horrible," 1900.

For nearly 300 years, from the day the first colonial weekly appeared in the coffee houses of Boston, newspapers were the principal source of news for the American people. Newsboys ran through the streets waving fresh copies and shouting "Extra!" when sensational news occurred. Stacks of late afternoon editions melted away on newsstands as crowds of urban commuters plunked down their pennies for copies to read on train or streetcar rides home. The raucous theatrical hit, *The Front Page*, depicted reporters and editors in their ramshackle newsrooms as hard-driving cynics scheming to outwit news sources and their journalistic competitors.

All that has changed. The days when newspapers were virtually the public's only source of news, except for sparse radio newscasts in later decades, are long gone. Television with its appealing visual images and glamorized personalities has become the principal source of news for millions of people. The "Extra" edition with its huge headlines has given way to the special news bulletin that interrupts TV programs.

Nevertheless, newspapers remain at the bedrock of journalism in the United States and other countries. They are the medium of record, providing permanent files for reference. They cover major stories in more detail than television does, report far more local stories than television, and provide editorial commentary. After watching television's often vivid visual coverage, serious students of events turn to their newspapers for detailed information. In that sense, the media complement each other. Radio and television are faster, newspapers are fuller. Reading the news on a page requires greater mental concentration than hearing it on radio or watching it on television. This fact puts an extra burden on newspaper editors to provide a stimulating product, easily comprehended and conveniently organized.

The fundamental principles and reporting techniques of today's journalism developed during three centuries of newspaper publication.

This chapter provides an overview of newspaper history, describes how newspapers operate, and explains how newspapers are trying to supplement their traditional role as a print medium with new electronic production and distribution methods.

## The Audience for Newspapers

Each day approximately 60 million copies of daily newspapers reach the hands of American readers. Each week more than 10,000 weekly newspapers publish issues filled with news and advertising about their local communities. When speaking of "the newspaper," people may be talking about the bulky New York *Sunday Times* with its million-plus copies or referring to a free-distribution weekly publication thrown on the driveway of every home in a community of 3000 people.

Most debate about newspapers' performance focuses on nationally known metropolitan newspapers such as those in New York, Washington, Chicago, and Los Angeles. Yet, in fact, 85 percent of the more than

1550 American daily newspapers are published in small and medium-sized cities and have circulations below 50,000. Less than a third of all dailies have circulations above 25,000. Some dailies in rural centers have barely 5,000 circulation, but they are vital elements of the local social fabric. Despite differences in appearance, size, and type of audience served, all newspapers have similar goals.

## Three Basic Functions

The contemporary newspaper has three fundamental functions and several secondary ones. The fundamental ones are:

- to inform readers objectively about what is happening in the community, country, and world.
- to comment on the news in order to bring the developments into focus
- to provide the means whereby persons with goods and services to sell can advertise their wares.

The newspaper's secondary roles are (1) to campaign for desirable civic projects and to help eliminate undesirable conditions; (2) to give readers a portion of entertainment through such devices as comic strips, cartoons, and special features; and (3) to serve readers as a friendly counselor, information bureau, and champion of their rights.

When a newspaper performs all or most of these tasks well, it becomes an integral part of community life. Television "sells" its news by developing on-the-air personalities whose mannerisms and aura at times have more impact on the viewer than the content of the news they are delivering. Newspapers lack that personality advantage; a familiar byline on a story carries the impress of authoritative knowledge to the steady reader but cannot match the congenial smile or the cynically lifted eyebrow of the TV news commentator. Therefore the newspaper must build a personality of a different sort based on its complete contents and tailored to its audience.

The printed word has a lasting power and precision beyond that of the spoken word or the visual image, although it has less ability to startle and shock. Readers can refer to it again and again. Stories may be clipped and saved by readers for many years and be readily examined in the newspaper's files decades later. This fact increases the reporter's feeling of writing history. It contributes to the newspaper's position as a stabilizing, continuing force in the community.

In the self-examination by the newspaper industry, editors as a group came to realize that too often the history they were recording was only the surface manifestation of the day's events—there was too much emphasis on who said this or did that and not enough attention to why this had happened. This has led to an upsurge in *investigative reporting*, frequently by teams of reporters, in which the newspapers try to report frankly how our complex society is actually working. Reporters are given time to probe into such situations as conditions inside mental hospitals and nursing homes, the devious and sometimes illegal deals between political leaders and contractors, and the manner in which charitable institutions actually spend the money they receive from kindhearted donors. The possibilities are almost endless.

# The Colonial Press

## Skimpy News Reporting

News as we know it today was rarely found in the first American newspapers published during the colonial era. The publishers were primarily printers, not editors. Although they had a sense of what interested people, most lacked reportorial instincts and the ability to write interesting stories. Moreover, their access to news sources was extremely limited; transportation was inadequate, and communication poor. Invention of that basic instrument of modern reporting, the telephone, was more than a hundred years in the future. It is not surprising, then, that most newspapers were incomplete, often inaccurate, and, to our contemporary taste, dull reading.

The publishers mostly printed information brought to them; they did not have local reporters as we know them today. They copied many stories from other newspapers and periodicals, especially those brought from London on voyages that lasted several weeks. Despite these handicaps and inadequacies, citizens read the colonial papers avidly. They had little other choice.

Benjamin Harris, with his ill-fated *Publick Occurrences* of 1690 in Boston, was banned because he did not have permission from the government to publish. James Franklin and Benjamin Franklin were early publisher-printers who were also journalists. James, in his *New-England Courant*, gave Boston readers of the 1720s the first readable and exciting American newspaper. Benjamin Franklin carried on the traditions in his *Pennsylvania Gazette*.

During the Revolutionary War period, publishers such as Benjamin Franklin and Isaiah Thomas of the *Massachusetts Spy* were alert to forward the patriot cause, but even a well-to-do publisher such as Thomas did not attempt to have his own correspondent with Washington's army.

## The Political Pamphleteers

Political pamphleteers—writers who used the early-day newspapers to advocate their causes—were more important during the 1700s than the editor-printers. Three of them in particular heavily influenced the desire for self-government that stirred among colonists in the years before the American Revolution.

**John Dickinson.**  Although he opposed revolution, John Dickinson's "Letters from a Farmer in Pennsylvania," published in the *Pennsylvania Chronicle* of 1767–1768, strongly advocated home rule for the colonies. Instead of representing agrarian interests, as the title implied, Dickinson spoke for the colonial business class. This group opposed the commercial restraints on colonial trade imposed by the British government, which prevented development of colonial industry and trade. Although Parliament imposed these restrictions, the Americans had no voice in that governing body.

**Samuel Adams.**  A genius at stirring popular emotions, Sam Adams was the great propagandist of the Revolution. He twisted every possible incident or administrative action of the British rulers in Massachusetts into an argument for revolt. In today's journalistic-political jargon he would be called a "spin-master"—an expert at bending facts to promote his cause. His enemies called him an "assassin of reputations," and undoubtedly he was.

Only briefly an editor himself, Adams worked with a group of Boston patriots assembled in the office of the Boston *Gazette*—a group that included the engraver Paul Revere. If news was dull and the fires of dissatisfaction needed fanning, Adams turned minor scrapes into events of seemingly major import. When British rifles fired to restrain a street crowd, the *Gazette* called the affair the Boston Massacre. In times of crisis, such as the passage of the Stamp Act or imposition of the tax on tea, Adams worked with others to stir up resistance throughout the colonies. His Committee of Correspondence, organized in 1772, was a major channel of communication among patriot editors.

**Tom Paine.**  A political philosopher, Tom Paine arrived in the colonies from England in time to make two great pamphleteering contributions to the patriot cause. His *Common Sense*, which sold 120,000 copies in three months in the spring of 1776, was a hard-headed, down-to-earth argument for independence that the common citizen could understand. That December, when Washington's discouraged army was camped on the Delaware River across from Trenton, Paine was drafted to write the first of his *Crisis* papers for a Philadelphia weekly:

> These are the times that try men's souls. The summer soldier and the sunshine patriot will, in this crisis, shrink from the service of their country; but he that stands it NOW, deserves the love and thanks of man and woman. Tyranny, like hell, is not easily conquered; yet we have this consolation with us, that the harder the conflict the more glorious the triumph. What we obtain too cheap, we esteem too lightly; it is dearness only that gives every thing its value. Heaven knows how to

put a proper price upon its goods; and it would be strange indeed if so celestial an article as FREEDOM should not be highly rated.

Paine's words lived to be broadcast to occupied Europe during World War II; at the time, they helped to spur the first American victory.

## Press of the New Republic

**The Political Newspapers.**   Vituperative, bitterly personal journalism in which editors of opposite political views attacked each other with biting sarcasm marked the years following the birth of the United States. The *political newspapers* of the period were more concerned with getting readers to accept their views than with the quality and completeness of their news coverage. The struggle over the adoption of the Constitution and the establishment of the new federal government were the chief objects of this rancorous debate.

Yet, out of this period of mudslinging journalism came the historic *Federalist Papers,* one of the best expositions of political doctrine ever conceived. Largely the work of Alexander Hamilton, the brilliant leader of the pro-Constitution party, this series of 85 articles was written for the newspapers of New York State. They were reprinted throughout the country and remain today as a source of study for political science students.

On the anti-Federalist side with Thomas Jefferson were his personally-sponsored poet-editor, Philip Freneau of the *National Gazette,* and other masters of partisanship such as Benjamin Franklin Bache of the *Aurora.* The opposing editors heaped invective not only on each other, but on their political sponsors as well.

The climax in this feuding came when Bache accused George Washington of being a "front man" for the Federalists. He wrote, "If ever a nation was debauched by a man, the American nation has been debauched by Washington."

The traditions of partisan journalism that developed in the 1790s, with all their excesses, continued for several decades into the 1800s.

**The Mercantile Newspapers.**   At the same time, however, another form of journalism was developing and prospering. It consisted of the *mercantile newspapers* published in the seaboard towns, primarily containing shipping news and reprints of articles from European newspapers. Although their circulations rarely exceeded 2000, they reached an important clientele and, excelling in their specialties, they played a role in the development of the news function concept.

Competition was tough. In 1800 there were six dailies in Philadelphia (but only two in 1990) and five in New York. The individual papers began to go out after the news. Correspondents covered sessions of

Congress in Washington as early as 1808 and were well established by the late 1820s. Seaport dailies hired boats to meet the incoming ships out in the harbor so their editors would have a head start on digesting the foreign news.

## The Penny Press

An exciting element entered American journalism in 1833 when Benjamin Day founded the New York *Sun*, the first of the East Coast big-city newspapers that collectively became known as "the penny press." Aimed at the common people, they emphasized the same titillating news elements that some mass-circulation tabloid newspapers do today. Highly sensational human interest stories filled their pages, overshadowing important news. Crime and sex stories were written in full detail.

When the *Sun* appeared on the streets of New York, it had a tremendous advantage: it sold for one cent, compared to six cents for its competitors. Readers found it to be tiny, bright, and readable. Within four years, the *Sun* was printing 30,000 copies a day—more than the combined total circulation of its competitors on the day it first appeared.

As could be expected, the *Sun* soon had imitators in its own city and elsewhere. James Gordon Bennett brought out the New York *Herald* (1835), and printers from New York founded the Philadelphia *Public Ledger* (1836) and the Baltimore *Sun* (1837). These four sheets all became famous newspapers.

News dispatches were transmitted for decades by dot-and-dash Morse code tapped out by operators such as these telegraphers at the White House in 1903. (Library of Congress)

## Bennett and News Enterprise

James Gordon Bennett serves as the symbol of the penny press news enterprises. He had been a Washington correspondent, reporter, and editor for other dailies before he launched the *Herald*. He more than matched the *Sun* with sensational coverage of crime and court news while challenging the more sober journals with detailed coverage of Wall Street affairs, political campaigns, and foreign news.

Bennett matched his rivals in establishing pony express services to carry the news from Washington and other points. One *Herald* courier service reached all the way from Newfoundland, carrying European news by pony rider, boat, and train to the first telegraph point. He hired locomotives to race presidential messages from Washington and used the telegraph as soon as Samuel F. B. Morse's invention proved itself in 1844. By the 1850s he had made the *Herald* the leading newsgathering paper.

Bennett's competitors included two new papers, Horace Greeley's New York *Tribune*, founded in 1841, and Henry J. Raymond's New York *Times*, founded in 1851. Greeley's managing editor, Charles A. Dana, directed a reportorial staff of high quality.

**Stereotyping**
Converting a flat newspaper page form into a semi-cylindrical metal plate to fit a rotary press so multiple copies can be made quickly

The Civil War called for great efforts in news enterprise. The *Herald* sent its own small army of correspondents into the field; other leading papers followed suit. Printing advances of the previous two decades—the flat-bed cylinder press, the type-revolving press, and *stereotyping*—were needed to handle increased circulations. Sunday editions of daily papers came into being. The illustrated periodicals, *Harper's Weekly* and *Frank Leslie's Illustrated Newspaper*, led the way in using woodcut illustrations and maps. The traditions of news enterprise and emphasis on the news function were well established.

## Greeley and the Editorial Page

Horace Greeley is recognized as one of the most influential editors in the history of American journalism. His New York *Tribune* was the first American newspaper to develop an editorial page that was the product of the thinking of a group of individuals. What the *Tribune* printed represented a dramatic change from the tradition of the pamphleteer.

Greeley was deeply conscious of his responsibility to the reader. He knew the *Tribune* had to be enterprising in reporting the news if it was to compete successfully for readers. But he felt it his responsibility to be just as enterprising in seeking to influence public opinion by devoting much space to serious discussion, editorial argument, and interpretation of events. The *Tribune* examined issues and debated ideas; it did not follow a set party line or insist that there was only one solution to a problem. It made the opinion function the key to its popular acceptance. Its weekly edition, in which the best of the daily news and opinion was reprinted for mail circulation, had the largest circulation of any contemporary publication.

William Cullen Bryant, who joined the New York *Evening Post* staff in 1825 and remained to edit it for a half-century, also fell into this category of the personal editor. Another was Joseph Medill, builder of the Chicago *Tribune*, who was one of Lincoln's firmest supporters.

In the post–Civil War years, the name of Edwin Lawrence Godkin stands out. Godkin founded the *Nation* magazine in 1865 and succeeded Bryant as the driving force of the New York *Evening Post* in 1881. Born in Britain, Godkin decided the United States needed a high-grade weekly journal of opinion and literary criticism similar to those in England. His distinctive style of writing and skill in ironic analysis made the *Nation* a favorite of other intellectuals.

## The New Journalism

During the 35 years between the end of the Civil War and 1900, the United States achieved enormous industrial and political growth. Its population doubled. Inventions such as the telephone and electric light and creation of a railroad network contributed to a period of dynamic expansion. So did the arrival of masses of European immigrants.

As chroniclers of this ferment, newspapers too underwent notable changes, both physically and in content. The era is known as the time of the "new journalism." All around them, editors saw fascinating things to report and social pressures to examine.

Newspapers grew swiftly during the period, in both number and circulation. Daily newspapers quadrupled in number; by 1900 there were 1967 general-circulation dailies—more than 400 above today's figure. Weekly papers tripled to more than 12,000 by the turn of the century, and at that point the country had more than 3500 magazines. The publications were able to respond to the hunger for the printed word through use of new machinery and processes such as the rotary press, mechanized typesetting, photoengraving, and color printing. A new cycle of sensationalism also arose.

**New journalism** Term originally applied to 1880s newspapers that were low-priced, entertaining, and objective in basic hard news, and supported social and economic reform

## Giant Figures of the Era

Three aggressive personalities—Joseph Pulitzer, William Randolph Hearst, and Edward W. Scripps—stand out as dominant leaders of the "new journalism" era. All were regarded as champions of the people.

**Joseph Pulitzer.**   This immigrant who became an editor and publisher serves as the principal symbol of the era. He had a rare ability to blend solid news and stimulating editorial opinion with sensational headlines, eye-grabbing graphics, and human interest stories, the stuff of which street circulation is made.

Pulitzer founded the St. Louis *Post-Dispatch* in 1878 and within five years made it the city's leading newspaper by giving readers what they wanted. Both his news and editorial columns reflected a fierce crusading spirit, reinforced by his insistence on accuracy, a search for facts, and

The Linotype machine, on which an operator sets lines of type in hot metal by fingering a keyboard, appeared in the 1880s and largely replaced hand-setting of type. The machines greatly increased the speed of preparing news for publication. The double row of Linotypes is producing type in the Los Angeles *Times* composing room. (Los Angeles *Times* photo)

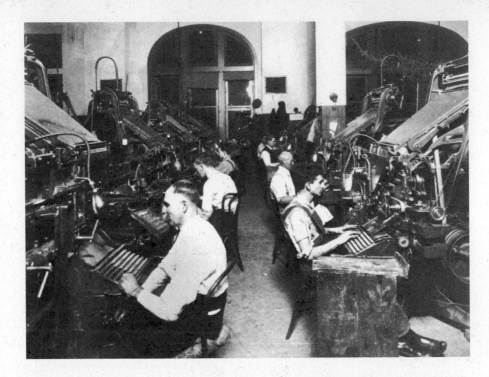

good writing. He created the coordinated crusade using both the news and editorial columns and tenaciously attacked wrongdoers in public and business life.

Two of Pulitzer's famous commands to his staff were:

"Accuracy! Accuracy!! Accuracy!!!"

"Terseness! Intelligent, not stupid, condensation."

Added to these orders was a reminder to his reporters that while seeking significant stories they also should watch for news that was "original, distinctive, dramatic, romantic, thrilling, unique, curious, quaint, humorous, odd, and apt to-be-talked-about."

Five years after starting the *Post-Dispatch*, Pulitzer invaded New York in 1883, buying the run-down *World*. Again his formula worked spectacularly. Within four years the *World* built a record-breaking circulation of 250,000 and eclipsed the *Herald* in advertising. It became the most talked-about paper in the country.

The key to Pulitzer's success was that behind the flash and sensationalism lay a solid body of news coverage and a strong sense of responsibility in the opinion function. This 1907 memo about the *Post-Dispatch* explains why his colleagues of this century have named him as the leading American editor of modern times:

I know that my retirement will make no difference in [the paper's] cardinal principles; that it will always fight for progress and reform, never

President Harry S Truman grins triumphantly at the Chicago *Daily Tribune* headline that falsely reports his defeat by Thomas E. Dewey in the 1948 presidential election. The *Tribune* strongly opposed Truman, an underdog for reelection, and drew the embarrassingly wrong conclusion from scattered early returns.

tolerate injustice or corruption, always fight demagogues of all parties, never belong to any party, always oppose privileged classes and public plunderers, never lack sympathy with the poor, always remain devoted to the public welfare, never be satisfied with merely printing news, always be drastically independent, never be afraid to attack wrong, whether by predatory plutocracy or predatory poverty.

**William Randolph Hearst.** The son of a rich Californian who gave him the San Francisco *Examiner*, Hearst traveled to New York in 1895 and bought the *Journal*. Soon he and Pulitzer were engaged in a ferocious circulation battle in which sensationalism ran rampant. Hearst, however, like some other competitors, never sensed the total character of Pulitzer's journalistic product and assumed wrongly that the *World* succeeded by sensationalism alone.

In the *Journal* and his other newspapers, Hearst likewise was a crusading champion of the people. His editorial platform at the turn of the century called for nationalization of the railroads and telegraph lines, a graduated income tax, and extensive new financial support for the public schools. To this he added an active support of labor unions that made them regard his papers as their champions.

Nevertheless, the liberals of the time distrusted Hearst's own political ambitions, which extended to the White House; they disliked the bitterness of his editorial attacks on his opponents, the sensationalism and near-cynicism of his news policies. But undoubtedly Hearst had great influence on the ordinary reader of the pre-World War I generation. By the

Three leaders of the "new journalism" who crusaded for reforms on behalf of all people. Top left: Edward W. Scripps on his yacht. Top right: Joseph Pulitzer, as depicted by John Singer Sargent, American portrait and mural painter. Bottom: William Randolph Hearst, at the height of his career.

1920s, however, the Hearst papers were much less progressive in outlook, and by the 1930s their position was almost reversed from the one they had held in 1900. The Hearst papers became bitterly isolationist by the time of World War I and remained so until their founder's death in 1951.

**Edward W. Scripps.**     Scripps was the third of the great people's champions of the new journalism era. He set his circulation sights on the work-

## "YELLOW JOURNALISM" IS BORN

Graphic, often humorous drawings were a key tool in the turn-of-the-century circulation battle in New York between Joseph Pulitzer's *World* and William Randolph Hearst's *Journal*. Especially popular were Richard F. Outcault's drawings in the *World*, in which the central figure wore a yellow outfit, as described at the opening of this chapter.

As New Yorkers grew disenchanted with the excesses of the battle, they applied the word "yellow" to the entire content of the newspapers—and "yellow journalism" was born.

The term is such a deeply imbedded cliché, that a hundred years later critics who dislike something they have read in a newspaper often sneer at "yellow journalism!"

ing people of the smaller but growing industrial cities of the country as he developed his chain of newspapers from his headquarters at the Cleveland *Press*. His social goal was to improve the position of the mass of people through better education, labor union organization, and collective bargaining, and a resulting reasonable redistribution of wealth. In this way, he reasoned, a peaceful and productive society could emerge in an industrialized America.

Scripps viewed himself as the only real friend of the "poor and ill-informed." He said his newspapers were the only schoolroom the working person had; the public school system did not serve him or her adequately, and other newspapers were either capitalistic in outlook or too intellectual in their appeal. He pictured himself as a "damned old crank" who was instinctively rebellious against the status quo in any field of human activity. Politically, the Scripps papers were strongly liberal. This pattern continued after Scripps' death in 1926 and until the late 1930s, when, under the influence of the late Roy W. Howard, the Scripps-Howard papers became substantially more conservative.

## Twentieth-Century News Trends

Impartial gathering and reporting of the news were generally recognized to be the basic obligation of newspapers by the early 1900s. The editor who put views ahead of news, and who tied his newspaper to a political machine, had pretty well gone out of style. Slanting of news to fit the prejudices or political preferences of a publisher was also recognized as a detriment, although some newspapers continued the practice. The Canons of Journalism adopted by the American Society of Newspaper

Editors in 1923 contain the following two paragraphs, which summarize the aspirations of modern journalistic leaders:

> The right of a newspaper to attract and hold readers is restricted by nothing but considerations of public welfare. The use a newspaper makes of the share of public attention it gains serves to determine its sense of responsibility, which it shares with every member of its staff. A journalist who uses his power for any selfish or otherwise unworthy purpose is faithless to a high trust.
>
> Partisanship, in editorial comment which knowingly departs from the truth, does violence to the best spirit of American journalism; in the news columns it is subversive of a fundamental principle of the profession.

The mass media made a reasonable effort to fulfill their increased responsibilities for interpreting the news. Professional standards had to be raised to meet the challenge. Better-trained and more knowledgeable men and women came to occupy key reportorial assignments and news desk posts. The range of subject matter with which a Washington correspondent had to be familiar in the 1920s was narrow indeed compared to the complexities of Washington news in the 1990s. And since all news tended to become local in its impact with the narrowing of geographic barriers in the atomic age, every general assignment reporter had to know far more about such areas as international affairs, science, and economic trends than did his or her predecessors.

## The New York Times

The editors of the New York *Times* built what is generally conceded to be the greatest single news machine of this century, publishing what was called by its admiring competitors a "newspaper of record." The story of the growth of the *Times* since Adolph S. Ochs rescued it from bankruptcy in 1896 illustrates the trend in acceptance of the news function responsibility, even though it is the story of an atypical journalistic leader. For what the *Times* did in its methodical completeness was done at least in part, and in some respects as successfully, by other responsible newspapers. Ochs told his readers in 1896: "It will be my aim . . . to give the news impartially, without fear or favor." What made the *Times* great was not so much its excellent special sections as its persistence in gathering and printing the news in all its varied aspects. One of the great managing editors, Carr V. Van Anda, was given control of the *Times* newsroom in 1904 with the understanding that he should do whatever it took to do a comprehensive job with the news. World War I gave Van Anda an opportunity to show his ability. Using the cables and wireless almost with abandon, the *Times* added the reports of its own correspondents to those of news services. Most important, the paper began to publish the full texts of documents and speeches. This policy, combined with the publication of the annual *New York Times Index*, made the *Times* the lead-

Copyreaders of the New York *Times* telegraph desk in about 1940 edit stories received from other U.S. cities. Use of computer terminals has virtually eliminated such piles of paper from contemporary newsrooms. One editor wore his hat because of a draft. (Library of Congress)

ing newspaper for librarians, scholars, government officials, and other newspaper editors. If there was any other complaint to be registered against the *Times* of the Van Anda period, it was that the paper presented a voluminous amount of news without sufficient interpretation or screening for the average reader.

## "Jazz Journalism"

One more wave of sensationalism was to precede the "era of interpretation." The 1920s were known as the Jazz Age, and the papers that catered to a new group of readers won the dubious honor of being identified as "jazz journalism." Their sensationalism was accompanied by the two identifying techniques of the period: the tabloid format and great emphasis on photography.

Leading the sensationalist tabloids was the New York *Illustrated Daily News*, founded in 1919 by Joseph Medill Patterson, cousin of Robert R. McCormick and partner with him in the publishing of the Chicago *Tribune*. Patterson, unlike his ultraconservative Chicago cousin, was unconventional in his socioeconomic beliefs—socialistic, his wealthy friends said. He wanted to reach and influence the lowest literate class of Americans and was attracted to the tabloid format by the success Lord Northcliffe was enjoying with it in England. The *Daily News* appeared with a photograph spread across its front half-page and was well stuffed with pictures, human interest stories, and entertaining features. By 1924 it had the largest circulation of any newspaper in the country, a position it held until surpassed by the *Wall Street Journal* in 1980.

Close behind in reflecting the Jazz Age were Bernarr Macfadden's New York *Graphic* and Hearst's *Daily Mirror*. For all three papers, the most important news involved gangsters, murders, illicit love nests, bootleggers, and flappers.

### Interpretive Reporting

This type of more skillful, yet impartial, handling of the news was not unknown before the 1930s. But by then the socioeconomic revolution known politically as the New Deal, coupled with the impact of international crises, forced editors to emphasize "why" along with "who did what." Old-style objectivity, which called for the reporter to stick to a factual account of what had been said or done, did not give the reader the full meaning of the news. The new concept of objectivity was based on the premise that the reader needed to have a given event placed in its proper perspective if truth was to be served. Also discarded were older assumptions that subjects such as science and economics could not be made interesting to a mass readership. Reporter-specialists who could talk both to their subjects and to a popular reading audience emerged.

## Another New Journalism

In the late 1960s, the literature of the mass media began to herald a "new journalism" that borrowed the title of the innovations of the 1880s. Its reportorial and writing techniques were variously described as tell-it-as-you-see-it, impressionistic, humanistic, investigative—and even interpretive. Its more controversial characteristic was described as advocacy, activist, or participatory. The latter trend merely reflected the widespread frustration of the era and the demand that the conservative establishment give heed and power to others—youth, minorities, and women. The mass media should be used, the argument ran, to further such reforms.

Perhaps the leading spirit of this new journalism was Tom Wolfe, although he viewed his efforts as a revolt against old-fashioned book writing rather than news writing. Other major figures were Truman Capote, Norman Mailer, Gay Talese, and Jimmy Breslin. Their work appeared in *Esquire*, the *New Yorker*, *Harper's*, and the fast-rising *New York*. Those magazines, the old New York *Herald Tribune*, and such underground papers as the *Village Voice*, founded in 1955, served as vehicles for the new style of reporting, perhaps best described as "saturation."

The best-known example of *advocacy journalism*, the *Chicago Journalism Review*, was founded in October 1968 in the wake of disillusionment among young Chicago newspeople over management and public reaction to the role of the press in the riots at the Democratic convention of that year. The sexual revolution of the 1950s and 1960s helped to spawn the "underground" publications.

There was an alternative press famed for radical dissent, antimilitary stances, and pungent arguments. *I.F. Stone's Weekly* (1953–1971) cut a swath through status quo politics and Vietnam war policies. Dorothy Day founded the *Catholic Worker* in 1933 and edited it as a champion of social justice and pacifism until her death in 1980. Deidre English's *Mother Jones* was an irreverent organ of women's rights.

**Advocacy journalism**
Writing in which reporters inject strong personal opinion, advocating social change. Popular especially during the 1960s

## The Minority Press

Publications written specifically for minorities in the multicultural American society, including those in foreign languages, long have had a significant role. As the American population becomes more diverse, and the total percentage of minority population continues to increase, their importance grows. The 1990 census showed nearly 30 million blacks, 22 million Hispanics, and 7 million Asians living in the United States. The Census Bureau predicted that by the year 2010 African Americans and Hispanics each will make up 13 percent of the nation's population, a total of 26 percent, while Anglos will be 58 percent. Asian Americans and Native Americans will provide the remaining percentages.

The minority press helps minorities to retain their cultural heritages and at the same time introduces newcomers from abroad to the ways of the American mainstream. Especially in times of crisis, such as the Los Angeles riot of 1992, these papers and local minority radio stations serve as vital communication channels. Because they represent the familiar and support the special interests of their audiences, some of their readers find them more believable than the mainstream newspapers, even when the two sets of publications report identical news.

### The Black Press

More than 3000 newspapers owned and edited by African Americans for African Americans have appeared since the first, *Freedom's Journal*, in 1827. "We wish to plead our cause. Too long have others spoken for us," said the editors of *Freedom's Journal*, John B. Russwurm and Samuel Cornish.

Unfortunately, the black community has had few socioeconomic resources to support a press. Obtaining sufficient revenue from advertising has been a problem. Historically, the average life span of a black newspaper has been nine years. Yet, collectively, this struggling press has made its impact on the country.

Black newspaper circulation peaked during the World War II period, when the Pittsburgh *Courier* achieved a national circulation of 286,000.

# Ethnic Media Serve as Lifeline Amid the Chaos

As the regular press more fully covered stories involving racial matters, black newspaper readership declined and community-based weeklies replaced the nationally circulated papers.

Black publications in 1995 consisted of 209 newspapers, most of them weeklies, and 71 magazines, according to the *Gale Directory of Publications and Broadcast Media.* Among the best-known black newspapers are the Atlanta *Daily World,* Baltimore *Afro-American,* Chicago *Defender,* Los Angeles *Sentinel,* and New York *Amsterdam News.* Most leading black newspapers are moderate in tone, heavily local in news coverage, strong in sports and social news, and occasionally crusading.

If there was a single major voice in black publishing, it was *Ebony,* the monthly picture magazine founded by John H. Johnson in 1945 in full imitation of *Life,* with circulation around 1.8 million. Johnson also published a popular news weekly, *Jet;* a woman's magazine, *Essence;* and other periodicals.

## The Hispanic Press

As the Hispanic population expands in the United States, so does the Spanish-language press. The 1995 *Gale Directory* listed 124 Hispanic newspapers and 85 magazines, largely published in regions where the Hispanic population is concentrated—primarily Miami, southern California, the Southwest, Chicago, and New York City. This list includes several large daily newspapers such as *La Opinion* in Los Angeles and *El Nuevo Herald* in Miami, both with more than 100,000 daily circulation. Most of the publications, however, are weekly or monthly.

The first Spanish-language newspaper in the United States was *El Misisipi,* printed during 1808–1810 in New Orleans. More than 100 Spanish-language publications came and went before 1900 as the centers of the Hispanic population developed.

Some publications for Hispanic audiences are bilingual, printed in both Spanish and English. Also, some mainstream dailies have special sections written in Spanish, which usually appear once a week. Another variation of the bilingual approach is found in Denver, where copies of a Spanish-language paper, the *Weekly Issue,* appear on Thursdays as a supplement to the Denver *Post* in neighborhoods with a large Hispanic pop-

ulation. The *Weekly Issue* also is distributed free at selected locations in the city.

Since a large percentage of the U.S. Hispanic population understands both Spanish and English, bilingual publications offer unusual possibilities. (See Chapters 8 and 10 for minority broadcasting.)

## Native American and Other Special Media

The first Native American newspaper, the *Cherokee Phoenix*, was published in 1828. Six years later soldiers shut down the newspaper and threw its press down a well. From that time until now, the Native American press has faced difficulties, including lack of funds and small circulation with a limited tribal audience. Nevertheless, it continues to serve an

# TWO FAMOUS BLACK JOURNALISTS

Two men in particular figure prominently in the growth of the black press during the nineteenth and early twentieth centuries: Frederick Douglass and W. E. B. DuBois.

*Frederick Douglass.* This remarkable ex-slave who founded *The North Star* in 1847 became the symbol of hope for blacks in his day. He rallied public opinion against slavery; through his writing and speaking he helped white men and women to see the degradation of slavery through black eyes. *The North Star*, published in Rochester, New York, had a circulation of 3000 in the United States and Europe, particularly among influential readers. It was renamed *Frederick Douglass' Paper* in 1851 and survived until the Civil War. Douglass then edited magazines for 15 years and wrote three autobiographies tracing his exceptional career.

*W. E. B. DuBois.* In 1910 DuBois founded *The Crisis* as the protest voice of the National Association for the Advancement of Colored People.

"Mentally the Negro is inferior to the white," said the 1911 *Britannica.* To DuBois this belief was the crisis that had to be eliminated before discrimination in education, housing, and social status could be overcome. Under his militant leftist leadership, *The Crisis* passed the 100,000 circulation mark. He retired as editor in 1934. Later he moved to the African country of Ghana, where he died at 95 in 1963.

Frederick Douglass shown in a Daguerreotype made between 1850 and 1855. (Smithsonian Institution)

Undaunted by the lack of electricity, staff members of the San Francisco *Chronicle* use flashlights as they write and edit their newspaper's issue of October 18, 1989 reporting the severe earthquake that struck the Bay area. The issue appeared only a few hours after the tremor shook the region. (Steve Ringman, San Francisco *Chronicle*)

important purpose in reporting tribal activities and goals. The Native American Journalists Association functions as a unifying force. Members report that they often are under heavy political and social pressures from tribal councils that seek to control them.

Best known of the Native American papers is the weekly *Lakota Times* of Rapid City, South Dakota. Established in 1981, it has a paid and free circulation of 26,000 with some national and international readership, and a correspondent in Washington to cover Native American affairs. The paper has been assisted by a $100,000 loan from the Freedom Forum.

As a further indication of U.S. ethnic diversity, the Gale directory lists publications in 45 foreign languages, from Swahili to Welsh.

## Newspapers Today

### A Perplexing Dilemma

Editors and publishers of American daily newspapers face a disturbing situation.

Today's daily newspapers are more attractive in appearance, with color photography and eye-catching graphics, than those of 25 years ago. Generally, they are better written. They cover a substantially wider

**Table 5.1**

**Trends in Newspaper Circulation: How the Sale of Newspapers Has Failed to Keep Pace with Growth of U.S. Households**

|      | Number of U.S. Daily Newspapers | Total Circulation | Total U.S. Households |
|------|-----------------|--------------------|------------------------|
| 1960 | 1763 | 58,881,746 | 52,799,000 |
| 1970 | 1748 | 62,107,527 | 63,401,000 |
| 1980 | 1745 | 62,201,840 | 80,776,000 |
| 1985 | 1676 | 62,766,232 | 86,789,000 |
| 1989 | 1626 | 62,694,816 | 92,630,000 |
| 1992 | 1570 | 60,083,265 | 93,347,000 |
| 1995 | 1538 | 59,024,805 | 96,301,000 |

*Sources: Newspaper Association of America*, Editor & Publisher, Statistical Abstract of the United States.

range of subjects that are more relevant to their readers' lives than their previous emphasis on politics, crime, and tragedy.

Yet fewer papers are being sold than even a decade ago, and scores of daily newspapers have gone out of business.

Why has this happened? What can be done to reverse the trend? Abundant, often contradictory, answers have been offered to both questions as the newspaper industry subjects itself to self-examination, but no single clear solution has emerged.

Newspaper executives face these basic facts:

1. *Television news coverage* has replaced newspaper coverage in the minds of many Americans. Although television news presents fewer facts, fewer stories, and less interpretation than newspapers do, it provides visual impact with a "you-are-there" feeling and "sells" its news with personalities.

2. *Total sales of newspapers* have failed to keep pace with the nation's population growth. The percentage of American homes receiving a newspaper has been declining, although the newspaper industry as a whole remains profitable.

3. *In this age of lightning-fast electronic delivery* of information, newspapers must find ways to supplement their traditional print delivery of news with electronic delivery methods, because much of their news is "old" before the paper is delivered. In some instances this might eventually result in electronic delivery, entirely replacing print delivery of the newspaper.

The newspaper industry's difficulty is much more complex than competition from television, because the industry is heavily influenced

**New York Newsday** EDITION

SATURDAY, JULY 15, 1995 • 50 CENTS

# So Long, New York

**After 10 Years, New York Newsday Is Closing Down** / Pages A2-3

When New York *Newsday* ceased publication in 1995 after 10 years as a combatant in the city's tabloid newspaper war, it said farewell with a jaunty headline. Its death left two New York tabloids, the *Daily News* and the *Post,* to fight it out.

by changes in lifestyles that tend to shut newspapers out of people's lives. Among them are: (1) a large percentage of women now hold jobs and are away from home much of the day; (2) disaffection from conventional society among many persons in the lower socioeconomic groups in big cities, especially youths, has caused them to reject newspapers as irrelevant; and (3) the distressing amount of illiteracy and semiliteracy in the country limits the potential number of readers.

Some researchers fear that if the current trend continues, daily newspapers may become information resources primarily for the well-educated, more affluent segments of the population, rather than for the mass market at which they traditionally have been aimed.

Of the problems facing the newspaper industry, perhaps the most distressing is widespread illiteracy. Estimates of the extent of "functional illiteracy" among American adults range from 20 to 30 percent or more.

The shutdown of a daily newspaper creates emotional scenes among staff members, saddened by loss of jobs and newsroom camaraderie. After the Houston *Post* told its employees it was ceasing publication, Adrees Latiff, a photographer, and Leanne Reidy, a researcher, comfort each other with an embrace. (AP Photo)

Functional illiteracy generally is described as the inability to read a newspaper, understand the warnings on a bottle of medicine, or fill out a job application.

The United States ranks 49th in the world in literacy, according to the United Nations Educational, Scientific, and Cultural Organization (UNESCO). It ranks 24th among nations in book sales per capita. School dropouts have reached alarming proportions in many urban districts. Eighty-five percent of the juveniles who come before the court system are illiterate.

Many programs to promote reading skills and interest in reading are being conducted by print media organizations, as well as educators, librarians, business executives, and others.

## General Organization of Newspapers

No matter what their size, from small weeklies to metropolitan dailies, newspapers have a common organization. Each has five major departments: *editorial*, which gathers and prepares the news, entertainment, and opinion materials, both written and illustrated; *advertising*, which solicits and prepares the commercial messages addressed to readers; *production*, which turns the editorial material and advertisements into type and prints the newspapers; *circulation*, which sells and delivers the newspapers to the readers; and *management*, which oversees the entire operation.

## THE CREATION OF A NEWS STORY

This is how a news story is born, edited, and put into print at a large newspaper:

*Covering the story.* A reporter covers a beat such as police or the environment, being responsible for all the news that happens in that territory, or is sent out by the city desk on a specific assignment. He or she uses the telephone extensively to gather and cross-check information. A metropolitan paper may have as many as 100 reporters.

*Writing the story.* The reporter writes the story on a computer in the office or perhaps on a personal computer in the field. On an urgent story, the reporter may telephone the facts to a writer in the office.

*Editing the story.* The story is transferred to a computer terminal on the city desk, where the city editor or an assistant reads it on the screen. The editor corrects errors, smooths out the writing, and looks for story "angles" that should be included. When approved, the story is moved by computer to the news desk.

*Writing the headline.* The news editor assigns the story a headline size and style and marks it into position on a designated page. The editor then turns over the story by computer to one of the editors on the copy desk. The copy editor gives it a final polish, writes the headline, and returns the story to the news editor.

*Putting the story into type.* After receiving final approval, the story is moved through the computer system to the production department. There it flashes through electronic typesetting machinery and emerges as printed words on strips of paper. A printer pastes the story into the designated position on a cardboard page form. This form is sent to the platemaking department, where it is transferred onto a thin metal sheet that is locked onto the press for printing.

At papers that have adopted full pagination, the paper typesetting stage is eliminated, and the story moves electronically from the news editor's computer directly onto a laser-produced printed page.

## The Newsroom

There are two main divisions of newsroom work—*reporting*, which includes gathering and writing news and feature stories and the taking of news and feature photographs, and *desk work*, which is the selection and preparation for printing of the written material and photographs submitted by reporters, photographers, news services, and syndicates. Those who do the desk work are the editors.

The local reporting staff operates under direction of the city editor, sometimes called the metropolitan editor. Much reporting is done by staff members working in teams. Sports, business, and lifestyle departments operate as separate entities and answer to the managing editor, as does the city editor.

A very important area of work is the editorial page. Editorial page staffs run to eight or ten members on metropolitan papers that pride

Virtually all writing and editing in newsrooms today is done on computers such as the ones shown here in the sports department of *USA Today,* situated near Washington, D.C. (Conklin, Monkmeyer Press Photo)

themselves on the quality of their opinion offerings. The editorial page director coordinates their work and consults with the publisher on major policy decisions. At the smaller daily level there may be only one editorial writer. Most weekly newspaper editors write editorial columns or more informal "personal columns."

Efforts to make newspapers more appealing in appearance through use of color photography and page layouts employing eye-catching artwork have led to the addition of a graphics editor in many newspaper offices, sometimes with the rank of assistant managing editor. (See Chapter 13.)

**Diversity in the Newsroom.**    Once the almost exclusive domain of white male staffs, the newsrooms of the United States have undergone a striking change during the last generation. By the early 1990s, more than 35 percent of newsroom workers were women, and the male–female ratio continues to improve.

The complaint remains that too few women hold high editorial posts on newspapers—19.4 percent in 1992, according to the National Federation of Press Women. That problem is diminishing slowly as the current generation of senior male executives retires and a large pool of skilled, experienced women journalists has become available to replace them. The excellent performance by the growing number of female managing editors and city editors, as well as editorial writers and columnists, has helped to overcome the traditional inertia against newsroom change.

## REPORTING THE END OF THE WORLD

Headlines often reveal the character of a newspaper—serious, sensational, or aimed at an audience with special interests.

Participants in a chat forum on the Internet had fun with this fact recently by suggesting the headlines certain newspapers might use in reporting the end of the world. Here are some of them, as published in *Editor & Publisher:*

*Wall Street Journal:* "Dow Jones Plunges as World Ends"

Washington *Post:* "Republicans' Triumph Short-Lived as World Ends"

New York *Times:* "Turmoil in Mideast as World Ends"

New York *Post:* "Nude Coed Found as World Ends"

*USA Today:* "We're Dead"

Suggested headlines from magazines:

*People:* "Charles and Diana: It's Really Over"

*Money:* "Ten Great Extremely Short-term Investments"

*Mother Jones:* "The End of the World: Who Profits?"

*Playboy:* "Girls of the Apocalypse"

Achievement of multicultural balance on newsroom staffs has been much slower, despite diligent work by some elements of the newspaper industry to achieve it. The goal of the American Society of Newspaper Editors (ASNE) is to achieve a minority ratio equal to that in the general population by the year 2000. Although improvement has been made, ASNE remained well short of its goal.

By 1996, minority employment in newsrooms had risen to 11.02 percent. More than half of U.S. newspapers employed African Americans, Hispanics, Asians, or Native Americans. Many small newspapers in predominantly white communities reported difficulty in employing and retaining young minority journalists, because larger papers offered bigger salaries and more attractive living conditions. Total newsroom employment was 55,000.

## Advertising

Newspaper advertising is divided into two types, *display* and *classified.* The former ranges from inconspicuous one-inch notices to multiple-page advertisements in which merchants and manufacturers proclaim their goods and services. Classified advertisements are the small-print, generally brief announcements packed closely together near the back of the paper; they deal with such diverse topics as help wanted, apartments for rent, used furniture and automobiles for sale, and personal notices.

Most newspapers receive about 80 percent of their income from advertising and 20 percent from circulation.

Approximately 50 to 60 percent of every daily newspaper consists of advertising, an important service that gives readers information for purchasing goods and services, seeking employment, and filling other needs. Traditionally, newspapers prepared all display advertising in their own composing rooms, employing large staffs of printers for that purpose. Today, colorful "preprints" supplied by chain stores and other companies with sales outlets in many cities have replaced much of this locally composed advertising.

These multiple-page sections, usually on slicker paper than newsprint, are printed in a commercial plant and distributed to newspapers in numerous cities for simultaneous distribution. As a result, newspaper composing rooms have far fewer employees than previously. When an advertiser wishes to reach every home in a city with its message, it either places its preprint in a free circulation publication or arranges for the daily newspaper to distribute free copies to nonsubscriber homes. This is called *total market coverage*.

The advertising department provides the basic plan for each day's issue by marking the sizes of scheduled advertisements on page "dummy" sheets. Editors then use the blank space on the dummies.

## Production

Electronic typesetting revolutionized the mechanical processes of producing a newspaper when it replaced the old "hot type" system, in which large numbers of printers put together pages by assembling lines of lead type. Only a few persons are needed now to paste strips of paper type onto page-size cardboard forms.

The phototypesetting machine contains a whirling disk of type letters in different faces or a cathode ray tube device. The flowing electronic commands of the computer cause the phototypesetter to record the indicated letters in sequence on fast film; this film produces a positive print of the words on a sheet of coated paper that emerges from the darkroom through a slot, ready to be pasted up in page form. This is called *cold type*.

When a newspaper computer sends local stories to a news service computer for possible regional or national distribution, or to another computer elsewhere, these transmissions are called *electronic carbons*.

The cold type process will in turn be overshadowed by the *pagination* system, now being used by many newspapers, as it becomes more commonplace. Further refinement of pagination to remove technical "glitches" is in progress.

In the pressroom, offset printing has replaced the traditional system, in which type contained on a semicircular revolving plate makes direct contact with the newsprint.

Offset printing is based on lithography, an older process in which printing was done from a smooth flat surface of stone. In surface print-

---

**Total market coverage**
System under which newspapers on occasion supplement their paid circulation by distributing free copies to nonsubscribers

**Electronic carbon**
Copy of a news story transmitted from one computer to another for publication or reference; for example, from a member newspaper to an Associated Press office

**Pagination**
Process of making up an entire newspaper page on a video screen, ready for transmission to a printing plate

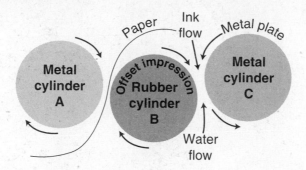

**Figure 5.1**

How offset printing works. The impression on the plate affixed to cylinder C is "offset" onto rubber cylinder B, then printed on paper passing between cylinder B and cylinder A. Because of the lack of wear on a metal plate, thousands of additional pages may be printed, and more clearly, with this method.

ing the image is placed on the stone by a greasy substance that has an affinity for ink. The nonprinting surface is covered with a thin film of water that repels the ink. Thus only the image is printed on paper when pressure is applied. The image is transferred from the printing plate cylinder to a rubber blanket attached to a second cylinder. It is then transferred to the paper, which is carried by a third impression cylinder (Figure 5.1). Development of offset presses capable of printing on a continuous web of paper was a major step in adapting this process to newspaper printing.

Competing with offset printing is another method recently adapted for newspaper work called *flexography*, long used in certain kinds of commercial printing. Flexography uses water-based ink rather than the traditional oil-based variety. Since this dries quickly, the vexing problem of ink rub-off onto readers' hands is virtually eliminated. Color reproduction is vivid.

## Circulation

For many decades newspapers used boys and girls to sell and deliver their daily issues. These carriers purchased papers wholesale and were paid by customers at a retail price. Thus they were known as independent "little merchants." The idea of a newspaper with millions of dollars invested in equipment, and with a skilled professional staff, leaving the selling of its product to boys and girls seemed crazy to many management specialists. Yet it worked fairly well.

Recently, many newspapers have replaced their youthful carriers with adults, at least in part. To give these adults more income, and to make a profit, numerous newspapers have added a supplementary service that delivers magazines, samples, and advertisements as well as the daily paper.

The circulation department handles the stuffing of preprinted advertising sections into the paper, a major task. Most dailies belong to

A system called pagination, just coming into general use, enables an editor to lay out a news page electronically, speeding up production and reducing the role of the composing room. Robin Fulton Manly of the Pasadena, California, *Star-News,* seated at a makeup station, designs a news page with graphics. (Reprinted with permission from *Presstime,* the journal of the Newspaper Association of America.)

the Audit Bureau of Circulations, which examines their books to certify that the circulation figures they report are accurate. This is crucial, since a newspaper's advertising rates are based on the size of its circulation.

## Management

The task of overseeing all aspects of a newspaper, coordinating work, stimulating the generation of revenue, and setting goals falls on management.

The top official is the publisher. He or she frequently is assisted by a business manager, to whom the advertising, circulation, and production departments answer. The editor, as head of the news and editorial department, often answers directly to the publisher. In some group operations, the editor has a strong independent role in matters of news judgment.

Publishers and editors confer often with colleagues in other cities. The major trade organization of the industry is the Newspaper Association of America (NAA), created in 1992 by unification of the former American Newspaper Publishers Association with several specialized groups. News executives belong to the American Society of Newspaper Editors.

The corporate groups that own a large majority of newspapers have created a professional class of media managers who frequently are moved from one member newspaper to another to solve problems. Below are some of the areas they examine.

## The Evolving Newspaper Pattern

### Switch to Morning Publication

One result of the newspaper industry's intensive self-examination, in an effort to stay abreast of social changes and electronic developments, is the switch of many dailies from afternoon to morning publication.

Traditionally, evening newspapers have dominated the field. They still do numerically, about 5 to 3 over morning newspapers, but a substantial and accelerating switch of papers into the morning field has occurred since the early 1980s. Although outnumbered, morning papers have substantially more total circulation than evening papers.

The shift to morning publication probably will continue. Nine of the ten largest circulation American dailies are morning publications, and the other is a 24-hour publication (see Table 5.2). The numerical superiority of afternoon papers persists because most small-city papers cling to their traditional patterns.

The most striking evidence of change is found in the great cities of the northeastern section of the country. Especially in the afternoon field, falling advertising and circulation income has forced one famous newspaper after another to quit publication, leading poorly informed observers to the false conclusion that the American newspaper industry is dying. Less noticed, however, is a strong offsetting trend.

**Table 5.2**

**Ten Largest U.S. Daily Newspapers**

| Newspaper | Circulation |
| --- | --- |
| *Wall Street Journal* (morning) national edition | 1,841,188 |
| *USA Today* (morning) | 1,617,743 |
| New York *Times* (morning) | 1,157,656 |
| Los Angeles *Times* (morning) | 1,021,121 |
| Washington *Post* (morning) | 834,641 |
| New York *Daily News* (morning) | 758,509 |
| Chicago *Tribune* (morning) | 667,908 |
| *Newsday* (all day) | 555,203 |
| Houston *Chronicle* (morning) | 551,553 |
| Chicago *Sun-Times* (morning) | 501,115 |

*Source: Audit Bureau of Circulations report, May 11, 1996.*

Earlier in the century metropolitan populations lived close to the center of the city, so the newspaper's newsgathering, circulation, and advertising efforts were concentrated near that center. As population spread to the suburbs, the problems of distribution grew, especially for evening papers. Many people no longer commuted downtown. Higher purchasing power was concentrated around the fringes of the city, not in the core area.

Quickly, suburban daily newspapers in the largest metropolitan areas were created to serve this new audience. Their growth has been one of the major publishing success stories of the last quarter-century. The local newspaper's greatest advantage over larger "invaders" from out of town, and over local television and radio news broadcasts, is its more detailed presentation of hometown news.

## Public Journalism

As they examined the future role of newspapers, editors discussed a concept called *public journalism*. Although it is loosely defined, the concept means basically that local newspapers should be vigorous leaders in promoting civic projects and setting the political agenda. Coupled with advocacy is stimulation of public participation in shaping the newspaper's direction.

Some editors embraced the idea. Others hesitated, concerned that they would be sacrificing the traditional newspaper role of objectivity. Still others said, "So, what's new? Our newspapers have been advocating and promoting civic improvement for years."

## A National Newspaper: USA Today

The success of *USA Today* as a national daily morning newspaper marks another significant change in the American newspaper pattern. Until the arrival of satellite transmission, publication of a general-interest national daily newspaper—one delivered simultaneously in all portions of the United States—was physically and financially impractical.

Then, in 1982, the Gannett Company launched precisely that kind of newspaper, *USA Today*. Assembled at a plant near Washington, D.C., the contents of *USA Today* are sent by satellite to 34 plants around the country, and to others abroad, for printing and distribution. By the end of its third year, *USA Today* reported net paid circulation of about 1.1 million and availability in more than 2000 towns and cities nationwide. By the start of the 1990s, it had added another quarter-million copies daily but was still losing money. The paper lost heavily during its early phase, perhaps as much as $70 million in its first year, and failed to meet the forecast of Allen H. Neuharth, then the head of the Gannett Company and founder of *USA Today*, that it might break even in 1988. *USA Today* finally earned a profit in 1994, after a decade of losses estimated by Wall Street analysts at $600 million.

USA Today's busy, colorful front page with its numerous photographs, brief stories, graphics, and summaries has influenced the appearance of other American newspapers. The national newspaper's content is designed to deliver news in print with the same brevity TV newscasts employ.

The impact of *USA Today* on American newspaper publishing has been intense. Abundant use of color and graphics, emphasis on brevity with short main stories and numerous capsulized summaries, unusually detailed and up-to-the-minute sports pages, a distinctive editorial opinion policy, and a full-color weather page are among its most conspicuous features. The paper is edited for an audience accustomed to the color and brevity of television news stories. Almost immediately, editors of other newspapers began to imitate its color charts, weather layout, and other features.

Critics called *USA Today* shallow and flimsy, with more flash than substance, and doubted that it would find a sufficiently large permanent audience. Its publishers and admirers asserted that it would change the nature of American newspapers because it was in tune with the times. *USA Today*'s impact on the traveling public is especially strong. Designed for a mobile audience with limited time to read, it is readily available in hotels, airports, and similar public places through the efforts of an extremely efficient distribution system.

Using satellite techniques, a few other American newspapers are distributed nationally on day of publication, but they are designed for more specialized audiences.

## The Electronic Newspaper

After three centuries of producing publications on paper, newspaper publishers in the new electronic age are searching for ways to deliver information on computer screens as well.

Some futurists see the day when the electronic newspaper will completely replace the familiar newsprint form. In their forecasts, subscribers would receive the entire publication on a home computer or television screen, never soiling their fingers with ink from a printed product.

Others call this concept unrealistic. Experiments so far seem to support their doubts. Americans have shown little enthusiasm for an exclusively on-screen newspaper. Subscribers apparently prefer to hold a newspaper in their hands in the familiar way. Display advertisers, perhaps from habit, still prefer the printed form.

Yet publishers recognize that millions of individuals ignore newspapers. Can these nonreaders be reached electronically—and if so, how?

The prevailing concept in the newspaper industry is that the printed newspaper will continue to appear and will be supplemented electronically with frequently updated news and sports reports plus much additional background and reference material from the newsroom. These reports will be made available to those who desire them through online computer database services, the World Wide Web, and automated phone-in requests to the newspaper offices.

Newspaper publishers will in effect assume the broader role of multimedia information providers.

Two basic facts underlie the emerging change: (1) newspapers are the most voluminous gatherers of news, especially at the local level, of all the mass media, and (2) they have far more information on hand every day than they have space to print, just as television and radio newscasts are limited by air-time restrictions. The online computer services, on the other hand, have virtually unlimited capacity.

The Los Angeles *Times* and the Cox newspapers of Atlanta, to cite two examples, have created regional electronic supplements on Prodigy, a commercial online computer service. By paying a monthly fee in addition to the basic subscription to Prodigy, an online user may call up background on news stories; up-to-the-minute news, sports, and financial bulletins; statistics; government programs; entertainment listings; transportation schedules; material for children; and other information not found in the printed editions of the newspapers. Some online programs contain newsphotos, graphics, and classified advertising from the newspaper, as well. In Richmond, Virginia, the concept has been taken further by combining a local television station's visual material and the local newspaper's supplemental material in an online service. Many newspapers opened home pages, offering late information, on the Internet.

Publishers hope that eventually their electronic online supplemental services, and further in the future two-way television newspapers, will be profitable. In the early stages, however, limited public participation makes them losing investments.

## Audiotex

A simpler form of electronic news supplement called *audiotex* already is offered by numerous newspapers. An individual may telephone a newspaper, indicate the category of news desired—late baseball scores or stock quotations, for example—and hear a recorded voice give the information. Some newspapers offer the service free of charge and recover their cost by including brief advertisements in the recorded messages; others charge a small fee for each call.

Expansion into electronic news delivery is creating jobs. Papers offering such service usually have an additional staff to prepare the material. Changes in the reporter's role may result, as well. Some planners suggest that a reporter in the field on assignment might write a story in the regular way, take photographs for the online service, and prepare a voice report for the audiotex service. Whether one person could do all these things efficiently is in doubt, but a person trained in multimedia reporting and editing should find additional opportunities in the future.

## The Weekly Newspaper

In thousands of American towns, the weekly newspaper is at the core of community life. It is the chief source of information about the activities of individuals and organizations, and the merchants look to its advertising columns as a weekly tool for selling goods. In the files of a small-town weekly are recorded the vital statistics of the town's life—the births and deaths, marriages, social events, and tragedies, and the ludicrous moments that give life zest. Even when it is overshadowed by a big-city daily a few miles away, the weekly newspaper often has a secure place in the heart of its community and can continue to thrive. The chief stock in trade it has to offer is names—subscribers reading about their neighbors and about themselves.

The weekly newspaper illustrates editing and publishing in its simplest form, although anyone who believes that putting out a weekly is easy has been badly misled. All the jobs involved in any newspaper must be done: getting news and editing it, selling advertising, handling circulation, and seeing to it that the paper is printed on time. On a weekly everything is done by a handful of workers. After the day's work at the office is finished, the weekly editor covers civic meetings, attends social functions in the hope of getting news, and listens to the complaints of fellow townspeople. Weekly newspaper publishing is a risky enterprise for a person who thinks only in editorial terms; unless the publisher quickly learns the business tricks of obtaining revenue from advertising and circulation, the paper won't live long.

Weekly newspaper publishing as a whole is thriving in the United States. Many weeklies earn excellent profits, while others in less desirable locations struggle to survive. A large majority of weeklies, especially in urban areas, give their papers away in order to reach concentrated audiences for advertisers. In order to prosper they must attract sufficient advertising, not always easy in small markets. Total circulation of weekly newspapers, paid and unpaid, was 78 million by 1994, according to the National Newspaper Association, their trade organization.

The range of editorial excellence among weekly newspapers is wide. Splendidly edited weeklies are to be found throughout the United States, along with others that barely qualify for the label "newspaper." Weeklies are rarely of the crusading type, again with outstanding exceptions. Most weekly editors see their role as that of printing constructive, orthodox news without dealing in what is often called sensationalism. In some cases the newspaper's profit margin is so thin that the publisher cannot risk irritating an important advertiser by printing something the person dislikes. Frequently a weekly newspaper has no editorial page at all. Without resorting to big-city street sensationalism, many weekly editors could serve their communities better if they dealt more bluntly with local problems, despite the pressures not to do so. The American weekly press as a whole is conformist and conservative, although some unorthodox "alternative" weeklies have a lively impact in their communities.

## Desktop Publishing

A simplified method of creating type and laying out pages, called desktop publishing, has recently come into wide use on newspapers. The system, discussed in Chapter 13, consists of one or more personal computers, some specialized software for layout, and a laser printer. Far cheaper than other typesetting equipment, it enables publishers to produce small newspapers profitably even in markets with limited advertising potential.

## Sunday Papers—World's Largest

By far the bulkiest newspapers published anywhere are the Sunday editions of American metropolitan newspapers. These mammoth publications wrapped in sections of color comics often contain more than 300 pages, nearly four pounds of reading matter covering everything from the current world crisis to interior decorating advice, theatrical notices, baseball scores, and weekly television logs.

Sunday newspapers have been growing in popularity with American readers, and the number of Sunday papers published has been increasing. The total was 889 "Sundays" in 1995, up 303 since 1970, with total circulation of 62.4 million.

More than 20 U.S. Sunday newspapers have circulations above 500,000, and several sell more than 1 million copies. Even these mammoth figures are greatly exceeded by the circulation of several Sunday papers printed in London and circulated throughout the British Isles. They do not, however, have the advertising bulk of their American counterparts.

The Sunday paper is designed for family reading and is distinguished from the daily editions by two elements: a large feature package and bulk retail advertising. As a medium for late spot news, the Sunday paper is less important than the daily editions because less news occurs on Saturday (which it is covering) than on weekdays. Most newspapers print part of their Sunday editions well in advance because of the difficulty of printing such huge issues on the available press equipment on the publication date.

The Sunday editions of most newspapers have substantially higher circulation than the daily editions and sell at a price often more than double that of the daily paper.

## Sunday Supplements

Most Sunday newspapers include magazine supplements, either nationally syndicated or created by their own staffs. Some give their readers both national and local magazines.

The two principal nationally distributed supplements are *Parade* and *USA Weekend*. These slick, colorful magazines, distributed only through newspapers, are edited for family readership, with upbeat emphasis on personalities, home hints, personal achievement, entertainment, and recreation. *USA Weekend* closely resembles *USA Today* in approach; both are published by the Gannett Company, Inc. It contains brief articles and abundant illustrations, with stress on television and sports. *Parade* tends to run longer, somewhat deeper articles. Each magazine is carried in more than 350 newspapers.

Locally edited Sunday supplements, once a fixture in many papers, have dwindled in number recently because of high publishing costs and inadequate advertising support.

## The News Services

Much of the material published in newspapers and included in radio and television newscasts does not originate from local staffs, but is created hundreds or thousands of miles away by global news services, supplemental news services, and syndicates that sell their material to clients.

Most American daily newspapers and broadcasting stations obtain the bulk of their national and foreign news, and many feature stories as well, from the Associated Press. The gigantic cooperative newsgathering organization has offices in major American cities and in numerous foreign capitals as well. It also supplies news reports to newspapers and broadcasters around the world.

While the AP dominates news distribution in the United States, rival foreign news agencies have very strong positions in other parts of the world. Reuters, the British service founded in 1851, distributes its general news report in approximately 160 countries and is especially strong in financial news reporting. The French Agence France-Presse also serves approximately 160 countries. Both Reuters and AFP serve a limited number of clients in the United States. ITAR-Tass (International

# The International Scene:
# GLOBAL NEWSPAPER PUBLISHING

There are approximately 8,000 daily newspapers in the world, and far more weeklies and semi-weeklies. Europe, North America, and Japan account for four-fifths of the sales. Japan, Germany, and the Scandinavian countries have the highest per capita circulation of dailies, well over 500 for every 1000 inhabitants. Some large cities in the developing countries have high quality newspapers, but beyond those urban areas the quality of content and appearance falls off sharply.

As in the United States, the growth of chains and conglomerates characterizes much of the world's press. Most dailies are privately owned, but direct and indirect government controls are evident in many countries. Except where funding is inadequate or where resisted by unions, modern printing techniques increasingly are being employed. Newspapers in many less-developed nations, however, are still printed with nearly worn-out equipment on antiquated flat-bed presses.

Because of its mass nature, much of the world's press is sensationalist and somewhat superficial in its treatment of the news. With the exception of a few countries including the United States, where the *Wall Street Journal* now enjoys the greatest daily circulation of any newspaper, dailies with the largest circulations almost always are those that emphasize entertainment value. Most countries, however, with the exception of a few in Africa and Asia, do have at least one high-quality daily newspaper that deals primarily with social and political ideas and issues and reflects the best practices of journalism.

John C. Merrill and Harold A. Fisher, in their book, *The World's Great Dailies*, provide profiles of 50 newspapers that they consider, by reputation and the consensus of serious observers, to be the world's finest. To a considerable degree, the editors of these dailies read each other's newspapers and, with the serious magazines of their countries, help maintain a dialogue among themselves and their readers about important national and world issues.

An around-the-world traveler examining copies of these dailies might pick up the *Times* in Great Britain, *Le Monde* in France, *Corriere della Sera* in Italy, *Al Ahram* in Egypt, *Pravda* in the Commonwealth of Independent States (formerly the Soviet Union), *The Statesman* in India, *The Age* in Australia, *The Straits Times* in Singapore, *Renmin Ribao* in the People's Republic of China, *Asahi Shimbun* in Japan, *Estado de S. Paulo* in Brazil, and the Los Angeles *Times* in the United States. The tourist might not be able to read all these papers, but since English-language newspapers are published almost everywhere, the tourist could keep up with news developments of major importance reasonably well.

Thanks to satellite transmissions of completed newspapers to distant printing plants, a choice of major publications is available simultaneously on several continents. The oldest is the *International Herald Tribune*, established in Paris in 1887 and now printed in London, Zurich, Hong Kong, Singapore, Marseilles, The Hague, and Miami, the latter for distribution in Latin America and North America. The paper is owned jointly by the New York *Times*, Washington *Post*, and Whitney Communications Company. Others include the *Wall Street Journal*, in Asian and European editions; *USA Today*, in more than 80 countries; the international weekly edition of the *Christian Science Monitor*, in Europe and Australia; the Miami *Herald*, distributed throughout Latin America; and *The Stars and Stripes*, serving U.S. armed forces overseas. Other newspapers distributed internationally include the *Financial Times* of London, *Die Zeit* of Hamburg, the Toronto *Globe and Mail*, and several Chinese and Japanese dailies.

In 1990, Robert Maxwell, the late British media magnate, began publishing *The European*, a four-section color newspaper patterned after *USA Today* and printed mostly in English. The weekly is distributed mainly in European Common Market countries.

## Eastern Europe

Press freedom spread rapidly across Eastern Europe after the downfall of communism in the late 1980s. Some countries, such as Poland and Hungary, seemed well on the way to creating a diverse, private, and independent press environment. Others crept only slowly toward the goal.

Impediments to press freedom included a lack of training; a scarcity of hard currency; political pressures; monopolies over paper supply, publishing, and distribution; and the absence of updated, liberal laws governing the media, according to a survey by the International Media Fund, a private organization initially financed by the U.S. government.

Numerous foundations, journalism organizations, and other groups sent money, personnel, and equipment to help the media begin to work in a market economy, to recast press laws, to operate computers and other modern equipment, and to conduct research. Numerous scholarships and exchange programs were begun. Many newspapers were acquired by foreign publishers.

## Commonwealth of Independent States

In Russia, where the government had controlled and subsidized newspapers (gazeti) for decades, similar painful adjustments were under way. The government of President Boris Yeltsin subsidized only a few publications; most struggled financially. The thrice-weekly *Pravda*, once the official voice of the Communist party, received no help from the government, which it strongly opposed.

Among the most popular were youth-oriented *Komsomolskaya Pravda*, with more than 19 million circulation daily, and the weekly *Argumenty i Fakty* (*Arguments and Facts*), with circulation exceeding 25 million.

Weak advertising and monopolistic practices of printers, distributors, and paper suppliers were among problems plaguing almost all the Russian press. Such financial practices also caused the demise in 1994 of two collaborative ventures: the weekly *News in Review*, published jointly by the New York *Times* and the Moscow *News*, and a weekly called *We* in English and *Mb1* in Russian, a joint venture of the Hearst Corporation of New York and *Izvestia* of Russia.

Russian journalists have drafted an ethics code designed to discourage bribe-taking and "hidden advertising" in the nation of poorly paid reporters and widespread corruption.

Under a new press law, the only taboos on content were racism, pornography, and "war propaganda," an official said. In contrast with the pre-Yeltsin period, Western correspondents operated freely in covering news.

Telegraph Agency of Russia, combined with the former TASS news service) serves the countries of the former Soviet Union and some of its one-time satellite countries.

During the first three-fourths of the twentieth century, the Associated Press engaged in a vigorous news coverage battle with United Press International. Reporters and editors of the two American news agencies competed intensely to deliver big stories first and to provide better written, more comprehensive reports.

United Press International, however, suffered severe financial losses during the 1970s and 1980s. It went through a disastrous series of ownership changes, lost hundreds of clients, and now operates in only a limited way. Owned by Saudi Arabian interests in Great Britain, it no longer functions as a full-scale general news service.

## Historical Development

**The Associated Press.**    Shortly after the invention of the telegraph in 1844, six New York morning newspapers formed the Associated Press of New York, forerunner of the modern news service. The AP developed a factual, condensed style presenting news acceptable to all its members in that period of ardently personal, highly politicized journalism.

The telegraph was used extensively to convey news from Civil War battlefronts, supplementing the old-style pony express. Because the wires frequently were cut or downed during storms, and because every word cost money, reporters developed the so-called *inverted pyramid* style of transmitting the news. As many as possible of the five W's—who, what, when, where, and why—were placed in the first and immediately succeeding paragraphs. The details were given in later paragraphs, which local editors could delete and still give readers the gist of the story.

During the latter decades of the nineteenth century, the Associated Press was torn by battles to control its operation. In the 1880s, Western members, led by Melville Stone of the Chicago *Daily News*, broke the New York newspapers' control of the organization. Stone drafted arrangements giving the AP exclusive right to exchange news with European agencies.

**United Press International.**    AP rules permitted publishers to exclude rival papers from obtaining AP news. So in 1907 Edward Wyllis Scripps founded the United Press Associations to provide another source of news. Two years later William Randolph Hearst established the International News Service, built around his chain of newspapers. The three services competed until 1958, when United Press took over International News Service to form United Press International.

Under the AP system, newspapers became members of the cooperative and had to contribute their own stories to the service, United Press and INS sold their services as a commodity. Both began selling news to radio stations in 1935, and the AP followed five years later. In 1934, the Associated Press finally ended its restrictive arrangement of news exchange agreements with foreign agencies.

**Powerful AP Position.**    With the decline of UPI, the AP holds an extremely strong position. By 1995, it served approximately 1550 American newspapers. It also delivered news to approximately 600 radio and television stations, plus 850 newspapers and broadcasting stations in foreign countries. It also provided an AP newsphoto service and supplementary services such as graphics, audio news for radio stations, and news film for TV stations.

The AP distribution system for news is organized so that members may obtain varying daily quotas of news, depending on their size and location. Thus the AP report to a small newspaper in Arizona contains less volume than a major newspaper in Pennsylvania receives but Southwestern regional news is included.

## Rise of Supplemental News Services

Competition from the AP wasn't the only cause of UPI's decline. New competition arose from the supplemental news services provided by several large newspapers or groups of newspapers. Development of computerized and satellite transmission, through which these supplemental services distribute their news and feature material quickly nationwide, was an essential element in their growth.

A supplemental service is in effect a specially edited by-product of its parent newspapers. The daily package of news stories and features it delivers to its customers consists primarily of selected material from the sponsoring newspapers, plus in some cases stories from other contributing newspapers. Usually the material is made available to customers at the same time it is published in the parent papers.

The material fills a niche for the customers, with emphasis on news analysis and special reporting on health, science, food, and business news.

### Editors Cut Back

At one time it was standard practice for many medium-sized and large newspapers to purchase both AP and UPI reports. On important breaking stories, the newspaper editors went to press with whichever service's story arrived first. But as local competition diminished with the closing of many newspapers, and radio and television generally delivered the first word on big stories, editors found much less need to have both services.

Instead, newspapers frequently canceled one news service and bought a supplemental service, saving a substantial amount of money while obtaining stimulating fresh material. The service they dropped usually was UPI.

## SPECIALIZED AGENCIES SERVING THE THIRD WORLD

In response to protests by many less developed nations that news happenings in their countries were being inadequately reported (see Chapter 17), a number of national and regional agencies have been established in recent years to help serve their needs. Among the present agencies are the following:

The Inter Press Service, a Rome-based cooperative formed by journalists in 1964 to provide news services supporting political and social reform in Latin America but now also functioning in Africa, Asia, and Europe; its U.S. affiliate, Interlink, which also generates stories on its own; the Caribbean News Agency, founded in 1975 with United Nations aid and now serving 17 English-speaking countries; the Middle East News Agency; Pacific News Service; Asia-Pacific News Network; Gemini News Service; Pan African News Agency; and South–North News Service.

The Pool of News Agencies of Non–Aligned Countries was established in 1975 under the aegis of Tanjug, the news agency of the former Yugoslavia. Now the Tunisian news agency, Tunis Afrique Presse (TAP), using leased circuits, telex, and radio-teletype channels, daily distributes approximately 40,000 words of news provided by the governments of about 50 countries. Influential in the Third World are ITAR-Tass of Russia; China's Xinhua; and the Press Trust of India, that country's cooperative news agency.

The four best known supplemental services are:

- *Knight-Ridder/Tribune Information Services* (KRTN). This service combines the offerings of the Knight-Ridder newspapers and the Chicago *Tribune*.

- *Los Angeles Times–Washington Post News Service*. In addition to offerings from these two major newspapers, the LAT–WP includes material from all other Times Mirror newspapers except the Baltimore *Sun*, which operates its own service. The LAT–WP also runs an AllSports service.

- *New York Times News Service* (NYT). This service covers entertainment and lifestyle in addition to its political, foreign, and business coverage. NYT also includes stories from the Cox newspapers.

- *Scripps Howard News Service*. Combined with offerings from the group's newspapers and Washington bureau are stories from the Toronto *Globe and Mail* and the London *Observer*.

These supplementals provide graphics and in some cases photographs along with text. Their material is delivered by satellite. They design packages of material for small and midsize papers that cannot use their entire report. Other smaller services include those of the Cox, Copley, and Newhouse groups.

# Newspaper Feature Syndicates

The other major source of editorial material used by daily newspapers, and one that tends to bring uniformity to the American press, is the feature syndicate. Syndicates sell to the newspapers a multitude of material for the entertainment and education of their readers, edited and ready for publication on delivery. Comic strips and other features are provided in proof form for newspaper reproduction; text features are available in proof or duplicated form, or by transmission directly into the purchaser's computer system.

The newspaper editor tries to strike a suitable balance. There is no firm rule of thumb about this; one good newspaper of substantial circulation and a reasonably large editorial "hole" (the space left in a newspaper after the advertisements have been inserted) will publish 16 comic strips daily while a comparable one runs only ten or 12. The same is true of political columns and other material offered by the syndicates.

Examination of a typical well-edited newspaper with 50,000 daily circulation shows the following material purchased ready-made from national feature syndicates: 12 comic strips, 12 cartoon panels, five political columns, a medical column, a personal advice column, a crossword puzzle, an astrological forecast, a political cartoon, two entertainment columns, and a juvenile information feature.

**The Comics.** Certain features, especially comics, have run in newspapers so many years that they are household words. Some comic strips such as "Blondie" and the newer "For Better or Worse" reflect everyday life, often in exaggerated form. The purpose of most strips and panels is entertainment, not social or political commentary. In numerous strips fantasy plays an important part. This is evident especially in endowing animals with the ability to think and talk. Some English teachers used to call the act of giving animals human abilities "the pathetic fallacy." Pathetic or not, the technique has been highly successful with the dog Snoopy in "Peanuts" and Garfield, the cat, among four-footed characters.

By far the most significant in terms of political and social relevance is "Doonesbury," by Garry Trudeau. Because "Doonesbury" contains often

The U.S. Postal Service commemorated the 100th birthday of the comic strip in 1995 by issuing sheets of 20 comic strip stamps featuring famous characters who have made readers smile or chortle at their antics and adventures. These are some of the stamps.

biting political satire, some newspapers publish it on their editorial pages. Among other strips that employ subtlety and sophistication are "Peanuts" and "The Wizard of Id." The popular "Cathy" is drawn from the female point of view.

"Peanuts," drawn by Charles M. Schulz, became the first comic strip to appear in more than 2000 newspapers; it is published in 23 languages and is a repeat winner in *Editor & Publisher* magazine's annual poll of most popular comics. Its character Snoopy even appears on a blimp that flies over sporting events.

**Trends in Comics.** Newspaper editors usually select the strips and panels in their comic sections by demographic target categories—some for children, older readers, families, teenagers, and the like. They have learned to be careful, however, about dropping longtime mass appeal strips. When the Washington *Post* replaced several older strips with five designed for children, it received 30,000 phone calls and letters, heavily in protest, and had to reinstate the old familiar "Mark Trail."

Breaking away from the virtually all-white sets of characters that dominated comic pages for so long, artists have introduced numerous minority characters and designed strips for ethnic appeal. Editors also are looking for humorous new strips for children, in a sense turning back to the original concept of comic pages as "the funny papers."

**Comic Books.** Closely related to comic strips and cartoons are comic books. These colorful publications may be collections of popular newspaper cartoons or, more dramatically, highly imaginative fantasy, horror, and science fiction stories. Collecting old comic books has become a cult activity; some hard-to-find ones bring surprisingly high prices.

Although the original, and still primary, goal of the comic book is to entertain, educators have found it a successful tool for delivering information to poorly educated adults as well as children. Its visual impact can hold the attention of individuals who are intimidated by regular books.

**Columns.** Among text features, the personal advice columns by Ann Landers and "Dear Abby" (Abigail Van Buren), who are sisters, have had extremely strong readership. Political columnists run the full spectrum of opinion. To provide balance, the majority of newspaper editors publish both liberal and conservative columnists on their editorial and commentary pages.

Fewer than ten major syndicates provide the bulk of the features appearing in American newspapers, although there are about 340 smaller companies, some of which operate in specialized fields such as boating and book serializations. The major syndicates have from 25 to more than 100 features on the lists they offer for sale to editors.

Features are sold to newspapers for prices scaled to the paper's circulation. Although some are sold for specific contract periods, many are on a "till forbid" (t.f.) basis, meaning that the feature runs until the editor sends in a cancellation, usually on 30- to 90-day notice.

Competition among the syndicates is intense. There are more than 250 daily comic strips on the market, many of which are also issued in color for Sunday comic sections.

**Tie-ins to Television and Films.** The system of selling features to individual clients, practiced for decades by the newspaper industry, now functions in a similar manner in television. Series that have finished their runs on the networks, as well as programs created specifically for syndication, are sold by television firms to individual stations nationwide.

Comic strip cartoon characters who have become household words through newspapers, such as Dick Tracy and Superman, have had an additional life starring in movies and TV shows as well. Some, such as characters from "Peanuts," also appear in commercials. Screen and TV producers watch the mass market comic books for characters and story lines they can adapt—Batman, for example.

## Points to Remember

1. What are the three basic functions of a newspaper?

2. How did Samuel Adams use the press to stir up the revolutionary spirit in the American colonies?

3. James Gordon Bennett employed ingenious ways to cover the news in his New York *Herald*. What were some of them?

4. Joseph Pulitzer has been called the leading American editor of modern times. How did he achieve this honor?

5. How do you explain the fact that sales of U.S. daily newspapers have fallen and the number of daily newspapers published has decreased?

6. Why are many newspapers experimenting with ways to distribute news to customers electronically?

7. What are some of the ways in which publication of *USA Today* has influenced other newspapers?

8. Can you describe the process of creating a news story, from original reporting until it appears in print?

9. What advice would you give an editor about the types of material readers would like to see in a newspaper?

10. In general, what are the characteristics of newspapers around the world?

11. When did the first comic strip appear? Who was the chief character?

## Media Questions to Think About

1. Do you read a daily newspaper regularly? A Sunday newspaper? If not, why not?

2. What is the first section you read when you pick up a newspaper? What section interests you the least?

3. Have you ever used a newspaper's audiotex service or read a newspaper on an online computer service? If so, did you find the experience satisfactory?

# CHAPTER 6
## Magazines

## The Essence of Success

A woman of deep spirituality, Susan L. Taylor caught the essence of what black women wanted to read and helped move the circulation of *Essence* magazine from 600,000 to 1 million after rising to editor-in-chief in 1981. Readership in 1995, the monthly's 25th year, was estimated at 5.3 million.

When Taylor succeeded Marcia Ann Gillespie, now editor of *Ms.* magazine, she de-emphasized the political to focus more on the personal. "She began calling her monthly editorial 'In the Spirit,' a reflection of her own spiritual journey," the New York *Times* Magazine reported.

Being profiled in *Essence,* receiving an *Essence* Award on TV, or being featured on the cover is a goal coveted by many of the nation's black women leaders.

Taylor commands a $10,000 lecture fee. A collection of her editorials, *In the Spirit: The Inspirational Writings of Susan L. Taylor,* was published in 1993, with more than 300,000 copies in print.

The editor told her staff about a visit to a juvenile detention center. "These sisters who are incarcerated are facing such great challenges," she said. "But I'll tell you something. God is soooo good." The staff responded in kind. Reported the *Times:*

"It's hard to imagine a similar scene at *Vogue,* with Anna Wintour saying, 'I just saw the spring fashion shows and you know, God is soooo good.'"

The richly diversified world of magazines is undergoing a stimulating change, with imaginative graphics, a proliferation of "niche" publications serving specific interests of their readers, and expansion into cyberspace through online periodicals. Even staid trade journals appear in lively new dress, thanks to computer design techniques.

More than 12,000 magazines provide information and entertainment for Americans. They serve virtually every age, occupation, hobby, and lifestyle. More than 500 new magazines are started every year. Only one in four survives beyond the fourth year, but new publications, especially special-interest magazines, take their place, and the growth rate, despite increases in single-copy and subscription costs, far exceeds that of a decade ago.

About 75 magazines have circulations exceeding 1 million, but the trend is toward magazines that focus their editorial content and advertising on carefully identified groups of readers that comprise their chief present and potential buyers of advertised products.

Many relatively small-circulation magazines have developed in response to the economies possible through use of desktop publishing, which is discussed in Chapter 13. Almost all publishing houses also have reduced production costs through use of new copy preparation and printing techniques.

In this chapter we discuss these developments and others, delve briefly into the history of American magazines, describe the categories into which they fall, including the business press, and discuss editing and marketing processes.

## The Role of Magazines

Much of the communication of ideas, information, and attitudes among American people is carried on through magazines. They range from the slick-paper, four-color monthly with circulation in the millions down to the small, special-interest quarterly that, though virtually unknown to the general public, may have very strong influence within its field.

Like most other media, magazines seek to inform, persuade, and entertain their audiences and put before them advertising messages of national, regional, state, and city scope. Magazines never appear more frequently than once a week; thus their writers and editors, although generally part of small staffs with firm deadlines, often have more time to dig into issues and situations than do those on daily newspapers. Consequently, they have a better opportunity to bring events into focus and interpret their meaning.

Magazines are a channel of communication halfway between newspapers and books. Unlike newspapers or books, however, many of the most influential magazines are difficult or impossible to purchase at

Magazines create eye-catching covers to attract buyers at newsstands. This cover of *Elle* includes basic elements found in magazines for women—a photograph of a glamorous model and headlines luring readers inside for articles about diet and makeup, six fashion "looks," and a Hollywood celebrity feature.

newsstands. With their color printing and slick paper (in most cases), magazines are a showplace for exciting graphics. Until the late 1940s, most consumer magazines offered a diverse menu of fiction, nonfiction, and miscellany such as poetry and short humor selections. With television providing a heavy quotient of entertainment for the American home, many magazines discovered a strong demand for nonfiction articles, their almost exclusive content today.

There is another basic difference between newspapers and magazines. Except for the *Wall Street Journal* and the zoned editions of some metropolitan newspapers that reach specific neighborhoods, a newspaper must appeal to an entire community and have a little of everything for almost everybody. Yet hundreds of successful magazines are designed for reading by computer operators, dentists, poultry farmers, and model railroad fans. Therein lies the richness of diversity that makes the magazine field so attractive to many editorial workers and to advertisers.

From 1965 to 1993, while the U.S. adult population grew by 54 percent, magazine circulation increased 72 percent, according to studies

## Table 6.1

## U.S. Magazine Circulation and Advertising Revenue Leaders

| Largest Circulation | | Advertising Revenue (in Millions) | |
|---|---|---|---|
| 1. *Modern Maturity* | 21,875,436 | 1. *People Weekly* | $405.7 |
| 2. *Reader's Digest* | 15,126,664 | 2. *TV Guide* | 391.7 |
| 3. *TV Guide* | 14,037,062 | 3. *Sports Illustrated* | 385.3 |
| 4. *National Geographic* | 9,203,079 | 4. *Time* | 372.0 |
| 5. *Better Homes and Gardens* | 7,613,661 | 5. *Newsweek* | 278.9 |
| 6. *Good Housekeeping* | 5,223,935 | 6. *Business Week* | 233.8 |
| 7. *Ladies' Home Journal* | 5,048,081 | 7. *U.S. News & World Report* | 221.1 |
| 8. *Family Circle* | 5,005,301 | 8. *Better Homes & Gardens* | 221.0 |
| 9. *Woman's Day* | 4,724,500 | 9. *Good Housekeeping* | 218.6 |
| 10. *McCall's* | 4,611,848 | 10. *Forbes* | 189.2 |

*Sources: Audit Bureau of Circulations and Publishers Information Bureau. Figures are averages during the last six months of 1994.* Modern Maturity *is a membership publication of the National Retired Teachers Association and the American Association of Retired Persons. As reported in AdWeek Feb. 27, 1995.*

made for the Magazine Publishers of America. Advertising revenues increased 627 percent from $1.10 billion in 1965 to $7.63 billion in 1993. Leaders in both of these categories are shown in Table 6.1.

Adult Americans buy about 34 magazine copies per year on average, compared to only 31 copies per person in 1980. Characteristics of the average reader of the average magazine copy are shown in Table 6.2.

## Table 6.2

## Profile of Average Reader of Average Magazine Copy

- Median age: 40.2 (U.S. median = 41.2)
- 36.7% are at least high school graduates
- 41% attended and/or graduated from college
- 59.4% are married
- 58.1% are the head of household
- 56.6% live in a 3-or-more-person household
- 55.7% are employed full-time
- Median household income: $37,161
- 67.5% own their home with a $92,878 median value
- 71.6% live in a metropolitan area

*Source: Magazine Research Institute, spring 1994.*

# The Growth of Magazines

In 1741, Benjamin Franklin published one of the first two short-lived colonial magazines. Fellow colonials preferred London publications to his *American Magazine*. But before the Revolutionary War, Tom Paine was selling articles to the *Pennsylvania Magazine*, and publishing genius Isaiah Thomas was printing his *Farmer's Weekly Museum* in New Hampshire. Mathew Carey's *American Museum* of 1787 was the best of the new country's efforts.

Forerunner of the news magazine was *Niles' Weekly Register*, a remarkable compendium of American events (1811–1849). Intellectual fare was offered by Harvard writers in the *North American Review* (1815–1914). But the splashiest and best selling was *Godey's Lady's Book*, which won 150,000 circulation with hand-colored engravings of fashionable clothing, fiction, and poetry. Sarah J. Hale, its editor from 1836 to 1877, wrote 50 books and promoted women's rights, but won her greatest fame for a poem, "Mary Had a Little Lamb."

The Harper book publishing house founded *Harper's Monthly* in 1850, introduced extensive woodcut illustrations, published the writings of English and American authors, and ran up a world-record circulation of 200,000 before the Civil War. *Harper's Weekly* (1857) and *Frank Leslie's Illustrated Newspaper* (1855) used artists' drawings for woodcuts and maps to bring the war to 150,000 readers each.

Most influential in shaping American political and social life were the opinion magazines. An Englishman, Edwin Lawrence Godkin, began publishing the *Nation* in 1865 as a journal of opinion and literary criticism that won influence far beyond its 10,000 circulation. The *Independent*, *Forum*, *Outlook*, and *Review of Reviews* all discussed the rapidly changing political and social environment of the 1890s. The *Literary Digest* began summarizing contemporary editorial opinion in 1890.

Helped by cheap postal rates and expanding delivery service, magazine publishers struck out to win mass readership. Cyrus H. K. Curtis founded the *Ladies' Home Journal* in 1883 and soon won a half-million circulation with Edward W. Bok as his editor. In the low-cost weekly field, *Collier's* appeared in 1888 and Curtis put George Horace Lorimer in charge of the *Saturday Evening Post* in 1897. Both rode to success with current affairs and fiction. Other low-priced popular monthlies were *Munsey's*, *McClure's*, and *Cosmopolitan*.

Nearly all these magazines took part in the "muckraking" era of exposure and reform during the Theodore Roosevelt administration. *McClure's* led the way in 1902 with Ida Tarbell's "History of the Standard Oil Company" and Lincoln Steffens' "Shame of the Cities." In 1906, Tarbell and Steffens joined Ray Stannard Baker, Finley Peter Dunne ("Mr. Dooley"), and William Allen White at the *American*

**Muckraking**
Theodore Roosevelt's term to demean crusading magazine article writers and adopted by them as a badge of honor

Ida M. Tarbell's revelations in print about the Standard Oil Company won her national renown. She was a leader among the early twentieth century investigative reporters whose magazine writing led to reforms in industry practices. Note her distinctive hat placed near the upright telephone on her desk. (Historical Picture Service, Chicago)

*Magazine* to continue the muckraking movement, forerunner of today's investigative reporting. The *New Republic* (1914) featured the political philosophy of Herbert Croly and Walter Lippmann. For those less concerned with idealism there were George Jean Nathan's *Smart Set* and H. L. Mencken's *American Mercury*, favorites of collegians of the 1920s.

Of all the magazines mentioned in this account, only a handful remained by the 1990s. The *Nation* and *New Republic* survived as magazines of opinion; *Harper's* and *Atlantic* continued as literary and public affairs magazines; and the *Ladies' Home Journal* and *Cosmopolitan* still appealed to women. But the 3500 magazines of 1900 had become the more than 12,000 of 1993.

## Specialization: Seeking Target Audiences

**Specialization**
Seeking a carefully identified audience

Mass-circulation figures mean far less than they once did because many marketing and advertising specialists prefer to use "niche" magazines, especially suitable for their particular products or services. Others use magazines such as *Time* and *Sports Illustrated* that have developed methods of reaching individual subscribers with personalized and often local advertisements, even including the subscribers' names and other selected information. Individualized editions of magazines with the editorial matter custom-tailored to certain demographic groups are being tested.

"People have highly specialized interests in certain areas," says Professor Don E. Schultz of the Medill School of Journalism at Northwestern University. "The magazines say they know who these people are and what their interests are, and they're getting things of interest to them."

Noting that 679 new consumer magazines were begun in 1992, Professor Samir A. Husui of the University of Mississippi, expressed the opinion that specialization had peaked. "There is hardly any subject or part of a subject that does not have a magazine," he wrote in *Folio* magazine. "What used to be considered specialized publications—sports and music, for example—have given way to specific sports (e.g., paddle sports) and specific music (e.g., rap) titles. They are taking the lead in this new age of ultraspecialized publications."

For decades, advertisers and magazine editorial directors have relied on demographic information, such as age, sex, and educational level, to identify and analyze readers. As discussed in Chapter 4, a research firm, SRI International, in the 1970s devised a psychographic approach to augment the demographic information. This Values and Lifestyles Program (VALS) was followed in the 1980s by a VALS 2 system that further analyzed specific subgroups of consumers.

In 1974, Jonathon Robbin, a computer scientist, devised a revolutionary target-marketing system while seeking business applications of the U.S. Census. As described by Michael J. Weiss in his 1989 book, *The Clustering of America*, Robbin programmed computers to analyze each ZIP code according to hundreds of census characteristics—like affluence, ethnicity, and family life-cycle—sorting each into one of the 40 lifestyle clusters. Claritas Corporation, which he founded, collated the clusters with dozens of media, product, and opinion surveys to create PRIZM (Potential Rating Index for ZIP Markets). The PRIZM system, says Weiss, can accurately predict the lifestyle of its residents—from the brands of bread likely to be found in the pantry to the political bent of books and magazines in the den.

"Like many statistical concepts that prove effective," Weiss writes, "Robbin's geodemography is based on a handful of simple principles, the key being, 'Birds of a feather flock together.' Although no neighborhood is strictly homogeneous in all respects, the system works because the differences between the neighborhoods are more significant than the differences between households within the neighborhoods. 'People are all different,' says Robbin, 'but clustering predicts where you can find more of one kind.'"

Using such information, many magazine publishers have directed printers such as R. R. Donnelley & Sons Company, America's largest, to place special pages and insert cards into magazines as they are being

The concept of magazines aimed at special audiences has long existed, as evidenced by this cover of a *Mother's Magazine* of 1919, but target audience magazines have proliferated in recent years.

bound, while omitting them from others. Computerized ink-jet printing permits localizing national advertisements.

Under Time Warner's TargetSelect program, editions of *Time*, *People*, *Sports Illustrated*, and *Money* with these features began reaching subscribers in 1990. The program was expanded when the company's magazine, *Entertainment Weekly*, made its debut shortly thereafter.

Avidly sought by magazine publishers and advertisers are people who are heavy readers of magazines and light viewers of TV. According to researchers, they account for a third of U.S. adults but a much larger share of professional people and managers.

# Types of Magazines

Generalizations about the content, style, and appearance of magazines are dangerous because so many variations exist. Not all appear in magazine format; quite a few resemble tabloid or regular-size newspapers. Newsstands across the nation are crowded with almost 3000 consumer (general) publications. In addition, more than 8000 trade, technical, and professional periodicals are published, as well as, among others, about 730 in the field of religion and more than 550 agricultural publications, according to the 1995 *Gale Directory of Publications and Broadcast Media.*

Not included in these figures are about 10,000 industrial, or company, publications designed for employees, customers, stockholders, dealers, and others. Because they are primarily public relations vehicles, these periodicals are discussed in Chapter 16. Also not included are Sunday newspaper supplements, discussed in Chapter 5.

Although all magazines share certain basic problems of production and distribution, their editorial content and advertising are of many hues. Even trying to group them into categories becomes difficult because inevitably there is overlapping, and a few magazines almost defy classification. Most magazines fall into the following general categories.

## General Family Interest

Two mass-circulation magazines, *Reader's Digest* and *TV Guide*, lead the general family interest group.

*Reader's Digest*, begun in 1922 by DeWitt and Lila Wallace as a compilation of nonfiction articles, is the centerpiece of a giant, expanding publishing enterprise. Its 21.7 million worldwide circulation (15 million in the United States) exceeds that of any other magazine. Publication of about 400 million condensed and general books each year accounts for a substantial part of the firm's approximately $2.9 billion in revenues. Its record, tape, and videocassette division augments that income.

In an effort to halt declining sales, largely on newsstands, Rupert Murdoch, who heads an international communications empire, instituted staff and content changes and advertised strongly after buying *TV Guide* in 1988 from Walter Annenberg. Nevertheless, circulation declined by more than 12 percent, to 14 million, in 1994. Blamed, in part, were the recession and competition from an increasing number of guides carried by Sunday newspapers and a handful of other publications aimed at cable subscribers.

Television's diversion of advertising revenues from general family interest periodicals doomed such formerly great magazines combining nonfiction and fiction as *Collier's* and the *American*, which ceased publication in the 1950s, and the *Saturday Evening Post*. After being abandoned as a weekly in 1969, the latter was reinstituted as a monthly "nostalgia" publication. In the 1970s, confronted with a lack of advertising

and rising postal rates, the enormously successful weekly picture magazines *Life* and *Look* disappeared. *Life*, however, reappeared as a monthly,
and had 1.6 million circulation in 1994.

Into the void created by the loss of these magazines came *National
Geographic*, established in 1888 by the National Geographic Society as a
travelog journal that blossomed out as a slickly edited, superbly illustrated monthly with a current circulation of 9.2 million in 167 countries. The society was the first American publisher to set up a color
photo lab (1929), the first to feature underwater color photographs
(1927), and the first to print a hologram, or three-dimensional photograph (1984).

Photographers from *Life* and *Look* also found their way to the Smithsonian Institution, whose *Smithsonian* magazine, founded in 1970, soared
beyond 2.2 million circulation by 1994.

*Ebony*, an African-American picture magazine founded in 1945 by
John H. Johnson, had a comfortable 1.9 million circulation in 1994.

## News Magazines

Close behind these magazines in general family appeal are weekly publications designed to summarize and interpret the news. They publish articles on news situations, examine headline personalities, and discuss
trends in diverse fields.

*Time*, founded in 1923 by Henry R. Luce, was the first magazine to
organize and departmentalize the news of the week in a style "written as
if by one man for one man," whom *Time* described as too busy to find
the time necessary to peruse the other media. The magazine developed a
large research staff as well as its own large news-gathering organization
that supplemented the news services. With this approach *Time* helped to
drive the older *Literary Digest* out of business.

*Newsweek* appeared in 1933 with an almost identical format. *U.S.
News & World Report* grew out of a combination of two of David
Lawrence's publications in Washington and took its present title in 1948.

For decades the newsweeklies had little competition. In the 1980s,
however, the Washington *Times* began publication of *Insight*, a fair-
minded weekly with a clearly conservative outlook. In addition, Americans get news digests and interpretations from a variety of other sources.
As a result, circulation of the newsweeklies has risen only marginally
since the 1970s. During the last two decades newsstand sales dropped
more than 25 percent and, during the last decade, the number of advertising pages declined about 20 percent, mostly from the loss of advertisements formerly taken by cigarette and liquor companies.

*Newsweek* boasts a circulation of almost 3.2 million and *U.S. News &
World Report* 2.2 million. In 1989 *Time*, as part of its new cost-conscious
Time Warner ownership, reduced its advertiser-guaranteed circulation
base from 4.6 million to 4 million, largely by eliminating marginal circula-

Susan Taylor, editor-in-chief of *Essence,* stands in front of a collection of the inspirational beauty and fashion magazine's covers. (See p.153.)

tion and drastically de-emphasizing its electronic giveaways such as telephones in television subscription drives. Its 1994 circulation was 4 million.

In the 1990s, worried newsweekly editors continued to ask themselves, "What are we giving readers that they can't get anywhere else?" *Time* sought to answer the question by redesigning itself in 1992. The result included a crisp eight-page section of news items, a large middle section of longer and more in-depth articles, and a final section devoted to cultural reviews. Also redesigned, *U.S. News & World Report* emphasized service journalism, described by owner Mortimer B. Zuckerman as "stories that affect the everyday lives of our readers." For an additional $5 a year, *Newsweek* offered subscribers 12 additional eight-page sections tailored to their individual interests.

*Jet*, a Johnson Publications newsweekly serving African Americans, seems to have found the answer to reader interest: its circulation increased by one-third to a record 956,000 during the last decade. Another Johnson publication, *Emerge*, a monthly news magazine for black professionals, began publication in 1989.

## Sophisticated Writing Quality

Possibly the most distinctive of American magazines has been the *New Yorker*, founded in 1925 by Harold Ross and carried on from 1951 to 1987 by William Shawn. E. B. White long conducted its "Talk of the Town"; it has had writers of the quality of James Thurber, Wolcott Gibbs, A. J. Liebling, and Frank Sullivan; artists such as Helen Hokinson, Peter Arno, Otto Soglow, and Charles Addams. It also gives its readers—along with the cartoons, whimsy, and fiction—penetrating "Profiles" and lengthy, incisive commentaries on public affairs. The magazine was acquired in 1986 by Samuel E. Newhouse, Jr., chairman of Condé Nast Publications. Robert E. Gottlieb replaced Shawn as only the third editor in the magazine's history. His tenure was short-lived, however. In 1992, Tina Brown, who as editor had transformed *Vanity Fair* after arriving in the United States from her native Britain in 1984, was named to succeed Gottlieb.

*Esquire*, founded in 1933 by Arnold Gingrich, ran the top bylines of American writing: Wolfe, Hemingway, Faulkner, Steinbeck, Capote, Mailer, Talese. It had 1 million readers but faltered and was sold in 1977 to Clay Felker. In 1979 the magazine was acquired by Philip Moffitt and Christopher Whittle, who had achieved remarkable success with their 13–30 Corporation, a Knoxville, Tennessee publisher of student giveaway magazines. In 1986 Whittle and Moffitt, both not yet 40 years of age, ended a 20-year business partnership that had begun when they were students at the University of Tennessee. Their assets were divided into two corporations, Whittle Communications and the Esquire Magazine Group. At year's end the Hearst Corporation purchased *Esquire*, and the American Express Publishing Corporation bought the group's six-month-old magazine, *New York Woman*, which ceased publication in 1992.

After ensuing business dealings, Whittle Communications by 1993 was owned primarily by Time Warner, Inc., Philips Electronics N.V., and Britain's Associated Newspapers Holdings PLC. Christopher Whittle and other Whittle executives held minor shares. The imaginative but ultimately unsuccessful efforts of Whittle, who continued as manager, to make the firm one of the dominant media companies in the 1990s, are described later in this chapter.

## Quality Magazines

Two quality literary magazines, *Harper's* and *Atlantic*, both nearly 150 years old, veered toward nonfiction and public affairs several decades ago. *Vanity Fair,* founded in 1859 and one of the most celebrated avant-garde arts and literature magazines of the 1920s, merged with *Vogue* in 1936. Condé Nast Publications resurrected it in 1983. The magazine wavered under two editors but finally reached 6.9 million circulation under the editorship of Tina Brown. *Vogue* was challenged in the 1980s by *Elle,* to be discussed shortly.

The quality journal *Ms.,* founded by Gloria Steinem and Patricia Carbine, chronicled the feminist movement for more than 17 years before it suspended publication in 1989. Dale Lang, the new owner, dropped all advertising, thus freeing its editorial staff of pressure from advertisers, said to have been a recurring problem. The bimonthly thrived on subscription and newsstand sales, with circulation approaching 200,000 in 1995.

**City, State, and Regional Magazines.**  Also ranking high in quality of writing are most of the approximately 500 city, state, and regional magazines, aimed at sophisticated audiences. According to the City and Regional Magazines Association, the average city magazine subscriber is 30 to 50 years old, married, college-educated, and childless, with a household income of between $50,000 and $75,000 a year. Mixing stories about million-dollar homes, dining-out guides, and features on the local singles scene and high society with frequent investigative pieces, these magazines became a strongly competitive force in the nation's journalism, mainly during the 1980s, along with a rapidly growing number of city, state, and regional business publications.

*San Diego Magazine,* founded in 1948, is reputed to be the oldest. *New York,* started in 1968 and now owned by Rupert Murdoch, has offered such talented writers as Tom Wolfe, Jimmy Breslin, and Judith Crist. *Texas Monthly,* begun in 1973, has featured an iconoclastic, investigative style of reporting. The *Washington Monthly,* founded in 1969, scrutinizes the city's political scene with what one observer described as "the precision of an anthropologist."

### Opinion Magazines

Seeking new readers and advertisers in the conservative political and social climate of the 1980s and 1990s, two magazines noted for their combative left-of-center opinions, *Mother Jones* and the *New Republic,* developed new marketing approaches and instituted changes in editorial content. *Mother Jones* introduced a dramatic redesign that included celebrity covers and columns aimed at older readers. The *New Republic,* founded as a vehicle of the intellectual left, appointed a conservative editor.

While the *New Republic* and the still-liberal *Nation* waged a circulation battle in the 95,000 range, William Buckley's *Conservative Review* attained circulation exceeding 150,000.

Examples of some women's interest magazines. (Grunnitus Studios)

## Women's Interest Magazines

The almost instant acceptance by readers and advertisers of the U.S. version of the French fashion magazine *Elle* after its introduction in 1985 sparked significant makeovers of American fashion publications and the addition of more to the crowded field.

*Elle*, a Hachette publication, offered bright, colorful pictures of models in unretouched, informal poses. They were shot with strobe-like clarity and printed on high-quality paper and oversized pages. The formula ended the era of artsy photography and heavily influenced older magazines, such as *Harper's Bazaar*, *Mademoiselle*, *Seventeen*, and *Vogue*, as well as those created in recent years, including *Sassy* and *Model*.

*Elle*, aimed at a younger and more hip audience, threatened the long-time dominance of *Vogue*, which ousted its editor of 16 years. Grace Mirabella, in favor of a younger, more hip editor, Anna Wintour. Rupert Murdoch's News Corporation hired Mirabella and started an upscale fashion monthly called *Mirabella*. Bauer Publishing, the U.S. division of a German company, introduced *First for Women* with a plan for reducing advertising clutter within its pages.

Among numerous other magazines seeking to hold or gain niches in the shifting women's interest field are *Working Mother*; *Cosmopolitan*, for the "sexually liberated woman"; and, as reported earlier in this chapter, *Essence*, for black women.

*Sassy* debuted in 1988, but encountered complaints about its frank treatment of sexual topics for 14- to 19-year-old girls. After *Liberty*

---

## THE "SEVEN SISTERS"

These traditional women's magazines, with circulations ranging from 3.4 million to 7.6 million, are moving from reliance on homemaking articles to emphasis on such matters as health, nutrition, and the environment in the face of competition from newer magazines such as *First for Women*.

- *McCall's*
- *Ladies' Home Journal*
- *Family Circle*
- *Woman's Day*
- *Better Homes and Gardens*
- *Good Housekeeping*
- *Redbook*

---

*Report*, a newspaper published by the Rev. Jerry Falwell, sparked a letter-writing campaign to major advertisers, *Sassy* toned down its editorial content.

The sensationalized *National Enquirer* (3 million), *The Star* (2.75 million), and *National Examiner* (900,000) also are aimed at female buyers. Although printed in newspaper format, in their feature content these publications more nearly resemble magazines. Sold mostly at supermarket checkout counters, the weekly publications have been noted for their "hoked-up" headlines; medical, science, and parascience stories; revelations about celebrities, usually TV stars; and first-person testimonials of an inspirational nature. Confronted with libel suits as well as competition from televised celebrity shows and magazines such as Time Warner Inc.'s highly successful *People Weekly* (circulation 3.4 million) featuring news of celebrities, the *National Enquirer* turned increasingly to reader service stories such as how to cope with cancer and how to care for pets. After the death of its founder, Generoso Pope, Jr., the publication was sold in 1989 to Macfadden Holdings, Inc., whose magazines include *True Story* and *True Confession*. (See Chapter 2, about *The Star*.)

### Men's Interest Magazines

Leaders in the men's interest category include a half-dozen magazines, such as *Outdoor Life* and *Popular Mechanics*, with circulations ranging from 1.5 to 3.4 million. A number of men's interest publications have become increasingly popular with women. Chief among these is *Sports Illustrated*, a Time Warner Inc. publication that has increased its advertising and circulation substantially in recent years through heavy marketing and promotion. The magazine's 25th anniversary swimsuit issue reached 41 million adult readers, 13 million of them women, as compared with 20 million readers of its regular issues. The 286-page issue contained 118 pages of advertising worth about $15 million.

*Playboy* and *Penthouse* are one-two leaders in circulation among a dozen or more sexually oriented publications intended for men (euphemistically called "gentlemen's sophisticates"). *Playboy*, established by Hugh Hefner in 1953, approached 7 million circulation, but later declined to 3.4 million. *Penthouse*'s 4.6 million circulation of 1980 has fallen to 1.3 million.

Publishers attributed the magazines' decline largely to a change in cultural mores, the increase in sales and rentals of adult-oriented video-cassettes, and an intimidating letter sent to retailers in 1986 by then-Attorney General Edwin Meese's Commission on Pornography, which caused a number of chain drug and convenience stores to remove the magazines from their shelves (see Issue 1).

Hugh Hefner's daughter, Christie Hefner, assumed command of Playboy Enterprises in 1988. She instituted changes designed to make the magazine acceptable to more advertisers and also, noting that 3 million women were among its readers, to many homes where it was once barred. The Playboy cable channel was renamed and a pay-per-view service was instituted.

## Special Interest Magazines

The thousands of periodicals intended for special audiences increased during the 1990s, particularly with the advent of desktop publishing. Many are little known to the general public because they are infrequently displayed on newsstands; others fall within major circulation categories.

**Shelter magazine**
Specialized publication that focuses on home and family

The latter include the *"shelter" magazines* about family living, such as *Better Homes and Gardens;* a greatly expanded array of travel magazines, including *Travel & Leisure;* farm publications such as *Successful Farming;* such science interest magazines as *Discover;* youth-oriented magazines such as *Boys' Life;* and such diverse publications as *Popular Photography* and *Outdoor Life.*

The movie, music, and television fan magazines form still another special-interest area. Typical is *Soap Opera Digest*, for afternoon viewers. *Premiere*, named after its French counterpart, began publication in 1987 as an upscale movie magazine. It has been promoted as "a *Rolling Stone* for motion picture fans," tapping into the same kind of passion for movies that *Rolling Stone* does for music. Once required reading for the counterculture, the latter has broadened its coverage to include public affairs.

The *Advocate*, for many years the only national gay magazine, faced competition in the 1990s from *Genre* and *Out.*

Religious magazine publishing is an influential field. There are denominational and nondenominational publications, the largest of which—*Catholic Digest* and *Christian Herald*—circulate to hundreds of thousands of readers.

Circulation of the bimonthly *Modern Maturity*, founded in 1958 and distributed to members of the American Association of Retired Persons, is approximately 22 million.

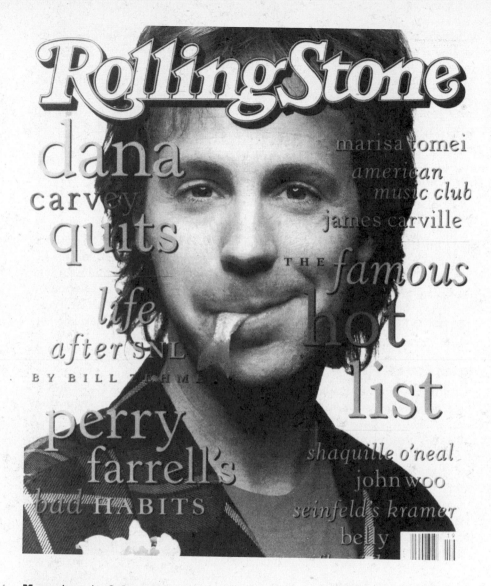

**Rolling Stone**

dana
carvey
quits

life
after SNL

BY BILL ZEHME

perry
farrell's
bad HABITS

marisa tomei
american
music club
james carville

THE
famous
hot

list

shaquille o'neal
john woo
seinfeld's kramer
belly

Primarily a magazine of protest in its earlier years, *Rolling Stone* now emphasizes news about popular music and interviews with rock stars and television entertainment personalities.

## Magazines in Cyberspace

Hundreds of magazines provide information, photographs, and graphics through computer online services. Many publish multimedia magazines that exist only in CD-ROM format, offering a combination of text, graphics, full-motion video, audio, and animation. Print publishers are providing material that can be repackaged and sold to different audiences. The CD-ROM market reached about 17 million computers in 1996.

Time Inc., a unit of Time Warner Inc., in 1994 created Pathfinder, a new advertiser-supported Internet site that provides text, photos, and graphics from eight Time Inc. magazines. The following year Condé Nast created CondéNet, a subsidiary that develops material for the World

Wide Web from its 14 core magazines. The first of these magazines to go on line, *Condé Nast Traveler*, offered detailed reports on 250 islands and rated more than 1000 hotels, with monthly updates of material.

These are only examples of the movement into cyberspace of a large segment of the industry.

Covering the explosive growth of commercial online services, such as Prodigy, CompuServe, and America Online, are new magazines, including *Boardwatch*, *Online Access*, *Connect*, *BBS*, *Online*, *Link-Up*, *Wired*, and *Internet World*. *Wired* created *Hotwired*, an online service that blends electronic publishing and the interactive power of the personal computer with a style of participatory reporting that provides sound and video clips on request.

Three new magazines are aimed at computer families with children (an estimated 23 million): *Home PC*, *Family PC*, and *Family Computing*. They join an established group of computer publications such as *PC Magazine* and *PC Week*. In addition, hundreds of smaller, independent electronic magazines, often called *digizines* or *e-zines*, have developed on the Internet, with varying degrees of quality, interest, and usefulness. Three of these titles: *Holy Temple of Mass Consumption*, *Spontaneous Combustion*, and *Armadillo Culture*.

**Digizine**
Electronic magazine. Also called an *e-zine*

## Retail Store Magazines

A number of giant retail chains followed the lead of the Great Atlantic & Pacific Tea Company (A&P) and began publishing their own magazines in the 1980s, some with outside advertising as well as feature stories and photos. Termed *magalogs*, the publications have helped build customer loyalty and defray the high cost of direct-mail marketing.

Examples are Waldenbook's *Kid's Club* and *Geoffrey's Toys Я Us Magazine*, of *Toys Я Us*, Inc. In 1988, *McCall's* magazine and K mart Corporation teamed to attract future readers and buyers with a promotional magazine for 6- to 12-year-old girls. It was called *Betsy McCall*, after the magazine's paper doll character of the 1950s. The minimagazine was given away at K mart stores, and copies were inserted in some issues of *McCall's*.

**Magalog**
Publication that combines the features of a magazine and catalogue

## The Business Press

A distinctive part of the magazine field, little known to the general public, is the *business press*. In 1995, according to the *Gale Directory of Publications and Broadcast Media*, this rapidly growing field was represented by more than 8000 specialized publications. The American Business Press calls the field "the unique and primary source of highly specialized technical, professional, and economic information." Its editorial matter and advertisements constitute *must* reading for managerial and professional personnel in commerce, industry, and the professions.

Julien Elfenbeim, in his pioneering book *Business Journalism*, described the business press as "the most potent kind of *continuing education*

**Business press**
Specialized magazines published for managerial and professional personnel in commerce, industry, and the professions

in our adult world." Unlike other media, Elfenbeim pointed out, the business press is a teacher, not an entertainer, and its publications circulate only among business and professional people whose income and education are far above that of the average magazine reader.

The field is divided into two distinct branches:

*Horizontal* publications, which serve readers such as chemical engineers and traffic managers who have similar duties or functions regardless of their industries or professions.

*Vertical* publications, which serve all aspects and functions of a particular industry or profession, such as oil and dentistry.

Not numbered among the specialized business press are such publications as *Business Week* and *Forbes,* classified as consumer (general) publications.

A little more than half of the business press consists of *controlled circulation* publications, sent without charge to readers who are active buyers of the product and service advertisements they contain. About a third are sent to subscribers at prices ranging from $40 to $400 a year, and a relatively small number are sold on newsstands.

The *trades,* as business publications are known, serve approximately 175 industries and professions. Combined circulation exceeds 72 million, and more than $3 billion is received in gross advertising revenues each year.

The business press has grown significantly since World War II. As in other media, mergers and, more recently, international consolidations have characterized the field. For example, a longtime leader, Harcourt Brace Jovanovich, sold its business papers to Robert Edgell as a result of heavy indebtedness in fending off acquisition by Britain's Robert Maxwell during the 1980s.

Firms such as McGraw-Hill produce scores of magazines and newsletters and sponsor equally profitable trade and consumer shows and conventions. Global networks of correspondents feed information to the publications.

So fierce is the competition and so rich the rewards, with pretax profits as high as 35 percent, that, whereas a major publication could be started in the 1970s for $200,000 to $500,000, today the cost ranges up to $5 million. America's "best-kept media secret," as one publisher termed it, is indeed a thriving field.

**Controlled circulation** Distribution of a publication free and only to a select group of desired readers

**Trades** Jargon for specialized business publications

## How Magazines Are Marketed

The magazine industry obtains its revenues from circulation and advertising, built on strong editorial content. The primary sources of advertising revenue are shown in Table 6.3. For decades publishers sold each copy for far less money than it cost to produce it, making their profit through the sale of national and regional advertising. During recent

**Table 6.3**

**Primary Sources of Magazine Advertising Revenue**

| Classification | Percent of 1993 Total Revenue |
|---|---|
| Automotive, Automotive Accessories, and Equipment | 13.9 |
| Toiletries and Cosmetics | 10.7 |
| Direct Response Companies | 9.4 |
| Business and Consumer Services | 8.1 |
| Apparel, Footwear, and Accessories | 6.7 |
| Food and Food Products | 6.2 |
| Travel, Hotels and Resorts | 4.9 |
| Drugs and Remedies | 4.8 |
| Computers, Office Equipment, and Stationery | 4.8 |
| Publishing and Media | 2.8 |

*Source: Publishers Information Bureau. Courtesy of Magazine Publishers of America. These ten classifications accounted for 72 percent of all magazine advertising revenue in 1993.*

years, however, the rising costs of paper, printing, payrolls, and home and newsstand deliveries greatly increased subscription and single-copy prices. Consequently, readers now pay about three times as much for a single copy or a one-year subscription as they did during the 1970s. Publishers obtain 52 percent of their net income from these sources.

Production costs fell substantially with the advent of new copy preparation and printing techniques in the mid-1980s. Especially helped were publications using desktop publishing methods. (See Chapter 13.) Few magazines own their own printing facilities; large firms with high-speed color presses do the printing.

## Subscription Sales

Three of every four magazine copies are delivered by mail. The second-class postal rate for magazine delivery increased substantially in the late 1980s and the 1990s. Direct-mail marketers also experienced sharp advances in rates; many of them also sell magazine subscriptions. Each year Magazine Publishers of America firms deliver more than 5 million copies, and Direct Marketing Association members distribute more than 150 billion units. The latter constitute about 50 percent of the Postal Service's load.

Of the 296 million magazine subscriptions sold in 1994, agents such as Publishers Clearing House, originator of the $10 million sweepstakes scheme known to every householder, accounted for about half.

Publishers have sought alternative delivery systems for decades. Tests have included using a milk company in Providence, Rhode Island,

and *Wall Street Journal* delivery people in Washington, D.C. Savings in cost, however, have generally proved insufficient to make the change.

## Single-Copy Sales

The proliferation of magazines in recent years has precipitated a crisis over the limited space available at supermarkets, airports, bookstores, convenience stores, and other outlets. In all, almost 2700 titles battle for the few hundred rack locations available at even the largest retailers. When the new magazine *First for Women* saturated supermarket checkouts, capturing as many as 190,000 newsstand pockets for its 8-million-copy launching, a reshuffling of titles occurred and some marginal sellers were eventually dropped from the racks.

Display space is obtained or kept on the basis of both sales and incentives provided to dealers, such as the longstanding retail display allowance (RDA) of about 10 percent given in compensation for good display positions. Retailers tally the sales and bill national distributors, who have dispatched the magazines through wholesalers. Some magazines, such as *Woman's Day* and *Family Circle*, bypass the wholesaler system and deliver copies directly to retailers, thus providing greater revenues and making dealers reluctant to bump them. The "safest" magazines, of course, are the big sellers, such as *People*, *The Star*, and *National Enquirer*.

## Redesigning Magazines

In order to stand out amid the increased competition on newsstands, gain more readers, and woo new advertisers, a large number of well-known consumer and trade journals have redesigned their styles and formats. Magazines recently redesigned include the *New Yorker*, *Harper's Bazaar*, and *Time*. Most sought affluent readers. Celebrities replaced traditional models on many covers.

## Innovative Marketing

Whittle Communications, discussed earlier in this chapter, developed a number of precisely targeted media vehicles that garnered millions of dollars in advertising revenue and shook up the advertising and magazine industries. These ventures included the following:

- *Special Reports TV*, a magazine and video venture for 32,000 doctors' waiting rooms.
- *Best of Business*, containing articles from a wide range of publications and sent to 350,000 executives but including advertisements for only one business.

Other Whittle niche publications included those tailored for both expectant and new mothers, distributed free at hospitals; posters and pamphlets placed on the walls of 4700 pediatricians' offices, advertising only Johnson & Johnson products; wall posters for hospitals and elementary schools; an American Airlines-supported magazine for travel agents; and a magazine given to girls in junior high schools, advertising feminine hygiene products.

Whittle also published books containing advertising unrelated to the content.

In 1994, as investors began to question the company's finances, Whittle Communications disintegrated through sell-offs and closings. In 1995, Whittle sought additional funding for its lone remaining enterprise, the Edison Project, an education experiment to build private schools that would make money.

Whittle's former cable news-in-the-classroom venture, Channel One, is discussed in Chapter 11.

## Editorial Content and Operation

The editorial operation of magazines varies greatly, depending on size, type, and frequency of publication. Generally, editorial staffs are small. A magazine selling 4 million copies can be prepared editorially by a smaller staff than one needed to put out a newspaper that sells one-half million copies. This is possible because much of the material published in many magazines is written by free-lance writers, either on speculation or on order from the editors.

The editors decides what kinds of material to publish, arranges to obtain it, and then presents it in as pleasing a manner as possible. Assistants screen free-lance material, conceive ideas, edit copy, and prepare layouts. On many magazines staff members write a substantial portion of each issue. During frequent conferences editors plan the next issue, examine proposed layouts and covers, and agree on projects for future issues. Magazine content generally is planned three to six months before publication.

News magazine staff members write some original material, but most of their work consists of rewriting and condensing stories received from bureaus in the United States and abroad as well as from the major news services.

Only a few magazines have their own professional photographers. Free-lance photographers, often working through agents, provide most of the pictures.

The articles in most magazines are provided by the 250 to 300 free-lance writers who work full-time in their enterprises. In addition, a large volume of unsolicited material arrives daily in magazine offices; most is never published because it is poorly written or does not fit the publication's formula or needs. Professional writers usually submit their articles in outline form or offer a brief proposal called a *query*. *Writer's Digest* and *The Writer* provide information about the needs of thousands of magazines, including rates of payment.

**Query**
Brief proposal made to a magazine with an idea for an article

# The International Scene:
# GLOBAL DISTRIBUTION OF MAGAZINES

An increasing number of magazines, both U.S. and foreign, provide advertisements and editorial content that residents outside their publication sites want to read. Their striking circulation spread accompanies the rapid global development of corporate business and the spread of Western ideas.

*Reader's Digest* distributes approximately 11.5 million copies abroad—44 national editions in more than a dozen languages, as well as books in 26 languages and videocassettes. The magazine's European editions alone have a circulation base of 6.7 million, about four times larger than that of any other European edition.

*Time* sells about 1.5 million copies abroad, including 400,000 in Europe, where 37 editions with regional advertising are published. *Newsweek*'s foreign circulation approaches 2 million.

In strong demand abroad also are *Business Week*, *Fortune*, *National Geographic*, *Cosmopolitan*, *Playboy*, and *Penthouse*. The latter garners more than $10 million annually in foreign newsstand sales alone.

## News Magazines

In addition to *Time* and *Newsweek*, the United Daily News group of 12 newspapers and magazines translates weekly editions of *U.S. News & World Report*. More than 45,000 copies are distributed in 18 countries and areas on four continents. Bilingual versions of five regular features of the magazine are especially useful for language students. The editions include a four-page supplement about Chinese people and events, also translated into Chinese.

Other top news magazines include *L'Express* of France; *Der Spiegel* of Germany and *Asiaweek*, circulating throughout the Orient. News magazines with strong economic emphases include *The Economist* of London, one of the world's great quality periodicals, and the *Far Eastern Economic Review* of Asia. One of the best picture magazines is *Paris-Match* of France.

Distribution is not always assured. In reaction to materials adjudged critical or offensive, countries from time to time ban the import and sale of publications, or confiscate issues after arrival. Editors avoid most problems of this sort by tailoring articles, photographs, and advertisements to the mores of the nations to which the magazines are sent.

## Russian Federation

Because laws prohibit taking rubles out of the former Soviet Union, foreign magazine publishers have not yet established a firm foothold there. Printing and distribution hurdles also have been difficult to overcome.

In 1995 American magazines with Russian-language editions included *Reader's Digest*, with a circulation of 100,000; the U.S. Information Agency's *America Illustrated* (150,000); Rodale's *Novii Fermer* (75,000); *Business Week* (50,000); *Scientific American* (25,000); and *Omni* (20,000).

*Omni* appeared on Moscow newsstands under an exchange agreement that brought
*Continued*

## GLOBAL DISTRIBUTION OF MAGAZINES
### Continued

the English-language magazine, *Science in the USSR*, to U.S. readers. *Scientific American* was distributed under a royalty arrangement with Russia's ministry of books and magazines. *Time* and *Newsweek* were permitted to distribute English-language editions.

Karz Publications of New York planned to provide a magazine supplement, *America, America,* for the daily newspaper, *Komsomolskaya Pravda*.

### Other Collaborations

Hachette Filipacci Presse, the French publisher of *Elle*, in 1994 tripled from two to six the number of times a year it publishes the Chinese-language version of the fashion magazine. Hachette and Time Warner Inc. publish a French version of *Fortune*, and an Italian version of *Time* is published in collaboration with a Milan company.

These are examples of a number of copublishing ventures around the world.

### Mergers

Acquisitions of magazine properties have been widespread. "Publishing is worldwide now, especially in the business press," Paul Beatty, vice president/marketing for International Thomson Retail Press, told *Folio* magazine, "it's rare to find a publishing company without an international operation."

In the same special report, publishing consultant David Oylow declared: "Factually, much more foreign ownership has occurred than people realize—they [foreign corporations] own billions of dollars in U.S. publishing." According to various estimates, between 15 and 25 foreign corporations have holdings in the U.S. magazine industry, as compared with only one or two a decade ago.

Foreign mergers with, and acquisitions of, U.S. magazine firms have been made chiefly by publishing houses in Great Britain, France, the Netherlands, Canada, and Australia. Their U.S. purchases included such consumer magazines as *TV Guide* and *Woman's Day* and such business titles as *Personal Computing* and *Medical World News*.

## Points to Remember

1. What systems are used to help identify the target audiences of magazines?
2. How many categories of magazines, including at least one example of each, can you name?
3. What challenges do news magazines face today?
4. How have women's interest magazines changed in recent years?
5. Why have the circulations of sexually oriented magazines, intended chiefly for men, declined in recent years?

6. What makes the business press different from other types of publications?

7. Through what methods are magazines sold? What are some of the problems?

8. What types of computer online services are offered by magazines?

9. From what sources do magazines obtain their articles?

## Media Questions to Think About

1. What is there about magazines that makes them appeal to you? What does your favorite magazine contribute to your life that other media do not?

2. When you look through a fashion magazine, do you have trouble finding a particular article? If you were editor, would you make it easier to distinguish the articles from the advertisements?

3. Investigate the specialized business-press publications of a profession in which you are interested. Are they horizontal or vertical publications? How can you tell?

# CHAPTER 7
## Book Publishing

## Book Talk: Over Coffee or in Cyberspace

In the mid-1990s, book buyers increasingly socialized in lavishly stocked super-stores with club chairs and coffee bars or, perhaps surprisingly, at book publishers' sites or at Bunnell's Book Channel on the Internet.

Reported *Time* magazine:

"The old-fashioned bookstore has been transformed into a convivial hangout spot where customers can get cappucino, conversation, and a cushy chair for pe-rusing the latest Elmore Leonard or the earliest Dostoyevsky." (More later in this chapter.)

The online service was started in 1995 by David Bunnell, a 47-year-old multimil-lionaire entrepreneur. During the 1960s, Bunnell was a member of the radical orga-nization, Students for a Democratic Society. He founded some of the most success-ful computer magazines, starting with *PC* magazine in 1961, followed by *PC World* and *Macworld*.

A gathering place for book lovers, Bunnell's Book Channel provided online fo-rums, discussion, and information.

"It's the early '80s again," remarked Stewart Brand, founder of the Whole Earth catalogues and the Well, an online service based in San Francisco. "There is the feel-ing again that computers are going to change the world, but this time it's on the Net."

Book publishing provides a stimulating environment for creative as well as business-minded people. To publishing houses throughout the United States, but particularly in the Northeast, are drawn thousands of writers, editors, advertising and public relations specialists, designers and other production workers, computer and accounting experts, sales men and women, and—each year—hundreds of young people anxious to enter what they perceive as a glamorous field of endeavor.

And indeed it is, because of the opportunity to mingle with authors and other bright people and to find and develop skills in such diverse publishing fields as trade books of interest to almost everyone, mass market paperbacks, professional books, and textbooks for elementary and secondary schools and for colleges and universities.

Their work, under the direction of top management executives, enabled publishers to gross $19.6 billion in sales in 1995 while providing knowledge and entertainment for millions of readers.

In this chapter we discuss these matters and tell how book publishing has developed to its present state, in which giant conglomerates, many international in nature, dictate the bottom-line financial decisions that characterize much of the industry. We describe how books are made and sold, the role of major bookstore chains, and the tie-ins of trade books with the movie, television, video, and computer industries. The field is indeed both glamorous and rewarding.

## The Role of Books

Books are a medium of mass communications that deeply affects all our lives. Books convey much of the heritage of the past, help us understand ourselves and the world we live in, and enable us to plan for the future. They are a significant tool of our educational process. They stimulate our imagination, and they provide entertainment for people of every age.

Whether they are paperbacks or hardcover volumes, books provide a permanence characteristic of no other communications medium. Newspaper reporters and broadcast commentators address large audiences, but their materials soon disappear. Videocassettes, audiotapes, recordings, motion pictures, and microfilm may deteriorate through the years. Magazines, especially those printed on high-quality paper and bound into volumes, may have extremely long lives, but most get thrown out with the trash. If cared for properly, however, books, such as the superb copies of the Bible produced by Gutenberg in the fifteenth century, last virtually forever.

For the mass communicator, books perform several important functions. They not only serve as wellsprings of knowledge but, through translation and reprinting and through conversion to movies, television productions, live performances, audiotape, and electronic "books" (to be discussed shortly), convey vital ideas to millions of people throughout

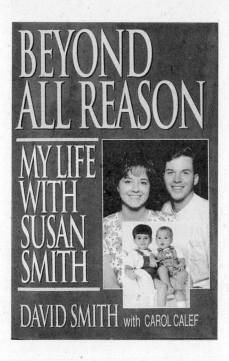

Weeks before Susan Smith was convicted of murdering their two sons by drowning them in an automobile, her husband David published this book, *Beyond All Reason,* about their life. "Quickie" books based on sensational trials and other headline-making events frequently achieve large sales.

the world. In publishing itself the mass communicator may find a rewarding outlet in writing, editing, and promoting the distribution of books.

Journalists such as Tom Wolfe, Jimmy Breslin, Gay Talese, and Anthony Lewis have written books that vastly increased the audience for their reports, and each has made an impact on the world of ideas that almost invariably accompanies the creation of a widely read book.

In the wake of news events that command great attention, some books are rushed into print. Warner Books published *Mad Genius: The Odyssey, Pursuit and Capture of the Unabomber Suspect*, only one month after the suspect, Theodore J. Kaczynski, was apprehended April 3, 1996. Warner won over Pocket Books, whose "quickie" book was delayed by an FBI review. (See "A Terrible Dilemma," Issue 1.) And *Beyond All Reason: My Life With Susan Smith*, by her ex-husband David Smith, was published by Kensington prior to the trial of the Union, South Carolina, woman convicted of murdering her two sons.

Even so, because of the relative slowness of writing, editing, and publishing a manuscript, books lack the immediacy that other media enjoy in conveying their messages. What may be lost in timeliness is often more than compensated for by the depth of coverage and analysis and by the care that editors and writers take in checking facts and rewriting copy for maximum effectiveness. This sustained, systematic exposition of a story or an idea (with the reader's opportunity to reread, highlight, and study at leisure) is afforded only by books.

## The Growth of Book Publishing

The world's oldest preserved book was printed from wood blocks in China in A.D. 968. Similar block-printed books, beautifully illustrated with handwritten texts, adorned European church altars and libraries in the 1450s, when Johann Gutenberg's introduction of the use of movable type in printing revolutionized the process. Between 1450 and 1500, thousands of crudely printed "cradle books" spewed from European presses, along with countless pamphlets and single sheets that acted as agents of change for the Renaissance and Reformation.

The first book published in the English colonies in America was Boston's *Bay Psalm Book* of 1640. The Revolutionary War spurred colonial enterprise in printing; Noah Webster's speller of 1784 eventually sold 60 million copies. By 1825, the United States had more than 1000 printing houses, but England still supplied 70 percent of the books sold. Best sellers were James Fenimore Cooper's frontier stories; New England authors Bryant, Hawthorne, and Emerson won intellectual acclaim.

The first great burst of American literature came around 1900 with the "age of realism" ushered in by Frank Norris, Theodore Dreiser, Jack London, and Upton Sinclair—journalists as well as great novelists.

Well-established American book publishing houses produced their wares. In New York City, Harper & Bros. dated from 1817, Charles Scribner's from 1842, and Macmillan from 1869 (a branch office imported from London). Boston's historic Little, Brown opened in 1837, and Houghton Mifflin in 1848.

The most exciting era for both the authors and their book editors was the 1920s and 1930s. And the most legendary figure was Maxwell Perkins, editor-in-chief of Scribner's from 1914 to 1947. It was Perkins who first recognized the writing skill of F. Scott Fitzgerald and who edited his *This Side of Paradise*. Perkins followed with Ernest Hemingway's *The Sun Also Rises* and Thomas Wolfe's *Look Homeward, Angel*—all in a single decade!

Two other noteworthy editors appeared in the 1950s. Bennett Cerf of Random House had Truman Capote and Moss Hart among his authors; Cass Canfield of Harper & Bros. scored with Robert Sherwood's *Roosevelt and Hopkins*. The Henry Holt house boasted Norman Mailer and Ernie Pyle on its authors' list. Doubleday & Co. was the largest house.

Conventional book publishers were challenged in 1939 by the first successful paperback publisher, Pocket Books. The firm sold 23 million copies by 1942 for 25 cents each. Two enormously successful titles were Dale Carnegie's *How to Win Friends and Influence People* (1940) and Dr. Benjamin Spock's *Baby and Child Care* (1946). Bantam Books was founded in 1945; the New American Library made quality paperbacks its specialty in 1948. By the 1950s, sales of Pocket Books alone reached 160 million annually.

The traditional world of book publishing turned topsy-turvy after 1960. The acquisition of Alfred Knopf by Random House that year marked the beginning of an extensive period of mergers and consolidations, some of the effects of which will be discussed later in this chapter.

## The Changing Book Publishing Industry

By dollar volume, book publishing is a dwarf among American industrial giants. It makes up only a tiny fraction of the nation's economy. Approximately one of every three of the approximately 22,500 publishing houses is situated in New York City, Boston, or Philadelphia. Although many of the 10,000 or so publishers that began operations during the 1980s and early 1990s were situated on the West Coast and in the South, New York City remained the center of the publication of trade books (general consumer titles), literary agents, and even of authors (about 37 percent of the total), as well as the one city visited by almost every foreign publisher during trips to the United States.

### Categories of Books

Approximately 90,000 books are published in the United States each year, including more than 50,000 new titles. The major divisions of the industry include:

- *Trade books*, marketed to the general consumer and sold mainly through bookstores and to libraries.
- *Religious books*, including Bibles and hymnals.
- *Mass market paperbacks*, sold mainly through newsstands and chain retail stores.
- *Professional books*, such as medical, technical, legal, scientific, and business works.
- *Book clubs*, actually a marketing channel for books issued by other publishers.
- *Mail-order publications*, created to be marketed by direct mail to the consumer, frequently as part of a continuing series related to a particular topic.
- *University or academic presses*, nonprofit adjuncts of universities, museums, and research institutions, mainly concentrating on scholarly or regional topics.
- *Elementary and secondary textbooks* (called elhi or school textbooks), hard- or softcover texts and manuals, maps, and other items for classroom use, mainly sold in bulk to school districts.
- *College textbooks*, hard- or softcover volumes and audiovisual materials; the texts are sometimes similar to trade books.

**Table 7.1** ━━━━━━━━━━━━━━━━━━━━━━━━━━━━

**Estimated Book Publishing Industry Sales in 1995**

| Division | Sales ($ Million) | Compound Percent Increase, 1982–1995 |
|---|---|---|
| Trade | 5,655.2 | 6.6 |
| Professional | 3,869.3 | 7.6 |
| Elementary and secondary text | 2,466.2 | 5.8 |
| Higher education | 2,324.8 | 3.7 |
| Mass market paperbound | 1,346.5 | 2.1 |
| Religious | 1,036.2 | 4.5 |
| Book clubs | 938.6 | 8.1 |
| Subscription reference | 670.8 | 5.4 |
| Mail-order publications | 564.5 | –3.6 |
| University presses | 339.7 | 6.6 |
| Standardized tests | 167.3 | 6.0 |

*Source: Courtesy of Association of American Publishers.*

- *Standardized tests*, for schools, colleges and universities, and industry.
- *Subscription reference books*, mainly sets of encyclopedias sold through the mail or door-to-door, as well as dictionaries, atlases, and similar works.

A survey showed that Americans bought more than one billion books in 1994, a record number that reflected a 31 percent increase since 1991. The annual survey, sponsored by several book industry trade groups, is compiled by market researcher NPD Group, based on purchasing diaries by 16,000 households.

Americans continued to spend more on books than on almost any other medium, paying an average of $49.22 for books each year, compared with $56.35 for recorded music and $72.97 for home videos, according to a 1995 study by Veronis, Suhler & Associates, an investment banking firm. A growth rate of 6.9 percent per year until 2000 was predicted.

As shown in Table 7.1, in 1995 publishers achieved almost four-fifths of their sales in five divisions, which brought in $15.7 billion of the total estimated sales of $19.4 billion. Book clubs registered the greatest increase during the 13-year period.

College textbooks were the third most productive category for many of those years, but their unit sales increased only 5 percent as compared with an increase exceeding 50 percent in sales of used texts during this period. One reason is the substantially higher price of a new college text, up well over 50 percent and much higher than the increase in the nation's

Consumer Price Index during the period. Sharply increased production and marketing costs, as well as the fact that bookstores return to the publisher about one of every six new texts, are among reasons for the advance.

The sales of publisher-originated audiovisual materials and computer software have increased substantially in recent years. Audio programs, pitched at the large number of home cassette and CD players, car audio systems, and Walkmans, showed marked increases. The products ranged from audio versions of popular books, some read on tapes by their authors (for example, Stephen King reading his novel *Needful Things*) to tapes on how to lose weight, stop smoking, and become a better manager.

## Distribution Channels

Books are marketed through six main channels: (1) retail stores; (2) college stores; (3) directly to consumers through mail order, book clubs, and door-to-door sales to individuals; (4) libraries; (5) schools and institutions; and (6) in miscellaneous fashion to industry, government, foundations, and research institutions. In addition, almost $1 billion in books from U.S. publishers are sold annually in more than 140 other countries where English is read. Translations provide additional income. Canada accounts for about 40 percent of this total.

Although book publishers constitute one of the few consumer industries that sell many products directly to users, most sales are made through wholesalers and jobbers, who stock the goods, mostly trade books, of many publishing houses and sell them locally and regionally. Wholesalers also sell nationally to retailers and through independent distributors, known as IDs, who supply retail outlets with mass market paperbacks and magazines as well.

### Retail Chains and Superstores

As reported earlier in this chapter, in recent years giant bookstore chains have transformed much of the book retailing industry and driven many independent bookstores out of business. In 1972, the four largest chain operations accounted for about 11.5 percent of all trade book sales. By 1995, however, the four largest chains sold 38 percent of all such books.

Largest of the chains was Barnes & Noble, which had merged with B. Dalton. Second was the Borders Group, into which the large Waldenbooks chain, owned by K mart Corporation, had been absorbed. Many Waldenbooks stores, most of them in malls, were downsized after suffering losses during the early 1990s recession. Other major chains were Crown Books and Books-A-Million.

Meanwhile, chain *superstores*, the phenomenon of the early 1990s, increased in number dramatically. Wrote John Mutter in *Folio* magazine: "Now chain superstores are huge book/music/video/software and CD-ROM coffee and food stores. . . ." Averaging 35,000 square feet in size,

**Superstore**
A large bookstore that carries 100,000 titles or more

the typical store, according to Mutter, stocked 125,000 book titles, up to 75,000 music CDs, another 10,000 videotapes, several thousand computer software titles, and other electronic goods. Competing most fiercely, often in the same neighborhoods, were Barnes & Noble and Borders Books & Music.

Many publishers, however, complain that the increasing size of the chains has produced some inefficiencies that endanger the industry. As one example, Alberto Vitale, chief executive of Bantam Doubleday Dell, cited the chains' high rate of return of unsold books, as much as 50 percent for some, which, he said, threatens "the very economics of publishing."

## Technological Improvements

The first electronic "books" were produced in the early 1990s. Among a number of firms experimenting with the idea, the Voyager Company of Santa Monica, California, published on floppy disks a series of Expanded Books, designed to be read on an Apple Computer Macintosh Powerbook screen. Using what was termed a Hypercard, readers could jump immediately to an index of all references to particular characters in the books, along with sound effects, background music, pictures, and graphics.

The first Voyager books included Martin Gardner's annotated version of *Alice in Wonderland*, Douglas Adams's *The Hitchhiker's Guide to the Galaxy*, and Michael Crichton's technological parable, *Jurassic Park*. Each disk was priced at $19.95.

Sony Corporation of America introduced the Data Discman, a $550 hand-held device with a keyboard and a 3.5-inch screen that allows users to consult reference and guide books produced on small disks.

Nathaniel Lande, a former Time Inc. executive, formed the Book-link company to develop a device called Bookmark, with a large flat screen and three buttons for turning pages. Books were encoded on a magnetic storage device called a Smartcard. Lande planned vending machines into which readers could insert cards on which a book would be encoded in as little as 15 seconds.

Multimedia CD-ROM disks were marketed. The disks store up to 100,000 pages of text, along with sound, music, animation, and video footage.

In 1993, a service called the OnLine BookStore was set up on the Internet. Users could browse through books on their PCs for $5 an hour and, for another $5, could "download" a book's contents onto a PC. Buyers could order traditional books from OnLine, or even converse with authors by computer. Project Gutenberg, also on the Internet, offered a similar service involving mostly texts that have reverted to the public domain.

Book publishing houses are making extensive use of other new technologies to reduce costs and improve customer service. Most firms accept author manuscripts on computer disks. Computer-formatting devices are widely used to prepare manuscripts prior to typesetting, among other benefits providing easier access to the product for storage and retrieval.

Few publishing houses print their own books. They rely mainly on the more than 900 major printing and composition establishments in this country, a third more than the number in 1970.

The recent trend to laser printing technology is expanding through use of desktop publishing techniques. Computers are often used in designing book jackets, covers, and catalogues; in producing additional graphic material; and in book printing itself. Avon Books produced the first rack-size mass market paperbacks from copy typeset on nonphotographic paper, thus significantly reducing composition costs. Because of technical limitations, however, most books are still printed on traditional typesetting machines. (See Chapter 13.)

New electronic equipment has given publishers the ability to tailor college textbooks and teaching aids to fit the needs of individual professors.

Electronic ordering systems are moving books into the hands of readers much more quickly than in the past. In 1988, Harper & Row introduced the first computer-ordering system used in the field by sales representatives. Their use of laptop computers has eliminated postal delays, reduced errors, and provided information on the status of titles at warehouses. An electronic ordering system called PUBNET, sponsored by the Association of American Publishers, is speeding orders from bookstores and, increasingly, from trade stores. Facsimile machines also are widely used.

## Ownership Developments

A relentless trend toward concentrating the ownership of individual publishing houses into ever-larger corporate organizations began in the 1960s. As part of inexorable economic trends that have transformed much of American business during the last century, and also because of near-confiscatory personal inheritance taxes, many privately owned companies have been converted into publicly held corporations and they, in turn, often have become absorbed into huge conglomerate organizations.

Today, with a handful of giant companies controlling much of the industry, a new and more complex corporate and finance environment has replaced the once leisurely and often inefficient atmosphere and practices of the major firms. Publishing decisions are based almost entirely on bottom-line financial considerations. Favorable accounting methods and a cheaper U.S. dollar have helped some international companies,

Clint Eastwood and Meryl Streep talk near a covered bridge in a scene from *The Bridges of Madison County,* the motion picture made from the runaway best-seller romantic novel. (Copyright © Warner Bros.)

primarily those in Great Britain, France, and Germany, to buy and merge American trade houses (see Issue 3.).

Nowhere have these consolidation and management trends been more apparent than in the mass market paperback field. Formerly, as consultant Carolyn Anthony has pointed out, publishing was divided into two camps: on one side, those that produced hardcover books and sold them through bookstores; on the other, mass market paperback houses that did cheap reprint editions of hardcover books and sold them through many other outlets in addition to bookstores. The staggering sums paid to hardcover houses by the reprinters (for example, $3.2 million for Judith Krantz's *Princess Daisy*) and hardcover firms' recovering the rights to successful books when the paperback license expired, produced a change. Many mass market houses either disappeared or found their lines, or identities, absorbed into other firms. Today many paperback houses are producing their own hardcover editions, and a number of hardcover publishers are publishing their own rack-size paperback editions, using the facilities of mass market paperback organizations for manufacturing and distributing. Like banks in the 1990s, they have become providers of one-stop services, able to publish and sell in all formats.

In the mass market paperback field in particular, management people of a new breed now build images, plan marketing, and set production and performance standards. Their work is closely akin to that of advertising people, TV producers, talk show hosts, and Hollywood producers and packagers. Literary agents remain the power brokers, and publishing decisions are increasingly made with movie, television, video, and audio subsidiary earnings in mind as well as the author's ability to "hype" a book on television talk shows.

## Steps in Book Publication

**Hype**
Promotional efforts in behalf of personalities, entertainment events, and other activities

All books begin with an idea germinated by the author or by an editor employed by a publishing house. If the author has an idea for a nonfiction book, he or she generally prepares a précis and perhaps several sample chapters and submits them to a literary agent or publisher. Generally, unless the author is well known, the entire manuscript of a novel must be submitted. If it is the editor's idea, the editor seeks out the writer who can best develop the book based on the concept.

Publishing houses vary in the number and level of responsibility of the editors they employ. In general, however, an acquiring editor works closely with an author in the development of a manuscript, and may also shepherd the work through various business and production stages. The editor must keep abreast of matters of public taste and interest and be able to intuit the types of books that will find markets in the years ahead. Reference, technical, and textbook editors who deal with specialized subject matter often employ professional critics. Trade book editors, especially those dealing with fiction, are less likely to employ outside advice.

A common fallacy held by each summer's crop of job applicants in book publishing is that a publisher or an editor is simply a person of taste who sits waiting for hungry authors to arrive with best-selling manuscripts. But book publishing is like an iceberg. The part that shows, mainly books that are reviewed in mass media journals and magazines, often touted on TV talk shows, and sold in general bookstores, constitutes only about 8 percent of the total dollar volume in books. For every editor who breaks bread with Norman Mailer or Shirley McLaine, there are hundreds who edit reference books or work with college and school textbook authors. For most publishing houses, the unsolicited manuscript is rarely publishable, as many disillusioned beginning writers can testify.

Manuscripts accepted for publication are turned over to copyeditors, who may rewrite considerably as well as search for grammatical, spelling, and punctuation errors. They corroborate facts, correct discrepancies in style, and perhaps help cut the copy to a predetermined length. The copyeditor must also coordinate entries in the bibliography with the citations in footnotes (if the book has them); ensure that chapter headings correspond to tables of contents; relate pictures, tables, charts, and the like to the text; query the author when necessary; read the proofs (material returned from the compositor), including indexes; check corrections made by the author in the proofs; and in general ascertain that the text is as accurate as possible.

The production department, which may consist of from three to two dozen or more persons, normally serves as the book publisher's liaison with the compositor and printer. Highly specialized employees oversee the production process. They design the book, including selection of the type, and oversee preparation of the cover and jacket; produce or commission art work, if necessary; estimate length; select the paper; and order the typesetting, printing, and binding. Every book presents an individual problem and every stage of production must be worked out carefully in advance, the schedule often requiring a full 12 months to complete.

At the time the book is contracted, plans are made for its marketing and sale. The marketing department, increasingly important in this competitive industry, helps to determine the direction and the form of advertising and promotion, with the acquiring editor acting as supervisor. Marketing also monitors the information to be sent to the salespeople. Trade sales representatives are called together usually twice a year for conferences involving the entire list of books being prepared for sale. In accordance with the advertising and promotion budget established for the book, based on anticipated sales, media are selected and advertisements and dealer aids, such as posters, circulars, and mail enclosures, are prepared.

The trade publicity department writes and mails news releases, arranges author interviews on television and radio and other personal appearances, sends copies of the book to reviewers, announces the publication of the book in trade magazines such as *Publishers Weekly*, arranges for exhibits at conventions attended by booksellers, and works in other ways to promote sales. The primary responsibility of the publicity department is to establish a climate of acceptance for the new book by employing every possible means at hand.

General sales representatives, calling on major bookstores, visit the largest stores perhaps 15 to 20 times a year. These persons normally work on salary or commission or a combination of the two, and sometimes carry the lines of two or more publishing houses. In addition, some sales personnel call on booksellers on behalf of jobbers and other wholesalers.

College textbook sales representatives, employed by the publishing house, perform a distinctly different function. Calling on the nation's college and university professors or telephoning those at institutions with low-volume potential, they make certain that their clients are acquainted with or receive examination copies of textbooks appropriate to the courses the professors teach. Textbook salespeople seldom, if ever, sell directly to bookstores. They must hope that the professors they visit, who usually have freedom of textbook selection, will give them a share of business via the college and off-campus bookstores. Sales representatives also act as manuscript scouts, since most college textbooks are written by college professors.

Hundreds of elhi school textbook agents work through state, county, and city adoption systems. Most school textbooks and audiovisual mate-

The abundance of titles available in a large book store encourages browsing by patrons. Some stores promote a leisurely "bookish" atmosphere by providing lounging areas and serving coffee. (Rogers, Monkmeyer Press Photo)

rials are written and prepared by the staff at a publishing house with professional advisers and teachers.

There are many other aspects of the production and sale of books not covered in this sketch of publishing. It is an intricate, fast-paced business, and many years of practical experience are required to learn the ground rules.

## How the Mass Communicator Fits In

The kinship of book publishing activities to those of other mass media should be apparent. Writing and editing must be done, as well as copyediting and proofreading; illustrating and designing; printing; marketing; advertising; and publicizing; distributing and selling. The editor must have shrewd insight into what interests the public, and when. The book editor identifies with the tastes and needs of various segments of

# The International Scene:
# GLOBAL DISTRIBUTION OF BOOKS

A post–World War II revolution in book production and distribution techniques, with emphasis on the paperback, has characterized the world book publishing industry. Between 1955 and 1976, world book production more than doubled in number of titles published annually and tripled in number of copies printed. It is estimated that about 600,000 titles and eight billion copies per year are now marketed.

In many countries, publishing is primarily a private enterprise, although governments of almost all nations have their own printing departments and some subsidize private operations. In communist nations, publishing is part of the planned public economy; this is true, for example, in the People's Republic of China, where books are published only after a public need has been established.

Although some U.S. book publishing firms have been largely inattentive to world markets, the industry exports about $1.7 million in books each year, while importing almost $1.1 billion. Approximately 82 percent of the exports are sent to other industrialized nations, with Canada, the United Kingdom, and Australia the largest markets.

The leading countries from which books are imported into the United States are the United Kingdom, Hong Kong, and Japan. Even so, American foreign book sales, comprising less than 10 percent of the total, are far below those of the British, who sell almost a third of their books in other countries.

## European Foreign Market

When some trade barriers among the major West European nations were largely erased at the end of 1992, a vast, commercially unified book market of about 320 million people began to be opened. The market was especially inviting to American and British publishers because the use of English is increasing both in daily discourse and as a preferred language of business, science, technology, and the social sciences. The use of English by educated people worldwide is a growing phenomenon.

United States publishing leaders fear that British companies will acquire exclusive rights for the entire Common Market, where American book sales have been almost $75 million per year not counting educational and professional titles. The battle for marketing rights is especially intense among the 15 to 20 international trade book conglomerates that have developed in recent years.

## Other Markets

United States publishers and authors' agents have strongly increased the sale of foreign rights to their books in recent years. Many of the sales are to previously inaccessible markets: China, Taiwan, Korea, and the countries of Eastern Europe.

## Global "Piracy"

Before the United States joined the Berne Convention for the Protection of Literary

## GLOBAL DISTRIBUTION OF BOOKS
### Continued

and Artistic Works in 1988 and threatened trade sanctions against offending countries, it was estimated that foreign publishing firms reaped profits of $2 billion each year by reproducing books and audiovisual materials without authorization. Of this sum, 70 percent represented revenues that should have accrued to American publishers and authors. U.S. losses in the People's Republic of China, for example, were estimated conservatively in excess of $100 million a year.

Because of conflicts with its own copyright laws, the United States long had refused to join the copyright convention, which was established more than 100 years ago.

The threat of U.S. trade sanctions in recent years has caused a number of nations to enact copyright laws, thus enabling American firms to market their products more successfully in such countries as Korea, Singapore, the People's Republic of China, and the Republic of China on Taiwan, where piracy had been rampant.

the book-buying population, just as the newspaper city editor maintains a sense of rapport with the newspaper's readers.

Book publishing is a step removed from the operations of some of the other media, which mostly deal with a mass audience. Books are often read by highly selective groups. Yet work in other mass communications fields can provide an ideal background for the responsibilities of book publishing.

Writers for newspapers, magazines, and radio-television, for example, inevitably gain insights that can be drawn on to advantage at the book editor's desk. With their attention to craft, they can quickly spot good or poor writing in a manuscript. As journalists they have learned to respect facts and to insist on documentation.

The knowledge of graphics that mass communicators obtain in school or on the job will be of use in ordering printing for a book and supervising the production of its cover and jacket. Advertising staff people, too, will find that the same principles of copy, layout, illustration, color, and selection of paper and ink apply in the preparation of advertisements for new books.

## Points to Remember

**1.** In what ways do books differ from other print media in communicating to the public?

2. How many major book categories can you name? Which produces the most income?

3. Through what major channels are books sold?

4. How has the growth of bookstore chains affected the industry?

5. What advantages does an electronic "book" offer that a printed book does not? What are the disadvantages?

6. In what other ways is the industry using new technology?

7. On what grounds are most book publishing decisions made today? Why?

8. Through what process must a book go from idea to distribution?

9. Is global "piracy" of books declining? Why?

## Media Questions to Think About

1. Which appeals more to your imagination—a book or a movie based on a book?

2. What's going on here? Americans bought a record one billion books in 1994. What is causing such a phenomenon when television, radio, recordings, and computers occupy so much of our time?

3. Have you read a book excerpt or a magazine article on a computer? Are you as comfortable doing so as reading the printed page?

# ISSUE TWO

## Ethics

## Do the Media Maintain Satisfactory Standards of Social Responsibility?

Can, or should, the mass media be held responsible for actions that many persons believe are harmful to society? Is such accountability possible under the First Amendment? If so, to whom would the media be accountable? Is self-regulation the ultimate answer?

In this Issue we explore complaints made against the media, examine media codes of ethics and how they are working, and review other ways in which the media seek to improve. Read the discussion and make your own decisions about media accountability. For example, how would you answer the following questions?

1. How does the moral law control the media and their practitioners?
2. Are the recommendations made by the Commission on Freedom of the Press in 1947 still applicable?
3. In terms of ethical standards, how do Americans generally rank mass communicators as compared with professional practitioners such as doctors and lawyers?
4. What are some of the charges of ethical lapses that have been leveled against each of the following: newspapers, magazines, television, radio, and popular music?
5. What are the principal ethical goals of the Canons of Journalism of the American Society of Newspaper Editors?
6. Why do some media practitioners object to codes of ethics?
7. What have surveys conducted by newspaper managers ascertained as the main lapses in ethical conduct of their reporters and editors?
8. What ethical problems may be involved in using a computer to gather information?
9. Why did the National News Council cease operation?

## The Moral Law

Of all the laws that the mass media and their supporting industries, advertising, and public relations, must obey, the moral law is the strongest. Public opinion produced the First Amendment, and public opinion can take it away. Not only does moral law impose a greater restriction on the media than any purely legal restraint, it also functions as a force that can overturn legal restrictions and bring greater freedom for most of the press today. A monumental example is the manner in which public opinion slowly overturned laws against the right to print and the right to criticize in the fifteenth through eighteenth centuries. A more familiar, specific example is the John Peter Zenger case in 1735, when an aroused public prevented the government from punishing an editor for criticizing it.

Moral law has grown principally out of religion and may be found embodied in the precepts of all major religions. In Christianity, for example, it is found in the Old and New Testaments, most notably in the Ten Commandments and the teachings of Jesus Christ; in the Muslim world, moral law is set forth in the Koran of the Islamic religion.

### Circles of Control

Examine in Figure 2.1 the five concentric circles, each succeeding one placed within the other, much like the bull's-eye used in target practice. These may be termed the "circles of control affecting the mass media" (or, for that matter, most other human activities).

1. The innermost circle represents the professional standards and ethical practices of *individuals*—publishers, reporters, editors, station and network owners, news directors, and film and videotape editors—the *gatekeepers* of what we read, see, and hear. In all that they do, these people must keep in mind the other four circles of control that surround them.

2. The second innermost circle represents the standards of practice and the codes of ethics established by the *individual media*. All the mass media—newspapers, magazines, broadcast stations, and so forth—operate under certain guidelines, whether these guidelines consist of written codes or simply unwritten assumptions, lore, and traditions. The persons who work for these media—those in the innermost circle—must subscribe to the standards and practices of organizations for which they work, or look elsewhere for their employment.

3. The third circle, moving outward, consists of *professional and industrywide* standards of conduct as embodied in the statements of sound practice affecting radio, television, film, newspapers, magazines, and books, and the codes of ethics of groups such as the American Society of Newspaper Editors, the Radio Television News Directors Association, and the Society of Professional Journalists. Broadcast standards are enforced—only in part, however—by the Federal Communications Commission; print codes are entirely voluntary. Professionalism and peer pressure are the major forces leading to compliance by individual media

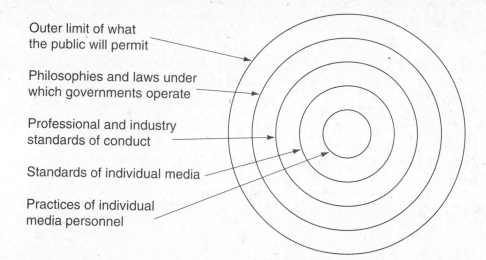

Outer limit of what
the public will permit

Philosophies and laws under
which governments operate

Professional and industry
standards of conduct

Standards of individual media

Practices of individual
media personnel

**Figure 2.1**

Circles of control of the
mass media.

and those working for them. There are other pressures, of course, economic considerations being among the strongest. Stories that an editor or news director regards as socially responsible and significant may strike some readers or listeners as indecent, or certain advertisers as harmful to their business. They may try to strike back economically by canceling their subscriptions, withdrawing their advertising, or, in the case of perceived lapses in good taste by broadcasters, filing a complaint with the FCC. Theoretically, such protests should not influence news decisions and most of the time, on better newspapers and broadcast stations, they do not directly influence them. But the pressure exists.

4. The fourth circle represents the *basic press philosophies and the laws of individual governments*. In Chapter 3, we discussed two theories of the press—authoritarianism and libertarianism—and a variant concept called the social responsibility theory. Under the latter concept, so strongly insisted on by today's press critics, it is the obligation of owners and managers of the media to be socially responsible, to ensure that all public issues are presented fairly and fully so that the people may form their own opinions about the issues. Should the media fail to do so, its proponents insist, it may be necessary for some other agency of the public to enforce this concept. The threat of such action by the public—which would draw us dangerously back toward authoritarian control of the press—illustrates how important it is that the three innermost circles of control function as they should.

5. The fifth circle represents the *limits that people will tolerate regarding all types of human activity*. No individual or organization can pass beyond that outer limit without reprisal; history shows that even the most powerful governments eventually fall (as did that of ancient Rome) if they exceed the outer limit of what the people will permit. And those in the three inner circles also fall if they disregard that outer limit circumscribing their conduct.

These circles of social and legal control are not fixed, immutably, for all time. They shift from century to century, from generation to generation. For example, in the Western world the relative social permissiveness of the Chaucerian and Shakespearian eras may be contrasted to the puritanical restraints and Victorianism of the nineteenth century, and they, in turn, may be contrasted with the permissiveness of the latter half of the twentieth century.

The outer limits vary, as do the inner circles. Governments rise and fall, greatly affecting human rights, including the freedom of the press. Governments in Portugal, Spain, and Greece provide examples. Codes of conduct stiffen, then relax, then stiffen again. The standards of the individual media respond to changing social mores as do the decisions of our media gatekeepers concerning what will be printed, filmed, or broadcast.

## Commission on Freedom of the Press

In 1947, the report of the *Commission on Freedom of the Press*, whose chairman was the late Robert Maynard Hutchins, then chancellor of the University of Chicago, set forth twentieth-century America's requirements of the mass media. Although denounced by much of the media because no newsperson was a member of the commission, these requirements reflect the code of ethics enacted in the 1920s by the American Society of Newspaper Editors, and they have been incorporated in codes of ethics subsequently established by other media organizations. The press, the commission declared, should provide the following in a democratic society:

1. A truthful, comprehensive, and intelligent account of the day's events in a context which gives them meaning

2. A forum for the exchange of comment and criticism

3. The projection of a representative picture of the constituent groups in the society

4. The presentation and clarification of the goals and values of the society

5. Full access to the day's intelligence.

The communications media, of course, may choose not to attempt to fulfill these obligations: Indeed, the First Amendment permits irresponsibility as well as responsibility. But, as we have emphasized, they may do so only at their own peril—and ours.

## Media Ethics

Criticism of the press has been commonplace in America since the publication of the first newspaper. However, since they gained widespread public attention as a powerful force not only reporting but also

## WAS ARTHUR ASHE'S PRIVACY INVADED?

As a world-renowned tennis player, Arthur Ashe set high standards both on and off the court. He was widely admired as a role model, especially for black youths.

The public was shocked when an inquiry from a *USA Today* reporter prompted Ashe to announce that he had AIDS. His illness resulted from a transfusion of infected blood.

Ashe protested that his privacy had been invaded. "It put me in the unenviable position of having to lie if I wanted to protect our privacy," he said. "No one should have to make that choice. I am sorry that I have been forced to make this revelation at this time."

*USA Today* editor Peter Pritchard told *Editor & Publisher* magazine that he did not "see any public service accomplished by sweeping this under the rug."

Other editors and members of the public both attacked and defended the newspaper's decision to publish the story. As an editor, would YOU have run it?

helping to shape the social and political upheavals of the 1960s and 1970s, the mass media have come under increasing attack for their perceived lapses in ethical and professional conduct. By almost any standard of measurement, the press today is more ethical and more responsible than in any previous period. Nevertheless, large money awards by unfriendly jurors in libel cases document some of the current public antipathy to the media. In this section, we discuss some of the criticisms of media actions as well as the codes of ethics that have been established and the extent to which some of these codes apparently are enforced.

### Criticism of Media Practices

Truth, honesty, and fairness are bedrock public expectations of all business and professional practitioners. But in poll after poll Americans rank the clergy, doctors, and police above mass communicators in terms of honesty and other ethical standards. That was the finding, for example, of a poll reported by the American Society of Newspaper Editors. Television anchors achieved fourth place, the highest ranking for a communicator. Television reporters ranked sixth, newspaper editors seventh, and newspaper reporters eighth. Near the bottom of the list were advertising executives, just ahead of used-car salespeople.

Among other perceived faults, the media are blamed for invading personal privacy, smearing reputations, practicing deception, unduly criticizing government and business leaders, emphasizing "bad news" over "good news," sensationalizing stories, reporting gossip and rumors, developing conflicts of interest, and failing to correct errors promptly and conspicuously or even admitting that mistakes had been made.

Extensive criticism of the media followed the explosion of the Challenger shuttle in 1986. Some critics said safeguards were not taken in part because newspaper and television coverage had heavily and unfairly criticized delays in the launch. Leslie H. Gelb, a New York *Times* correspondent, wrote that, through a barrage of TV and print reporting, the media, "almost without exception, quickly transformed tragedy into gruesome voyeurism and soap opera by its gross overcoverage." And when 300 reporters and camera operators converged on Concord, New Hampshire, to cover memorial services and to interview grieving family members and students of Christa McAuliffe, the schoolteacher victim, George Wilson, publisher of the Concord *Monitor*, termed the spectacle "a very ugly scene . . . a classic horror show."

The Miami *Herald* was accused of unethical conduct after it reported in 1987 that Democratic presidential candidate Gary Hart had spent the night with a young woman, precipitating Hart's withdrawal from the race five days later. Hart angrily denied the report, denounced the *Herald* for spreading "false" information, and accused the media of harassing people in public life. Many criticized the paper for basing its account on a haphazard stakeout of Hart's Washington, D.C., residence and for printing the story hurriedly against a deadline without giving Hart a full chance to explain himself. Others questioned the propriety of media inquiries into a candidate's sex life. A number of editors defended the *Herald's* action as legitimate, coming as it did on the heels of widespread accounts of Hart's social activities including a report in *Newsweek* magazine that Hart "had been haunted by rumors of womanizing." Said Heath J. Meriwether, executive editor of the *Herald:* "We think the issues raised by our stories are germane to any consideration of a presidential candidate."

In what former Arkansas Governor Bill Clinton termed "cash-for-trash journalism," Gennifer Flowers, a TV reporter, singer, and state employee, sold an account of her alleged affair with the future president to the *Star*, a national celebrity tabloid. The story spread to the mainstream media, most of which berated the tabloid for publishing the account. Columnist Gelb pointed out that "journalists . . . say the sleazy tabloids are smearing candidates and the candidates deserve and need the chance to clear their names but, if a legitimate news organization repeats sleaze, it necessarily magnifies and legitimizes the sleaze."

Comparing the situation with the Hart case, Charles Krauthammer, a Washington *Post* columnist, praised the mainstream papers for playing down the story. Said Everette Dennis, executive director

## "LIKE FISH IN THE OCEAN"

"We have a new kind of food chain in journalism. If a sensational story appears anywhere, it appears everywhere.

"We're like fish in the ocean, feeding off each other. If the bottom-suckers find something down there in the muck, they dredge it up and we gobble up their story, because we know the whole hungry school of media fish is right there in the feeding frenzy with us."

—James P. Gannon, Washington bureau chief, Detroit *News*

of the Freedom Forum Media Studies Center: "High-caliber professional coverage of public officials . . . requires that serious, ethical journalism establish a zone of decency that effectively distinguishes rigorous, responsible reporting from sleazy, haphazard rumormongering and reckless endangerment of the quality of information reaching the public, not to mention the rights of individuals involved in such stories."

After being sharply criticized for, as one critic put it, "sinking to tabloid levels" with the Flowers allegations, the mainstream media were wary in reporting a charge by Paula Corbin Jones that Clinton had made sexual advances to her in a hotel room. It was not until Jones filed a sexual harassment lawsuit against Clinton several months later that the major media heavily covered the story.

Condemned by mass communicators and the public alike are deceptive practices such as fabricating stories, quoting nonexistent sources, impersonating people when other means to obtain a story could be used, plagiarizing, unexpectedly confronting persons being interviewed on television with accusations, and preoccupation with dramatic TV or still pictures at the expense of accuracy and fairness.

Washington *Post* reporter Janet Cooke admitted that her sensational account of "Jimmy," an eight-year-old heroin addict, was a hoax, prompting her dismissal and the return of a Pulitzer Prize. Darrow "Duke" Tully resigned as publisher of the *Arizona Republic* and Phoenix *Gazette* after admitting that for more than 30 years he had lied about being a decorated Air Force pilot with extensive combat service in Korea and Vietnam. Writer Michael Daly admitted that he had used questionable journalistic techniques in "300 columns over two years." Revelations of fraud based on the incognito operation of a Chicago bar, "The Mirage," by a team of Chicago *Sun-Times* reporters won some acclaim but not a Pulitzer Prize because of some

## AN ETHICAL DILEMMA?

An emotionally troubled 18-year-old college student murdered his mother, father, and sister. Found mentally incompetent to stand trial, he underwent many years of intensive psychotherapy and subsequently was found not guilty of murder on grounds that he was insane at the time.

The student obtained his college degree, married, and rose through journalistic ranks to become president of a large group of suburban weekly newspapers.

*Twenty-one years* after the slayings, however, a competing weekly paper disclosed his past. No other news medium picked up the story, and many condemned the action.

This story illustrates a cardinal principle of journalism—*never* publish unsavory information about a long-ago happening without cause, such as a person's seeking public office. People, it is almost universally agreed, have a right to "live down" their past.

Probably no other editor would have run this particular story. But newspeople *are* confronted with ethical decisions almost daily: Does the public interest override individual privacy? Should a news source go unnamed? Should a "leak" possibly affecting national security be used? Should a rape victim's identity be disclosed?

General journalism codes call for truth, accuracy, impartiality, fair play. Most news media also have their own codes, generally enforced. Many decisions, however, test individual judgment and conscience.

Would *you* have run this story?

judges' objections to the method employed. These are only a few of innumerable examples of deception troubling editors and the public alike.

Conflicts of interest, such as using unpublished information for financial gain and accepting gifts from news sources, represent another area of ethical concern. R. Foster Winans was found guilty of "insider trading" under the Securities Act of 1934 when he "leaked" advance word of his *Wall Street Journal* columns to a stockbroker. A number of journalism organizations, although not condoning Winans's breach of journalistic ethics, argued unsuccessfully that extending "insider trading" prohibitions to journalists intruded into First Amendment rights of free speech.

Approximately 5000 media representatives accepted an expenses-paid trip to Disney World for an $8 million, 15th anniversary party outside Orlando, Florida in 1986. Some print and broadcast people paid their own way. The Society of Professional Journalists condemned the acceptance of gratuities as "a breach of ethical conduct that inescapably creates the appearance of journalists being bought in return for favorable publicity."

**Photographs.**  Manipulating photographic images in order to deceive the viewer is strongly denounced by the National Press Photographers Association. Michael T. Martinez, association president, said that, with the advent of new technology, "the handling of wire pictures will take place without the benefit of dry silver paper. It will only be a matter of time until darkrooms as we know them will become a thing of the past and local photos will also be handled electronically, thus banishing wet darkrooms to the land of 4 × 5 Speed Graphics. The ethical principles we, as photojournalists, have always adhered to must be reinforced to deal with the new tools. . . ."

*Digitexing,* as it is termed, involves the manipulation of tiny pixels on a computer screen to alter images (see Chapter 13). Photo and graphics editors and educators attending a conference at the Poynter Institute for Media Studies concluded that even the alteration of an image in photo illustration and nondocumentary feature material was bad practice unless it was immediately obvious to anyone that it was merely an art concept.

**Digitexing**
Altering images on a computer screen

Legal as well as ethical aspects also are involved. Photographers whose work is altered may sue for copyright violation, it was pointed out, and photo subjects whose images are changed could bring libel or false-light suits against publications that portray the subjects in distorted or fictionalized ways.

In addition, whether to publish newsworthy pictures that are sure to offend some readers constitutes a continual dilemma for editors. A minority of publications ran a photo showing a Pennsylvania state official shooting himself in the mouth during a news conference. A relatively small number of newspapers printed a close-up of a 15-year-old boy whose jaw had been impaled on a metal spike on a fence he had been climbing (he recovered); the Associated Press photo editor termed it a classic, but some editors called it gruesome.

Other examples, although not so extreme, abound. Editors anguish over such decisions, which inevitably are questioned by some readers on grounds of ethics, taste, and invasion of privacy.

**Magazines.**  Guidelines of the American Society of Magazine Editors restrict editorial involvement with a publication's advertising. However, a panel of *Esquire* editors and Carillon Importers executives judged a short story contest that required the inclusion of a sentence about Absolut vodka. The winning entry was published as an advertisement in the magazine. *Family Circle* ran stories about the renovation of an old house by Martha Stewart, a contributing editor of the magazine and a paid consultant for K mart Corporation. K mart advertisements surrounded the articles and Ms. Stewart appeared in the company's television commercials endorsing some of the products. Advertisements for J & B scotch that mimicked the look and editorial tone of *Spy* were also published in the magazine; use of *advertorials* in other publications is not rare. Critics also

**Advertorial**
Coined term for an advertisement that resembles the news or editorial content of a publication

charge that some magazines containing tobacco advertisements will not publish anti-tobacco articles.

Among other dubious practices, some magazines permit editorial staff members to accept free tickets and trips from advertisers, and others occasionally use composite characters and fictional situations to make a point in nonfiction articles.

**Re-creation**
In television the dramatic reenactment of a news event using actors

**Television.**    Use of the technique of *re-creation*, in which actors dramatize news events, evoked protests in 1989. The strongest criticisms were directed at the reenactment by ABC News of American diplomat Felix Bloch's allegedly handing over a briefcase to a Soviet KGB agent without labeling the faked scene a simulation in its first "feed" to stations. Even though the footage subsequently was so labeled, news directors of other networks said such an action blurs the lines between news and entertainment.

Reenactments continue to blur the line between "straight" news programs and syndicated tabloid shows such as "Hard Copy" (see Issue 1). In 1993, the credibility of NBC News suffered a severe blow when the network admitted that it had rigged the fiery test crash of a controversial General Motors pickup truck on its "Dateline NBC" program by placing incendiary devices in the truck and exploding them by remote control, without explaining the faked setup to its viewers. As a result of the admission, GM withdrew a defamation suit it had filed against NBC five days after an Atlanta jury fined it $105 million for the death of a young man when a similar GM truck caught fire. NBC fired three producers and reassigned a correspondent on the program, and NBC News President Michael Gartner resigned. "When questions arose during editing, the usual systems for checks and balances failed to operate," an NBC report explained.

Television programs that feature heroes and villains drawn from the toy store shelf or developed in conjunction with the marketing of goods unfairly exploit children, the American Academy of Pediatrics (AAP), a congressional committee chairman, and a consumer group have charged. "What the shows do is hook kids into these program-length commercials that in fact offer an engaging story but are designed to sell the product," Dr. William H. Dietz, chairman of the AAP's task force on children and television, said.

Other critics complain that broadcast stations have reduced the amount of air time devoted to public affairs and news programming as a result of federal deregulation and the industry's changing economics. TV news coverage has been criticized for "its superficiality, its choppy brevity for fear of dial turners, its preoccupation with visual excitement (fires, hurricanes, riots)," as *Time* magazine essayist Thomas Griffith put it. Television production executive Norman Lear, at a Boston conference on TV and ethics, charged that, "The manufacturers of television entertainment, news, and public affairs proceed with very little consideration for the ethics involved. . . . Commercial television's north star, from which nearly all bearings are set, is quite simply, 'How do I win Tuesday night at 8 o'clock?'" "Trash TV" is discussed at length in Issue 1 and Chapter 10.

**Radio and Recording.**  With commercial success of a record so dependent on radio exposure, promoters sometimes resort to unethical tactics to obtain air play. The result has been the recurring *payola* scandals. In its simplest form payola is under-the-counter payment of cash to a radio program director or disc jockey to play certain records frequently. Payola may take more subtle forms as well, such as free trips and other favors paid for by a record company. Another device is including the radio decision makers in profits on "backdoor sales," an industry racket. Stacks of new records are slipped out of the normal commercial distribution system and given to a radio executive or disc jockey; that individual sells them at a reduced price to a retail music store and pockets the proceeds. It should be emphasized, however, that most radio personnel reject such practices.

The litany of complaints about media ethical practices seemingly is endless. When the subject arises, nearly everyone, it seems, is eager to attest to some media failing.

**Payola**
Under-the-counter payment of cash or favors to radio station personnel who play certain records frequently

## Codes of Ethics

The model for modern codes of ethics is the Canons of Journalism, established in 1923 by the American Society of Newspaper Editors, Accuracy, fair play, and responsibility are its hallmarks. The Society of Professional Journalists adopted the code as its own in 1926 and revised it in 1973. Public criticism of media practices developed strongly during the 1960s, culminating in Vice President Agnew's attacks on the press in 1969. The report of the professional standards committee of the Associated Press Managing Editors Association in 1972 was the first salvo in a barrage of attention to the problem of media ethics during and after the Watergate era, when public distrust of all institutions mounted. Today almost all national organizations and the vast majority of individual print and broadcast media have developed ethical guidelines for their news-editorial operations.

Practitioners and mass communication educators have mixed feelings about codes of ethics. Most media people seem to maintain that codes are useful as standards against which to measure their own value systems; others, steeped in the individualistic tradition, take a cavalier attitude toward codes, supporting conscience and principle but disdaining formalized strictures. Others fear that courts will use written codes as a measure for deciding right and wrong in suits against media personnel. Codes are criticized by others as containing internal contradictions and also as the products of managers who, as Professor Richard A. Schwarzlose of Northwestern University puts it, "tend to focus on things reporters cannot do (as a protection for corporate and product credibility) rather than on ways of uplifting the reporters' self-image."

## Society of Professional Journalists

# Code of Ethics

SOCIETY of Professional Journalists, believes the duty of journalists is to serve the truth.

We BELIEVE the agencies of mass communication are carriers of public discussion and information, acting on their Constitutional mandate and freedom to learn and report the facts.

We BELIEVE in public enlightenment as the forerunner of justice, and in our Constitutional role to seek the truth as part of the public's right to know the truth.

We BELIEVE those responsibilities carry obligations that require journalists to perform with intelligence, objectivity, accuracy, and fairness.

To these ends, we declare acceptance of the standards of practice here set forth:

### I. RESPONSIBILITY:

The public's right to know of events of public importance and interest is the overriding mission of the mass media. The purpose of distributing news and enlightened opinion is to serve the general welfare. Journalists who use their professional status as representatives of the public for

### IV. ACCURACY AND OBJECTIVITY:

Good faith with the public is the foundation of all worthy journalism.

1. Truth is our ultimate goal.

2. Objectivity in reporting the news is another goal that serves as the mark of an experienced professional. It is a standard of performance toward which we strive. We honor those who achieve it.

3. There is no excuse for inaccuracies or lack of thoroughness.

4. Newspaper headlines should be fully warranted by the contents of the articles they accompany. Photographs and telecasts should give an accurate picture of an event and not highlight an incident out of context.

5. Sound practice makes clear distinction between news reports and expressions of opinion. News reports should be free of opinion or bias and represent all sides of an issue.

6. Partisanship in editorial comment that knowingly departs from the truth violates the spirit of American journalism.

7. Journalists recognize their responsibility for offering

The Code of Ethics issued by the Society of Professional Journalists is one of the basic guidelines used by editors and reporters in deciding how to handle difficult problems that arise in their daily work. (Society of Professional Journalists)

Nevertheless, codes of acceptable practice by professional communicators continue to be developed and to a substantial extent are enforced, especially among newspapers.

In 1992, the Society of Professional Journalists developed a handbook designed to teach the skill of ethical decision-making to journalists. The manual is titled *Doing Ethics in Journalism: A Handbook with Case Studies.* By using real-life examples from current journalism issues, the manual outlines the basic questions journalists can ask themselves to reach an ethical solution.

**Plagiarism**
Copying or imitating the language, ideas, or thoughts of another author and passing them off as one's original work

**Newspapers.**   Action against plagiarism has been taken by a number of newspapers during the last several years. Examples: Laura Parker, chief of the Miami bureau of the Washington *Post,* was fired when she lifted major portions of a story about mosquito and grasshopper infestations in Florida from stories by the Miami *Herald* and the Associated Press; Chicago *Tribune* Middle East correspondent Jonathan Broder was forced to resign for plagiarizing a Jerusalem *Post* article; Bob Wisehart, a Sacramento *Bee* television columnist, was suspended indefinitely without pay for plagiarizing parts of a book by best-selling author Stephen King; David Hawley, drama critic of the St. Paul *Pioneer Press*, was reassigned after he plagiarized parts of a six-year-old New York *Times* review in his own review of a play; and Denver *Post* art critic Irene Rawlings was fired for plagiarizing two *New Yorker* magazine pieces.

In addition, Mark Hornung resigned as editorial page editor of the Chicago *Sun-Times* after admitting he plagiarized a Washington *Post* editorial in a column, and Bob Wisehart then resigned as Sacramento *Bee* television critic after he plagiarized an Orlando *Sentinel* column.

Plagiarism was cited as one of the three most serious ethical violations in an informal mail survey conducted by the American Society of Newspaper Editors. Using unpublished information for financial gain and receiving discounts for personal purchases made from companies the reporter or editor handled in news stories were the other two types of offenses. The replies from 226 editors disclosed that at least 48 newspaper journalists were fired and 30 suspended for ethical violations during a two-year period.

"The [thin] line between ethical use and plagiarism is drawn on the border that separates following known rules from cheating," Deni Elliott, director of the Ethics Institute at Dartmouth College, wrote in *Quill* magazine. ". . . A reporter who passes off some other reporter's reporting as her own cheats her boss by violating a rule of research that she knows she is expected to follow. She cheats the original author by not recognizing her claim of ownership. Most importantly, she cheats her reader because she doesn't have the background that she implicitly promises with her byline or on-air appearance."

Conflict of interest problems were addressed by the Associated Press Sports Editors in an ethics code adopted in 1991. Issues include serving as official scorers, using unnamed sources, sharing notes or quotes, accepting free or discounted tickets, voting for awards and all-star teams, and paying for travel, accommodations, and food supplied by teams being covered.

Faced with increasing pressure by advertisers to influence the content of business stories, the Society of American Business Editors and Writers in 1992 reaffirmed its code of ethics with emphasis on four points:

1. A clear-cut delineation between advertising and editorial matters should be maintained at all times.

2. Material produced by an editorial staff or news service should be used only in sections controlled by editorial departments.

3. Sections controlled by advertising departments should be distinctly different from news sections in typeface, layout, and design.

4. Promising a story in exchange for advertising is unethical.

The society represents 1200 business and economics journalists from U.S. newspapers, magazines, and TV-cable operations, as well as free-

# ETHICS ON THE INTERNET

A protocol to help newspeople make ethical decisions about intrusion and privacy when they use computers to gather and analyze information was drawn up at a seminar at the Poynter Institute in 1994.

Participants raised the following questions, according to the *Bulletin* of the American Society of Newspaper Editors: What of the co-worker who routinely reads the messages of his or her colleagues? Or distributes salary lists? Or logs onto a system and sends inflammatory e-mail to a news group under another's ID? Or taps into a Pentagon database with a stolen password? Or takes information that another person improperly retrieved from a computer? Or asks a source to provide access to a corporate database?

Some news organizations forbid such "hacking" practices while others often make ethical decisions in ad hoc fashion while pursuing a story, the writers explain. Agreeing on a protocol—a process and a framework for making good decisions—is recommended. The following principles were incorporated into the protocol:

- We are committed to truth-seeking, full and fair reporting, independence from news sources, and to minimizing harm to all who are touched by our actions. This standard does not change with the mode of news gathering. . . .
- We respect the property of others, regardless of the forms it takes: ideas, words, physical possessions. This includes files, messages, data, and other electronic property.
- We respect the privacy of other persons, including the privacy of their electronic persona.
- Truth-telling is enhanced by truthful news gathering. Using deceptive methods to gain information, including the failure to reveal one's identity as a journalist while using a computer or the use of false identification to obtain access to a computer system, is corrosive to truth-telling.
- We respect the importance of law in a democratic society. Directly breaking the law, including laws relating to computer access, in the pursuit of news, or asking others to break laws on our behalf, erodes institutions and should be avoided.

En route to deciding on a course of action, the journalist consults a checklist of questions, such as, "Who would benefit and who would be harmed by our actions?"

"The principles provide reference points on your moral compass, represent 'what you stand for,' and guide you in ethical decision-making," the writers point out. "The checklist of questions is a pathway to follow to resolve conflicting principles and to help determine your actions."

lance journalists. Said the ethics committee chairperson, Gary Klott, a syndicated writer: "Newspapers' survival depends on editorial integrity. Readers turn to us for fair, objective, critical reporting, and fair, objective, critical information on how to spend their money. Readers will turn away if we compromise that."

The Associated Press Managing Editors in 1994 adopted a revised code of ethics that, among other items, declared that a newspaper "should reasonably reflect, in staffing and coverage, its diverse constituencies" and encouraged newspeople "to be involved in their communities to the extent that such activities do not create conflicts of interest."

**Magazines.**    Magazine journalists disagree significantly on how they would handle specific ethical dilemmas, Professor Vicki Hesterman of Point Loma Nazarene College, San Diego, found in a survey of consumer magazine editors. Forty-nine of 100 editors responded to her questionnaire.

> Some take free trips, some take free tickets, some allow composite characters, some experience editorial-advertising collaboration. . . . Considering the fact that consumer magazines comprise a mere fraction of the magazine industry . . . arriving at any kind of a common code will probably not be a simple process.

**Public Relations.**    The Public Relations Society of America (PRSA) is the only professional communications group that has created a grievance procedure taking action against members on ethical grounds. A compilation by the Foundation for Public Relations Research and Education (now called the Institute for Public Relations Research & Education) found that in a 33-year period the ethics board received or initiated 165 complaints about code violations by PRSA members, mainly charging account piracy and job infringement. Of these, the society warned two members, censured three, suspended two, and expelled two.

The International Association of Business Communicators (IABC), comprised mainly of publications editors and information specialists, in 1985 replaced its code of standards with a code of ethics. Sanctions against a member found in violation of the code primarily consist of warnings that IABC considers "informative and educational." If the offense is considered extremely flagrant or the individual has shown no serious commitment for improvement, suspension for up to one year can be imposed.

## News Councils

With the financial aid of the Don R. Mellett Fund of the Newspaper Guild, community news councils were established during the late 1960s in several states including California, Oregon, Illinois, and Colorado. The councils, composed of both public and media representatives, were intended to provide a forum for public criticism of the media and to enable editors and managers to respond. The idea, however, met with only limited success. Today, only the statewide Minnesota News Council, the Northwest News Council in Washington and Oregon, and the Honolulu Media Council are in operation. In 1985, and again in 1994, the Kentucky Press Association rejected a proposal to establish a news council.

Similar media and public apathy marked the operation of the National News Council from 1973 to 1984. The council was funded by several foundations and about 40 news media and was composed of prominent journalists and laypeople. In all, 249 complaints were investigated and the findings reported in journalism periodicals. Media reaction was mixed. Lacking visibility and hobbled by insufficient funds, the council ceased operation.

## Organizations Seeking Media Improvement

Almost every mass communicator in the United States either is a member of one or more journalism and mass communications associations or is represented by the organization for which he or she works. Generally, the managers fulfill institutional member responsibilities and staff personnel belong to craft organizations. Thousands are active in local groups. The purposes of almost every organization are to exchange ideas in order to advance professional ideals and practices, and to work collectively to solve common problems.

**Trade Associations.**   Representative of these organizations are the Newspaper Association of America, National Association of Broadcasters, Motion Picture Association of America, and Magazine Publishers of America. There are also numerous state and regional associations.

**Organizations of Individuals.**   Representative of these groups are the Society of Professional Journalists, American Society of Newspaper Editors, Radio Television News Directors Association, Public Relations Society of America, and American Academy of Advertising.

**Centers, Institutes, and Action Groups.**   In this category are the Reporters Committee for Freedom of the Press, World Press Freedom Committee, American Press Institute, Poynter Institute for Media Studies, Freedom Forum Media Studies Center, and many others.

**Other Aid Programs.**   Millions of dollars are provided in scholarships, research grants, and other awards to students, faculty members, colleges and universities, and other groups and individuals in mass communications. They are given by such organizations as the Ford Foundation, William Randolph Hearst Foundation, Dow Jones Newspaper Fund, and the National Association of Broadcasters.

Almost all these organizations publish magazines, newsletters, and other educational and informative materials. Because of the strong support provided, the steady but at times uneven improvement in media performance that has characterized the last several decades seems certain to continue.

# PART THREE
# Radio and Popular Music

## ROLES OF THE MEDIA—RECORDER

History is recorded first in haste by the news media, then after greater reflection by magazines, books, film, and electronic methods for later study.

*"The camera should be like the notebook of a trained reporter, to record events as they happen, without trying to stop them to make a picture."*

*—Stefan Loren, photojournalist*

*"There is now and will be a monster explosion in the means of disseminating material . . . but there still is something to be said for sitting on the stoop reading a daily newspaper."*

*—Chuck Ward, publisher*

*"Some books are to be tasted, others to be swallowed, and some few to be chewed and digested."*

*—Francis Bacon, English essayist, 1612*

# CHAPTER 8
## Radio

## Limbaugh Speaks; His Listeners Act

His program is unabashedly biased. He sneers at liberals as "dittoheads" and worse. He calls other members of the media liars. He brags about himself on the air.

Millions of his fans love it. They devour his liberal-bashing and accept his statements as political gospel.

That is Rush Limbaugh, the glib commentator who has been called the "800-pound gorilla of talk radio." He is heard on more than 600 radio stations.

Limbaugh's influence on his listeners is enormous. Claiming that the media were distorting the Republican plan in Congress to transfer the federal school lunch program to the states, he urged listeners to call their newspapers, the national networks, and the news magazines to protest.

"All you say is, 'Stop lying about the school lunch program' and hang up," he told them.

Thousands from coast to coast immediately did so, many using his exact words. Typically, Cable News Network in Atlanta received more than 300 calls.

Critics of Limbaugh's bombastic style recognize his power but contend that he is preaching to the converted. William Rentschler observed in *Editor & Publisher:* "His program is largely a love feast of like-minded listeners massaging the giant ego of their hero."

Radio is almost everywhere—at home, in the automobile, at the beach, on the street. For every person in the United States, there are more than two radio sets. In some foreign countries ownership is nearly as high. This abundance of receivers makes radio perhaps the most pervasive of all the mass media.

In the 1920s, radio brought a new dimension to American life. A magic box in the living room delivered music, comedies like "Amos 'n' Andy," and soap operas like "One Man's Family." Sound effects made the backgrounds sound real.

Today satellite transmission as a means of distributing programs has brought fresh vigor and innovation to radio.

In this chapter we examine the history of radio, how the industry operates, and the economics involved. We see how stations project "personalities" aimed at focused, specialized audiences.

One section discusses the role of radio news—how it is prepared and broadcast, its strengths and weaknesses. We also examine radio talk shows, whose abundance and aggressive style created a communications phenomenon in the 1990s.

## The Lure of Radio

Former President Jimmy Carter once recalled to a group of broadcasters his boyhood days on a farm in Georgia that had no electricity, and how the family gathered outdoors at night to hear a radio hooked up to the battery of his father's automobile. The music, drama, comedy, and political talk they listened to opened the world to them, as they did to millions of other persons.

From a fascinating novelty in the early 1920s, radio grew swiftly into an essential element in family life. It created an almost instantaneous nationwide distribution system for urgent information about major events, adding a significant new element of unity to the American social fabric. At first, listeners used earphones and brought in programs by meticulously moving a "cat-whisker" wire across a crystal. Many sets were homemade; equipment in the broadcasting stations was almost as amateurish. On certain nights, local stations would remain silent so listeners could tune in distant stations. Call letters of stations east of the Mississippi River were designated to start with the letter W, and those west of the Mississippi with a K. Two pioneer exceptions were KDKA in Pittsburgh and KYW in Chicago. When the loudspeaker was developed, radio's place in the living room was assured.

Families were transported in their imagination to far-off places by clever use of sound effects. As the Lone Ranger and Tonto rode off in pursuit of bandits, the hoofbeats of their horses echoed from the loudspeaker, made by studio technicians drumming a half-dozen toilet plungers on pebbles. When Sergeant Preston of the Royal Canadian Mounties stalked killers through the snow with his dog King at his side, listeners thought they heard King's heavy breathing; what they actually heard was an actor panting into a megaphone close to the microphone. Although radio performers at work were only disembodied voices to the listeners, their physical features became nationally known through newspaper and magazine publicity and public appearances.

In the world before television, radio's clever use of sound effects created images in the minds of listeners.

The first glimmerings of radio's future disc jockeys came during the 1930s, when a few stations offered "Make Believe Ballroom" programs. During those shows an announcer played records and pretended to be broadcasting from a ballroom, simulating the live performances of orchestras broadcasting from hotels and nightclubs that were a staple of local and network radio programming. Expanded from terse telegraphic reports, play-by-play descriptions of baseball games in distant cities were simulated by imaginative studio announcers, including a young Midwestern sportscaster named Ronald Reagan.

## Blending News and Entertainment

Alexander Graham Bell's demonstration of his newly invented telephone at the Philadelphia Centennial Exposition made it apparent that the telephone could be used to transmit music and talk. Edison's phonograph and Eastman's Kodak of 1888 were other milestones in communication.

Guglielmo Marconi's transmission of dot-and-dash messages through wireless telegraphy in the 1890s was a crucial advance toward broadcasting. Reginald A. Fessenden improved on the process by using continuous waves (instead of Marconi's bursts) to carry a voice or music. On Christmas Eve 1906, Fessenden broadcast to ships offshore. But it was Lee De Forest's key improvement in the vacuum tube in 1906 that ensured radio's future. He used Columbia Phonograph Company records to broadcast concerts for wireless enthusiasts in 1907 and recorded famed tenor Enrico Caruso's voice at the Metropolitan Opera House in 1910, transmitting it to nearby homes.

On November 7, 1916, the New York *American* ran a wire to De Forest's experimental station at High Bridge, New York, so that the "father of radio" could broadcast to a few amateur radio enthusiasts the returns from the Wilson-Hughes presidential election. Like the *American* and other newspapers misled by the early returns from that closely contested election, De Forest signed off with the statement that "Charles Evans Hughes will be the next president of the United States."

The inventive and engineering resources of wireless and radio were subsequently needed for military purposes during World War I, and private broadcasting was banned until 1919. Even then, few saw the possibilities of mass radio listening. One person who did was David Sarnoff, who got his start as a Marconi wireless operator. When three big companies of the communications and electric manufacturing industries—Westinghouse, General Electric, and American Telephone & Telegraph

(AT&T)—pooled their patent rights interests in 1919 and formed the Radio Corporation of America (RCA), Sarnoff became RCA's spark plug. His active career extended to 1970.

It was a Westinghouse engineer, Dr. Frank Conrad, who offered the first proof of Sarnoff's contention that people would listen to radio. His broadcasts of music in Pittsburgh in 1919 stimulated sales of crystal sets and led Westinghouse to open KDKA on November 2, 1920, as the first fully licensed commercial broadcasting station. The featured program consisted of returns from the Harding–Cox presidential election, one whose outcome was more easily predictable. Newspaper publishers thought radio newscasts stimulated sales of newspapers; by 1927, 97 papers presented small amounts of news over the air and 48 radio stations were owned by newspapers.

**Entertainment.** But despite these evidences of concern for news, radio's pioneers were more intent on capturing the public's interest by entertaining it than by informing it. Dramatic news events and on-the-spot sports coverage combined both objectives. News summaries themselves remained infrequent in the 1920s because they excited little advertiser interest, because radio itself did not collect news, and because news merely read from the newspaper sounded awkward and dull on the air. Meanwhile, in 1921, KDKA broadcast accounts of prize fights and major league baseball games. The next year, AT&T's New York station, WEAF (now WNBC), used phone lines to bring to its listeners the Chicago–Princeton football game from Stagg Field in Chicago. By 1924, the number of stations had grown from 30 in 1921 to 530. Twenty-one stations from New York to California joined in a March 1925 hookup to broadcast President Calvin Coolidge's inauguration.

### The Networks Emerge

The development of networks was vital for radio's progress. In early 1924, the Eveready Battery Company bought time on 12 stations for its Eveready Hour performers—the first use of national radio advertising. By 1925, AT&T had organized a network headed by WEAF with 26 outlets, reaching as far west as Kansas City. RCA, Westinghouse, and General Electric had a competitive network led by WJZ, New York, and WGY, Schenectady.

In 1926, the big companies reached an agreement under which AT&T would retire from the broadcasting business and in return would control all forms of network relays. RCA, Westinghouse, and General Electric bought WEAF for $1 million. They then formed the National Broadcasting Company as an RCA subsidiary. The station group organized by AT&T and headed by WEAF became the NBC Red network at the start of 1927, while the group headed by WJZ became the NBC Blue network. Regular coast-to-coast network operations began that year. Sarnoff emerged in full control of RCA and NBC in 1930.

Dolly the elephant rehearses a "song" at Madison Square Garden for radio broadcast of the Ringling Brothers Barnum and Bailey Circus over WJZ New York in 1925. Such novelty shows were frequent during the early days of radio. (Library of Congress)

Some rivals organized a network service with the support of the Columbia Phonograph Record Company in 1927, which became the Columbia Broadcasting System. In 1934, it had 97 station affiliates, compared with 65 for NBC Red and 62 for NBC Blue.

**FRC's Role.**    Passage of the Radio Act of 1927 strengthened the two big networks, since the number of stations on the air was reduced by the new Federal Radio Commission to avoid interference in receiving programs, and a group of about 50 powerful "clear-channel" stations was authorized. By 1938, all but two of the clear-channel stations were either network-owned or -affiliated. The two independent clear-channel stations, the Chicago *Tribune*'s WGN, and WOR, New York, formed the loosely organized Mutual Broadcasting System in 1934 but found competition difficult. Mutual's complaints to the Federal Communications Commission (the regulatory body was renamed in the Communications Act of 1934) brought about the sale by NBC in 1943 of its weaker Blue network to Edward J. Noble, who renamed it the American Broadcasting Company in 1945.

The growth of the networks after 1927, and their success in winning advertising revenues, made radio a more disturbing challenger to the newspaper industry. Radio's increasing interest in broadcasting news and public affairs also provided competition. In 1928, Republican Herbert Hoover and Democrat Alfred E. Smith took to the air, spending $1 million on campaign talks over NBC and CBS networks that reached many

Silent screen stars Mary Pickford and Douglas Fairbanks aboard the S.S. *Paris* in mid-Atlantic listen in the wireless room to a 1921 broadcast from the American mainland. (Library of Congress)

of the nation's 8 million receiving sets. That year the press associations—Associated Press, United Press, and International News Service—supplied complete election returns to the 677 radio stations. Radio's success in covering that bitter presidential election whetted listeners' appetites for more news broadcasts. In December, KFAB in Lincoln, Nebraska, responded by hiring the city editor of the Lincoln *Star* to produce two broadcasts daily of what it called a radio newspaper. Other stations developed similar programs.

## The Radio–Newspaper War

A bitter war then broke out between radio and newspapers over the broadcasting of news. Radio, as a new medium, was winning an increasing, if yet small, advertising investment. Why let radio news broadcasts attract listeners who would become the audience for advertisers' commercials, asked some publishers. This argument gave more weight to public interest in news than it deserved, considering the demonstrated interest in listening to such entertainers as Kate Smith and Eddie Cantor. But after both 1932 political conventions were aired on coast-to-coast networks, and after the Associated Press furnished 1932 election returns to the networks to forestall the sale of United Press returns, the American Newspaper Publishers Association cracked down. The news services should stop providing news to radio; broadcasting of news should be confined to brief bulletins that would stimulate newspaper reading; radio program logs should be treated as paid advertising. After a majority of AP members voted in 1933 for such restrictions, all three services stopped selling news to radio stations. Radio now had to gather its own.

The Columbia Broadcasting System set up the leading network news service, opened bureaus in leading U.S. cities and in London, and developed a string of correspondents. Hans Von Kaltenborn, a former Brooklyn *Eagle* managing editor, joined CBS in 1930 to become the first of a long line of radio commentators. NBC organized a less extensive news service.

A compromise was soon proposed. This was the Press-Radio Bureau, which would present two five-minute newscasts daily on the networks from news supplied by the press associations. Bulletin coverage of extraordinary events would also be provided. In return, the networks would stop gathering news. The bureau began operating in March 1934, but was doomed to quick failure. Stations wanting more news bought it from five new agencies that jumped into the field, led by Transradio Press Service. A year later, UP and INS began selling full news reports to stations. UP began a wire report written especially for radio delivery, which AP matched in 1940. The Press-Radio Bureau stopped functioning in 1940; Transradio closed in 1951.

Radio, meantime, was developing a blend of entertainment and news. The trial of Bruno Hauptmann in 1934 for the kidnap-murder of the Lindbergh baby attracted more than 300 reporters, including many with microphones. President Roosevelt's famed "fireside chats" and the presidential nominating conventions and campaigns were major events. In December 1936, the entire world listened by shortwave broadcast as Edward VIII explained why he was giving up the British throne for "the woman I love."

## Radio Comes of Age

Radio fully met the challenge of diplomatic crisis and world war that began with Adolf Hitler's annexation of Austria and ultimatum to Czechoslovakia in 1938. Beginning with a patched-together but striking coverage of the Munich crisis, the radio networks expanded their news reporting tremendously during World War II, especially after the 1941 Japanese attack on the American naval base at Pearl Harbor in Hawaii plunged the United States into the global conflict. At the station level, newscasts took a place of prime importance.

In 1937, CBS sent a then-unknown Edward R. Murrow to Europe as news chief. For an assistant he hired William L. Shirer, a news service man. They did human interest stories and cultural programs for shortwave broadcasts that were rebroadcast by United States stations. Then came Hitler's invasion of Austria and the *Anschluss*. Murrow hurried to Vienna. On March 12, 1938, the first multiple-pickup news broadcast in history went on the air. Shirer spoke from London, Murrow from Vienna, and newspapermen whom CBS had hired gave their impressions from Berlin, Paris, and Rome. The pattern was set for radio's coverage of the fateful 20 days in September, beginning with Hitler's demand that the Czechs cede him the Sudetenland and ending with the Munich Pact.

**The Munich Crisis.** American radio listeners heard news broadcasts from 14 European cities during the Munich crisis period, including the

Edward R. Murrow, shown here on a rainy London street in 1941, first won fame as a broadcaster with his CBS radio reports on the German bombing blitz of the British capital. He opened each report with a slow and solemn, "This . . . is London." (UPI/Bettmann Newsphotos)

voices of Hitler, Benito Mussolini, Neville Chamberlain, and other leaders in the quarrel that set the stage for World War II. CBS alone devoted 471 broadcasts—nearly 48 hours of air time—to the crisis.

In his "Studio Nine" in New York City, Kaltenborn spent the 20 days catnapping on a cot, analyzing the reports, and backstopping the CBS European correspondents with commentary. Max Jordan of NBC had a memorable 46-minute beat on the text of the Munich pact, which he broadcast from Hitler's radio station. When Shirer and Jordan broadcast from inside the Berlin Sportspalast, the background of hysterical oratory and frenzied Nazi crowd reaction gave American listeners a personal conception of the warlike Nazi mood.

After World War II began in August 1939, Americans became familiar with the stirring oratory of Winston Churchill. Murrow's graphic descriptions from London as German bombers smashed the city did much to awaken a still-neutral United States to the world's danger. After Pearl Harbor, radio newsmen, using mobile units and shortwave, joined the coverage of American forces in the Pacific and Europe.

The demand for war news seemed inexhaustible. As the war drew to a close, radio expressed the sorrow of the people by devoting three days of programming solely to solemn music and tributes to the late President Roosevelt after his sudden death.

## Radio's Postwar Expansion

The war years were exceedingly prosperous ones for radio. When the FCC returned to peacetime licensing procedures in 1945, there were 909 licensed commercial standard (AM) radio stations. Sixteen months later there were approximately 600 new stations, and the number of communities with radio stations had nearly doubled. By 1950, there were 2086 AM radio stations on the air and 80 million receiving sets.

**AM radio**
Amplitude modulation transmission sent high into the air

But television was casting its shadow over radio. Television's breakthrough year was 1948, the one in which the value of time sales for the national radio networks reached an all-time high. (See Chapter 10.) Competition among the four networks was intense. The smaller stations found plenty of local advertising revenues in newly exploited markets, fortunately, and after 1947 radio had more revenue from local advertisers than from network advertisers. The networks were already shifting their attention to television. CBS forecast the fate of network radio when it made its famed 1948 talent raid on NBC to capture such stars as Amos 'n' Andy, Jack Benny, Burns and Allen, Edgar Bergen, and Bing Crosby for future television shows. While network radio dwindled in favor of music, news, and sports programming, radio continued to expand as an industry.

### The Growth of FM Radio

When FM broadcasting began to develop experimentally in 1936, the industry treated it as a minor novelty. Few sets were equipped to receive FM (frequency modulation) signals. Those AM (amplitude modulation) stations that also had FM licenses regarded them as a sideline of little consequence or potential. The poor relation has grown tremendously, however, and now dominates its onetime big cousin. Between the mid-1970s and mid-1980s, the FM share of the audience increased 38 percent. FM's appeal was exceptionally strong to younger listeners. FM continued to grow, especially after the FCC in 1984 decided to proceed with a plan to license 1000 or more new FM stations.

**FM radio**
Frequency modulation transmission along the line of sight to the horizon

AM stations have longer range and in most cases greater power than FM stations, but are subject to static interference. In some instances, government regulations require them to reduce their power or sign off at sundown to avoid conflict with other station signals, which carry farther at night. FM stations can be heard only for relatively small distances but are virtually static-free and transmit music with greater fidelity in stereophonic sound.

At first, FM stations played semiclassical or classical recordings without commercial interruptions. Stations with both AM and FM licenses often transmitted their AM programs on FM, as well as in simulcasts, just to keep the FM signal on the air at virtually no cost.

Gradually, broadcasters and advertisers became aware that FM could be an effective commercial medium. New sets for homes and automobiles were built with both AM and FM bands. Many FM stations took on much the same mixture of advertising and entertainment heard on AM stations.

**Narrowcasting**
Designing a radio station's programming to serve the interests of a limited, closely defined audience

From the advertiser's point of view, FM is attractive because stations can target the content of their broadcasts to audience segments with special listening interests. Use of demographic studies enables the FM stations to shape their programs for specific age ranges and listening preferences. This technique is called *narrowcasting*. Thus an advertiser may choose a station that features progressive rock, to reach the young liberal audience with a message, or one that plays softer, easy-listening music, to appeal to an older, more conservative group with different purchasing desires. Because of their generally larger audiences, AM stations cannot specialize as much as FM stations can. FM stations outnumber AM stations by a seven-to-five ratio.

The popularity of AM stations made a substantial recovery during the mid-1990s, however, because of the profusion of radio talk shows about political, sports, and social issues, most of which appeared on AM stations. Because the stations were able to increase their audiences, the sale prices of AM stations rose sharply. Sales and trades of both types of radio stations at very high prices occurred at a furious rate after the Telecommunications Reform Act of 1996 removed the limits on the number of stations a company could own. (See Issue 3.)

Prime AM stations in major markets have sold for more than $22 million. Top urban FM stations have been purchased for as much as $79 million.

AM stereo transmission has been developed, but adoption has been complicated by confusion over which of four available systems is most desirable. The FCC has refused to select one system as a standard.

## A Changing Medium

Radio's pervasive impact on American life today is due primarily to its immediacy and flexibility. It is present all around us: the mail carrier walks a route with a transistor fastened to the mail bag, the crowd on the beach listens to a singing group, the carpenter on a roof nails shingles in time to a rock beat. There are half a billion radio sets in the United States.

The majority of radio programs consist of popular recorded music, frequently emphasizing rock groups, interspersed with brief news summaries, sports, chat, commercials, and relatively little dramatic or intellectual content. Others offer all-talk formats and religious programs. Although radio delivers generally undistinguished fare, it obviously has

## Intriguing Prospect
# NATIONWIDE SATELLITE RADIO MAY BE NEXT

Something to watch for: coast-to-coast radio broadcasts that deliver programs by satellite directly to cars and homes, using digital signals captured by receiving discs only $1\frac{3}{4}$ inches wide.

Development of this revolutionary digital system is in progress. The Federal Communications Commission has assigned a portion of the radio spectrum to such broadcasts. Owners of regular radio stations, however, fear that such a nationwide satellite system would ruin them by drawing away their audiences and reducing income from national advertisers. The National Association of Broadcasters sought to block FCC approval of the plan.

Developers of the digital audio radio satellite (DARS) say it will deliver music of compact disc quality and other material on up to 50 channels.

First, they must overcome regulatory, political, and technical problems, as well as the opposition from the terrestrial broadcasting industry. Four companies developing the service hoped to have it in extensive operation by the end of the century.

Once satellite broadcasting becomes a reality, extensive changes in the radio industry as Americans have known it can be expected.

Technical specialists foresee a time when digital audio broadcasting receivers also will have a liquid crystal display screen on which the digital data will appear as visual data—weather reports, for example.

broad popular appeal. While cynics describe much radio programming as that of an on-the-air jukebox with commercials, in fact radio not only provides mass entertainment but serves a vital function as a swift disseminator of information.

Because of its diversity of programming, radio offers something for virtually everyone. Urban commuters tune in for freeway traffic reports, farmers for livestock prices, and families for lists of school closings when winter storms hit the northern states. Radio is quicker than any other communication medium in providing such service material. The bulk of radio listeners, however, tune in their sets to be entertained—and have strong, widely varied tastes in what they wish to hear.

The configuration of U.S. broadcasting stations today is shown in Table 8.1.

Radio's capacity to serve the nation as a channel of instant communication in an emergency and the cultural impact its outpouring of music has, especially on the nation's youth, are two principal aspects of its role in contemporary American life.

Having survived one basic change during the 1950s, when television replaced it as a medium for general entertainment, radio today is in the

**Table 8.1**

**U.S. Broadcasting Stations**

| Type of Service | Stations on Air |
|---|---|
| **Radio** | |
| Commercial AM | 4906 |
| Commercial FM | 5285 |
| Educational FM | 1810 |
| *Total radio* | 12,001 |
| **Television** | |
| Commercial VHF | 559 |
| Commercial UHF | 622 |
| Educational VHF | 123 |
| Educational UHF | 240 |
| *Total television* | 1544 |
| **Low-power television** | |
| VHF LPTV | 561 |
| UHF LPTV | 1211 |
| *Total LPTV* | 1772 |

*Source:* Broadcasting & Cable, *January 29, 1996.*

midst of another major evolution. This has been brought about by satellite transmission of radio signals, discussed elsewhere in this chapter. The recent removal of many federal regulations controlling operation of radio stations also has influenced the reshaping of programs.

As a commercial industry, radio is uneven. Many of the more than 10,000 commercial stations on the air flourish, with strong staffs and generous profits. Hundreds of others with low power and limited audience potential scramble to stay alive, hunting constantly for a magic programming formula to increase their share of the listeners and bring in greater advertising revenue. Three of every ten American radio stations lose money. Stations in the cluttered radio spectrum are as varied as vehicles in a crowded parking lot where glossy limousines stand bumper-to-bumper with dented, aging compacts and muddy pickup trucks. All function but with vastly differing images.

Radio stations range from extremely strong, clear-channel, 50,000-watt transmitters whose signals can be heard for hundreds of miles to low-powered noncommercial stations with a range of only a few miles. While many stations operate under joint ownership with television stations, hundreds of small ones are unaffiliated with television or other media. In metropolitan areas, competition among radio stations for audiences has created a jungle. Approximately 65 stations broadcast in the New York metropolitan area, for example; Los Angeles has nearly 100.

**Radio's Advantages Over TV.** For several years in the 1950s and early 1960s, radio floundered under the shock of television's visual competition. Then industry leaders began to realize that radio has several advantages over television in the competition for listeners. Chief among these is mobility, brought about by development of the small transistor radio. One can either listen to a program attentively or have the music playing as background with almost a subliminal effect. Millions of people drive with their car radios turned on. Radio stations outnumber television stations approximately eight to one, providing a broad choice of programs to hear around the clock. Hardly a square mile exists in the United States—this applies to most other countries too—where the sound of radio cannot be heard.

Every radio station must hold a license from the Federal Communications Commission, authorizing it to broadcast on a specified band with designated power, at certain authorized hours. If the government did not allocate the wavelengths in this manner, the broadcast spectrum would become a chaotic jumble of sound as station signals overlapped and the strong stations overpowered the weak. Station licenses must be renewed every seven years.

For several decades, radio operated under strict federal regulation of its procedures. Station owners chafed at the limitations and the paperwork burden the government imposed on them. Finally, in 1981, came partial deregulation by the FCC.

The commission removed its requirements that stations must (1) devote a portion of their air time (8 percent for AM, 6 percent for FM) to nonentertainment programming, (2) restrict the number of minutes in each hour devoted to commercials, and (3) keep detailed program logs in their public files. Requirements for license renewal were greatly reduced; however, if challenged, a station must still defend its performance in dealing with the needs of its community, presenting reasonable evidence to support its case.

In making this decision, the FCC majority emphasized its belief that competition in the marketplace would exercise sufficient control over behavior of the stations.

## Radio Program Styles

Approximately three-fourths of the U.S. radio audience listens to FM broadcasts. The once-dominant AM stations are fighting hard, primarily with talk shows, to increase their remaining 24 percent in the face of FM's important advantages. These facts need to be borne in mind as we examine today's radio styles.

### Talk, Talk, Talk

Talk shows are the hottest commodity on radio today. They range from the liberal-bashing Rush Limbaugh to the "shock jock" mouthings of

Howard Stern, to advice from psychologists on the sex problems of their phone callers, and the second-guessing of sports commentators. The interplay between talk show "hosts," male and female, and listeners who call in makes provocative, if not always informative, listening. Some urban stations offer talk and news programs 24 hours a day.

Talk radio is raw public opinion, and, as such, a valuable tool of democracy. Persons who believe they can't be heard otherwise find an outlet in these shows. Radio's speed and flexibility make the shows one of the quickest ways for public opinion to be expressed after a major political or social news story breaks.

It is dangerous to assume, however, that opinions heard on talk shows necessarily represent the true shape of general public opinion. Many citizens never would call a talk show; others may not be able to make a phone call when the show is on the air, and a highly partisan host can manipulate the types of phone calls aired. A host with an obvious political bias tends to attract listeners who hold the same views and can limit opposition views by brusquely cutting off the callers or insulting them.

Talk has always been part of radio. For decades it was dominated by commentator-to-listener broadcasts by such national figures as Elmer Davis and Raymond Gram Swing on politics and Walter Winchell, who delivered Broadway gossip at a machine-gun speed. The veteran Paul Harvey, a survivor of changing radio styles, continued this tradition. National programs based on two-way talking between radio host and listeners who phoned in developed slowly until syndicated distribution by satellite emerged. Local versions of the format proliferated.

The personality of the talk show host is the key to a program's success. Only a relatively few follow the concept of cool, objective discussion in search of truth. Many are opinionated and confrontational. Some come across as aggressive know-it-alls ready to pronounce opinions in strident fashion on almost any topic. Others resort to gimmicks, such as the Minneapolis hostess who broadcast each Friday from her hot tub, where guests were invited to join her. Some attempt to confront their celebrity guests with scandals about themselves.

A San Francisco host—who keeps two American flags by his microphone and pounds the table as he proclaims his conservatism—spoke for many other hosts when he said, "I am a radio entertainer."

Politically oriented hosts are predominantly conservative, riding the wave of conservatism that gave the Republicans control of Congress in the 1994 election. Aware of Limbaugh's phenomenal success, many local station hosts have tried to emulate him. In doing so, some have crossed the line of good taste and common decency. A Los Angeles talker, for example, said on the air shortly after O. J. Simpson was charged with murdering his wife and a young man that Simpson should be lynched. Vehement public complaints forced him to apologize on the air.

Such extreme incidents are rare. Most stations operate their shows with a seven-second tape delay, during which an obscene or libelous

Bob Grant, a New York radio talk show host for more than 30 years, says the medium has become "more opinionated and less inhibited" while turning into . . . "almost a national obsession." (AP Photo/Kevin Larkin)

statement by a listener can be deleted before the caller's voice goes on the air. This does not prevent the broadcasting of obviously false information by callers; that is the host's job to correct. But that does not always happen. Callers usually are identified only by their first names.

President Clinton in a 1995 interview commended the democratic role of talk radio but added, "I cannot defend some of the things some of these more extreme talk-show hosts have said." He urged them to reject statements "that are just purely fostering hatred, division and encouraging violence."

Talk shows on black, Hispanic, and Asian radio stations have especially strong social impact, surmounting language and cultural barriers to deliver important information to their audiences. For example, after Earvin "Magic" Johnson, the Los Angeles Laker basketball star, disclosed that he had tested positive for the HIV virus, which frequently leads to the fatal AIDS illness, urban black radio stations conducted AIDS Awareness Days and similar campaigns to warn listeners about the disease.

## Music Programming

The key figure in music programming is the disc jockey, whose talking between recordings helps to create a station's personality and brings it

**Disc jockey** Broadcaster whose introduction of recordings gives a radio program cohesion and personality

Wilbert Begay, program director of radio station KNDN, Farmington, New Mexico, broadcasts in their native language to residents of the Navajo reservation. With its slogan "All Navajo All the Time" and emphasis on tribal news, KNDN binds together this far-flung community of Native Americans. (Eric Draper, Los Angeles *Times* photo)

closer to its listeners. Lonely listeners in particular come to regard favorite disc jockeys as companions.

A disc jockey's on-the-air job is to package several hours of record playing in a lively manner, so that it seems to the listener to have recognizable form. Usually the disc jockey's broadcast time is listed under the performer's name as, say, the Jim Nelson Show. Jim Nelson does not simply introduce the records and read the commercials. He gives traffic reports, announces the time and temperature, offers free tickets and gifts as promotional tie-ins with advertisers, and chats on the air with listeners who call in. Since his voice is the only tool with which to sell personality, Jim Nelson cultivates a tone that is easily recognizable—jovial, confidential, aggressive, or theatrical—whatever is effective.

The disc jockey's manner changes according to the time of day—a peppy "wake-up-and-be-happy" style for the morning drive-time audience going to work, a more leisurely manner for midday listeners, and a confidential, intimate tone for the after-midnight hours.

**Use of Play Lists.**　Radio stations exploit Americans' tendency to value numerical superiority by playing tunes that are ranked as the Top Forty of the current week. The ranking of records in descending order from the week's number one favorite is done by trade publications such as *Billboard* and *Cash Box*, based on sales in stores. Indeed, in this age of spe-

**Play list**
Names of tunes chosen by management for play on a radio station, frequently based on national Top Forty polls

cialization, separate Top Forty lists are compiled for contemporary-rock, country-western, and soul single-record categories, and for albums of multiple selections.

In making up the list of songs a station will play each week, its program and music directors consult several nationally published music tip-sheets and listen to sales pitches from record company promoters pushing new releases. Then, typically, the local directors talk to the station's programming consultant by phone. The consultant keeps a close watch on what is being played in each popular format in numerous cities. The resultant playlist decisions on each station thus reflect national patterns. That is why a cross-country motorist hears the same songs on rock stations in half a dozen states, and the same country tunes. The music that local radio stations offer in the various formats to a considerable extent shapes the taste of American listeners, rather than reflecting it.

Some stations follow the Top Forty lists so dogmatically that they will play only those songs. A few have reduced their play list even further, to the Top Thirty, having their DJs play the same few tunes again and again. Their theory is that when a record is a hot new favorite, listeners want to hear it repeatedly. Constant on-air exposure of a song that has just reached the lower rungs of the Top Forty ladder helps it to climb to a higher position. Some stations vary the Top Forty diet by interspersing "golden oldies" and "extras."

Radio and the recording industry are tied together in a relationship of convenience and mutual need. Radio depends on the recording manufacturers for a constant flow of new material to broadcast. The recording industry must have exposure of its products to promote their sale, and radio play to bring new recordings to the attention of potential purchasers. The relationship between radio and recording companies will be examined more closely in Chapter 9.

Program directors usually strive for a special *sound* that will make their stations distinctive. Often this means broadcasting music of a special type. A station may air only country-western, hard rock, or reggae and soul, hoping to build a loyal following from devotees of the genre. Or it may stress a blending of styles, such as folk rock, and emphasize the play of albums rather than single records. Extremes in specialization are found most often in urban FM stations. The easy-listening format of heavily stringed background music, sometimes called wallpaper or Pablum music, is heard on FM. At the other extreme, some FM stations feature the fast-talking, often raunchy, rap artists. Religious programs, often featuring music, are frequent fare on smaller stations.

**Sound**
In radio, the choice of music and vocal technique that makes a station's programming easily recognizable

The abundance of program variations offered by American radio stations is apparent from this list of formats used by the National Radio Broadcasters Association in taking surveys: adult contemporary, urban contemporary, country, religious, easy-listening/beautiful music, contemporary hit radio, album-oriented rock, news talk, classical, oldies, soft rock, ethnic, and big band/nostalgia.

Year after year, adult contemporary has been reported as the most programmed format, usually followed by country and contemporary hits, with album-oriented rock strong on FM stations.

## The Satellite Era Arrives

The recently acquired ability of radio stations to receive program material by satellite from syndicates and networks has caused a major change in both music and talk programming. A trend toward automated broadcasting, in which a station puts on the air taped programs prepared by someone other than itself, already was in progress when satellite transmission began. That has greatly enlarged the automated approach.

**Automated broadcasting** System under which scores of stations play identical, satellite-transmitted music simultaneously hour after hour

Today a radio station can be on the air 24 hours a day broadcasting programs it receives on a satellite dish from a supplier and then retransmitting them from its own tower. These satellite programs sound to the listener as though they originated at the station, because they contain local station identification announcements and local commercials. Yet virtually no local station on-air talent is involved, just station engineers.

Except for the local cut-ins, the identical program may be on the air simultaneously from a hundred or more other stations around the country. Some critics call this homogenized radio.

This method is possible because at certain points during the satellite transmission warning tones are sounded. These cause local station identifications, prerecorded by the satellite disc jockey for every station, to be inserted by computer between songs. Local commercials are handled similarly.

From an economic point of view, use of satellite programs saves a station large amounts of money in salaries, because it doesn't need its own on-the-air talent. The satellite producer's "Jim Nelson" is performing as disc jockey on all hundred or more stations simultaneously. The stations also can eliminate their record libraries.

A station using a satellite service is free to cut into it with its own live material, such as news, whenever it desires. The usual arrangement is for the station to pay the program supplier a monthly fee, and in addition the supplier reserves two minutes each hour in which it inserts the national commercials its staff sells.

Satellite programming is broadcast most heavily by small stations; for some its use means the difference between losing and making money. Many large stations refuse to use it because they believe it destroys a station's "personality."

Capital Cities/ABC is the largest supplier of satellite programming, both music and talk. Second is the Unistar Radio Network, formed by the merger of the Transstar and United Nations networks. Another major competitor is Westwood One, Inc., which owns both the Mutual Broadcasting System and the NBC Radio networks. Each supplier offers several different carefully targeted types of programs, from country to rock.

## News Coverage

When an event of tremendous national or global significance occurs, such as a presidential assassination or a great natural disaster, news of it often is delivered faster by radio than by any other medium. Radio's programming flexibility enables news bulletins to go on the air immediately. During a hurricane, tornado, or other continuing crisis, radio is invaluable in delivering information and instructions over a wide area.

Unfortunately, routine daily news reporting on radio frequently fails to achieve a similar high standard. Some of the larger AM stations are noted for the scope and excellence of their local news operations and national affairs reporting, but many AM and FM station managements regard news as a costly nuisance. Radio stations operating under joint ownership with television stations tend to have better-quality newscasts than those without TV ties. Staff-prepared news stories are broadcast on both outlets, and often TV news reporters do some radio broadcasts. About 5000 radio news operations exist in the United States, some of them serving joint AM-FM station organizations.

Hundreds of stations offer their listeners little more than rip-and-read news summaries that their announcers take from the news service machines, plus in some cases brief hourly network news summaries of national and world headlines. All stations have pronunciation guides that announcers are supposed to use, though some do not, and it is evident that they have not read the copy before going on the air. At many smaller stations coverage of local news consists primarily of stories rewritten from the local newspaper or obtained from police sources, plus announcements of meetings or events submitted by community organizations. Local news reports are especially sparse on weekends.

There are wide differences in types of news broadcasts. Some announcers deliver the news in strident, excited tones, a fashion sometimes referred to as the "town crier syndrome." This occurs especially on rock and roll stations, whose managements believe that their young audiences are not interested in news at all. Newscasts designed for this audience emphasize soft items about lifestyles and rock stars, instead of heavier, hard news about world and national affairs.

Some networks supplement their hourly headline summaries with five-minute commentaries. Using these services and on-the-scene audio *actualities* from the news services, an alert station with an able news director can keep its audience well abreast of major news. Hundreds of stations, however, have no network affiliation.

**Actuality**
Brief on-the-scene report, live or on tape, inserted into a broadcast news program

**Financial Restrictions.**  News staffs are expensive to maintain; yet without enough reporters, a station cannot cover the police, municipal, school, and other beats fundamental to comprehensive newsgathering. As a result, many small stations tend to abandon all but the most cursory local news coverage to the television stations and newspapers. Some FM stations offer news only during the morning commuting "drive-time" hours.

While this minimizing of news is regrettable, it is also understandable. The financial resources of many radio stations, especially in small cities, are sparse because the revenue they generate from a limited market is not great. If they invested heavily to build a large, competent news department, the effort might wipe out the annual profits. So a small station may try to do the best it can afford to do with a news director and possibly one assistant. The news director also may have other on-the-air responsibilities. The management of a lucrative station that gives little more than lip service to news coverage because it does not find such programming profitable could be considered more open to censure.

A continual turnover among news directors tends to weaken the quality of radio news. Many of these directors move rapidly from job to job; this shuffling undercuts the consistency of news coverage. They may step up the career ladder to a larger station; perhaps they leave because of disputes with station management; quite frequently they leave in frustration over budget restrictions. A recent survey by the Radio Television News Directors Association showed that the median tenure of radio news directors was less than two years. Forty-nine percent held their jobs a year or less, while only 6 percent held the same position for more than 10 years. Although this turnover creates frequent job openings, the goal of reliable, enterprising news coverage suffers.

Closely linked to news on radio is sports. Sometimes the news director carries the title of sports director as well, or may also be a disc jockey. For example, a help-wanted advertisement published in a broadcasting trade journal read: "Small market adult contemporary AM needs morning drive announcer to jock and anchor news block." Play-by-play reports of baseball and football games attract large radio audiences, and sports call-in shows are growing in popularity.

## The Economics of Radio

Radio stations have only one thing to sell, and that is an inventory of time, intangible and perishable. The majority of each hour a station is on the air is devoted to entertainment and information. The rest is cut into small segments and sold to advertisers as commercials. A station's financial success depends on the number of commercials it sells each day and the prices it can charge for them, based on the size of its audience. When a station broadcasts a network program containing commercials, the network pays the station an agreed-upon fee.

In the older days of radio, before television, sponsors commonly bought 15- or 30-minute portions of air time during which their commercials alone appeared. Today, stations fill the hours with brief spot commercials paid for by many advertisers.

## STATION STUCK WITH HONEYED MONEY

Wacky contests for prizes are widely used by radio stations to attract audiences and create public awareness.

WYHY-FM in Nashville staged a far-out contest and ran into unexpected trouble.

The station filled a swimming pool with $100,000 in dollar bills. Then it invited 10 listeners covered with honey to roll in the money and keep whatever stuck to them. Among them, they emerged from the pool with $8000.

When the station attempted to return the remaining $92,000, the Federal Reserve Bank demanded that the money be cleaned. It wouldn't take back sticky bills.

About 20 staff members spent two days washing the $1 bills in pillow cases, drying them in a clothes dryer, ironing them, and stacking them face up while an armed guard watched.

The laundering team saved the station's chief accounting office from a threat of jail for defacing U.S. currency.

This practice of scheduling commercials at such frequent intervals influences the recording industry; it holds the length of its popular song releases to about three minutes. Between these brief segments of music the disc jockey can work in two or three commercials, keeping a staccato pace to the program and accommodating many advertisers. The heavy loading of AM programs with commercials turned many irritated listeners to FM stations. However, many FM stations now follow the same practice of loading their air time with commercials.

A station's sales staff seeks to convince clients that radio is an effective medium on which to spend advertising dollars and that its station is the place to spend them. Having achieved this objective, the sales staff works with the advertiser to select the programs and times of day best suited for the client's commercials. The station's rate card shows the price it charges for commercials at different hours, depending on the size and type of audience it reaches at those times. Combinations of time slots and prices can be agreed upon. When a station has difficulty selling its available commercial minutes and its income is suffering, it may go "off the rate card" and make cut-rate deals giving advertisers special bargains, such as including one or several free commercials.

Sales representatives stress demographics, to show an advertiser the size and nature of the audience that can be reached. This information includes income, education, occupation, ethnic background, marital status, and buying behavior. Program and sales directors have been especially anxious to reach the audience of young adults born after World War II. By the early 1990s, they had entered their forties and their tastes were changing. Many stations have shifted their focus to a younger generation.

A station cannot identify and count every listener in the way a newspaper can determine its audience by the number of copies sold each day and the addresses of its subscribers. Thus, radio depends on surveys and polls, along with statistical research. The Arbitron rating service provides information to many stations. Researchers for large stations also make contact with a limited number of individuals, by telephone or mail, or in person, then project the results to cover the entire population of the station's listening area. The return addresses on cards and letters the listeners send to the station in response to a gift offering made by a disc jockey can be analyzed by researchers. So can the originating locations of phone calls to local talk shows.

The primary advantage that radio offers to advertisers compared with television is lower cost, both for air time and for preparation of the commercials. Radio is more flexible, too, in time availability and the speed with which it can accommodate new advertising copy. Radio, however, lacks the visual appeal that helps television sell goods.

## Public Radio

In one form of broadcasting, taxpayers underwrite part of the operating costs, along with institutions, foundations, and corporations. This is National Public Radio (NPR), a not-for-profit organization based in Washington, D.C., that supplies programming, largely of a cultural and informational nature, to approximately 400 noncommercial radio stations.

The federal Corporation for Public Broadcasting gives money to NPR member stations, which in turn pay membership fees to NPR. Member stations receive more than 50 hours of programming a week, most of it produced at NPR headquarters. "All Things Considered" has been one of the most popular NPR programs.

Public Radio International, formerly named American Public Radio (APR), which grew out of Minnesota Public Radio, is a competitor of NPR with more than 275 stations, a large percentage of which are also NPR members. APR says it distributes more programming hours than NPR does; it does no producing of its own, however, but distributes programs created by stations.

## Points to Remember

1. How did Lee De Forest acquire the title "the father of radio"?
2. When and how did the ABC, CBS, and NBC radio networks come into existence?
3. During the Munich crisis, what did CBS and its commentator Hans Von Kaltenborn do to keep the American public informed?
4. What are the principal reasons FM stations now dominate radio, while the older AM stations have lost audience and influence?

5. In what way do play lists influence the selection of music radio listeners receive?

6. How do radio stations use satellite transmission of programs?

7. Can you cite an example of the potential political power of talk radio hosts?

8. What do digital audio broadcasting and the compact disc have in common?

## Media Question to Think About

G. Gordon Liddy served a prison term in the 1970s for his part in the Watergate burglary that forced President Nixon to resign from office.

He became a combative conservative national talk radio star in the mid-1990s. On the air he advised one caller that the most effective way to shoot a federal agent in self-defense was to aim at the head or groin. He also discussed in a broadcast using cardboard figures of President Clinton and his wife Hillary for target practice.

The National Association of Radio Talk Show Hosts gave Liddy its 1995 "Freedom of Speech" award, despite protests from many members. Other critics called Liddy an example of hate broadcasting.

Another talk show host, Gloria Allred of Los Angeles, told *Broadcasting & Cable:* "Clearly Mr. Liddy had a right to his free speech, but rights also carry responsibilities. If he used speech that inflames and that may encourage some extremists to rationalize confronting or harming law enforcement, that is not speech that should receive an award."

Convention chairman Michael Harrison, who supported the award, said: "We saw it as our role to protect the role of talk radio and the right of its people to free speech."

Did Liddy deserve a "Freedom of Speech" award?

# CHAPTER 9
## Popular Music

## "Dark Side's" Record Run—741 Weeks

Rock bands often zoom into prominence with a hit record, gather an enthusiastic following, then slip back into obscurity. Yet Pink Floyd rocks-and-rolls along year after year, the possessor of extraordinary longevity.

The band won a place on the record charts in March 1973 with its album "Dark Side of the Moon." After 303 weeks on *Billboard*'s Top 200 album chart (almost six years), "Dark Side of the Moon" became the longest-charted rock album ever. After 490 weeks, it became the longest-charted album of any kind. When it finally fell off the chart in 1988, it had been there for 741 weeks, almost $14\frac{1}{2}$ years.

Even that wasn't the end. In the mid-1990s, the album still sold more than 500,000 copies a year.

Nobody knows for certain why the album was so popular. Roger Waters, one of its composers, told *Entertainment Weekly,* which tracked the album's record, he believed that "Dark Side's" "humanity" was responsible.

Pink Floyd continued to draw large crowds. Its 1994 tour grossed $103 million.

Those facts are the stuff of dreams for players in bands in small night clubs everywhere.

Sold by the millions and played on the air incessantly, recordings are not only a form of popular entertainment but a channel for expression of opinion as well. Songs deliver the messages of love and protest, most often to a rock and roll beat.

Because popular tastes are ever-changing, the recording business is risky and full of surprises. Some music personalities develop huge followings that endure, while others soar to prominence, then disappear almost as quickly.

This chapter explains how the recording industry functions. It examines the sudden emergence of the compact disc (CD) and the growing role of the CD-ROM, the computer technology that adds video and the written word to the sound. Also it discusses the close ties between those who produce recordings and the radio stations that play them, as well as the influence of music videos on the marketing of records.

Among other aspects examined are the threat of home recording to the producers and the appeal of rock festivals.

Concert tours to college campuses and large cities by recording stars are another method of dramatizing popular music. We show how these tours are organized and the problems involved in them.

## The Power of Popular Music

The impact of popular recordings on the public consciousness is insufficiently recognized as a means of mass communication. Tape cassettes and compact discs form crucial channels of communication in the youth culture. Through them, desires, anger, ideas, attitudes, and fads spread around the country and across the oceans.

The electric guitar does not yet rank with the word processor as a tool for distributing ideas. However, the recordings, music videos, and stage performances of such stars as Madonna and Bruce Springsteen have a strong impact on youthful thinking. For teenagers in particular, popular musicians often become role models.

"Hot" individual performers and groups sing fervently of youth's yearnings for love, freedom from restraints, popularity, and peace. The voice of protest and defiance is prominent in the lyrics. The music is vibrant, beat-driven, insistent—and usually loud.

Unorthodox ideas and uninhibited language that challenge codes of conventional social conduct have found an audience through recordings. In earlier years musicians were prominent in the anti-Vietnam war movement. Today their voices are raised in the campaign against AIDS, in the environmental crusade, in the women's movement, and in the form of gangsta rap against governmental authority. The upsurge in the popularity of rap singers has increased attention to social issues.

Some people regard popular music lyrics as seductive propaganda for a hedonistic attitude toward life that encourages the use of drugs, vio-

Michael Jackson made a heavily promoted comeback effort with a new album in 1995 after avoiding prosecution on child-abuse charges, but the eccentric pop singer-dancer failed to regain fully the superstar status he had before the incident. (AP Photo)

Popular singer Stevie Wonder performs at the keyboard in his recording studio while a technician watches and listens. (Mr. Bonzai, courtesy of *Mix* magazine)

## MICHAEL JACKSON, LOVING HUSBAND, TRIES COMEBACK

How well can an eccentric rock star forced into hiding by charges of child abuse regain public favor as the result of a shrewdly calculated marketing campaign?

For Michael Jackson and his corporate sponsor, Sony Corporation, that is a multi-million dollar question.

Highly publicized charges were leveled against Jackson by parents of a boy who had been a guest at Jackson's Neverland Ranch in California. Jackson hid out in Europe while his attorneys negotiated. No public testimony ever was taken in the case. Jackson made a large payoff to settle the civil suit against him, and the boy then refused to testify in a criminal action.

Jackson stayed in seclusion, his career at a standstill and possibly ended.

Then Sony began its $30 million marketing effort to build a fresh image for Jackson and sell his new album "HIStory." The singer disclosed that he had married Lisa Marie Presley, daughter of Elvis. They appeared as a loving couple in an intimate hour-long interview by Diane Sawyer on the ABC television network. A movie trailer appeared in 1000 theaters. Television commercials ran nationwide. A 32-foot-high statue of Jackson was pulled by a barge up the Thames in London to promote the album there.

A Sony official said the company would be "disappointed" if the album didn't sell at least 20 million copies. Rather slow early sales indicated that it might be. And the Jackson-Presley marriage broke up.

---

lence, and casual sexual relationships. (Questions of sex and good taste are discussed in Issue 1.)

Although popular music is heavily oriented toward teenagers and young adults, other types of recordings have devoted followers, mostly among somewhat older groups. Heartbroken country singers with their plaintive laments sell millions of records. Jazz, blues, classical music, and the sweet saxophone sounds of the big bands lure recording customers to the cash register.

### Rock and Roll Arrives

Until the early 1950s, popular music consisted primarily of ballads, comedy songs, Broadway show tunes, jazz, and country. Then rock and roll burst into prominence, and the popular music scene was revolutionized. *Grove's Dictionary of Music and Musicians* defines rock and roll as "a commercial amalgam of the styles of American white country music and black rhythm and blues."

Quickly, recordings by early rock stars such as Chuck Berry, Little Richard, and Jerry Lee Lewis became big hits. So did those by Bill Haley and his Comets, whose "one, two, three o'clock, four o'clock rock" came to symbolize the pulsing, rhythmic pace of the new music.

Rock's first spectacular star was Elvis Presley, a young Tennessee truck driver who made his first amateur record in 1954, was heard on a Memphis radio station, and quickly became a national, even international phenomenon. By the time he died in 1977, at 42 years of age, Presley had become a legendary figure, leaving an estate of $15 million derived from the sale of more than 500 million records. His death touched off mass mourning. Years later, Presley remains a cult hero and sales of his records continue to be high. Thousands of visitors tour his mansion in Memphis, spending large sums on Elvis ashtrays, scarves, statuettes, and other souvenirs. A U.S. postage stamp was issued in his honor. Elvis imitators abound.

Although rock and roll began in the United States, many of its most popular groups came from Great Britain. The exuberant Beatles made a spectacular American tour in 1964, followed by the more arrogant Rolling Stones, who proclaimed and practiced a lifestyle involving drugs, violence, and blatant promiscuity. Country-western music, always popular on small-town radio stations in the West and South, enjoys strong national popularity today. "Crossover" blends of rock, folk, and country have emerged, producing such stars as Garth Brooks, Kenny Rogers, and Dolly Parton, while the more traditional ballad singers such as Barbra Streisand and the aging Frank Sinatra remained popular.

The American public was jarred into realization of the impact rock and folk music had on its young listeners by what happened on a muddy farm near Bethel, New York, during a humid August weekend in 1969. Known as the Woodstock Music and Art Fair, this three-day marathon performance by rock and pop stars drew an amazing throng of 400,000 people who swarmed around the grounds in an unfettered demonstration of independence from their parents' social norms. The participants camped out in the fields, sang, drank, swam in the stream, used drugs, listened to the bands on the stage, and talked defiantly against the Vietnam war. Three persons died of drug overdoses and hundreds were treated for drug illnesses. The crowd itself was as much an event as the music it had come to hear. Woodstock became the historic symbol of the counterculture. Rock festivals patterned after Woodstock became a part of American life, even though many other manifestations of the youthful revolt dwindled into the greater conformity and conservative political trend of the 1980s and 1990s. A 25th anniversary Woodstock festival in 1994 drew a large crowd but lacked the uninhibited zest of the original.

**Woodstock**
Famous three-day rock festival in 1969 attended by 400,000 persons

## The Compact Disc

A revolutionary form of recording, the compact laser disc, commonly called a CD, suddenly became popular in the latter part of the 1980s. It passed the traditional vinyl recording in sales so dramatically that

An unused ticket for the original 1969 Woodstock Music and Art Fair, now a collector's item. Caught in a chaotic traffic jam stretching dozens of miles, the owner failed to reach the festival grounds and was forced to sleep in a field overnight. (Courtesy of David Born)

**WOODSTOCK MUSIC and ART FAIR**
**SATURDAY**
**AUGUST 16, 1969**
**10:00 A. M.**
**$7.00**   Good For One Admission Only
**0 01306**
**NO REFUNDS**   GLOBE TICKET COMPANY

by the start of the 1990s some stores had stopped selling long-playing vinyl records.

After decades in which purchasers could buy recorded music only in vinyl form, the portable tape cassette appeared. Tapes have the great advantage of flexibility and small size: they can be carried everywhere and played on small tape players. Quickly they came into wide use. When compact discs with their far superior sound reproduction were introduced in stores in 1983, a new upheaval in music marketing began. Today, sale of vinyl recordings has virtually ended. Compact discs and cassette tapes are being produced in approximately equal numbers.

**Compact disc** Small recording whose content, encoded in digital form, can be heard when "read" by a laser beam, in contrast to a grooved recording played with a needle

The digital laser disc coated with plastic is slightly less than five inches wide and extremely durable, easy to transport, and convenient to store, requiring only a fraction of the space occupied by a 12-inch long-playing vinyl record. Between one and two hours of music are contained on the single playing surface of a CD. Digital recording involves the coding of sound waves into binary digits etched on the disc surface. As the disc is played, a laser beam "reads" the digits and translates them into sound.

Recording companies dug into their files of master recordings to reissue earlier selections in CD form and recorded new releases in the same way. They also offered a new, smaller version of the compact disc, three inches in diameter, called the CD-3, aimed at buyers who once purchased the vanished 45-rpm vinyl singles records.

### Digital Audiotape

**Digital audiotape** Recording by a digital method on tape that can be erased and used again

Still another new form of recording, digital audiotape (DAT), was developed in Japan, but the powerful Recording Industry Association of America (RIAA) fought vehemently against its sale in the United States. The recording companies feared that use of DAT would hurt the sale of their compact discs.

This high-stakes commercial quarrel boiled down to these basic facts:

Thousands of rain-drenched fans crowd around the North stage of Woodstock '94, the 25th anniversary celebration of the original Woodstock rock festival, on a farm at Saugerties, New York. (biob/Joe Traver Reuter)

- Tapes sold in the current popular cassette form can be erased by the purchaser and rerecorded with new material, or they can be purchased in blank form. Music recorded on these tapes, however, lacks the fine sound quality of compact discs.

- Compact discs cannot be erased and rerecorded with new music or purchased in blank form. A recordable compact disc was under development.

- Digital audiotapes record with the same excellent quality as a compact disc and, like the traditional tapes, can be erased and rerecorded. DAT recorders produce almost perfect copies of

Axl Rose, controversial rock recording and concert tour star, right, visits Michael Monroe during a New York recording session. Rose credits Monroe's old band, Hanoi Rocks, with influencing the style of his Guns n' Roses. (AP/Wide World)

CDs. Efforts to create a device that would prevent copying of a compact disc with DAT were unsatisfactory.

The recording industry worried that if ownership of digital audiotape became common in the United States, home tape copiers and professional "bootleg" operators would undercut the compact disc market. The RIAA threatened to sue any company that introduced a DAT with recording capabilities into the United States.

Finally, a compromise among the Japanese, American, and European electronics industries in 1989 opened the door for the sale of digital audiotapes in the United States and elsewhere. The agreement approved a microprocessor device that permits a consumer to copy music from a compact disc onto a digital audiotape but prevents that tape in turn from being copied. Thus copyrighted music is protected from mass piracy. High cost and lack of recorded tapes to play, however, delayed marketing of digital audiotape and tape decks in the United States. Meanwhile, a competing system, the digital compact cassette (DCC), has emerged from the laboratory with bright prospects. The advantage of the DCC player over the DAT deck is that it can play both standard audiotapes and the digital ones.

## The CD-ROM

CD-ROM (Compact Disc-Read Only Memory) is the multimedia version of the compact disc. While the CD gives the listener only music or voice, the CD-ROM delivers visual and printed material as well. By combining these forms of communication, the CD-ROM is a splendid method for delivering information. Full-color photographs, graphics, supporting text, music, and voice, put together, create an educational tool, as well as an entertaining one. A CD-ROM can display up to 300,000 pages of information.

The CD-ROM disc is played on a specially equipped computer. As such, it is much less easily available for use than the ordinary CD. The discs themselves are expensive, from about $35 to $100 in most cases. The limited sales outlets and relatively small number of CD-ROM offerings available, along with the high cost, have restricted expansion of CD-ROM sales, but active marketing efforts are developing.

A modification called the CD Plus permits a user to put the CD-ROM disc on a regular CD player to hear music or to place it on a properly equipped computer to see the visual material and text as well.

## Music Videos

An electronic phenomenon of the 1980s, the *music video* has greatly increased the impact of rock music in particular by bringing its vivid sights and sounds to television. Other forms of popular music are receiving similar, if less abundant, exposure on the home screen.

The music video is a taped performance, usually three to five minutes in length, in which a group or a single performer offers a song while the musicians or other performers act out the song's story or meaning. Some videos have a narrative thread. In others, the pictures merely create an atmosphere or a mood, often erotic. These hybrid sound-and-sight minimovies found a swiftly growing audience. They introduce new acts and new songs. Also, they project contemporary pop music to an entirely new audience, the stay-at-home television viewers who are not traditional purchasers of recordings or tickets to concerts.

**Music video**
Enactment of a musical number on video

Created as a promotional device to sell recordings, the video has taken on a life of its own—an art form, its enthusiasts call it.

Cable television music programs, especially the Music Television Network (MTV), are the primary outlet for video releases. MTV plays rock, rap, and pop music videos 24 hours a day. The visual portion may be a videotaped excerpt from a live performance by the group or it may be conceptual—a piece of fantasy, drama, or comedy, often using computer graphics and animation. These videos are introduced, disc-jockey fashion, by a new kind of performer called a *veejay*.

**Veejay**
Video disc-jockey

Virtually every important recording made today has a video version. These usually cost about $40,000 to make, with occasional ones running as high as $250,000. Producers regard this expense as a good investment in most instances because the appearance of an attractive new video on television has an immediate impact on record sales. Repeated play on MTV's special program featuring cutting-edge music, the Buzz Bin, can

The ability of CD-ROM recordings to combine large amounts of audio and visual material makes them an excellent method for explaining complex topics. This cover of a multimedia CD-ROM about France suggests the wide range of material covered.

produce sales of several million records. Approximately 1500 music videos a year are produced in the United States.

Recording companies provide videos to stations, frequently without charge, and urge their use in the same way they "push" recordings at radio stations. MTV gives air time to little-known groups and unknown selections. In the cable television field, in which scores of entrepreneurs are hunting a successful formula, MTV claims to reach 58 million homes with its multiple channels. Aware of MTV's impact, other networks and stations have packaged similar music-and-visual services, often playing country-western and other categories of music that MTV does not offer.

Enthusiasts for music videos contend that they appeal to a "television generation" that responds to sense impressions without needing a narrative line. Videomakers use at least 30 visual changes a minute, with no static shot exceeding two seconds.

## Recording: A Volatile Industry

Making and marketing recordings is a large and volatile industry, far less structured than the print media, radio, and television. Approximately 1200 American companies produce as many as 700 million records and tapes each year, according to figures supplied by the Recording Industry Association of America (RIAA). Many of these companies are small, some handling only one performer or category of recordings. More than 90 percent of the recordings sold in the United States are made by the 45 companies belonging to RIAA. The industry's gross sales in a typical year are around $4 billion, an estimate based on listed retail prices of records; net sales are difficult to ascertain because of price discounting and heavy returns of unsold records.

Success in the industry depends on one's ability to exploit the quicksilver changes in public taste, indeed to stimulate those changes through the production of new sounds and the promotion of fresh performing groups and individuals. The pursuit of novelty in sound and performance style is endless. A common pattern is for an unknown band to assemble enough material for a demonstration tape, then make a recording for a small independent producer. With luck this catches the attention of scouts for the major labels who travel around the country searching for a band that can produce what industry people call the Next Big Sound. The hope that lightning will strike in this manner keeps thousands of performers struggling along on obscure stages.

This is a business for quick-witted individuals who can recognize trends, make deals, and take risks for the "big buck"—those who know how to practice the art of "hype," the tricks of providing an exciting buildup for the performers they are selling. They must be able to sense which performers have the magical ability to stir audiences. An industry built on such an ephemeral base inevitably contains an element of chaos.

Electronic recording techniques using tape, developed in and after the late 1950s, provide great flexibility in making recordings. No longer is a studio recording session a simple act of a group or an individual singer performing a piece of music before a microphone. Now a record is an intricate melding of several taped sound tracks into a master recording. The skill of the studio sound mixer is as important as the ability of the performers. The use of electronic musical instruments expands the variety of sound effects achievable.

## Recording and Radio

Producers of popular recordings have four principal ways to introduce their new numbers to the public: "play" on the radio, advertising in youth-oriented publications, live concerts by performing groups, and music videos on television. The most important of these is radio. Without it, the mass marketing of discs and cassettes would collapse.

Not only do record distributors provide copies of their new products to radio stations free of charge, but their promotion staff members try to encourage the stations to play them. If a new record is introduced on a major Top Forty station in a metropolitan market, listeners in search of something fresh will buy it in the stores. Industry trade magazines and tip sheets report that the record is "hot" in that city. By telephone calls and personal visits, promoters spread the word and cajole stations in other cities to add the song. If it catches on, sales flourish in those cities also, and onto the Top Forty charts it goes.

In the dizzy promotional milieu of the recording world, a valuable accolade for an album or single recording is to be certified "gold" by the RIAA. This means that an album or single record has sold 500,000 copies. To be declared "platinum," an album or single must sell 1 million units. Competition in the recording industry is so intense and production costs so high that 75 percent of the recordings produced fail to earn a satisfactory profit for their creators.

## Multicultural Channels

Recordings provide a significant channel for spreading minority cultures, especially the music of the black and Hispanic communities.

Distinctively black music is such a major product of the recording industry that *Billboard*, the industry's trade paper, each week publishes full-page charts of the 100 Top Black Albums and Hot Black Singles. It carries a similar listing for Latin music.

The songs of such famous black performers, past and present, as Diana Ross and the Supremes, Michael Jackson, Ray Charles, and Whitney Houston have done much to spread awareness of the black perspective.

The recent popularity of rap music, a raucous form of fast-talking and singing commentary on social injustice, crime, and sexual prowess, is a major trend. Begun on the urban streets—called "ghetto" music by *Billboard*—rap has created mainstream awareness of such black performers as Chubb Rock and Queen Latifah.

## The Concert Circuit

Groups and individual performers in the pop-rock world whose records have sold well enough from radio exposure to earn them a reputation frequently capitalize on this achievement by doing live concert tours. These tours stimulate sales and build the performers' followings.

An intricate public appearance circuit has developed. Famous stars play the circuit of arenas in cities and on university campuses that seat 10,000 or more people. Performers with a growing reputation, but who are not yet at the top, are booked into smaller houses that seat 2000 to 5000. If the touring performer demonstrates drawing power at this level, a promoter may risk booking the act onto the arena circuit. Another way in which a group promotes itself is to perform as the opening act in a big-name show. Opening-act performances are watched closely by promoters. If the openers please the crowds—not an easy task before a restless, often boisterous throng waiting impatiently for the main act—promoters may finance the act on a tour as a headliner on the small-house circuit.

Tours by big-name performers draw much publicity and often very large audiences. Michael Jackson's 15-month world tour ending in 1988 played to more than four million people, The Rolling Stones' 60-concert North American tour in 1994 grossed $121.2 million, an all-time tour record.

This glamorous picture, however, has another side. Newspaper notices report from time to time that so-and-so's scheduled concert in that city has been canceled because of poor ticket sales. Concert touring is a high-risk enterprise because of extremely heavy operating costs. For example, for its 1995 tour the group R.E.M. traveled with six huge equipment trucks and nine buses, a 47-person road crew, and four chefs. Their stage setup included 128 speakers and eight movie projectors.

Recognition of music's role led to the creation of the Black Radio Hall of Fame. At its first dinner, 20 black disc jockeys who performed before 1959, in the days when acceptance of black music was less widespread, were inducted into the hall.

Few Latin performers have attained the national followings of black stars, but many radio stations in areas with large Hispanic populations play Hispanic music exclusively.

## The "Free" Market

Although they sell huge quantities of recordings, record producers are angry about unknown millions of recordings made annually from which they and the performers collect no income. These either are taped by amateurs for personal use or "bootlegged" at cut rates by professionals who evade payments of royalties. The simplicity of electronic copying makes this situation possible. The intensity of the RIAA's fight against importation of digital audiotapes shows how strongly the producers feel about record "piracy," which it says costs makers and artists $400 million a year.

When moderate-priced home recording machines came onto the market, the industry uttered cries of corporate pain. Alarmed by loss of sales, music recording companies joined videotape producers in shouting, "Unfair!" The U.S. Supreme Court ruled in 1984 that home videotape recording of television shows does not violate copyright regulations

**Record piracy**
Unauthorized copying and illegal sale of recordings protected by copyright

## ROLLING STONES ROCK THE AIRWAVES

When the Rolling Stones broadcast a concert live on radio, millions of their fans listen. The veteran rock band, led by strident Mick Jagger, has built an enormous following with its records. So, live broadcasts of some performances on their recent world tour were splendid promotion for the group's latest songs.

The Stones' concert in New Orleans was broadcast by satellite simultaneously by 225 radio stations over a Westwood One network put together specifically for the show.

This simulcast required elaborate preparation and technical detail. As *Broadcasting & Cable* described the setup, Westwood One staff members made hundreds of phone calls to stations nationwide, promoting and arranging the broadcast. Two dozen microphones carried the sound from the stage into a mobile recording studio outside the arena, then by satellite to participating stations.

The broadcast wasn't quite "live," however. To eliminate possible technical mishaps such as a dead microphone, the music was taped, then put on the air 10 to 15 minutes after the actual performance. If a delay occurred during a performance, Westwood One engineers filled the air time by playing taped segments from previous Rolling Stones shows.

This tape delay gave New Orleans concertgoers an odd bonus. Listening to local WENO-FM as they drove home, they heard the closing portion of the concert they had just attended.

(see Chapter 12), a decision that affected the music recording industry similarly. The two groups continued to ask Congress for a law requiring the manufacturers of blank tapes to pay them a fee for each tape sold, as compensation for lost recording sales.

The appearance of small personal cassette machines has created the phenomenon of men and women walking city streets, jogging, cycling, and riding on buses with small headsets covering their ears. Tuned out from the world around them, even though surrounded by people, they listen to taped music and conversation that sometimes is packaged in cassette "magazines." Often they listen to home-recorded tapes.

## Points to Remember

1. How do compact discs differ from traditional vinyl recordings?
2. Why did the recording industry resist introduction of digital audiotape into the United States?
3. How does a recording win a "gold" rating? A "platinum" rating?
4. Can you name two early rock stars other than Elvis Presley?

## Media Questions to Think About

1. How do you explain the continued fascination with Elvis Presley that has made his home a tourist attraction and created so many Elvis impersonators?

2. Why, in your opinion, do some famous rock and roll groups emphasize exaggerated gestures, odd clothing, and shouting in their on-stage performances?

3. How significant do you believe the MTV channel is in creating hit songs and shaping the course of popular music?

# ISSUE THREE

## Who Owns the Media?

Major owners of mass media have prestige, power, and the possibility of enormous profits—so much so that collectively they spend tens of billions of dollars in the new electronic age to build their empires. Some of these reach around the globe. In the owners' hands lies the ultimate power to decide what users of the media see, hear, and read.

In less complex times half a century ago, most newspapers, radio stations, and the newly created television stations were owned by relatively small companies, families, or individuals. So were magazines. Much book publishing was in the hands of families, partnerships, or privately held companies. Motion picture corporations concerned themselves only with making and selling movies.

Today everything is different.

The rush toward group and conglomerate ownership that has swept through the entire fabric of American business has significantly altered the ownership of the mass media.

Huge multimedia corporations own or control interlocking media outlets. Only 22 percent of U.S. daily newspapers are independently owned. A single corporation publishes magazines and books, owns a major motion picture studio, operates cable television systems serving 11 million homes, and makes programs to show on its own premium cable channel.

Basic policy and financial decisions affecting local media are made in distant corporate headquarters. Foreign companies have purchased numerous American media firms.

## Aspects to Examine

As you study the following discussion, these are some aspects of the huge changes taking place in media ownership that you should consider in deciding whether the changes are good or bad:

1. Has something vital in American life been lost with the replacement of many local media ownerships with managements far away? On the other hand, are local residents better served? How?

2. Should the U.S. government impose restrictions on the purchase of more media properties by large corporations? If so, how could this be done without violating the First Amendment?

3. Is the switch of control over some U.S. media properties to foreign ownerships likely to have a helpful or harmful effect on American viewers and readers? Or do you anticipate no change?

4. How does ownership of media in the United States differ from that in some other countries?

5. The hundreds of mass media purchases and combinations in recent years fall into four broad categories. Can you name and describe them?

6. Why did Rupert Murdoch find it necessary to change his citizenship from Australian to American?

7. Can you list three major developments in electronic transmission that have made the creation of global media corporations physically possible?

## Products of Free Enterprise

The owners of broadcasting stations, newspapers, and other mass media outlets expect them to earn a profit, an expectation that many of them fulfill handsomely. Some outlets, however, although important to the audiences they serve, have difficulty in providing a return on the investments their owners have made. The annual profit is not the sole motivation driving many media managers, who think also of their responsibility to provide the truth and serve their communities, but the necessity to survive in a competitive market makes profitable operation vital.

Even most of the noncommercial radio and television stations get into the money scramble because they must find financial grants and underwriting gifts to remain on the air. So the demands of the marketplace influence and often determine the decisions of those who distribute the printed and spoken word: which books to publish, what type of films to produce, what kind of programs to televise, and what size each day's newspaper should be.

In this respect the American concept differs from that of many other parts of the world. The federal government neither finances nor operates any of the media in this country, although it assists some noncommercial stations with subsidies. Nor do the political parties underwrite daily newspapers to enunciate their points of view. An American broadcasting station or publication survives only if it provides a product its audience likes and manages its finances prudently.

Contrast this to the practice in much of Africa, for example, where it is commonplace for television and radio networks to be owned by the government. In many countries, especially the remaining communist-governed ones, newspapers are published by the government, with the censorship and manipulation of news such control implies.

Because the United States is so vast and its population so diverse, American media have historically and proudly lacked uniformity, both in content and ownership. Newspapers born as the frontier moved westward were the products of individual enterprise, reflecting the views of the editor-proprietor. So were the magazines. When commercial radio came into being, stations were established by a potpourri of owners anxious to play with the new toy, among them newspaper executives, automobile dealers, manufacturers, and amateur engineers. Licenses for television, when that medium's turn came, were obtained in many instances by companies already involved in radio. Thus the American media truly consisted of many thousands of voices, often highly individualistic.

Frequently these individual proprietors were more concerned with exercising influence in their communities than with drawing the last dollar of profit from their operations. Since they answered only to themselves or to small groups of private stockholders, they were free to function in that way.

## Consolidation Disturbs Critics

Critical students of the media are concerned that the concentration of ownership may weaken the editorial independence and individuality of the media. They distrust what they see as excessive emphasis on profit-making by the multimedia giants, in part because some of them are burdened by debts in the billions of dollars, built up as they acquired more and more properties.

Some critics perceive the danger that the large corporate owners may manipulate the content of their media outlets for selfish purposes, or at least to defend the status quo to protect their own interests.

These critics have cited, for example, the fact that the NBC television network is owned by the General Electric Company, a manufacturer of defense equipment with close contractual ties to the Pentagon. NBC, a traditional over-the-air service, also operates the CNBC cable television channel.

Leonard A. Grossman, former president of NBC News and of the Public Broadcasting Service, summarized the concern over concentration of ownership thus in a *Columbia Journalism Review* article:

> While the number of TV channels and media outlets is burgeoning, ownership and control of the mainstream media, both print and electronic, are becoming increasingly concentrated. . . . Today, a few conglomerates, which have no direct responsibility to the American public, wield extraordinary power over the ideas and the information the public can receive.

Some of the more cynical critics even foresee the possibility that a huge multimedia owner might coordinate its many print and electronic outlets to promote or defeat a political cause, on a far more grandiose scale than William Randolph Hearst did with his newspapers many

**Conglomerate** Corporation that owns companies in several fields of endeavor

## Table 3.1

### Increase in Media Voices

| | 1959 | 1965 | 1970 | 1975 | 1981 | 1987 | 1990 | 1996 |
|---|---|---|---|---|---|---|---|---|
| Commercial TV stations | 520 | 672 | 690 | 709 | 864 | 1000 | 1099 | 1181 |
| Educational TV stations | 43 | 115 | 182 | 242 | 292 | 297 | 349 | 363 |
| AM radio stations | 3377 | 4058 | 4269 | 4436 | 4729 | 4867 | 4981 | 4906 |
| FM radio stations | 776 | 1301 | 2471 | 3571 | 4350 | 5209 | 5707 | 7095 |
| Daily newspapers | 1755 | 1763 | 1761 | 1768 | 1745 | 1674 | 1626 | 1538 |

*Sources:* FCC, Broadcasting & Cable *magazine,* Editor & Publisher *magazine, compiled in* Les Brown's Encyclopedia of Television. *1996 figures as of Jan. 29.*

decades ago. No evidence to support such fears has been cited. In reality, the possibility that a community could be forced to depend on a single corporate source for its news is almost nonexistent. Much competitive news delivery is available to its citizens through other *media voices,* including radio and television newscasts, neighborhood newspapers, national newspapers, magazines, and newspapers published in nearby larger cities. (See Table 3.1.)

**Media voices**
Those of all separate ownerships of media seen, heard, and read in a community

### Huge Media Deals

As the multimedia corporations maneuvered to build profitable competitive positions in a communications revolution whose final form nobody could define with certainty, they carried out massive takeovers and mergers.

This high-stakes dealing reached astonishing proportions in the mid-1990s. According to the Associated Press, such transactions totaled $40.1 billion in 1994. Then, in a frenzied nine-day period during midsummer 1995, four huge deals totaling $28.4 billion were announced. One of them was by far the most costly combination in media history. They were:

- Walt Disney Company bought Capital Cities/ABC Inc. for $19 billion. Under this deal the motion picture producer obtained the ABC broadcasting network, over which it can show its new films and rerun its long-time favorites. Details of the combination appear later in this chapter.

- Westinghouse Electric Corporation announced the purchase of CBS Inc. for $5.4 billion. The takeover included the CBS television and radio networks, plus ownership of eight television stations and 21 radio stations. Westinghouse is an electronics manufacturer, defense contractor, broadcasting owner, and cable TV program producer.

- Tele-Communications Inc., already the largest operator of cable television systems, bought Viacom's cable systems for $2.3 billion.

- The Gannett Corporation, the largest U.S. newspaper group, purchased Multimedia Inc. for $1.7 billion. The deal brought Gannett more newspapers, television stations, and the Multimedia syndication operation.

A few weeks later, Time Warner Inc. added to the list of massive mergers by announcing the purchase of Turner Broadcasting System for $7.5 billion. This merger combined Time Warner's facilities for creating motion pictures, television programs, magazines, and books with Turner's elaborate satellite distribution system. Completion of the deal was delayed, however, by federal antitrust concerns and demands of secondary stockholders.

The flurry of combinations came before Congress in early 1996 enacted telecommunications legislation to remove most federal regulation of broadcast ownership (see box on p. 258).

## Four Giant Waves

Understanding the complexities of the surge toward ever-greater dominance of the media by a small group of corporations is a perplexing task. Remembering who owns what is even more difficult because media units constantly are being traded or combined.

To simplify the problem, we shall group the multitude of sales and combinations into four waves. These waves have followed one another during the past 20 years; although they overlap somewhat, they form a sufficiently distinct pattern for our purposes. They are:

1. Growth of newspaper groups
2. Growth of multiple-media ownerships
3. Foreign purchases of U.S. media
4. Formation of international media giants.

The following sections examine each of these phases.

## Growth of Newspaper Groups

Group ownerships gobbled up independent daily and weekly newspapers with voracious appetite during the 1970s and 1980s. Most of the small percentage of dailies remaining under local ownership are in the under-50,000 circulation class.

**Newspaper group**
Two or more dailies in different markets under common ownership

# 1996 TELECOMMUNICATIONS ACT BRINGS GREAT CHANGES

Passage of the Telecommunications Reform Act of 1996 by Congress will lead to immense changes in the shape and ownership of communications systems in the United States.

The complex act was expected to consolidate media ownership increasingly in the hands of a few huge corporations, while opening new channels of communication for consumers.

The principal elements of the act include:

- *Cable service.* Allows local telephone companies to deliver video service to homes and offices. Removes all controls on cable TV rates within three years.
- *Telephone.* Permits long-distance, cable, and other companies to provide local telephone service and allows the regional Bell systems to offer long-distance service.
- *Television.* Authorizes a single company to own an unlimited number of television stations, so long as those stations do not reach more than 35 percent of the U.S. population. Gives existing TV stations free additional channels on which to develop high definition television service.
- *Radio.* Removes limits on how many stations a company may own.
- *Ownership combination.* Permits a company to own a television station and a cable system in the same market.
- *Violence chip and control of indecency.* Outlaws transmission of sexually explicit and other indecent material to minors on computer networks. Requires manufacturers to equip new television sets with V-chips so parents can block shows they deem offensive. (See Issue 1.)

Preceding the surge of group ownership, and contributing to it, was the rise to predominance of "one-newspaper cities" as a result of economic attrition of second and sometimes third newspapers in a city. Today, fewer than 30 American cities have fully independent, competing dailies. Critics fear that, in a city with one daily newspaper, the publication will print only the news and opinion it wants its readers to see. On the other side, there are frequent instances in which a monopoly publisher, sensitive to the charge, has made extra effort to provide the city with more extensive, deeper news coverage than was previously available in a competitive situation.

Closely connected is the charge that advertisers dictate a newspaper's coverage, or at least exercise veto power over certain kinds of stories that might damage their trade. Numerous episodes exist to document this complaint, in which stories went unreported because advertisers requested that they be dropped. Yet many newspapers consistently reject such pressures, rebuffing all attempts to have stories suppressed.

Organizations and readers who do not want to hear the truth also at times exert extreme, unpleasant pressure against newspapers in revenge for stories they print. In Texas, the Fort Worth *Star-Telegram* lost 1200 subscribers and endured vitriolic attacks from the Bell Helicopter Corporation, a hometown company, other business firms, and Bell employee unions because it published articles disclosing a long-standing fault in the construction of Bell helicopters. This fault had contributed to crashes in which about 250 military servicemen died. A blue ribbon military–civilian panel subsequently confirmed the newspaper's findings, and 600 Army helicopters were grounded for repairs. The *Star-Telegram* won a Pulitzer Prize for the series.

Similarly, when the Lexington *Herald-Leader* disclosed years-long illegal payments to University of Kentucky basketball players by school boosters, the newspaper was attacked vehemently for "disloyalty" to the school. The *Herald-Leader* received bomb threats and angry petitions and lost 369 subscribers. The editor's home was festooned with toilet paper. This paper too won a Pulitzer Prize.

Publication of columns called "Action Line" or some similar name, in which a newspaper acts as its readers' problem-solving agent, often causes it to print facts that show its advertisers in a poor light. The completeness of a newspaper's coverage of controversial issues and sensitive stories depends largely on the moral courage and journalistic integrity of those who run it.

So many newspapers have ceased publication in competitive markets, especially in the metropolitan field, that fewer than 2 percent of daily newspaper cities and 5 percent of weekly newspaper towns have competing newspaper ownerships. Some new newspapers have begun publication, especially in areas of fast population growth around the fringes of metropolitan centers. Usually these newspapers are without competition in their cities of publication but face heavy inroads in circulation and advertising from nearby large-city papers.

While the presence of two daily newspapers in a city gives readers the benefit of rival coverage effort, a substantial argument exists on the other side. One strong newspaper in a city, if the publisher and editor are conscientious persons sensitive to their responsibilities, often can provide better news coverage and community service than two weaker ones. Also, a financially strong paper may be more willing to attack entrenched and harmful interests in a city because it can absorb the financial retaliation aimed at it.

## Rising Costs Cause Shutdowns

The chief immediate reason for the disappearance of newspapers is the constantly rising cost of production. The wages of those who write, edit, and print the newspapers; taxes; the cost of newsprint and gasoline for the delivery trucks—these and many other expenses have risen precipitously. An especially sharp rise in newsprint prices in the mid-1990s caused even the strongest newspapers to take retrenchment measures. The expense problem has caused publishers to raise the price of their newspapers and their advertising rates, attempting to keep the papers profitable.

Where a newspaper's hold on its readers and advertisers is not strong, or where its area of distribution loses population at the same time that radio, television, and competitive newspapers cut into its circulation and advertising revenue, the salvage effort fails and the paper must cease publication. This has been especially true of some papers in Northeastern metropolitan areas, whose inner cities have become depressed areas.

The Newspaper Preservation Act was passed by Congress in 1970 after lively controversy within the newspaper industry. This act created exemptions in the antitrust law so that a struggling newspaper might join forces with a healthy publication in the same city. The newspapers were allowed not only to operate joint production facilities but to combine business departments and have joint advertising and circulation rates. Their editorial departments remained separate. An argument for the measure is that it would preserve a second newspaper voice in the city. Publishers who testified against it, especially those from aggressive suburban newspapers, asserted that it would increase the trend toward monopoly.

## Size of Newspaper Groups

The acquisition trend reached the stage at which large groups were buying out small ones, thus increasing their holdings at a wholesale rate. By the mid-1990s, 13 groups had aggregate weekday circulations of more than 1 million copies each and published approximately half of the newspaper copies sold daily in the United States. Table 3.2 shows the ten largest U.S. newspaper groups in circulation.

By early 1995 Gannett owned and operated 82 newspapers, including the national five-day-a-week *USA Today* (see Chapter 5). The company also owned 10 television stations, 15 radio stations, and a large outdoor advertising company. Then in midsummer 1995 its announced purchase of Multimedia Inc. added 11 daily newspapers, 5 television stations, and a radio station to its list.

Although little known to the public, Thomson Newspapers Ltd. of Canada actually publishes more newspapers in the United States than any other company. At its peak, Thomson owned 143 daily and several nondaily newspapers in the United States and Canada. It announced plans to sell 39 of its small properties in a regional reorganization plan. Thomson's total circulation was about one-third of Gannett's.

Next in size to Gannett is Knight-Ridder, Inc. Although Knight-Ridder has far fewer newspapers than Gannett, 28 to 82, many of them have large circulations.

Among other major newspaper groups are Dow Jones & Company (the *Wall Street Journal*), the Tribune Company (Chicago *Tribune*), the

Table 3.2

## Ten Largest Newspaper Groups in Circulation

|  | Daily Circulation | Sunday Circulation |
|---|---|---|
| Gannett Co. Inc.* | 5,830,579 | 6,072,313 |
| Knight-Ridder Inc. | 3,605,770 | 5,109,471 |
| Newhouse Newspapers | 2,960,366 | 3,832,894 |
| Times Mirror Company | 2,624,426 | 3,349,296 |
| The New York Times Company | 2,436,436 | 3,357,236 |
| Dow Jones & Company Inc. | 2,365,615 | 534,468 |
| Thomson Newspapers Inc. | 2,071,469 | 1,902,574 |
| Tribune Company | 1,348,455 | 1,985,086 |
| Cox Enterprises Inc. | 1,315,319 | 1,792,815 |
| E. W. Scripps Company | 1,295,234 | 1,341,339 |

*Before purchase of Multimedia Inc. newspapers

Source: Facts About Newspapers 1995 by the Newspaper Association of America.

Times Mirror Company (Los Angeles *Times*, *Newsday*), Newhouse Newspapers, Scripps Howard, and Harte-Hanks Communications. Well-known companies that began as newspaper operators but have become huge multiple-media firms are examined in the next section.

## Why Newspaper Owners Sell

Ownership of a newspaper group, sometimes supplemented by broadcasting stations, can be extremely profitable. Pretax profits of American and Canadian newspaper publishers long averaged about 18 percent, fell sharply during the recession of the early 1990s, then recovered.

Why do owners of independent newspapers succumb to the lures of group corporations and surrender ownership that in some cases has been in their families for more than a century? The answer lies primarily in a bedeviling economic headache for them, caused by the federal income tax and inheritance tax laws, compounded by inflation. The individual publisher who heads a family-owned newspaper, and who perhaps owns a majority of the stock, faces the distressing fact that upon death the inheritance taxes will be so high that any heirs may be forced to sell their stock in order to pay them. Because of the income tax laws, the family members cannot afford to receive high dividends from the paper's comfortable earnings. The family newspaper plant is growing obsolete and needs new electronic and press equipment in order to remain profitable. Yet inflation has made the price of that equipment extremely high, and the cost of borrowing money for it frightens the publisher.

Along comes a group publishing corporation whose stock is publicly owned. By using part of its profits to purchase additional newspapers, the corporation reduces the federal income taxes it otherwise would be required to pay. It has additional tax advantages and financial resources not available to the individual owner and never faces an inheritance tax problem. Thus it can offer the perplexed individual owner an extremely lucrative price for the newspaper; the publisher and other family stock owners may receive large cash payments which, after payment of capital gains tax, they may place in tax-free bonds. The publisher and heirs in turn are made financially secure instead of facing the likelihood of a forced sale of the paper for inheritance taxes. So the publisher sells to the highest bidder, after running up the price as far as possible. Competition among purchasers has been intense. When family owners put up for sale one small Midwestern city daily, 14 companies sought to buy it.

Quarrels among the younger generations of publishing families, and the desire of some family members to obtain cash for their stock holdings, also cause the sale of newspapers. Such a dispute among members of the Bingham family in Kentucky led to the sale of the distinguished Louisville *Courier-Journal* to Gannett, the highest bidder in an intense competition among giant groups.

As a result of these circumstances, the prices at which newspapers have been sold approach the astronomical. In 1993, the New York *Times* purchased the venerable family-owned Boston *Globe* for an estimated $1.1 billion.

The great surge of newspaper buying subsided by the mid-1990s, however, because most of the desirable, available large newspapers had been acquired by groups.

A primary difference between contemporary newspaper groups and the newspaper chains of an earlier era, of which the Hearst newspapers under the personal direction of William Randolph Hearst were an example, is the local editorial autonomy generally practiced today. In Hearst's heyday, his newspapers from coast to coast looked almost alike, with the same screaming headlines, heavy typography, and crowded front pages. They took the same editorial positions on national issues and played up Hearst's personal campaigns, such as antivivisection.

Group managements today as a rule permit each newspaper to have an individual appearance and personality and to set its own editorial policy. Such diversity is practiced by most group ownerships largely in order to alleviate disapproval of absentee ownership among local readers and advertisers.

## Book Publishers, Too

The same rush to group ownership that swept the newspaper industry has hit book publishing, once known for its large number of family-run companies. Publishers have taken over other publishers, and multimedia concerns have in turn swallowed them.

As one example, Random House, one of the largest general-interest publishing houses, acquired Crown Publishing Group, another large general publisher. Each of these houses published books under several imprints obtained through earlier purchases of small publishers—one was prestigious Alfred Knopf. Random House in turn is owned by Advance Publications, Inc., a firm owned by the Newhouse family, publishers of newspapers and magazines, including the *New Yorker*.

## Growth of Multimedia Groups

The first, most natural, diversification was for one form of print media, newspapers, to acquire or create other types of print publications, magazines, and books. The Times Mirror Company, for example, added a dozen magazines to its newspaper properties. Among its periodicals are *Sporting News*, *Popular Science*, and *Skiing Magazine*. It also acquired an art book publisher and higher education publishing houses. The Hearst and Newhouse organizations also coupled lists of well-known magazines to their newspaper base.

Soon the lure of ownership in the electronic field became almost compulsive, first in the ownership of television stations, then cable television systems. Visions arose of interlocking services, in which a multimedia corporations could use the same set of news and entertainment material in the several television, film, print, and ultimately online computer services it owned or shared.

Typically, Cox Enterprises Inc., publisher of the Atlanta *Constitution* and *Journal*, built up a string of newspapers, primarily in the South, an array of radio and television stations, *Palm Beach Magazine*, and cable TV systems. Then it took over the cable TV systems that Times Mirror had acquired and later decided to divest.

Today newspapers, television and radio stations, cable TV systems, magazines, book publishers, motion picture studios, video production firms, and makers of popular music recordings have been tossed together into a gigantic financial grab bag.

As we try to understand the thinking behind the billion-dollar deals, a basic fact should be kept in mind:

> Mass communication consists of two fundamental elements, distribution and content. That is, the methods of delivering news and entertainment to consumers and the material that is delivered. Each is meaningless without the other.

Commenting on the current churning of ownership, the *Wall Street Journal* reported:

> The mantra for the big distributors like cable companies, TV networks, publishers and phone companies has become, "Content is king." No matter how large or powerful a distribution system, the programming and other content that will be offered to consumers will drive sales. Thus the recent frenzied bidding war for filmed entertainment and publishing. . . .

### Telephone Companies Enter the Picture

As the regional Bell telephone companies pushed aside the political and legal barriers to their entry into the television business, they realized the critical need for programming to show on the channels they planned to develop. They too entered the content scramble. They made deals with TV program producers and syndicates that distribute popular shows.

Three of the Baby Bells, for example, teamed with the Walt Disney studios to produce movies for their planned TV channels. The Baby Bells also purchased interests in various cable companies to strengthen their competitive positions. Three examples illustrate the emerging pattern the scramble has produced:

**Walt Disney Company.**   The motion picture company's purchase of Capital Cities/ABC Inc., mentioned earlier, combined its highly respected film production operation and theme parks with the Capital Cities/ABC lineup of television network, TV stations, newspapers, and magazines. The combination added numerous new outlets to Disney's formidable marketing capability.

Already a strong international presence with its films and its theme parks in France and Japan, Disney positioned itself to become a global multimedia giant by acquiring the ESPN sports network and other international elements of the Capital Cities/ABC organization.

The growth of Capital Cities/ABC before its purchase by Disney exemplifies the process of media diversification.

Once primarily a newspaper group, CapCities purchased the ABC television network and built it into a highly profitable operation. Next it diversified into cable television with a controlling 80 percent ownership of the ESPN sports channel. In addition to newspapers and broadcasting stations, the company owned Fairchild Publications, including *Women's Wear Daily* and scores of periodicals covering everything from stamp collecting to hardware; *Los Angeles Magazine*; a music publishing house; and a record club. ABC produces numerous TV programs for distribution.

**Tele-Communications Inc.**   TCI is the world's largest owner and operator of cable television systems, which delivers cable channels to 17 million homes, 27 percent of the country's 65 million cable subscribers. It also has ownership shares in 12 companies that make and supply programs TCI can distribute through its cable systems. It creates other programs through its Liberty Media programming unit. TCI established a joint venture with Sprint Corporation, a long-distance telephone company, and two other cable companies to pay $2.1 billion for 29 mobile phone licenses. Sprint in turn announced a $4.1 billion joint venture with Deutche Television of Germany and French Television to provide international data, voice, and video services.

Because TCI was worried that direct broadcast satellite service (DBS) might capture a significant portion of cable TV customers, it and five other cable companies combined to establish a direct satellite system of their own, called Primestar. Thus by hedging its bets, TCI in a sense went into competition with itself.

**Viacom.** When Viacom, a power in the television industry, won a bidding war and purchased Paramount Communications Inc., it formed a gigantic creator and distributor of motion pictures, books, TV programming, and video entertainment, with various spinoff supplements.

Paramount is among the most famous names in Hollywood as a moviemaker. It has an enormous storehouse of hit films from the past. Viacom, less known to the public, has numerous cable television interests, including The Movie Channel, and produces popular TV programs. It sold its cable TV systems to Tele-Communications Inc.

Among results of the combination were plans to star Viacom's MTV characters, Beavis and Butt-Head, in Paramount movies and to put child characters from Viacom's Nickelodeon cable channel into Paramount's theme parks.

The largest media elements in the combined Viacom-Paramount conglomerate include:

Paramount motion picture studio

Blockbuster, the country's largest video and music retail store chain.

Simon & Schuster, Macmillan, and Prentice Hall publishing houses. Combined, they form the world's second largest book publishing empire, behind Bertlesmann A.G. of Germany.

The MTV and Nickelodeon cable channels

Motion picture theaters

The United/Paramount Network, opened in 1995

Radio and television stations

Viacom has announced its goal of becoming a global media power.

The tangled skein of interwoven financial and operational threads depicted in these three examples will become even more complicated as the large media companies continue to buy smaller companies that no longer can afford to compete in the high stakes game.

## Concentration of Broadcast Ownership

The aggressive growth of multimedia corporations was restricted for many years by federal rules limiting the number of broadcasting stations a company could own.

For decades the limits on broadcasting station ownership were enforced by the licensing authority of the Federal Communications Commission. The principle underlying these restrictions was that the number

# TED TURNER STRIKES IT RICH

Daring, innovative, and flamboyant, Ted Turner won a reputation as an aggressive maverick in the corporate world while building the Turner Broadcasting System. People called him "Captain Outrageous." His publicly stated desire was, "I want to be bigger."

Then, unexpectedly, he sold out in 1995 to Time Warner Inc., a media giant with five times the revenue of Turner's system. He accepted a second-place role as vice-chairman of the merged corporation.

Before the merger, Turner created the first satellite television superstation, developed the Cable News Network (CNN) into a world power, operated six TV networks, and owned the world's largest movie library. As sidelines he owns the Atlanta Braves baseball and Atlanta Hawks basketball teams as well as the world's biggest buffalo herd.

Although putting a corporate harness on Turner's free-wheeling methods, the Time Warner agreement brought him a huge personal profit in stock prices and made him Time Warner's largest stockholder with a 10 percent share. The deal also allowed him to retain control over his Turner Broadcasting businesses, plus operation of Time Warner's famous HBO pay entertainment channel.

In 1986, Turner took his greatest gamble by purchasing the giant Hollywood motion picture studio, MGM-UA Entertainment Company, for $1.5 billion. This deal saddled him with an enormous debt, but it gained him ownership of MGM's magnificent collection of 3300 vintage movies. Later he sold all parts of MGM except the film library. At the time, critics maintained that Turner had been taken as a "sucker" by Hollywood financiers. He further angered industry traditionalists by colorizing some famous black-and-white films.

Turner opened his fourth cable satellite network, Turner Network Television (TNT), successfully in 1988, primarily showing the MGM movies.

When Turner got into financial trouble, he was forced to sell a minority interest in his company to a group of cable system operators. One of these was Tele-Communications Inc. Another was Time Warner, a fact that Turner publicly resented. He claimed before a National Press Club audience that Time Warner had blocked his deal to buy NBC for $5 billion. He said, "I had to go almost to war with them," before he could buy the Castle Rock and New Line movie companies.

Watching "Captain Outrageous" play second fiddle under these circumstances, media analysts kept their ears tuned for sour notes.

of broadcasting channels available formed a limited national resource that needed to be regulated by the government. Opponents argued that an enormous increase in channels, first through development of cable television, then recently by the impending creation of several hundred new channels through digitalization and the entry of the telephone companies into the cable television business, made such restrictions obsolete. Congress accepted their arguments.

Ted Turner.

*Radio.* For more than 30 years, beginning in 1953, the FCC limited a company to ownership and operation of seven AM radio stations, seven FM stations, and seven television stations. This was called the 7-7-7 rule.

Permissible ownership of radio stations was increased gradually by the FCC in 1992 and 1994. By the time Congress considered the telecommunications reform bill in 1995, a single company could own 40 radio stations, 20 AM and 20 FM. This limit was lifted completely in the 1996 communications act.

*Cable television.* Unlimited ownership of cable TV systems by a company is permitted.

*Broadcast television.* Breaking away from the 7-7-7 rule in the 1980s, the FCC permitted single ownership of 12 television stations, providing that the owner's TV stations did not reach more than 25 percent of American households with television sets. The 1996 act gave a company the right to own an unlimited number of television stations, provided that the stations did not reach more than 35 percent of the nation's television viewers.

### Foreign Ownership of TV Forbidden

An important government rule forbids foreigners from owning U.S. broadcasting stations. Rupert Murdoch, the international media entrepreneur discussed later in this chapter, switched his citizenship from

Australian to American so that he could purchase seven U.S. television stations. No such restrictions against foreign ownership exist in the other media.

An industry drive to win elimination of all controls on cable rates from a divided Congress was made in 1995 during consideration of the massive telecommunications reform bill.

## Foreign Purchases of U.S. Media

Numerous well-known American media companies have fallen under foreign ownership in recent years, in part because the cheap American dollar created prices favorable to foreign purchasers. No restrictions exist on foreign ownership of U.S. print media, motion picture, and recording companies, unlike the U.S. government-licensed broadcasting stations.

Some foreign purchasers acted in order to obtain a foothold in the rich American market and create an international foundation for sale of their products. Others have a greater ambition—one that is shared by several American corporations—to build multiple-layer worldwide media operations. Such an ambitious goal requires a strong American base.

The foreign incursion has been intense in book publishing, in which ownership of several old-line publishing houses passed from American hands. The huge Doubleday & Company is now owned by a German firm, Bertlesmann A.G.; Harper & Row was purchased by Rupert Murdoch; Macmillan by Robert Maxwell; and the Grolier, Inc., encyclopedia firm by Hachette S.A. of France, the world's largest publisher of encyclopedias and magazines, whose U.S. holdings include about a dozen magazines. After Maxwell's mysterious drowning death, Macmillan ultimately came into the hands of Viacom, the huge U.S. multimedia corporation.

Many American advertising agencies also have passed into foreign ownership, primarily British (see Chapter 15).

### Overseas Owners Invade Hollywood

Motion pictures made by Hollywood dominate the world market and are regarded as a depiction of American culture, but in fact a substantial portion of the U.S. film industry now is owned by Japanese companies. Two other major Hollywood studios are owned by French and Australian firms.

All this transfer of ownership from American to foreign ownership occurred during the late 1980s and early 1990s.

Sony Corporation, a huge Japanese electronics firm, now owns Columbia Pictures, TriStar Pictures, and CBS Records. Its Japanese rival, Matsushita Electric Industrial Company, through its purchase of MCA, Inc., owns Universal Pictures, MCA Records, and G. P. Putnam's Sons book publishers. Another Japanese electronics maker, Toshiba, and a trading firm, C. Itoh & Co., bought a 12.5 percent share in Time Warner's Warner Bros. film studio and cable TV operations, including HBO.

Sony Corporation, a Japanese electronics company, purchased Columbia Pictures as part of a trend to foreign ownership of Hollywood studios. In this Columbia picture, *Desperado,* Antonio Banderas stars as the Mariachi without a name. (Copyright © Columbia Pictures)

The principal purpose of these deals totaling $11 billion was to "marry" Japanese-made "hardware" such as TV sets and videocassette recorders with American entertainment "software"—that is, movies and recordings—for global distribution.

Global strategy also underlies purchase of the 20th Century Fox studio by Rupert Murdoch's News Corporation of Australia, and control of the MGM-Pathé studio by Credit Lyonnais, the French bankers.

The Japanese venture in Hollywood was disastrous. The film colony's creative culture and often byzantine financing did not mesh with the Japanese business culture. After five years of difficulty, Mitsushita in 1995 sold MCA to Seagrams, transferring it from Japanese to Canadian ownership. A few months earlier, Sony had announced a $3.2 billion loss writeoff resulting from five years' ownership of Columbia.

## Global Media Giants

Global communication companies that deliver news and entertainment in many forms virtually everywhere in the world, only a vision a few years ago, have become a reality. They have come about through a combination of two forces: the explosive growth of electronic communication and a group of media entrepreneurs with foresight and financial daring.

In building their worldwide systems, these companies have taken heavy risks and acquired monumental debts. They gather profits from fees paid by users of their satellite systems, admissions to movies they make, and advertising purchased by the growing list of corporations that sell goods and services on the international market.

The two global companies described here are leaders in the field but are being challenged by others.

### Rupert Murdoch's News Corp.

The headline of a *Business Week* article about Rupert Murdoch catches the essence of the Australian-born magnate's media empire: MAN BUYS WORLD.

His News Corp., an Australian corporation, began with newspaper holdings Down Under. Murdoch migrated from his native land to Great Britain. There he accumulated newspaper holdings that include both racy tabloids and the prestigious *Times of London.* Then he moved to the United States. From his American base, he reached out around the world.

**Vertical integration**
Ownership in several media fields, interlocked so they may serve each other and multiply overall profit

A fundamental precept of Murdoch's operations is to provide *both* a global distribution system and the content distributed through it.

By the mid-1990s his ever-expanding company had these principal media properties and was negotiating for additional ones:

Motion pictures—Twentieth Century-Fox studio

Broadcasting—Fox Broadcasting Network; seven television stations; Star-TV satellite system for Asia, the Middle East, and India; and BSkyB satellite system for Britain (40 percent ownership)

Newspapers—New York *Post;* In Britain, the *Times,* the *Sunday Times, News of the World,* and the *Sun;* in Australia, 100 newspapers

Magazines—*TV Guide* and free-standing inserts for newspapers

Book publisher—HarperCollins

Multimedia—Delphi Internet Services; a joint venture with MCI, the long-distance telephone company that invested $2 billion in Murdoch's company. The joint venture planned to distribute information worldwide.

One simple hypothetical example shows how the interlocking nature of Murdoch's multimedia companies can operate. A book published by HarperCollins could be made into a movie by Twentieth Century-Fox. The movie could be shown on the Fox TV network in the United States and over Murdoch's satellite system in Asia, the Middle East, Britain, and India. It could be publicized in *TV Guide* and reviewed in his newspapers in Britain, Australia, and the United States.

### Time Warner Inc.

When two giants combine, they become a behemoth. That is what happened in 1989 when Time Inc. purchased Warner Communications Inc. for $14 billion. With the 1995 purchase of Turner Broadcasting System

Rupert Murdoch is surrounded by reporters as he arrives for a hearing of the Federal Communications Commission in Washington. (AP Photo/Kathleen Beall)

from Ted Turner for $7.5 billion, including the worldwide CNN network, Time Warner sought to expand its position as a global media empire.

Time Warner's lineup of famous magazines is based on the original *Time* weekly news magazine, whose foreign editions reach many countries. Also on its list are *Sports Illustrated*, *People Weekly*, *Fortune*, *Life*, and others.

In the print world, Time Warner also owns the Book-of-the-Month Club, Time-Life Books, Warner Books, the Little, Brown publishing house, and *Entertainment Weekly*.

The conglomerate's cable television systems group, second largest in the country, serves 11.5 million homes. It owns Home Box Office (HBO) and Cinemax premium cable channels, and Lorimar Television. In 1995, it opened its own television broadcast network, WB, on a part-time basis and gradually expanded its hours of programming.

The Warner Brothers movie studio is one of the oldest and most productive institutions in Hollywood. It distributes its films around the globe and also produces situation comedies and other programs for international distribution.

In popular music, Time Warner's recordings are heard worldwide. Time Warner Music International distributes recordings in 58 countries. The company owns Warner Brothers Records, Atlantic, and Elektra Entertainment. Another subsidiary, Warner/Chappell Music Publishing, owns or administers copyrights to more than 800,000 music titles.

Among its other operations, less known to the public, Time Warner has media investments in Japan, Hungary, Germany, Taiwan, Australia, and Great Britain.

Added to these holdings in 1995 were the following Turner Broadcasting System holdings:

Cable television—CNN, Headline News, Cartoon Network, Turner Network Television (TNT), TNT Latin America, TBS superstation

Filmed entertainment—New Line, Castle Rock Entertainment, Turner Pictures, Turner Entertainment (film library), Hanna-Barbera animation

Other properties—Turner Publishing (books), Turner Home Entertainment, Goodwill Games, World Championship Wrestling, Atlanta Braves and Hawks, Omni Coliseum.

## Media Control by Minority Groups

In 1978 the Federal Communications Commission adopted policies, later endorsed by Congress, that encouraged minorities and women to own broadcasting stations. One allowed a broadcaster in danger of losing its license to avoid that risk by selling its license to a minority-controlled business. Another gave minorities and women extra credit in the evaluation of their applications for new licenses. Even so, by 1993 minorities controlled only 3.5 percent of radio and television stations. As part of the Bush administration's examination of affirmative action policies, the Justice Department argued before the Supreme Court in 1990 that the FCC policies were unconstitutional. The Court, in a five-to-four decision, disagreed. "It is of overriding significance in these cases that the FCC's minority ownership programs have been specifically approved—indeed, mandated—by Congress," noted Justice William J. Brennan, Jr., writing the majority opinion.

An increasingly conservative Supreme Court reversed that decision in 1995. In a five-to-four decision it ruled that the FCC policy was too broad. Earlier in the year Congress killed the minority tax certificate program. These two actions virtually ended federal government efforts to stimulate minority ownership.

## A Look to the Future

From this examination of who owns the media come two inescapable conclusions:

- The ultimate decision-making power over the media in the United States rests in distant corporate offices and board rooms. The day of the small local media owner, independent and sometimes cantankerous, is vanishing. The psychological atmosphere of ownership has changed.

- Concentration of ownership into fewer and fewer hands will continue.

Ted Turner, given to sweeping statements, predicted recently, "We're going to end up with four or five mega-companies that control just about everything we see."

In more measured tones, *Advertising Age* commented editorially:

How much hope is left for the dissemination of diverse, offbeat opinions? TV already is feeding the public a homogenized news diet; just listen to the three nightly network newscasts if you have any doubt about it.

It's sad to see print journalism traveling this same route as the entrepreneurial companies sell off their proud possessions.

Leaders of the ownership consolidation movement depict it in benign terms. They say that it brings greater efficiency through application of skillful management techniques, infusion of fresh capital, and use of bulk purchasing power—and, for the consumer, additional sources of information and entertainment.

Critics fear that the "bigger is better" mentality that pushes the huge corporations will squeeze out provocative individual expression and cultural presentations that appeal to limited numbers of persons and generate no profit. Optimists hope that the proliferation of new channels, on-line services, and other distribution systems will provide space and time for an abundance of materials that appeal to all tastes.

Which will it be? The twenty-first century brings intriguing questions. The media will pour out information and entertainment in volumes almost beyond comprehension. How well will individuals discipline themselves to make wise, focused selections from the flood engulfing them? Perhaps that is a greater question for media critics to worry about.

# PART FOUR
## The Visual Electronic and Film Media

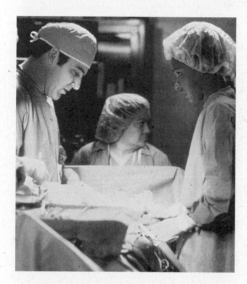

## ROLES OF THE MEDIA—ENTERTAINER

A world once dominated by the printed page now turns to the visual media for entertainment and news, and to computers as well for information.

*"Television has proved that people will look at anything rather than each other."*

—Ann Landers, columnist

*"Is society being enlightened by a new freedom of speech or coarsened by a new license to offend? We fear the latter. . . . The issue is responsibility. Broadcasters have it when it comes to the programming they air. They must not hide their heads in the sand, covering their tails with a copy of the First Amendment."*

—Broadcasting & Cable

*"Most rock journalism is people who can't write interviewing people who can't talk for people who can't read."*

—Frank Zappa, musician

# CHAPTER 10
## Television

## Part 1 ✳ Television Entertainment

### Slices of Life

Bored with your chores? Come, turn on a television soap opera and enter the world where pulses throb, hearts palpitate, tragedy strikes, and evil women connive to destroy their rivals.

See, for example, what happens in just one week on "As the World Turns," as summarized by *TV Guide:*

After getting bad news about Jeremy's father, Dawn asked Tom and Margo to take Jeremy when she dies. Holden returns to the farm. Lilly was shocked by what she found in Damien's desk drawer. Mike heads for prison.

Or turn the dial to "The Young and the Restless":

The family and Mamie welcomed John home. Paul and Chris flew to New York to do some surveillance. Nikki went to Kansas to have a woman-to-woman chat with Hope. In New York Jeri tried to seduce Cole. Vicki puts the moves on Brad.

Meanwhile, back in the real world. . . .

Of all the mass communication methods, television has the most impact on our lives. Ninety-eight percent of American homes have TV sets, and those sets deliver entertainment, news, and advertising into the average home about seven hours a day.

Television has expanded dramatically through the recent growth of cable television. Transmission of programs around the country by satellite and their delivery to the home TV screen by wire or microwave ("wireless cable") have opened dozens of additional channels for viewing. So has development of Direct Broadcast Satellite (DBS).

First this chapter traces the history of television, which has been a factor in daily life for almost 50 years. Television grew out of the technical advances of the first half of the twentieth century in the fields of wireless and radio, photography, motion pictures, and wire transmission.

Television is constantly in flux as new technologies and programming ideas develop. For convenience of study, this television chapter is divided into two parts. Part 1 covers the history and operation of the industry, with emphasis on the entertainment aspects. Part 2 covers television news. The swiftly expanding field of cable television is examined in Chapter 11, because it increasingly has become a separate entity.

## The Birth of Television

Experimental television broadcasting in the United States began in the 1920s. The scientific advances that preceded actual telecasting stretched back over a century. Between 1890 and 1920, a number of British, French, American, Russian, and German scientists suggested techniques for the transmission of images. John L. Baird, a Scottish inventor, showed live television pictures in London beginning in 1926 and televised pictures of the English Derby in a movie house in 1932. The British Broadcasting Corporation began the world's first regularly scheduled television service on November 2, 1936.

Baird and other early experimenters used a mechanical scanning disc that failed to scan a picture rapidly enough. The turning point came in 1923 with Dr. Vladimir Zworykin's invention of the iconoscope, an all-electric television tube. Zworykin then developed the kinescope, or picture tube, by 1926. This "electronic" method allowed the various elements of the image to be recorded all at once before being translated into the electrical charges that end up as the picture on the screen.

**Kinescope**
Picture tube in a television set that translates electrical impulses into visual images

Instrumental in television's reaching the public was David Sarnoff, brilliant son of a Russian immigrant family, who took full control of the Radio Corporation of America and its NBC subsidiary in 1930 when the three companies that had founded radio—Westinghouse, General Electric, and AT&T—dissolved their association. Sarnoff brought Zworykin into the RCA research team and began experimental telecasting in 1932. The Sarnoff team outmaneuvered television pioneer Philo Farnsworth, inventor of the electronic camera, and Allen B. Dumont, developer of receiving tubes and the first home television receivers.

Experiments in wire transmission of pictures during the 1920s led to the founding of AP Wirephoto in 1935. One of the researchers, H. E. Ives of AT&T, sent a closed-circuit television picture from Washington to New York in 1927. The next year General Electric's WGY began experimental telecasting. In 1930, NBC began operating W2XBS in New York; in 1939, it became the first station to offer regular telecasting schedules. Large numbers of people first saw television that year at the New York World's Fair. Hundreds looked up at a small screen as President Franklin D. Roosevelt talked to the nation. New York viewers watched major league baseball on 7-inch screen sets; coverage was restricted by limited camera range.

## 1948: A Watershed Year

The year 1948 was the crucial turning point when television changed from an experiment into a commercial force in the United States. From that time forward, its impact on daily life grew at an extremely rapid rate.

Commercial telecasting had been authorized by the FCC in 1941, a few months before the United States was plunged into World War II. Only six pioneer American stations had gone on the air before Pearl Harbor; the first two to receive licenses were NBC's WNBT and WCBS-TV, both in New York. Wartime restrictions, then equipment shortages in the immediate postwar years, delayed development of television until the sudden blossoming in 1948. Three significant events occurred that year:

1. *A sharp increase in the number of stations, from 17 to 41, and the number of cities with TV, from 8 to 23.*

2. *The appearance of star entertainers who were to become TV's first household names.* Milton Berle—"Uncle Miltie"—stepped before the cameras at NBC and Ed Sullivan at CBS. Jack Benny switched from radio in 1950, as did Lucille Ball.

3. *The Federal Communications Commission imposed a "freeze" on additional station authorizations for a four-year period, until 1952.* During that time, the FCC worked out a comprehensive policy for telecasting designed to give all areas of the country equitable service.

## FCC Sets Television Policy

During the freeze, more previously-authorized stations went on the air; the number of sets soared to 15 million. In 1951, the transcontinental microwave relay was completed, and on September 4 the first coast-to-coast audience saw the Japanese peace treaty conference in San Francisco. The World Series was telecast for the first time, too. Television was solidly establishing its grip on the public.

Ireene Wicker, a radio star known as the Singing Lady, conducts a pioneer television show for children for the American Broadcasting Company in 1948, the year commercial television began to gain popularity. (Library of Congress)

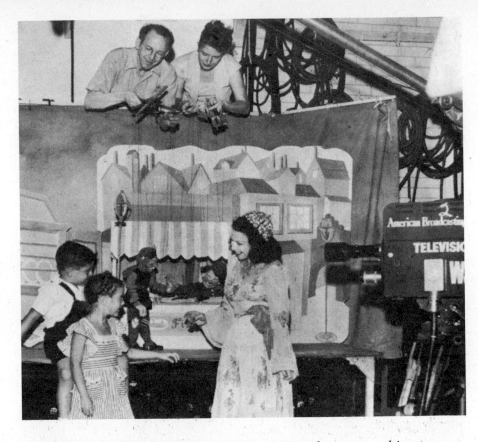

When the FCC lifted the freeze in 1952 and announced its comprehensive plan for American television, it established the basis that still exists for the industry.

The FCC plan created 2000 TV channel assignments in nearly 1300 communities. To make this possible, the FCC extended telecasting from the established very high frequency (VHF) channels (numbered 2 through 13) to 70 additional ultrahigh frequency (UHF) channels (numbered 14 through 83). There were more than twice as many UHF as VHF assignments. In addition, 242 channels were reserved for educational TV stations.

**VHF television**
Very high frequency transmission of signals

An upsurge in new UHF stations was not immediate, however, because different equipment was needed to tune a set to VHF and UHF stations. Not until 1964 did the FCC require manufacturers to include both VHF and UHF tuning equipment in the sets they made. After that, UHF stations multiplied, although their power was less than that of VHF stations with lower channel numbers.

**UHF television**
Ultrahigh frequency transmission of signals

A long technical dispute over the best method of color telecasting ended in 1953, when the FCC ruled in favor of the RCA compatible system permitting reception in either black and white or color. Table 10.1 shows the current distribution of U.S. television stations.

**Table 10.1**

| U.S. Television Stations | Number of Stations |
|---|---|
| Very high frequency TV | |
|     Commercial | 559 |
|     Educational | 123 |
| Ultrahigh frequency TV | |
|     Commercial | 622 |
|     Educational | 240 |
|     Total TV stations | 1544 |
| Low-power stations | 1722 |

*Source:* Broadcasting & Cable, *May 13, 1996.*

## Television as Entertainer

During television's "gold rush" expansion period from 1952 to 1953, networks and stations experimented with many program forms and entertainers, trying to gauge the expanding public's tastes. Some entertainers caught on immediately; others failed. Jack Benny's stingy, vain, harassed character, already familiar on radio, became an instant TV hit with the opening line on the premiere show. Playing off his reputation for stinginess against his reputation for vanity, he said, "I'd give a million dollars to know what I look like." Nationwide laughter!

Ed Sullivan, a dour-faced New York newspaper columnist, succeeded as master of ceremonies on his variety show because of the famous and soon-to-be-famous entertainers he presented. William S. Paley remarked in his memoirs, "He himself could not perform in any way. He never tried. All he had to do was talk, and he did very little of that."

Gradually, the television screen grew from 7 inches in diagonal to 12, to 17, to 21, and in some cases even to 24 inches. This larger viewing surface made possible more elaborate production techniques. The TV audiences became more selective, too, and in the early 1960s the average set remained on for more than six hours a day.

### Programming Problems

Having captured a very large portion of the entertainment-seeking audience, television found many serious problems. Program directors discovered that, operating as they did many hours a day, the television stations devoured good program material faster than it could be created. The writing and producing talent drawn into the television industry simply could not conceive enough fresh material of broad general appeal to fill the stations' program time.

As a result, the mass of television programming offered to the public was uneven in quality. Much of it was trite, inane, and repetitive. The critics denounced it vehemently, with good reason. Yet every week, at least during the winter months, a selective viewer could find many hours of literate, provocative, informative, and frequently very entertaining programs. Some of the best were the "spectaculars" or "specials" originated by Sylvester "Pat" Weaver for NBC to break the monotony of regularly scheduled series. The cost of these lengthy and star-studded productions also could be spread among several sponsors.

Television programming suffered from two major difficulties: (1) the tendency of many program directors and sponsors to underestimate the intelligence of the audience; and (2) a severe case of overexposure—too many hours of program time in relation to the amount of good-quality program material, even when old Hollywood movies were added to the fare.

New program ideas quickly attracted imitators. The public was subjected to cycles of entertainment, a number of programs similar in nature. For two or three seasons in the late 1950s, quiz programs were extremely popular; these gave away fantastic amounts of money to contestants who made the correct replies to many kinds of questions. But the public began to grow weary of these giveaways, and when revelations of unethical assistance to some contestants were made, most of the quiz programs disappeared. Western programs, a modification of the Western movie or "horse opera" that long was a standard item in the motion picture industry, came into vogue. Soon the obvious tales of the Old West were exhausted, and producers took to exploring many ramifications of life, transferred to a Western setting. At the peak of the Western craze, so many of these "oaters" (as the industry called such horse pictures) were being shot around the overcrowded Hollywood outdoor locations that the casts of competing shows had to wait in line for turns to perform their heroics before the camera.

Television viewers with long memories still talk about such outstanding programs of the late 1960s, 1970s, and 1980s as the family shows "The Waltons," "All in the Family," the warm-hearted Bill Cosby series; "M*A*S*H*," the Korean field hospital comedy whose final first-run episode after 11 years set a viewing record for a single show; "Cheers" for humor; the glittery "Miami Vice" crime series; and the international favorite "Dallas," erroneously believed by some foreign viewers to be typical of the American lifestyle. Some of these shows still appear occasionally as reruns.

The television industry today is divided into two primary areas: (1) Free *over-the-air television*, in which advertisers pay the cost of the programs; and (2) *cable television*, in which viewers pay monthly fees to receive programs. A third, growing but still minor, form of program delivery is *pay-per-view*, in which the subscriber pays fees to see movies and special programs of unusual merit.

**Over-the-air television**
Programs delivered without charge, paid for by advertisers

**Cable television**
Programs delivered to homes by coaxial or fiber-optics cable, for which subscribers pay monthly fees

**Pay-per-view television**
Delivery system under which a set-owner pays a special fee to view a program of unusual appeal

## Television Delivery Systems Multiply

The ways in which television viewers receive their programs are growing in number. For decades they received TV programs in just one way, over the air from local stations and the national networks. Now the proliferation of delivery systems created by electronic developments soon should bring programs into the home by five different methods, some of them still developing:

1. *Over-the-air reception of network and local station programs.* Picture quality of these traditional broadcasts should improve as high density television (HDTV) comes into operation. (HDTV is discussed later in this chapter.)

2. *Cable.* Programs are delivered by satellite to local cable systems, which distribute them to homes by underground cable or on overhead wires, the standard cable system of the 1990s. (See Chapter 11.)

3. *Digital cable.* This is part of the "information superhighway." Local cable systems and their telephone company competitors expect to deliver programs to subscribers largely by underground fiber optics cable instead of the traditional coaxial cable. Fiber optics cable has extremely high capacity, potentially capable of carrying 500 or more channels. This system will make two-way television communication possible. Installation of fiber optics cable is progressing nationwide at enormous cost.

4. *"Wireless cable."* Some cable systems deliver programs to their subscribers by microwave transmissions instead of underground cable. This method eliminates the cost of installing fiber optics cable and requires special equipment on receiving sets. It provides fewer channels than digital.

5. *Direct broadcast satellite (DBS).* Programs are transmitted by satellite direct from their point of origin to 18-inch-diameter receiving dishes on home roofs. This method bypasses cable television systems completely. It began in the United States in 1994 and gained favor rapidly.

As pointed out in Chapter 1, huge multimedia and telephone companies are investing heavily in these rival systems. It is uncertain which methods will dominate after the year 2000 and which companies will control them.

**Digital cable**
Fiber optics cable, laid underground

**"Wireless cable"**
Microwave transmission of television programs

## The Impact of Television

The power of television to influence contemporary life is astounding. A prime example of this fact is found in the Senate Judiciary Committee hearing in 1991 in which Anita Hill accused Supreme Court nominee Judge Clarence Thomas of sexual harassment. The American people were plunged into emotional turmoil, often arguing passionately as they tried to decide who was lying.

The hearing created a national debate about sexual harassment in the workplace and greatly increased male consciousness of the problem. The explicit testimony carried into family living rooms a host of sexual terms and descriptions previously forbidden on television, contributing to a further loosening of traditional language taboos. The judge's claim that he was being subjected to a high-tech racial lynching also opened a frankness of racial debate previously avoided on television.

As the Thomas episode indicates, what viewers see and hear influences their attitudes, their manners, their speech, and often their daily habits. Thomas was confirmed. Anita Hill, a law professor, became a frequent spokesperson for the feminist movement.

Television's impact is strong in other areas as well, especially in sports. It often dictates the hour at which events take place and when the game action will halt for commercials. National political conventions are staged and timed like theatrical performances to lure a TV audience. Protest demonstrations that would pass almost unnoticed gain national exposure when a television news crew arrives and photographs protesters shaking their fists at the camera. In the home, the program listings influence meal-and bed-times. Parents may use the TV set as a babysitter, relieved that it keeps the children quiet, and too often unconcerned about the ideas and images they are absorbing. According to A. C. Nielsen statistics, the average American family watches television about seven hours a day.

A large percentage of viewers have not yet developed a discriminating attitude toward television. In its finest hours—coverage of the explosion of the space shuttle Challenger and the Los Angeles race riot, to cite two examples—television with its enthralling visual immediacy gives its audience a feeling of participation far more powerfully than any other medium. Each season, a limited number of dramatic programs rise above the tightly packaged limits of commercial television, stirring viewers' emotions.

Television's spokespersons cite a long list of distinguished accomplishments. But these are almost obscured in the daily TV grist. The monotonous succession of game shows, soap operas, reruns of old movies, inane situation comedies, talk shows, sexually oriented "reality" programs, and violent police shows, interrupted relentlessly by commercials, becomes an opiate for some adults, an escape from the reality of daily life while purporting to be reality. It is an artificial reality: in the television world, hardly anyone grows old, even the poor are well dressed, the private detective hero always finds a parking place, and the emotional impact of tragedy is blunted by the bouncy, cheerful toothpaste and laundry detergent commercials that follow it.

In 1961, when Newton N. Minow, then chairman of the Federal Communications Commission, labeled much of television programming "a vast wasteland," he drew praise from critics and criticism from TV industry leaders. In his speech he said:

> You will see a procession of game shows, violence, audience participation shows, formula comedies about totally unbelievable families, blood and thunder, mayhem, violence, sadism, murder, western bad men, western good men, private eyes, gangsters, more violence, and car-

toons. And, endlessly, commercials—many screaming, cajoling and offending. And most of all, boredom.

Twenty-five years later, John J. O'Connor writing in the New York *Times* recalled Minow's description, then commented:

> Yet, while getting bigger and more pervasive, and periodically laying claim to accomplishments of unquestioned value and stature, the television landscape remains essentially and distressingly the same as that described by Minow. Substitute "disease of the week" movies for the westerns, and the picture is still all too familiar. . . . As one analyst after another has pointed out over the decades, commercial television is in the business not of creating programs but of supplying audiences to advertisers who generally do not want their potential customers to be unduly upset.

As long as measurements of audience size—the ratings—determine whether a program stays on the air and the cost of commercials in it, the quality of television programming will continue at approximately the same level. Networks rarely risk showing a notably innovative program, because if it fails to attract a large audience, the price the network can charge for commercials in it must be reduced. So they play safe. Year after year they present the same familiar types of programs whose audience ratings, and hence advertising revenue, are predictable.

## Big Money at Stake

A basic fact to bear in mind as we examine the television industry is the huge amount of money involved in costs, profits, and occasional losses. A few examples indicate the scope of financial risks and profits in television:

- NBC paid $1.27 billion for television rights to the 2000 Summer Olympic Games at Sydney, Australia, and the 2002 Winter Olympic Games at Salt Lake City, Utah.

- Ted Danson set a salary record of about $450,000 per episode to star in the comedy series "Cheers." Cost of producing a one-hour television drama is about $1 million per episode.

- The networks and some metropolitan stations pay their star anchors more than $1 million a year each because their personalities attract viewers.

- ABC lost more than $20 million on its lengthy miniseries, "War and Remembrance." In contrast, the "Wheel of Fortune" game show takes in an estimated $125 million a year in advertising and licensing fees but costs only $26 million to make, sell, and distribute.

These massive figures come about because advertisers have found that commercials on television often sell merchandise in enormous quantities. So they pay very high prices to broadcast their commercials on popular programs. When corporations pay $900,000 for 30-second spots on the annual Super Bowl professional football championship broadcasts, they expect, and usually get, big results.

It is easy to see what a tension-ridden business television is and why TV executives put heavy emphasis—excessive emphasis, critics say—on presenting programs that make a profit. Indeed, their readiness to risk large sums makes possible the televising of major events and projects. Critics recognize this fact but contend that commercial television has a social obligation to temper its drive for profits by providing audiences occasionally with stimulating cultural and intellectual fare. Caught in a fierce competition to be "number one," network decision-makers only rarely break away from their slavish adherence to the ratings to do so.

## Decline of the Networks

The three traditional television networks—ABC, CBS, and NBC—dominated American television for four decades. Most of the larger U.S. stations and many of the smaller ones were affiliated with one of the three, each of which has more than 200 affiliates. Today these networks are suffering a severe decline in audience size, and subsequently in income, and haven't yet found a way to halt the slide.

**Affiliate**
Television station that distributes a network's programs under contract in a specified area

Once the three networks fought only among themselves for audience leadership. That fight continues, as shown in news stories about which had the most popular programs the previous week. But since the early 1980s the Big Three networks have faced five dangerous competitors whose combined and growing strength has stolen many of the networks' viewers. These are:

1. Cable television.
2. A growing number of independent TV stations, which have developed strong audience appeal. These stations have access to popular shows that programming syndicates deliver to them by satellite for a fee. Such programs may be reruns of network series or made-for-syndication features that rival network material in quality.
3. Home video, which many viewers watch instead of television.
4. The aggressive, young Fox network.
5. Appearance in 1995 of two additional broadcast networks, WB Television (Warner Brothers) and UPN, United Paramount Network. They began with part-time schedules.

At the peak of their power in 1978, the three networks drew 93 percent of the viewing audience in the prime-time evening hours. Ten years later this figure had fallen to 68 percent, and by 1996 to 53 percent.

Industry leaders, however, predicted that purchase of the ABC and CBS networks by new owners would bring fresh vigor to network operations. Network officials emphasize that, with their competition fragmented among many cable channels and independent stations, each network program continues to draw a much larger audience than any of the individual competing programs.

Lost viewers mean a severe loss of income, because advertising rates for each program are determined by the size of its audience. This in turn has led to vigorous cost-cutting in the networks' news and other departments. The companies, once so profitable, actually have lost money on network operations with affiliated stations in some financial periods. The large stations each network owns and operates, popularly called O and Os, continue to be very profitable, however, with some profit margins as high as 50 percent before the recession of the early 1990s sharply reduced advertising revenue.

**A Fourth Network.**    The problems of ABC, CBS, and NBC increased when Rupert Murdoch, the international media tycoon, established Fox Broadcasting as a fourth entertainment network in 1987. Murdoch used his own seven big-city TV stations as a base and his Twentieth Century Fox studio as a program supplier.

At first the network operated only on Sunday evening, but it gradually expanded to every-night programming. Fox aimed at a youthful, multiethnic audience with unconventional shows such as "The Simpsons," "Married . . . with Children," and "In Living Color." Murdoch also planned a TV news service.

**. . . And Two More.**    By starting the WB and UPN networks, Warner Brothers and Viacom Paramount, both giant producers of motion pictures and television programs, created outlets on which they can show their film products without first making deals with the Big Three and Fox networks. Early programming on the new part-time networks emulated the Fox appeal to youthful and multiracial audiences. Despite low initial viewership, WB and UPN programs cut somewhat into the older networks' audiences.

## Networks Fight Back

With their advertising revenue curtailed, the major networks sought other ways to improve their finances.

One method was to approach cable television with an "If you can't lick 'em, join 'em" attitude. Both NBC and ABC made substantial investments in the cable business. NBC started the Consumer News and Business Channel (CNBC) and entered a joint venture with Cablevision Systems Corporation, a major cable TV program supplier. ABC owns 80 percent of the ESPN sports channel.

Second, the networks tried to change the traditional financial arrangements with their affiliates in ways to save themselves money (see How a Television Station Operates section, p. 288).

**O and Os**
Jargon for VHF stations owned and operated by television networks

Their third move involved a head-to-head battle with the Hollywood studios and production companies that make most of the entertainment programs seen on the networks in prime time.

For more than a quarter century, ABC, CBS, and NBC were severely restricted as to the number of prime-time entertainment programs they could make and show on their own networks under a consent decree signed with the federal government. Also, they were forbidden to syndicate their own shows. Each network had to purchase performance rights for most of the prime-time programs they showed from program producers who made and owned the shows. Thus, for example, ABC did not own "Roseanne" but leased its episodes from the Carsey-Werner Company. The networks under this arrangement paid about $2 billion a year for programs.

**Syndicated show** Program leased by its producer for re-run showing after it has appeared on a network

The purpose of the decree was to prevent the networks from getting a stranglehold on TV entertainment by controlling the production, selling, and showing of programs.

As broadcasting economics changed, largely through the growth of cable television, the networks sought relaxation of these restrictions. The Hollywood studios in turn tried to keep the strongest financial control possible on TV program-making. They said that because the cost of making a half-hour show was so high, often around $500,000, the fees they received from the networks frequently didn't cover their production costs. They made most of their money from subsequent syndication to local stations. They pointed out, too, that a TV series must stay on the air about five years to accumulate a sufficient number of episodes to justify syndication.

With hundreds of millions of dollars at stake in the long run, a fierce legal struggle ensued, involving the Federal Communications Commission and the U.S. Circuit Court of Appeals. Ultimately, the financial and syndication rules restricting the networks were allowed to expire in late 1995. These rules had barred the networks from holding a financial interest in a company that syndicated television programming and prevented the networks from syndicating their own programming. Removal of the restrictions was a motivating factor in Disney's purchase of ABC. With the legal doors opened, the networks increased production of their own programs. Nevertheless, because of complex talent contracts and financial concerns, the Big Three networks continued to obtain a substantial portion of their prime-time programming from the Hollywood studio TV production divisions.

## How a Television Station Operates

Unlike most of the printed media and the commercial motion picture industry, a television station gives its product away. Anyone possessing a television set may watch hour after hour of programs free of charge. The station, of course, must earn money to cover its high cost of operation and return a profit. It does so through the sale of commercial advertising time.

Examination of the operation of a successful TV station of medium size, affiliated with one of the three major networks, shows how American television functions. In most respects this station is typical of many in the United States, although it has a considerably larger news operation than many of its size.

The station is headed by a general manager. Reporting to the manager are four major department heads—chief engineer, program director, news director, and sales manager. The head of the production department reports to the program director. The promotion director is closely linked to the sales department but also reports to the program director.

Although it is on the air 24 hours a day, the station creates only about three or four hours of programming in its own studios, mostly local news. The rest is obtained from the network and from independent suppliers of filmed shows. To do this job, the station has a staff of nearly 100 people, plus eight to ten part-time employees. Some of the latter are local college students who usually help with live show production. The station offers a full hour of local news, weather, and sports at the dinner hour preceding the evening network news program and another 30 minutes of news in the late evening and at noon. During the week it presents other local background news and discussion programs. Twenty-five people of varying degrees of experience comprise the news staff.

The necessary income with which to operate the station is obtained from three primary sources: the network, national spot commercials the station puts on the air during station breaks, and local and regional commercials. Traditionally, each network has paid its affiliated local stations to carry its programs, with payments based on the size of the station's market. Most of the commercials in a network program are put on the air by the network, which keeps the money. During station breaks, the station inserts its own commercials.

The networks, however, are trying to change the longtime network-affiliate relationship by reducing or eliminating the money they pay to stations. Various alternatives have been negotiated.

NBC was first to introduce a new system, based on a station's performance. The network increased or decreased its payments to an affiliate station depending on its ratings on early-evening local programs leading into network prime time and the size of its 25–54-year-old audience, deemed by advertisers to be the most desirable. CBS's announcement of a sharp reduction in payments to affiliated stations in 1992 met such vehement opposition that it had to reduce the amount of cuts by half.

WPBF in West Palm Beach, Florida, shook the industry by agreeing to pay ABC for the network programs it broadcast. It did so in order to obtain affiliation with the network in a competitive situation. This was the first reversal of the traditional method; how many more might follow was uncertain.

Oprah Winfrey gestures to the audience during the taping of her television talk show. Despite a growing number of aggressive competitors, her ratings have remained high. (AP Photo)

The local station we are examining, like others, also obtains programs from syndication firms under various plans. One is a straight fee arrangement, such as used in the former Phil Donahue show; all commercial time slots in the show were open for local commercials.

The widely used barter system has several variations. A station may obtain a syndicated program without charge, but the syndicator retains control of half the commercial spots as its source of income. Under a barter-purchase plan, the syndicator sells a show to the station for a fee but retains possession of one or two 30-second spots for sale to national advertisers.

An affiliate may decline to carry a specific network program, either because it finds the show objectionable or in order to present a local or syndicated show in its place. Most stations carry about 90 percent of the programs a network offers.

Figure 10.1 shows the complex interplay of forces in the television industry.

## High-Definition Television

Television pictures spectacularly more detailed and brilliant than those seen today may appear soon on home screens as digital technology replaces over-the-air broadcast signals. This system is known as *high defi-*

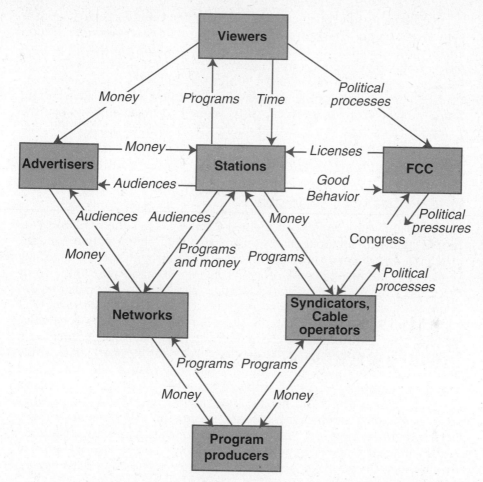

**Figure 10.1**

Organization of the television industry. (Source: Reprinted by permission from *Television Economics* by Bruce M. Owen, Jack H. Beebe, and Willard G. Manning, Jr. Lexington, MA: Lexington Books, D.C. Heath and Company, 1974.) Figure updated to reflect the new role of Congress due to the competition between broadcasting (FCC-regulated) and cable (not FCC-regulated).

*nition television* (HDTV). After years of development and legal haggling, HDTV finally was submitted for final testing. It might be seen in many American homes before the year 2000.

By all accounts, the new picture will be broader and razor-sharp. A television picture consists of hundreds of lines of dots. Conventional screens have 525 lines. HDTV uses more than 1000 lines, with more dots per line.

While the HDTV picture is almost ready for use, practical problems remain concerning its widespread adoption. Today's TV sets cannot receive the digital HDTV signal, and new sets that can will be very expensive at first. Will the public be willing to buy them? Broadcasting stations cannot afford to shut down their present service and convert their channels to HDTV when only a few sets are available to receive the new signals. Industry experts speak of a 15-year transition period during which the public replaces old sets with the new type.

**High-definition television**
High-resolution television system that uses more than 1000 scanning lines instead of the traditional 525

Recognizing the problem, the Federal Communications Commission announced a plan to give each existing television station a second channel on which to broadcast HDTV signals while continuing to provide a traditional signal on its original channel. Some stations wanted to use the second, free channel for additional old-style broadcasting or transmission of data for sale, rather than for quick HDTV installation. Some members of Congress, in turn, wanted to make stations pay the federal government a high fee to obtain the second channel. The 1996 communications bill gave the stations these extra channels free of charge, although Congress reserved the right to later reconsider the issue.

## Entertainment on Television

With fanfare, every September the major networks put their fall lineup of prime-time entertainment shows on the air. Each new program is publicized as a sure winner, yet relatively few survive through the winter. Many vanish after the first 13-week programming cycle, some after only two or three episodes. Since the network executives know this will happen, they are continually ordering replacement programs to be tossed into the breach.

The odds against any specific program being placed on a network schedule are enormous. In the process of program development, on which millions of dollars are spent every year, the network staffs study audience demographics, programming and advertising sales goals, and the programming desires of affiliated stations. They weigh proposed program ideas in this light. For example, in a recent season one network examined 2500 program ideas, studied scripts for 150 of them, and underwrote production of 37 pilot films. Out of this mass the network actually obtained 9 new programs, most of which did not last beyond that first season. Occasionally, a network will show a pilot film it has made, but never developed into a series, as a single freestanding program.

The hour at which a program is shown and the nature of the programs the rival networks put on the air against it may be the deciding factors in its survival. Like generals maneuvering their battle forces, network program executives move the programs on their lists around from time slot to time slot. On the offensive, a programmer may place a promising new show at a time when the competition's offerings are weak, giving it favorable audience exposure. As a defensive act, a well-established program may be shifted into a slot opposite a popular show on another network, in the hope that it will siphon off some of the rival's rating. It is common practice to have a new show follow an established hit in order to pick up the lead-in audience, viewers who watched the previous show, then decided to take a look at the new show rather than turn the dial. Another device is to *hammock* a show, placing it between two hits.

ABC's scheduling of the comedy "Coach" illustrates what a time slot can do. Apparently believing that a situation comedy about a football

**Hammocking**
Positioning a new network program between two proven prime-time shows

# The new world of high-definition television

**High-definition television technology (HDTV) may have wide-ranging effects in coming years. Here are some possible results of its growth.**

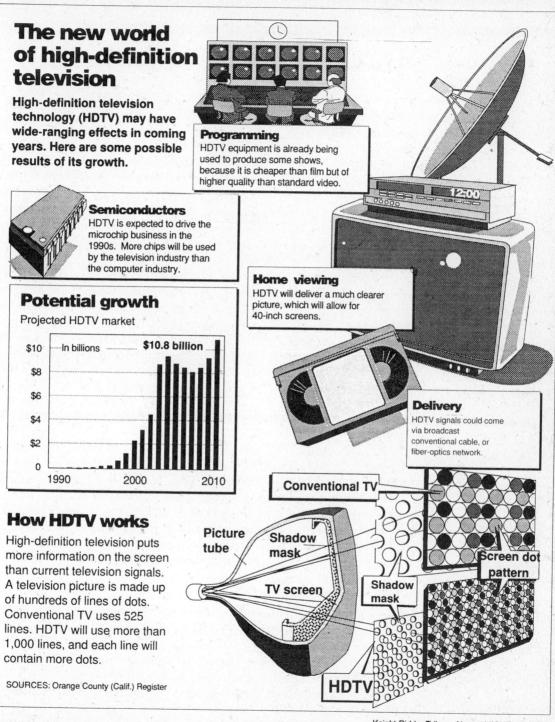

## Programming
HDTV equipment is already being used to produce some shows, because it is cheaper than film but of higher quality than standard video.

## Semiconductors
HDTV is expected to drive the microchip business in the 1990s. More chips will be used by the television industry than the computer industry.

## Potential growth
Projected HDTV market

$10 — In billions — $10.8 billion
$8
$6
$4
$2
0
1990        2000        2010

## Home viewing
HDTV will deliver a much clearer picture, which will allow for 40-inch screens.

## Delivery
HDTV signals could come via broadcast conventional cable, or fiber-optics network.

## How HDTV works
High-definition television puts more information on the screen than current television signals. A television picture is made up of hundreds of lines of dots. Conventional TV uses 525 lines. HDTV will use more than 1,000 lines, and each line will contain more dots.

SOURCES: Orange County (Calif.) Register

Conventional TV

Picture tube
Shadow mask
TV screen
Shadow mask
Screen dot pattern

HDTV

Knight-Ridder Tribune News / MICHELLE WISE

This graphic explains in simple visual form the electronic principles of high-definition television and projects potential growth of the HDTV market. (Knight/Ridder Tribune News/Michelle Wise)

## SPANISH TV—A SEPARATE WORLD

Millions of American viewers are unaware that a thriving television world exists in their country in addition to the English-language programs they watch. It consists of Spanish-language networks and local stations.

Two over-the-air Spanish networks and one principal cable network serve millions of Spanish viewers with wide-ranging programming built around novellas, sports, situation comedies, and an increasing amount of news. They are:

*Univision.* This is the dominant, more prosperous of the over-the-air networks. It owns and operates 11 full-power stations in major Hispanic markets, such as Miami, Los Angeles, and New York, and delivers programs to affiliates elsewhere. One of its primary attractions is the Mexican novellas it shows. These continuing dramatic stories are the most popular programming among Hispanic viewers.

*Telemundo.* Much smaller in audience size and handicapped by financial and programming difficulties, this over-the-air network is making a comeback after emerging from Chapter 11 bankruptcy. It owns and operates seven full-power and nine low-power stations. Like Univision, it concentrates on building a younger audience.

*Galavision.* This cable network serves more than a million households, providing a schedule of entertainment, news, and Mexican football.

The Nielsen organization now produces rating information for the Hispanic networks that reflects their growth as the Hispanic population increases.

---

coach would do well as a lead-in to its popular Monday night football broadcasts, the network switched its previously highly rated "Coach" from Tuesday to Monday at the start of the 1994–1995 season. The result was disastrous. "Coach" fell to 66th place among 94 prime-time shows in the weekly Nielsen ratings. Late in the season, the network moved "Coach" to 8:30 p.m. Wednesday, surrounded by other comedies. The ratings of "Coach" skyrocketed, from 66th place to 6th place.

### Talk, Soaps, and Scandal

Soap operas, with their provocative fictional exploration of personal relationships, have long dominated daytime television. Recently they have been challenged by an upsurge of talk shows and tabloid TV "reality" programs whose chief stock in trade is supposedly "inside" stories about scandals involving so-called celebrities.

Daytime television talk shows generally differ from radio talk shows. The radio shows deal heavily with political issues and consist of dialogue between host and listeners who phone in their opinions. The TV shows have a studio audience and a panel of guests whom the female or male host leads, or sometimes goads, into raucous arguments on a previously announced topic. Confrontation makes lively visual fare, and the hosts are skillful at provoking it.

The longtime stars of daytime talk—Oprah Winfrey, Geraldo, and Sally Jessy Raphael—face intense competition from a younger, youth-oriented group such as Ricki Lake, Jenny Jones, and Montel Williams. In the frantic battle for ratings the topics discussed have become more and more intimate, salacious, and trivial. Oprah Winfrey, who has kept her show at a higher level than the others, holds a substantial lead in the ratings.

**A Typical Day on the TV Talk Shows.**   These are among the topics covered on one actual day: Jenny Jones, fantasy kisses; Montel Williams, cheating men confronted; Jerry Springer, beautiful men who live as women; Ricki Lake, pregnant women whose habits endanger the fetus; Oprah Winfrey, the Judds; Geraldo, jealous rage; and Charles Perez, lesbian mothers.

These talk shows have been accused of exploiting emotions without concern for the long-range effect on show participants. *Broadcasting & Cable* magazine commented editorially, "For years, the talk program genre has been an escalating war of the sensational versus the bizarre. Adultery, incest, transvestism and other muck are the daytime currency."

Participants in the shows are recruited by displaying an 800 telephone number on the screen during a program and through the National Talk Show Guest Registry. Although guests often are subjected to intimate questioning and sometimes humiliation, the desire to appear on national television generates an abundance of volunteers. Some participants show up on more than one show.

Television tabloid magazine shows such as "Inside Edition" generally appear in early evening. They pay high fees to persons involved in scandals or dramatic news events to reveal titillating "secrets." Their subject matter and approach parallel those of supermarket tabloid publications. (Also see Issue 1.)

## Rating the TV Shows

When a network claims that 30 million viewers saw a show, it is obvious that the viewers have not been counted one by one. Television viewership is determined by monitoring the viewing habits of a small, scientifically selected sample, then extrapolating the percentage results into nationwide statistics. Although these projected statistics have built-in potential for error, television producers and salespeople quote them as though they are completely accurate. The fact is that the viewing preferences of a few American families determine the national ratings for a show.

Two firms provide most of the ratings reports—the A. C. Nielsen Company and Arbitron. Arbitron specializes in monitoring local TV markets. Programs are dropped or renewed, executives keep or lose their jobs, and advertising revenues rise and fall, depending on what the "Nielsens" and Arbitron ratings reveal. These reports give two kinds of

**Rating**
Percentage of all households having television sets that viewed a particular program

Nielsen ratings showing the size of audiences for network television shows heavily influence purchase of advertising, selection of talent, and placement of shows on network schedules. *Broadcasting & Cable*, a trade magazine, publishes the report as a weekly feature.

sumers free with two proofs of purchase. The hour video features classic clips from *Seinfeld*'s first five seasons. The grand prize for the contest will be an all-expense paid trip to Hollywood for two and a tour of Sony Pictures Studios.

Coca-Cola/Packer Plastics in its promotion will offer *Seinfeld* collector's cups at retail outlets where there is Coca-Cola fountain service.

The cups will feature memorable quotes from the series' characters and will be customized with the market's

local station and time period for *Seinfeld*-syndicated broadcasts. C-C/PP will support the campaign through point-of-purchase materials and will look for local cross-promotion opportunities with *Seinfeld* stations and local retail outlets. ■

**PROGRAMING**

**Share**
Percentage of households with television sets having their sets tuned to a given program at a given time

**People meter**
Instrument installed in selected homes by rating services to measure size and demographic elements of television audiences

data about a show, its *rating* and its *share*. The rating of a show is the percentage of all households having TV sets that viewed the particular program. Nielsen placed the number of television-owning households at 95.9 million in 1996.

As an example, the Nielsen ratings for the week of May 8–14, 1995, at the close of the 1994–1995 network season, showed "E.R.," the NBC medical drama, to be the most-watched show. Its rating was 22.9. Since Nielsen estimated the total TV households at 95.4 million, one rating point equalled 954,000 homes. That figure multiplied by the 22.9-point rating, gave "E.R." an audience of 21,846,600 households. In contrast, the Fox program "Sliders" ranked 80th for the week with a 5.6 rating. By the same multiplication method, "Sliders" was reported to have an audience of 5,342,900, less than one-fourth of those who watched "E.R."

The share figure is based on the number of households having their sets turned on at a given time; it measures a program's audience against other shows on the air at the same time. The networks believe that, to be called successful, a show needs at least a 20 share. At the high end, Super Bowl football telecasts sometimes win a 60 share or a little more.

Nielsen uses two principal measuring devices:

1. The "*people meter*," introduced in 1986 for nationwide measurement of audiences. This device is a small hand-held instrument with eight numbered buttons, one for each family member among the 5000 randomly selected test families.

Users feed their sex and age information into the people meter. Individual viewers are supposed to punch in when they begin watching and punch out when they stop. This method provides more specific personal information about viewers than the old Nielsen system of small electronic boxes, which showed only when a set was turned on and to what channel. The introduction of people meters upset network executives because they showed somewhat smaller audiences for some programs than the old box system had shown.

2. The *weekly diary*, in which participating viewers record what they watched during each 15-minute segment of viewing time. This method supplements the people meter in order to obtain demographic information for local ratings in some cities. In the New York metropolitan area, for example, the 500 Nielsen diaries in use are supposed to represent the viewing in 6.9 million homes with TV sets. Thus, as a *Wall Street Journal* reporter pointed out after filling in a diary for a week, his report was supposed to speak for nearly 14,000 persons. Some advertising specialists point out that more than one-third of the households Nielsen invites to participate in its survey refuse to do so. These researchers express concern that as a result the survey group used may not truly reflect the viewing habits of the total television audience.

Nielsen announced that it is developing a "passive people meter" to provide even more detailed information about TV viewers. This computerized, camera-like scanner atop a TV set will detect how many people are in the room, who they are, and whether each individual is watching the TV set. Since it produces computerized images, not actual photographs, the device cannot record what else the individuals are doing beyond watching TV. Thus it doesn't quite fit into the "big brother is watching" category.

Critics of television and its manner of measuring its own success emphasize that, huge as the viewership figures are, many people watch very little television. They argue that an important difference exists between having a TV set turned on and watching the program attentively. Surveys indicate that many persons turn on a set primarily for the companionship the voices and pictures provide as background for their other activities.

## Public Television

Viewers who prefer more educational and cultural programs than commercial TV usually offers can find them on the more than 360 nonprofit (noncommercial) public television stations operating in the United States. Their programs are presented without commercial interruptions.

These nonprofit stations obtain operating funds from several sources, including government grants, underwriting grants from large corporations trying to build a good public image, foreign partners in co-production, and public subscriptions. Well over $50 million a year is contributed by the public to the nonprofit stations. A federally funded organization, the Corporation for Public Broadcasting, established by Congress in 1967, provides money for production and distribution of programs through the Public Broadcasting Service.

Programming on public television long has been condemned by conservative Republican Party forces as being "too liberal." When the Republicans took control of Congress in 1995, many of them proposed elimination of all federal funding for the Corporation for Public Broadcasting. Substantial public support for the system became apparent, however, and a compromise was discussed that would reduce the federal funding immediately and possibly phase it out entirely over several years.

Viewers who rallied to the support of PBS did so because they admired such special PBS presentations as the Ken Burns Civil War history, as well as the science series "Nova," the children's programming including "Sesame Street," and the MacNeill-Lehrer News Hour (now the Lehrer News Hour).

A frequently heard criticism is that public TV shows are dull at times, elitist in tone, and intended for the well-educated upper middle class. Viewers complain about the frequent on-the-air fund drives, but station executives insist that these are essential in order to provide sufficient operating money. Still another problem for public television's future is the inroads some cable television networks are making into its audience. A growing number of cultural, historical, science, and nature programs—areas traditionally covered by public television—are appearing on certain cable channels. Just what long-term impact this competition will have on public television's role is not yet clear.

## A Look Ahead

Television is such a complex, ever-shifting, and expanding industry that forecasting what will happen in it in the next ten years is risky, indeed. But these trends seem probable:

- Use of high-definition television will spread slowly during a transition period. The cost of the new-type sets will be high for a few years.

- More programs, especially sporting events, that viewers have been accustomed to viewing free on broadcast television will be shifted to pay cable, at times on a pay-per-view basis.

- Expansion of satellite transmission and the growth of international media companies will lead to distribution of much more American programming abroad and of some additional foreign-produced and -financed programming in the United States.

- The success of the regional Bell telephone companies' campaign to become owners and suppliers of information and entertainment, not merely the operators of systems delivering other companies' material, may lead to significant ownership changes and an increase in programming brought to homes.

- The nature of over-the-air network programming probably will remain much as it is today, with a continued gradual lowering of network program restrictions to meet the more liberal social and moral standards applied to cable TV and home video movies.

No conclusive answers to long-debated questions about television's impact on the fabric of society and on the lives of individuals are likely to emerge soon, if ever.

- Does televised murder and mayhem, when watched hour after hour, induce violent behavior in juvenile and adult viewers?

- Does TV news with its emphasis on brevity and personality provide sufficient substance to inform the electorate adequately?

- Do the unrealistic, glossy, simplistic solutions, and implausible plots of many TV shows cause viewers to believe in an artificial dream world dangerously at odds with their own daily lives? Indeed, has television become an opiate that lulls some viewers into mental stagnation and dulls their lives?

- Or, just the opposite, does television enliven dull lives and provide welcome escape from depressing realism?

The questions are many, the answers subjective and difficult to document. The one obvious truth is that television, ever more pervasive, shapes contemporary politics, news coverage, the form and timing of public events, the nature of family life, and, in many respects, the quality of our national thinking—remarkable power for a medium whose critics, often with good reason, dismiss much of its programming as "mindless."

## Points to Remember

1. What was Dr. Vladimir Zworykin's basic contribution to the development of television?

2. How did the Federal Communications Commission's policy established in 1952 affect the growth of television?

3. Can you name three popular TV shows of the 1970s and early 1980s?

4. Explain why Newton N. Minow once called television programming "a vast wasteland." Do you believe this description is accurate today?

5. What factors have caused the decline in the size of audiences watching the ABC, CBS, and NBC networks?

6. Three broadcasting networks compete nationally with the traditional Big Three—ABC, CBS, and NBC. What are they?

7. How does the television ratings system operate?

8. The Nielsen "people meter" is a key device in measuring the size and nature of television audiences. Explain how it works.

# Part 2 ✳ Television News

Television newscasts are the primary source of news for a large percentage of Americans and virtually the only source for many of them. Leaders of the television industry concede, however, that most TV news programs are only a headline service with little depth. Nevertheless, television newscasts have made tremendous strides since the industry's early days.

The first efforts at news shows on television often consisted of newsreel excerpts and black-and-white still photographs shown while the on-camera announcer read the script. There is little comparison visually between those pioneering efforts and today's colorful presentations with their shots from helicopters, two-way on-camera discussions between a show's anchor and field reporter, and similar devices.

In Part 2 of the television chapter, we examine the development of TV news and how it functions today. At the networks, the news departments traditionally have been regarded as separate entities unrelated to the entertainment side of the business. As we shall see, however, that distinction has begun to blur.

## Early-Day Newscasts

During the first decade of telecasting, TV newspeople did far better with on-the-spot broadcasts of major news events, public affairs programming, and documentaries than they did with scheduled daily newscasts. Development of mobile units and magnetic tape gradually enabled them to get out of the studios and into the field.

In 1951 Edward R. Murrow turned from "Hear It Now" on radio to "See It Now" for CBS. NBC's early-morning "Today" show with Dave Garroway, a mixture of news and entertainment, opened in 1952.

Television news broadcasts in the early 1950s also gave viewers a sense of up-close participation with live broadcasts of an atomic blast at Yucca Flats, the political conventions and the inauguration of President Eisenhower, and the dramatic confrontations during the McCarthy–Army hearings in Congress that exposed the unproven claims of the Wisconsin senator that a communist conspiracy existed in the U.S. gov-

President John F. Kennedy is laid to rest in Arlington National Cemetery. The funeral climaxed three days of mourning during which the nation was bound together by television as never before. (UPI/Bettmann)

ernment. At least 65 million Americans saw one of the "Great Debates" between John F. Kennedy and Richard M. Nixon in 1960 with the U.S. presidency at stake. Some 135 million people watched at least part of John Glenn's pioneering orbital space flight in 1962.

**Mourning for Kennedy.** If proof were needed of television's ability to report great events magnificently, it came on November 22, 1963, when President Kennedy was assassinated in Dallas, Texas. Within minutes, the networks began a four-day vigil ending with the burial at Arlington. Many heard the first bulletins on radio, then rushed to watch the unfolding drama and hear news summaries on television. Viewers saw the new president, along with Jacqueline Kennedy and the casket, returning to Washington. They went with the cameras into the White House, saw the Sunday ceremonies at the Capitol. Sunday viewers on NBC (the only network "live" at the precise moment) saw Jack Ruby lunge forward in a Dallas police station to shoot fatally the alleged assassin, Lee Harvey Oswald. On Monday, the funeral of President Kennedy drew a 93 percent viewership figure, the highest known level in television history.

With full involvement of American troops in Vietnam after 1965, the ugliness of the indecisive war was brought into American living rooms by television news crews. Public reaction against the war led to President Lyndon Johnson's decision to retire from the 1968 election race—an announcement made live to a Sunday evening television audience. There were even greater public shocks in 1968: the assassinations of the Rev. Martin Luther King, Jr., and Senator Robert F. Kennedy, and the turmoil and rioting accompanying the Democratic convention in Chicago. In each event, television played a major news coverage role.

**Camera on the Moon.**   In July 1969, however, television played a happier role when it brought to a worldwide audience the flight of Apollo 11 and direct transmission of the pictures of humankind's first steps on the moon. Viewers saw black-and-white pictures originating from the moon for five hours, including two hours with the astronauts on the moon's surface. Some 125 million Americans saw the climactic nighttime broadcast, and a satellite network carried the pictures to an eventual audience estimated at 500 million. Truly a "See It Now" triumph of immediacy, the pictures from the moon gave all viewers a sense of participation in a great feat of exploration. But in 1986, television viewers watched with disbelief and horror as the space shuttle Challenger, carrying five astronauts, exploded a few moments after takeoff, disintegrating in great plumes of smoke.

**CBS.**   After Murrow left CBS in 1958, Walter Cronkite became that network's leading personality. A United Press war correspondent, Cronkite joined CBS in 1950 and became the star of many of its documentaries. He took over the major CBS news program from Douglas Edwards and transformed it into a 30-minute dinnertime show in the fall of 1963, with Eric Sevareid as commentator. Mike Wallace, Dan Rather, Morley Safer, Harry Reasoner, and Diane Sawyer made the documentary "60 Minutes" a "top ten" show. Rather succeeded Cronkite on the evening news show in 1981, and Connie Chung became a co-anchor with Rather in 1993. Two years later CBS fired her abruptly from the evening news program and her own "Eye-to-Eye With Connie Chung" show.

**NBC.**   NBC's stars were two seasoned newspapermen, Chet Huntley and David Brinkley, whose mixture of news and comments between 1956 and 1970 made them a top-ranking television team. When Huntley retired in 1970, John Chancellor emerged as the chief NBC newscaster, with Brinkley continuing to contribute his wry commentaries. Tom Brokaw became the evening show anchor in 1982.

**ABC.**   With fewer resources, ABC kept pace by offering such top-flight commentators and news anchors as John Daly, Frank Reynolds, Howard K. Smith, and Barbara Walters, who came from NBC in 1976 and continued to excel in interviewing famous personages. ABC's fortunes began to turn upward in 1979 when Ted Koppel began his "Nightline" broadcasts following the local late-night newscasts. Koppel focused first on the Iranian hostage crisis, blending late-breaking news with live interviews by satellite of newsmakers, politicians, and correspondents. Koppel also developed programs treating domestic social and political problems. Peter Jennings scored a success as the evening anchorperson after 1983, and by the early 1990s placed first in the ratings among the network anchors. Sam Donaldson, a controversial White House correspondent during the Reagan years, was called "Jumping Sam" as he leaped into the air

Ted Koppel casts a skeptical glance at a guest on his provocative ABC "Nightline" show before pouncing with a hard question. (Laurel Luth)

to shout questions at the retreating President. Later he became co-host of ABC's "Prime Time Live" with Diane Sawyer.

Industry observers speculate that ABC's news programs might become more entertainment-oriented under its new owner, the Walt Disney Company.

**PBS.** Favored by serious followers of the news was the one-hour show produced for Public Broadcasting Service by Robert MacNeil and Jim Lehrer. They first won attention as PBS anchors for the Watergate hearings and began their hour-long program in 1983 with Charlayne Hunter-Gault and Judy Woodruff (formerly of NBC) as staff reporters. MacNeil's retirement in 1995 created a temporary period of uncertainty for the program, quickly overcome.

**Satellites.** News by satellite became television's most sensational achievement of the 1960s. The successful launching of AT&T's Telstar on July 10, 1962, permitted the first live transmissions between the United States and Europe. These were "staged" shows of only a few minutes' duration, but they thrilled TV audiences. RCA's Relay carried pictures of events surrounding the Kennedy assassination to 23 nations. Howard Hughes' efforts to launch a satellite that would achieve a fully synchronous orbit (an orbit and speed that keep the craft directly over one point on earth) met success with Syncom III in 1964.

## Television News Today

Despite television's impact and almost seductive visual appeal, critics believe that television news often falls short of what it should be as a channel for informing the public. They argue that "show biz" entertainment values too frequently take priority over news values to the point that presentations sometimes border on the irresponsible. The criticism applies more to local news shows than to the networks.

The relentless fight among stations and networks for audience ratings, plus time restrictions, create programs that make audiences aware of news developments but only skimpily informed about them. The fault lies in part with the audiences. Producers have discovered how short the attention span of many viewers is, and in order to hold them use quick-cut techniques that omit background and explanations of why things have happened. Fortunately for serious viewers, notable exceptions to these shortcut techniques do exist. On massive news stories, such as the terrorist bombing of the federal building in Oklahoma City that killed 168 people in 1995, national TV coverage often is impressive in both impact and background. The network evening news shows have sought to combat the "just headlines" image by adding interpretive and background segments.

MacNeil contends that the assumptions behind many TV news programs are that "bite-sized is best, that complexity must be avoided, that nuances are dispensable, that qualifications impede the simple message, that visual stimulation is a substitute for thought, and that verbal precision is an anachronism."

Writing in the *Christian Science Monitor,* Rushworth M. Kidder reaches much the same conclusion: "Television, unlike print, favors movement over stillness, simplification over complexity, specificity over abstraction, personality over conceptualization, and the present over both the past and future."

Despite the shortcomings cited by these and other critics, annual surveys by the Roper organization have found that a large percentage of those questioned—usually about half—regard TV news as more believable than newspapers. The explanation for the power of TV news lies in the threefold advantage television news has over newspapers:

1. Its ability to tell stories visually from the scene of the action, making viewers feel as though they are at the scene themselves.

2. The ease with which viewers can receive the news. Reading a newspaper story requires more concentration than watching a news item on television.

3. The fact that TV news is delivered by attractive men and women whose carefully nurtured personalities create an aura of intimacy impossible in print reports and only partially achievable in radio news. For many viewers, the TV messenger who brings the news has more impact than the news itself.

In weighing these criticisms of television news as essentially a headline service, one must remember that many purchasers of newspapers merely scan the headlines; "bite-size" TV news stories satisfy their limited appetites for news as much as or more than newspaper headlines do. Individuals who desire to learn *why* things have happened almost always must supplement TV news viewing by reading printed accounts.

## The "Sound Bite"

Knowing the impact of television news, political leaders from the White House down plan their actions and time their statements in an effort to obtain a 30-second appearance on evening news shows. They create quotations that sound punchy as 10-second "sound bites," about which John E. Frohnmayer, former chairman of the National Endowment for the Arts, said: "The sound bite, which has become so pervasive in political fisticuffs, is to the First Amendment as bumper stickers are to philosophy."

The impressions formed by these brief glimpses strongly influence the opinions Americans develop about their leaders, many of whom they never see in person or listen to at length. As President, Ronald Reagan was especially skillful in creating an image of amiability through carefully controlled "photo opportunity" appearances.

Although heavy use of talk shows by candidates decreased emphasis on the sound bite during the 1992 presidential campaign, it continued to

Larry King comes head-to-head with Marlon Brando as he probes for answers during his popular "Larry King Live" interview program, on which many prominent entertainment and political leaders appear.

be an important tool for officeholders and TV news editors on regular TV news programs.

For extended coverage of Congress in session and other significant political meetings, viewers of many cable systems can watch C-SPAN, the Cable Satellite Public Affairs Network. This in-depth coverage provides details and nuances not shown on commercial newscasts.

## TV News Makes Profits

Once regarded more as a service to viewers than as a source of profit, television news today is a strong moneymaker, for both the Big Three networks and local stations. Management's drive for profits is apparent. It influences the content of newscasts and their style of presentation.

Osborn Elliott, former dean of the Columbia University Graduate School of Journalism, warned against this trend at an awards ceremony. He asserted that broadcast journalists "feel the wash of an accelerating tide away from news business and toward just plain show business. News divisions, which once may have enjoyed some kind of special standing within their companies, may now be perceived as just another chicken in the corporate hothouse, to be stuffed or starved as may serve the corporate purpose."

According to unofficial figures published by *Broadcasting & Cable*, ABC News was the most profitable and largest network news operation in 1994. It earned more than $100 million after spending about $400 million to produce its news programs. Its "Nightline" program with Ted Koppel produced much of the profit. Its news magazine programs contributed, too, just as "60 Minutes" was a major source of CBS News profit.

During the same year, 82 percent of American commercial television stations reported earning a profit on news; only 7 percent lost money on it. These results were obtained in a survey by the Radio Television News Directors Foundation and Ball State University.

One result of the bottom-line emphasis has been the appearance of the previously mentioned "reality" programs such as "Hard Copy." These cheaply produced shows with their emphasis on sex and crime are condemned by critics but draw large audiences. Citing the influence of so-called trash television on other news programming, Fred Friendly, famous CBS producer and educator, commented, "I believe television has lost its ethical compass."

Much criticism of TV news focuses on local newscasts. Many are loaded with crime reports and often inane chit-chat among anchorpersons, weather reporters, and sportscasters. Stories about homicides, traffic deaths, and fires dominate these programs, while local government and background stories get little attention. Crime coverage is played up so much on some stations that industry cynics use the expression, "If it bleeds, it leads."

CBS News anchorman Dan Rather broadcasts from the site of the San Francisco Bay earthquake in 1989. For dramatic effect, the networks frequently send their anchor men and women to the scene of major disasters and international events such as summit meetings. (Sacramento *Bee*/Sygma)

Contrasting to all this, certain stations especially in major markets set excellent examples with programs built around enterprising reporting in depth and a well-balanced range of topics.

## A Question of Ethics

Was the story you saw on the TV news about a clever new toy or a physical therapy device a genuine news story covered by a local or network reporter? Or was it a *video news release* from a manufacturer subtly tilted for commercial purposes but presented by the station as its own work?

If used properly, the growing number of video news releases being delivered to stations by satellite or videocassette form a valuable additional source of information, just as printed news releases do. Too often they are not.

Some releases contain pictures and voice-over commentary; others consist of pictures only but have an accompanying script written by the public relations firm, which can be read by a staff reporter as if it were original work. The networks and many stations carefully identify the sources of such material on the air, but other stations, trying to impress viewers with what far-reaching staffs they have, fail to do so.

The program-length commercial or "infomercial," an extended form of the video news release, has created controversy. Running most often 40 minutes, it purports to be an objective presentation of a situation, often in a news show format, when in fact it promotes a product. Some sta-

**Video news release**
Videotaped news story in words and pictures sent to television stations by a public relations source

tions and cable channels fill early or late hours by running these commercials, with no cost to themselves, thereby misleading viewers.

Children's cartoon programs supplied by toy companies in which they promote their own products are a conspicuous form of the program-length commercial. Congress undertook some reform of children's programs by passing the Children's Television Act of 1990. (See Chapter 15.)

### Importance of Personality

So important is personality for TV newspersons that on-camera people may hold or lose their jobs on the basis of measured physiological response by sample audiences.

**Anchor**
Person on a television news program who reads news items and introduces stories taped in the field

TV journalists chosen to anchor news programs—to read news items and introduce stories from the field—are particularly subject to personality testing and shaping. Self-assurance, charm, a resonant voice, and the ability to ad-lib smoothly are key ingredients. In addition to having these physical attributes, the best anchors are skillful newsgatherers, often with long experience as reporters. Walter Cronkite, longtime anchor on the "CBS Evening News," projected such an avuncular presence that one survey found him to be the most trusted man in the United States. The chief anchors at the three general networks—Dan Rather at CBS, Tom Brokaw at NBC, and Peter Jennings at ABC—reached their positions against fierce competition because of polished personalities that generate confidence in those who watch them.

The nation received an inside glimpse of how television anchorpersons are chosen and molded when Christine Craft sued station KMBC-TV in Kansas City after it dismissed her as its anchor newscaster. She charged that station management told her she was being hired for the job because of her journalistic abilities. But when she was dismissed, the management told her she was "too old, unattractive, and not deferential enough to men." Trial testimony told how the station had called in a specialist to alter her image by changing her hair, makeup, and wardrobe. When asked for his list of qualifications for an anchorperson, the station's general manager testified that he "would put appearance at the top of the list." A jury awarded Craft $500,000 in damages but she lost the award on appeal.

## Mass News Coverage

The battle for audience supremacy in news programs among the three traditional networks is ferocious. In addition, their combined monopoly on national and world news coverage has been challenged from two directions.

First, Ted Turner's Cable News Network (CNN) with its 24-hour coverage has emerged as a fourth major television news source (see Chapter 11). Second, numerous major stations around the United States are extending coverage in their own shows beyond local areas by use of satellite transmission. They dispatch correspondents to distant news events, exchange stories with other stations, and operate mobile satellite uplink vans in the field, either on their own or in cooperation with their affiliated national networks. More than 50 television stations have their own news bureaus in Washington, concentrating on local angles.

Satellite transmission made possible instantaneous live coverage of the Persian Gulf War in 1991. TV viewers worldwide watched incoming Iraqi Scud missiles being destroyed in the air by U.S. Patriot missiles—combat action that looked liked scenes from a movie. Yet, despite such split-second transmission, the hundreds of TV and other reporters in the war zone could not give well-rounded coverage of the war because U.S. military officials restricted their movement so much. (See Issue 4.)

The upsurge of almost-instant transmission facilities has added to the mob-scene news coverage of big events that many observers find distasteful. When a tragedy occurs and the TV crews and other newspeople swarm in, they often trample lawns, invade the privacy of individuals, and virtually take over the area. Little of this is apparent to TV viewers, but it leaves anger and bitterness in its wake.

**Satellite newsgathering**
Use of satellite transmission units by reporters in the field to send stories quickly to their home studios

## "Welcome to Somalia"

Aggressive pack journalism, especially by television crews, that puts getting the picture above the restraints of good judgment, reached a new height when U.S. military forces arrived in Somalia in 1992 to safeguard delivery of emergency food supplies to starving Somalis.

Grim U.S. Marines, with faces blackened to reduce visibility to an enemy, jumped from their landing craft onto the Somalian beach in a predawn landing—straight into the glare of floodlights erected by a throng of TV camera operators. Obviously this put the Marines in a dangerous position as brilliantly lighted targets, in case enemy gunmen were waiting for them.

The television networks said they had been invited by the Pentagon to have camera crews at the scene, because the U.S. government wanted to publicize the troops' arrival. Even so, the lack of self-discipline among the press corps raised fresh demands that the media, especially TV crews, be even more stringently restricted in military operations.

## Points to Remember

1. Television covered important national events during the 1950s and 1960s. Can you name three of them?
2. When did the use of satellites for news transmission begin?
3. List three advantages television news has over newspaper reporting.
4. Describe a "sound bite" and "trash television."

Television trucks form clusters of satellite transmission dishes at big news events. These trucks are at New Madrid, Missouri, to send out stories about a projected earthquake in the region that did not occur. (AP/Wide World)

5. Do you agree or disagree with Fred Friendly that "television has lost its ethical compass"?

6. How much restriction, if any, should be placed on the media in covering military operations?

## Media Questions to Think About

1. Can you explain why television talk shows such as those of Ricki Lake, Oprah Winfrey, and Jenny Jones draw such large audiences?

2. Watch a local television newscast for a few days. If you were appointed news director of that program, what are the first two changes you would make to improve it?

3. Analyze your own television viewing. Approximately how many hours each week do you watch television? Roughly, how do you divide that time among situation comedies, newscasts, drama, sports, talk shows, and soap operas? How many of the channels available on your set do you actually watch?

# CHAPTER ELEVEN
## Cable Television

## Sci-Fi, Popcorn, and Cupid on Cable TV

Want to improve your putting? Try watching the Golf Channel on cable television. Worried that it might rain on your game? Turn to the Weather Channel. Rather go fishing? Click to the Outdoor Life Channel.

They are among an expanding list of cable channels known collectively as niche cablecasting. Each niche channel aims at an audience with a special interest or provides one-topic information for the general cable audience.

You may choose the History Channel, the Sci-Fi Channel, Comedy Central, or the Popcorn Channel (movie information). Perhaps you prefer to watch well-dressed women sell clothing on a home shopping channel or less-dressed women on the Playboy Channel. You might combine these interests by watching Cupid Network Television, an adult home shopping channel.

Where do you find these channels on the cable dial? That's the problem. Dozens of new channels such as those above have been started or announced, yet few slots are open for them on most current cable systems. Owners of these channels hope to gain a foothold in the TV spectrum, control their losses for a few years, then make it big when the digital TV system, now under construction, provides channel space for hundreds of programs. Meanwhile, depending on where they live, viewers can surf around the dial and find some of these niche-fillers.

Television programs delivered by cable already provide a large proportion of daily viewing in 65 million American homes. This profusion of cable programming will increase enormously as adoption of digital TV technology, now in progress, makes possible the creation of 500 or more channels.

How different this is from the days when the broadcast television industry regarded cable TV as a weak offspring! At its beginning nearly 50 years ago, cable television delivered a limited number of programs to isolated areas plagued by poor over-the-air reception.

When television owners connect their sets to a cable system, they no longer are restricted to receiving a maximum of 12 over-the-air stations for which the standard dial originally provided space. In many cities, only five or six over-the-air channels are available. With cable these same sets may receive 40 or more additional channels, depending on facilities provided by the local cable system.

With abundance comes cost. Cable users must pay monthly service charges, just as they pay their water and electricity bills.

In this chapter, we describe the growth of cable television, what it offers, how it operates, and its economic structure. We also discuss Direct Broadcast Satellite (DBS), a new delivery system that some analysts believe may threaten cable TV, just as cable TV threatens traditional over-the-air television.

## Growth of Cable

Because rugged terrain interferes with over-the-air transmission of television pictures, a method was devised in 1949 to carry TV signals by cable into regions with poor reception. The first Community Antenna Television (CATV) systems were constructed in eastern Pennsylvania and Oregon. Only three to five channels were provided in early CATV operations.

In the intervening decades, technical improvements have revolutionized the TV-by-cable concept. The growth of cable television is inextricably tied to development of satellite transmission.

The cable boom began in 1975 when Time, Inc. leased space on a communication satellite to distribute Home Box Office service, mostly motion pictures at that time, to participating cable system operators. After being plucked from the sky by earth receiving dishes, Home Box Office programs were fed over local cable systems and could be viewed by set owners willing to pay extra for the service. A special connection on the set made viewing of the HBO scrambled signals possible.

Quickly, other cable program producers came into being and distributed their offerings by satellite. Since all television sets manufactured after 1972 were required to have reception capability of at least 20 channels, sufficient positions existed on them to receive numerous additional programs. By the mid-1990s, more than 100 cable television services of varying nature were offered nationwide. The average household can receive about 40 channels.

Figure 11.1 shows how the U.S. cable industry has grown since 1952.

The pioneering role in cable television played by entrepreneur Ted Turner of Atlanta is described in Issue 3.

## Cable TV Programs

Viewers of cable television find two things more evident than when they watch over-the-air stations:

1. A rich variety in programming, with many cable channels aimed at segments of the audience interested in specialized subject matter,

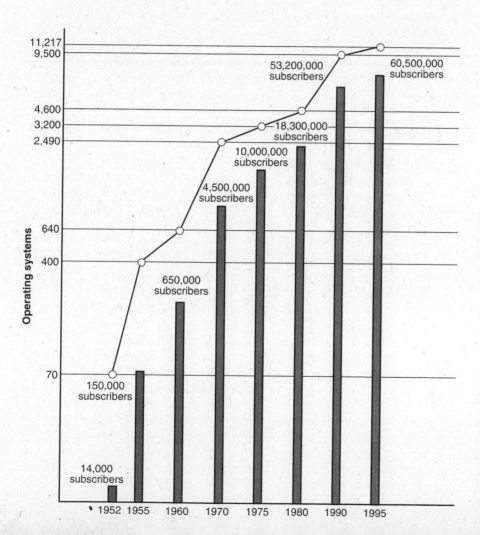

**Figure 11.1**

Growth of the cable TV industry in the United States. (Sources: *Television Fact Book,* National Cable Television Association, Television Digest, Inc., *Broadcasting & Cable Yearbook,* and *Broadcasting & Cable.*)

**Table 11.1**

**Ten Most-Watched Basic Cable TV Channels**

This table reports viewership of the highest-rated basic cable television channels during evening prime-time hours.

|  | Households watching |
|---|---|
| 1. USA | 1,622,000 |
| 2. TBS | 1,260,000 |
| 3. TNT | 997,000 |
| 4. Nickelodeon | 968,000 |
| 5. ESPN | 876,000 |
| 6. CNN | 855,000 |
| 7. Lifetime | 788,000 |
| 8. Discovery | 762,000 |
| 9. TNN | 684,000 |
| 10. A&E | 680,000 |

*Source: A. C. Nielsen, first quarter 1995, published in Broadcasting & Cable.*

ranging from rock and roll music to financial news. So-called narrowcasting to carefully researched portions of the total available audience is playing a growing role in cable TV.

2. Franker sex scenes and more uninhibited language. New viewers of cable wonder how the steamy scenes and strong obscenities contained in some cable shows can be shown on family television screens.

In the answer lies an important point about the difference between broadcast and cable television. Because broadcast television is distributed on the public airwaves, it is subject to such restrictions as the Federal Communications Commission chooses to impose. Cable television has far fewer restrictions.

In addition, the broadcast networks traditionally have sought to avoid public criticism, in particular organized pressure from self-proclaimed morality organizations that might affect their advertising income. When the broadcast networks show R-rated theatrical-release motion pictures, they edit them carefully to remove offensive language and nudity. Cable channels show the films uncensored. Their operators contend that the programs come into the home by invitation and the subscribers pay to obtain them. If subscribers dislike the pay channels that show so-called adult fare, they are free to cancel them. Opponents of such openness attempt to curb it by urging municipalities to file charges under local or state obscenity laws against cable operators that show objectionable material. These efforts have had little success. Efforts to legislate controls at the local, state, or federal levels are challenged vigorously in court.

Aware that such adult programming contributes to cable's popularity, the broadcast networks have loosened their own standards gradually—intensifying sexual situations in comedy series, for example—to determine today's limits of acceptable on-screen conduct. The popular ABC network police drama "NYPD Blue" contains partial nudity and certain obscenities previously banned on the networks. Each show opens with a warning about adult content. After an initial flurry of criticism, the material draws only limited complaints.

In the early years, old movies and reruns of former broadcast network series were the most important aspect of cable TV programming. As more channels developed and competition increased, however, the number of made-for-cable movies and other original programming increased substantially. For example, USA Network committed $140 million during the 1995–1996 season to creation of original programs, including a Saturday night block of comedies. These programs were aimed at the highly prized 18-to-49-age viewers. Other networks announced similar plans.

Motion pictures, both recent releases and old films drawn from the vaults of Hollywood studios, still form a large portion of programming on some channels. So do former network situation comedies obtained from suppliers in the highly competitive syndication market.

## Pay Cable Channels

Cable TV channels fall into two categories, those that include commercials just as over-the-air channels do, and those such as the Disney Channel and Showtime that are free of commercials. The latter, supported entirely by subscriber fees, are known as premium or pay cable channels. About 80 percent of the cable channels carry advertising.

Best-known of the premium channels is Home Box Office, with 17.3 million subscribers. Its owner, Time Warner Inc., also operates the Cinemax channel, with 6.3 million subscribers. Together, the two have revenues of more than $1 billion a year. Showtime is HBO's strongest competitor, with 7.3 million subscribers. The Movie Channel also is a premium channel.

HBO and Showtime show recent theater-release motion pictures, often before the broadcast networks do; taped concerts by popular entertainers; and special events. They also produce their own motion pictures, as well as comedy and drama series that usually are more free-swinging in content than the traditional broadcast series. The Disney Channel, which emphasizes family viewing, is built around films from the Disney studios. The Disney Channel is listed as a basic channel by some local systems and as a pay channel by others.

### Special-Interest Channels

As described at the opening of this chapter, many cable television channels are aimed at target audiences. Their programming appeals to viewers with a special interest or to those who fall into a demographic group particularly appealing to certain advertisers.

Popular music enthusiasts can get their fill of rock and roll and rap on MTV, and advertisers selling goods to a youthful audience find it a splendid selling tool. Country music fans, whose demographic pattern is somewhat older, are reached through the Nashville Network. The Discovery Channel specializes in programs about nature; Nickelodeon appeals to children. Among others are Black Entertainment Television, Fashion Channel, Travel Channel, Interfaith Satellite Network, and Consumer News Business Channel.

**Channel One.**   One special-interest channel, Channel One, sends a daily 12-minute newscast to 12,000 American secondary schools. Since media entrepreneur Christopher Whittle started the project in 1990, it has been a controversial operation, mainly because inside each program it packages two minutes of commercials for products such as Pepsi and Reebok shoes. In return, the present owner, K-111 Communications, leases to each school without charge, a satellite dish, 24-inch color TV set, and videocassette recorder, all valued at $80,000.

The channel employs nine correspondents, ages 18 to 28, to cover social issues of interest to young people. The program is credited with reaching 8 million students, or 40 percent of all teenagers in the country. (See Chapter 6.)

Cable News Network provides a free 15-minute daily newscast without commercials to more than 7000 other schools. Some other cable operators also link the schools to cable without charge.

With so many channels available, competition is intense among them for the limited space available on local cable systems. Many of the newer special-interest channels have difficulty in building an audience.

### More and More Sports

One of cable television's strongest attractions is coverage of sports. Indeed, the ESPN sports network reaches more American homes than any other channel, having become in 1990 the first channel to enter 60 percent of the U.S. homes with TV sets—a total of more than 55 million homes. It covers everything from football games to bodybuilding contests in which heavily muscled women in bikinis flex their biceps.

Regional cable sports networks also operate, primarily to cover professional and college games.

As more and more sporting events are moved from the over-the-air stations to cable outlets, sports enthusiasts have begun to complain that they must pay for TV coverage of games they formerly received free of charge. The most cynical of these critics foresee a day when even the World Series and the Super Bowl will be shown only on cable.

## Cable News Network (CNN)

Discussion of news on cable television focuses automatically on the spectacular success of the Cable News Network (CNN), Ted Turner's 24-hour-per-day newscasts worldwide that equal, and in certain ways exceed, the services provided by the ABC, CBS, and NBC networks.

CNN's around-the-clock operation enables it to offer almost immediate and continuing coverage of breaking stories. Being all-news, it is free from a problem faced by the general networks' news departments—competing for air time with entertainment programs.

The stature of CNN was magnified by its intense coverage of the Persian Gulf War, especially on the first night when CNN reporters broadcast from their Baghdad hotel room vivid audio descriptions of the city being bombed. Its coverage of the O. J. Simpson murder trial earned very high ratings. On major international and domestic stories alike, CNN commits large staffs—for example, 75 people to cover the first South African election after the end of apartheid and 70 to cover the bombing of the Oklahoma City federal building.

Established in 1980 with headquarters in Atlanta, CNN has 1800 employees and 19 foreign bureaus. It is seen in 60 million American homes and in 140 other countries.

The Turner Broadcasting System expanded its Cable News Network International (CNNI) service around the world in the 1990s while facing a new, strong challenge from the highly respected World Service of the British Broadcasting Corporation, which had been mainly a radio operation. CNN opened a financial news network called CNNfn at the start of 1996 in competition with NBC's CNBC business service. Rupert Murdoch's Fox network announced plans for a 24-hour cable newscast in competition with CNN. NBC and Microsoft, the software manufacturer, disclosed plans for an MSNBC network to deliver 24-hour newscasts on a cable channel and simultaneously on the Microsoft online service for computer users. A scarcity of available cable channels presented a difficulty for all these projects.

By the time of its 15th birthday in 1995, the organization was operating the CNN Domestic service, CNN International, Headline News (a 30-minute repeating news summary), Airport Network, CNN Spanish, and CNN Radio (both English and Spanish), and had partial ownership of the German NTV service in Berlin. It operated 20 foreign bureaus and nine in the United States. More than 3 million homes in the United States were receiving the CNN International service.

CNN began its international programming in 1985 when it beamed its 24-hour service to Great Britain and Western Europe. Developing close ties with the former Soviet government, Turner in 1989 reached an agreement to uplink CNN programs on Intersputnik's Stratisoner 12 satellite in stationary orbit over the Indian Ocean, thereby reaching the Indian subcontinent, Africa, and Southeast Asia. CNN already had been carried on the Pan American satellite to Central and South America, and to Europe and the Far East on Intelsat satellites.

Soon CNN was being received by an estimated 75 million households via paid cable or satellite subscription. Millions more viewers picked up its signals illicitly or in excerpted form via commercial TV stations that had contracts with CNN. CNN and sports channel ESPN began using an Indonesian satellite to expand coverage even farther.

Because of CNN's near-global coverage, high credibility, and ready access to important newsmakers, its reports were viewed regularly by high government officials in many countries; they frequently provided reactions to international news happenings before turning to diplomatic channels. "We're part of the agenda-making process," said Ed Turner, executive vice-president for newsgathering.

### Local News Shows

Cable's possibilities as a purveyor of local news and advertising remain largely unfulfilled, although a few cable systems have begun to make greater efforts in this area.

**Electronic newspaper**
Delivery of a newspaper's content on a television or computer screen rather than on newsprint

Numerous newspapers, hoping to establish a foothold in cable, leased channels on cable systems and offered news in various forms. Mostly they drew on the pools of news gathered by their newspaper staffs, offering it on the screen either in text block form or with live reporters. Some developed advertising on cable tied to their newspaper advertising. In general, these programs failed to attract sufficient followings, and few newspapers have continued their efforts. In New York, however, Time Warner opened a 24-hour news channel in 1992 that included a 45-minute newscast by the New York *Times*.

Some enthusiastic futurists foresaw the day when the *electronic newspaper*—that is, news delivered on the home TV screen—would replace printed newspapers. Since many American newspapers now put their contents on online computer services, an upsurge in cable TV newscasts seems unlikely.

## The Economics of Cable Television

The fundamental differences between a television station and a local cable system are these:

- The television station, licensed and rather loosely regulated by the Federal Communications Commission, broadcasts programs over the air on a single channel. It must have its license renewed by the FCC every seven years.

- The local cable system is essentially a distributor, not a creator. Although not subject to FCC licensing, it must obtain a franchise to operate in a designated area from the city council or similar government agency.

The system receives programs by satellite or over-the-air antenna from the various networks and stations with which it is associated. It funnels these signals into its delivery system of underground cables or overhead wires, through which they are carried simultaneously on numerous channels to homes. The number of these channels each family can view on its TV screen depends on the fees it is willing to pay.

Creating a cable system is expensive because of the cost of laying its wires and cables, as much as $100,000 a mile in some urban areas. For the right to distribute a program service, the system usually pays the originating network an agreed fee per subscriber, often 10 to 15 cents. Some networks may give their programs to cable systems in order to increase the audience for the commercials they carry.

More than 11,000 cable systems serve the United States, ranging in size from a few hundred subscribers to many thousands. A system's income is obtained from the fees it charges subscribers, plus money received from sale of local advertising.

## Wireless Cable

Because installing underground cable costs so much, some cable systems use a method called *wireless cable*, a contradiction in terms. How can a cable system exist without wires? It can't. Instead of delivering programs to homes by underground cable, these systems transmit them through the air by microwave. Subscribers have set-top decoders that transform the incoming microwave signals into TV pictures. Federal law permits these wireless cable systems to use regular cable TV programming.

How much use the wireless cable method will receive is uncertain. It can carry fewer channels than the digital TV method now under development, but may attract numerous users as an interim method. One factor aiding the system is the investments made in it by the regional Bell telephone companies, which seek economical ways to break into the video delivery business in competition with established cable systems. The telecos, as they are nicknamed, like the fact that the wireless system saves the cost of laying cable. (The telephone companies' effort to enter the video business is discussed later in this chapter.)

## Cable Service Packages

Cable services are sold on an add-on basis. First comes a basic package of channels for a fixed monthly fee; this is the bread-and-butter business of

Main studio of the Cable News Network in Atlanta, Georgia, from which news is broadcast worldwide by satellite. CNN's around-the-world service has enabled it to break important stories and provide continuous coverage of them. The network won praise in particular for its coverage of the Persian Gulf War. (Photo courtesy CNN)

a cable operator. On top of this package, the subscriber may purchase one or all of the supplementary channels for an additional fee. In addition, the subscriber may subscribe to one or all of the premium channels such as HBO. This is known as *tiering*.

**Tiering**
System under which a cable subscriber purchases a basic package of channels, then pays extra for additional channel reception as desired

Here is how the system works, as exemplified by a system serving a Western urban area:

1. *Limited Basic Service*. Consists of 16 channels, including local network and independent broadcasting stations, C-Span, a national entertainment channel, two superchannels, a Spanish language channel, and a religious channel.

2. *Standard Service*. Adds 12 national entertainment and information channels.

3. *Expanded Plus*. Adds four entertainment channels.

4. *Premium Channels*. HBO, Showtime, The Movie Channel, and Cinemax, at an individual additional charge.

A subscriber receiving all services, including the premium channels, pays a monthly charge of $66.69, based on fees under the federal rate control law of 1992, described in the following section. In addition, the system offers pay-per-view programs such as professional basketball games on a fluctuating fee basis.

## Control of Cable Rates

Under the Cable Communications Policy Act of 1984, the control local governments once had over fees charged subscribers by the franchise holders in their jurisdictions was eliminated. Congress permitted the cable systems to charge whatever they desired.

The cable industry contended that this freedom would enable it to pay for better programming. Its spokespersons point to the broader range of programs developed since the act was passed as proof that deregulation of pricing was beneficial to viewers.

Three other trends, however, developed so strongly after deregulation that critics charged the cable industry with creating an uncontrolled monopoly that gouged subscribers and placed the power to decide what would be shown on cable into the hands of relatively few corporations. These developments were:

1. Cable system operators raised their prices. Nationwide, basic cable rates rose from $10.60 to $18.84 in the six years following deregulation in 1984.

2. Large corporations purchased scores of cable systems around the country, enabling only a few executives to choose what channels millions of subscribers could see. The largest of these multiple-system operators (MSOs), Tele-Communications Inc., has 14.7 million subscribers—nearly 25 percent of all the cable customers in the United States. Time Warner is second with 11.5 million.

3. Cable system operators became investors in the networks that produced the programs their systems showed. Called *vertical integration*, this arrangement was seen by critics as part of a monopoly system. (See the discussion in Issue 3.)

**Multiple-system operator**
Company that operates more than one cable television system

Thus it was to the operators' advantage to provide a place on their systems for channels in which they had a financial interest, possibly squeezing out other networks whose product might be of greater value to viewers. Also, these system operators could give their own networks the choice low-numbered positions on the dial.

Despite heavy pressure by the cable industry, Congress overrode a veto by President Bush in 1992 and enacted a law giving the Federal Communications Commission authority to regulate basic cable rates on a regional basis. The purpose was to stop the steep rise in basic rates, increase competition, and improve service. Charges for premium channels such as HBO were left unregulated. Under industry pressure, Congress agreed in the 1996 telecommunications bill to eliminate all restrictions on cable TV rates within three years. Cable systems with fewer than 50,000 subscribers were immediately freed from rate controls.

## The Must-Carry Dispute

**Must-carry**
Former FCC rule, struck down by the courts, requiring a cable system to carry programs of all over-the-air stations in its area

At one time the FCC required each cable system to carry the programming of all broadcast television stations within its area. On smaller systems with only a dozen channels, this requirement left little room to include popular cable networks in their service.

The U.S. Circuit Court of Appeals threw out this "must-carry" rule in 1986 as a violation of the systems' First Amendment rights. Soon after that, switching their position as TV economics changed, network affiliates and other local stations that had supported the "must-carry" rule asked Congress for the right to collect fees from cable systems for use of their programs.

The 1992 cable re-regulation law decreed that cable TV systems must carry most major local over-the-air station transmissions at the request of the broadcasters. It offered local stations the alternative of negotiating with their cable system a license fee, called a retransmission consent, that the cable system would pay for carrying a local station's programs. Legal challenges were filed against this plan, complicating even further the complex battle for future control of the industry. Some broadcasting stations have solved the problem by launching local cable channels over which they retransmit their network and other programs.

## Advertising on Cable

Large national advertisers were slow to use cable because its audience is so fragmented that they have difficulty in reaching the mass audiences they need. Advertising volume has grown, however, as the cable audience expands and certain popular programs have begun to draw audiences that approach those of the lowest-ranked broadcast network shows in size. Advertisers also like the ability to reach target audiences such as the youth market through the MTV music channel, and sports enthusiasts through the ESPN sports channel. Some cable channels leave brief gaps in their programming, during which cable system operators can insert commercials from their local merchants. This puts them in competition with radio and television stations, and newspapers as well, for the local advertiser's dollar.

In order to give advertisers better information about cable audiences, Nielsen has added some cable channels to its people-meter rating service. (See Chapter 10.)

## The 500-Channel Vision

As explained in Chapter 1, the massive expansion in the number of television channels eventually will be achieved by the process of digital compression. This requires nationwide installation of fiber optics, a huge and extremely expensive construction operation already in progress.

Anticipation of eventual availability of 500 channels or even more is the force driving the multibillion-dollar jockeying for position on the information superhighway by multimedia corporations, discussed in Issue 3. The fully realized dream lies in the future, however, well into the 21st century.

Behind the hype and the sweeping predictions of interactive wonders lie three large problems:

- Technical difficulties and construction time
- Cost

A Time Warner executive estimated at a 1995 National Cable Television Association panel that a cable system would spend between $900 and $1,000 to deliver the digitalized fiber optic TV service to each home served, plus another $600 to deliver personal computer service.

To recover such an investment, the cable company obviously would need to charge its subscribers high fees.

- Consumer acceptance

How many cable subscribers will desire the galaxy of services the cable systems eventually will be able to deliver? Small-scale preliminary trials by companies have not disclosed overwhelming consumer demand. Industry experts generally predict slow expansion of the superservices, in compact urban areas at first, governed by consumer demand.

## Ownership Consolidation

More and more cable systems have fallen into the hands of fewer and fewer corporations. By 1995, the ten largest cable system operators served 44.5 million of the almost 61 million cable TV subscribers, or 72 percent. These figures were published by *Broadcasting & Cable*.

As the big multiple system operators (MSOs) bought out smaller operators, they found themselves owning widely scattered properties. This led to a move called *clustering*. This is an effort by a company, through trading and buying, to consolidate the systems it owns into contiguous groups in urban and adjacent areas. Such clustering improves administration and strengthens a company's competitive position.

The Big Three television networks, ABC, CBS, and NBC, long were forbidden by the Federal Communications Commission from owning cable television systems. That ban was cancelled by the FCC in 1992.

## The "Baby Bells" Move In

Hanging over the cable system operators as they maneuvered and expanded was realization that the regional Bell telephone companies soon would compete with them in delivering television programs to the home.

Strenuous opposition by cable operators before the Federal Communications Commission delayed actual delivery of video programs by the telecos. The FCC, however, showed its intention to let the phone companies compete with the cable systems.

Simultaneously, cable system operators developed plans to enter the telephone business, using their newly installed fiber optics lines. By 1995, an estimated 40 percent of the cable system lines still were old-style copper, and parts of the new fiber optics lines needed additional upgrading. The time was within sight, however, when a home consumer might receive phone calls through a cable company or cable TV programs through a telephone company.

These are the basic elements in the complex situation:

1. A federal court in 1984 broke up the gigantic American Telephone and Telegraph Company in an antitrust action, removing its local telephone operations from its long-distance service and equipment manufacturing. The local services were assigned to seven independent regional phone companies known as the "baby Bells." The consent decree forbade the regional companies from originating and delivering their own information over their wires and from manufacturing telephone equipment. They were limited to being common carriers of other people's information.

2. Subsequently, the court order was changed, permitting the regional companies to enter the information service business. In addition, the U.S. Senate voted to allow them into manufacturing.

3. The Federal Communications Commission in 1992 permitted telephone companies to offer a "video dialtone"—that is, to carry television programming created by others over telephone lines. The FCC urged Congress to repeal a restriction in the 1984 Cable Communications Policy Act that prohibited phone companies from creating and transmitting their own TV programs. The commission also moved to permit cable TV operators to enter the telephone business.

4. Fearing the loss of advertising revenue because the phone companies would deliver their own electronic Yellow Pages advertising into homes, the newspaper industry lobbied Congress for legislation forbidding the phone companies from entering the information business. Such legislation would override the court order. The prospect of having phone companies become electronic newsgatherers and dispensers also disturbed newspaper publishers.

The first actual baby Bell entry into the news field occurred in 1992 when Pacific Bell began its Daily Reporter service. For a small monthly fee, telephone subscribers could call in for headline reports of recorded, updated international, financial, and sports news over their regular telephone lines. Significantly, Pacific Bell's partner in the project was a newspaper organization, Dow Jones & Co., publisher of the *Wall Street Journal*, which supplied the news information.

At Tele-Communications Inc.'s National Digital Television Center near Denver, video and audio signals are compressed into digital form for worldwide transmission by satellite. (Courtesy National Digital Television Center)

One charge by the cable operators was that the telephone companies might use income from the regular telephone service to subsidize development of their video service. The FCC said it would guard against such a move.

Before they could develop their video service fully, the baby Bells, like the cable operators, faced the problem of laying fiber optics lines. In the interim they could use wireless cable or some other method. They also had the problem of obtaining television programs to deliver through their video dialtone.

## Direct Broadcast Satellite—Cable's Rival

Within eight months of its 1994 introduction in the United States, direct broadcast satellite (DBS) service had signed up a million subscribers. That wasn't much compared to the 61 million cable television subscribers, but enough to establish DBS as an attractive, growing competitor of cable TV.

As explained in Chapter 1, in DBS service, programs are beamed up to a satellite, just as in cable television. The satellite bounces them down directly to home rooftop receiving dishes only 18 inches in diameter. This eliminates the middleman role of the cable TV delivery systems.

Direct broadcast's digitalized signals use the high-powered K-band satellites rather than the C-band variety used by the older style 10-foot-diameter receiving dishes familiar in rural areas. DBS delivers 175 channels, far more than normal cable TV is capable of before completion of the fiber optics system.

One negative factor for DBS is that it cannot deliver local cable channels, so the subscriber must have a rooftop antenna or subscribe to basic cable service. Another problem is the cost of receiving equipment. Efforts to solve this problem were being made.

DIRECTV, owned by the Hughes Electronic subsidiary of General Motors, was the first DBS service in operation. Competitors soon followed as public interest in the direct-to-the-home service grew.

## Other Transmission Methods

### Teletext and Videotex

Two more sophisticated methods of cable information delivery now under development, with a few experimental systems in existence, may enlarge cable's role as a news medium. They are *teletext* and *videotex*.

**Teletext**
System of delivering news and other information to a television screen from which the viewer can select certain portions to watch

**Teletext.** This one-way service transmits text news, graphics, advertising, and service information over a cable channel or over the vertical blanking interval of a standard television signal. The vital difference is that teletext adds the element of *viewer selectivity*. Viewers have special keypads. By punching certain keys, they can call up on the screen the type of news or information they desire, chosen from an index shown on the screen. Hundreds of pages of material are in the electronic bank, awaiting the viewer's selection. Each page is kept up-to-date.

A viewer may, for example, wish for a current report on stock market prices. He or she can call up the stock pages immediately without having to wait for other news and information to scroll past first. Teletext viewers pay for the service. Usually they are billed according to the number of pages they call up.

One unanswered question about teletext is both economic and psychological: Will enough viewers be willing to pay a substantial price to receive on-the-screen information that in considerable part will be available to them in print when the next edition of the newspaper is delivered? So far they have not been.

**Videotex**
Two-way interactive television service in which the viewer can respond to material shown on the screen and conduct business or other transactions

**Videotex.** This more complex and expensive system provides viewers with *two-way interactive* service. Using either cable or telephone lines, the viewer can connect the home television terminal to a central computer and either call up a broad range of news and information or conduct business transactions.

*Broadcasting & Cable* illustrates the difference between teletext and *videotex* with this example: "A teletext service might allow a user to access [call onto the screen] an airline's schedule, but a videotex user could not only access that schedule but also make his reservation, transfer money from his bank account to pay for the ticket, then buy a new wardrobe for his planned trip—all without leaving his seat."

The videotex customer is charged for the amount of use made of the system. Videotex has been called the Cadillac of cable information systems and teletext the Chevrolet. Although several major corporations have spent millions of dollars in developing videotex systems, participation by consumers and advertisers has been disappointing so far. The Times Mirror Company and Knight-Ridder Newspapers, Inc., closed their Gateway and Viewtron projects in 1986 because of heavy losses. Representatives of the two companies agreed that their subscribers were more interested in exchanging messages with each other electronically than in receiving news.

Videotex has failed as a news medium in the United States because of public apathy. It does have a role, perhaps eventually a substantial one, in providing special services such as banking and commercial transactions and certain categories of limited-interest information.

### Satellite Master Antenna Systems (SMATV)

These operate as cable television systems do, with one exception. The ordinary cable system obtains a local government franchise to serve an extended area, while an SMATV system operates only on private property such as an apartment building complex or mobile home park. The system distributes programs only within the confines of its private property zone, picking up signals directly from satellites.

### Low-Power Television (LPTV)

As mentioned earlier, recent FCC rulings make possible new low-power television stations permitted to relay TV signals and to originate programming. These stations have secondary status with power too low to interfere with existing UHF and VHF stations. Their role is to serve small areas and supplement present television programming. About 1700 low-power stations were on the air by 1996, most of them offering old syndicated series and movies.

### Videoconferencing

By using temporarily leased satellite circuits, companies can hold press conferences or business meetings at one site and have them seen and heard at numerous points, perhaps in several countries. Two-way telephone connections, or even two-way satellite transmissions, allow participants at distant points to respond to those at the point of origin. Use of videoconferencing (also known as teleconferencing) has been growing steadily.

**Videoconferencing** Linking groups of people by satellite television, usually for business purposes. Also called *teleconferencing*

## Points to Remember

1. What was the original purpose of cable television?
2. Why may cable television show more nudity and carry heavier profanity than over-the-air television does?
3. What pay-cable channel has the largest number of subscribers? How many does it have?

4. Can you name three cable channels targeted to serve a special interest of an audience segment?

5. Discuss some reasons for the success of Cable Network News.

6. Cable systems use a "tiering" method in charging their customers for service. How does this function?

7. What is the difference between wireless cable and regular cable television?

8. Why have the cable television and newspaper industries opposed allowing the telephone industry to deliver its own TV programs and news into U.S. homes?

9. Why is direct broadcast satellite (DBS) regarded as a rival of cable television?

## Media Questions to Think About

1. Should warnings about obscene language, violence, and sexual situations be shown at the start of possibly offensive cable television programs?

2. Which do you find more convenient and satisfactory for your needs, CNN newscasts or the half-hour evening news programs of the three major broadcast networks?

3. Are you willing to pay substantially higher cable TV bills to receive a large number of cable channels beyond the number you now receive?

# CHAPTER TWELVE
## Video

## "Let Me Outta Here"

Do you want to teach your parrot to talk? Simple! Just place its cage five feet in front of the TV screen and show the bird a training video.

According to its advertising, the parrot-prattle tape coaxes the bird to repeat 12 popular phrases by showing it bright images of macaws and cockatoos while repeating the words continuously.

If the vivid plumage and sassy slang motivate your parrot, it will graduate from video school able to squawk such sentences as "Give me a kiss" and "I'm melting." If an A student, it also will proclaim, "Go ahead: make my day."

"Your bird can have a blast," the advertisement assures the video purchaser, "and you'll have hours of fun listening to your pet."

Video educates people, too. If you are tired of kissing your parrot and your muscles ache from video exercises, pop a tape into the VCR and the world widens. A few learning opportunities await you: "Do You Want to be a Gambler?," *Cosmopolitan*'s weight-loss "Seven Pounds in Seven Days," Renee Taylor's "Yoga, the Art of Living," and "Jazzercise" with Juli Shapperd Missett.

Or maybe it would be easier to slump back and watch a video movie.

Videotape was a mass communications phenomenon during the 1980s. It turned the family living room into a private movie theater with "free" popcorn. It brought the gleam of dollar signs to the eyes of Hollywood producers when they found that their archives of old films were like gold mines. For television fans, the videocassette recorder (VCR) created the handy tool of time-shifting. With it they could record favorite TV programs while away from home, then play them at their convenience.

The abundance of home videos available for rental or purchase has given seekers of entertainment an enormous range of choice. Video also has emerged as a significant form of education for those who desire information and guidance in many fields. Approximately three-fourths of American homes have VCRs.

## Video Bursts Forth

Introduced in 1976, the VCR at first was an expensive novelty for electronics enthusiasts. But as the price per set fell from $1000 to $200 and the number of available taped movie cassettes multiplied, sales soared. Within a period of about five years, a major method of mass communication developed, its limits still undetermined.

Video is a hybrid of more traditional methods of communication. The name itself, which derives from the Latin word *vidére* (to see), was used originally to describe the visual portion of broadcast television. Now it has taken on a life of its own. Video uses the equipment of television to show products of the motion picture industry. Because video offers the same movies as pay television, often sooner and more cheaply, it has cut heavily into the growth of the cable television industry. The tapes video stores rent and sell are packaged to resemble books and increasingly contain material transferred from books (see the discussion later in this chapter).

Yet video is more than a borrower. A body of original material available only on videocassettes is growing steadily, going direct from the creator to the home viewer. This is where the most intriguing potential of video lies. Its possibilities as an educator and persuader are still being explored.

For viewers, video is alluring because it enables them to watch what they wish, when they wish, and to view their favorite tapes over and over again. They can do so in the privacy and comfort of their homes. With video, users control their own viewing without being subjected to the dictates of television programmers.

## How the Market Grew

Many television enthusiasts began to build libraries of TV programs they had recorded on their VCRs. Innovative entrepreneurs wondered, would VCR owners also play and collect videotaped versions of popular movies if they could rent or purchase them? The marketeers obtained rights to a few motion pictures and to some films no longer covered by copyright restrictions, converted the movies to videotaped form, packaged the tape cassettes attractively, and offered them to the public. Results were spectacular.

The boom was stimulated by a U.S. Supreme Court decision in 1984 stating that Americans are legally entitled to videotape shows and movies from television for personal use. With a mass market thus hastily created, producers of VCRs and videotapes scrambled to fill the demand. Similar upsurges in popularity of video occurred in Great Britain, on the European continent, in Japan, in the Middle East, and in other areas around the world.

There was a product and a demand. But no obvious sales outlets for videotapes existed in the traditional pattern of American retailing. This void did not last long as video shops blossomed in every city. Supermarkets and department stores installed video departments. Some 27,000 retail video sales outlets soon opened, many of them of the small "mom-and-pop store" variety. As in other fields of retailing, mass market operators and chain stores moved into the business, and many small shops were squeezed out because they could not afford to carry sufficient inventory.

## Hollywood Cashes In

Video versions of motion pictures have become a critical part of the moviemaking business. According to statistics gathered by *The Economist*, home video provides 48 percent of Hollywood's revenue. Americans rent 90 million videos a week, and foreign rentals are huge as well. The financing of a motion picture is based in part on predictions of its video sales. Films that lose money at the boxoffice frequently are turned into profit-makers by their video sales.

Film stars also are trying to get pieces of the video action. Those with big names and boxoffice clout sometimes demand a percentage of video sales as part of their compensation.

Both the planning and production of today's movies are influenced by the home video market. Stories are selected and shaped with the demographics of the home audience in mind as well as those of the theater audiences. Some directors shoot movie scenes in a form that can easily be cropped for the small TV screen. Often video rights to a picture are sold by the producer before the cameras roll and help pay for the film's production.

With VCR owners hungry for movie tapes to view, motion picture studios and television show producers dug deep into their files for old material to package and release. Hundreds of long-forgotten movies returned to life. Adventure series, situation comedies, and collections of

A customer decides which motion picture videotape to rent for playing at home on a videocassette recorder. Thousands of video stores opened during the mid-1980s to rent or sell tapes when the VCR won swift acceptance as a home entertainment machine. (Monkmeyer)

music videos that had disappeared from the television screens were resurrected and distributed as videocassettes. In fact, a two-hour videotape of the popular NBC police show "Miami Vice" appeared while the TV series was still running in network prime time.

The raid on the motion picture libraries largely depleted the backlog accumulated for 50 years or more. Theatrical releases today are mostly of recent films.

**Window**
In video trade talk, length of time between release of a movie to theaters and its first release for home viewing

While producers enjoyed their bonus profits, theater operators grumbled about the "window," the length of time between the original release of a movie to theaters and its subsequent release for home viewing. Filmmakers established a six-month window, and for a while this time span was quite well observed.

Warner Home Video broke the pattern in 1989, however, by releasing its spectacularly successful movie *Batman* as a video less than five months after its appearance in theaters. With an October release at a sale price of $24.95, Warner aimed to cash in on the Christmas trade. This angered theater owners, who wanted a window longer than six months, not shorter.

Some studios release their films to cable operators for showing on a pay-per-view basis on the same date they release them to video stores. Others wait 30 to 60 days.

## Classic Films Saved

The studios' rush to release old pictures has had the valuable cultural benefit of making classic films easily available to today's audiences. As an example, in 1995 on the 60th anniversary of Ingrid Bergman's first film, World Artists Home Video released videos of eight Bergman movies in a package called "Ingrid Bergman in Sweden," a treat for film students.

Today, shoppers in video stores find videotapes of motion pictures that were never shown in movie theaters. Such straight-to-video marketing, done at first with low-budget films of marginal value, is being used now for better-quality pictures. The practice reduces the marketing expense of a film and sometimes has striking success. Disney released *The Return of Jafar*, a sequel to *Aladdin*, direct to stores, and the film sold so well that it made the list of all-time top ten videos in sales.

Sex-oriented movies, the outright X-rated pornographic pictures as well as softer R-rated ones, are big attractions in video. Renting or purchasing porn films for home viewing can be done at many video stores, although some do keep their X-rated films in semi-enclosed areas restricted to customers aged 18 and over. The availability of pornography in the parlor has caused a widespread closing of adult movie theaters from lack of business and a dropoff in street sales of magazines featuring

Deviating from normal industry procedures, Walt Disney released the motion picture *The Return of Jafar* direct to the video stores without a previous showing in theaters. The film, a sequel to *Aladdin,* had strong video sales.

nude photographs. *Playboy* has attempted to offset this loss by issuing monthly videocassettes of its nude centerfold Playmates simultaneously with their appearance in the magazine. It also has a cable TV network.

Of course, movies have been coming into homes for more than 30 years over the broadcast television channels, and more recently over cable television. Movies shown on regular TV are interrupted by commercials, however, and often reduced in length to fit broadcast requirements. Although movies on pay channels usually are uncut, uncensored, and free of commercials, on any given evening the choice of films is limited.

**Time-shifting**
Recording a television program on a videocassette recorder for viewing at a later time

Even when VCR owners record broadcast TV movies for later replay—an action called *time-shifting*—they can avoid the commercials by "zapping" them with the fast-forward switch that skips over them. This practice disturbs advertisers, who see their expensive messages being blacked out by the audience.

## How the Industry Operates

"Going to the movies" at home is easy for VCR owners. They rent or purchase tapes, pop the cassettes into the VCR, and watch the film on the television screen. Behind this simple act, however, is a complicated system of marketing that continues to evolve as the potential of the video field becomes better understood.

Film producers sell the video rights to their pictures to distributors, many of which are divisions of major motion picture companies. A distributor prepares the videotape version of a movie, packages it, and sells copies through wholesalers to the retail video shops. The shopkeeper either sells copies of the film to customers or rents them for a daily fee. As competition has intensified and the supply of available films has multiplied, rental prices have dropped as low as 99 cents per day for nonprime pictures. The film producer usually receives nothing from the rental fees. After it has earned substantial rental fees, the store may offer the used tape for sale for as little as $7.95.

At first, sale prices for new movie releases were high, around $80 per copy, but prices dropped precipitously and sales volume rose. *Beverly Hills Cop*, starring Eddie Murphy, was the first videocassette to sell more than a million copies. Rental fees substantially exceed the sales market, but the gap is shrinking as greater emphasis is placed on sales promotion (Disney in particular encourages the purchase of its family videos such as *The Lion King* and *Pocahontas* as gifts and as an addition to home video libraries). (See Advertising and Marketing later in this chapter.)

Moviemakers complain about widespread pirating of their films on videocassettes, especially in foreign countries. Highly organized gangs of pirates make illegal prints either by gaining possession of a theatrical print or taping the movie as it is shown in a theater. For example, unauthorized videotapes of major new American movies have been distributed in Thailand within four days after the movies opened in the United States.

With a strenuous marketing campaign, Walt Disney studios promoted sale of the videotape of its motion picture *Pocahontas* for family video libraries.

Placing a secret code marking on each theatrical print has enabled producers to gain some control over the pirating. By checking the code marking, which shows through in pirate copies, detectives can discover which theatrical print has been stolen or duplicated.

## Video's Other Roles

Video is best known for entertainment, through the showing of movies and television programs. Its potential goes much further, however. As videomakers expand their craft, it is playing increasingly significant social roles as educator, stimulator of psychological and physical self-help, and commercial and political persuader.

An upsurge in special-interest videotapes is occurring, with material drawn from a wide range of fields. Often these informational tapes are viewed in meeting rooms by professional, student, community service, and other groups concerned with the particular subject matter.

Frequently videotapes of this nature are sold not in video stores but at points where persons with a particular interest gather—Esther Williams's "Swim Baby Swim" is available in swimming pool equipment shops, for example.

### Videos As News

An unanticipated bonus of the video boom has been creation of thousands of amateur camera operators who, with their ever-present camcorders, happen to be at the scenes of shootings, fires, wrecks, and other unscheduled news events. Often they turn their tapes over to TV news

## BRIDE SAYS "I DO" TWICE

Mrs. Rita Lockett of Torquay, England, was such an enthusiast for video that she restaged her daughter's $35,000 wedding and reception two months later because she hated the video made of the first ceremony.

She asked the 200 guests at the original wedding to wear the same clothes for the replay. Every aspect of the wedding in a luxury hotel was repeated exactly, except for one thing. She hired a new camera operator.

organizations. The tape of the Rodney King beating by Los Angeles police is the most famous example of an amateur's work. The fatal explosion in the gun turret of the battleship U.S.S. Iowa provided another opportune videotape that, when it appeared on television, helped the world to visualize what happened.

ABC's "America's Funniest Home Videos" has become a highly popular weekly television show. The show contains choice excerpts from more than 1000 tapes contributed each day.

Terrorists have used videotape for propaganda and ransom tools. One grim example: the videotape showing U.S. Marine Lieutenant Colonel William R. Higgins dangling from a rope after being hanged by his abductors in Lebanon. International uses of video are discussed in Chapter 17.

### Self-Help and How-To Tapes

Jane Fonda scored the first mass market success in nonentertainment video with her "Jane Fonda Workout" tape. That and eight more Fonda exercise programs together sold more than 4 million copies. Competing exercise leaders soon sought portions of the lucrative market. A videotape of O. J. Simpson leading an exercise class became important evidence in his trial. The prosecution showed it in court to rebut a defense claim that Simpson was too crippled with arthritis to have committed a double murder.

Other typical videotapes of this nature include "Golf My Way," sold in pro shops; Phyllis Diller's "How to Have a Money-Making Garage Sale"; and "Let's Learn How to Dance."

### Training Tapes

Corporations have found videotapes to be excellent tools for training new employees, as well as for delivering annual reports, corporate messages, and the like to staff members. Trade associations use them to instruct and stimulate their members; medical organizations use them to demonstrate new techniques. Additional uses are being created constantly.

Companies with predominantly young employees, such as McDonald's, deliver their training messages in music video form—for example, McDonald's "Clean It," which, set to a fast beat, reminds the food chain's workers to maintain specified cleanliness standards.

## Children's Programs

Inevitably called *kid vid*, thousands of video titles for children are available on store shelves. Although many of these are cartoons from TV and visual versions of traditional children's stories such as "Cinderella," a growing body of material is designed to instruct young viewers, usually with entertaining graphic and story-telling techniques.

**Kid vid**
Slang description of videotapes designed for viewing by children

## Education and the Courts

The use of videotape as a teaching tool is obvious, and its appearance in the classroom, in study at home, and before professional groups is expanding.

A frequent criticism of the televised or videotaped classroom lecture is that students cannot interrupt with questions, as most instructors permit them to do in live lectures. This difficulty has been overcome in some classes by having instructors or teaching assistants stop the tapes at critical points for questions and discussion.

Video distribution houses offer in-depth taped studies of issues and techniques for classroom use to supplement or replace printed material. Typical of these are a five-part examination of the Watergate scandal, narrated by Daniel Schorr, and the BBC TV Production Training Course, a 13-part series. Single-tape presentations on subjects ranging from Winston Churchill's leadership methods to collections of outstanding TV commercials are on the market.

Closely related to education is use of videotapes in legal proceedings. Forty-seven states permit cameras to record courtroom action; also, numerous judges will accept carefully prepared videotapes of depositions, reconstructions of incidents, and summaries of a plaintiff's case. Such taping can save the courts' time. Often it is expensive, however, and critics are concerned that affluent plaintiffs who can afford the expense may have an advantage over opponents who cannot. Videotape of the crime scene, taken by TV news photographers, was admitted as evidence in the Simpson trial to show movements of the police investigators.

Use of videotaped testimony by child victims in molestation cases, in order to spare them the psychological ordeal of testifying in open court, has been sharply debated by the legal profession. Some attorneys contend that this method is unfair to defendants because their attorneys lack adequate opportunity to discredit the children's testimony in face-to-face questioning. Trial judges face a delicate problem of balancing the welfare of child witnesses against the rights of defendants.

## Video and Books

The wedding of book publishing (printed words and still pictures) to video (spoken words and moving pictures) has taken place, but the partners are uncertain how the marriage will develop. Stakes are high, but many persons involved in the world of books are unenthusiastic about the pairing. Because viewing and listening require less mental challenge than reading, they worry that children will fail to develop reading skills and adults will allow theirs to stagnate.

Simon & Schuster became the first major publishing house to enter the video market, in 1984, with taped versions of books, especially of the how-to variety. The publishing house also created new material for video, including a 45-minute tape made in association with the American Cancer Society titled "How to Quit Smoking."

Experiments in marketing book videotapes through bookstores have been made, with varying results. Publishers have searched their backlists for titles that might effectively be converted to video form.

Public and academic libraries began circulating videocassettes in the mid-1980s, and their patrons responded enthusiastically. Public libraries circulate informational cassettes and some entertainment cassettes just as they do books, except that loan periods are shorter. Some libraries do so without charge. One typical library in a medium-sized city reported that the 1000 cassettes it stocks account for 14 percent of items checked out; the tapes are taken out 70,000 times a year.

Some more traditionalist librarians are less than enthusiastic about providing this service, although it draws patrons who have not previously used a library.

## Advertising and Marketing

Once they realized the potential of the video market, advertisers sought ways to deliver their sales messages to the captive audience it represents. Fearing that insertion of direct, hard-sell commercials might irritate home viewers who had paid to see the videotapes, the advertisers at first used a soft approach intended to create awareness without stirring resentment.

The soft sell turned hard in 1987 when Pepsi Cola placed a direct sales commercial in the video version of Paramount's popular movie *Top Gun.* Consumer resistance proved to be slight.

That opened the doors for heavy advertising and mass marketing in video. More and more videotapes contained commercial messages. Companies that placed advertisements helped to promote the videos. Tapes for children sometimes contained two minutes of advertising, primarily for toys.

This trend led to the marketers' spectacular success with the video of *E.T.: The Extra-Terrestrial.* The cassette version of the movie sold 15 million copies in three months after its release, more than double the sale of any other home video. The video contained a Pepsi commercial, and Pepsi offered buyers a $5 rebate on the video's already low $24.95 price. Pepsi and MCA Home Video, the distributor, together put $25 million into promoting the video.

Distributors of video movies often place promotions for other films at the start of the tapes, much like previews in a theater.

## Politics and Video

Since politics involves persuasion, and video's potential as a persuader is high, use of videos as campaign tools has become widespread. Some political videos are informative and fair, others grossly slanted and filled with misrepresentations. They resemble other campaign materials in this respect. Use of videos, some of them with quite sophisticated production values, was widespread in the 1994 election at both state and federal levels.

Many campaign directors planning videos studied a controversial early use of videos to defeat a candidate in California, where voters in 1986 rejected state Supreme Court Chief Justice Rose Bird's re-election attempt. Bird was unpopular because the court she led had overturned many death sentences.

Some of her opponents distributed 10,000 copies of a 28-minute videotape that included vivid descriptions of murder cases in which death sentences were overturned. The tape quoted a county prosecutor about the court: "It's the laughingstock of the United States."

The tapes were distributed to video rental outlets, libraries, private individuals, and law enforcement agencies. Anti-Bird campaigners organized private parties to see the tape. How much that videotape hurt Bird's campaign is uncertain.

This episode also raised a question of propriety. Almost certainly no commercial television station would show such a politically biased program. Yet this "attack" video when shown on a home TV screen to politically inexperienced viewers took on the aura of a genuine television show, with no possibility of a rebuttal. In fact, the tape did include one serious factual error.

### Principal Uses

Today political videos are used for three main purposes:

1. *Recruit volunteer campaign workers.* These videos are used to stimulate possible workers' enthusiasm for the candidates and to demonstrate how they can assist them.

2. *Present the candidate in the most favorable light possible.* Bill Clinton's campaign for the 1992 Democratic presidential nomination achieved a fast start when he won a straw poll at a Democratic

meeting in Florida. Clinton's organization sent copies of a 16-minute video introducing him to all 2000 delegates, hand-delivering copies to hundreds of them known to be undecided. The victory drew national attention to Clinton and stimulated his fund-raising. The video copies cost about $1 each.

3. *Raise campaign money.* Candidates and their aides who solicit funds frequently show 10- to 15-minute videos when they call on potential givers. These videos presenting the candidates and their policies can be crafted for target audiences with variations designed for political action committees, unions, wealthy individuals, and the like.

## Unanswered Questions

The explosive growth of video inevitably has created unanswered questions of a social nature, as well as commercial and technical ones, some of them partially concealed by the excitement surrounding the form.

*Will excessive watching of electronic material in private isolate viewers from normal participation in the affairs of society?* At a time when almost fanatical involvement in single-purpose political and social causes strains our national fabric, the retreat of large numbers of individuals into static nonparticipation could seriously undercut the breadth of citizen action that traditionally has brought balance to the democratic system of government. Those who sit in isolation at home receiving their impressions of the world primarily from packaged electronic entertainment, lose community awareness and personal contact with persons outside the family circle.

*Will dependence on packaged electronic visual material for entertainment and instruction deprive children and adults alike of the desire to read?* The amount of illiteracy already is distressingly high in the United States, for a country so richly endowed, and millions of people are functionally illiterate, barely able to conduct the simple business of everyday life. This situation will become worse if today's children are lured away from the stimulation and pleasure of reading by a surfeit of visual material that requires minimal mental exertion to watch.

*Will marketing methods improve?* Except for some large chain stores, retail video shops carry a relatively small range of tapes for rent or sale, those being predominantly popular movies. Persons wishing to obtain specialized videotapes often have difficulty in doing so. Catalogues, direct mail offers, and television commercials are in use as marketing methods.

*Can a satisfactory ratings system be devised?* Home video companies have had only a vague idea about how many people watch the tapes that are rented or sold, and what kinds of people they are. Advertisers and commercial underwriters of videotapes want this information. Trying to solve the problem, the A. C. Nielsen Company undertook an experimental program of marking a limited number of popular movie videos with an electronic code. When a marked copy was played by one of the families participating in Nielsen's tests, the fact was recorded for analysis. Further refinement and expansion of the Nielsen system is being carried out. Although *Variety* publishes a weekly list of the Top 50 Video Titles rented in stores, the tabulation does not report how many viewers actually watched each tape or their demographic backgrounds.

## Three Trends

To summarize, now that videocassette recorders can be found in a substantial majority of American homes, three trends in the video industry seem to be fairly certain during the late 1990s:

- Original programming—that is, material created especially for VCR viewing as contrasted with repackaged movies and television shows—will increase markedly. Much of this will be for educational, sales, and promotional purposes. Some producers who release their films direct to the video market without prior release in theaters have begun to improve the quality of the pictures they make.

- Advertisements will be contained in many videotapes that viewers rent or purchase, although viewers will often skip over them by pushing the fast-forward button.

- Growth of pay-per-view television may cut into the home video market. If families can see a popular new movie on pay-per-view before the videotape is released, for roughly the rental price, and can order it by telephone from home rather than going to a store, the video business could suffer. Much of this remains problematic, but video store owners are worried.

## Points to Remember

1. A U.S. Supreme Court decision stimulated growth of the video industry. What was it?

2. Approximately how many videotapes do Americans rent each week?

3. How long is the usual time period between a movie's first appearance in theaters and its release in video form?

4. From your own TV viewing, can you cite an example in which an amateur video played a role in reporting a news story?

5. In what ways do corporations use videotapes in their business?

## Media Questions to Think About

1. Do you watch videotapes only for entertainment, or do you sometimes use them for instructional purposes, such as exercise programs or how-to-do-it demonstrations?

2. How often do you purchase videotapes as gifts or as part of a home library? Or do you rent them only for one-time viewing?

3. How important in your life is your videocassette recorder, compared to your radio, computer, television set, and telephone? If necessary, which would you eliminate first?

# CHAPTER THIRTEEN
## Photographic and Graphic Communications

## "Coming Alive" for Chanel No. 5

In a TV commercial viewed around the globe in 1995, a model eating popcorn watches Marilyn Monroe singing in a film.

Suddenly, the model's blouse pops open, her hairline changes, and her face is transformed into Miss Monroe's. The spot turns to color, and the popcorn box becomes an oversized bottle of Chanel No. 5 perfume.

The 30-second commercial, part of a multimillion-dollar campaign, showcases a computer technique known as morphing, so named because one image metamorphoses into another. Researchers spent about 900 hours looking through newsreels of the late actress to obtain the appropriate seconds' worth of footage.

Marketers such as Coca-Cola, Gap Inc., Hershey Foods, and Levi Strauss pay royalties to heirs to use likenesses or re-creations of deceased celebrities. A 1991–92 campaign by the Lintas New York agency for Diet Coke featured Louis Armstrong, Humphrey Bogart, James Cagney, Cary Grant, and Groucho Marx.

A Chanel Inc. official would not discuss the Monroe commercial's cost except to say that it ran into seven figures.

The advent of electronically operated cameras accompanied a surge in the use of striking and informative graphics in the newspaper, magazine, television, video, and movie industries during the 1980s and 1990s. The computer was the primary transforming agent.

Swirling, bouncing, three-dimensional and other special effects brought new excitement to many movies and video and to television commercials and logos.

Digitized photographs and artwork, as well as textual materials, were sent around the world in seconds. Computer operators learned that they could effect almost any changes in the images on their screens. At the same time, newspapers and magazines improved their visual appearance through expanded use of graphics and color.

Modern still photography, and the motion picture as well, had come into being a hundred years earlier. The invention of small cameras in the 1920s enabled photographers to take many pictures, rapidly, in low-level lighting conditions. Picture magazines flourished. Other inventions, including magnetic videotape, new cameras and lenses, laser technology, and digital processing, transmission, and storage, brought photocommunication to its present stages.

In this chapter, we trace the development of photography and photojournalism, describe modern techniques in both photography and graphics, and discuss the phenomenon known as desktop publishing.

## The Visual Dimension

The art of telling a story with still and motion pictures, and with graphs, maps, and other such devices, developed centuries later than the technique of telling it with words. Photographic equipment was relatively slow to become available, and those who used visual techniques needed time to develop the editorial methods of photo and graphic communication. The rapid development of new technologies, particularly in the 1980s, and of comprehension of how to use these sophisticated new tools, however, have made pictorial and design creations a fundamental mode of mass communication.

*Photojournalism* for newspapers and magazines developed rapidly during the 1930s, keyed by the development of the 35-mm camera and the birth of the picture magazines *Life* and *Look*. Film was first used in the motion picture theater to provide entertainment, news, and documentaries. In the mid-1950s film was joined by videotape, which gradually became the tool for televised news, public affairs, and documentary communication. Photojournalism thus has expanded in concept and function and today is part of the larger field known as *photographic communication*, which serves advertising and other purposes as well.

Fewer than 150 years elapsed from the moment when the first photographic image was produced until a fascinated world watched astro-

**Photojournalism**
Combination of words and photograph(s) designed to communicate information or attitudes

**Photographic communication**
Transmission of ideas, information, and attitudes through one or more photographs for all types of purposes, including news and advertising

Firefighter Chris Fields holds 1-year-old Baylee Almon, a victim of the Oklahoma City federal building terrorist bombing. Minutes later the child was pronounced dead. This tragic photograph symbolized the horror of the bombing for millions of readers and viewers around the world. (Charles H. Porter 4th/Sygma)

nauts Neil Armstrong and Edwin Aldrin transmit a live television picture from the surface of the moon. During that period, the growth of photography as a medium of communication was spectacular. But in the years after that 1969 event, the image became even more important both in print media and on the screen. A new wave of picture agencies gave newspapers and magazines spectacular, on-the-spot coverage. Presidential elections hinged on the perceptions Americans gained from television screens—images rather than words. New graphic art forms enhanced movie and television presentations. And by 1995 individual Americans, according to industry sources, were taking more than 15 billion of the approximately 58 billion pictures taken each year worldwide.

## How Photography Developed

### Pioneering Photography

Joseph Nicéphore Nièpce, a retired French lithographer, began searching for a method to capture the photographic image in 1813. Three years later he is believed to have succeeded in producing a negative image, but he could only partially fix the image after exposure—that is, desensitize it to light. In 1826, he made a photograph on a pewter plate showing a view from his workroom window. He called this process Heliographie (sun drawing).

Photography took a significant step forward with the creation of the Daguerreotype by another Frenchman, Louis Jacques Mandé Daguerre, in 1839. In this process, an invisible (latent) image was developed by using mercury vapor. The exposure time was reduced from eight hours to 30 minutes, giving photography a practical application. The Daguerreotype image was a negative, coated on a mirrored metallic surface, so a viewer could see it as a positive only if the mirror reflected a dark background.

A major advance was the collodion wet plate process, developed in 1851 by Frederick Scott Archer, an English sculptor. The process required the coating of a glass plate with a light-sensitive solution that had to be kept wet until exposed in the camera and processed in a darkroom. Very sharp paper prints could be made from a collodion negative. A photographer could use this process outdoors to record exposures of only 10 seconds to a minute, a spectacular improvement in photographic speed. The photographer was required, however, to work from a portable darkroom on location.

It was with this wet plate process, so clumsy by modern standards, that Mathew Brady and his assistants produced magnificent photographs of the Civil War. For the first time, photography proved its value as a news and documentary medium.

In 1912, the famous portable Speed Graphic $4 \times 5$ press camera, which was to become the workhorse for news photographers for a half-century, was introduced. The small camera came into use in America in the 1920s. Ernst Leitz's Leica, a German camera using 35-mm film, was followed by another German make, the Rolleiflex, a larger $2\frac{1}{4} \times 2\frac{1}{4}$ camera.

**Candid photography** Photographs taken without flash in low-level lighting conditions

The small camera freed photographers from carrying bulky film or plate holders. It enabled them to operate less obtrusively, to take 36 pictures in rapid succession, and to use the fast lens to take pictures without flash in low-level lighting situations, a process known as *candid photography*. A German lawyer, Dr. Erich Salomon, who declared himself to be the first photojournalist, began using such a camera in 1928, photographing European nobility. Two other Europeans influenced the development of photojournalism: Stefan Lorant, who edited German and English illustrated publications, and Alfred Eisenstaedt, a West Prussian, one of *Life* magazine's first photographers.

Color photography became a commercial reality when the Eastman Kodak Company announced development of its Kodachrome color film in 1935. In the same year, the first motion picture in Technicolor, a high-fidelity color process, was presented on the American screen.

Two more fundamental breakthroughs followed World War II. In 1947, Edwin H. Land introduced the Polaroid system for producing a positive black-and-white print 60 seconds after exposure, a time soon reduced to 10 seconds. In 1963, a 50-second *color* print process opened new avenues for amateurs and professionals alike. The second breakthrough, as previously stated, came in the mid-1950s: the recording of moving pictures on *magnetic videotape*. This was an electronic approach; all the other advances in the photographic process had depended on chemistry.

## Early Newspaper Photography

From a mass communications viewpoint, taking good photographs during the 1860s was not enough: a way had to be found to reproduce them in newspapers and magazines. The woodcuts in use were slow to produce, inexpensive, and inexact.

Working separately, two men developed a *halftone photoengraving* technique. Frederic Eugene Ives produced a halftone engraving in his laboratory at Cornell University in June 1879, and Stephen Horgan published a photograph "direct from nature" in the New York *Daily Graphic* in March 1880. By the mid-1890s, halftone engravings were appearing in the New York newspapers.

During the early years of the twentieth century, pictures in newspapers generally were used singly, to illustrate important stories. The newspaper picture page, making use of special layouts and unusual picture shapes, was developed during World War I. A major new force in American journalism, the *picture tabloid*, came into being shortly after World War I. In these newspapers, with their small page size and flashy makeup designed to appeal to street sale readers, the photograph was given the dominant position, often overshadowing the text of the news stories.

During the 1920s, experiments were carried out in transmission of a photographic image by wire and by radio. The first American photos sent by wire were transmitted from Cleveland to New York in 1924. A decade of development passed before the Associated Press established its Wirephoto network in 1935. Distribution of newsphotos by wire enabled newspapers across the country to publish pictures from other cities only a few hours after they were taken.

## The Picture Magazines

The expanded interest in all forms of photographic communication in the 1930s led Time, Inc. to establish the weekly picture magazine *Life* in November 1936. *Life* was patterned after photographic publications developed in Germany and England. In 1937, the Cowles organization established *Look*, published every other week and more feature-oriented

**Halftone**
Engraving produced by photographing a picture through a screen onto a plate so that small dots of varying size will display lights and shadows when printed

**Picture tabloid**
Newspaper with about half the dimensions of a standard-size newspaper emphasizing photos, often sensational

than *Life*. Both magazines emphasized editorial research and investigation preceding assignment of photographers to all but spot news stories. Photographers were well briefed as to the significance of a story before arriving on the scene. In that sense, photographers controlled a mind-guided camera.

From the mid-1930s into the 1960s, a small group of well-known magazine photographers contributed to the development of the photographic essay and interpretive picture story. Dorothea Lange's sensitive images of America's condition during the Great Depression stand as examples of still photography at its finest. So do the pictures of Margaret Bourke-White, Gordon Parks, and Henri Cartier-Bresson, a French photojournalist, who defined the *decisive moment* to capture an image. Robert Capa and David Duncan demonstrated how the still camera could record the reverberations of war.

**Decisive moment**
An instant out of many when a photograph will capture the essence of an action

## The Picture Agencies

When the great photographic teams developed at *Life* and *Look* dissolved in the wake of the financial crises that forced the closing of the magazines in the early 1970s, there was a slump in photojournalism in America. Some of the photographers and editors migrated to the *National Geographic*, which became a center of photographic communication during the next decade. Others made the *Smithsonian* magazine of the Smithsonian Society a superb example of photographic communication. Neither magazine, however, provided an outlet for the on-the-spot news photography that had made both *Life* and *Look* so memorable and which was still seen in *Paris-Match* and other European picture magazines.

Filling the gap in the 1970s and 1980s was a group of new picture agencies, strongly European-based, devoted both to photojournalism and to high-level action photography. Contact, Sipa, Black Star, Gamma, Sygma, and others placed their photographers on call for assignments from *Time*, *Newsweek*, and the revived *Life*, now a monthly. Their picture essays were marketed at high prices; for example, Matthew Naythons's Guyana mass suicide photos earned $250,000 for Gamma.

## Television

When television became a commercial force in the late 1940s, the tools and techniques developed by the motion picture industry were adopted for presenting news on television. A motion picture camera was relatively small and portable, and film shot at news events could be shown on the television screen. Until remote telecasting became practicable, visual presentation of on-the-spot news had to be done with motion picture film, but this medium, as previously stated, has been almost entirely replaced by videotape.

The television documentary became an established part of network programming. Under the tyranny of the ratings system, however, the number of documentaries on the networks declined during the 1980s. An exception was the Cable News Network (CNN), which redefined the documentary by using the material first as daily news inserts and then in its entirety on weekends. CNN also returned to the roots of the documentary process by focusing on the story itself rather than on highly paid anchors and reporters who described the issues involved instead of letting the material do the telling.

Documentaries made by individual stations and those shown on public television stations comprise the overwhelming majority of the more than 200 documentary entries submitted annually in the prestigious George Foster Peabody awards competition administered by the University of Georgia College of Journalism and Mass Communication.

## The Electronics Revolution

As the photographic world moved from its mechanical and chemical base into the electronic era, a multitude of inventions and new processes strongly affected individual photography and the field of mass communications.

### The Electronic Camera

The pace of change in camera technology continued to accelerate in the 1990s. The 35-mm still cameras could do everything—load the film, wind it to the next picture, set the exposure, focus, and unwind the film. Infrared beams focused in the dark, and built-in zoom lenses provided wide-angle and telephoto shots with a flash unit that narrowed or widened its beams accordingly. *Single-lens reflex* cameras, with operators looking through the lens to focus on a subject, were in wide use. The automatic features relied heavily on sophisticated electronic circuits and motors built into the camera. Next came the *filmless camera*.

**Single-lens reflex** Camera with only one lens and a viewing system using a mirror to reflect the image entering the lens and viewfinder

An estimated 15 million Americans own *camcorders*. Introduced in the early 1980s, these video recording cameras are in wide use throughout the world (see Chapter 17). Their amateur owners are venturing into journalism, selling tapes to television stations with unpredictable outcomes. Millions viewed George Holliday's camcorder scenes of Los Angeles police beating Rodney King; their acquittal in the first of two court trials sparked riots in several cities. In 1992, however, camcorders were found in only 15 percent of U.S. homes, as compared with 20 percent penetration in Japan. Efforts were being made to reduce the price below $500.

**Filmless camera** Electronic camera with digitized circuits and motors

**Camcorder** Videotape camera that can also be used as a VCR

Introduced in the 1980s, Eastman Kodak's line of cameras, recorders, and accessories that adapt the television set to a range of new roles found increased favor. The set serves as a screen for viewing photographs and home movies made with a camcorder, a substitute for the darkroom that makes prints electronically; a movie lab for adding sound to home videotape and creating programs that mix still and video pictures; an electronic family album or picture archive of still and video motion pictures; a utilizer of the floppy disc; and a source of near-instant still photographs. In 1992, Kodak marketed a system that allows customers to store their photos on compact discs and display them on TV sets and computer screens.

Sony aimed for the mass market with its Consumer Mavica (MAgnetic VI-deo CA-mera) system. Images are recorded on miniature diskettes by *analog* video, not *digital*, means. No processing is required. Users slip the diskette into a viewer for display on a TV monitor, after which a printer can produce a color picture in about a minute. The images also may be transmitted over telephone lines anywhere in the world.

Cardboard cameras containing a single roll of film have become increasingly popular; well over 15 million were sold in the United States in 1991. After shooting the roll, the user turns over the entire camera to a photofinisher, who removes and develops the film and returns the camera to its maker for recycling.

A number of other companies were marketing cameras capable of similar or other new electronic operations.

## The Electronic Picture Desk

The global news services for many years have conducted and sponsored research into the making and transmission of photographs, as well as news stories and other materials, by digital means. A breakthrough occurred in the late 1970s when Bell Laboratories invented a computer chip capable of recording images electronically.

As research accelerated, the Associated Press introduced its *electronic darkroom*, also known as an *electronic picture desk*. Under the system, a picture can be sent electronically to the AP's offices or directly to the print and broadcast media. There, under a system known as *image processing*, an editor can crop (by maneuvering horizontal and vertical lines on the screen) and enlarge or reduce the desired portion. The photo can also be enhanced by brightening or darkening certain portions and can even be combined with other photos to produce composite pictures. The refining of the image may be carried on at the level of the individual *pixel*, the tiny dot that by the multithousands comprises the image. (See box, "Skating on Thin Ice?")

The electronic darkroom is part of a larger system, rapidly being developed, whereby a photographer processes 35-mm film into electronic data (unnecessary if an electronic camera has been used) on a portable photo transmitter. Captions are inserted and the photos are transmitted over phone lines to a newspaper. There, the picture editor calls up the photos on a screen and makes such color corrections as may be necessary. After a phone conversation with the photographer, the editor crops and sizes the photos and sends them to other editors to view on their terminals. If an editor is making up the front page on a *pagination* terminal

**Analog**
Mechanical method of using changes in electrical voltage to create sound and pictures

**Digital**
Electronic method of translating signals into binary and decimal notations

**Electronic darkroom**
Computerized processing of photographs and other graphic material, in contrast to processing by chemical means

**Image processing**
Enlarging, enhancing, or otherwise transforming a representation on a computer screen

**Pixel**
Definable location on a computer screen used to form images

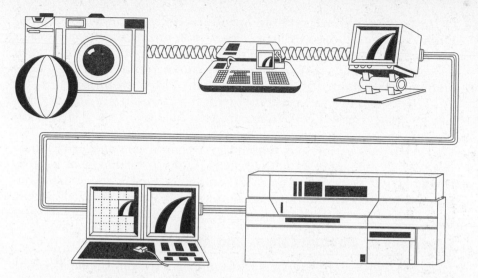

**Figure 13.1**

How a picture moves from the camera to the printing press by use of electronic technology is explained in this graphic published in *Presstime,* the magazine of the Newspaper Association of America.

(capable of laying out an entire page), color pictures may be placed on the front page and others in black-and-white on inside pages, along with a story also transmitted electronically from the scene.

Benefits of the system include the rapid transmission of late-breaking news events just before deadline, the bypassing of traditional darkroom procedures, and better reproduction through use of Scitex and other electronic imaging systems. Figure 13.1 illustrates the method.

The Associated Press announced in 1990 that it was switching to electronic darkrooms as its basic photo receivers. The action accelerated conversion of the nation's newspapers to PhotoStream, AP's picture-a-minute digital photo delivery highway. Replacement of LaserPhoto receivers at 950 newspapers with the AP Leaf Picture Desk, developed in cooperation with Leaf Systems of Natick, Massachusetts, was completed in 1992.

Other major news agencies also are using advanced camera technology and electronic picture desks.

A landmark event in the movement away from the use of film occurred in January 1989, when the AP, within 40 seconds, began transmitting an image of the swearing in of President George Bush. It was not a normal photo made on light-sensitive silver-emulsion film. There was no film processing and no printing. Using a Nikon electronic camera, Ron Edmonds captured the image on a magnetic disc. It was previewed on a tiny screen and transmitted directly from the photographers' platform via AP's Laserphoto network. The action was the first live transmission of an electronic newsphoto direct from the scene to newspapers and broadcast stations.

A filmless camera designed specifically for news photographers was introduced in 1994 by the Eastman Kodak Company and the Associated Press. A year later, the Vancoucer (Canada) *Sun* and *Province* purchased 20 of the AP NewsCamera 2000 cameras and became the first North American newspaper company to convert wholly to digital news photography.

In 1995, the Associated Press opened its collection of 55 million images to electronic access by its members. The images date as far back as the Civil War. Members dial into the database; after viewing thumbnail images and making a selection, they may automatically order high-resolution files transmitted via phone lines or the PhotoStream satellite.

The AP planned to create four regional archives to store images specific to those areas. The service currently files well over 2000 photos each week.

Kodak and Sprint were setting up a central computer that could store digital versions of millions of photographs that could be ordered by telephone and delivered to personal computers. Kodak also sought consumer markets with the introduction of a $1000 computerized camera.

## Functions of Photographers and Editors

Daily newspaper photographers perform one of the fundamental tasks in photojournalism. On a typical day they receive three or four assignments, usually to events fairly close to the office. They most likely will use a staff car, equipped with a two-way radio. The photographer will take a number of pictures, gathering names and important caption material. On most assignments, only one of the pictures taken will be published; in fact, frequently none will be printed because of space limitations or the development of later, bigger news stories. The introduction of digital photographic equipment at many newspapers has freed hundreds of photographers from time-consuming chemical processes, so they can spend more time on assignments or processing electronic images in the newsroom.

*USA Today* employs more than 580 freelance photographers, who receive precise technical instructions for each assignment. The newspaper transmits about 100 color photographs in an average week and processes approximately 1000 rolls of color film each month. Transmission time of a color photograph is $3\frac{1}{2}$ minutes by telephone wires and 30 seconds by satellite.

A photographer on a general magazine staff works on more elaborate projects than does the daily newspaper staff member, often taking several weeks or even months to complete a single job. Assignments at times range far from home. The photographer is well briefed by researchers and receives large research folios as "homework." On a major assignment, the photographer will shoot from 1000 to 5000 images, sending them in "takes" to the editors. After all this effort, 12 to 20 of the pictures most likely will appear in print.

Most television stations cover breaking news live. Pictures are transmitted either by line-of-sight microwave from the ground, from helicopters within a 50-mile radius from the station, or by satellite from expensive vans equipped with motorized dishes. On ordinary assignments, the photographer works in a manner similar to that of a daily newspaper colleague. The TV photographer has four to six assignments a day, usually travels in a radio-equipped staff car, and carries lightweight videotape camera equipment. The photographer takes notes ("spot sheets"), including the names of those appearing in various scenes. Camera operators may work alone, with a reporter, or with a full crew to handle lighting and sound. After their return to the station, the tape is edited and a script is written.

Many photographers also are employed by advertising agencies, public relations firms, and other organizations.

## The Graphics Revolution

Innovative uses of the computer have helped convert thousands of newspapers, magazines, books, and advertising and public relations materials such as newsletters and annual reports into intriguing, highly informational, and well-designed publications. New computer uses also have transformed aspects of television, video, and the movies into a kaleidoscope of movement and illusion. Color, long resplendent in film and television, has found increased use in all these print media, much of it made possible by the steadily improving color capabilities of the personal computer. Figure 13.2 shows predicted pictorial uses.

### Desktop Publishing

The phenomenon known as *desktop publishing* (DTP) has markedly changed much of the publishing world since its advent in 1984. Today the process is being used to produce newspapers, magazines, books, newsletters, school yearbooks, and other materials at substantial savings in cost and time over methods formerly employed. Almost anything that appears in print can be produced with this technology. Corporate communications departments, art directors, graphic designers, and persons with no prior production experience are steadily expanding its uses.

**Desktop publishing** Writing, editing, setting textual material, preparing artwork, and laying out a letter-size page on a computer that can be sent to a printer for multiple reproduction

Desktop publishing resulted from the simultaneous merging of three significant technological developments: (1) affordable, graphically-based personal computers (PCs); (2) lower-cost laser printers; and (3) new computer languages (software) specifically designed to describe entire pages at once, such as PostScript.

With only a PC, software, hard-disc drive, and a basic laser printer, one operator can write (or edit copy provided by others), set type, prepare artwork, and lay out an entire publication. The result is camera-ready copy that can be sent to a printer to be reproduced in thousands of copies.

Desktop publishing got its big boost early in 1985 when Apple Computer's Laserwriter plain-paper printers were made available. Further impetus came a few months later when Aldus introduced its Apple Macintosh-compatible Pagemaker software. Other manufacturers, including IBM, followed with hardware and software of their own.

# SKATING ON THIN ICE?

Should a newspaper have published a composite photo of Tonya Harding and Nancy Kerrigan practicing together during the Winter Olympics? The caption said the two skaters "appear to skate together in this New York *Newsday* composite."

*Newsday* editors defended the photo, pointing to the caption. Stephen D. Isaacs, acting dean of the Columbia University School of Journalism, told the New York *Times* that the picture represents the "ultimate journalistic sin," because a composite picture "is not the truth. It is a lie and, therefore, a great danger to the standards and integrity of what we do."

In light of the technology that allows manipulation of such images, the National Press Photographers Association, Durham, N.C., has issued the following guidelines:

It is our policy that changing content is unacceptable using past or present techniques and/or technology. If significant reason exists to challenge this policy, it will be addressed in the following manner:

## No Discussion Needed

Dodging and/or burning areas that do not change content, such as lightening football players' faces in a contrast photo or toning down a hot spot from a strobe. Correction of technical defects in a photo, such as dust spots, line hits in a transmission, color shifts.

## Discussion Recommended

Photos that may offend community standards. For example, gruesome photos or those showing overwhelming grief and/or distress.

## Discussion Required

Photos with potential to breach community standards. These include shots with the accidental inclusion of genitals, obscene gestures or language and offensive cultural elements.

Also, photo alteration and/or manipulation used in photo illustrations. Discussions should include:

- Photographer when possible
- Top newsroom executive available
- Picture-desk representative
- Section editor where photo will appear
- Ombudsman

The group should be expanded to include gender and/or cultural diversity if it doesn't exist in the above group.

Questions to consider:

- Do we have all the necessary information on the photo and story available?
- Is there any information missing in the content of the photo?
- What is the news value of the photo?
- What is the motivation for publishing?
- What are the ethical, legal concerns?
- Who will be offended?
- What are the possible consequences from publishing the photo?

## Photo Credit/Labeling

All photo illustrations should be labeled as such. When possible and/or feasible, we encourage the inclusion in the cutline of an explanation of any special effect used in the creation of a photo illustration when the technique may cloud the reader's understanding. The underlying purpose of this explanation would be to eliminate the reader's perception of any intent to deceive.

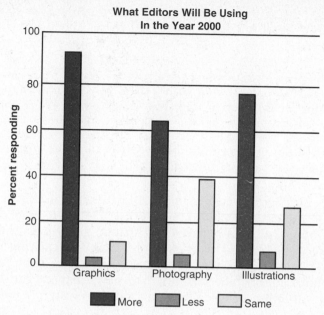

**Figure 13.2**

Striking increases in newspapers' use of graphics, as well as photographs and other illustrations, by the end of this decade is shown in this chart.

Accelerating the adoption of the new equipment was its relatively low cost of about $10,000, far less than the cost of a traditional phototypesetting machine. One user prepared a trade magazine for 60 cents a page, whereas a professional typesetter would have charged from $5 to $6 a page. Another produced a book at the cost of about 30 cents a page, as compared with professional typesetting charges ranging from $10 to $30 a page.

Desktop publishers, using a wide variety of type styles and sizes, prepare the text and headlines and then, with the aid of a hand-held "mouse" or other device, expand or reduce the copy, arrange it into columns, and perhaps decorate the computer page with rules and other embellishment. Photos may be refined and exact color combinations determined simultaneously on four-part screens.

## Newspapers

Confronted with an upsurge in the use of striking graphic displays in other media, a steadily increasing number of newspapers during the late 1980s and the 1990s hired designers, trained their staffs, and began using computers and picture-scanning systems in much more creative ways than formerly. As once-somber pages were converted into attention-getting and much more immediately informative displays, *infographics* (informational graphics) became the order of the day.

**Infographics**
Jargon for graphic materials that provide information

"Indeed, the entire appearance of many newspapers is being re-designed from coast to coast," wrote staff writer David Shaw in the Los Angeles *Times*.

> New typefaces. More drawings and charts and graphs. More news summaries and "chronologies" of major events. Fewer stories on the front page. More (and bigger) photographs. Wider (and fewer) columns on a page. A more complete index. New headline and byline styles. Front-page "teasers" referring to stories inside the pages. Provocative quotations lifted out of a story and displayed separately, in larger type, to catch the reader's eye and lure him into the story itself.

A large number of weeklies and small dailies began producing newspapers with the desktop publishing process. On many large dailies, the linking of individual PCs replaced the former "front-end" central computers. Even reporters and editors with little or no training found that they often could produce the graphics accompanying their stories. Designers, photo editors, and text-oriented newsroom executives merged their responsibilities, and the traditional slots of illustrator and photo retoucher began dying out. The Society of Newspaper Design, begun in 1979 with only 22 members, soared to a membership of 2300, including artists, newspaper designers, editors, and publishers.

**Advertising and Promotion.**   The graphics computer also made heavy inroads into newspaper advertising and promotion departments. Speculative advertisements were prepared on the computer in connection with computerized clip-art services, which provided drawings that could be displayed on the screen and then manipulated. Although ads that call for sophisticated illustrations, such as fashion layouts, often were still drawn by artists, many finished ads were designed on the screen in complete form and sent to a laser printer, bypassing paste-up of various components. Many promotion departments used computer graphics systems to produce elaborate slide promotions and to transfigure dry statistics into appealing graphics.

**Clip-art**
Illustrations provided commercially for use in advertising and other materials

### Magazines

Countless specialized magazines began using the new technology, partly accounting for an upsurge in the number of magazines (see Chapter 6). Among the first magazines produced in such a fashion were *Balloon Life*, *Western Horse*, *Professional Locksmithing*, and *Vintage Motorsport*. A number of new do-it-yourself magazines appeared, including *Publish!* and *Desktop Publishing*.

### Books

With the new technology, the production of books, as well as other publications, no longer was exclusively a specialized business. The rise of the

# Toxic air pollution state by state

**The federal government has conducted a state-by-state accounting of toxic material released into the atmosphere. The U.S. total has reached 2.4 billion pounds a year. Figures are based on industries' estimates of their own emissions, not on actual monitoring. Data may underestimate releases.**

Emissions by millions of pounds per year:

☐ 0–10    ☐ 10–30    ☐ 30–80    ■ 80 or more

Maine
N.H.
Vermont
Wash.
Mont.
N.D.
Minn.
Mass.
Ore.
Wisc.
N.Y.
Idaho
S.D.
Mich.
Pa.
R.I.
Wy.
Iowa
Ohio
Conn.
Nev.
Neb.
Ind.
W.Va.
N.J.
Utah
Col.
Ill.
Del.
Calif.
Kansas
Mo.
Ky.
Va.
Md.
Ariz.
N.M.
Okla.
Ark.
Tenn.
N.C.
S.C.
Miss.
Ala.
Ga.
Texas
La.
Fla.

Alaska    Hawaii

Worst state:
**TEXAS**
230 million pounds per year

## Most polluting industries

| Industry | Millions of pounds |
|---|---|
| Chemicals | 887 |
| Primary metals | 215 |
| Paper | 208 |
| Transport. equip | 192 |
| Rubber, plastics | 132 |
| Metals products | 110 |
| Electrical equip. | 90 |
| Oil, coal products | 76 |
| Printing, publishing | 47 |
| Non-electrical equip. | 46 |

Total toxic releases into air, in millions of pounds

SOURCE: U.S. Environmental Protection Agency

Graphic presentations such as this provide easily absorbed information and simultaneously give newspaper pages a lively appearance.

PC and the digitization of type democratized the publishing and printing industries, putting the necessary tools into the hands of people who once were merely the customers of printers and typesetters.

The biggest problem to be surmounted in book publication involved the quality of the typeface. Viewed closely, the images produced by the technology were not quite as sharp as regular type. Advances were being made, however, to approach the quality of the 1000-dpi or higher resolution typical of commercial typesetters.

## News Services and Syndicates

Many graphics are provided by the news services and syndicates to supplement the work of newspaper staff artists.

Delivery of these materials by satellite is gradually replacing their transmission by mail and phone lines. The Associated Press and United Press International accelerated their transmission of graphics during the latter half of the 1980s. AP began a graphics retrieval service, called AP Access, that swiftly delivers original, camera-ready art to its members over land lines. The service was available to AP LaserPhoto II members with Macintosh computers and a modem. It features computer-to-computer digital transmission, original quality art, 24-hour telephone retrieval of graphics, constantly updated weather maps, the ability to edit text and manipulate typefaces and other images, and the ability to store graphics locally for future use.

The AP provides a wide range of charts, maps, photo and color separations, and feature packages. In addition, with a service called AP GraphicsBuilders, the AP offers Apple Macintosh diskettes to its members, updated monthly.

In order that syndicates and the alternative news services could transmit their own graphics by satellite, the AP opened its Graphics-Net satellite to others. The Independent Network Systems, owned by Maxwell Communication Corporation, provided a similar service.

A broad range of graphics services is offered by the Knight-Ridder/Tribune Graphics Network. It provides breaking news graphics created on the Macintosh computer and transmitted via PressLink communications software.

## Television, Video, and Film

The use of computer animation, three-dimensional, and other special effects became commonplace during the 1980s and 1990s in the production of movies, television programs and logos, videos, and commercials. Three-dimensional colorful objects now bounce or fly around screens at will.

A computer operator, for example, enters a 3-D design of a building, then tours its interior while it rotates on its axis. Another blends 3-D animation with two-dimensional effects, flying a 3-D object over a giant two-dimensional logo or rotating a large 3-D logo over an entire city. The possibilities seem endless for creating in Americans, as one observer put it, "a sweet tooth for eye candy."

It was a Frenchman, George Melies, however, who produced the first special effects movie, *A Trip to the Moon*, in 1902. Over the years techniques were improved in such landmark films as *King Kong* (1933)

**Logo**
Abbreviation of logotype, a symbol depicting a company, product, or service, designed to project an affirmative image

Special effects in the motion picture *Batman Forever,* starring Val Kilmer, were achieved by developing a computerized "Batman" to perform superhuman feats that look real.

and Stanley Kubrick's *2001: A Space Odyssey* (1968). Industrial Light & Magic (ILM), the special effects division of George Lucas's Lucasfilm, Ltd., broke new ground with the first of the three *Star Wars* epics in the late 1970s.

In 1982, electronic animation dramatically occupied a full 53 minutes of Walt Disney Studio's 96-minute *Tron,* thrusting the protagonist via laser beam into the flowing grids of a vast computer system. Handmade backdrops and miniature objects abetted computer magic in such ILM-assisted films as Steven Spielberg's *Raiders of the Lost Ark.* Boss Films Corporation created the special effects for *Ghostbusters* and *Poltergeist II.* Lucas's *Captain Eo,* a 17-minute, 3-D musical science-fiction movie starring Michael Jackson, won high praise in 1986 for its spectacular effects. Allowing the imagination to run wild, these and other movies, including Spielberg's *Jurassic Park,* have enormously expanded the limits of storytelling.

Image *morphing,* in which one image may be digitally changed into another by a computer, made its debut in the movie *Willow* in 1988: a reclining tiger is smoothly transformed into a sleeping woman. Morphing has been widely used in advertising: A car changes into a tiger in an Exxon commercial; a bear turns into a bull for a Merrill Lynch ad; for Diet Coke ads, James Cagney and Louis Armstrong are reanimated on screen, seamlessly blended and colorized. (See the vignette opening this chapter.)

Virtual reality, a cyberspace development described as "just like being there," emerged in the mid-1980s as an offshoot of three-dimensional graphics and computer-aided design, known as CAD. A virtual reality system requires as its base a computer workstation, a monitor, and

**Virtual reality**
An artificial computer world experienced through sight, sound, and touch by use of electronic goggles, earphones, gloves, and body suit

special software. But what distinguishes the system from just fancy computer graphics are the goggles and controller.

With the goggles, wearers get a sense of being in the computer image, looking left or right, up or down, and seeing the corresponding change in perspective on the goggles' two screens, one for each eye. A separate controller, described by the *Wall Street Journal* as a type of computer-game-like joystick, controls movement within the computer-generated "world."

An electronic glove is often used as a controller, with the added benefit of being able to reach out and "grab" items on the screen; it is shown in the computer graphic as a floating hand.

With this system, a prospective home buyer can sit in a Realtor's office and "walk through" houses for sale. Or a surgeon may perform a complicated operation on a computer-generated virtual patient. Other applications are endless.

**Desktop video**
System enabling an operator to produce videotaped materials by computer

**Desktop Video.** Desktop video systems sharply reduced the cost of producing animated films and videotapes, from $20,000 per minute in 1987 to $6,000 per minute in 1988, with other drops following. As the power of desktop computers grew, companies built plug-in circuit boards for computers that can quickly convert pictures into digital data. These circuit boards are widely used to prepare commercials, animated logotypes for television stations and corporations, and many other elaborate graphic images, including 3-D, for video and broadcast presentations. Quicktime, mouse-driven Apple software, allows video and sound to be incorporated in Macintosh computers. The program is interactive, enabling the user to cut among film scenes, songs, and animated graphics.

## Functions of Artists, Designers, and Editors

As increasing attention was paid to a newspaper's appearance, a new era of teamwork among reporters, editors, artists, photographers, and designers gradually came into being on major newspapers.

During most previous decades, it was word-conscious, nonvisually-oriented subeditors who more often than not laid out the portions of pages alloted to them by the advertising department. Often scant attention was paid to the dynamic possibilities inherent in the proper interplay of white space, body and headline type, color, photos, and other illustrative material to capture the reader's eye. On many papers, photographers held second-class status in decisions about the taking and display of pictures, and artists were used mainly to retouch their work, accentuating lines and airbrushing unsightly backgrounds from pictures, and for other illustrative purposes. Such a situation is still true on some newspapers.

During the 1970s, some newspapers hired specialists to redesign typefaces and improve the overall appearance of their pages. The advent

## DEPICTING A CRIME SCENE ELECTRONICALLY

One night in April 1987, a gunman went on a rampage in Palm Beach, Florida, shooting at two boys in his neighborhood and killing six people at two shopping centers before taking hostages at a grocery store. When reports of the shooting spree reached the newsroom at the Miami *Herald*, 180 miles away, an editor decided to send a staff artist on a chartered plane to capture the scene in a drawing.

Artist Dan Clifford arrived as police were trying to coax the hostage taker out of the store. At 2 A.M., they blew out the door with a bomb and subdued the gunman. Clifford then climbed on a rooftop to draw some sketches of the scene and subsequently pinned down details of the chronology of events.

Back at a motel, the artist first drew a locator map on his personal computer, eyeballing a local road map as a guide. The image appeared on the computer screen as he rolled a "mouse" over a tabletop. Then he took on "the big graphic," a diagram of the crime scene showing the path of the gunman as he shot his way through town.

Using a modem, he sent the two graphics via telephone lines to a mainframe computer. They were pulled up on a personal computer for editing, then sent to a laser printer that generated camera-ready copies within minutes. The artwork made the first edition.

*Presstime*, February 1989. Courtesy of the Newspaper Association of America.

---

of computer technology, including pagination, heightened the movement. But disagreements frequently arose. Some designers, with no journalistic background or training, proposed display ideas incompatible with production deadlines.

At a number of major newspapers today, however, graphics personnel and photographers meet with editors to plan immediate and future coverage and presentation. Under this new arrangement, major newspapers have (1) a top editor committed to the importance of attractive design; (2) a staff designer with authority and a title, generally "assistant managing editor for graphics"; (3) an ongoing design review; and (4) a practice of treating artists and photographers as partners in the journalistic process rather than as service personnel.

## Points to Remember

1. What relation does photojournalism have to photographic communication?

2. What principal inventions were essential in the development of photography?

3. What was required before photographs could be reproduced in the print media?

4. What role did picture magazines play in the development of photojournalism?

5. How does the electronic camera differ from other types?

6. How does the electronic picture desk operate? What are its benefits?

7. How has the graphics revolution affected (a) the print media and (b) the electronic media and the movies?

8. What is desktop publishing? What are its advantages and disadvantages?

9. What changes have newspapers and magazines made in the use of graphics?

10. What roles regarding graphics do the news services and syndicates play?

11. How has computer graphics changed the staff operations of many newsrooms?

12. What are some of the uses of computer graphics by corporations, not-for-profit organizations, advertising agencies, and public relations firms?

## Media Questions to Think About

1. Now that photographs may be altered electronically, how can you believe what you see in a photograph or a motion picture? Why has this development made ethical standards and professionalism so important?

2. Examine the drawings, charts, and graphs in a newspaper. How do these graphics help you understand a news or feature story?

3. Why have artists and designers become so important in preparation of the printed page in recent years?

# CHAPTER FOURTEEN
## The Film

## Film Computer Plays Historical Trick

In the Oscar-winning motion picture *Forrest Gump,* the lead character, played by Tom Hanks, shakes hands with President John F. Kennedy. The audience is baffled. How could that happen, since Kennedy had been dead for more than 30 years?

Electronic magic made it occur.

Here is how Steve Starkey, the film's producer, explained it:

Researchers studied many reels of historical film, searching for a suitable shot of Kennedy shaking hands with another man. They cut the chosen shot of Kennedy out of the stock footage.

Hanks then was photographed against a blue screen, shaking hands with a nonexistent person. Blue was used because the color does not show up on a final print.

Hanks was placed in the setting to be used in the scene. The photos of Hanks and Kennedy were put together by computer. The matchup had to be done meticulously, frame by frame. The audience saw, or thought it saw, the two men shaking hands in a continuous motion.

The movies aren't always what they seem to be.

Motion pictures are a dominant form of visual mass communication around the world. More than a hundred million people watch them every week in movie theaters, on television, and on videocassettes. In the United States and Canada alone, more than one billion movie tickets are sold each year.

American motion pictures, produced in that rather nebulous place called Hollywood, flood the global market. They influence the attitudes, behavior, and expectations of people worldwide.

In this chapter we examine how the motion picture industry was born and developed, how Hollywood operates today, the economics of filmmaking, and why producers make the kinds of pictures they do. We discuss the ratings system and the criticisms of sex and violence in motion pictures.

The chapter cites the intimate ties between the motion picture industry and television. Also, it examines the less glamorous but vital role of nonentertainment filmmaking—documentaries and sponsored films—and the function of film criticism.

## The Role of Motion Pictures

From the capture of a moving image on a strip of film was born a form of communication that, surmounting language barriers, soon carried visual messages to the remote places of the world. When sound was later added, the motion picture became an even more powerful mass medium for entertainment and the transmission of ideas. Today, in its many forms, film projects reality and the illusion of reality on theater screens, on television sets, in school classrooms, and on building walls in isolated villages.

As motion picture critic Stanley Kauffmann observed, "Film is the only art besides music that is available to the whole world at once, exactly as it was first made." And film, like opera, can be enjoyed despite the viewer's ignorance of the language employed in the dialogue or narration. Kauffmann contends, "The point is not the spreading of information or amity, as in USIA or UNESCO films, useful though they may be. The point is emotional relationship and debt."

Although the advent of sound tended to nationalize film and reduce film's claim to being an international art as in the days of the silent movie, the widespread distribution of American films in foreign markets demonstrates the primary role played by a film's visual elements, and the lesser importance of language as a communications device. In fact, when a motion picture is subtitled for distribution in a foreign market, the subtitles convey little more than one-third of the dialogue. Yet the meaning of the film is seldom, if ever, impaired, and its beauty is often enhanced.

A note of warning: *Film and its close cousin, television, constitute the most powerful propaganda media yet devised.* As a consequence, their potential for aiding or injuring civilization is enormous. In addition to supplying a

Forrest Gump, an imaginary character, shakes hands with President John F. Kennedy in a motion picture made 30 years after Kennedy's death. The "meeting," in the film *Forrest Gump* starring Tom Hanks, was achieved through the use of digitalized video technology.

verbal message through dialogue, narration, or subtitles, they provide an instantaneous, accompanying visual message—supplying the viewer with a picture to bulwark what is being learned through language. Thus the imagination need not conjure a mental image to accompany the words; the viewer receives both a concept and its substantiation. If a picture is worth 1,000 words, a picture together with three or four carefully chosen words is worth 10,000 words. Makers of television commercials know this; so does anyone who has ever thought carefully about these compelling and contemporary media of communication.

The power of the motion picture and television to stir emotion has been vastly extended by development of satellite transmission. By use of electronic transmission methods the barriers against distribution in authoritarian countries have been sharply reduced, although not fully eliminated.

## The Movies Are Born

The motion picture preceded radio and television as an entertainment medium. The illusion of movement created by the motion picture projector, and the sense of reality felt by a viewer of the film, made "going to the movies" a popular activity for Americans by the 1920s and kept them going in great numbers until 1950.

**Persistence of vision**
Concept that the human eye retains an image slightly longer than it actually appears, creating an illusion of continuous motion

Inventors worked steadily on the motion picture concept after Peter Mark Roget (of *Thesaurus* fame) advanced his theory of *persistence of vision* in 1824. Roget contended that the human eye retains an image for a fraction of a second longer than it actually appears. Thus a series of still pictures printed on a ribbon of celluloid film, and projected at 16 or 24 frames per second, will create the illusion of continuous motion.

The work of Joseph Nièpce and Louis Daguerre in France created a photographic process that enabled Edward Muybridge and John D. Isaacs to use 24 cameras to conduct their famous 1877 demonstration of the gait of a galloping horse (all four legs *are* off the ground simultaneously). "Magic lantern" shows became commonplace on lecture circuits. George Eastman's marketing in 1888 of his Kodak camera, which used a roll of film, enabled Thomas A. Edison and his assistants to develop a 50-foot "peep show" in a 4-foot box called the kinetoscope.

Louis and August Lumiere presented the first public performance of a motion picture for pay in the Grand Cafe of Paris in 1895. The first public showing in a theater in the United States, using Edison's improved Vitascope, occurred in 1896. *The Great Train Robbery*, Edwin S. Porter's eight-minute film of 1903, was the first to tell a unified story, utilizing camera angles, film editing, and parallel development of story themes. It was also the first of untold Westerns to follow. Earlier films merely had shown fragments of motion.

Edison's jerky, primitive pictures of President William McKinley's inauguration in 1896 and Admiral George Dewey at Manila in 1898 showed the motion picture's potential as a recorder of history.

**Newsreel**
Once-popular short film containing pictures of current news events with commentary which was killed by television

These pioneer efforts at recording news events led within a few years to creation of the newsreel, a standard short item on virtually every motion picture theater program for half a century until television's faster coverage drove the last one out of business in the 1960s. The first regular newsreel series is credited to the Pathé "Journal" of 1907. Among other familiar newsreel names in American theaters were Fox Movietone News, Metrotone, and International Newsreel.

## Three Filmmakers

In the second decade of the twentieth century, three men led in the rise of filmmaking. David Wark Griffith, a director at Biograph, in 1915 produced *The Birth of a Nation*, the first American film "epic." The 12-reel film took nearly three hours to show. The story was of a victimized Southern family, told in a setting of Civil War battles, renegade blacks, and Ku Klux Klansmen. While controversial, the film's emotional impact, and its excellence in filmmaking artistry, gave it a permanent place in motion picture history.

Mack Sennett made a major imprint on film history. In 1912, he founded the Keystone Film Company in Los Angeles. A master of slapstick, he created the Keystone Kops, starred comedienne Mabel Nor-

mand and frozen-faced Buster Keaton, and discovered a young English actor named Charlie Chaplin.

Chaplin, the third of this eminent trio, rose to fame with *The Tramp* (1915) and *Shoulder Arms* (1918). In 1919 he, Griffith, Douglas Fairbanks, and Mary Pickford formed the United Artists Corporation so they could control their own careers and earnings. Chaplin used pantomime to tell the story of "the little fellow" who never fitted in. He captivated his audiences with his tramp's costume and orchestrated mannerisms in such films as *The Gold Rush* (1925) and *City Lights* (1931). He was the wistful little tramp who shuffled off into the night.

Hollywood produced three-quarters of the world's films in the early 1920s at studios with such renowned names as Metro-Goldwyn-Mayer and Paramount. Memorable among the producers of that era were Sam Goldwyn, Louis B. Mayer, and Jesse Lasky. The stars included comedian Harold Lloyd; William S. Hart, the Western hero; romantic heroines Lillian Gish and Gloria Swanson; and "The Sheik," Rudolph Valentino. Still remembered and occasionally replayed today are such films as Cecil B. DeMille's *The Ten Commandments, What Price Glory?, All Quiet on the Western Front*, and *The Covered Wagon*. Among the famous stars imported from Europe were Greta Garbo, Marlene Dietrich, and Maurice Chevalier.

Today, viewers of some major silent films, preserved on videotape, note the strength of many story lines, their emotional impact, and the skillful black-and-white photography often displayed. Equally impressive is the craft of the caption writers, whose brief clusters of words printed on the screen kept the story moving, as spoken dialogue does today.

Clark Gable and Vivian Leigh in a romantic scene from *Gone With the Wind,* one of the most famous motion pictures ever made. Released in 1939, the film is still being shown on television more than a half century later.

**Talkies**
Popular term for talking motion pictures after their introduction in 1927

**The "Talkies."**  The "talkies" arrived in 1927, when Al Jolson sang "Mammy" in *The Jazz Singer.* The addition of the sound track doubled weekly movie attendance from 46 million persons in 1925 to 90 million in 1930. In the Great Depression years, the movie houses offered double bills, even triple bills, for as little as a quarter, along with warmth for the underpaid and unemployed. An antidote for the Depression came in the form of humor, provided by Mae West, W. C. Fields, and the Marx Brothers, among others. Frank Capra directed Clark Gable and Claudette Colbert in the 1934 smash hit, *It Happened One Night.* The Thirties closed with Gable playing Rhett Butler to Vivien Leigh's Scarlett O'Hara in *Gone With the Wind,* the Civil War story that led the list of box office successes from 1939 to 1965 and, with its color refreshed, had a critically acclaimed fiftieth anniversary in 1989.

The art of animation was revolutionized by Walt Disney, whose artists created Mickey Mouse, Donald Duck, and other favorites, then produced the memorable *Snow White and the Seven Dwarfs* (1937). The 1930s also featured lavish musicals, gangster films, and the performances of child stars, particularly Shirley Temple and Judy Garland, the latter of whom reached stardom in *The Wizard of Oz* (1939).

Widely regarded as among the top motion pictures ever made is *Citizen Kane,* filmed by Orson Welles in 1941 as a psychological study of publisher William Randolph Hearst. It reflected exciting experimentation, particularly in the technique of narration. Director John Ford's production of John Steinbeck's *The Grapes of Wrath* in 1939 set another standard for examination of significant social issues. Audiences of the

## 25 FILM CLASSICS

These classic motion pictures were selected by the Library of Congress in 1989 to be preserved as "national treasures." Seventy-five other noteworthy films were added later, making a list of 100 films deemed worthy of preservation in the Library of Congress.

| | | |
|---|---|---|
| 1. | *The Best Years of Our Lives* | 1946 |
| 2. | *Casablanca* | 1942 |
| 3. | *Citizen Kane* | 1941 |
| 4. | *The Crowd* | 1928 |
| 5. | *Dr. Strangelove* | 1964 |
| 6. | *The General* | 1927 |
| 7. | *Gone with the Wind* | 1939 |
| 8. | *The Grapes of Wrath* | 1940 |
| 9. | *High Noon* | 1952 |
| 10. | *Intolerance* | 1916 |
| 11. | *The Learning Tree* | 1969 |
| 12. | *The Maltese Falcon* | 1941 |
| 13. | *Mr. Smith Goes to Washington* | 1939 |
| 14. | *Modern Times* | 1936 |
| 15. | *Nanook of the North* | 1922 |
| 16. | *On the Waterfront* | 1954 |
| 17. | *The Searchers* | 1956 |
| 18. | *Singin' in the Rain* | 1952 |
| 19. | *Snow White and the Seven Dwarfs* | 1937 |
| 20. | *Some Like It Hot* | 1959 |
| 21. | *Star Wars* | 1977 |
| 22. | *Sunrise* | 1927 |
| 23. | *Sunset Boulevard* | 1950 |
| 24. | *Vertigo* | 1958 |
| 25. | *The Wizard of Oz* | 1939 |

1940s saw Humphrey Bogart and Ingrid Bergman in *Casablanca* and enjoyed sophisticated comedies with Cary Grant, Katharine Hepburn, and Spencer Tracy. William Wyler's *The Best Years of Our Lives* was a postwar hit. Alfred Hitchcock had come to the United States in 1940 after making *The 39 Steps* (1935) in England, foreshadowing his thrillers of the 1950s, *Rear Window* and *Vertigo*.

Hollywood had become a symbol of high living, sex, and sin; its stars had fan clubs and endless publicity. In order to offset public complaints about the film colony and its movies, the studios named Postmaster General Will H. Hays to be their czar, as head of the Motion Picture Producers and Exhibitors of America. The Hays Office wrote a 1930 production code that restricted moviemakers, along with city and state censors and the 1934 Legion of Decency movement. The Hays code contained restrictions against strong language, any depiction of sexual intimacy, use of drugs, excessive violence, and plots in which crime paid. The bad guys always lost in the end.

## The Entertainment Film

### Hollywood: 1945–1965

The late 1940s found "old" Hollywood at the peak of its prosperity. With World War II ended, the market for Hollywood films was huge worldwide. Television had not yet developed as a rival medium of mass entertainment. The major studios churned out a flow of movies, from low-budget B films to big-name epics, using the actors they kept under contract. They were assured of distribution for their products through the theaters they owned, under the block-booking system (to be discussed later in this chapter).

**Block booking**
Practice formerly used by studios of forcing a theater operator to show a poor film in order to obtain rights to a popular one

During 1949, more than 90 million tickets were sold weekly in American movie houses, compared with 21 million in 1968. In 1949 the major studios—among them Metro-Goldwyn-Mayer, Twentieth Century Fox, Columbia Pictures, RKO, and Warner Brothers—released 411 new motion pictures. By the early 1960s, their annual output had decreased to barely 200. Still administered by the people who had established them, the studios turned out romantic comedies, emotional dramas, and horror-thrillers, along with occasional provocative and candid films such as *Crossfire* (1947), to a receptive and apparently uncritical American audience.

Then, around 1950, two developments staggered the motion picture industry. Television rocketed into prominence; millions of families watched free TV shows at home instead of making one or two trips a week to the neighborhood movie house. The second blow to the old order came from the federal courts. Bowing to government pressure and a lawsuit charging them with restraint of trade, the major studios signed consent decrees in which they agreed to sell their chains of theaters and to end the practice of block booking. In doing so, they lost the automatic outlet for the pictures they made. Instead of arbitrarily booking their pictures—good, bad, or indifferent—into hundreds of theaters, the moviemakers were required to sell pictures on their merit, one by one. With their audiences shrinking because of TV, the theater operators did not want to show the shoddy "program" films being ground out. The result was a severe reduction in the number of pictures made, leading to the death of the contract player system, under which a studio paid a performer a salary and assigned him or her to whatever picture it desired.

During the Reagan presidency in the 1980s, the Justice Department allowed exemptions to the consent decree, and several large studios quickly purchased large chains of theaters. Their purpose, in addition to making money as exhibitors, was to control the manner of their films' release. These exemptions were part of a general Reagan policy of removing government controls on industry; also, because of his movie actor background, Reagan as president strongly supported the film industry. By 1989, six large chains owned 40 percent of all U.S. movie screens. The Twentieth Century Fox Film Corporation, however, was found guilty of block booking and was fined $500,000.

Hunting for ways to save itself in the 1950s, Hollywood made drastic alterations in its films, both in appearance and in content. The great change in appearance came with the introduction of the wide screen, called the most significant innovation in film technology since the ad-

Colorful poster publicizes the motion picture *High Sierra,* starring Humphrey Bogart and Ida Lupino, first released in 1941 and later re-released. Such posters are a traditional tool of movie promotion. (Bettmann Archive)

Movies drew attendance during the 1940s never since equalled. Fans crowded theaters to see such glamorous stars as Clark Gable, Spencer Tracy, Claudette Colbert, and Hedy Lamarr. Theaters in large cities offered continuous all-day showing. *Boom Town* was released in 1944. (Library of Congress)

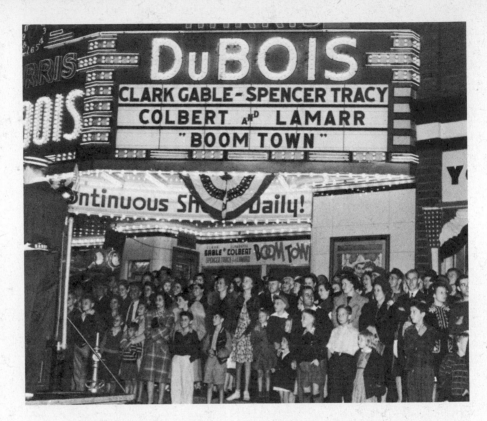

vent of sound. Since the pictures on early TV sets were so small, the massive scope of the wide screen was intended to entice audiences away from their living rooms and into the theaters. Until the appearance of the first wide-screen motion picture, *The Robe* (a $5 million Cinemascope film produced and distributed by Twentieth Century Fox in 1953), the standard screen shape had been a rectangle 20 feet wide and 15 feet high; this represents a ratio of 4 to 3, or 1.33 to 1—a proportion determined by the width of the film, and going back to Thomas Edison and the kinetoscope. Cinemascope settled its wide-screen proportion at 2.55 to 1. Regardless of trade name, most new screens are at least twice as wide as they are high.

Initial critical reactions to the wide screen were mixed, with some filmmakers insisting that the new screen size signaled the end of the close-up and rendered established directorial and cutting techniques ineffective. In time, however, the advantages and possibilities of the wide screen became apparent to filmmakers, who have used its new dimensions to experiment with new kinds of visual compositions and new uses of the close-up.

In response to the wide screen and as a further effort to bring the American public back into the movie theaters, Hollywood in the late 1950s began to produce longer and more expensive movies with casts of thousands and an abundance of well-known stars.

As a further lure to their audience, the filmmakers lowered the censorship barriers of their self-imposed Production Code and made pictures about topics and situations they knew would not be shown on home TV screens. Films about drugs, adultery, prostitution, and abortion—social issues previously banned—appeared bearing the Motion Picture Seal of Approval. This new freedom led to a few artistic successes, but Hollywood soon used it to create new clichés in plot and character.

At first, the Hollywood studios tried to shun television, hoping that it was merely a novelty. However, they soon changed course. Hollywood executives decided to do business with the new electronic medium, recognizing a potential for immense profits. Television needed a continuing supply of programs, and the studios had masses of material available: the old movies stored in their vaults. The studios sold rights to this backlog of films to the TV networks and individual stations for high prices—a windfall not anticipated when the movies were made. Between 1955 and 1958, Hollywood sold almost 9000 pre-1948 feature films to television, and by 1960 the major studios were vying with each other for sale of films produced after 1948. This bonanza for the studios began a relationship of interdependence between them and television that continues to grow.

Although Hollywood studios profited from old work in this manner and created a fresh source of income by renting out sound stages and equipment to TV companies shooting television series, the major studios' basic business of making movies continued to dwindle. Foreign films found increasing popularity in the United States, and American experimental filmmakers gained attention, but the traditional Hollywood film, lavishly produced, lost much of its audience appeal. The audience itself was changing. It grew more sophisticated and was weary of shallow, innocuous fare. By 1965, boxoffice receipts in the domestic market had fallen to barely half what they were in 1946, despite such smash hits as *Dr. Zhivago* and *The Sound of Music*, with Julie Andrews. Three studios—RKO, Republic, and Monogram—stopped production entirely. Approximately 6000 movie houses closed their doors.

## Hollywood Today

The conception held by many people that Hollywood is a closely knit community in which most American movies are made is false. Hollywood, like many of the pictures it turns out, is largely an illusion. The famous corner of Hollywood and Vine is merely a dingy, noisy commercial intersection. Yet the word is a convenient label to identify the American film industry.

Actually, "Hollywood" film production is spread throughout the Los Angeles area, through many other states, and indeed around the world. Most of the complex financial aspects of filmmaking are centered in Los Angeles and New York.

**Table 14.1**

**All-Time Boxoffice Champions**

These ten motion pictures are the largest revenue producers in film history, based on film rentals in the United States and Canada markets.

| | |
|---|---|
| E.T.: The Extra-Terrestrial (1982) | $399,804,539 |
| Jurassic Park (1993) | 356,748,415 |
| Star Wars (1977) (estimate) | 322,000,000 |
| The Lion King (1994) | 298,879,911 |
| Forrest Gump (1994) | 298,096,620 |
| Home Alone (1990) | 285,761,243 |
| Return of the Jedi (1983) | 263,734,642 |
| Jaws (1975) (estimate) | 260,000,000 |
| Batman (1989) | 251,188,924 |
| Raiders of the Lost Ark (1981) | 242,374,454 |

*Source:* Variety, *January 1995.*

Motion pictures made by Hollywood dominate the world market today, as always, but both the films and the industry that produces them are far different from what they were in the 1960s. The industry has found a profitable new course.

No longer are movies produced for a single audience, those people who buy tickets at the boxoffice to see films in theaters. Now films are aimed at two additional audiences as well—those who watch movies on television and those who watch them spun out of a videocassette onto home TV screens. Yet, although some films earn more money from video and television "play" than from their showings in theaters, theatrical release traditionally has come first and is the foundation for all further distribution. Recently, however, some producers have begun releasing pictures direct to the video stores and in certain cases to television after that. Thus the theaters are bypassed completely.

Sales of movie tickets dropped significantly during the early 1990s but then rebounded. Ticket sales in the domestic market (United States and Canada) reached an all-time high of $5.25 billion in 1994. Added to this was the income from showings in foreign markets, television, and video. Approximately 1.21 billion tickets were sold in the domestic market, the largest number in the past quarter century. Inflated ticket prices, some above $7, contributed to the record gross. The increase in the actual number of tickets sold lags behind the rate of U.S.-Canadian population growth.

**Changing Emphasis in Film Types.** During the 1980s Hollywood film producers aimed a large proportion of their output at the youth market, persons under age 25 with emphasis on teenagers. The young audience was more liberal in its attitudes toward sex, profanity, and violence than the older age categories, and more fascinated with fantasy.

Catering to these tastes, producers chose stories and ways of telling them that ignored previous restraints. Few family pictures were produced, except by the Walt Disney studio. As the 1990s progressed, a shift in focus developed. Films closer to traditional values began to appear. Some of them such as *Driving Miss Daisy* were boxoffice and artistic hits.

Filmmakers realized that members of the post–World War II baby boom generation were aging and their tastes were changing. They had children of their own to be entertained. The trend toward films with a broader appeal accelerated. It reached a financial high point in 1994 when two smash hits—*The Lion King*, an animated Disney family film, and *Forrest Gump*, a story about a lovable but slow-witted man that won the Oscar for best picture—were one–two in boxoffice sales. Two other family films, *The Santa Clause* and *The Flintstones*, were also among the top five boxoffice winners. Many film executives noted the correlation between sales improvement and the type of pictures being made.

The balance of movies offered today is considerably better than a decade ago. Action films loaded with violence and sexual situations continue to have strong appeal. Pictures created specifically for the youth market also appear frequently, such as a 1995 film, *Tank Girl*, of which one reviewer said, "*Tank Girl* aims silly, R-rated salvos at teens . . . the film flashes with violence, nudity, profanity and sex."

### Special Effects Intrigue Viewers.

A notable development in recent motion pictures is spectacular special effects created by computer manipulation. Dinosaurs clump around, frightening humans in *Jurassic Park*. Buildings explode and fill the screen with massive balls of fire and debris. Speeding trains overturn in jumbled wreckage; automobiles crash on top of each other. Such ingenious effects have great boxoffice appeal.

For years, special effects were accomplished by trick photography. Perhaps the most memorable such scene was achieved in *King Kong* in 1933, when the 50-foot-tall lovesick ape stands atop the Empire State Building, holding a lovely blonde woman in his arms. Four Navy planes sweep past, raking him with bullets. Gently he places the terrified woman on a ledge, then, bleeding, plunges to his death. Fascinating as that scene is, it is dwarfed in scope by what Hollywood experts accomplish today with computers.

Often enormous scenes in "blockbuster" movies are created on a small scale, then expanded by computerization. In *Interview With the Vampire*, for example, one scene shows a wharf, moving ships, and burning buildings. To achieve the appearance of a massive fire, technicians built a miniature model of a few waterfront buildings. They ignited the model and photographed the small fire. They scanned this picture into a

Action-thriller motion pictures with dramatic special effects draw large audiences in foreign countries as well as in the United States. Copley Square in Boston is the site of one of the many explosive scenes in the MGM film *Blown Away*. (Copyright © Metro-Goldwyn-Mayer)

computer and multiplied it electronically until several blocks of structures appeared to be ablaze. (See Chapter 13.)

### Upsurge of African American Films

The 1990s have seen a striking increase in the number of films about blacks made by an expanding group of African American directors in Hollywood. The commercial success achieved by such movies as *Boyz N the Hood* and *New Jack City* has opened the film capital's door to additional films about the African American experience. During 1991, for example, 19 movies by black directors were released, and the trend continued.

Most of these films focus on urban inner-city life, with strong social messages of anger and frustration. Gang violence is frequently featured but usually with an anti-gang message. Unfortunately, gang members drawn to the openings of several black pictures have committed shootings inside and outside theaters, frightening away some moviegoers.

Spike Lee is the best known of the black male directors. Others winning increased attention include John Singleton, Robert Townsend, Doug McHenry, and George Jackson. Black women directors, however, have been struggling to break into the major studios.

### Changes at Studios

The power structure of Hollywood also has undergone a transformation. In the bygone days of the movie moguls—men such as Louis B. Mayer,

Harry Cohn, the Warner brothers, Samuel Goldwyn, and Darryl F. Zanuck—the major studios dominated the industry. A studio created a story, arranged financing for it, cast it with performers from its roster of contract players, and filmed the story on its back lot. Then it booked the movie into the theaters it controlled. Its overhead was tremendous, especially the salaries of stars under contract.

Today, about two-thirds of Hollywood films are independent productions. This is the era of the package deal, in which the outside talent agent or producer has in a sense replaced the old-time studio czar. Independent companies avoid excessive overhead investment by having neither costly studios nor large production staffs. Often they have major studio organizations handle distribution of their films on a percentage basis.

By accepting the lesser roles of financier, promoter, and distributor, even at times leasing their own facilities to the independent production companies, the major studios relinquished artistic control over the films they were underwriting. Control passed to the independent producer, creating a situation that allowed a film to have a style impressed on it by those who created it, rather than by a studio boss who would oversee a dozen or more films simultaneously.

An independent company's success depends not only on the popularity of the film it produces but also in the financial deals it can arrange. Although they do not see their names on the marquees, accountants and deal makers keep the wheels of Hollywood turning.

The production situation is changing once again as enormous multimedia corporations buy into the Hollywood scene. Their purpose is to combine filmmaking with marketing their films through an interlocking complex of theaters, cable and network television, worldwide satellite distribution, and the telephone companies' emerging television services. Some independent producers may be squeezed out in this developing battle of the giants. (See Issue 3, Who Owns the Media?)

## Changes in Theaters

As the movie industry has changed, the old picture palaces have been replaced by hundreds of new, small cluster theaters, in which different pictures are shown simultaneously in two or more relatively small auditoriums that one enters through a central lobby. Often these theaters are located in shopping centers. Despite competition from television and home video, a record number of 24,000 motion picture screens are in use today in the United States, only a few of them large screens. Recently a trend has begun for construction of more ornate theaters.

## The Ratings System

Since motion pictures have such strong worldwide impact, the question of social responsibility in the situations they depict, and the manner in which they depict them, is a matter of deep public concern.

## WHAT HAPPENED TO DRIVE-INS?

Teenagers on dates and families with a carload of children and a dog once thought that outdoor drive-in theaters were wonderful places to watch movies. Admission was cheap. They could see and hear the shows from their cars, with a portable loudspeaker in the window. If the movie was dull, they could amuse themselves by socializing.

The first drive-in opened at Camden, New Jersey, in 1933, the middle of the Great Depression. Hundreds more screens popped up quickly in fenced fields at the edge of cities. By 1958, 4063 drive-in theaters were operating. Jokingly they were called "passion pits," "ozoners," and "un-derskyers." Indoor theaters were "hardtops."

So, why have thousands of drive-in theaters vanished?

Two principal factors caused the precipitous decline of the drive-ins. Urban sprawl created housing tracts at the edge of cities. Owners found they could make a big profit quickly by selling their theater land to developers. Also, the appearance of videocassettes enabled people to watch movies at home at less cost and bother than going to the drive-in.

By the mid-1990s, the number of operating drive-ins in the United States had dwindled to 837 and was still falling.

**Ratings system**
Series of letters from G to NC-17 indicating the degree of sexual boldness, violence, and/or profanity in a motion picture

For nearly 40 years, from 1930 to 1968, the film industry policed itself with a form of self-censorship enforced by its Production Code Administration. Censors reviewed new films submitted by producers and ordered cuts made. The code was so strict that a husband and wife could not be shown together in the same bed. Mention of narcotics was forbidden. Criminals could not emerge as victors, although the studios produced gangster movies full of violence by having the bad guys lose at the last moment.

American-made films grew bolder during the early 1960s. Sexual situations that had been only hinted at a few years earlier were shown explicitly. The imported Swedish film *I Am Curious (Yellow)* showed actual scenes of sexual intercourse. Actors casually used language in films that was forbidden in polite conversation a decade earlier. Homosexuality became an open topic on the screen.

As a result, criticism of excessive emphasis on sex and violence in films grew. Producers were accused of going too far, exploiting their new freedom for quick profits. Demands for government censorship were heard.

So in 1968, the Motion Picture Association of America (MPAA), the industry's major trade association, abandoned its Production Code and adopted a new ratings system in its place. That system, somewhat modified, still operates today.

In doing so, the MPAA neatly shifted responsibility for what movie-goers see away from the filmmakers and onto the customers. Movie producers are free to put anything they want onto film, without censorship. An industry rating board places a letter symbol on each movie submitted to it, indicating the degree of boldness the film contains. Guided by these symbols, individuals can decide whether a picture is suitable for their children to see—and for themselves as well.

The ratings system is based on the classic "let the buyer beware" concept, with the assumption that the letter classification makes a person an informed buyer.

A few films are shown without a letter rating, because their producers do not submit them to the ratings board. That is true of hardcore pornographic films shown in adult theaters and on home videos. (See Issue 1, Sex and Violence.)

## What the Letters Mean

This is the ratings code, with an explanation by Jack Valenti, president of MPAA, of what each rating means.

- G: *General audiences.* All ages admitted. This is a film which contains nothing in theme, language, nudity and sex, or violence that would be offensive to parents whose younger children view the film.

- PG-13: *Special parental guidance.* Parents are strongly cautioned to give special guidance for attendance of children under 13. Some material may be inappropriate for young children. (Category added in 1984.)

- PG: *Parental guidance suggested.* Some material may not be suitable for pre-teenagers. . . . There may be profanity in these films but certain words with strong sexual meaning will vault a PG film into the R rating. There may be violence but it is not deemed excessive. Fleeting nudity may appear in PG-rated films, but anything beyond that puts the film into R.

- R: *Restricted.* Under-17s require accompanying parent or guardian. . . . This is an adult film in some of its aspects and treatment of language, violence, or nudity and sex. . . . The language may be rough, violence may be hard, and while explicit intercourse is not found in R-rated films, nudity and lovemaking may be depicted.

- NC-17: *No children under 17 admitted.* The NC-17 rating, introduced in 1990, replaced the X rating included in the original code (*No one under 17 admitted*). The MPAA said it made the change because the X rating had come to stand for hardcore pornographic films; this prevented the showing of certain films with substantial artistic merit that contained scenes of sex or violence too strong to permit an R rating. Only a few films, such as *Henry and June*, *Showgirls*, and *Tie Me Up, Tie Me Down*, have received the NC-17 rating.

On the twentieth anniversary of the ratings system, Valenti asserted in *Variety* that the symbols had become part of the American social fabric. He conceded that the system is flawed and subject to criticism both from those who want a stricter method with more specific warnings and from those, mostly producers, who desire fewer restraints.

"...The rating system strives to do the very best that can be achieved, to offer parents some guidance, some counsel," he wrote, adding, "Ratings are not surrogate parents. They are parent helpers."

During the first two decades, the review board rated 8460 feature films, as follows:

R—47.8 percent

PG—33.4 percent

G—11.1 percent

X—4.3 percent

PG-13—3.4 percent

As a group, G films do poorly at the box office, being regarded by many moviegoers as too bland. So producers often add rough language or nudity to a film in order to obtain a more marketable PG or R rating. During a typical year in the early 1990s, 58 percent of the films made by Hollywood were rated R.

Over the years, the ratings board has slightly loosened its restrictions on nudity and slightly tightened those on violence. Even so, the principal complaint about American films is the excessive violence many of them contain.

## The Big Gamble of Making Movies

News stories reporting the large box office receipts earned by major motion pictures from their opening weekend showings look impressive, but they give only a hint of the often byzantine financial operations in filmmaking.

Hollywood has a few rules of thumb that help laypeople understand how a movie becomes a big moneymaker or a financial disaster. These include:

- The average feature film costs $28 million to make, and spectaculars may cost more than $50 million.

The total expense of making the movie, including interest charges on money borrowed to finance the film, is known as the "negative cost."

- Approximately $12 million more is spent to promote the average picture and make film prints for theaters. Thus $40 million or more has been spent by the time the picture opens.

Current marketing technique on a major picture is to release it simultaneously in 800 to 2000 theaters in order to obtain maximum impact from the advance publicity and advertising. That requires an expensive print for every theater.

- No picture is expected to earn back all this cost in the domestic theater market of the United States and Canada. A producer is happy with 80 percent recovery.

The remaining 20 percent, plus any profit, must come from foreign showings, television, and home video sales and rentals. Foreign rentals usually range from 30 to 50 percent of what a picture earns in domestic theaters. Occasionally a film that fails in the domestic market hits a bonanza abroad, a fact that keeps producers eternally hopeful.

- Published weekly boxoffice statistics are gross figures, the total amount customers paid for tickets. The theater operator keeps about half and returns the other half to the film's distributor as a rental fee.

The theater operator keeps 100 percent of the food and drink concession revenue, an important source of income.

- According to Hollywood's conventional wisdom, a film must earn two and a half times its negative cost in domestic rentals to break even.

Even more costs are added to a film's expense ledger, reducing its prospects for earning a final net profit. The studio or other organization that distributes the picture to theaters charges the producer 30 percent of the rental income for doing so.

The huge risks in making movies are well illustrated by Hollywood production figures for 1994. *Variety* tracked the fate of more than 450 films in the domestic market that year. Of these, 11 grossed more than $100 million each at the boxoffice. Two of the 11, *The Lion King* and *Forrest Gump*, each grossed nearly triple that amount. Yet virtually every major filmmaker spent $40 million or more on at least one picture that flopped at the boxoffice, with losses of many millions.

Investors who have agreed to accept a percentage of a movie's *net* profit sometimes find themselves getting nothing, even though the film achieved powerful boxoffice success, because so many high costs have been charged against its gross income. These include large percentage payoffs to the director and top stars that may total tens of millions of dollars. Given these facts, telling the winners from the losers is difficult.

The odds against any single film script reaching the screen are heavy. In a recent typical year, the Writers Guild register contained 27,000 scripts, concepts, and outlines. That year, 5000 scripts (movie and television) began production. Of these, 455 feature movies were released, and 200 cable movies and 100 TV movies were produced.

## Hollywood, Capital of Hype

The motion picture industry lives on publicity. Producers must lure customers to the boxoffice. Actors must keep their names before the public and the casting directors. Men and women who strive for attention and "celebrity" status yearn to see their pictures on the screen and in print. As a result, a legion of publicists bombards media offices with news releases and phone calls promoting their clients.

For the studios, publicity and marketing are crucial. They depend on other forms of mass media to inform the public about the forthcoming releases of new movies.

Elaborate marketing and publicity campaigns are focused on the crucial opening weekend for a film. Most of the carefully orchestrated publicity occurs during the final two weeks before opening day. If the first three days bring favorable reviews and strong boxoffice receipts, word-of-mouth support usually gives a picture "legs," as the jargon goes.

In the advance promotion, publicists select a selling strategy. What element in the film is most likely to pull in the audience? Story? Stars, action, and drama? Startling special effects?

*The Bridges of Madison County*, for example, was based on a hit novel; its story of a love affair between an itinerant photographer and a lonesome farm wife was well known. So promotion concentrated on the film's stars, Meryl Streep and Clint Eastwood. Speculation was encouraged: did they strike an electric spark in the film as the characters did in the book? The stars appeared on broadcasts, saying how exciting it was to work together. They gave magazine interviews. Newspaper stories discussed their careers using material from the producer.

In contrast, *Apollo 13*, a competitor for summer audiences, concerned the perils of U.S. astronauts in space. So, its promotion emphasized tension.

Spectacular opening nights with sweeping searchlight beams and celebrities arriving in limousines are a long-time Hollywood staple. Disney topped this approach, however, by opening *Pocahontas* with a public showing in New York's Central Park attended by 100,000 people. Nationwide TV and newspaper coverage was intense.

Even such spectacles don't guarantee favorable reviews. While most reviewers praised the film's brilliant animation, many complained about its historical inaccuracy. The *Wall Street Journal* referred to the Indian princess as "Disney's cartoon squaw" and commented, "*Pocahontas* marks Disney's ill-advised entry into the teaching profession, where the pitfalls are many and the rewards problematical."

## Ties with Television

Once separate camps suspicious of each other, the motion picture and television industries have been drawn close together through interlocking ownerships and mutually beneficial financial deals.

For example, media tycoon Rupert Murdoch owns both Twentieth Century Fox studios and a group of metropolitan stations, part of his Fox television network, that show the studio's films. Through a series of complicated deals, Ted Turner now owns more than 3000 old motion pictures from major studios, including black-and-white classics such as *King Kong*. He adds color to these old films, then releases them for a new life on television and home video. Traditional movie enthusiasts maintain that computerized colorization destroys the artistic values of black-and-white photography but have been unable to block use of the process.

Those who control a new film manipulate the sequence of its appearance on various outlets to generate the largest sums possible. A common sequence is to release the film initially in first-run movie houses; second, on videocassettes for the home audience; third, on pay-per-view television, in which the viewer pays a special added fee to see the new picture; fourth, on regular pay cable television, in which the viewer sees it as a part of basic cable service for which he or she pays a monthly fee; and fifth, on free television.

The fabulously successful *Jurassic Park* followed that pattern, with one exception. It grossed $913 million at the theater boxoffice worldwide, then sold 21.5 million video copies. The picture ran successfully for several weeks as a pay-per-view attraction. Next, the NBC network paid a reported $50 million to show the movie three times on its television network, drawing a huge audience for the first showing in 1995. Industry observers believed that NBC paid the exceptionally high price in order to get the picture on network TV ahead of its cable appearances.

Knowledge that a movie will be shown on the small home screen as well as the large theatrical screen influences the way in which it is shot. Differing close-up techniques and camera angles are considered. So is plot development, to permit breaks for commercials at convenient intervals. Television has long borrowed program ideas from motion pictures. For example, the enormously popular TV series "M*A*S*H" was derived from the earlier movie of the same name. Recently, the process has worked in reverse; motion pictures borrow ideas and material from television shows and blow them up into big-screen productions—more evidence that the two industries are inextricably tied together.

**The International Movie.**    Part of the lifestyle that characterizes the new Hollywood involves the international movie. A step toward internationalization occurred in the 1950s. The independent producers, not shackled to particular film studios, made movies in Europe and other foreign locations to profit from cheaper labor costs and national subsidies, to use authentic locales and to please the movie stars who, by establishing residence in a foreign country, at that time could avoid paying U.S. income tax on money earned while working abroad.

An international movie is not the output of the film industry of a single foreign country; it is a melange of performers, production concepts, and scenery from several countries. To cite one example, most of the

# HUGH GRANT'S LUCKY ESCAPE

Protecting clients who get into trouble is part of a Hollywood publicist's job. The careers of some movie stars are ruined by scandal. Others, such as Hugh Grant, a youngish British actor just becoming known in the United States, have escaped virtually unscathed from their misdeeds.

Los Angeles police vice officers arrested Grant for lewd conduct with a prostitute in public near Sunset Boulevard. He was taken to jail and booked, two weeks before the opening of his film, *Nine Months*.

The classic Hollywood damage-control operation began immediately. Through his publicist, Grant issued a brief apology for doing something "completely insane." The publicist canceled all the actor's scheduled media interviews promoting the film. Grant flew to England and went into hiding. When the case came up in court, an attorney appeared in his place and entered a guilty plea.

Two days before *Nine Months* opened, Grant made a carefully staged appearance on Jay Leno's late-night NBC television show. He turned on the smiling "aw shucks" boyish style he uses in films and said he couldn't explain his behavior. He took the same sheepish apologetic line on "Larry King Live." In Hollywood, Grant was greeted with smiles and hugs at the premiere party for the movie. His longtime girlfriend Elizabeth Hurley, reportedly angry with him, clung to his arm.

Grant was fined $1108. His new film took in $16.3 million at the boxoffice during the first 10 days of showing. The prostitute received a reported $150,000 from the *News of the World*, a London Sunday scandal newspaper, for an interview describing their meeting. She said she had never heard of Grant before he picked her up. Many moviegoers said they hadn't, either, but bought tickets because they were attracted by the publicity.

filming of the Home Box Office made-for-pay-TV film, *The Far Pavilions*, was done in England, with location shots made in New Delhi and Jaipur, India. Featured in the cast were three English performers, an Italian, an Egyptian, and an American.

The mobility of contemporary moviemakers has been aided by certain technological developments. Lightweight cameras and sound recording equipment, as well as ministudios capable of being airlifted, are allowing movie producers to set up shooting wherever whim and geography dictate.

The many film festivals prevalent today are additional evidence of the internationalism of the film industry. Festivals in Cannes, Berlin, Venice, San Sebastian, New York, Moscow, Montreal, Cork, Chicago, and Mexico City have provided showcases for films from every nation and a meeting site and marketplace for actors, directors, writers, and producers.

Other international aspects of filmmaking and distribution are discussed in Chapter 17.

## American Experimental Filmmakers

Stimulated by the innovations in filmmaking coming from Europe in the years soon after World War II, numerous young Americans turned to film to give shape to their feelings and ideas, as their predecessors (and many of their contemporaries) had chosen the more traditional vehicles of drama, fiction, poetry, painting, and sculpture.

Much of the credit for publicizing and organizing the work and aesthetic doctrines of America's experimental filmmakers goes to Jonas Mekas, himself a filmmaker, in addition to having served as editor of *Film Culture*, occasional film critic for the *Village Voice*, and organizer of the Film Makers' Cooperative and Distribution Center. In describing his own work and that of other independent filmmakers, Mekas said:

> Our movies come from our hearts—our little movies, not the Hollywood movies. Our movies are like extensions of our own pulse, of our heartbeat, of our eyes, our fingertips; they are so personal, so unambitious in their movement, in their use of light, their imagery. We want to surround this earth with our film frames and warm it up—until it begins to move.

Of extreme importance to the experimental filmmakers is the noncommercial and intensely personal nature of their films. The actors are often friends, and usually nonprofessionals. In many instances, desire and budget dictate that the film be the result of one person who functions as producer, director, cameraperson, editor, and often distributor. Because video is less expensive, the camcorder largely has replaced the 16-mm camera. There is an absence of chronological continuity and carefully plotted story lines, along with considerable use of improvisation and emphasis on spontaneous action and reaction rather than on stagy performance.

The many purposes and styles of American experimental films and videos range from social criticism using documentary techniques to embodiments of the subconscious through surrealism and myth to psychedelic experiments with light and color. At their best, the films of the avant garde are exciting, fresh, sensitive, and fully able to transmit their maker's vision.

## Film Criticism

As film's potential for personal and artistic expression was realized, and as its capability for being more than a cheap entertainment medium was understood, an accompanying aesthetic developed to explain and analyze the form and content of motion pictures. Vachel Lindsay's *The Art of the Moving Picture* (1915) and Rudolf Arnheim's *Film* (1933) are early examples of enlightened film criticism. Later, James Agee achieved even greater acclaim for his work.

Good film criticism, like good literary criticism, serves two functions: (1) It explicates the work at hand, and (2) it elevates the public taste. The first function is the more obvious. As film techniques have become more complex, as film has probed deeper into human sensibility and experience, and as films have become identifiable as the work of individual directors who use personal symbols in the manner of contemporary poets and novelists, effective film criticism seeks to explain this heightened complexity by clarifying techniques, images, and relationships of time, place, and character.

The second purpose is perhaps best explained by Walt Whitman's often-quoted remark that great audiences make great poets. An audience knowledgeable about film history and techniques is in a position to recognize the second-rate, the false, the vacuous, the film that appears to be saying something but in reality says nothing, and the slick directorial tricks that attempt to hide the untrue. Advances in film technology and subject matter have occurred and will continue to occur because film artists and film audience have become knowledgeable together.

At its best, good film criticism is informative, expanding the reader's knowledge by relating the film at hand to other works of a particular filmmaker, or to other films of similar or dissimilar genre. It bears the stamp of its creator's mind by possessing a distinctive style; it bridges epochs and nations by linking past with present achievement regardless of country of origin.

In all this, the film critic must be distinguished from the film reviewer, who serves a reportorial function. Whereas the film critic seeks to analyze and explain, the film reviewer seeks to ascertain the merits of a particular film with the intention of warning audiences against an inferior, boring, or morally degrading film, or touting those films with a high entertainment value. The commentaries of both critic and reviewer, however, are influenced by their aesthetic judgments and broad knowledge of film history.

## The Documentary Film

**Documentary**
Photograph(s) or film depicting real life

In both England and America, the documentary film came of age in the 1930s through direct patronage by national governments, and matured, still under government auspices, during the troubled years of World War II. Perhaps this is not surprising, as a documentary's purpose is always partially social—setting forth public and private crises and victories, showing us where humanity has been and what, inevitably, humanity will become unless proper action is taken.

The documentary film had its start in 1922. Hired by a New York fur company to film the life of an Eskimo family, Robert Flaherty overcame great technological difficulties in the Arctic climate to produce *Nanook of the North*. From this film developed the documentary tradition that has given filmmaking some of its finest products.

During the Depression years, Pare Lorentz produced *The Plow That Broke the Plains* for the Farm Security Administration (FSA) in the same spirit as the FSA team of photo documentarians who, under the guidance of Roy E. Stryker, made more than 272,000 negatives and 150,000 prints of the United States and its dust bowls and migratory workers. Lorentz's 1937 film, *The River*, visualized the problems of erosion in the Mississippi River basin with more power than had his previous documentary.

A third form of factual story-telling on film, halfway between the newsreel and documentary, was *The March of Time*, a weekly *news magazine of the screen*. Started by Time Inc. in 1935, it played for 16 years. At its peak in the late 1930s and the early years of World War II, it was seen by audiences of nearly 20 million per week in more than 9000 American theaters. Louis de Rochemont, the producer, used real events and actors, skillfully blended, to present an interpretive account of an event in relation to its background.

World War II gave impetus to increased documentary film production, ranging from training films for U.S. service personnel to informative films for a civilian population needing instruction in wartime procedures. Hollywood directors such as John Huston, William Wyler, and John Ford began making films for the military, as well. *San Pietro* (1944), *Memphis Belle* (1944), and *Battle of Midway* (1944) are memorable documentaries filmed on and around battlegrounds.

In England, the documentary filmmakers working under the aegis of the Ministry of Information also turned their attention to wartime subjects, producing films such as *London Can Take It* (1940), depicting London during a Nazi air raid; *Target for Tonight* (1941), documenting an air force bombing mission; and *Desert Victory* (1942), an account of the North African campaign.

## Documentaries on Television

Television has largely replaced the motion picture industry as the creator of documentaries. One fine example of a 1960s television documentary, and one that used cinemá verité techniques, is *Royal Family*, produced by a consortium of BBC and England's independent television companies and shown on American television. Richard Cawston served as producer-director, working with an eight-person crew throughout nearly a full year of shooting 43 hours of film. Cawston has attributed the success of this film to the royal family's willingness to talk without restraint, ad-libbing in front of the cameras, with the knowledge that Queen Elizabeth and Prince Philip had the right to veto any sections they found unacceptable in retrospect.

The use of television to throw a spotlight on serious social and political issues through well-researched documentaries produced what some observers call "the golden age of television documentaries" during the 1960s and 1970s. Such national network programs as "The Selling of the Pentagon," "Pensions: the Broken Promise," and "Harvest of Shame" are examples. Gradually, however, the costs entailed in researching and

**Cinemá verité**
Film format using a camera to record reality in an unbiased and unmanipulative manner. Also known as spontaneous or direct cinema

producing these documentaries and, particularly, the revenues lost to competing entertainment shows diminished the number of documentaries shown by the networks.

CBS-TV's "60 Minutes," an hour-long show consisting of three or four short documentary pieces, has continued to draw top ratings, and, in its weekly "48 Hours" magazine-style news documentary with Dan Rather, CBS-TV has provided powerful coverage of timely topics. ABC-TV's "20/20" has done well, and NBC-TV has scored with "Date-line NBC." Today's outstanding documentaries generally are shown not on the traditional networks, but on Cable News Network, PBS, HBO, Discovery and Arts and Entertainment, and on a surprisingly large number of independent stations (see Chapter 10).

## The Sponsored Film

**Sponsored film**
Motion picture provided by a company or organization seeking to deliver information or a message

The term *sponsored* is used as a catch-all description for the thousands of films made for showing to industrial and sales groups, schools and universities, government and community organizations, the armed forces, and professional and religious groups.

A commercial entertainment film is made to earn money at the box office; a sponsored film is created to inform or influence viewers on a special topic. Usually, sponsored films are shown free to audiences. Production and distribution costs are borne by the sponsor, whose cause, whatever it may be, is advanced by showings of the picture. In theatrical films, advocacy is uncommon and when present is incidental to the primary purpose of boxoffice profit. In sponsored films it frequently is the primary purpose. Such advocacy may promote a commercial product or may urge such noncommercial goals as better health practices and in-plant safety.

While not widely publicized, this area of production is booming. It presents substantially greater opportunities than does Hollywood for newcomers with skill and creativity. About 600 established producing and marketing firms for sponsored films operate worldwide; numerous others, often not much more than one-person operations, exist on the fringes. Federal and state governments make many such films. About 15,000 nontheatrical films are produced each year.

The cost of making and distributing a good company film averages $200,000, with some major productions exceeding $500,000. As many as 200 prints are made for some films to satisfy the demand. The average total audience for such a film is estimated to be 1.5 million. Many educational and instructional films are produced on far smaller budgets, some of them only a few thousand dollars, and are shown to more limited audiences. There are 2600 film libraries in the United States distributing 16-mm films. *The H.W. Wilson Educational Film Guide* lists more than 20,000 films that can be borrowed.

## Points to Remember

1. Why was *The Great Train Robbery* so significant in the early development of motion pictures?

2. In what year did talking pictures appear? Who was the first performer to be heard on the screen?

3. What two major developments contributed to a sharp decline in the motion picture business after its peak attendance in the late 1940s?

4. After 60 years as fixtures on movie house programs, why did the newsreels go out of business? Name two of the best-known newsreel companies.

5. How does today's independent film production differ from the methods employed by major studios in the days of such moguls as Louis B. Mayer?

6. What are the letter categories in the motion picture rating system, and what does each mean?

7. How is film criticism distinguished from film reviewing?

8. How do theatrical motion pictures and sponsored films differ in purpose and financing?

## Media Questions to Think About

1. How frequently do you go to the movies? What prevents you from going more often—mainly time, price, or lack of films that attract you?

2. If you have seen any black-and-white films recently, how do you compare them with current hit movies in terms of story content, dramatic approach, taste, and star personality?

3. Does the rating of a movie, from G to NC-17, influence your decision about attending it?

# ISSUE FOUR

## Credibility

## Can We Trust the Media?

Do the news media have substantial public support as to believability? How bitter are the media critics?

How strongly does the public agree with journalists' belief that the press is needed as a "watchdog" of government?

Does the public feel that the media overemphasize the personal scandals of public figures?

What do the polls tell us about the trust placed in public figures and officeholders? Which is more cynical and distrustful—the media or the public?

Would most Americans give unqualified support to the First Amendment if voted on today?

How did Presidents Reagan and Bush fare in their dealings with the media? How did President Clinton seemingly harm his image?

Did the military unduly restrict the news media in their coverage of the Persian Gulf War?

The answers to these questions will be found in the following pages, which begin with a report of several major studies of press credibility and public support for the media made during 1995 and the preceding 10 years. These reports showed a more substantial public support of the media in terms of believability than many journalists had estimated; they also showed shortcomings in press performance that fan criticism. Most important, they demonstrated that the "watchdog" function of the press is highly regarded: 67 percent of respondents to one survey said press criticism keeps leaders from doing things that should not be done, while only 17 percent thought press criticism keeps leaders from "doing their job."

If the role of the press is to serve the governed, not the governors, as Justice Hugo L. Black declared, then the self-assigned role of the press to act as censors of the government is vitally necessary in a democracy. In the past three decades or so there has been a credibility duel between government and the press, with the public alternating its support between a particular president and the media.

## Measuring Media Credibility

The American public feels that the news media have become too focused on reporting the misdeeds and other failings of public figures, according to a 1995 survey conducted by the Times Mirror Center for the People and the Press. Nearly three-quarters of the public, the report disclosed, feel journalists drive the personal scandals of politicians rather than just report facts.

"What it says is the public still wants the press in a watchdog role, but it wants a better-mannered one with not so much blood lust," said Andrew Kohut, center director. "The press has to convey that it is protecting the public interest, not merely uncovering wrongdoing for the sake of uncovering wrongdoing."

For example, the public considers that the media have spent too much time doing stories on President Bill Clinton's character, but only 39 percent of members of the national news media feel so, according to the poll.

Indeed, the survey found some surprising results when comparing the public's view of journalism with the views of journalists. Among them:

- Journalists turned out to be much less cynical about politicians and officeholders than the public, with 59 percent of the general public distrustful versus about 25 percent of journalists.
- While 22 percent of the public felt the national media were sensationalistic, only 11 percent of journalists agreed.
- Forty-eight percent of the journalists felt there was too little coverage of the Clinton administration's achievements, while

## THE BARKING WATCHDOG

The Advertising Council conducted a public service campaign with the title "The Barking Watchdog" to increase public awareness of the First Amendment in the late 1980s.

The Watchdog name was adopted from a speech by Alan Barth, former editorial writer for the Washington *Post*. Barth drew an analogy between the press and a barking watchdog. He said, "If you want a watchdog to warn you of intruders, you must put up with a certain amount of mistaken barking. Some extraneous barking is the price you must pay for his service as a watchdog."

President Clinton has a soft drink in a field with two voters during a speaking tour. His ability to mingle easily with strangers is an important aspect of his political technique. (Time Life Photo)

only 25 percent of the public agreed, with 22 percent saying there had been too much coverage.

- More than half the public agreed with House Speaker Newt Gingrich that the press had been too cynical and negative in covering the 1995 Congress, but eight in ten national journalists disagreed.

"There appears to be a cultural divide that the press itself acknowledges," Kohut said. "The public is saying the national media is part of the problem. They identify more of the 'gotcha' journalism and out-of-control journalism with national news organizations."

One more example of the "cultural divide": more than half of the public says homosexuality should be discouraged, but eight in ten journalists believe it should be accepted.

Responding to the survey were 515 journalists and 2000 others.

**Previous Polls Support Findings.**   How much credibility, then, do the mass media have in the eyes of the public? More credibility than the most vehement critics believe, judging from the results of polls during the past decade, but less than ardent supporters of the media contend.

Most Americans support the principle of the First Amendment to the U.S. Constitution guaranteeing freedom of speech (see Chapter 3). Many, however, are ready to abandon aspects of its guarantee if the principle of the First Amendment gets in the way of their personal beliefs

**Public opinion study**
Method of determining the prevailing frame of mind publicly expressed by a significant number of people on an issue of public concern

about political or social situations. About two-thirds or more of Americans fail to give unqualified support for certain press rights, according to a major survey commissioned by the American Society of Newspaper Editors in 1991, the 200th anniversary of the First Amendment.

Several conclusions that run counter to the conventional wisdom concerning public opinion and the nation's press resulted from an in-depth study titled *The People and the Press*. It was commissioned in the mid-1980s by the Times Mirror Center for the People and the Press and carried out by the Gallup Organization.

If credibility is defined as believability, the report says, then there is no credibility crisis for the nation's news media. Nor are journalists' concerns that public perceptions characterize them as inaccurate and arrogant folk borne out by the data. But the study offers cautions. Overall measures of favorability reveal a reservoir of public support that is wide but not deep. The public appreciates the press far more than it approves of news media performance. Its marks for believability are good, not excellent. Its approval is asymmetrical: critics are more critical than supporters are supportive. But, says the Times Mirror study, emphatic public appreciation of the press's watchdog role against the government and an inherent desire to get the news are two factors washing out dissatisfactions with press performance.

**Residual Public Support.**   In one area the public already stands solidly on the side of the press. When the issues involve the rights of news organizations versus the rights of the government, the public usually sides with the press. As a Times Mirror survey concluded:

> The public says "no" to formal censorship and says "no" to prior restraint. The public says "no" to the government requiring fairness in news coverage. The public says "no" to the government requiring equal advertising time on television or space in newspapers for political candidates. And the public says "yes," emphatically, to publishing a story such as the Pentagon Papers [to be discussed in this Issue].

Seventy-nine percent of respondents agreed with this statement in an ASNE study: "I may not be happy with everything the press does, but if the government tried to close down a newspaper and stop it from publishing, I'd be upset enough to do something."

Nevertheless, a 1992 Times Mirror survey titled "The Generation Divide" found that younger Americans know less—and care less—about public affairs than their elders. The survey confirmed a disturbing parallel trend linking apathy and ignorance to young people's growing dependence on television as their primary information source. Only about 35 percent of those over 35 say television is their main news source.

To all the people who think the press goes too far sometimes, consider the alternative.

WASHINGTON (AP) — New details about the Navy's 1965 lo...

...device. It was lost in ...waters about 80 miles from the closest point of the Okinawa island chain ...about 200 miles ...

comment.

...d an associate. Joshua ...said their...

To learn more about the role of a Free Press and how it protects your rights, call the First Amendment Center at 1-800-542-1600.

If the press didn't tell us, who would?

A public service message of The Ad Council and The Society of Professional Journalists.

The impact of censorship on the press is demonstrated dramatically in this advertisement prepared by the Advertising Council as part of a campaign supporting the First Amendment.

## Media Influence on Politics

Media coverage of politics, especially at the national level, is massive, both in news reports and commentary. Newspapers, magazines, and broadcasts flood the public with news about what happens in Congress, at the White House, and on the campaign trail.

Columnists take radically conflicting positions in appealing to different segments of the political spectrum, from liberal to ultraconservative. Radio talk show hosts, the majority of whom are ardently conservative, discuss political developments voluminously. With all this exposure, however, uncertainty remains as to the extent that media coverage influences the outcome of elections.

One problem with political coverage is the tendency of reporters, hunting in packs, to emphasize personal conflicts and scandal reports at the expense of substantial coverage of issues. They do this because the public's appetite for such information is, or appears to be, immense. An example: the Republican majority that took over Congress in 1995, for the first time in 40 years, prepared an elaborate opening-day schedule that introduced legislation they had promised to bring up. Much of the media coverage that day, however, focused on the disclosure by newly elected House Speaker Newt Gingrich's mother, in a broadcast interview with CBS television anchor Connie Chung, that Gingrich had called President Clinton's wife Hillary "a bitch." Probably this remark caused far more dinner table conversation than the day's legislative actions.

Displeasure with the often nasty, extremely negative 1994 congressional election was extensive. In fact, however, editors and broadcast news producers have been blamed wrongly for much of what happened.

The most vicious, misleading campaign claims appeared in "attack" television commercials purchased by candidates, portraying their opponents as incompetent and often dishonest. Editors and reporters had no control over these advertisements, which were accepted by media managements. Rarely in such 30-second commercials did the candidates tell the public specifically how, if elected, they planned to achieve socially desired results.

Postelection surveys generally showed that this barrage of demeaning negative campaigning, while decried by many viewers, helped numerous congressional and state candidates to win elections. This outcome encouraged candidates to use these same tactics in the 1996 campaign.

## The Presidency and the Media

Every U.S. president seeks media support for his policies and recurring fights with Congress. Each chief executive, aided by public relations advisers, tries to manipulate members of the White House press corps and to reach the public over their heads. Some achieve quite good results; others fail wretchedly.

## Nixon and Watergate

**Watergate**
Word characterizing illegal actions by Nixon administration officials, including the 1972 break-in at Democratic Party offices in the Watergate Tower

Conflict between a president and the media reached unprecedented proportions during the terms of Richard M. Nixon in the early 1970s. Vindictive and secretive, Nixon put some Washington reporters on his private "enemies list" and tried to take punitive action against publications and broadcasters opposed to him.

The animosity between press and president climaxed during the Watergate scandal. This began when a bungled burglary attempt in the Democratic National Committee headquarters at the Watergate Building complex in Washington was revealed as a White House-instigated

# THE PENTAGON PAPERS

When the New York *Times* began in June 1971 to publish a series of news articles summarizing the contents of a 47-volume study of the origins of the Vietnam War, the "Pentagon Papers case" erupted. The study had been made for Defense Secretary Robert McNamara by the RAND Corporation. It was historical and revealed no military secrets or strategy, but it was highly explosive in terms of political and diplomatic interest.

When the first installment appeared, Attorney General John Mitchell asked the *Times* to stop the series. The newspaper refused, and the Nixon administration went to court to seek a prior restraint order forbidding further publication. The government obtained a temporary restraining or-der but was refused a permanent one. It engaged in a second duel in the courts with the Washington *Post*.

The case finally reached the Supreme Court, which by a five-to-four vote continued the temporary prior restraint order, a shocking setback to the free press concept. The newspaper lawyers then avoided a historic showdown on the absolute nature of the constitutional ban on prior restraint and argued only that the government could not prove any involvement of national security in the banned publication. To this, the Supreme Court agreed, six to three, and the series resumed.

In 1995, in a reversal of his policy during the war, McNamara confessed that the Vietnam war was a bad mistake.

attempt to steal the opposing party's secrets. As evidence of White House complicity in the crime and the cover-up emerged—largely provided by the splendid investigative reporting of two Washington *Post* staff members, Carl Bernstein and Bob Woodward—tension heightened between Nixon and the White House press. At one news conference, Nixon blurted out under intense questioning, "I am not a crook!"

Finally, evidence was produced that Nixon had indeed participated personally in the Watergate conspiracy. Facing impeachment, Nixon resigned from the presidency on August 9, 1974.

## Reagan and Bush

During the 1980s, Ronald Reagan, a longtime motion picture and television actor, had a generally smooth eight-year relationship with the media, with one striking exception. He limited his exposure to reporters to a relatively few well-rehearsed news conferences; brief, carefully staged "photo opportunities"; and speeches, usually before friendly audiences. At these appearances, he exuded amiability, made quips, told sentimental stories, and delivered patriotic lines. His wife Nancy, a former actress, played the role of admiring supporter at his side. Criticism seemed to slide off Reagan so easily that he was jokingly called "the Teflon president."

Reagan's stature as the "great communicator" was damaged, however, by the Iran-Contra crisis. He professed lack of knowledge about his administration's secret sale of arms to Iran in exchange for American hostages and illegal diversion of the arms sale profits to the Contra forces in Nicaragua. Many of his critics doubted his claim.

**Iran-Contra**
White House scandal of 1986 involving secret sale of government-owned munitions to Iranians as a step toward release of U.S. hostages; profits were then diverted illegally to aid Contra forces in Nicaragua

Reagan's successor, George Bush, lacked Reagan's acting skills but enjoyed relatively good relations with the media through much of his term. He held many news conferences and gave individual interviews. The flurry of good news he reported near the end of the Cold War showed him in a good light. Bush received severe criticism from the media during the Persian Gulf War, however, for his policy of restricting and manipulating reporters trying to cover the conflict. (See "The Media and the Military" section of this Issue.)

## Clinton's Personal Problems

No modern-day president has had his private life so closely scrutinized as President Bill Clinton. Unfavorable, controversial stories about a White House occupant usually involve his policies. In Clinton's case, they dealt as well with his personal affairs, both sexual and financial.

When Clinton, then governor of Arkansas, emerged as a prominent candidate for the 1992 Democratic presidential nomination, the press along with his opponents in both parties searched intently through his home-state record.

Published reports alleged his sexual misconduct and improper participation in a land development project called Whitewater. Although legally unsubstantiated and unrelated to his conduct as president, these innuendo-laden reports have plagued him throughout his campaign and presidency. They were compounded by Republican assertions that the White House staff interfered improperly in the Whitewater investigation. An Arkansas woman sued Clinton during his presidency, alleging intimate details of sexual abuse. A federal judge postponed any trial on the charges until after Clinton left office but allowed development of evidence during his presidency. (See Issue 1.)

From these stories came the so-called "character issue" in White House politics. Clinton's most vehement foes denounced him as a philanderer, a friend of homosexuals, and a dishonest businessman. The result was a wave of "I hate the man in the White House" talk much more intense than most presidents faced. The "religious right," strong in the South, was especially vocal in its condemnation.

What marred Clinton's image so greatly? Political analysts and psychologists point to a convergence of causes. As the first of the post–World War II "baby boomers" to reach the White House, and a Washington outsider as well, he disturbed entrenched political forces in the capital. His effort to bypass the Washington press corps and reach the public directly through radio talk shows and similar means aggravated the situation.

As an activist president with a list of social legislative goals, Clinton almost automatically stirred up vocal, powerful detractors. His support for homosexuals in the armed forces angered the Christian right and the veterans lobby, already upset because he had avoided the Vietnam war draft. His support for abortion did the same to the Roman Catholic hierarchy and some other church groups. When he introduced a sweeping health care reform plan, he encountered ardent resistance from insurance companies, the medical profession, and hospital owners, all fighting to protect their positions in the health care system. These groups spent millions of dollars in advertising and lobbying to block passage of the Clinton plan. Many of the president's opponents on political issues were quite content to see the "character issue" kept alive to undercut his popularity.

The fact that Clinton placed his wife, Hillary Rodham Clinton, in charge of the health care reform campaign also stirred resentment among traditionalists. Americans were accustomed to seeing their First Ladies in the role of dutiful helpmate, presiding graciously in the White House and supporting a noncontroversial social service cause. The exception was Eleanor Roosevelt, who served as her husband Franklin's "eyes and ears" before and during World War II. Mrs. Clinton expressed great admiration for Mrs. Roosevelt. As a successful attorney, Mrs. Clinton epitomized the ambitious young professional career woman. Although many First Ladies had exercised strong backstage influence, having a presidential wife placed in active charge of a major political program created some public uneasiness.

Media concentration on Clinton's private life contributed to deterioration of the traditional aura of dignity and reserve surrounding the office of the president. The right of privacy long accorded to a chief executive when not dealing with official business has dwindled before the "anything goes" aggressiveness of tabloid newspapers and broadcasters. This has caused many observers to worry that the stature of the presidency has been eroded.

Republicans kept trying to exploit the "character" issue after Clinton took office, primarily through a Senate committee's prolonged, repetitious investigation of the Whitewater land deal in which Clinton was involved in Arkansas while governor. They talked "character" again during the 1996 presidential campaign. When the Republicans became the majority in the 1995 Congress, they sought to enact their "Contract with America" into law over Clinton's objections. One GOP congressman even called the president "irrelevant." Much of this program failed to become law, however, either from presidential veto or resistance in the Senate.

As the 1996 election neared, a decided shift in public opinion emerged in Clinton's favor. When the Republicans twice caused shutdowns of the federal government, in an attempt to force their will on the president in their argument about balancing the budget, a large portion of the electorate blamed the GOP for the unprecedented closures and inconvenience.

These developments were coupled with Clinton's dignified, articulate public performance as president, an upsurge in the economy, and the apparent success of his dispatch of U.S. troops as a peacekeeping force in Bosnia. As a result, Clinton entered his campaign for reelection with a strong lead in the polls over retired Senator Bob Dole, especially among female voters.

## The Media and the Military

American journalists have a good record of delaying broadcasts or publication when lives are at stake, especially during wartime. Even so, in the aftermath of the Vietnam conflict, the Pentagon and several administrations tried repeatedly to restrict or prevent battlefield reporting whenever possible. When U.S. troops invaded Grenada in 1983, the press was excluded entirely. When troops were landed in Panama in 1990, a press pool of reporters and photographers was brought in four hours after the fighting started and held in restricted circumstances for another six hours.

**The Persian Gulf War.**   The news media's battle for access to war news continued throughout the Persian Gulf War and long after it ended. "Free press falls victim to war," was the headline of an article in *Quill*, a magazine for journalists, in October 1991. U.S. Secretary of State James Baker even told as a joke what many of his government colleagues told as a truth: "After Desert Storm who could not be moved by the sight of that poor demoralized rabble—outwitted, outflanked, outmaneuvered by the U.S. military. But, I think, given time, the press will bounce back!"

Department of Defense guidelines for war coverage included (1) a pool system strictly controlling the number of journalists covering combat units; (2) review of stories, photos, and video by military officials before the reports were dispatched to the United States; and (3) restrictions on reporting in the States. Said Paul McMasters, Freedom of Information chairman for the Society of Professional Journalists:

> These restrictions were accompanied by a carefully prepared public information strategy that included military briefers handpicked for their abilities before TV cameras; elaborate rehearsal of briefers; forbidding Pentagon spokesmen from appearing on programs with any of the 16 plaintiffs in a lawsuit challenging the pool system; and polite forgetfulness of journalists' requests for video footage and other information.

Most complaints centered on operation of the National Media Pool.

- Once hostilities began, the pools should have been dropped in favor of independent coverage. This didn't happen when the air war began January 17, nor when the ground war began February 23.

United States General Norman Schwartzkopf, commander of coalition forces in the Persian Gulf War, points to a troop position during a press briefing in Saudi Arabia. Much of the war news was released at such press briefings, while restrictions were placed on correspondents who sought to observe the fighting first-hand. (AP/Wide World)

- During the air war, pool reporters were accompanied by military public affairs officers who often interrupted interviews to object to what was being said or asked, and whose presence inhibited sincere responses.
- During the 100-hour ground war, pool reports from battle scenes were delayed, often for hours and sometimes days.

Secretary of Defense Dick Cheney defended the pool system, saying it was impossible to handle up to 1600 news staff members in a war zone. Reporters termed that figure cumulative over seven months and said that midway through the war no more than 300 journalists were trying to get slots in pools.

Peter Arnett, a Cable News Network reporter and former Pulitzer Prize-winning Associated Press reporter, was the only U.S. journalist to broadcast from Baghdad during most of the war. That distinction re-

# Unconditional surrender of the U.S. press

Restrictions placed on U.S. correspondents during the Persian Gulf War were condemned by numerous writers and broadcasters.

sulted in some characterizations of him as an Iraqi sympathizer. In a Washington *Post* opinion piece, Arnett termed such comments vindictive and slanderous:

> The reason I stayed . . . is quite simple. Reporting is what I do for a living. I made a full commitment to journalism years ago. If you ask, are some stories worth the risk of dying for, my answer is yes—and many of my journalist friends have died believing this.

Eighty-three percent of Americans polled by the Times Mirror Center for the People and the Press said the press did a good to excellent job of covering the war. About 83 percent of respondents said they viewed military restrictions on war news coverage as a good thing, and about 58 percent chided the press as "going too far" in breaking away from the pool to report independently. Four of five persons polled by the Roper Organization said they got most of their news about the war from television.

In 1992, chief news executives and defense officials agreed on guidelines for future conflicts. Included were provisions for training, equipping, and staffing military units to accommodate reporters on the battlefield. The Pentagon, however, retained its option to review news material that might endanger troop safety or the success of a military mission.

The pool was already in place and planes and ships were en route to invade Haiti when former President Jimmy Carter negotiated a peaceful solution to the return of President Jean-Bertrand Aristide to the island nation in 1994. Citing "strong planning" and "good faith" on the part of the military, Jon Wolman, Washington bureau chief of the Associated Press, said, "It looked as if it could have been a successful combat pool."

# PART FIVE
## The Persuasive Professions

## ROLES OF THE MEDIA–PERSUADER

Persuading people to accept ideas and products, and to approve institutions and companies, is the goal of advertising and public relations.

*"The trouble with us in America is not that the poetry of life has turned to prose, but that it has turned to advertising copy."*

–John Kronenberger, critic

*"The hand that rules the press, the radio, the screen, and the far-spread magazine rules the country; whether we like it or not, we must learn to accept it."*

–Learned Hand, U.S. jurist

*"Cheek to cheek . . . they meant to be . . . the lights went out . . . and so did she . . . he needed . . . Burma Shave."*

–Jingle from famous highway small-sign advertising campaign of 1930s

# CHAPTER FIFTEEN
## Advertising

## Advertising Women "Pay Dues," Rise to the Top

It's an "old boys' club" no longer. After about 20 years in the trenches, women in increasing numbers have been moving into the advertising industry's executive suites in the 1990s. Calling the trend a "phenomenon driven by changing attitudes among male agency executives—and clients," the *Wall Street Journal* listed a half dozen such top appointments during a single year. Among them: Mary Lou Quintas, chief executive of N.W. Ayer & Partners; Susan Gianinno, head of the New York office of WPP Group's J. Walter Thompson Company; and Linda Kaplan Thaler, executive vice president and executive creative director of Wells Rich Green/BBDO.

The critical factor in the rise of women, according to a senior male executive, is that they are finally being accepted by the clients. Prejudices are falling, such as a former view that women shouldn't work on automotive accounts.

It really hasn't taken so long for women to break into the senior ranks, said O. Burch Drake, president and chief executive officer of the American Association of Advertising Agencies.

"Women had to work their way through the system," he added. "Women didn't start to actively join the business until the past 20 years. It's a slow rise to the top. Now they've paid their dues."

**A**dvertising is indelibly woven into the fabric of our society. It is credited with raising our standard of living, lowering unit costs of mass-produced goods, providing information, and helping new firms enter the marketplace. Without advertising we would pay far more for most of the mass media that we enjoy.

Despite the fragmentation of the mass market into hundreds of smaller markets and the development of new ways of communicating with consumers, business firms still spend well over $150 billion to advertise their goods, services, and ideas in the United States each year.

In recent years, advertising by U.S. corporations in other nations has increased dramatically with the spread of business internationally, fueled by new communication technologies. The formation of giant transnational advertising agencies has greatly affected the industry.

In this chapter, we discuss the development, function, regulation, trends, and problems of the industry, including the present and prospective role of advertising on the Internet.

## The Role of Advertising

Advertising plays a unique and central role in the American economic system. Along with other forms of marketing communication, it helps to sell ideas, goods, and services. As a large part of the environment in which we live, advertising both reflects and affects our very lifestyles and thus plays a substantial social role. And, particularly since the advent of television, advertising figures prominently in our political decisions.

The American Marketing Association defines advertising as *any paid form of nonpersonal presentation and promotion of ideas, goods, or services by an identified sponsor.* Thus, advertising is distinguished from publicity in that the medium using publicity does not receive payment for its use, and the sponsor is not always identified.

Advertising has become a workhorse that serves many communication needs of society, including needs other than goods and services. Business firms, labor unions, government agencies, and political leaders, among others, are successfully employing advertising to inform and persuade preselected audiences about major issues.

Americans live in an advertising environment. Advertising is so much a part of our lives that no one can count the number of such exposures, demanding or subtle, that seek our attention each day; one study estimated the figure at 1800 per adult. Ads are found on athletic shoes and even in the names of sporting events, such as the Outback Steakhouse Gator Bowl football game. Commercials are viewed in school classrooms and doctors' offices. Airline passengers thousands of feet in the air hear them on the Gannett Company's *USA Today* Sky Radio. Most mass media would cost us a great deal more were they not filled with advertising; even specialty items, now distributed so freely, would bear a price.

6.0, 6.0, 6.0, 6.0, 6.0! If I had to rate milk as an after-sports drink, it would definitely get the gold. Besides being a better source of potassium than the leading sports drink, it has more vitamins and minerals per ounce. And how do I like it? On ice, of course.

**MILK**
What a surprise!™

As part of a campaign promoting the nutritional value of milk, the milk industry published this alluring magazine advertisement featuring skating star Kristi Yamaguchi. The text advocates use of milk as an after-sports drink.

Stanley E. Cohen, an authority on consumer–government relations as well as on advertising–government relations, stated the following in *Advertising Age:*

It is hardly strange that advertising has become a focus for so much attention. It comes uninvited into the home. Sometimes volunteering useful information, often probing into hidden feelings and yearnings. Sometimes subtle, sometimes harsh. Often useful. Occasionally brash and offensive. It brings championship football into the living room but breaks the spell as the action nears the climax. It provides TV programs which keep children occupied on rainy afternoons, but it encourages them to want a multitude of things, some of which don't especially appeal to their parents. It encourages contributions to a multitude of causes; pleads the diverse viewpoints of politicians, causes and special interests. It exercises a powerful, but undefined, influence on the life cycle of products and companies, ringing in the new, while silently marking the passage of the old.

Name a problem and someone will almost surely find a way to link it to advertising, whether it is the wasteful use of energy, changing moral standards, bad eating habits, or the poor quality of TV programming. For advertising is a communications tool which influences our attitudes toward products, companies, lifestyles, and public issues. Advertising helps determine which styles are fashionable, which resorts are "in," what music we hear, which public figures are our next folk heroes.

Because so many other factors contribute to purchasing decisions it is difficult to measure the effectiveness of any single advertising campaign and impossible to determine the overall impact of advertising on the marketplace. For decades, economists generally ignored advertising and its influence on the economy. Today, some maintain that advertising people have not proved their claims of advertising's value to society. Writing in *Advertising Age*, Dr. Richard H. Holton of the University of California at Berkeley, an authority on marketing and economic development, says that the proponents of advertising would like to have economists agree on at least four points:

First, because of advertising, *the country's gross national product is greater and the standard of living is higher than they would otherwise be.* Advertising creates generic demand as well as demand for individual brands and thus assists in the marketing of more and better products. So advertising creates jobs, the argument runs, and provides us with a greater variety of products, while the quality of goods is improved over time in part because of advertising.

A second argument put forth by advertisers is that *advertising plays a major role in informing the consumer so that more intelligent choices are made in the marketplace.* Thus advertising aids the competitive process.

A third rationale for advertising is that *the firm's cost of production per unit of output is lower because advertising increases demand for the firm's output.* Thus substantial plant economies or economies of scale are achieved; fixed costs are spread over a larger number of units of output. So advertising leads to a more efficient use of resources in the economy.

Finally, advertising's proponents ask economists to recognize that because of advertising, *new firms have an easier time entering the market than would be true if advertising were restricted or prohibited.* Advertising helps the new firm, or the firm with a new product, take on the giants in the industry and carve out a niche in the marketplace. Thus, advertising, again, is procompetitive.

Since the 1950s, with better data on advertising, the refinement of analytical techniques, and the introduction of the computer, economists have seriously studied the economics of advertising. The results have been inconclusive, but Holton asserts that economists today are much more likely to have a balanced view of advertising than before these inquiries were undertaken.

## U.S. Advertising Expenditures

Advertising expenditures in the United States totaled $161 billion in 1995, an increase of 9.3 percent over the preceding year. Table 15.1 shows how U.S. advertisers allocated their expenditures in the various media during those two years. Newspapers barely led the way, with only one-tenth of a percentage point edge over television, in which cable television continued to advance. Direct mail was the third strongest competitor for advertising dollars followed, in order, by miscellaneous, radio, the Yellow Pages, and magazines.

The expenditures include commissions as well as the art, mechanical, and production expenses that are a part of advertisers' budgets for each medium. *Spot* refers to commercials sold by local broadcast stations.

## How Advertising Developed

### In the Nineteenth Century

Advertising is as old as civilization itself. In the ruins of ancient Egypt, explorers have found papyrus posters offering rewards for the return of runaway slaves. In the ruins of the Roman city of Pompeii, archaeologists have discovered political advertisements painted on walls along streets bearing such entreaties as, "Vote for Cicero, the friend of the people." However, until the advent of mass selling in the nineteenth century, advertising played only a minor role in the conducting of business. In early Greek and Roman days, signboards were placed above the doors of business establishments, and town criers proclaimed that merchants had certain wares for sale. These were merely means to attract customers to a shop, however; in contrast with modern advertising and sales techniques, the display of merchandise and personal selling were depended on to make the sale.

After the invention of movable type accelerated printing in the mid-fifteenth century, handbills, posters, and then newspapers were used in increasing quantities to advertise products. Advertisements appeared in early American newspapers, but the volume did not grow to sizable proportions until trade began to flourish in the metropolitan centers in the early days of the republic. Almost all selling was local until about 1840. Then the development of railroad transportation enabled industry to send its products to consumers far from the manufacturing plants. National advertising resulted as businesspeople used both magazines and newspapers to broaden their markets.

The first advertising agency in the United States was organized by Volney B. Palmer circa 1840. His agency, and those that followed his, did not prepare copy but served primarily as publishers' representatives. By 1860, approximately 30 agencies were selling space for more than 4000 American publications. Since there were no public lists of these publications and no way of substantiating circulation claims, the agents

**Table 15.1**

## U.S. Advertising Expenditures in 1994 and 1995

| Medium | 1994 Millions of Dollars | Percent of Total | 1995 Millions of Dollars | Percent of Total | Percent Change |
|---|---|---|---|---|---|
| NEWSPAPERS | | | | | |
| National | 3,906 | 2.6 | 3,996 | 2.5 | 2.3 |
| Local | 30,450 | 20.3 | 31,321 | 20.1 | 6.1 |
| Total | 34,356 | 22.9 | 36,317 | 22.6 | 5.7 |
| MAGAZINES | | | | | |
| Weeklies | 3,140 | 2.1 | 3,347 | 2.1 | 6.6 |
| Women's | 2,106 | 1.4 | 2,236 | 1.4 | 6.2 |
| Monthlies | 2,670 | 1.8 | 2,997 | 1.8 | 12.2 |
| Total | 7,916 | 5.3 | 8,580 | 5.3 | 8.4 |
| FARM PUBLICATIONS | 262 | 0.2 | 283 | 0.2 | 8.0 |
| TELEVISION | | | | | |
| Four networks | 10,142 | 7.3 | 11,600 | 7.2 | 6.0 |
| Big 3 Minus Fox | 9,959 | 6.6 | 10,263 | 6.4 | 3.1 |
| Cable networks | 2,321 | 1.5 | 2,670 | 1.7 | 15.0 |
| Syndicates | 1,734 | 1.2 | 2,016 | 1.2 | 16.3 |
| Spot (national) | 8,993 | 6.0 | 9,119 | 5.7 | 1.4 |
| Spot (local) | 9,464 | 6.3 | 9,985 | 6.2 | 5.5 |
| Cable (non-network) | 713 | 0.5 | 856 | 0.5 | 20.0 |
| Total | 34,167 | 22.8 | 36,246 | 22.5 | 6.1 |
| RADIO | | | | | |
| Network | 463 | 0.3 | 480 | 0.3 | 3.7 |
| Spot (national) | 1,902 | 1.3 | 1,959 | 1.2 | 3.0 |
| Spot (local) | 8,164 | 5.4 | 8,899 | 5.5 | 9.0 |
| Total | 10,529 | 7.0 | 11,338 | 7.0 | 7.7 |
| YELLOW PAGES | | | | | |
| National | 1,314 | 0.9 | 1,410 | 0.9 | 7.3 |
| Local | 8,511 | 5.7 | 8,826 | 5.5 | 3.7 |
| Total | 9,825 | 6.6 | 10,236 | 6.4 | 4.2 |
| DIRECT MAIL | 29,638 | 19.7 | 32,866 | 20.4 | 10.9 |
| BUSINESS PAPERS | 3,358 | 2.2 | 3,559 | 2.2 | 6.0 |
| OUTDOOR | | | | | |
| National | 648 | 0.4 | 701 | 0.4 | 8.2 |
| Local | 519 | 0.4 | 562 | 0.4 | 8.2 |
| Total | 1,167 | 0.8 | 1,263 | 0.8 | 8.2 |
| MISCELLANEOUS | | | | | |
| National | 13,928 | 9.3 | 15,041 | 9.4 | 8.0 |
| Local | 4,884 | 3.2 | 5,191 | 3.2 | 6.3 |
| Total | 18,812 | 12.5 | 20,232 | 12.6 | 7.6 |
| National total | 87,325 | 58.2 | 94,280 | 58.6 | 8.0 |
| Local total | 62,705 | 41.8 | 66,640 | 41.4 | 6.3 |
| GRAND TOTAL | 150,030 | 100.0 | 160,920 | 100.0 | 7.3 |

*Source: Prepared for* Advertising Age *by Robert J. Coen, McCann-Erickson Worldwide.*
*Reprinted courtesy of* Advertising Age, *67:21 (May 20, 1995).*

Hat Conformature for taking shape of Heads.

# H. DICKSON,
## HATS, CAPS & FURS,
### No. 60 STATE STREET, ALBANY.

Some early newspaper and magazine advertisements were illustrated with drawings such as this one from Albany, New York, in 1855, in the days before photographic reproduction in print was possible.

could manipulate the buying and selling of space to substantial personal advantage.

In 1869, however, George P. Rowell began publishing *Rowell's American Newspaper Directory*, a rather complete list of newspapers, together with careful estimates of circulation. The same year, F. Wayland Ayer and his father founded N. W. Ayer & Son, Inc., to buy space in the interest of clients rather than to sell it for newspapers. In 1880, the agency began publishing a directory of all periodicals, predecessor of the current *Gale Directory of Publications and Broadcast Media*. Soon other agencies were started along professional lines of providing planning and space-buying services for their clients. There was an upsurge in the use of pictorial art in advertisements. The nation began to be conscious of the first widely quoted slogans such as Ivory Soap's "99$\frac{44}{100}$ Per Cent Pure" and "It Floats," Eastman Kodak's "You Press the Button—We Do the Rest," and "Good Morning, Have You Used Pears' Soap?"

Strongman Charles Atlas used coupon advertising in magazines effectively during the 1930s to sell his body-building courses to weak-muscled men. Atlas called himself "the world's most perfectly developed man."

"Here is my la graph exactly as took it—without retouching to 'buil or anything else. tells its own story what I have done No physical instru for you any more able to prove he with his own me HIS OWN body."

*Charles* C

Holder of the "The World's Mo. Developed M

Won in open com the only national national contests h the past 15 y

## Send for
## FREE BOOK

MAIL the coupon right now for full details and I'll send you y illustrated book, "Everlasting ealth and Strength." Tells all about my *ynamic-Tension* method. Shows actual photos men I've made into Atlas champions. Sup es the facts you need to know about your ndition. It's a valuable book! And it's FREE. Send for your copy *today*. Mail the coupon to me personally:
**CHARLES ATLAS, Dept. 28-9**
133 East 23rd Street, New York City

**RAY HOWEL'S**
**BUILD**

From head to foot n ready to give you body like Howel's.

**DAVID BONACO'S**
**CHEST**

How many chests can you show me that will begin to stack up with this strapping development I've built for David Bonaco. Here's the kind of real-man strength that means business in any crowd, anywhere.

**BILL SPEEC'S**
**BACK**

Big-muscle arms and a chest that makes people look at you twice are mighty important—but don't forget the back. Here's where you get extra strength, long endurance, real tough stamina. The back I've built for Bill Speec, is the kind that walks off with also prize every time. Muscles rippling, not an ounce of flabby flesh—solid, tiger-man power!

## CHARLES ATLAS
**Dept. 28-9, 133 East 23rd Street, New York C**

I want the proof that your system of *Dynamic-Tension* will make of me—give me a healthy, husky body and big muscular developmen your FREE book, "Everlasting Health and Strength." This reque under no obligation.

Name.................................................
(Please print or write plainly)
Address..............................................
City.............................................State......

© 1933—C. A. Ltd.

# ALBERT D. LASKER

Known as "the father of modern advertising," Albert D. Lasker did more than anyone else to change advertisements from dull lists of items for sale into what he called "salesmanship in print."

At the age of 18, the Texan began work in 1898 with the Lord and Thomas advertising agency in Chicago, which he later acquired.

From about 1900 to 1940, when American industry produced a cornucopia of new products, many became household words because of the advertising campaigns that Lasker ran for them after creating the first copywriting department in an advertising agency.

Lasker was a gregarious, loquacious, emotional man with a subtle mind. An instinctive psychologist, he and his creative team produced catchy advertising headlines and slogans. Among the latter were "Keep That Schoolgirl Complexion" for Palmolive soap and "Reach for a Lucky Instead of a Sweet," which probably did more to convince women to smoke than any other promotional effort by the tobacco industry.

Lasker helped to develop the use of test markets, sampling, and the distribution of coupons. Words meant much more to him than pictures, so the agency paid little attention to graphics. At one point during the 1930s the agency purchased 30 percent of all radio network time on behalf of its clients and packaged many of the most famous evening comedy and dramatic shows as well as afternoon soap operas.

After more than 40 years in the business, Lasker closed the agency and transferred most of its clients to the newly created Foote, Cone & Belding agency. He then turned to philanthropies and art collecting. He died in 1952, a legend among his peers and one of the most influential shapers of modern mass communications.

## Early in the Twentieth Century

As newspaper and magazine circulations increased and new technological advances were made, at the turn of the century advertising developed new slogans, better copywriters and artists, and improved methods of analyzing products, media, and markets. Because much advertising was deceptive and grossly exaggerated, a strong movement to regulate advertising was begun in the 1910s. This involved both federal and state laws and control systems initiated by responsible advertising leaders. (The history of this movement is described later in this chapter.)

The advent of radio and a further improvement in the techniques of advertising, such as copy-testing, the study of psychological appeals, and plans for integrated campaigns, characterized the 1920s. Advertising fought to hold its own during the depression years of the 1930s against both the near-paralysis of business and organized consumer objections to improper practices. During that decade, advertisers increasingly used research methods, such as readership studies and audience measurement.

### Advertising Council

During World War II, the War Advertising Council was established by advertising agencies, media, and advertisers as a voluntary contribution to the war effort. So successful was the council in promoting the sale of war bonds, donation of blood, rationing, and the like, it was continued as the Advertising Council, Inc., headquartered in New York. This private, nonprofit organization conducts almost 40 major public service campaigns each year.

During the past half-century, Smokey the Bear has told Americans that forest fires cost them money as well as the loss of recreational facilities and the natural beauty of the country ("Smokey Says: Remember, Only You Can Prevent Forest Fires!"). More recent council campaigns have borne slogans such as: "Help Stop AIDS. Use a Condom," "Take a Bite Out of Crime," "A Mind Is a Terrible Thing to Waste," and "If the Press Didn't Tell Us, Who Would?"

Major American advertisers provide volunteer coordinators. The agencies rotate in conducting the campaigns, and the media offer free time and space for the ads. Each year the media donate more than $1 billion in time and space in support of these campaigns. The media's total dollar contribution since 1942 has exceeded $20 billion.

### After World War II

The booming economy after World War II produced rapid growth in all areas of advertising. Staffs were enlarged, branch offices of agencies proliferated, and small agencies formed networks to provide reciprocal services for their clients across the country. Television—described by industry leaders as the most important development affecting advertising in the twentieth century—accelerated the trend toward larger agencies because it increased the complexities of advertising. Advertisers turned increasingly to research to provide facts about their products and services and to discover the motivations of consumer markets.

During the 1960s and 1970s, advertising faced the staggering task of helping to move into the hands of consumers an unprecedented volume of manufactured goods. Periodic recessions made this task more difficult. Management demanded more efficient methods of measuring the effectiveness of advertising as distinguished from other marketing functions. Many large agencies went public—that is, converted their proprietorship to shares that were traded and priced on the stock market. Some agencies diversified into side businesses, such as retail stores and product manufacturing.

The computer came into more sophisticated use. It helped management, advertising, and marketing people understand the new world of product proliferation, market segmentation, automated distribution, population shifts, and the profit squeeze. National and international computer networks were established by large agencies using high-speed data transmission telephone lines, satellites, and other communications facilities. The computer was used to analyze consumer surveys, to assist in media buying, to help in predicting the effectiveness of one media plan as opposed to another, to calculate television program cost efficiencies in relation to client objectives, and in numerous other ways.

Increasingly large amounts of money were allocated to marketing and advertising research. The emphasis on research resulted from high entry costs into markets, high costs of new product development, market failures, the rapidly changing marketing environment, changing lifestyles of consumers, and the urgency of having more information for decision making. Companies found it necessary to involve specialized outside consulting groups as well as their own in-house groups to analyze the changing market.

## Creativity

As an increasing number of advertising specialists drew on their imagination and instinct, grounded in experience and research, to produce attention-getting print and broadcast messages, a widely discussed "cult of creativity" swept the industry. Early examples included the highly entertaining creations of satirist Stan Freberg for Jeno's Pizza and Chung King products. Later came the television commercials of Clairol's Herbal Essence Shampoo, launched with an animation technique that included warm humor; Morris the 9-Lives Cat commercials; and those portraying the Keebler elves. Humor began playing a larger role in slice-of-life commercials as consumers became more sophisticated and more critical of their portrayal in advertising. Many new agencies were established as the most creative advertising personnel went into business for themselves.

Some advertising people decried the extensive use of wit and humor, contending that it might be entertaining but that it does not always help to sell goods and services. During recessions, many commercials of a humorous, awareness, and image-building variety gave way to "hard-sell" advertisements.

Creativity returned in force during the 1980s. Advertisers vied for the attention of consumers whose attention was splintered among over-the-air and cable television, videocassette recordings, and a myriad of other media and leisure-time pursuits. Striking print and video graphics augmented the novel approaches.

Eroticism characterized the print and broadcast commercials of Calvin Klein, the designer whose suggestive series of underwear ads first appeared in 1982. ("Nothing comes between me and my Calvins," cooed the then-15-year-old beauty Brooke Shields.) Erotic advertising sold everything from after-shave lotions to exercise machines. Nostalgia for the 1950s was the theme of advertisers who turned to black-and-white television to attract attention in the color-dominated medium.

Humor was everywhere. Dancing raisins sing "I Heard It Through the Grapevine." Men waddling in penguin costumes buy Coors' Colorado Chillers. In a "time machine" commercial a man heads back 100

Television advertisers often create symbols or personalities to provide quick product identity and continuity in their commercials. The whimsical Putterman family, shown here, achieves that goal for Duracell batteries.

years in time inadvertently holding a can of Pepsi; as he moves through time, Coke and Pepsi dispensing machines come into view but the Coke machine slowly disappears and a Coke delivery truck and bottling plant suffer the same fate. On a radio commercial, a woman offers Laughing Cow cheese from France as a snack for her husband in bed and declares: "Then he ate all 10 mini-cheeses and said it was the best treat he ever had in bed. So I smacked him."

Creative people faced an enormous challenge in the 1990s: they were called on to devise advertising to run on the new media and offer consumers interactivity. Said Meredith Flynn of U S West: "It's a bigger challenge than ever to cut through the clutter and make the creative compelling enough for someone to actually select it."

## Cycles in Advertising

Many observers have noted the apparent trends that have characterized advertising during the post–World War II decades, all of them continuing today.

**1950s: The Product Era.**  For the Ted Bates agency, Rosser Reeves sought the "unique selling proposition" for each product: "Wonder Bread builds strong bodies 12 ways." "Rolaids absorb 47 times its weight in stomach acid." David Ogilvy, founder of Ogilvy & Mather, offered finely crafted ads for products such as Hathaway shirts, Schweppes tonic, and Rolls Royce motor cars. Leo Burnett, founder of the so-called "Chicago school," ascertained the "inherent drama" of each product and sold it in folksy, down-to-earth style or created figures such as the Jolly Green Giant and the Marlboro Man.

**1960s: The Image Era.**  Setting the dominant tone, William Bernbach brought together creative teams at Doyle Dane Bernbach agency to combine words and images in memorable campaigns such as those for Avis Rent-a-Car ("We're number two, but we try harder") and the Volks-wagen Beetle ("Think small").

**1970s: The Era of Comparative Advertising.**  Manufacturers and market-ing people have always sought to identify in the public mind the unique position of their products in the marketplace. The advertising door to this practice, known as *positioning*, was opened wide in 1972 when the Federal Trade Commission (FTC) strongly advocated the use of com-parative advertising—naming the competing product(s) instead of refer-ring to "brand X" or bleeping the names. The FTC reasoned that the direct comparison of brands provides additional information for con-sumers and thereby increases competition. By the mid-1980s compara-tive advertisements, based on objective data or subjective tests, ac-counted for 35 percent of all television commercials. Pepsi announced it had found that "more people prefer Pepsi to Coke" and mounted "the Pepsi Challenge." The confrontations included Schlitz versus Michelob, and Whopper versus Big Mac.

    With only mixed results, some injured defendants mounted counter-campaigns. Others sought relief from the networks, the National Adver-tising Division of the Council of Better Business Bureaus, the FTC, and the courts, the latter under provisions of Section 43(A) of the Lanham Act, which prohibits "any false description or representation . . . of any goods or services." In 1986, a federal appeals court awarded U-Haul a record $40 million from the rival Jartran rental company on the basis of false advertising.

    The Trademark Law Revision Act became effective in 1989. Whereas the Lanham Act applied to a company's own products, the 1989 law prevented advertisements from misrepresenting the qualities or characteristics of "another person's goods, services, or commercial activities." Many leaders contended that comparative advertising, with its attendant litigation and negative publicity, was harming the indus-try. Nevertheless, the practice grew during the era of precise, niche marketing.

**Positioning**
Differentiating a product or service, mainly through marketing and ad-vertising, from those of its com-petitors

**Comparative advertising**
Advertising that refers specifically to a competitor's prod-uct or service

### 1980s: The Era of Target Advertising and Marketing, and of Advocacy Advertising.

Carrying positioning a step further, advertisers began marketing more by how their products—fast foods, soft drinks, and automobiles, for example—fit into different lifestyles than by dwelling on specific details of the products. Often this "targeting" was based not on customary demographics but on psychographics—the grouping of people by values and lifestyles as well as by age, sex, and income. Intensive research, including a wide variety of tests, studies, and interviews, formed the basis of the campaigns.

**Target marketing**
Aiming a marketing campaign at a special demographic or psychographic group

**Advocacy advertising**
Advertising in which companies and nonprofit organizations take positions on important issues

*Advocacy* advertising, in which corporations run paid ads that take sides on important issues, became popular. In the historic case of *First National Bank of Boston* v. *Bellotti*, the Supreme Court in 1978 had stated that the government may not limit the range of issues on which a corporation may express itself. The Court, however, did not define the outer boundaries of such expression. When the broadcast networks, because of their access policies, refused to carry commercials telling the major oil companies' side of the energy story, the firms inserted their advertising messages in newspapers and magazines. Other corporations used print advertising to respond to what they considered unfair treatment in such network programs as "60 Minutes" and "20/20."

### 1990s: The Era of Adjustment to the New Media.

Advertising agents and their clients experienced difficulty in finding ways to use new media such as online computer services and CD-ROMs. In the mid-1990s advertising people generally adopted a "wait and see" attitude, a condition that some compared with the apprehension accompanying the early years of television. Advertising on the Internet will be discussed later in this chapter.

## Current Problems and Trends in Advertising

The advertising industry faces other problems and trends in addition to those previously cited. Among them are the following:

1. *Audience fragmentation.* To a large extent the mass market is splintering into hundreds of smaller markets, requiring new ways to communicate with them. In television, the growth of cable and the number of independent stations, coupled with the heavy use of videocassette recorders, has reduced the impact of conventional TV programming and commercials. Network television's share of the prime-time audience dropped to 53 percent in 1996 from 93 percent in 1978.

2. *Clutter.* Hundreds of new products crowding supermarket shelves and aisles have greatly increased advertising clutter, making creative breakthroughs difficult to achieve. Fifteen-second TV spots, rare a few years ago, now constitute about 25 percent of all television advertising. Countless network and station promotional spots exacerbate the problem.

3. *Zapping.* Millions of viewers are zappers, switching channels repeatedly to avoid commercials or to shop for a more inviting program. A

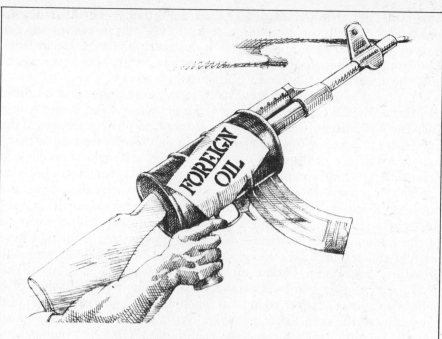

AMERICA'S NEXT HOSTAGE CRISIS?

According to the latest figures, America is now importing almost 50 percent of all the oil we use. If our oil imports continue to rise, another energy crisis could be triggered, one that could hold America's economy hostage again.

But the more we use nuclear energy, instead of imported oil, to generate electricity, the less we have to depend on foreign nations.

Our 112 nuclear electric plants already have cut foreign oil dependence by 4 billion barrels since the oil embargo of 1973, saving us more than $115 billion in foreign oil payments.

But 112 nuclear plants will not be enough to meet our growing electricity demand. More plants are needed.

We can help keep America from being held hostage and maintain our energy indepen-

dence by relying more on our own resources, like nuclear energy.

For a free booklet on nuclear energy, write to the U.S. Council for Energy Awareness, P.O. Box 66103, Dept. RF16, Washington, D.C. 20035.

Nuclear electricity and energy independence

U.S. COUNCIL FOR ENERGY AWARENESS

Nuclear energy means more energy independence.

©1989 USCEA

An example of advocacy advertising, published in several American magazines.

new experimental rating system developed by R. D. Percy & Co. measured the zapping frequency of 1000 New York City households. It showed that zapping reduced a prime-time audience by 10 percent or more. A. C. Nielsen studies, however, have indicated that zapping is not widespread.

4. *Dazzling special effects.* Using computer devices or software with names such as Flame and Harry Paintbox, special effects companies are turning real objects and scenes into digital images, or they create new

ones, and then manipulate them, or combine them with other objects and scenes. "Whatever an agency can dream up, we can now put on the screen," said Jim Morris, president of Industrial Light & Magic, in 1994. The companies are in growing demand as advertisers seek new ways to hold the attention of fidgety TV audiences.

5. *Loss of advertising revenues.* Sales promotion firms, such as those that devise the 25-cents-off coupons for supermarkets and invent games enabling customers to win prizes, have become permanent fixtures in the marketing budgets of large companies, draining money from advertising budgets. The use of bar-code scanning devices has enabled retailers to determine customer preferences and put pressure on manufacturers to shift money from advertising into discounting, shelf-space fees, and other promotions. Studies show that promotions now constitute two-thirds of marketing expenditures and advertising one-third, the reverse of the traditional percentage. At the same time, many companies have learned the art of "value added" advertising, insisting that print and broadcast media offer flexible rates ("rate busting," as it is known) or marketing incentives to increase the impact of their advertising. In the belief that agencies were making too much money, many advertisers also have reduced the agencies' compensation packages, with incentive-based commissions and fees replacing the traditional 15 percent commission-plus-fee standard, discussed later in this chapter.

6. *More sophisticated targeting of market segments.* Advertisers are increasingly supporting innovative methods to reach only those consumers most likely to buy their products and services. Examples include the identification of clusters of like-minded consumers through psychographic and demographic studies, as previously mentioned, and through controlled-circulation and controlled-television-audience techniques such as those used by Whittle Communications, both discussed in Chapter 6.

7. *Growth in minority populations.* Minority groups in the United States are growing five times faster than the general population, and during the 1990s will account for more than 85 percent of all population growth, according to *American Demographics* magazine. By 2000, the magazine reports, 15 states will have minority populations equal to or above the national average of 28 percent, and California and Texas will have nearly 50 percent minority populations. Reaching these Asians, blacks, Hispanics, and Native Americans is an advertising necessity.

8. *"One-stop shopping" problems.* To combat the growth of "in-house" agencies within corporations as well as competition from boutique specialty shops, many agencies have become "communications supermarkets." They have acquired firms specializing in direct marketing (including mail operations on which almost half of all advertising dollars are spent), public relations, sales promotion, package design, and dealer aids and sales-meeting operations. Many advertisers, however, remain un-

convinced that one-stop shopping provides the high quality of services they desire.

9. *Global advertising.* The expansion of business worldwide has spawned giant transnational advertising agencies and forced a number of American agencies, many now foreign-owned, to become international in their operations. In the opinion of some leaders, the creative nature of the industry has suffered as a consequence of these management changes. Creativity was discussed earlier in this chapter and global advertising will be reviewed later.

10. *Talent hunting and "leaner" agencies.* In the wake of global mergers, the early 1990s recession, and the thinning of employee ranks, many agencies have become "leaner" in the sense of seeking to depend on senior, experienced people to service accounts, supported by a cadre of highly motivated junior employees. The goal of many is to hire fewer, better people who work harder in the right structure and are well rewarded. In particular demand are corporate marketing executives known as "business proprietors," who aggressively seek major new accounts, a field in which women have become especially proficient.

11. *Threats to commercial free speech.* Advertisers and agency and media leaders are concerned that a number of states are considering the imposition of a sales tax on advertising, as Florida did in the late 1980s before repealing a legislative measure. Of equal concern are state and federal proposals to make illegal the advertising of alcohol and tobacco products.

12. *Rise of the "New Puritanism."* Convinced that network TV has become too lenient in its treatment of sex and violence, individuals and organized pressure groups have boycotted or threatened to boycott advertisers who buy time on these programs. Congress has joined in the assault. (See Issue 1.)

## Criticisms of Advertising

Because advertising is so much a part of our lives, criticisms are rampant. Some of the more common complaints and the replies that have been made to each of them are:

1. *Advertising persuades us to buy goods and services we cannot afford.* Persuasion is present, but never coercion; it is up to each of us to exercise self-control and sound judgment in our purchases.

2. *Advertising appeals primarily to our emotions, rather than to our intellect.* Since all of us are motivated by emotional drives, it is only natural that advertisers should make such appeals. Again, a cautious buyer will avoid obvious appeals to the emotions.

3. *Advertising is biased.* This, too, is natural; all persons put their best foot forward in whatever they say or do. Being aware of this bias, we can discount some of the superlatives used in advertising.

4. *Advertising involves conflicting competitive claims.* But advertising is "out in the open," never hidden as are some forms of propaganda, and we can decide for ourselves.

5. *Advertising is unduly repetitious.* This is because the public is essentially a passing parade, not a mass gathering; there are always new users whom the appeal has never reached. Slogans such as "It Floats" have sold goods successfully for generations.

6. *Much advertising is vulgar, obtrusive, and irritating.* Actually, only a handful of advertisers employ poor taste in their appeals; their excesses damage the higher standards of many other advertisers. The very nature of radio and television accounts for much irritation; this complaint is seldom voiced in relation to printed advertising, which may be ignored.

Some years back, Morton J. Simon, Philadelphia lawyer and author, cited six principal reasons for unfavorable government and public attitudes toward advertising. Five of the reasons are still valid:

1. *Advertising is a horizontal industry.* It cuts across almost every business and service, so an attack on any industry almost always includes advertising.

2. *Advertising represents a lot of money.* It spends billions of dollars annually, and some persons view these funds as apparently untaxed and outside the grip of government (a complaint expressed by many Third World countries in their quest for a New World Order of Communications).

3. *Advertising lives in a glass house.* By its nature, it cannot hide its sins.

4. *The gray flannel suit image is pervasive.* Many consider that advertising people live lavishly and improperly on tax-deductible expense accounts (a view that led to President Carter's attack against the "three-martini lunch" as a tax-deductible business expense).

5. *Advertising is not constitutionally protected.* Some persons in government believe that advertising is somehow tainted by its commercial purpose and therefore is not protected by the First Amendment; its legal status has still not been made wholly clear.

Simon also pointed out that advertising had rarely lobbied; during the last several decades, however, the industry has maintained a Washington lobby to protect its interests.

## Regulation of Advertising

Businesspeople and consumers alike agree that advertising should provide information on which the public can rely—that it not be false or deceptive. Central among the issues are the following:

1. How much regulation is reasonable and necessary?

2. How much can be accomplished through *self-regulation*—that undertaken by the advertising industry itself?

3. Can *federal* agencies, during the current era of government deregulation, still be depended on to enforce existing regulations or should *state* law-enforcement officials take more vigorous action?

Among many federal agencies, the Federal Trade Commission took the lead in regulating national advertising and marketing practices until the early 1980s. Since then, as the FTC became increasingly lax in exercising enforcement powers, the National Association of Attorney Generals has led efforts by the states to regulate interstate commerce, using antitrust suits and legislation, to fill the breach. Many states have taken additional steps to protect consumers against perceived *in-state* fraudulent and deceptive practices, especially in such fields as nutrition and health advertising.

Because of the complexities of dealing with numerous state laws, national advertisers generally have expressed a desire that the FTC again take the lead.

## Early Regulatory Actions

The first legal restraint on advertising in the United States was enacted more than 100 years ago. It was designed to ensure that persons ordering goods from mail-order catalogues received what was promised.

During the progressive reform era after the turn of the century, business abuses, including the gross exaggerations and misleading claims of some advertisers, prompted a flurry of actions supported both by consumer groups and by various advertising organizations determined to elevate the ethics of the advertising business. They included the following:

1. Many states, beginning in 1911, enacted a model Truth in Advertising law proposed by *Printers' Ink*, a magazine formerly published for advertising people. State controls, however, were weak, so pioneer advertising leaders supported federal legislation to deal with interstate advertising.

2. Advertising organizations adopted codes of behavior, and some publications established guidelines for accepting or refusing advertising. The *Good Housekeeping* Seal of Approval is a notable, more recent, example of evaluations of advertising by magazines.

3. The first Better Business Bureau was organized in 1913. Bureaus have since been established in major cities across the nation to promote ethical practices and to help consumers with problems.

4. The Audit Bureau of Circulations, a nonprofit organization making unbiased periodical audits and statements concerning a publication's circulation, was established in 1914.

5. Congress enacted the Federal Trade Commission Act of 1914, establishing the agency (FTC), which steadily increased the extent and nature of its regulation of advertising until the early 1980s.

In 1931, the Supreme Court ruled that the FTC could restrict deceptive advertising only if it could show that such advertising injured competition. With the passage of the Wheeler-Lea Act in 1938, however, the FTC was given a clear-cut mandate to deal with advertisements that deceived consumers.

**The 1950s.** During this decade the FTC—well before the Surgeon General's warning condemning cigarette smoking—challenged the use of cigarette advertising that implied that smoking was harmless. In addition, the agency attacked "bait and switch" advertising, misleading discount offers, misleading use of the word "free," extravagant claims for indigestion products and headache remedies, and other such practices.

In all, more than 20 federal agencies, including the Internal Revenue Service and the Securities & Exchange Commission, took steps to regulate advertising. At least 12 states had begun to tax advertising.

The first serious attempt to regulate broadcast commercials began in 1952, when the National Association of Broadcasters (NAB), under pressure from the Federal Communications Commission, established advertising and program standard guidelines for radio and television stations. For three decades, the professional staff of the NAB's Code Authority cleared commercials prior to airing and the networks, operating independently, reviewed commercials for truth, taste, and fairness to children. It was a major undertaking; each year NBC, for example, processed about 16,000 commercials.

In 1982, the U.S. District Court for the District of Columbia ruled that parts of the NAB television code, relating to the number and length of commercials within certain time periods, violated the Sherman Antitrust Act. In response the NAB suspended all of its code activities. Thereafter, the clearance of commercials was undertaken by the networks and individual stations; the burden of regulating children's commercials was partially assumed by the National Advertising Review Board, a trade-sponsored, self-regulatory body; and some oversight was provided by agencies that regulate on a case-by-case basis after the commercials have been broadcast.

**The 1960s.** Another wave of consumerism occurred during the 1960s, and the FTC vastly enlarged its operations. It began to require factual substantiation of advertising as well as factual disclosures in future ads and, in some cases, corrective statements to offset previous misstatements. In the belief that consumers would benefit if advertisers argued with each other in their ads, the FTC, as previously discussed, vigorously urged comparative advertising. The agency asked the FCC to require the airing of *counter-commercials*, particularly regarding those addressed to children, so that consumer groups could reply to advertising claims. The FCC declined to do so, contending that such action would amount to "a tortured or distorted application of Fairness Doctrine principles." (The Fairness Doctrine is discussed in Issue 5.)

In 1966 Congress passed the Fair Packaging and Labeling Act, covering food, drug, and cosmetics packages. A Department of Commerce program to reduce the proliferation of package sizes followed. In 1968

**Counter-commercials**
Broadcast advertising by consumer groups responding to claims made in other commercials, which aired briefly in the 1960s before the FCC declined to require them

came the Truth in Lending Act, requiring disclosure of the annual interest rate on revolving charge accounts.

## Later Regulatory Actions

**The 1970s.**    As the consumer movement continued, Congress banned the broadcasting of cigarette commercials in 1971. The direct-mail industry began cooperating with postal authorities in a plan that enabled recipients of direct-mail advertising to have their names removed from mailing lists. Guidelines of ethical business practice were established by the direct-mail industry in 1978.

In that same year the advertising industry sought to forestall further legal action with a two-tiered system of self-regulation. A permanent professional staff working within the structure of the Council of Better Business Bureaus began receiving complaints from the public and from business and started doing its own monitoring. In addition, the National Advertising Review Board was created. Fifty persons, including ten public members with no advertising connections, were designated to consider complaints in five-member panels throughout the country. The board considers about 400 complaints each year. Although no penalties are imposed, findings are published.

In 1975, Congress extended even broader powers to the FTC through passage of the Moss-Magnuson Act.

The Supreme Court ruled in 1973 that advertisements are entitled to a degree of First Amendment freedom-of-speech protection. In a landmark case, *Bigelow* v. *Virginia*, the Court overturned the conviction of a newspaper editor for publishing an advertisement for an abortion referral agency.

Three years later the Court also overturned a Virginia ban against prescription-drug advertising, flatly asserting First Amendment protection for *commercial speech.* "Speech is not stripped of First Amendment protection merely because it appears in the form of a paid advertisement," wrote Justice Harry Blackmun. However, in this landmark decision, *Virginia State Board of Pharmacy* v. *Virginia Citizens Consumer Council,* the Court pointed out that commercial speech is different from other types of expression and may be regulated under certain circumstances. The Court did just that in 1990. It upheld a Michigan law that placed strict limits on political campaign spending by corporations, ruling that free-speech rights are outweighed by the need to reduce big-money influence over elections. The six-to-three decision did not affect corporate spending to promote political issues submitted to voters in ballot referendums.

The Supreme Court ruled in 1986 that states may ban advertisements for products that have "serious harmful effects" on citizens. At issue was a Puerto Rican law that authorized gambling casinos but prohibited casino owners from advertising their establishments on the island. They were permitted to run advertisements on the U.S. mainland with

**Commercial speech**
The First Amendment right of a company to express its views through advertising and other means, subject to legal regulation

the hope of attracting tourists. The Court upheld the law by a five-to-four margin. "The particular kind of commercial speech at issue . . . may be restricted only if the government's interest in doing so is substantial," Justice William Rehnquist wrote for the Court majority.

The decision was criticized by the Newspaper Association of America and other groups that contend that no advertising ban should be placed on any legal product or service. It was hailed as a victory by the American Medical Association and other groups attempting to ban print cigarette advertising. They also applauded the Court's 1986 decision to ban broadcast commercials for smokeless tobacco products and to require warning labels on print tobacco ads.

The consumer drive was finally blunted in 1978, when the House of Representatives defeated a bill that would have established an Agency for Consumer Representation.

**The 1980s.**   Responding further to business complaints of too much government interference, in 1980 Congress subjected FTC regulations to two-house congressional veto. So began a decade when, as a *Wall Street Journal* reporter put it, "health and nutrition claims spun out of control, virtually unchecked by the federal government. When else could marketers promote candy bars as health foods or potato chips as a source of high fiber?"

**The 1990s.**   In 1991, the FTC resumed cracking down on misleading advertising claims. The agency found that Kraft General Foods ran deceptive advertising for its Kraft Singles and, further, prohibited the company from misrepresenting any nutrient in any cheese-related program. The FTC signaled that it would go after advertising agencies as well. "The FTC is back in the game," an advertising lawyer noted.

In addition, the Federal Communications Commission began a crackdown on those *infomercials*, program-length commercials, that misled many viewers into thinking they were consumer programs, not paid advertising.

**Infomercial**
Lengthy commercial on cable TV often mistaken for a regular program

Soon, however, new guidelines were instituted by NIMA International, the Washington, D.C.-based trade association representing nearly 500 companies in the infomercial and television shopping business. The guidelines require disclaimers not only at the beginning and end of the programs, but immediately before ordering information as well.

As consumer trust was re-established, the format expanded from direct-selling methods into informative, entertaining corporate-image infomercials, fictional stories, and other such forms. The association estimated that infomercial-driven revenues exceeded $1 billion in 1994.

After Action for Children's Television and other groups had lobbied for more than a decade, Congress in 1990 passed the Children's Television Act, major elements of which President Reagan had vetoed in 1988. The Federal Communications Commission subsequently required TV broadcasters and cable operators to limit advertising on children's shows to 12 minutes an hour on weekdays and 10.5 minutes an hour on weekends. They also were charged with maintaining records summarizing efforts to provide "educational and informational" programs to children under 16 years of age. The commission, however, refused to limit shows based on popular toys such as G.I. Joe and He-Man, which many parents and educational groups have characterized as 30-minute commercials.

Led by ABC, the networks, facing pressure from advertisers who were allowed greater freedom on cable channels, loosened their standards for competitive claims and doctor endorsements. The rules, dating back to the late 1950s and early 1960s, were supposed to battle false and misleading advertising claims, but officials said they were hopelessly outdated for today's more sophisticated viewers. The changes also made it easier for diet-product marketers to show before-and-after pictures, and relaxed restrictions on such commercials as those dealing with fortune-telling and astrology.

## What Advertising People Do

Advertising people disseminate messages through purchased space (print) or time (television and radio), or through expenditures in other media, in order to identify, inform, and/or persuade. How some of these people accomplish this objective can be described by examining briefly the roles they play in agencies, in advertising departments of the mass media, and in retail store and company advertising departments.

### Advertising Agencies

An agency first studies its client's product or service to learn the advantages and disadvantages of the product itself in relation to its competition. It then analyzes the present and potential market for which the product or service is intended. Taken into consideration next are the distribution and sales plans of the client, which are studied with a view toward determining the best selection of media. A definite plan is then formulated and presented to the client.

Once the plan is approved, the agency staff writes, designs, and illustrates the proposed advertisements or prepares the broadcast commercials; contracts for space or time with the media; produces the advertisements and sends them to the media with instructions; checks and verifies the use of the ads; pays for the services rendered and bills the client; cooperates in such merchandising efforts as point-of-purchase displays; and seeks to measure results.

Advertising agencies range in size from small operations to full-service agencies employing 1000 persons or more. The executive heads of an agency usually are people who have proved they can achieve results for clients and who are capable of procuring new business for the agency. These executives may be organized into a plans board, giving general direction to such departments as research, planning, media, copy, art and layout, television production, print production, traffic, merchandising, checking, and accounting.

The key persons in servicing an account—that is, in providing a liaison between the agency and the client—are the account executives. These executives must have a general knowledge of all phases of advertising, merchandising, and general business practices, as well as the ability to be creative in solving a client's special advertising problems and in planning campaigns. Account executives call on the agency's various departments for assistance and correlate their efforts in behalf of clients.

Copy and art chiefs are responsible for the actual creation of advertisements. Copywriters are salespeople, inventors, interpreters, and perhaps artists, but always competent writers. Art directors are salespeople, inventors, interpreters, perhaps writers, and sometimes producers, but also are visually-oriented persons who usually can draw. They consolidate visual elements at every phase of the work from rough layouts to finished ads. They supervise every aspect from the graphic approach to selection of type. For television they begin by making a storyboard, the series of pictures representing the video portion of the commercial. Often they help choose the film techniques, music and other sounds, and models.

From the moment a print ad is designed and written to the time it appears in magazines and newspapers or on billboards, it is in the hands of the print production people. They know what is practical for reproduction and help to guide the creative departments in planning their work. They buy graphic arts services and materials and see assignments through to completion.

Because so many agency functions are involved in the same assignment—that of producing a single ad or commercial or an entire campaign—it is vital to keep everyone working smoothly and on schedule. Planning the flow and timing of all the work is the function of traffic control, which sees that media deadlines and closing dates are met.

The marketing research department gathers the facts that make it possible to solve sales problems. Facts—for instance, about what type of people use a product and why—may help to provide creative people with the central idea for an advertising approach. Or media people may plan an entire advertising campaign based on research about the way consumers read certain magazines or which television programs they watch. Most agencies depend on their clients to supply most of their marketing information.

Media people select and buy print space for ads and air time for commercials, using facts and figures from the research department. They must know the tones and attitudes of magazines, the psychological environments of TV shows, and the editorial tone of any given newspaper. From daily and weekly newspapers, magazines, radio and television stations and cable outlets, outdoor posters, and direct mail lists, they choose the most effective combinations for each advertisement and product. And they must be able to stay within a budget.

In 1984, many newspapers adjusted their mechanical formats and billing procedures, under an expanded Standard Advertising Unit system. The resulting conformity made it easier for agencies to place national advertising in papers throughout the country. Much national advertising is transmitted via satellite by the AD/SAT company.

Agencies also have people who handle such matters as sales promotion, merchandising, public relations, fashion, home economics, and personnel.

## Online Services

A number of advertising agencies gradually established sites on the Internet, the global computer network, during 1994 and 1995. Most targeted the portion known as the World Wide Web, an information-retrieval system that allows for the use of multimedia. Their databases presented graphics and sound, despite the fact that, at the time, only 2 million to 3 million of the Internet's estimated 25 million users could access these functions. All, however, could browse, and the agencies could learn more about these early adopters of new technology.

In 1994, the New York office of BBDO Worldwide, the world's fourth-largest agency, became the first to establish a presence on a big online service. During a three-week test of the BBDO Tech Setters Hotline area on CompuServe, more than 3200 people logged responses and an uncounted number browsed. Subscribers participated in surveys on subjects such as interactive television; read about advertising, marketing, and media trends; entered contests; and took part in conferences.

After the Interpublic Group formed a joint venture with Time Warner's interactive unit in 1994, the two companies created and produced information and entertainment products using new technology. Many other such ventures were under way.

In order to help its advertisers feel comfortable, the electronic magazine *Hotwired* contracted in 1995 with Nielsen Media Research to evaluate its audience measurement systems.

**Compensation.** Traditionally, most of an agency's compensation came from commissions received from the media in which the advertisements appeared. This usually was 15 percent of the medium's national rate; if the advertising space or time cost $1000, the agency collected that amount from the client and paid the medium $850. This system came under severe advertiser attack during the late 1980s, and by 1995 only 14 percent of advertisers supported it, according to a survey by the Association of National Advertisers. Compensation based on performance was a popular alternative method.

Regardless of the system employed, agencies continued to bill clients for actual costs incurred in preparing the advertisements, such as typography, photostats, filmed commercials, artwork, and any special services plus a service charge, usually about 2.65 percent. After all expenses had been met, an agency wound up with a 2 or 3 percent net profit on its gross income each year (less during the 1990s recession). Verification that the advertisements have been used is accomplished by the Advertising Checking Bureau.

## Advertising Departments of Mass Media

All the media employ space or time sales personnel and almost all engage national sales representatives to obtain advertising for them. Let us consider several actual newspaper and radio operations.

One newspaper publishes both morning and evening editions with a combined circulation of 38,000. The combined retail advertising staff consists of six sales representatives and a retail manager. Advertisements handled by the department comprise 70 percent of the newspaper's total advertising volume, the remainder being in classified and national.

Each salesperson services between 75 and 100 accounts, ranging from department stores to small shops. Unlike the practice on large newspapers, these salespeople are not assigned to specific territories. After calling on the business firms that have accounts with them, they prepare semicomprehensive layouts by computer or they use artwork from one of several advertising layout service books. The layouts are then prepared for publication. Proofs are delivered to any retailer placing an ad that contains 15 or more inches of space.

In contrast, 32 salespersons are employed by a nearby morning, evening, and Sunday newspaper selling more than 350,000 copies primarily in a 15-county metropolitan area. Each must serve accounts only in a specified district. If the ad is too elaborate for the salesperson to prepare, the newspaper's art department lends assistance. After the copy and artwork are arranged on the dummy ad, it is printed on a proof sheet exactly as it is to appear in the newspaper. The salesperson checks the ad and may send it to the customer for signed approval before it is printed. The salespeople earn commissions above their base salary if they produce more sales than their monthly quotas.

A nearby 1000-watt medium-market AM station employs four salespeople. Among them is the commercial manager who doubles as station manager but spends most of her time calling on accounts. One salesperson also announces occasional play-by-play sports broadcasts. The station owner handles all national accounts as well as a dozen local ones.

A copywriter prepares the commercials and the station announcers tape them. The spots are played over the telephone for client approval before being aired. The traffic manager then schedules them on cartridge tapes ("carts"). Many of the commercials also are aired on the station's 5200-watt FM station.

All advertising personnel provide fresh, up-to-date information about the markets that their newspaper, magazine, or station covers and about the "pulling power" of the medium itself. These facts are provided regularly by their own research and promotion departments or by national trade associations or bureaus.

Most magazines deal directly with national advertisers or indirectly through national representatives. As is true with the other media, copywriters, artists, and production, promotion, and merchandising personnel supplement the sales force. And there is a similar ladder of promotion to executive positions.

## Retail Store Advertising

It is estimated that retail firms employ more than 80,000 persons in their advertising departments. These range from one-person staffs to those employing dozens of persons. In a large store, the advertising manager works closely with sales promotion and marketing specialists. In one large department store, the staff consists of a copy chief, production manager, and proofreader; an art director and assistant art director, together with six layout artists, five "finish" artists, and two apprentices; and five copywriters, people with a high degree of creativity who specialize in women's and children's apparel, men's apparel and accessories, and home furnishings. In addition, two copywriters are assigned to the basement store and suburban stores. Other journalistic personnel may be found in the public relations office and in the radio-television division preparing special product demonstrations.

Those charged with planning a store's advertising must be familiar with all aspects of the market, consumer behavior and attitudes, and such factors as product images and characteristics. The steps normally taken in planning a campaign include these: (1) setting a sales goal or budget, based to a large extent on sales the preceding year; (2) deciding how much advertising is needed; (3) determining which products or services to promote and when; and (4) preparing a day-to-day schedule. Store displays and other merchandising efforts are coordinated. The volume of sales produced during each advertising period is carefully monitored to determine the probable success of the advertising and to help in future planning.

## Industrial and Trade Advertising

The public is well aware of consumer goods advertising. We see and hear advertisements almost every moment of the waking day. Not so with industrial and trade advertisements, for they are not addressed to the general public. *Industrial* advertising is employed by producers of industrial goods, such as steel, machinery, lubricants, packaging, and office equipment, in order to sell these products to other industries. *Trade* advertising is employed by the producers and distributors of branded and nonbranded consumer goods in order to reach the retailers and wholesalers of consumer goods. They, in turn, sell these goods to their own customers.

**Industrial advertising**
That employed by producers of industrial goods to sell products to other industries

**Trade advertising**
That employed by producers and distributors of consumer goods to sell these products to wholesalers and retailers

# The International Scene
# GLOBAL SPREAD OF ADVERTISING

With the growth of transnational companies and new, expanding communications technologies has come the growth of huge *transnational* advertising agencies to serve *multinational* as well as domestic clients. As trade barriers have fallen, the manufacturing, distribution, and advertising practices of thousands of companies worldwide have become so international in nature that the old concept of home as distinct from overseas markets has become increasingly irrelevant.

The earlier American dominance of world advertising has been diminished by the global mergers and acquisitions that created mega-agencies and rocked the advertising world during the last two decades. British firms, in particular, acquired a number of U.S. agencies.

The WPP Group PLC of London bought America's giant Ogilvy Group, not long after acquiring the United States' JWT Group, parent company of the J. Walter Thompson Company. WPP thus became the world's largest marketing operation, with 21,000 employees serving more than 5000 clients in 50 countries. Its global gross income in 1995 exceeded $3.1 billion.

Other firms and their rankings in the top ten in gross income in 1995 were, in order, the Omnicom Group, New York; Interpublic Group of Companies, New York; Dentsu, Tokyo; Cordiant (formerly Saatchi & Saatchi, London); Young & Rubicam, New York; Hakuhodo, Tokyo; Havas Advertising, Levallois-Perret, France; Grey Advertising, New York; and Leo Burnett Co., Chicago. Billings increased 11.1 percent over the previous year to $130.5 billion worldwide.

The firms provided integrated marketing services, largely on a regional basis, that included advertising, public relations, product design, promotion, and direct marketing. In all, more than $500 billion was spent annually on marketing around the world.

Mass communications—primarily satellite television—fueled the new age of marketing. David Miln, business development director of Saatchi & Saatchi, said that it is now possible "to produce the same product, in the same packaging, with the same name, at the same price, wherever you want within the world markets, in the cheapest place probably, and, if there are enough people out there who want it—terrific. But first comes finding the need and branding the product." The transmission of printed pages by satellite also enabled newspapers and magazines to be distributed worldwide.

Dozens of companies now market their products to vast portions of the world as if those regions were a single market. In 1992, the Coca-Cola Company began its first global marketing campaign when advertisements for Coke, Diet Coke, Sprite, and Fanta were shown around the world at the same time. Observed the Washington *Post*:

"For 60 seconds, the Atlanta-based soft drink company showered the planet with images of its disparate people—Asian children riding oxen, desert Bedouins, India women, African tribesmen, a Buddhist

## GLOBAL SPREAD OF ADVERTISING
### Continued

monk, a Catholic priest, a young blonde woman in a bikini. Mankind's common bond, the universal commercial suggested, is a soda pop. . . .

"Observers . . . foresee a cultural clash in the making as consumerism, carried everywhere by advertising, collides with other worldwide 'isms'—religious fundamentalism, environmentalism, the last outposts of communism."

Most advertising, however, still must be tailored to the vastly differing political, cultural, economic, and legal environments that characterize regions and countries. Some of the transnational business firms that operate numerous subsidiaries centralize their marketing and advertising operations, while others assign much decision-making to foreign managers.

In the former USSR, after decades during which the "vulgarity" of Western capitalism and advertising was condemned. In 1988, Soviet television for the first time carried commercials by Visa, Pepsi, and Sony during a five-part series examining life in the United States. In 1989, *Izvestia* began running advertisements weekly in its foreign and Moscow editions. The Soviet Union even offered ad space on one of its space shuttles.

Some Third World countries have established guidelines regarding advertising content and the values and attitudes it fosters, often in conflict with national cultural values. A number of countries tax advertising to fund national media development.

As in the United States and Canada, the consumer movement has gained momentum in recent years in most industrialized nations. Legislation to regulate and control advertising has been proposed or passed in Australia, Canada, Finland, Germany, Japan, Norway, the United Kingdom, the United States, and other countries. Cigarette and children's advertising, along with that considered dishonest, have been primary concerns. Statutes vary from country to country. Some countries, such as the United Kingdom and Ireland, rely on self-discipline by business itself. Most companies subscribe to the International Chamber of Commerce code of advertising practice.

The International Advertising Association, composed of about 2500 individual members and more than 300 international companies and other groups, states that, in order to gain acceptance for self-regulation, its members should eliminate abuses in the marketplace and champion the public's interests in quality and performance of goods and services.

The industrial or trade advertising department may employ only one person, the advertising manager, or as many as 400 or more persons. The typical department, however, has about six. These are likely to include the advertising manager, a secretary, a writer, perhaps an artist, and one or two persons engaged in marketing research, media evaluation, or production work.

## BIG BUCKS FOR STAR POWER

Celebrities sell soft drinks, beer, personal computers, even underwear on television—but not for peanuts. Celebrity endorsement fees exceed $300 million annually, according to industry statistics. The stars appear on almost 35 percent of all commercials, and are especially popular in Japan.

Insiders say sponsorship deals start at $500,000 and run up to more than $10 million. Matching product and star is essential. "Murder, She Wrote" TV star Angela Lansbury cracked the top-10 list of favorite celebrities because of her appeal to older viewers who use Bufferin. Los Angeles Dodger Manager Tommy Lasorda ranked high because of his beer-belly reduction with the Ultra SlimFast diet.

Consumer attitudes toward celebrity endorsers turned negative in the mid-1980s when Cybill Shepherd, promoting the beef industry, said she didn't eat meat; National Beef Council spokesperson James Garner underwent bypass surgery; and Bruce Willis was rumored to have a drinking problem while touting Seagram's Golden Wine Cooler.

A Video Storyboard Tests, Inc. survey in 1994 ranked Cindy Crawford, endorsing Pepsi-Cola and Revlon, in top favor, followed in order by Candice Bergen, Sprint; Bill Cosby, Jell-O; Elizabeth Taylor, White Diamonds perfume; and Jerry Seinfeld, American Express.

During that same year, actress Marilyn Monroe, who died in 1962, was revived through a special effects technique known as morphing to endorse Chanel No. 5 perfume in a 30-second television commercial. (See Chapter 13.)

---

The department handles inquiries and prepares catalogues and technical data sheets, direct mail, exhibits, and sales promotion materials such as slide films, videos, movies, and props for sales meetings. It may engage in market research, but most departments obtain market data without charge through business paper research services.

Almost all industrial and trade advertising departments employ outside agencies to handle trade advertisements. More than half the advertising placed in business publications comes from general agencies. Others identify themselves as industrial advertising agencies, although most also handle consumer goods advertising. They specialize in industrial, technical, scientific, commercial, and merchandising products and services. A few agencies confine themselves to such fields as financial or pharmaceutical advertising.

### Direct Response Advertising

One of the fastest-growing fields of the industry, as target marketing has increased, is *direct-response* advertising. For decades this has included much of *direct-mail* advertising, and the publication of coupons in news-

**Direct response advertising**
Advertising message that attempts to obtain an immediate response from consumers

**Direct mail advertising**
Letters, catalogues, samples, and other product or service materials mailed to a selected group of actual or anticipated customers

papers and magazines as incentives for consumers to make purchases, sample products, and obtain additional information.

In recent years, cable television has stimulated growth in direct-response advertising through the use of 800 telephone numbers that consumers may use to order products. Examples are the sale of rock music records and discs on Music Television (MTV) and health products on the Lifetime channel. One or two channels have been devoted exclusively to telemarketing.

## Points to Remember

1. What economic benefits does advertising provide in our society?
2. What is the function of the Advertising Council?
3. How has each of the last four decades been identified in terms of cycles in advertising?
4. What principal trends and problems confront advertising?
5. In what ways is advertising often criticized? What reply can be made to each charge?
6. How is advertising regulated?
7. How does industrial and trade advertising differ from other kinds?
8. What principal functions are performed in an advertising agency?
9. To what extent has the advertising industry incorporated computer networks into its practices?
10. What problems are encountered when a firm advertises in other countries?

## Media Questions to Think About

1. Which recent advertising campaigns have been effective in drawing your attention to their products? What made them effective?
2. Have you ever encountered deceptive advertising? Who should help protect you against such an abuse—the federal government, the state government, the advertising industry itself, or some combination of these groups?
3. Do you receive much direct-mail advertising? What percentage of it do you read or respond to by buying a product?

# CHAPTER SIXTEEN
## Public Relations

## The Shape of Things to Come

Just informing Americans how to lose weight isn't enough, says former Surgeon General C. Everett Koop. You've got to motivate people to eat more sensibly and get at least some exercise. How? Through public relations strategies and tactics, on a massive scale.

Koop enlisted the help of Hill and Knowlton, which assigned Nancy Glick, director of the firm's Food and Nutrition Specialty Group, to head the "Shape Up America" campaign. Signing on as sponsors were Weight Watchers, Heinz Foundation, Kellogg Company, Campbell Soup Company, *Time* magazine, and others.

After a White House ceremony in December 1994 attended by First Lady Hillary Rodham Clinton, the 78-year-old surgeon embarked on a nationwide tour, preaching the importance of exercise and a healthful diet.

The campaign positioned obesity as a treatable disease and stressed that even a small change in diet and minimal physical activity could result in a 10-percent reduction in body weight.

Tools included a prime-time TV special, public service advertisements and special promotions, in-store information, and grassroots education.

The shape of things to come—silhouettes and waistlines—will reveal the success of the effort.

Public relations is a rapidly developing field of communications that has evolved into an essential link in much of the world's economic, political, social, and mass communications networks.

Some of its elements—publicity, persuasion, and press agentry—are as old as civilization itself. But as a recognized function in business and other areas of activity, public relations dates back only to the start of the twentieth century.

Public relations involves research and analysis, policy formation, communication, and feedback from the publics involved. Practitioners serve as advisers to their clients or to a company's management and as technicians performing a wide variety of functions.

As corporate mergers and joint ventures have crossed national borders, particularly during the last decade, major public relations firms have greatly increased their global operations. The Internet is now a useful part of those efforts.

In this chapter, we describe the various facets of public relations, outline its historical development, and discuss the increasing professionalism of its practitioners.

## A Growing Field

It is estimated that almost a quarter-million persons are employed in various kinds of public relations jobs, with an increasing number at high levels of management. More are being attracted every year, mainly from the mass media and from among graduates of journalism and public relations programs in mass communication schools. As society becomes more complex—and the need for effective relationships between the numerous institutions and the individuals they serve becomes more essential—the field of public relations is likely to continue its steady growth.

The term *public relations* means many different things to different people. It has been used to include a wide range of activities from legitimate attempts at persuasive communication to the bribery efforts of unscrupulous lobbyists. In its best and narrowest sense, public relations is *the planned and organized effort of a company or institution to establish mutually beneficial relationships with its various publics.* Publics, in turn, may be defined as the various groups of people who are affected by—or who can affect—the operations of a particular firm or institution. Each public is bound together by a common interest vis-à-vis the organization.

Thus, for a manufacturing corporation, such publics would include employees, stockholders, citizens of the community in which it is located, dealers who handle its products, and the ultimate purchasers or users of its products. Similarly, for a hospital, these publics include its professional staff, its employees, its patients and their families, the citizens in the community and region in which it is located, and its financial supporters.

Although many persons tend to consider public relations and publicity as synonymous terms, it should be obvious that more than effective communication is required to initiate and execute a sound public relations program. Effective public relations programming begins with the establishment of equitable policies by management. The essence of these policies must be explained, in varying forms of communication, to those who work for the organization or who represent it, and to the interested publics. In short, communication must explain the policies and actions of management, but the policies and actions must support the words. Finally, the responses of these publics to what the organization says and does must be reflected back to management so that—with recommendations—appropriate adjustments may be made in both policies and operations.

Public relations has been defined by *PR News*, a weekly newsletter in the field, as "the management function which evaluates public attitudes, identifies the policies and procedures of an individual or an organization with the public interest, and plans and executes a program of action to earn public understanding and acceptance." Many managements expect their public relations executives to analyze social, economic, environmental, and political trends that may have an impact on the operations of the business or institution so that future problems may be avoided or alleviated. Thus, the public relations people may be required to evaluate developments in such areas as consumer activism, the environmental protection movement, and government responses to minority problems. The practice is known as *issues management*.

In such areas public relations practice—at its best—affords genuine opportunities for meaningful service to society. As this function develops more fully, the value of public relations people to management and the social significance of the function will increase.

**Issues management**
Analyzing and seeking solutions to possible problems before they become critical

# The Growth of Public Relations

## Early Development

Although the concept of public relations as a systematic social activity, and the term itself, were not recognized until the first decades of the twentieth century, its more elementary functions of publicity, persuasion, and press agentry are many centuries old.

Archaeologists have discovered evidence of political communication, such as painted messages, in ruins of ancient civilizations. Just as thousands of communicators publicize today's Olympic Games, so did their predecessors promote the first contests in Greece. Caesar's *Commentaries*, glorifying the emperor, and the four Gospels of the New Testament represented other forms of publicity and persuasion. As Peter G. Osgood, president of the public relations firm, Carl Byoir & Associates, remarked, "St. John the Baptist himself did superb advance work for Jesus of Nazareth."

In colonial America, Samuel Adams and other agitators achieved a propaganda triumph in helping persuade the colonists to revolt against

The world's largest peanut butter and jelly sandwich was assembled in the little town of Peanut, Pennsylvania, by the Peanut Advisory Board to publicize the food product. The sandwich, nearly 40 feet long, contained 100 pounds of peanut butter and 50 pounds of jelly.

Great Britain. Their tools included a staged event, the Boston Tea Party; widespread publicity accorded the so-called Boston Massacre; and exhortations published in pamphlets and newspapers.

As the first presidential press secretary, former newspaperman Amos Kendall adroitly counseled and publicized Andrew Jackson. Those opposing Jackson glorified Davy Crockett as a frontier hero in order to draw political support from the rough-hewn politician.

When the nation expanded into the plains territories and states, almost every town was heralded as "the garden spot of the West" in pamphlets and newspaper copies sent back East and to Europe to attract settlers.

As a wave of industrialization, mechanization, and urbanization swept the nation after the Civil War, the public became concerned about many aspects of big business, including concentrations of wealth and control. In 1888, the Mutual Life Insurance Company sought to improve its image by employing newspaperman Charles J. Smith to write press releases. A year later, Westinghouse Corporation created what is said to be the first in-house publicity department. In 1897, the term *public relations* was used, perhaps for the first time, by the Association of American Railroads.

## Press Agentry

Nineteenth-century America also experienced the rise and popularity of *press agentry*, whose modern counterpart is found, among other places, in the *hyping* of movie and television stars, books, magazines, and the like, through shrewd use of the media and other devices. Press agents attracted thousands to the touring shows of Buffalo Bill and his sharp-shooter Annie Oakley, made a legend of frontiersman Daniel Boone, and promoted hundreds of other personalities, politicians, and theatrical performers with remarkable success. Today's press agent, usually called a publicist, rarely resorts to the outright fabrications that characterized the old-time promoter.

> **Press agentry**
> Promotion of an idea, product, service, or individual(s) through shrewd, often extravagant notices in the media, staged events, and other such devices

Phineas T. Barnum was the great showman of the century. He was the master of what historian Daniel Boorstin has termed the *pseudoevent*, the planned happening that occurs primarily for the purpose of being reported. Barnum provided the attractions and he and his own corps of press agents, headed by Richard F. "Tody" Hamilton, contrived immense buildups, planted "news" stories and letters in the press, and prepared advertisements containing gross exaggerations. Much of the public loved it, and it made Barnum a wealthy man.

> **Hype**
> Promotional efforts in behalf of personalities, entertainment events, and other activities

The Connecticut-born showman employed the public relations technique known today as *third-party endorsement*. He induced London society leaders and even royalty to view the midget "General" Tom Thumb; drew opinion leaders to the performances of Jenny Lind, billed as "the Swedish nightingale," by arranging for donation of part of the proceeds to charity; and persuaded the clergy to attend plays in his American Museum in New York City at a time when such performances were considered by many to be wicked.

> **Pseudoevent**
> Activity that would not have taken place except for the purpose of being reported

> **Third-party endorsement**
> Technique of associating a person, product, or organization with individuals or organizations of high credibility

Because of the exaggerations that characterized old-time press agentry such as Barnum employed, today's public relations practitioners strongly disassociate themselves from the practice and chafe under the heritage of distrust that persists among many journalists. Yet, in much more restrained fashion, the scheduling of pseudoevents and the hyping of celebrities and products do constitute one, albeit relatively minor, phase of public relations activities today.

## Twentieth-Century Developments

The first publicity firm, known as the Publicity Bureau, was established in Boston in 1900, with Harvard University as one of its clients. Within the decade a number of other such bureaus were established. Among them was the office of Ivy Ledbetter Lee and George Parker.

**Ivy Lee.**   Lee, a Princeton graduate and former newspaper reporter of business activities, soon branched out on his own to offer the first public relations counseling service. It was Lee's belief that much of the public's antipathy toward business at that time—an antipathy exploited by the muckrakers (publications and writers who exposed corruption and exploitation)—resulted from the fact that most businesses operated in secrecy and most business people would not discuss their policies or operations with the public.

Such was the case with the anthracite coal industry, which hired Lee in 1906 during a strike. Lee persuaded industry leaders to change their policy and release information to the public. Retained by the Pennsylvania Railroad Company after a rail disaster, Lee again was successful in changing management policies. Reporters were taken to the scene of the accident and given full information, after which the company received fairer press comment than on any previous such occasion.

Lee was hired by John D. Rockefeller, Jr., in the wake of the vicious strike-breaking activities known as the "Ludlow Massacre" at the Rockefeller family's Colorado mining operation. By arranging photographic and feature story coverage of the activities and generous philanthropy of the family over a period of several years, Lee gradually changed the public's image of the Rockefellers.

Among other counseling activities, Lee persuaded the Pennsylvania Railroad to beautify its stations, got the American Tobacco Company to install a profit-sharing plan, and persuaded the movie industry to stop its inflated advertising and form a voluntary code of censorship. Lee, who died in 1934, is remembered for four important contributions to public relations:

1. Advancing the concept that business and industry should align themselves with the public interest.
2. Dealing with top executives and carrying out no program unless it had the active support and personal contribution of management.
3. Maintaining open communication with the news media.
4. Emphasizing the necessity of humanizing business and bringing its public relations down to the community level of employees, customers, and neighbors.

**Public Relations in World War I.**   Another dimension was added to the public relations concept during World War I, when the Committee on Public Information was established by the federal government under George Creel, a former newspaper reporter. The committee conducted a massive and successful publicity campaign to mobilize the American public behind the war effort.

During World War I, this poster for United States government bonds was only one part of a large public relations campaign mounted by the Committee on Public Information to encourage public support for the war effort. (Brown Brothers)

The values of such massive communications efforts were impressed upon those who worked with Creel, and some of them became pioneers in the establishment of public relations firms designed to conduct similar campaigns for private clients. They included Edward L. Bernays, who in 1923 coined the term *public relations counsel* to describe a function that was to become the core of public relations, and Carl Byoir, whose previously mentioned firm became highly successful.

**Edward L. Bernays.**  In 1922, Walter Lippmann published his classic treatise, *Public Opinion*, in which he pointed out how people are moved to action by "the pictures in our minds." When it was followed in 1923

**Public relations counsel**
Specialist who advises clients and management on ways to deal most effectively with various publics

by publication of Bernays' book, *Crystallizing Public Opinion*, widespread attention was drawn to the subject of opinion formation. Bernays taught the first public relations course, at New York University, and spent the rest of his life counseling companies and individuals, writing books, and lecturing. (He died in 1995 at age 103.)

Bernays' first employee was Doris E. Fleischman, a talented writer, ardent feminist, and former assistant women's page editor and assistant Sunday editor of the New York *Tribune*. When Bernays and Fleischman were married in 1922, the two became equal partners in the firm of Edward L. Bernays, Counsel on Public Relations. The partnership continued until Fleischman's death in 1980.

Bernays aptly theorized that if the public relations practitioner has the responsibility for explaining management's policies and actions to the public, then the public relations specialist should also have a voice in advising management on the formulation of its policies and the development of programs affecting the public. Although some managements still have not recognized this aspect of public relations practice, in many of America's largest corporations today the public relations executive is a vice-president who participates in boardroom discussions and has strong influence on the development of management policy.

Bernays helped Procter & Gamble sell soap and heightened interest in art by promoting national interest in children's soap sculpturing. He helped publishers sell books by persuading contractors to build bookshelves in new houses. Many other such examples could be cited. Perhaps his greatest counseling feat, in the service of General Electric and Westinghouse, was attracting worldwide attention in 1929 to the fiftieth anniversary of Edison's invention of the electric light bulb.

**Other Pioneers.**    Among other notable public relations pioneers have been the following:

- Benjamin Sonnenberg, who proposed that the Texaco Company counter unfavorable publicity received after negotiating an oil deal with Hitler by sponsoring performances of the Metropolitan Opera Company on radio. The series sponsorship, begun in 1940, still continues.

- Rex Harlow, probably the first full-time public relations educator, who began teaching a public relations course on a regular basis in 1939 as a professor at Stanford University. Harlow founded the American Council on Public Relations that same year, and later founded the *Social Science Reporter* to demonstrate how social science findings directly benefit the practice of public relations.

- Arthur Page, former vice-president of the American Telephone and Telegraph Company, who advocated the philosophy that public relations is a management function.

- Paul W. Garrett, whose 25-year career as public relations counselor for the General Motors Corporation, beginning in 1931, was a model for corporate public relations practice.
- Earl Newsom, who worked behind the scenes (issuing no news releases and holding no news conferences) to bring public and press recognition to Henry Ford II after he assumed command of the Ford Motor Company.
- Leone Baxter and her husband Clem Whitaker, credited with establishing the first political campaign public relations firm in the United States. Among their first clients on a national level were Dwight Eisenhower and Richard Nixon. In 1996, Leone Baxter remained an active public relations consultant in San Francisco with an impressive array of corporate, government, and trade association clients.

In addition, no survey of the development of public relations would be complete without mention of the inventor Henry Ford, who staged events and solicited by mail customer opinions of his Model-T car; President Theodore Roosevelt, who exploited the news media in building his image as a trustbuster, Rough Rider, and Bull Moose; and President Franklin D. Roosevelt, the master of the radio "fireside chat" in communicating with the public.

**Behavioral Techniques.**  A major dimension was added to the public relations concept in the 1930s with the development of modern public opinion and marketing survey techniques by George Gallup, Elmo Roper, Claude Robinson, and others. This development provided a tool by which public relations counselors and executives could achieve some degree of objective measurement. Public opinion measurement techniques are still far from perfect and their results subject to error, but they have become more reliable as the result of refinements over the years. Public attitude surveys have become a standard tool of public relations practitioners.

**Public Relations in World War II.**  During World War II, the federal Office of War Information (OWI), headed by journalist Elmer Davis, enlarged upon the public relations practices of the previous Creel Committee. A number of the people who worked with Davis became public relations leaders after the war. The OWI was the forerunner of the U.S. Information Agency, established in 1953 "to tell America's story abroad."

**The Maturing of Public Relations.**  After World War II public relations developed rapidly, in business and industry at first and later in nonprofit institutions. The number of public relations workers soared, from only 19,000 in 1950 to about 250,000 in 1995, according to the U.S. Bureau of Labor Statistics. The *U.S. Employment Opportunities Handbook* has predicted a growth rate for public relations "much faster than average for all occupations through the year 2000."

Federal law prohibits the employment of public relations people by U.S. government agencies, but essentially the same function is carried out by "information officers." The Army, Navy, and Air Force all have designated public information officers especially trained in military public relations policy at service schools or who have been sent for the same purpose to universities with good public relations programs.

In its greatly broadened role, contemporary public relations, when practiced at the optimal level, involves four general responsibilities:

1. *Analyzing* the social, economic, political, and human environment in which the business or institution operates in order to anticipate developments and provide a basis for advice to management.

2. *Counseling* management on the development of policies and operations to develop sound relations with the various pertinent publics.

3. *Communicating* essential information about managerial policies and practices, products, and services to the concerned publics.

4. *Evaluating* the results against the stated objectives to learn what was done right, what was done wrong, how much progress was made, and how to perform more productively next time.

One popular way to describe the process, and to remember its components, is to use the RACE acronym, first articulated by John Marston in his book, *The Nature of Public Relations*. Essentially, RACE means that public relations activity consists of the following:

1. *Research*—What is the problem?

2. *Action* and *planning*—What will be done about it?

3. *Communications*—How will the public be told?

4. *Evaluation*—Was the audience reached, and what was the effect?

In short, the public relations function today—as foreseen in some of its important aspects by Ivy Lee, Edward L. Bernays, and others many decades ago—helps correlate the private interests of management with the overriding interests of various publics to facilitate the development of the particular organization. No public relations program can succeed if the private interests of the business or institution run counter to the interests of its publics.

## Public Relations and the Mass Media

Public relations at its best has a unique relationship with the mass media. The communicative function of public relations practice has become an inextricable part of the mass communications network in the United

## NEEDED: A CRISIS PUBLIC RELATIONS PLAN

For hundreds of delighted readers, the contest pieces matched—those in the Sunday newspaper flyer and those on the packages of Kraft Singles cheese slices.

Winners all—of a new Dodge Caravan LE.

No, replied embarrassed Kraft USA people as they canceled the contest. A printing error . . . sorry! Send in your matched pieces and we'll see what we can do.

Several days passed, as fuming "winners" sounded off—to the company, neighbors, lawyers, even state consumer fraud offices.

For lack of a crisis public relations plan, Kraft's image plummeted. Finally, letters of explanation and regret were mailed, along with $250 checks for the van "winners" and lesser amounts for others.

Public relations specialists said that, as Tylenol did in its poisoning crisis, Kraft top officials should have listened to their public relations people, not their lawyers, and explained in the media.

Said Pat Jackson, editor of *PR Reporter* newsletter:

"I don't know how many times businesses are going to have to learn this lesson: When Kraft ducks under the covers, it immediately sends the message. 'They are lying.' . . . The one thing that the public understands is that people screw up. Kraft should have gone majorly public. If they had carried it off with humility, they could have gotten the public on their side. . . ."

Cost to the company? In cash, $4 million, not including possible legal settlements. In good will, inestimable.

States and many other countries. It is not too extreme to state that, without the contributions of tens of thousands of public relations communicators, the print and broadcast media would not be nearly as accurate, or as well rounded in content, as they are.

Consider, for example, that no newspaper—not even the New York *Times* or the *Wall Street Journal*—nor any magazine, news service, or broadcasting station or network can afford a staff large enough to have experts in every major field of human endeavor. Even the largest media rely on the public relations persons representing companies and institutions to provide the expertise, the background, and the explanations and translations from the language of the experts to the language of the layperson that enable journalists to write about complex and arcane subjects with understanding. The smaller papers and the smaller news staffs of the broadcast media are even more dependent on public relations people for this kind of help. In one sense, then, public relations practitioners provide a necessary link between the media and many specialized areas of activity in our society, a link that the media usually could not afford to provide for themselves.

Government agencies issue an immense amount of public information. This advertisement by the U.S. Government Printing Office offers a free catalogue, listing nearly a thousand of the most popular books sold by the federal government.

# KEEP UP IN A CHANGING WORLD

Take advantage of the wealth of knowledge available from your Government. The U.S. Government Printing Office has just produced a new catalog. It tells about the most popular books sold by the Government—nearly 1,000 in all. Books on business, children, energy, space, and much more. For a **free** copy of this new catalog, write—

**New Catalog**
Post Office Box 37000
Washington, D.C. 20013

Public relations communications, however, are not limited to the mass media. Public relations staffs and counselors develop many specialized (or controlled) forms of communication, such as printed booklets or periodicals; exhibits; and motion pictures, slide films, video, and other audiovisual presentations aimed at specific publics. In this area also, public relations communicators are influenced not only by their innate sense of honesty but also by the knowledge that their long-range effectiveness must be built on a reputation for integrity.

## Fields of Public Relations Practice

As previously stated, corporations employ the greatest number of practitioners; a survey disclosed that 85 percent of the 1500 largest corporations have public relations or communications departments. Some, such as General Motors and U.S. Steel, employ scores or hundreds of people in numerous subdepartments specializing in different areas of public relations or in differing communications techniques. Thousands of smaller business firms each employ only a few public relations people.

About one-third of the large companies retain external public relations counseling firms. The number of such firms has mushroomed since World War II, and today there are well over 1500. Like an advertising agency, a public relations counseling firm may serve a number of clients on a fee-plus-expenses basis. Such firms range in size from those with

# Put Toxic Waste In Its Place.

Household Hazardous Materials Program — County of San Diego

**Stoorza, Ziegaus & Metzger has developed a program for San Diego County and its "Toxic Waste Gang" cartoon characters.**

Whimsical cartoon characters often are effective in conveying a public relations message. This poster was distributed by the County of San Diego, California, in a campaign to control hazardous household materials.

only one practitioner and a secretary to complex organizations with 2000 or more employees.

Trade associations as well as not-for-profit social and educational organizations use the services of public relations practitioners in many ways. Principal areas of not-for-profit public relations activity include:

*Trade and professional associations.* Approximately 4000 national organizations of this type exist, plus some 40,000 state, regional, and local associations, including chambers of commerce. The American Hotel and Motel Association is an example.

*Social and health agencies.* Areas include social service (American Red Cross); health agencies (American Heart Association); hospitals; religious organizations (Southern Baptist Convention); welfare agencies (Salvation Army, government offices, cultural organizations, and foundations).

*Entertainment, sports, and travel.* Publicists build the careers of television and movie stars, help to sell tickets for rock stars' concerts, and stimulate public interest in tourist attractions. Every major sports team has a public relations office.

*Colleges and universities.* Thousands of practitioners operate general news bureaus; write, edit, and design publications; produce broadcasting and audiovisual materials, and so on. Others do similar work in alumni and development offices, with emphasis on fund-raising.

*Public and private schools.* Public relations work at the elementary and secondary school levels, similar to that at the college level, requires the services of a large number of practitioners.

There are two types of public relations people in these jobs: *generalists* and *specialists.* The generalists, a definite minority, are usually at the executive or managerial level. They are responsible for analyzing problem situations, developing programs to resolve these situations, participating in management-level discussions of policy, and supervising the implementation of programs. The specialists, much greater in number, are the experts in various techniques of communication and in the specialized areas of public relations practice. These men and women work under the direction of the generalists. The specialists write news releases and speeches, prepare booklets, answer inquiries from the press, arrange press conferences and special events, develop audiovisual presentations and educational materials, and so on. Most public relations careers start at the specialist level—for example, in product news release writing or employee publications writing. After the individual gains experience and shows promise of generalist potential, he or she moves to a higher level.

**Generalist**
Experienced practitioner who functions primarily as a planning or policy-making adviser to clients and company managements

**Specialist**
Technician who primarily produces communication products such as news releases or brochures; who distributes messages to the media; or who serves in a liaison capacity between an organization and its publics

**Internal publication**
One designed for distribution primarily to employees

**External publication**
One designed to be read by persons not employed by the sponsoring company or organization

**Company Publications.** Most corporations and not-for-profit groups publish magazines and newsletters for customers, employees, salespeople, stockholders, and other groups that management wishes to inform or impress. These public relations vehicles are divided into *internal* publications, for distribution within a company, and *external* ones, which go to nonemployee readers. Many combine these approaches. The publications range from sleek, sophisticated-appearing magazines often with four-color covers and splashy graphics, such as *AT&T Magazine* and *Chevron World,* to four-page folders in black and white that resemble a small tabloid newspaper. The best available estimate puts the number of editorial employees on company publications at around 15,000. (See Chapter 6.)

## Professionalism in Public Relations

Like journalism and advertising, public relations is not—and cannot become—a profession such as medicine and law. Practice in these latter fields requires legal state certification following years of educational

# HOW PUBLIC RELATIONS PRACTITIONERS SPEND THEIR TIME

Practitioners on average spend more than one-third of their workweeks writing specifically for public relations purposes, according to a study conducted by Frank Stansberry, APR, manager of guest affairs for Coca-Cola USA.

Stansberry sent questionnaires to a random sample of 500 practitioners listed in the membership directory of the Public Relations Society of America. The 198 respondents averaged 12.2 years' experience. Principal findings:

## Time Devoted to Writing Tasks

| Writing Task | Percent of Total Time | Percent of Writing Time |
|---|---|---|
| 1. Releases | 7.1 | 19.5 |
| 2. Internal publications | 5.9 | 16.1 |
| 3. Counseling reports | 4.3 | 11.1 |
| 4. Speeches | 3.5 | 9.5 |
| 5. Community relations plans | 3.2 | 8.8 |
| 6. Research reports | 3.1 | 8.5 |
| 7. Advertising copy | 2.9 | 7.9 |
| 8. New business proposals | 2.8 | 7.7 |
| 9. Issues monitoring reports | 2.7 | 7.3 |
| 10. Financial reports | 1.1 | 3.0 |

preparation and the passing of examinations. Under the First Amendment no one can be prohibited from engaging in an occupation based on freedom to speak and to publish. Nevertheless, journalists and advertising and public relations people attain varying degrees of *professionalism*, in the broader sense, through the preparation, skill, and practice that distinguish them from amateurs in these fields. Such professionalism normally is characterized by a high degree of independence, a sense of responsibility to society, and an adherence to recognized ethical and other standards that supersedes their loyalty to an individual employer.

The 15,000-member Public Relations Society of America certifies the professionalism of practitioners through a program of accreditation. To become an accredited member of the society, a person must have at least five years of experience in public relations practice or teaching, must have two sponsors who will testify as to integrity and ability, and must pass written and oral examinations.

The PRSA accreditation program, instituted in 1965, has been a major step toward professionalizing the field. To be an associate member of PRSA, one need have only one year's experience in the field. For students who have just earned their college degrees and who have been

**Professionalism**
Acting with the standards and other characteristics normally associated with state-certified occupations such as those of legal and medical practitioners

## Table 16.1

### Time Devoted to Various Responsibilities

| Function | Percent of Time | Percent Active* |
|---|---|---|
| Product publicity | 11.6 | 85 |
| Media relations | 11.0 | 87 |
| Business administration | 10.4 | 75 |
| Internal communications | 9.0 | 72 |
| Management counseling | 8.7 | 68 |
| Community relations | 8.0 | 68 |
| Research | 5.4 | 67 |
| Advertising | 5.0 | 53 |
| Issues-monitoring | 4.8 | 54 |
| Speeches | 4.7 | 67 |
| New business development | 4.7 | 45 |
| Government relations | 4.1 | 43 |
| Entertaining | 3.9 | 57 |
| Development/fund-raising | 2.2 | 23 |
| Investor/financial relations | 2.1 | 23 |
| Formal education | 1.6 | 23 |
| Other responsibilities | 3.0 | NA |

*Percent of sample indicating some time on function.
Source: Public Relations Journal, March 1989.

members of the Public Relations Student Society of America, there is an associate form of membership in PRSA. The student organization, sponsored by PRSA, has chapters in about 175 colleges and universities. More than 80 percent of its approximately 6000 members are female.

Additionally, PRSA, the International Association of Business Communicators (IABC), and the public relations division of the Association for Education in Journalism and Mass Communication have worked to improve and standardize the curricula for programs of public relations studies at the bachelor's and professional master's levels. PRSA and IABC also have developed codes of professional standards for the practice of public relations. Although parts of the codes are phrased in general terms, such as requiring practitioners to adhere to generally accepted standards of accuracy, truth, and good taste, other clauses and interpretive supplements deal with specifics. For example, a PRSA member cannot represent conflicting or competing interests without the express consent of both parties, nor can the member reveal the confidences of present or former clients or employers.

PRSA is the only professional communications organization with an established grievance procedure that can lead to the suspension and censure of a member for illegal or unethical professional activity.

The Institute for Public Relations Research & Education, established in 1956 with the support of the society but now independent, seeks to advance professionalism through grants for research studies, publications, films, and videos such as its documentary, "Communications that Count."

The other organization for public relations practitioners, IABC, had approximately 11,000 members in more than 35 countries in 1995. IABC describes itself as "a professional organization for writers, editors, audio-visual specialists, managers, and other business and organizational communicators." The association sponsors student chapters at universities and has developed its own accreditation program. About 5 percent of IABC members hold the accredited business communicator (ABC) rating.

Approximately 1800 of its members are in Canada, where the Toronto chapter, with more than 600 members, is almost the size of the New York chapter, IABC's largest. Other chapters outside the United States in 1996 included those in the United Kingdom, the Philippines, Hong Kong, and Belgium.

The International Public Relations Association (IPRA) was organized in 1955 as an individual membership society for public relations professionals with international interests. IPRA has well over 1000 members in about 65 countries and is seeking further expansion. Every third year it sponsors a World Congress of Public Relations, which attracts 600 or more practitioners from the United States and Europe as well as from countries in Latin America, Africa, the Near East, and the Far East, where public relations is also growing rapidly.

## Public Relations on the Internet

Many public relations firms are, as *Publishers Weekly* put it, "leapfrogging over the media" to deliver their messages directly to consumers, and consumers are responding. A number of such firms have opened sites on the World Wide Web, beginning in the spring of 1995 with Edelman Public Relations Worldwide and Fleishman-Hillard.

"Anyone doing PR today who ignores the Internet is as shortsighted as the PR person in the late 1940s who ignored TV," declared Dick Martin, AT&T vice president for corporate advertising. "It's not only a terrific channel for telling a story, it can have a terrific impact on business. All you have to do is read the clippings to see what it did to Intel."

In early 1995, word of a flaw in the new Pentium processor chip produced an avalanche of disparaging comments throughout the Internet. The Intel Corporation, producer of the chip, at first kept quiet about the problem—a no-no in crisis communication tenets. By the time the company issued an Internet-wide message addressing computer users' concerns, considerable damage had been done to the company's image.

Partly to help companies fend off such situations, eWorks!, an electronics media adviser and producer, launched eWatch, which

# The International Scene
# GLOBAL PUBLIC RELATIONS

The international mergers and joint ventures that characterized much of American business during the 1980s and 1990s led to a corresponding increase in public relations activity abroad. With their clients opening plants and sales offices overseas and trading on stock exchanges in London, Tokyo, New York, and other centers, public relations firms have increasingly been called on to handle product publicity and government and employee relations work. Satellite, fiber optic, and computer networks, as well as facsimile machines and electronic mail, have enabled corporations and public relations firms to feed information simultaneously around the globe. As a result, all but the smallest firms have taken steps to serve their clients' international needs.

Much attention has been focused on opportunities and problems associated with the opening of the European Common Market. Public relations activity, however, also has increased substantially in other parts of the world, especially in Asia, and the giant public relations firms have adopted at least four strategies for expansion: (1) open their own offices and staff them with local people (Burson-Marsteller); (2) acquire local agencies but leave them untouched (Shandwick); (3) take equity positions (buy into) firms in other countries (MSL Worldwide); and (4) join an international network of independent firms (Padilla Speer Beardsley, Inc.).

According to *O'Dwyer's Directory of Public Relations Firms*, net fees of the top 10-ranked firms totaled $974.1 million in 1994. In order of income, the top ten were: Burson-Marsteller, Shandwick, Hill and Knowlton, Communications International Group (formerly Omnicom), Edelman Public Relations Worldwide, Fleishman-Hillard, Ketchum Public Relations, Ogilvy Adams & Rinehart, Robinson Lake/Sawyer Miller/Bozell, and The Rowland Company.

All these firms except Shandwick, Edelman, and Fleishman-Hillard are subsidiaries of large advertising agencies.

"Everyone realizes now that they have to be part of an international structure, because the big agencies are getting bigger and the small ones are disappearing," Edward M. Stanton, chief executive of MSL Worldwide, told the New York *Times.*

American managers of U.S. corporations provide the continuing, overall strategy, but—because every country's customs and values are different, and substantial variations often exist even within companies—its application must be carried out primarily by public relations employees and outside consultants native to each country. New technologies, however, are increasingly providing improved supervision. For example, the General Electric Company created an international telecommunications network that permits employees to communicate worldwide, using voice, video, and computer data, by simply dialing seven digits on a telephone. *Teleconferencing* has become an important marketing tool.

Companies everywhere are confronted with essentially the same public relations problems as those in the United States, in-

## GLOBAL PUBLIC RELATIONS
### Continued

cluding relationships with local and national governments, consumer groups, the financial community, and employees. For transnational firms these problems often are aggravated by, among other things, the differences in language, longer chains of command, evident and subtle differences in customs, and the varying levels of media and public relations development.

A number of American public relations firms help foreign industries attain their sales and investment goals in this country. These firms seek to (1) hold off protectionist moves threatening a company's operations, (2) defeat legislation affecting the sale of a client's products, (3) support the expansion of the client's markets, and (4) keep the foreign company informed about important developments that may affect its interests in this country.

U.S. counseling firms also are retained by foreign governments, at large fees. Among other things, they seek to (1) advance their client's political objectives, (2) advise regarding probable reactions to projected actions, (3) advance commercial interests such as tourism, (4) help the client communicate in English, and (5) modify laws and regulations inhibiting the country's activities in the United States. For example, Hill and Knowlton has represented Indonesia and Morocco; Burson-Marsteller, Argentina, Costa Rica, Hungary, and the former Soviet Union (the latter mainly in trade fairs); and Ruder Finn, El Salvador, Israel, and Japan.

Hundreds of not-for-profit groups depend on international support for their undertakings. Vigorous public relations programs are maintained by such organizations as the International Red Cross, World Council of Churches, International Council of B'nai B'rith, and the International Chamber of Commerce, along with numerous foundations, educational enterprises, labor unions, and government-support agencies.

Public relations associations have been organized in about 50 countries. In Great Britain, more than 2500 practitioners belong to the British Institute of Public Relations. Because the German language has no close equivalent, practitioners in Germany have formed an association known as the Deutsche Public Relations Gesellschaft. In Japan, where more than 1000 consultants practice, the Public Relations Society of Japan has been formed. Regional associations include the European Center of Public Relations, the Pan Pacific Public Relations Federation, and the Inter-American Federation of Public Relations.

tracks comments made about a company on thousands of electronic forums and discussion groups. The program is sold by PR Newswire, a leading distributor of corporate, association, and government news releases.

Scores of other interactive services have been established to aid public relations efforts. An example is Alumnet Services, which provides contact between colleges and universities and their alumni. Included are password-protected areas, which allow subscribers to pledge or make cash gifts; live chat opportunities; and links to hundreds of schools' home pages on the World Wide Web.

## Points to Remember

1. What roles does public relations play in our society?
2. What are the principal steps in the evolution of public relations?
3. Contemporary public relations, when practiced at the optimal level, involves four general responsibilities. What are they?
4. What relationship does public relations have with the mass media?
5. How do the activities of generalists and specialists in public relations differ?
6. List four areas of not-for-profit public relations.
7. What is meant by professionalism in public relations? How may it be achieved?
8. Why has much public relations activity become global in nature?
9. What are some of the ways in which the practice of public relations is affected by the Internet?

## Media Questions to Think About

1. Draw a wheel, and on each spoke identify one of the publics to which a particular business or institution is related, such as the faculty and students of a university. Now draw a wheel that shows the publics involved in YOUR life.
2. In a newspaper, see how many stories and photos you can find based on what historian Daniel Boorstin called "pseudo-events," activities that would not have taken place except for the purpose of being reported. In your opinion, how valuable are these stories and photos in building and maintaining good will for a business or institution?

# ISSUE FIVE

# Legal Environment

## Are the Media Restricted by Too Many Laws?

As has been emphasized in this book, the First Amendment to the U.S. Constitution protects basic rights of American citizens. Interpretations of that amendment, however, have produced a wide variety of laws that affect the media's rights to print, to criticize, and to report, with the Supreme Court the final arbiter.

While reading the discussion that follows, try to decide which restrictions strengthen the public's right to know and which seem unduly to hinder the media in fulfilling that obligation. For example, how would you answer the following questions?

1. Of the eight types of law that affect the media, which is the most powerful? Why?

2. Why is *Near* v. *Minnesota* considered a landmark Supreme Court decision?

3. How has the Supreme Court's *Hazelwood* decision affected the student press?

4. What are the media's principal defenses against libel lawsuits?

5. What are some of the consequences of the *New York Times* v. *Sullivan* decision?

6. Has the Freedom of Information Act worked to the satisfaction of the media and government? If not, why not?

7. To what does "government in the sunshine" refer?

8. Why must journalists disclose their sources of information in a criminal investigation? What protection may they be given?

9. What is the right of privacy?

10. What are the pro and con arguments regarding the Fairness Doctrine?

11. What legal issues involve the Internet?

## Laws Restricting the Media

Eight types of law affect the media in their relationships with society. Taken together, these laws create a significant barrier against unrestricted operation of the media and are an ever-present factor influencing the decisions media people make. They are, in summary form:

1. *Common law*—written and reinforced by court decisions through the centuries;
2. *Constitutional law*—both federal and state, including the crucial First Amendment to the United States Constitution;
3. *Statutory law*—that passed by legislative bodies;
4. *Criminal law*—which concerns the press largely in the areas of treason, criminal libel, and fraudulent advertising;
5. *Civil law*—dealing with such matters as libel, invasion of privacy, and unfair competition;
6. *Equity*—seeking relief from the courts, such as the government's suit in the Pentagon Papers case;
7. *Administrative law*—as enacted by such agencies as the Federal Communications Commission and the Federal Trade Commission;
8. *Moral law*—which has no distinct position in our modern legal system, but which imposes a greater restriction on the press than any purely legal restraint. Conversely, it functions as a tremendous force that can overturn legal restraints and bring greater freedom for the press. Moral law is discussed in Issue 2.

### The First Amendment Battlefront

Freedom to print without prior restraint has been a basic tenet of Anglo-American civilization since 1694. It was written into the First Amendment to the U.S. Constitution as a part of the Bill of Rights. The high watermark for this concept was reached in 1931 when the Supreme Court, by invalidating a state law, applied the press guarantees of the First Amendment to the states in the case of *Near* v. *Minnesota* (see Chapter 3). But as supportive of the freedom to print as that decision was, it did not establish an absolute prohibition of prior restraint. In giving his five-to-four majority decision, Chief Justice Charles Evans Hughes quoted from Blackstone on prior restraint and postpublication punishment:

> The liberty of the press is indeed essential to the nature of a free state; but this consists in laying no *previous* restraints upon publications, and not in freedom from censure for criminal matter when published. Every freeman has an undoubted right to lay what sentiments he pleases before the public; to forbid this is to destroy the freedom of the press; but if he publishes what is improper, mischievous, or illegal, he must take the consequences of his own temerity.

Hughes continued with a dictum, or observation, that weakened the case for absolute protection against prior restraint:

> The objection has also been made that the principle as to immunity from previous restraint is stated too broadly, if every such restraint is deemed to be prohibited. That is undoubtedly true; the protection even as to previous restraint is not absolutely unlimited. But the limitation has been recognized only in exceptional cases.

The chief justice defined some such cases: military secrets, overthrow of the government, and obscenity. But he excluded publication of censure of public officers and charges of official misconduct.

It was under this latter exclusion that the Supreme Court ruled six to three in favor of the New York *Times* in the Pentagon Papers case in 1971. (See Issue 4.)

In 1995, *Business Week* killed an investigative story an hour before the presses were ready to roll. A federal judge in Cincinnati had barred the magazine from printing information he said was under seal in a Procter & Gamble lawsuit against Bankers Trust New York Corp. *Business Week* anticipated that an appeals court would overturn the order on constitutional grounds.

## The *Hazelwood* Decision

In 1988, the Supreme Court ruled in *Hazelwood School District* v. *Kuhlmeier* that school administrations could censor some student "speech that is inconsistent with [the school's] basic educational mission." The controversial decision followed almost four years of dispute over administrative censorship of two pages of the Hazelwood East (Missouri) High School *Spectrum*.

Reaction to the *Hazelwood* decision was mixed. Many commercial newspapers supported the action editorially on the grounds that the school district constituted the "publisher," which could act to avoid possible libel and invasion of privacy suits and to maintain school order. Many other newspapers and media groups attacked the decision as repugnant to First Amendment guarantees and restricting the opportunities of student journalists to explore in their media social and political issues such as drug and alcohol abuse, AIDS, teen sex, and teen pregnancy.

Mark Goodman, executive director of the Student Press Law Center, reported that, according to telephone calls to the center, direct censorship of student stories, editorials, and cartoons was taking place throughout the country. Many principals, however, were adamantly opposed to any form of censorship, Goodman reported, and they joined students, teachers, and other citizens in appeals to school boards to enact clear-cut policies to protect student expression. California, Massachusetts, Iowa, Colorado, Kansas, and Arkansas were the first states to enact statutory or constitutional legislation providing such protection.

Pulitzer Prize winners George Rodrigue and Craig Flournoy of the Dallas *Morning News* show boxes containing one-third of the government documents they obtained under the FOI Act. Their stories revealed a pattern of racial discrimination and segregation in public housing in the United States. (Reprinted by permission from *Presstime,* the journal of the Newspaper Association of America)

BUILD THE NEWS UPON THE ROCK OF TRUTH AND RIGHTEOUSNESS CONDUCT IT ALWAYS UPON THE LINES OF FAIRNESS AND INTEGRITY ACKNOWLEDGE THE RIGHT OF THE PEOPLE TO GET FROM THE NEWSPAPER BOTH SIDES OF EVERY IMPORTANT QUESTION

The Journalism Education Association provides information about student press rights and related First Amendment issues through its World Wide Web home page: http://www.spub.ksu.edu/jea/.

## "Hate Speech" and the First Amendment

Declaring that the First Amendment prohibits the government from "silencing speech on the basis of its content," a five-member majority of the Supreme Court ruled in 1992 that legislatures may not single out racial, religious, or sexual insults as "hate speech" or "bias crimes."

Although divided in approach, the other four justices agreed with the Court in declaring unconstitutional a St. Paul, Minnesota, ordinance making it a crime to engage in speech or behavior likely to arouse "anger or alarm" on the basis of "race, color, creed, religion, or gender." In *R.A.V.* v. *St. Paul*, the four found only that the ordinance was "over-broad," posing too great a risk that it might deter speech or expression that deserved constitutional protection.

Observers said the decision likely invalidated many of the speech codes adopted at public universities; under such codes, students face punishment for insults or harassment on the basis of race, religion, or sex. Private universities are not affected because their behavior in this regard is not constrained by the Constitution.

## Libel and Slander

In their day-by-day work, editors and broadcasters probably worry more about libeling or slandering individuals in print or on the air than about any other form of law restricting the media. Laws designed to protect persons from unfair and damaging attacks create well-defined limits as to what may be broadcast or printed without risking legal action and possibly heavy financial losses.

*Defamation* is communication that exposes people to hatred, ridicule, or contempt; lowers them in the esteem of their fellows; causes them to be shunned; or injures them in their business or calling. Its categories are *libel*, mainly printed or written material; and *slander*, mainly spoken words. Because a person may be injured as greatly in a radio or television broadcast as in a printed publication, the courts have come to treat broadcast defamation as libel.

**Libel**
Mainly printed or written defamatory material

**Slander**
Mainly spoken defamatory words

Some defamation is considered privileged, such as statements made on the official record during court trials and public meetings of government bodies. For example, council member Jones may call council member Smith "a liar and a thief" during an official session, and the allegation may be safely broadcast or published because it is privileged by law. However, if Jones should make such a statement about Smith in the corridor after the meeting adjourns, the newspaper or broadcast station that reports it would risk a libel or slander suit from Smith unless it could prove that the charge was true.

The principal defenses against libel actions involving the press are provable truth, the privilege of reporting fairly and truly an official proceeding, the right of fair comment, consent, and the U.S. Supreme Court ruling in *New York Times* v. *Sullivan* that state libel laws must yield to the First Amendment freedom of the press guarantees.

Historically, the libel and slander laws have protected individuals or small groups of easily identified persons, but not large, amorphous groups. There is pressure now to enlarge protection to cover broader groups, such as ethnic minorities, but the difficulty in writing such laws has discouraged their adoption.

### Criticism of Public Figures

**The Sullivan Ruling.** A landmark case in broadening the media's right to comment was the Supreme Court ruling in *New York Times* v. *Sullivan* in

1964. Professor Don R. Pember, a media law researcher, has called it "one of the most important First Amendment cases ever decided." Civil libel law until that time had been governed by the doctrine of strict liability, which made it likely a plaintiff would win a lawsuit if he or she could prove identification in a published story and that the words were defamatory. Now the Supreme Court said for the first time that a plaintiff who is a public official must also show the defendant had been at fault when the defamatory material was published—that the defendant had known the material was false or had shown reckless disregard for its truth or falsity. Justice William Brennan used the phrase "actual malice" to describe the concept, which became known as the "*Times* rule."

In 1960, the *Times* had published an advertisement assailing police actions in Montgomery, Alabama, against followers of the Rev. Martin Luther King, Jr. Sullivan, a police commissioner, sued for libel and was awarded $500,000 in damages in a state court. Reversing the judgment, the Supreme Court held that errors contained in the advertisement were not malicious and that the First Amendment protects "uninhibited robust and wide-open" debate of public issues without any test of truth. Henceforth, public officials who sought to win a libel suit based on defamatory allegations about their conduct of public office would have to prove actual malice. *Sullivan* had "buried the common law crime of seditious libel."

## The Public Law of Libel

Legal scholars called the theory developed in the *Sullivan* case the "public law of libel." In this and related rulings, the Court broadened the interpretation of "public official" to include relatively minor public employees. It then included "public figures" such as former officeholders and prominent personalities. Finally it extended the "actual malice" requirement to include even private individuals who had been projected into the public interest area.

But in the 30 years since the *Sullivan* ruling was handed down, the Court frequently has altered its definitions of issues involved in libel cases, and sometimes has changed course perceptibly in its support of theories. The theory of the use of summary judgments to clear media defendants in cases where actual malice had not been proved became widespread.

**What Is a Public Figure?**   This question occupied the attention of the Supreme Court and First Amendment scholars for decades in the wake of the *Sullivan* decision. In 1967, the Court extended its theory to cover "public figures" as well as "public officials." In *AP* v. *Walker*, it reversed a $500,000 judgment that General Edwin A. Walker had been awarded against the Associated Press, ruling that Walker, a right-wing spokesperson, was a public figure subject to criticism. But it upheld a $460,000 award to another public figure, University of Georgia football coach

**Public figure**
Person defined by Supreme Court decisions whose ability to recover damages for defamatory falsehood is limited because of such status

Wallace Butts, for a story in the *Saturday Evening Post* charging Butts had thrown games. The Court said the *Post* had lost its "actual malice" protection by being highly reckless in not adhering to professional standards of investigation and reporting.

In 1971, the Supreme Court extended its "actual malice" requirement from public officials and public persons to include even private individuals who found themselves involved in a situation of public interest. The case, *Rosenbloom* v. *Metromedia*, involved a broadcaster's references to a book dealer's "obscene" literature.

### Limited Public Figures.

But beginning in 1974 the Court began to restrict its position, stating in several decisions a theory of "limited public figures" that developed two categories of those persons. In the key case of *Gertz* v. *Welch* in 1974, the Court held in a five-to-four decision that a "private person," regardless of involvement in a public event, might recover such actual damages as could be proved for injury or harm resulting from publication of a defamatory falsehood, without proof of actual malice by the libeler, but with proof of negligence as determined by a state standard.

The Supreme Court further modified its position on public figures in 1976 and 1979. Pember cites three basic points defining the phrase "limited public figures" that he found emerging from the three decisions: (1) Limited public figures normally must voluntarily step into the public spotlight, (2) a limited public figure is someone who plays a role in the resolution of an important or social issue, and (3) there must have been some attempt by the plaintiff to influence public opinion in the resolution of these issues.

In *Firestone* v. *Time Inc.*, the Supreme Court ruled in 1976 that the wife of Russell Firestone III, scion of a prominent industrial family, was not a "public figure," even though she was a well-known citizen of Palm Beach, Florida, society and held press conferences during her celebrated divorce trial. She was awarded $100,000 in a libel suit against *Time* magazine for incorrectly reporting that her husband had been granted a divorce from her on grounds of extreme cruelty and adultery.

The decision unnerved news media executives and lawyers, occurring as it did during a period when more than 500 libel suits were being filed each year and juries seemed willing to compensate plaintiffs for their injuries with large settlements. With expenses ranging up to $100,000 or more per case, even when won, fears mounted that the threat of such high costs would make the news media more timid in their pursuit of news. Mrs. Firestone, however, in 1978 dropped the case rather than pursued a second trial, ordered by the Supreme Court to determine *Time*'s degree of negligence (in order for her to collect the $100,000).

Things were made even more difficult for media libel lawyers when Chief Justice Warren Burger commented in his decision of 1979, in the case of *Hutchinson* v. *Proxmire:* "We are constrained to express some doubt about the so-called 'rule' [of summary judgment on First Amendment grounds in libel cases]. The proof of 'actual malice' calls a defendant's state of mind into question . . . and does not readily lend itself to summary judgment."

Another new rule for libel cases emerged from the decision in *Herbert* v. *Lando,* in 1979. This permits pretrial inquiry into the journalist's state of mind as a means of establishing the presence of actual malice in a libel action. Colonel Anthony Herbert, a Vietnam War veteran, sued CBS and producer Barry Lando of the "60 Minutes" program for falsely and maliciously depicting him as a liar (Herbert had agreed that he was a public figure). His attorneys asked for the right to explore the states of mind of CBS newspeople at the time they were making editorial decisions. A U.S. Court of Appeals held that requiring reporters to divulge their thoughts and to reveal the content of their discussions with colleagues would "strike to the heart of the vital human component of the editorial process." The Supreme Court, in a six-to-three decision, reversed the appeals court decision, saying such inquiries were valid and necessary if the plaintiff were to be able to prove actual malice.

Later, the Supreme Court bulwarked the "actual malice" standard when the Court let stand a U.S. Court of Appeals ruling affirming a summary judgment for CBS dismissing a libel claim by Colonel Herbert.

**Granting of Summary Judgments.**   In 1986, the Court gave further support to the *Sullivan* doctrine by ruling that a public-figure libel plaintiff must demonstrate "actual malice" by "clear and convincing evidence" to overcome a defendant's motion that a summary judgment dismissing the suit be granted by a trial judge.

### Multimillion Dollar Suits

The wave of libel suits against newspapers, broadcast networks and stations, and magazines, previously mentioned, swept through the courts beginning in the late 1970s. The Legal Defense Resource Center reported that juries awarded more than $1 million each to plaintiffs in 26 libel suits between 1976 and 1985. Seventy percent of the verdicts were reversed by appeals courts, however, on grounds the *Sullivan* standards had not been observed.

Among the largest cases were these:

- General William Westmoreland sought $120 million in damages from CBS for statements made in a Mike Wallace documentary, "The Uncounted Enemy: A Vietnam Deception." After 18 weeks of trial, Westmoreland withdrew his suit. CBS spent more than $4 million on its defense.

- *Time* magazine defeated a $50 million libel suit by former Defense Minister Ariel Sharon of Israel for statements linking

## FALWELL'S "EMOTIONAL DISTRESS" REJECTED

The biggest victory for the media in cases involving libel came in a 1988 Supreme Court decision. The Court, in an eight-to-zero vote, broadly affirmed and extended its rules protecting criticism of public figures as free speech, even if the criticism is "outrageous" and offensive.

The Court overturned a jury's $200,000 award to the Rev. Jerry Falwell for "emotional distress" over a *Hustler* magazine parody that portrayed Falwell as an incestuous drunk. The case was important because it could have opened the floodgates to suits by people claiming emo-tional distress in order to avoid the legal burden of proving libel.

Legal scholars viewed the decision as an unqualified endorsement of the prece-dent-setting "actual malice" standard of the *Sullivan* case—that public figures must prove the media knowingly published false or dubious information as fact. Chief Justice William Rehnquist's opinion said the Court had little choice because, if it ruled for Falwell, "there can be little doubt that political cartoonists and satirists would be subjected to damages without any showing that their work falsely defamed its subject."

him to a massacre of 700 Arabs. The jury, however, issued a statement that the magazine "acted negligently and carelessly in reporting and verifying" its information.

- The Alton, Illinois, *Telegraph*, caught in an editing error, was assessed $9.2 million in penalties, including $3.5 million in punitive damages. The owners settled out of court for $1 million to save the paper.

- The *National Enquirer* paid Carol Burnett $200,000 in settlement of a $1.6 million verdict for reporting her drunk in a restaurant.

In *Masson* v. *New Yorker*, the Supreme Court ruled in 1991 that fabricated quotations attributed to a public figure may be libelous if the alterations materially change the meaning of what the person actually said. The decision reinstated a celebrated libel suit by a psychoanalyst, Jeffrey M. Masson, who accused Janet Malcolm, a writer, of deliberately misquoting him in an unflattering profile in the *New Yorker* magazine—a profile that later appeared as a book. In 1993, a federal jury in San Francisco found that the writer had misquoted and libeled Masson, but the trial ended inconclusively when the jury deadlocked on damages. In 1994, a second jury found that Malcolm did not libel Masson.

In an extraordinary action in 1994, the U.S. Court of Appeals in Washington, D.C., retracted a controversial ruling that would have made it easier to file libel suits against publishers of negative book reviews and other critical works. Author Dan Moldea had sued the New

York *Times*, claiming that a harsh review of his 1989 book, *Interference: How Organized Crime Influences Professional Football*, ruined his reputation and harmed his ability to make a living. The court's reversal followed emotional attacks by reviewers, publishers, and media companies, who accused the three-judge panel of endangering constitutionally protected free speech.

Libel awards against the media reached an all-time high in the first two years of the 1990s, with six judgments each surpassing $10 million, according to the Legal Defense Resource Center. There were no libel awards in excess of $10 million during the next two years, however, and the 12 libel trials and 5.5 media losses each year were far fewer than the 25 trials and more than 15 losses per year during the 1980s. Even so, libel awards during that period still averaged more than $1 million, a "chilling phenomenon," according to the center's general counsel, Henry Kaufman.

## Legal Issues and the Internet

Can existing laws solve problems on the Internet that involve libel, privacy, censorship, and copyright? Is it possible, or desirable, to regulate the content of millions of communication acts that take place daily on this international highway? If so, to whom should the laws primarily apply—to the operators of the online services or to their users? And how can the rights of the creators of those materials be protected?

These are some of the questions still largely unanswered in the complex, almost anarchic, cyberspace world of the 1990s.

**Libel.**  In 1995, the New York Supreme Court ruled that a suit for libel by the Stratton Oakmont investment firm of Long Island, New York, against the Prodigy information service should proceed. A codefendant, Prodigy subscriber David Lusby of Key West, Florida, was accused of posting comments on the service stating that the firm had committed fraud and other criminal activities. Lusby asserted that his Prodigy account was inactive and that someone else must have used it without authorization.

In his decision, Justice Stuart L. Ain drew a distinction between Prodigy, which uses human monitors and automatic systems to remove objectionable material posted to its network, and other information services that merely act as conduits for unfiltered information. In 1991, a federal judge had ruled that the CompuServe information service could not be held accountable for messages posted on its system any more than a bookstore owner could be held liable for the contents of a book it sells.

The investment firm later agreed to drop its libel suit in return for an apology from Prodigy. Citing the "best interests of the parties as well as the online and interactive services industries," the firm also asked Justice Ain to set aside, or overturn, his earlier decision holding Prodigy liable for comments made by its users.

**Copyright.** The widespread copying of text, sound, and pictures on the Internet has fueled a debate on how, or whether, the nation's laws should be modified to protect the copyrights of the owners of those materials. A U.S. Patent Office task force has recommended to Congress changes in the Copyright Act to deal with this and other problems.

Among items most likely to be used without permission are the news service reports provided to publications and broadcast stations, musical content, and original materials such as electronic books and magazine articles.

The Frank Music Corporation has accused CompuServe in a U.S. district court in New York of enabling the downloading and uploading of unauthorized recordings of the copyrighted song, "Unchained Melody." The action was taken on behalf of 140 music publishers. The Internet Underground Music Archive has negotiated with various record companies to make music available over the Internet.

The fair use provision of the Copyright Law permits the unauthorized use of limited amounts of copyrighted material for comment and criticism, news reporting, and classroom teaching. Educating the public about copyright applications is a major task yet to be accomplished.

## The Right to Report

While the narrowing of constitutional defenses in libel suits, particularly in reporting those involving public figures, became a problem for the media of the 1980s and 1990s, erosion of the right to report was even more extensive.

Supreme Court decisions of the 1970s adversely affected the media in four areas: (1) requiring reporters to reveal their sources in certain situations or face fines and imprisonment, (2) allowing police raids of newsrooms, (3) allowing law-enforcement agencies access to telephone records of news organizations, and (4) closing pretrial hearings and in some cases courtroom trials. These decisions, along with the erosion of the Freedom of Information Act that was gaining strength, affected not only the rights of newspeople but also the public's right to know.

### The Freedom of Information Crusade

Throughout American history conflict has existed among the three branches of government—legislative, executive, and judicial. The acceptance of the principle of judicial review, making the Supreme Court the final authority on the constitutionality of legislative and executive actions, gave that branch relative freedom from conflict and attack. In the Watergate struggle, for example, President Nixon bowed to an eight-to-zero decision by the Court, which overruled his assertion of executive authority to suppress the Watergate tapes, and he submitted the tapes for review. But the dueling between Congress and the White House over the principle of "executive privilege" continues unabated. The privilege

of reporters to use public records and documents is involved in this in-fighting. (See Issue 4.)

**The FOI Act.**   After 11 years of wrestling with the problem of the people's right to know the facts of government, Congress passed the Freedom of Information (FOI) Act in 1966. The law states basically that any person may go to court to gain access to public records, and the burden of proof that secrecy is necessary is on the government.

Congress moved to strengthen the Freedom of Information Act in 1974, by enacting amendments into law over President Gerald Ford's veto. The amendments narrowed the scope of exemption that protected certain categories of government files from public disclosure.

After passage of the law, agencies such as the FBI and CIA provided copies of thousands of documents about individuals, companies, and events. Private citizens were able to obtain copies of FBI files about themselves.

Despite these advances, the huge volume of secrets protected by the government continued to mount. In 1994, the Information Security Oversight Office issued the following report:

- There are 5,798 people in the federal government authorized to wield the secrecy stamp. They wield it 17,000 times a day while classifying information.
- This totaled 6,349,532 classifications in fiscal year 1992.
- Each of these actions is duplicated and entered into computers to be replicated 300 to 400 times.
- The National Archives has 325 million pages of classified documents, and it is only one of 80,000 government repositories for classified material.
- The archives right now is awash in classified documents dumped there for declassification; it will take 19 years to clean up the mess.

That's the "dirty little secret of our open society," according to Paul McMasters, executive director of the Freedom Forum First Amendment Center in Nashville, Tennessee.

In 1995, President Bill Clinton issued an executive order declassifying hundreds of thousands of satellite images taken between 1960 and 1972. The public may view the images at the National Archives facility in College Park, Maryland, or via Internet.

**Computerized Public Records.**   Reporters encountered varying degrees of difficulty in gaining access to computerized government records during the 1990s. "The federal government is plunging pell-mell toward a paperless government by the year 2000, and it is in electronic chaos," charged McMasters.

**FOI**
Freedom of information; specifically, the FOI Act of 1966, which gave media and citizens access to many federal government agency files

Among other problems, McMasters said, "there is no overall policy . . . no index of databases . . . no uniformity in formats and software . . . no guarantee of access to even the most routine information . . . an obsession with privacy that goes beyond the legitimate concerns for individuals and confidential information."

The courts have uniformly ruled that electronically stored information is subject to public records laws, such as the FOI Act. Nevertheless, many government agencies resist releasing such information, said Dan Paul, a Miami attorney specializing in First Amendment law. "There's a real fear that technology could eviscerate the access right," he told a gathering of media lawyers. "It's a lot easier to hide those records. . . ."

**Privatization of Public Records.**   In addition, the accelerating trend for local, state, and federal governments to contract out their responsibilities to private business firms, in the name of cost-cutting and efficiency, led to increasing secrecy, FOI activists reported. Journalists in particular complained that privatization had become a convenient way for government to reduce the flow of information.

**Government in the Sunshine.**   An encouraging sign in the battle for the right to know, however, was the enactment by Congress of a Government in the Sunshine Law that took effect in 1977. This law requires more than 50 federal boards and agencies with two or more members to conduct most meetings in the open. The law allows closed meetings for certain specified reasons but requires that the reasons for any closed meetings be certified by the chief legal officer of the agency. In 1978, the House decided to open its debates to daily live broadcast coverage, and the Senate later took similar action. All states now have some form of open-meetings law as well as laws guaranteeing the opening of public records to reporters needing access to them.

### Reporters' Confidentiality

In 1972, the Supreme Court, by a five-to-four vote, decided that news reporters have no special immunity under the First Amendment not to respond to grand jury subpoenas and provide information in criminal investigations, even at the risk of "drying up" their sources.

One broadcast and two newspaper reporters, in separate appeals, urged the Court to make it clear that the First Amendment guarantee of a free flow of information gives reporters at least some degree of immunity to government subpoena powers. Justice Byron R. White, however, writing the decision with the support of four Nixon administration appointees to the Court, stated: "The Constitution does not, as it never has, exempt the newsman from performing the citizen's normal duty of appearing and furnishing information relevant to the grand jury's task."

Justice Potter Stewart, in an opinion in which he was joined by Justices William J. Brennan and Thurgood Marshall, said that the decision "invites state and federal authorities to undermine the historic independence of the press by attempting to annex the journalistic profession as an investigative arm of government."

In his dissent, Justice William O. Douglas wrote: "If [a reporter] can be summoned to testify in secret before a grand jury, his source will dry up and the attempted exposure, the effort to enlighten the public, will be ended. If what the Court sanctions today becomes settled law, then the reporter's main function in American society will be to pass on to the public the press releases which the various departments of government issue."

The justices, however, did leave open some avenues for relief to the media. They declared that state legislatures could enact "shield" laws preventing reporters from being forced to reveal sources of information to *state* courts and grand juries.

Shield laws were subsequently enacted in 26 states. Many journalists, however, declined to support campaigns to persuade Congress and the states to pass protective legislation, on grounds that the First Amendment guarantee of press freedom would be endangered by such action.

In 1980, the voters of California approved, by a 73 percent majority, a state constitutional amendment that included the exact language of that state's reporter shield law. Thus a statutory protection became a constitutional one in California.

The Senate asked Peter Fleming, Jr., a special independent counsel, to discover who leaked confidential documents relating to the charges of sexual harassment by Anita Hill, a University of Oklahoma law professor, against Supreme Court Justice Clarence Thomas during the justice's confirmation hearings in 1991. Subpoenaed were Timothy M. Phelps, a reporter, and Anthony Marro, editor and senior vice-president, both of *Newsday*, and Nina Totenberg, a reporter for National Public Radio. All refused to divulge additional information. The Senate Rules and Administration Committee rejected Fleming's request to compel the testimony of the journalists or the release of their records. "To do otherwise," said Chairman Wendell H. Ford, "could have a chilling effect on the media. . . ."

Attempts by tobacco companies to force the news media to reveal confidential sources and information are symptomatic of "a national subpoena epidemic," according to a 1995 report by the Reporters Committee for Freedom of the Press.

More than half of 900 news organizations surveyed reported that in 1993 they received 3,519 subpoenas from government agencies, lawyers, and private litigants demanding notes, outtakes, or other information, the report stated.

Broadcasters were especially hard-hit. News organizations complied with more than half of the subpoenas. But when the media fought back, they were likely to prevail: judges quashed 81.2 percent of the challenged subpoenas.

**Shield law**
State legislation preventing reporters from being forced to reveal sources of information to state courts and grand juries

Anita Hill accuses Clarence Thomas, nominee for a U.S. Supreme Court seat, of sexual harassment in a televised hearing before a Senate committee. Their conflicting statements created an emotional national debate. Despite her testimony, Thomas was confirmed. (Markel, Gamma Liaison)

## Searches and Seizures

When police raided the offices of the student-run *Stanford Daily* in 1971 seeking photographs of a campus sit-in, the incident set off a series of events culminating in the signing of legislation by President Jimmy Carter in 1980 that banned similar police raids on newsrooms. The legislative action was necessary because the Supreme Court's decision of 1978 in *Zurcher* v. *Stanford Daily* had declared that the First Amendment provides the press no special protection from police searches.

**Privacy Protection Act.** There had been two reactions to this Court decision. Police in various parts of the country carried out at least 27 similar raids in two years, armed only with search warrants, instead of subpoenas that required advance warning of their action. But the other reaction was a welcome rebellion in Congress against increasingly conservative decisions by the Supreme Court that negated basic individual rights as well as First Amendment rights. The result was the passage, virtually without opposition, of the Privacy Protection Act of 1980.

The bill requires federal, state, and local authorities either to request voluntary compliance or to use subpoenas—with advance notice and the opportunity for a court hearing—instead of search warrants when they seek reporters' notes, films, or tapes as evidence. It also covers authors, scholars, and others engaged in First Amendment activities. Searches are allowed only in very limited situations. The bill also calls for the attorney general's guidelines to limit the use of search warrants against nonsuspect third parties who are not covered by the First Amendment.

**Secret Seizure of Telephone Records.**   But in the case of *Reporters Committee for Freedom of the Press* v. *AT&T*, the Justice Department sided against the media in their effort to prohibit secret seizure of their telephone call records by law enforcement agencies. The case began with the disclosure in 1973 that various Nixon administration agencies had secretly subpoenaed both office and home telephone call records of columnist Jack Anderson and the bureau chiefs of the New York *Times*, St. Louis *Post-Dispatch*, and Knight-Ridder. The Reporters Committee for Freedom of the Press asked AT&T to agree not to permit such seizures without advance warning to the newspersons involved so that they could seek relief within the courts. AT&T refused. The Reporters Committee went to court, seeking First Amendment rights. But it lost in the U.S. district court and court of appeals trials, at which the Justice Department argued that, "the First Amendment does not permit reporters to withhold information about their news sources . . . in the course of a legitimate criminal investigation." In 1979 the Supreme Court refused to hear the case, leaving unanswered the question of how reporters could protect themselves against highly dubious seizures and searches such as those made by the Nixon administration merely to find out who was leaking news—a noncriminal offense.

In 1991, Procter & Gamble attempted to invoke an Ohio "trade secrets" statute to learn which of its employees had leaked company information to Alecia Swasy, a *Wall Street Journal* reporter. At the firm's request, county prosecutors subpoenaed records for 803,000 business and home telephones. The incident enraged journalists and citizens worried about invasion of privacy. Subsequently, the investigation was dropped.

## Reporters in the Courtroom

A Nebraska murder trial in 1976 brought about a press-bar confrontation when the trial judge entered an order restraining the news media from reporting the existence of any confession or admission made by the defendant until the trial jury had been impaneled. The order followed the guidelines developed after the Supreme Court had overturned the murder conviction in 1966 of Dr. Sam Sheppard in Ohio because he had been subjected to massive pretrial publicity. In the Supreme Court decision in *Nebraska Press Association* v. *Stuart*, Chief Justice Burger held that the press was entitled to report all evidence presented in an *open* preliminary hearing, including confessions and admissions. By that time the Nebraska trial had ended. It was noted that Burger's decision made it plain that the ruling did not prevent future "gag" orders, and that it did not cover the issue of First Amendment rights when pretrial hearings were closed.

After a period of confusion, the situation was clarified in 1980, to the satisfaction of First Amendment advocates, when Chief Justice Burger read a seven-to-one decision in *Richmond Newspapers* v. *Commonwealth of Virginia* declaring that the public has a constitutional right to attend criminal trials even when defendants want to exclude them. The decision overturned a Virginia judge's closing of a murder trial in 1978. Burger cited First Amendment rights in his decision, but, as usual, warned that "the constitutional right to attend criminal trials is not absolute." The decision left pretrial hearings still subject to closing.

The gap in the Supreme Court decisions about public attendance at criminal trials was closed in *Press Enterprise Company* v. *Superior Court of California* in 1986. The Court held seven to two in an opinion written by Justice Burger that the public has a First Amendment right to attend pretrial hearings in criminal cases over the objections of defendants.

## Cameras in the Courtroom

**State Courts.** The U.S. Supreme Court ruled unanimously in 1981 in *Chandler* v. *Florida* that states have the right to allow television, radio, and photographic coverage of criminal trials, even if the defendant objects. Although the decision did not guarantee news media a right to insist on such coverage, it clarified the fact that any state was now free to allow cameras and microphones into courtrooms as long as the defendant's right to a fair trial is protected.

By 1995, all but three states permitted cameras in their courtrooms. A four-year experiment in New York was renewed that year with greater restrictions designed to protect the privacy of witnesses.

Camera coverage of the O.J. Simpson trial in Los Angeles drew huge ratings. Some legal experts expressed the opinion that the trial was dragged out excessively by attorneys playing to the TV audience. "Sure, there's been posturing and pandering," said a *USA Today* editorial. "But the public still learns from televised trials. . . .

"TV coverage of the Simpson case, for all its excesses, has generated public debate over different racial views about police, money's effect on the quality of justice, and the ethics of lawyers and jurors alike." (See Chapter 1.)

While the trial was under way, a judge in Union, South Carolina, barred TV cameras from the trial of Susan Smith on charges she drowned her two young sons. "There is an absolute likelihood that broadcast coverage in the courtroom would interfere with the due process of the trial and pose a risk to the case," Circuit Judge William Howard said.

**Federal Courts.** A nearly half-century-old ban on cameras in federal courts seemed to be ending in 1991. Judge William C. Conner of New York allowed camera crews to cover a copyright dispute between the estate of the late actor James Dean and a photographer over fees for marketing Dean's image. At the same time, a three-year experiment was begun to allow still and video cameras and radio recordings, at individual judges' discretion, into eight civil trial and appellate courts in seven states.

In 1994, however, top federal judges comprising the Judicial Conference of the United States voted two to one to continue the restriction.

## The Right of Privacy

Closely allied to libel and slander is the question of which is more important, the privacy of the individual or the privilege of the press. The right of privacy, perhaps the most cherished right of all, is guaranteed, but more and more it is coming into conflict in the courts with the First Amendment right to report news freely.

As previously discussed, public figures such as politicians, entertainers, and athletes give up their right to privacy in return for being public figures. But how much right to privacy does a person who is not a public figure have when that right conflicts with the rights of the press? Privacy rights have been obtained through a series of judicial rulings in this century.

**Right of privacy**
Constitutional right of an individual, which comes in conflict with privileges of the press to report and comment

**Identifying Rape Survivors.** An individual's privacy may be violated if that person is depicted in a "false light," an action that is similar to but separate from libel law, and if private facts about private persons are publicly disclosed. In a case pertaining to the latter, in 1975 the Supreme Court struck down a Georgia law that made it a misdemeanor to print or broadcast the name of a rape victim. Following a court hearing for six youths accused of raping a 17-year-old girl who subsequently died, presumably from rape-related trauma, Atlanta station WSB-TV used the girl's name in a newscast. Claiming serious disruption of the family's privacy, the girl's father filed suit. The Georgia courts upheld the suit as a matter of law, and the TV station appealed.

Although the Supreme Court ruled in favor of the Cox Broadcasting Corporation, it would not go so far as to make truth an absolute defense in invasion of privacy cases. The Court held that "once true information is disclosed in public court documents open to public inspection, the press cannot be sanctioned for publishing it." The Court then dampened the ruling somewhat by stating that it was confining its judgment to "the narrower interface between press and privacy" involved in printing the name of a rape victim rather than "the broader question whether truthful publications may ever be subjected to civil or criminal liability."

The issue was reignited when William Kennedy Smith was accused of raping a Florida woman on Easter weekend in 1991. During the lengthy televised trial, the woman's face was obscured electronically. After the *Globe*, a supermarket tabloid, disclosed her identity, some other publications, including the New York *Times* and NBC News used her name in stories. Prosecutors charged the *Globe* with violating a 1911 statute that made identifying a rape victim a second-degree criminal misdemeanor.

Many community and women's rights organizations protested the disclosures, and lawmakers in at least six states introduced legislation making such action a crime. A dozen news and press freedom organizations urged the defeat of such efforts on First Amendment grounds. Smith was acquitted, and charges against the *Globe* were dropped. Media leaders said they would continue to exercise great care in deciding whether it is necessary to report the names of rape survivors.

**Federal Restraints.** Media lawyers hope that eventually the Supreme Court will permit the publication of any and all information about individuals unless clear and convincing proof can be shown that such information is false and that the communicator either knew it was false or acted in "reckless disregard" of the facts—the test laid out in the *New York Times* v. *Sullivan* case.

The Privacy Act of 1974 stipulated types of information about individuals that could not be disclosed by federal agencies and provided means whereby persons could determine the nature of information about themselves in official files. A Privacy Protection Study Commission, created by the act, submitted a report to President Carter in 1977. The report listed five "competing social values" that must be taken into account in protecting personal privacy: the First Amendment, freedom of information, law-enforcement interests, the cost of privacy protection, and federal–state relations.

The commission recommended that no action be taken that would affect the ability of the press to request or obtain information. The commission did suggest, however, that medical records be kept strictly confidential and that it be considered a crime to seek such information through misrepresentation or deception.

For many years most colleges and universities refused to release information about crimes involving students on their campuses. They contended that the 1974 Buckley Amendment to the federal Family Education and Privacy Rights Act, protecting the privacy of student educational records, extended also to reports of criminal activities. The U.S. Department of Education supported their stance. Traci Bauer, editor of the *Southwest Standard* student newspaper, sued Southwest Missouri State University for release of the records. In 1991, a federal judge ruled that "withholding criminal investigations and records is unconstitutional under Fifth Amendment due process and the First Amendment." The decision was a victory for the newspaper and many free press organizations, especially the Society of Professional Journalists, which financially supported the legal challenge. Subsequently, the Department of Education sought changes in the law that would mandate access to the records at public colleges and also give private institutions the option of doing so.

## Access to the Media

### Newspapers

In 1969, Jerome A. Barron, a law professor at George Washington University, proposed a new concept of the First Amendment in relation to newspapers. Pointing out that in the *New York Times* v. *Sullivan* case the

Supreme Court had created a new relative freedom from libel for newspapers by the way it had interpreted the First Amendment, Barron said that similar techniques could be used to fashion a right of access to the press for the public:

> If this approach does not work, then a carefully worded right of access statute which would aim at achieving a meaningful expression of divergent opinions should be attempted. The point is that we must realize that private restraints on free expression have become so powerful that the belief that there is a free marketplace where ideas will naturally compete is as hopelessly outmoded as the theory of perfect competition has generally become in most other spheres of modern life.

In 1974 the Florida Supreme Court, in *Miami Herald Co. v. Pat L. Tornillo*, upheld a state law requiring that newspapers give "right of reply" space to political candidates criticized by newspapers. The U.S. Supreme Court, however, unanimously overturned the decision, its opinion reading in part as follows:

> The Florida statute fails to clear the barriers of the First Amendment because of its intrusion into the function of editors. A newspaper is more than a passive receptacle or conduit for news, comment, and advertising. The choice of material . . . the treatment of public issues and public officials—whether fair or unfair—constitutes the exercise of editorial control or judgment. It has yet to be demonstrated how government regulation of this process can be exercised consistent with First Amendment guarantees of a free press as they have evolved to this time.

Newspaper editors long have sought to obtain replies from possibly maligned individuals, companies, and institutions both before and after the printing of controversial stories. Letters to the editor columns traditionally have been open to all readers. A number of newspapers have solicited articles from the public to run in the columns opposite their main editorial pages.

Recognizing the pressures for greater access to their publications, however, many newspapers more recently have employed persons called *ombudsmen*, or have assigned certain staff members, to consider complaints; have endeavored to establish local and state press councils; and have hired reporters and editors from minority groups. But the editors insist that the final decision as to what is printed must be theirs alone.

**Ombudsman**
Person employed by a news organization with independent authority to respond to reader complaints and to call attention to discrepancies in the handling of news

## Broadcasting

For many of the nation's broadcasters, one specific legal requirement—the "Fairness Doctrine"—has had the effect of discouraging coverage of many important social issues. Since 1949, broadcasters had been obligated to offer reasonable opportunity for opposing sides to respond to the coverage of controversial public issues. This statutory requirement to be fair was based on two legal philosophies not relevant to print media: (1) the airwaves are public property; and (2) broadcasters are licensed to operate in the "public interest, convenience, and necessity." Public interest is served, Congress and the FCC ruled, if the airwaves are made accessible to many differing viewpoints.

Most broadcasting leaders took issue with the Fairness Doctrine, charging that it abridged the principles of freedom of speech and press traditionally applied to electronic media by forcing the presentation of various sides of an issue, even when the views may be unfounded, untrue, or difficult to identify in a local community.

Even more annoying to broadcasters was the *personal attack* clause of the Fairness Doctrine. This clause stated that if an individual is attacked in an editorial or program, a script or tape of the attack must be sent to the individual, with an offer of a reasonable opportunity to reply. Furthermore, if the licensee endorsed or opposed legal candidates for office in an editorial statement, the same notice and offer of time must be made within 24 hours after the program is aired.

The industry considered the clause unconstitutional, a violation of freedom of the press. Its effect, it was argued, would be to curtail meaningful discussion of issues because of the expense involved in offering time for reply and because the licensee would avoid controversial issues if uncertain about the freedom to comment.

The Supreme Court did not agree with the broadcasters; in 1969 it held the personal attack rules constitutional, noting that "it is the right of the viewers and listeners, not the right of the broadcasters, which is paramount" in such instances. If broadcasters were not willing to present representative community views on controversial issues, Justice Byron White of the Court wrote, the granting or renewal of a license might be challenged. To make this threat of a license loss, he continued, "is consistent with the ends and purposes of those constitutional provisions forbidding the abridgement of freedom of speech and freedom of the press." In law circles, this became known as the *Red Lion* decision (*Red Lion Broadcasting Co.* v. *Federal Communications Commission*).

Broadcasters, and many print journalists as well, continued to oppose the Fairness Doctrine as inhibiting the free flow of ideas, and measures were introduced in Congress to eliminate the requirement. In 1987, an effort by Congress to turn the policy into law was vetoed by President Reagan. Two months later, however, the FCC voted unanimously to abolish the doctrine. Unaffected were the *equal time rule* and other regulations such as license requirements calling for local programming. Broadcasting was on its way to achieving First Amendment parity with print.

In 1989, the U.S. Court of Appeals for the District of Columbia upheld the FCC's repeal of the Fairness Doctrine in a three-judge panel opinion, and the U.S. Supreme Court in 1990 refused to review the decision. Meanwhile, the media's watchdogs were opposing efforts in Congress to reinstate the Fairness Doctrine as law.

Access to ownership of broadcast media by minorities and women is discussed in Issue 3.

# PART SIX
# Communications Worldwide

## ROLES OF THE MEDIA—
## GLOBAL COMMUNICATOR

A worldwide communications system is expanding, based on the growth of international corporations, the impact of the global Internet computer network, and the popularity of American films and videos in foreign countries.

*". . . being involved in television on a global level is very much a priority for us at Viacom Paramount. MTV is virtually everywhere and Nickelodeon is following in their footsteps . . . We are involved with HBO in Asia, with CineCanal in Latin America. We have U.S.A. Latina. We are in the process of gearing up to do a Sci-Fi Europe."*

*—Kerry McCluggage, chairman, Paramount Television Group*

*"We're doing some things with Viacom in Bangkok and have a cable system over there, and we're talking about expanding into China . . .*

*—Ivan Seidenberg, Nynex chairman*

*"I think that CNN will be reporting from virtually all nations of the world to all nations of the world. We will do it not only in English but in many other languages . . . "*

*—W. Thomas Johnson of Cable News Network, looking ahead to 2010*

# CHAPTER SEVENTEEN
## International Mass Communications

## "Personal Evangelism on a Mass Scale"

The Rev. Billy Graham used 30 satellites that covered 24 time zones when he preached to an estimated 8 million people at 2200 locations in 1995.

"This is not mass evangelism," said Graham spokesperson A. Larry Ross. "It's personal evangelism on a mass scale."

In a technological feat that experts said surpassed coverage of the Olympic Games and World Cup soccer competitions, Graham used technology to appear as if he were at each venue.

When the evangelist preached from San Juan, Puerto Rico, for three days, each sermon was translated into 45 languages and edited into one of eight preproduced culturally tailored packages.

"People in South America have different heroes and different music than people in Asia," Ross said.

The crusade packages then were transmitted to churches, town halls, soccer stadiums, and outdoor amphitheaters. Technicians at each site recorded the services for broadcast on 40-foot-high screens.

The Graham organization later broadcast an edited version about Easter on prime-time network television to an estimated 1 billion people in 100 countries.

Said Kimithy Vaughan, co-owner of Vision Accomplished, a California company that handled the extravaganza: "There's never been anything like this before."

In this chapter, we discuss the structure and expanding nature of international mass communications, including elements of the mass media and their supporting agencies not previously explored in this book.

We begin by discussing the roles played by radio, television, video, recordings, and facsimile transmissions in the exciting prodemocracy uprisings of the late 1980s. New widespread uses of the camcorder are reviewed.

After exploring other dimensions of world telecommunications, we focus on the impact that television is making elsewhere on global society through innovative use of satellites and the privatization of ownership of many stations, with emphasis on the establishment of the European Common Market.

We discuss the worldwide distribution of telefilms and the charges of cultural imperialism resulting from the almost universal showing of Western television programs and movies.

We explore how print communication developed internationally, including the global news cartel imposed by the news agencies and an online program that encodes all letters and characters of the world's languages into a single computerized standard.

We examine the role of foreign correspondents and the dangers they face, and the demands of many Third World countries for more equitable news reporting.

We end by noting the transformation of UNESCO from an agency largely promoting press control to one advocating press freedom.

## Telecommunications and Political Uprisings

Radio, television, video, and even facsimile transmissions played major roles in the almost incredible prodemocracy uprisings in the late 1980s. For decades, shortwave and mediumwave radio conveyed Western-style news and values to, among other countries, the former Soviet Union, other Eastern bloc nations, and the People's Republic of China. Millions living near the western borders of Eastern Europe viewed television programs from free world countries. Western records became highly popular. Thousands of videocassette recorders, videos, and camcorders were smuggled into communist countries. And when communication was hampered, facsimile copies of news stories and other messages got through.

Bombarding the Soviet Union were signals from the Voice of America (VOA), British Broadcasting Corporation (BBC), other European stations, and America's Radio Liberty, which transmitted programs in 14 languages from Munich, West Germany. Despite jamming that persisted into late in the 1980s, millions of Soviet citizens clandestinely listened. The effect of these efforts, as well as television transmissions, in helping to provide the climate for acceptance of Mikhail Gorbachev's *perestroika* and *glasnost* campaigns, in the midst of economic deprivations, may never be known, but many consider them substantial.

Uprisings in Poland followed the Soviet liberalization movement. Leader Lech Walesa attributed much of the success of the Solidarity movement in gaining control of Poland's government to imaginative uses of the camcorder. Just as Shiite Muslims had undercut the regime of the Shah of Iran in 1979 with the widespread, underground use of audiotape recordings. Solidarity members acquired an estimated 3 million videocassette recorders and smuggled tapes in and out of the country in their fight for recognition.

For decades, people throughout the People's Republic of China have listened to Western radio broadcasts, particularly those of the VOA and BBC. Western ideas were spread, of course, from many other sources, including international travel and study. So it was that activist-minded students and others were ready when Gorbachev visited Beijing in June 1989. Dramatic student-led demonstrations climaxed by the occupation of Tiananmen Square ended in a bloody massacre and the arrest of thousands.

Through it all the VOA's 24-hour service in English, but particularly its nearly 13 hours of Mandarin and Cantonese broadcasts each day, helped get the facts out to the Chinese population even as the state- and Communist Party-controlled media tried to hide them. The BBC supplemented its regular English-language broadcasts with two and one-half hours of programming in Chinese each day. And Chinese students throughout the country gained information and encouragement from several thousand copies of news stories and pictures sent surreptitiously on telephone fax machines each day by Chinese students in the United States and Europe.

With 80 percent of East Germans within range of West German television stations, the population had long been immersed in Western mass tastes and mass consumerism. Most youths enjoyed their own subculture, wearing blue denim clothes and listening avidly to rock and roll lyrics on radio and television and on records smuggled into the country, often extolling personal freedom. When thousands tried to hear the amplified hard-rock blasts of three British rock groups in June 1987 at the historic Brandenburg Gate by the Berlin Wall, they were chased away, only to chant "The Wall must go" and "Gorbachev, Gorbachev." Other factors including food shortages and the communist leaders' misuse of power undoubtedly were much stronger, but observers say East German youths were primed in part by rock lyrics to make their demands at the Gate in November 1989. The collapse of the Stalinist East German government quickly followed nationwide demonstrations led by those in Leipzig.

Other East European uprisings against iron-fisted communist rule, in which the media played a similar role, followed. In 1991, old-line communist military leaders attempted a Moscow coup, imprisoning Mikhail Gorbachev for several days. The coup failed, in part because many communication lines were left open but mainly because of popular support of Russian president Boris Yeltsin.

"In the days of Goebbels, they could enslave a people," observed James "Scotty" Reston, the late New York *Times* columnist. "They could fill them full of such lies and such deceptions. But then along came these new instruments, and they vault over boundaries and Iron Curtains. People begin to see that our standard of living is totally different. They see by television that tyranny is not inevitable but intolerable."

**Communications Development.**   In the wake of the liberalization movements, U.S. telecommunications companies, with visions of tapping new markets for consumers and developing low-cost manufacturing bases, proposed to lay fiber-optics lines across the Soviet Union, establish cellular telephone service in Budapest, give Hungary its first workable phone system, and take cable television to Poland. In a joint venture, Chase Enterprises began to wire in Warsaw and Cracow the first 1.8 million of Poland's 8 million homes. Numerous other arrangements followed.

**Camcorders.**   When the Israeli government tried to block television transmissions during its ongoing struggle with the Palestinian Intifada, scores of camcorders were given to young Palestinians. Recorded instances of alleged Israeli brutality were distributed to television networks in a number of countries.

A monthly video magazine distributed to churches and human rights organizations in Chile included the shooting of a female student, allegedly by government forces.

People almost everywhere are using camcorders not only to air alternative political views and organize subversive movements, but also to depict family and community experiences and record news events.

## A Telecommunications Explosion

So rapidly is world communications expanding that its growth may best be described not as a revolution but as an explosion. Telecommunications, as defined by international convention, is *any transmission, emission, or reception of signs, signals, writing, images, and sounds or intelligence of any nature by wire, radio, optical, or other electromagnetic systems.* Thus it includes, among other means, the telegraph, telephone, facsimile (fax) and data transfer among computers, and radio and television broadcasting.

Telecommunications takes place through the air, over land and oceanic cables, and, most dramatically, via satellite. It is used mostly for business and personal messages. Although by 1990 almost 80 percent of the well over 400 million telephones had been installed in only ten countries, the telephone links all nations. It is estimated that nearly 500 billion calls are made each year. Fiber-optics cables installed in 1989 beneath the Atlantic and Pacific Oceans can carry more than 40,000 calls simultaneously; another transatlantic cable, installed later, is handling double that many calls.

Computers capable of performing 1 billion operations a second are linking all parts of the world with a flow of electronic data that can be stored, processed, analyzed, and retransmitted in oral and visual forms. Data processing, in a field known as *informatics*, has transformed most industrial, scientific, commercial, and government operations. It is estimated that about one-half of the workers in the United States are now engaged in some form of information processing.

France has achieved a leading world position in several fields of advanced telecommunications. Its system includes digital switching equipment, electronic telephone directories, and a videotex operation known as Minitel. Several million terminals are in use throughout the country. Under a $6 billion plan, the nation has been linked with videophones and fiber-optics cables capable of handling vast quantities of information and images. The government has installed the videophones in more than 3 million residences, charging homeowners only for calls. The tabletop videophone incorporates a telephone, television screen, and movable video camera. Customers are automatically billed for all uses, including videotex services and video programs ordered from a library of more than 2000 titles.

**Informatics**
Communication field in which information and other data are processed, mostly by computer. Based on the French word *informatique*

## Television

### Direct Satellite Broadcasting

Efforts have been made in a number of countries in recent years to establish direct broadcast satellite (DBS) systems. Signals are transmitted from a high-power satellite directly to individual home sets or community receivers without the need of local stations to receive and rebroadcast. An 18-inch-diameter antenna, set-top box, and remote control unit, when mass-produced, could cost as little as $200. Economic and technical problems delayed development of the system in some countries.

Largely in anticipation of the spread of DBS, however, issues of *access* and *spillover* have been addressed in international forums. Because of the finite space available for satellites placed in geosynchronous orbit, less-developed countries have been seeking access to those already positioned by industrialized nations.

Spillover occurs when one country's signal creates what is known as a *footprint* in the territory of another nation. The problem has created spirited debate. The diffusion of standard satellite signals can largely be controlled from a few central locations, but DBS transmissions cannot be made to conform to nonoval-shaped national boundaries. Because a DBS signal can cover about 1 million square miles, an area about one-third that of the United States, problems related to spillover are especially acute in some regions.

**Access**
Ability to obtain use of a communications facility such as a satellite or cable television channel, to buy a broadcast station, or to obtain other such use

**Spillover**
Dissemination of a television signal into a region or country for which it is not primarily intended or authorized, resulting in a *footprint*

## Television in Western Europe

Driven by satellite technology, the desire of viewers for more varied programming, deregulation, and the move toward a unified European market, West European entrepreneurs have vastly expanded commercial television, both in satellite and conventional channels. More than 100 new channels were added by the mid-1990s.

The most striking changes involved the direct transmission of programming from satellites to homes, bypassing conventional networks, local stations, and cable systems. Rupert Murdoch's Australian-based News Corporation began sending signals into homes in Great Britain and Ireland in 1989; by 1992 Sky Broadcasting (BSkyB) was in about 12 percent of Britain's 22 million homes. In 1995, Murdoch owned 40 percent of the system. British Satellite Broadcasting Ltd., a consortium of British, French, and Australian companies and the German government, also launched satellites.

In Britain, more than 40 new channels via satellite greatly expanded the television scene. It had previously been limited to two BBC channels, carrying no advertising and funded by license fees, and two Independent Broadcasting Corporation (ITV) channels with a monopoly on TV advertising. Under a law designed to make ITV more competitive, the government auctioned franchises for the corporation's 16 channels; four leading companies lost their licenses.

A number of American cable and telephone companies joined in a venture to rewire Great Britain and give Britons a new system capable of nearly unlimited two-way TV programming and first-rate telephone service. U.S. companies involved included Tele-Communications Inc., U S

## TOP SATELLITE TV SERVICES IN EUROPE

Six satellite television channels provide much of the news, sports, and entertainment viewed in Europe, according to the January 16, 1995, issue of *AdWeek* magazine. The channels, countries of origin, and estimated number of homes reached by each are:

- CNN—Britain (via U.S.)—67 million
- NBC Super Channel—Britain—65 million
- MTV—Britain—58 million
- Eurosport—France—57 million
- TNT Cartoon Network—Britain (via U.S.)—23 million
- BBC Prime, BBC World—Britain—2.3 million

Viewing by hotel guests adds considerably to these figures. The NBC Super Channel estimates that it reaches 350,000 hotel rooms. Programming on the TNT Cartoon Network consists of cartoons (14 hours daily) and classic films (10 hours daily).

West, Nynex, Comcast, Jones Intercable, Southwestern Bell, and Cox Cable Communications.

The French government dropped one of its three state-owned channels and authorized four for private use. One was licensed to the late British publisher Robert Maxwell, who began transmissions to much of Europe. Another was assigned to a French-Italian consortium, with Silvio Berlusconi, the principal developer of Italian privately-owned TV, as a 40 percent owner. In 1992, France's Canal Plus pay-television giant joined Murdoch's News Corporation to develop European-wide TV services that exploit technological advances.

In 1995, Philips Electronics N.V. of the Netherlands and United International Holdings Inc. of the United States agreed to combine their European cable television interests to create Europe's largest cross-border cable company. The cable would reach 2 million households in 15 countries.

Providing video-on-demand and other interactive multimedia services was a major goal of Europe's media giants.

Government restrictions on advertising and programming in France hampered the channels' commercial success. Television advertising for tobacco and liquor was forbidden. Only one commercial break was permitted during movies, and half the programs shown on TV had to have been made in France.

The liberalization movement that transformed much of West European broadcasting contrasts sharply with the practice in most other parts of the world, where government ownership of radio and television is common.

**"Television Without Frontiers."**   The European Community in 1989 adopted a nonbinding plan that banned pornography, limited advertising, and stipulated that its member nations "shall ensure where practicable and by appropriate means that broadcasters reserve for European works" a majority of their transmission time, excluding news, sports, game shows, and commercials.

The new standard, known as "Television Without Frontiers," was part of the community's plan to build a unified, barrier-free market for goods and services. It sought to prevent domination of the airwaves by foreign entertainment shows—dramas, situation comedies, and films—most often purchased from the United States and to a considerable extent laden with sex and violence. These types of shows proliferated to the extent that during the 1990s European television systems paid an estimated $1 billion each year for American-made shows, triple the level in 1984.

Seeking to stimulate European production of films and television shows, the foreign ministers called for millions of dollars in government aid for production, including increased cooperation, and for film schools and state-owned television stations.

Reaching all of Europe with programming was a major problem. Explained Michele Martin, writing in *AdWeek:* "Europe may be the world's

**Television Without Frontiers** Term applied to television programs in the European Community that cross national borders by advance agreement of the countries involved

## WHY U.S. SHOWS ARE POPULAR

Pascal Fleury and Jorge Dana of France's state-owned Antenne 2 have compiled "five keys" to the success of American shows that European producers might copy, according to an article in the *Wall Street Journal*.

- Emphasize "how, not why."
- Put normal people in extraordinary situations rather than vice versa.
- Show lots of chase scenes, not long dramatic stories. (In a new TV show, "Eurocops" [called "Euroflics" in Francophone countries], seven Eurocops, one from each of the participating producing countries, pursue Eurocrooks in picturesque settings.)
- Use strong and simple characters, not complicated ones.
- Complete a story in each show rather than carry the story over several episodes.

French traditionalists, however, cringe at the thought of their dramas being transformed into a money-obsessed business that promotes the likes of Arnold Schwarzenegger. Says Pascal Rogard, general secretary of a French producers' guild: "French films are the cinema of creation. American films are products of marketing."

biggest television market, but it is also the most fragmented. It is divided culturally, linguistically, and technologically. Still, global players such as News Corporation, Turner Broadcasting, and NBC have eagerly entered the market over the past several years."

Zenith Media Worldwide predicted that 26.4 percent of all advertising spending in Europe would air on nonbroadcast TV by 2004. An "explosion" of new channels was foreseen, along with improved digitalization and increased interest in pay-TV services.

## Television in Other Countries

The revolution in television moved across Asia and the Middle East during the 1990s. Much as Free World broadcasting had penetrated tightly controlled media walls in the former Soviet Union and East European countries a few years earlier, millions of viewers watched news, music videos, and dramas that often presented a picture radically different from the views espoused by their leaders.

In 1990 Richard Li Ka-shing, a Hong Kong billionaire, founded Star-TV, a satellite service that projected a "footprint" stretching from Cairo, Egypt, to Hokkaido, Japan, and encompassing almost 60 countries with a potential audience of 2.7 billion people. In 1993, Li and his son Richard sold 63.6 percent of the company to the News Corporation, controlled by Rupert Murdoch.

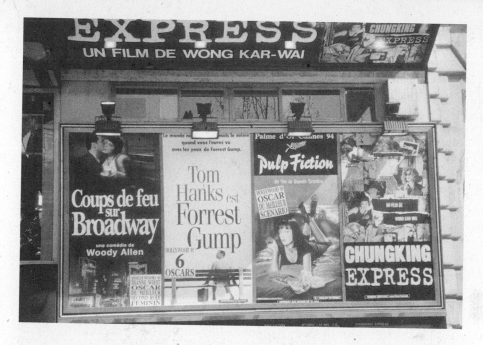

The impact of American motion pictures in foreign countries is illustrated by this advertisement in French on a Parisian billboard. Notice the emphasis on Oscar awards, which boost box office sales abroad as well as in the United States.

Murdoch boasted that satellite television posed "an unambiguous threat to totalitarian regimes everywhere." Alarmed by such a bold assertion, the Chinese government forbade satellite owners from receiving Star-TV, and blocked the News Corporation's plans to publish a magazine in Shanghai with a Chinese partner.

Bowing to pressure, the News Corporation announced in 1994 that Star-TV would no longer transmit the British Broadcasting Corporation's World Service Television news channel into China. Stung by CNN's global success and its prominence in covering the Persian Gulf War (see Chapter 11), the BBC had joined with Star-TV in starting the Asian edition of its news service, which for the first time carried commercials. In 1995, the Lis sold their remaining interest in Star-TV to the News Corporation.

On its five channels, Star-TV carried MTV, Mandarin Chinese soap operas, sports, American TV reruns and, to all countries except the People's Republic of China, the BBC World Service. Its biggest markets were Taiwan, India, and Israel.

In 1994, the BBC, already in Europe, beamed its 24-hour service to Africa and other regions.

Countries affected by Star-TV and a multitude of other satellite services, including Time Warner and Turner Broadcasting System, reacted in various ways to the transnational programming. Some, such as Singapore and Malaysia, banned home satellite dishes. Others, including India and Indonesia, accepted the explosion of satellite ownership. In Taiwan, where the three national TV stations are state-run, an estimated 300 cable television companies were operating even though cable TV was still technically illegal.

Meanwhile, Japan's semiofficial broadcasting giant, NHK, abandoned its plans to compete with CNN and the BBC. Aiming to provide a European perspective on the news, a dozen state-backed European TV stations created Euronews. The satellite channel planned news broadcasts in English, French, German, Italian, and Spanish. Other major satellite news services included Britain's Sky News and Mexico's Galavisa. NBC Cable spread its NBC Super Channel into 60 million homes and 32 countries. CNBC expanded into Asia, and Canal de Noticias, the company's 24-hour Spanish language news service, continued to grow in Latin America.

Hoping to dethrone Egypt's satellite channel as the number one pro-Arab television station, the Middle East Broadcasting Center (MBC) beamed its fast-paced programs to all Arab countries from studios in London. MBC's biggest attraction was its news programs, which pushed the limits of Arab press freedom. In 1992, MBC strengthened its news service by purchasing United Press International (see Chapter 4).

The government-operated network in India began accepting sponsored shows in 1985, thus enlivening programming. Approximately 60 million Indians, representing about 75 percent of the population, watched on more than 5 million TV sets. The number of people viewing Indian and other satellite channels increased spectacularly by the 1990s. "The imagination of the viewers has been fired. There is no stopping satellite television," said Lalit Mehta, who studied the trend in India. "For good or bad it is here to stay."

Japan, with more than 10,000 TV stations and 60 million sets, introduced pay-TV. And in the People's Republic of China, the nation's first communications satellite was sending programs to about 40 million TV sets. Beijing residents were reported to be viewing television an average of 90 minutes a day. Sports and other forms of entertainment comprised three-fourths of the programming. After prodemocracy demonstrations were crushed in 1989, news programs strictly followed the communist line.

Cartoons, soap operas, pop videos, and TV advertisements from the West were proving a huge hit with Russian viewers, according to research into Russian TV tastes, as reported by *Variety*. "Disney Presents," a showcase program that ran weekly on the first national channel, Ostankino, emerged as the highest-profile Western show. About a third of all Moscow viewers watched Western shows every week. A ban on tobacco and alcohol commercials on TV in 1995, however, dimmed the picture for stations and advertisers.

PanAmSat, which has provided cable service throughout much of Latin America, moved into direct-to-home satellite service in 1994. The company planned to enlarge its service with delivery of a new satellite in 1996, targeting Brazil, the Argentina/Uruguay region, and Mexico.

Competitors included Hughes Communications' DIRECTV service and Rupert Murdoch's News Corporation, which joined Brazil's Globo Organization in developing DBS service for Latin America and the Caribbean Basin.

## Export of Telefilms

Hollywood films had long dominated the world market, and in the early 1960s, U.S. motion picture and TV production companies turned increasingly to the expanding worldwide television market. They found ready acceptance because many countries had introduced TV and made heavy capital investments, but lacked the facilities and experience to produce much TV programming on their own. By 1990, approximately 160 major motion picture studios and both large and small independent producers and distributors were exporting programs to more than 100 nations, with revenues surpassing one-half billion dollars.

Videotaped game shows, as well as interview and variety programs, constitute only a small part of the exports. Because, except for Japan, U.S. videotape cannot be used in other countries without costly conversion, the programs are usually shot on 16-mm or 35-mm film for worldwide distribution, as well as on videotape for domestic TV consumption.

Approximately 85 percent of the total telefilm sales to other countries are programs produced by the nine members of the Motion Picture Export Association: MCA, Metro-Goldwyn-Mayer, Allied Artists, Avco Embassy, United Artists, Columbia, Paramount, Twentieth Century Fox, and Warner Bros. Six countries—Canada, Great Britain, Italy, Australia, Germany, and Japan—have accounted for three-fourths of the total dollar income from foreign distribution. Brazil, Mexico, France, and Venezuela comprise other large markets.

As a result of soaring production costs and increased import restrictions in many parts of the world, among other reasons, the cofinancing/coproduction of telefilms has become widespread. By placing quotas on imported products, countries seek to protect and develop their own film and television industries. Because U.S. outlets represent 50 percent of the worldwide market, at least one version of all American–European programs must be in English. The dubbing of voices, shooting of scenes twice, and other techniques increase costs but they are readily recouped by profitable U.S. syndication markets.

Great Britain, France, and Germany also export much programming. In Mexico, where the *novella* is highly popular, many programs are sold to other Latin American countries. Brazil also sends its novellas abroad, especially to Portugal. Nations in the Middle East obtain most of their programs from Egypt.

**Novella**
Latin term for a
soap opera

## Cultural Diffusion

Charges of cultural imperialism by the Western media have been advanced vigorously by many less-developed countries during the last four

President Clinton and the First Lady, Hillary Rodham Clinton, support American trade overseas by posing at the opening of the Coca-Cola refreshment plant in Moscow. With them, left, is Michael O'Neil, the company's manager in Russia. The sign says "Coca-Cola" in Russian. (AP Photo/Greg Gibson)

decades. Critics charge that the United States, in particular, is unduly imposing on other countries its set of beliefs, values, knowledge, and behavioral norms as well as its overall lifestyle. TV programs such as "Dallas," "Hill Street Blues," and, more recently, "N.Y.P.D. Blue" have been cited as most harmful. In response, media spokespersons point out that these countries are not forced to buy these products, although they recognize the scarcity of production facilities and expertise that would enable the nations to fill their TV and cinema screens. In some countries, the problem is slowly being rectified.

Long a powerful force in the world's film, TV, and home video market, the U.S. movie industry grew even more dominant. Hallmark Entertainment joined Germany's Taurus Film in producing 22 features per year for three years; MGM/UA and Tele Munchen of Germany signed a $100 million contract; and Discovery Enterprises Worldwide arranged deals with NHK of Japan, Canal of France, and SVT of Sweden to show its documentary series *Last of the Czars.* These are examples of countless such arrangements. Hollywood also ventured into such promising markets as Indonesia, South Korea, the Commonwealth of Independent States, and the People's Republic of China.

The United States is far from being the leader in theatrical film production. Of the estimated 3000 feature-length films produced worldwide each year, India makes the most, followed in order by Japan, the United States, France, Italy, and Russia. Almost one-half of the world's full-length entertainment films are made in 11 Asian countries, and about one-third in Europe and the Russian Federation. Language and cultural differences, as well as the expense of dubbing voices or placing limited translations at the bottom of film frames, are major problems.

Nevertheless, films as well as videos continue to cross international borders at a pace that has alarmed those concerned with preserving national and regional cultural identity. For example, the increased black market in X-rated entertainment has disturbed religious and cultural leaders in some Muslim countries. Pakistani soap operas have become popular in India, and Hindi musicals from India have attracted many video viewers in Pakistan. The growth of the video black market in the Republic of China on Taiwan has caused authorities there to relax their censorship of movies on grounds that the films would be seen uncut anyway. Chinese kung-fu films are popular in Indonesia. Overall, however, Hollywood entertainment fare dominates most world markets.

## Radio

Anywhere in the world a person with a shortwave radio may tune in voices in a multiplicity of languages, as well as music and Morse code signals, projected by powerful transmitters in many countries. Where boundaries are not far distant, regular mediumwave broadcasts from other nations may be heard.

International radio broadcasting is that which is intended, either exclusively or in part, for audiences outside the frontiers of the country from which the broadcast originates. About 400 million of the estimated 1.5 billion radio sets in the world can receive worldband broadcasts, so potential audiences are vast. The Voice of America broadcasts around-the-clock in 47 languages. It has a worldwide audience estimated at 100 million people and receives half a million letters each year from listeners. The British Broadcasting Corporation estimates that about 75 million adults listen to its programs at least once a week.

In 1922, Germany began daily propaganda news broadcasts to other countries in Morse code. During the mid-1920s, the Soviet Union became the first country to produce foreign language broadcasts in several languages, and Great Britain and other countries soon followed. During the early 1930s, several commercial stations in Europe, such as Radio Paris and Radio Luxembourg, began broadcasting on longwave or mediumwave in several languages.

In the United States, companies such as General Electric, NBC, and CBS built and operated shortwave transmitters, mostly relaying domestic programs but also transmitting some in foreign languages. Pearl Harbor convinced the U.S. government that it could not rely solely on commercial broadcasters for an international service, so the Voice of America was created in 1942 as a part of the Department of State.

After playing a vital role in ending the Cold War, the Voice of America focused its efforts on information-deprived countries. One step was the creation in 1994 of Radio Free Asia, beaming programs from the

# ATTACKING THE CYBERSPACE TOWER OF BABEL

Worldwide text communication on the Internet became much simpler in the mid-1990s: a computer industry consortium created Unicode, the first such program to encode all the letters and characters of the world's languages into a single computerized standard.

Banding together to produce the spectacular software advance were IBM, Apple, Microsoft, Xerox, Hewlett-Packard, and other companies.

News of the coding breakthrough was especially exciting to the Voice of America. "The implications of this are quite amazing," said VOA media analyst Ken Donow.

In 1994, the VOA started an Internet service that enabled users in 15 countries to download sound files containing agency broadcasts. The agency planned to have written transcripts of its broadcasts available in their original languages via a local service, from which Internet users worldwide could download them.

Downloading a sound file could take hours, a text file perhaps minutes on even a minimally efficient modem. Such accessibility is particularly important in less developed countries.

"In Africa, for example," said Donow, "only four countries on the continent have full Internet connections. So if we're doing only sound, that leaves most of Africa inaccessible to us via the Internet. If Unicode lets us make a connection that corresponds to their level of technology, we're able to make a major contribution to the local news environment."

United States into the Chinese mainland, Burma, Cambodia, Laos, North Korea, Tibet, and Vietnam.

The VOA also increased its programming to countries such as Iran, Iraq, and Cuba, where the United States was portrayed as a demonic country. Cuba and China were only partially successful in blocking the signals.

The main fare of the service is regional and local news, features, music, and English lessons. News reports and features are produced independently of the State Department, which offers editorial comment only. The VOA budget was reduced from $104 million in 1994 to $95 million in 1995, forcing cutbacks in programs to the former Soviet Union and Eastern Europe.

Radio Free Europe and Radio Liberty moved their operations from Munich to less expensive headquarters in Prague and trimmed their staffs from 1100 to 300.

Today the countries engaged in the most international broadcasting, ranked in order of number of programming hours each week, are Russia, the United States, the People's Republic of China, Germany, the United Kingdom, North Korea, Egypt, and Albania. In addition, many privately-owned stations seek international audiences for religious, commercial, and clandestine purposes, the latter often seeking to provoke revolutions. Most of the stations intend their broadcasts for particular portions of the world.

Why do so many countries broadcast internationally? The answer takes many forms: promoting national interest, enhancing national prestige, keeping in touch with nationals abroad, promoting understanding among nations, disseminating news with accuracy and objectivity, spreading a particular creed or doctrine, attempting to influence the internal affairs of another country, fostering the national culture including the teaching of the national language, and reserving a place in the broadcasting spectrum against a future need.

With an estimated 4600 shortwave stations in the world, audibility is a genuine problem, so some leading broadcasters send taped material to relay stations that boost their output, or they transmit programs to them directly by shortwave or by satellite.

## The Print Media and News Services

### Global Readership Factors

Circulation of the print media has declined in many countries during recent decades. The reasons most frequently cited are illiteracy, censorship, poor economies, competition from television and video, and increased leisure-time pursuits.

On the other hand, despite some of these problems, readership has remained relatively high in some other countries. They are the ones that enjoy high literacy, comfortable per capita income relatively evenly distributed among households, population homogeneity, keen interest in world affairs, good educational and transportation systems, and effective print media distribution techniques.

A multifaceted campaign to combat illiteracy in the United States reached major proportions in the 1990s. Newspaper, magazine, and book publishing leaders have joined business executives, educators, librarians, and many other individuals and groups in the massive effort.

Estimates of the extent of "functional illiteracy" among American adults range from 20 to 30 percent or more. In his book *Illiterate America*, Jonathan Kozol estimates that approximately 60 million adults "live in the dark nether world of functional illiteracy . . . [stumbling] through a colorless life, frequently not comprehending the ideas and expectations of the society in which they live."

Studies by the United Nations Educational, Scientific, and Cultural Organization (UNESCO) disclose that one of every four adults in the world is illiterate—nearly 1 billion people.

Illiteracy is more common in southern hemisphere countries than in those in northern regions of the world. For example, Sweden and Korea

The worldwide popularity of *Reader's Digest* is evident by its numerous foreign editions. (Copyright © 1986 The Reader's Digest Association, Inc.)

have literacy rates of 99 percent, while Syria has a literacy rate of 47 percent and Mozambique 14 percent. As reiterated by UNESCO publications, from which these figures were taken, "The world map of illiteracy is the map of poverty."

## Early Development

In the ancient world most communication was oral, augmented by signals, ceremonies, coins, and forms of architecture, and later by signs identifying places of business (the forerunner of advertising today). The earliest writing was done on stones, on walls of caves, or on primitive materials such as bamboo slips. Conquerors, traders, and missionaries gradually spread their own language and writing to other parts of the world. Books were first produced laboriously by hand.

International communication was accelerated by Gutenberg's invention of movable type and the introduction of the printing press. Newssheets, or *corantos*, relating the most wondrous of happenings, were carried from country to country by travelers. Important financial families such as the Fuggers and Rothschilds in Europe hired couriers to bring them news of political events and economic developments. Newspapers and magazines soon were printed and distributed by means of horseback and sailing ship, and later by means of steamship and train. When the telegraph, oceanic cable, radio, and improved newspaper presses ap-

**Coranto**
Primitive newssheet, the rudimentary prototype of modern newssheets; distributed early in the seventeenth century

peared in the nineteenth and twentieth centuries, international mass communication became an important element in modern world society.

## The Global News Cartel

In 1835, Charles Havas, a Frenchman, began collecting European news for French newspapers. A few years later, Paul Julius Reuter, a German, began using homing pigeons to beat the Rothschilds' couriers. Telegraph lines linked continental countries but could not traverse the Skagerrak and the English Channel. Reuter took his pigeons to London in 1851 and began gathering news for about a dozen newspapers in the British Isles. He then persuaded the British government to let him use government cables that were beginning to link the empire's outposts. Such an arrangement was mutually profitable: Reuter got his news, and his partner, the government, got favorable treatment in the news.

Finding that his service could not compete in world newsgathering with Reuter's use of the cables, Havas persuaded Reuter and Dr. Bernard Wolff, who founded a German agency in 1849, that the world should be divided into three parts for the purposes of newsgathering. Havas covered the French empire, southwestern Europe, South America, and parts of Africa; Reuter covered the British empire, North America, Mediterranean countries, and most of Asia; Wolff covered the rest of Europe and Russia. Each agreed to exchange news with the others.

In the United States, the New York Associated Press had been organized in 1849 as forerunner of the modern AP. Since the British government wished to avoid offending its former colony, the cartel decided to admit the AP, and the agreement was formalized in 1887. Nevertheless, the AP was confined to the United States until early in the twentieth century, when it was permitted to gather news in Canada and Mexico and, near the end of World War I, in Central and South America.

Dissatisfied with the cartel's method of newsgathering and reporting, major newspapers in the United States and other countries increased their number of foreign correspondents. Radiotelegraphy, a cheap alternative carrier, challenged the monopoly of the cables. By 1909, the United States had three press agencies, the AP, United Press, and International News Service.

The news cartel was finally broken by 1920, when through a friendship between a UP executive and the owners of *La Prensa* in Buenos Aires, the UP obtained contracts with a number of Latin American newspapers. At about the same time, several English provincial newspapers organized the British United Press and began exchanging news items with the UP.

Such major national news agencies as Stefani in Italy, Fabra in Spain, and the Press Association and Exchange Telegraph in England also had developed in the mid-nineteenth century. In the twentieth century, the Associated Press of India, the Canadian Press, Japan's Domei, and Nazi Germany's DNB all appeared before the start of World War II. So did three other important government-controlled agencies: the USSR's TASS (1925); the New China News Agency, now called Xinhua (1931); and Franco Spain's EFE (1938).

The Associated Press broke away completely from the weakened cartel in 1934. The Havas agency ceased its operations in 1940, and British newspaper proprietors took over the Reuters agency in 1941. Stefani was succeeded a year later by the Agenzia Nazionale Stampa Associata, modeled after the AP and the new Reuters. An independent Agence France-Presse was organized in postwar France. Deutsche Press-Agentur succeeded DNB in the Federal Republic of Germany and Kyodo replaced Domei in Japan. EFE, TASS, and Xinhua survived as official news agencies, joined by Tanjug of the former Yugoslavia. As the result of a merger in 1992, TASS joined ITAR (Information Telegraph Agency of Russia) to become ITAR-Tass.

## Foreign Correspondents

### Early Coverage

Two London newspapers, the *Times* and *Morning Chronicle*, pioneered the practice of individual newspapers sending correspondents abroad to supplement news agency services. They established foreign correspondence from the European continent in the 1820s, and by 1850 had extended coverage to Asia and the United States.

James Gordon Bennett reported Queen Victoria's coronation for his New York *Herald* in 1838. Horace Greeley's New York *Tribune* employed Charles A. Dana, Margaret Fuller, and Bayard Taylor as early European correspondents. Taylor was with Commodore Perry in Tokyo Bay in 1853. George W. Smalley opened the *Tribune*'s London bureau before 1870.

Major foreign news services, syndicated to other dailies, expanded rapidly in the 1920s, led by those of the New York *Times* and *Herald Tribune* and the Chicago *Daily News* and *Tribune*.

### Modern Coverage

In the 1960s, the New York *Times* and Chicago *Tribune* services were joined by the syndicate sponsored by the Washington *Post* and Los Angeles *Times*. Other U.S. media organizations maintaining bureaus abroad both then and later included the major broadcast networks, news and business magazines, and the news services; the *Wall Street Journal*, *Christian Science Monitor*, and Baltimore *Sun*; and the Hearst, Scripps Howard, and Knight-Ridder groups.

Mainly because of the expense of maintaining a correspondent in another country, currently estimated in excess of $200,000 annually, the number declined during much of the 1970s. Studies by Professor Ralph E. Kliesch of Ohio University for the Overseas Press Club revealed a 28 percent drop in the number of full-time persons employed abroad by the American media during the years 1969 to 1975.

During the 1980s, however, foreign coverage increased considerably. With such events as the Mid-East wars, the growth in terroristic activities, the African famine, and the democratic uprisings, Americans became much more interested in foreign news and feature stories. Accelerating the trend was a signal effort by Western journalists to respond to Third World demands for portrayal of their complex economic, political, and cultural problems along with traditional stories on "coups and earthquakes." (Third World demands will be discussed later in this chapter.) In addition, advances in telecommunications made it possible to transmit copy and televised and still pictures much more rapidly than in the past.

In 1990, almost 25 major U.S. dailies employed about 190 foreign correspondents. The New York *Times* had 40 in 30 bureaus, the Washington *Post* 22 in 18 bureaus, and the Los Angeles *Times*, which had only one in 1961, 25 in 24 bureaus. In a 1990 survey, Kleisch found that about 1735 Americans were working abroad full-time for news organizations, an increase of 150 percent in 15 years. There were more correspondents in Third World countries than ever before. In addition, middle-sized newspapers were expanding their network of "stringer" correspondents and were flying reporters and photographers on more frequent special projects abroad.

Global distribution of newspapers, magazines, and books has been discussed in earlier chapters.

## Violence Against Journalists

The lives of journalists have continued to be at risk in many countries. At least 72 journalists were killed—58 of them deliberately targeted—and 174 were imprisoned worldwide during 1994. The Committee to Protect Journalists said the number was the largest ever for one year. The most dangerous country was Algeria, where 19 journalists were assassinated by extremists. Fourteen were deliberately killed in Rwanda and another 14 killed while on assignment in battle zones in Bosnia, Somalia, Chechnya, South Africa, and Angola.

Despite the existence of democratic governments in most of the hemisphere's countries, the Inter American Press Association reported that 24 journalists were murdered, 223 were physically assaulted, and 38 media sites were attacked there in 1993.

Ten immigrant journalists were killed in the United States from 1981 to 1995 because of their reporting, the committee announced. The Vietnamese, Haitian, Chinese-American, and Cuban-American journalists worked for ethnic publications and radio stations. The report said such journalists were routinely subjected to intimidation, death threats, beatings, and arson that were part of organized terror campaigns by military or criminal organizations or foreign governments.

Peter Jennings was a foreign correspondent before becoming anchor of ABC-TV World News Tonight. (Courtesy, *Quill*)

The committee, founded in New York in 1981 in response to the murder of ABC camera operator Bill Stewart in Nicaragua, sent protest letters, called "interventions," to government leaders. The International Press Institute and the French organization Reporters sans Frontiers (Reporters without Frontiers) were similarly active.

The International Committee of the Red Cross operates a hotline, including a fax machine, to assist journalists on dangerous missions. The hotline was created in 1985 as a way for families, organizations, and employers to request intervention on behalf of journalists believed to be in danger.

## Organizations

### The United Nations

International communication has been a major concern of the United Nations since its founding in 1946. In that year, the UN issued a Declaration on Freedom of Information, which stated that "all states should proclaim policies under which the free flow of information within countries and across frontiers will be protected. The right to seek and transmit information should be insured in order to enable the public to ascertain facts and appraise events." Because of conflicting legal and ideological positions, a convention as to how this principle would be invoked was never worked out.

In 1948, the UN General Assembly issued a Universal Declaration of Human Rights, which, although not legally binding, carries great moral and psychological weight with UN members. Article 19 of the document proclaims that: "Everyone has the right to freedom of opinion and expression; this right includes freedom to hold opinions . . . and to seek, receive, and impart information and ideas through any media and regardless of frontiers." Article 2 extends the document's affirmation of basic human rights to every individual "without distinction of any kind" including the "limitation of sovereignty."

Resolution 110 (II), passed in 1947, condemns all forms of conflict-inciting propaganda, and Article 4 of the International Convention on Elimination of Racial Discrimination, passed in 1963, condemns all forms of racist propaganda. The issue of human rights was reaffirmed with the International Covenant on Civil and Political Rights in 1966 and by the Helsinki and Vienna agreements in 1975 and 1989, respectively.

With the launching of the first space satellites, the UN became involved in questions relating to outer space, and in 1959 the Committee on the Peaceful Uses of Outer Space was established. A declaration in 1963 was followed by passage of the Outer Space Treaty in 1967. It declared that outer space was to remain the "province of all mankind" to which all nations shall have equal access, that its uses should be nonmilitary but contributing to international peace and security. Two years later, with 102 nations in favor and the United States opposed, the UN called on its committee to "elaborate principles governing the use by States of artificial earth satellites for direct television broadcasting with a view toward concluding an international agreement or agreements."

**UNESCO.**   The involvement of the United Nations Educational, Scientific, and Cultural Organization (UNESCO) with mass communications was mandated in Article 1 of its constitution, which states that the organization shall "collaborate in the work of advancing the mutual knowledge and understanding of peoples, through all means of mass communication, and to that end recommend such international agreements as may be necessary to promote the free flow of ideas by word or image." UNESCO is composed of official delegations of all member nations, which convene biennially. Between these general conferences, UNESCO's work is carried out by its Secretariat, based in Paris. Its activities include research, field projects, meetings of experts, regional conferences, and seminars. Among its actions was a declaration in 1972 calling for the principle of prior consent to be applied to broadcasts from satellites. Until the 1990s, UNESCO was the primary forum for Third World communication complaints.

## Other Organizations

**Government.**   The governments of virtually every country have one or more departments involved in international communications. Almost all oversee broadcast operations, and many exercise direct and indirect control over the print media including fields such as news and editorial content, the acquisition of newsprint and equipment, the collection and dissemination of news by foreign correspondents in their countries, the news agencies that receive and transmit information, and their international information and propaganda activities.

The U.S. Information Agency (USIA) administers a wide variety of information, educational, and cultural exchange programs around the world. The agency reports to the president and receives policy guidance from the secretary of state.

USIA employs approximately 7600 persons, of whom about 4200 are non-Americans serving abroad. About one-half of the USIA's 3400 employees in the United States are engaged in the broadcasting operations of the Voice of America. Many of the others provide supporting services for 600 Foreign Service information and cultural affairs officers working overseas alongside colleagues from the Department of State and other U.S. agencies at more than 200 embassies, consulates, and other missions in 125 countries. Among other activities, USIA operates regional libraries, plans exhibits and tours of performing groups, produces radio and television programs and research reports, and provides opportunities for foreign residents to learn English.

In 1983, USIA established a one-way video, two-way audio WorldNet television service providing viewers in 75 countries with regular access to prominent American newsmakers as well as video-conferences on public diplomacy themes. Within five years, nearly 1000 interactive conferences had been conducted. Daily news and information programming was added in 1984, but in 1988 Congress suspended this service after questions were raised about the extent of viewership around the world and charges that the service's $36.9 million annual budget was taking dollars away from other USIA programs such as the Voice of America. The interactive conferences, however, continued.

In 1985, USIA began operation of Radio Marti, a mediumwave station in Florida, transmitting, according to its congressional mandate, "news, commentary, and other information about events in Cuba and elsewhere to promote the cause of freedom in Cuba," along with music. In 1990, TV Marti began sending programming into Cuba from a small island in the Florida Keys.

**Nongovernment.**   Hundreds of private mass communication organizations operate throughout the world. Among the leaders are the Federation Internationale des Editeurs de Journaux (FIEJ, in English), the International Federation of Newspaper Publishers, and the International

Press Institute, InterAmerican Press Association, InterAmerican Association of Broadcasters, International Federation of Journalists, and the World Press Freedom Committee.

## The Third World Communications Controversy

Not only is the majority of the world's news transmitted by Western news agencies, but the Western powers are also the most advanced in the use of telecommunications channels, including satellites. Many Third World nations view this dominance of communications channels as a vestige of colonialism that must be shaken off if they are to develop culturally, politically, and economically. Beginning in the early 1970s, these countries, strongly supported by the Soviet Union, worked through UNESCO and, to a lesser extent, the UN, to achieve their goals. Under Western pressure and the collapse of communist governments, however, policies advanced through UNESCO seeking government control of the press have been reversed.

**Third World**
The less technologically advanced nations of Asia, Africa, and Latin America

The demands of Third World countries were detailed in a document written by Mustapha Masmoudi, a Tunisian government official. They included the following.

- Establishing independence and equity in access to global communication resources in order that their own views, values, and developmental efforts might be reported more fully.

- Substantial help from the West to speed their own communication development.

- Western support of the Pool of News Agencies of Non-Aligned Countries, distributing mostly government press releases among Third World nations.

- Legitimizing the right of governments to limit access to news sources and the right to censor or restrict the flow of information across national borders.

- The adoption by UNESCO of resolutions proclaiming the right of governments to become involved in the licensing of journalists in order to "protect" them, and in the adoption of an international code of ethics and an international right of reply.

- Establishment of a supranational tribunal by UNESCO to monitor media behavior throughout the world.

The Third World complaints gained the full attention of the Western nations in 1976, when the Soviet Union's draft copy of a declaration proposed for adoption by UNESCO stipulated the "use" of the mass news media for certain purposes and made independent journalists subject to control by governments. Alarmed, Western governments and the independent news media mounted a strong defense that won a two-year delay, based mainly on promises of increased aid to Third World news media. A 16-person International Commission for the Study of Communication Problems was created under the chairmanship of the late Sean MacBride of Ireland, recipient of both the Lenin and Nobel Peace Prizes.

By making further pledges to help Third World countries develop their news agencies and media, and by skillful maneuvering, Western leaders again warded off the state control threat at the 1978 UNESCO conference. A declaration was adopted that dropped the phrase, "free and balanced flow of information," the antithesis of a free flow, and called for "a new equilibrium and greater reciprocity"—a balancing of news reports between the developed and developing countries and among the developing nations.

Through the World Press Freedom Committee (WPFC), American news organizations already had raised more than $500,000 toward an initial goal of $1 million and were engaged in spending almost $300,000, mainly for training programs on three continents, soliciting donations of used equipment, and sending consultants abroad from a pool of 900 volunteer consultants.

**The MacBride Report.** When the MacBride Commission released its final report in 1980, the World Press Freedom Committee noted the following *positive* aspects of the report, from its traditional democratic-capitalist point of view:

- Censorship in all forms is condemned.
- The right of access applies to private as well as public sources of information.
- Journalists should have no special protection; they will be protected when the rights of all citizens are guaranteed.
- Licensing of journalists is rejected because it would require stipulation by some authority as to who is eligible and on what basis.
- Employment of journalists by intelligence agencies of any country is condemned.

*Negative* aspects from the Western point of view included:

- A proposed International Center for Study and Planning of Information and Communications, to be established within UNESCO, conceivably could become a training ground for those challenging the Western concept of privately owned news businesses operating with traditional Western news values.
- News media (including the international news agencies and other transnational communication enterprises) would be pressured, or required, to promote government-set social, cultural, economic, and political goals.

- Private ownership of news media and communication facilities would be questioned.

After several weeks of wrangling, UNESCO delegates adopted a resolution calling for the free flow of information; expressing the need to safeguard freedom of opinion, expression, and information; supporting the widest and most democratic access possible to the functioning of the mass media; and repudiating censorship and licensing.

**Development Projects.**    A decision was made at the 1980 UNESCO conference to establish the International Program for the Development of Communications (IPDC), designed to mobilize financial and technical support to help meet the communications needs of developing countries. By 1990, the IPDC council had dispensed about $25 million to more than 325 Third World projects. Especially helped was the Pan African News Agency, composed of 45 government press agencies on the continent. IPDC money also helped establish government-run news agencies in the Caribbean and Asia. The Arab states received money for a broadcast training center and communications planning.

Because only a handful of projects directly benefited independent media, many Western nations provided only limited support for IPDC. Instead, they continued to aid Third World communications projects through such government organizations as the U.S. Information Agency and the U.S. Agency for International Development, and through nongovernment groups including the World Press Freedom Committee and International Press Institute. Other nonprofit, professional groups such as the Center for Foreign Journalists in Reston, Virginia, provided education and training for Third World journalists.

The concept of the Third World faded with the collapse of communism. Said Roberto Savio, managing director of Inter Press Service, founded as a Third World news agency in 1965 (see Chapter 4): "With the fall of the Berlin Wall, a new process of realignment was activated, in which the Third World lost its strategic importance which stemmed from East-West confrontation."

The fall of communism severely reduced funding for development projects in the 1990s. The World Press Freedom Committee, however, headed a group of six free press organizations that provided equipment and other aid for the emerging independent news operations in Eastern Europe. The committee's $400,000 allocation in 1992 included $100,000 from Gannett's Freedom Forum.

**Current Status.**    The United States and Great Britain withdrew their UNESCO memberships in 1984 in protest to an expanded budget and limited response to Western demands for policy and operational reforms. Having lost about 30 percent of its funding, UNESCO fired more than 2000 staff members and canceled or phased out a number of its programs. United States and British funds previously allocated to UNESCO instead were sent directly to developing countries to aid UNESCO-type objectives.

Federico Mayor Zaragoza of Spain was elected director-general of UNESCO in 1987. Pledging to make the organization a "house of freedom," Mayor effectively silenced debate on the New World Information Order. He was succeeded in 1995 by Boutros Boutros-Ghali.

In 1991, UNESCO adopted a policy supporting "free, independent, and pluralistic media" in both public and private sectors and increased IPDC support for nongovernment media. The agency approved an international charter for a free press endorsed by the World Press Freedom Committee and celebrated the first annual International Press Freedom Day at UNESCO headquarters in 1992. The charter, formulated in London in 1987, set forth principles rejecting censorship, licensing of journalists, and discrimination against media, and supporting free access to information, freedom to operate across borders, and protection for journalists. "The international agenda has been turned from press control to press freedom," said WPFC executive director Dana Bullen. Nevertheless, free press leaders continued to monitor UNESCO's activities.

## Points to Remember

1. Why is knowledge of the international aspects of mass communications essential for many practitioners today?

2. What are some of the problems and opportunities occasioned by the international diffusion of satellite transmissions?

3. What dramatic changes are taking place in mass communications in Western Europe? In Eastern Europe? In Asia?

4. What is the current global reach of television and radio programming from a single source?

5. What is meant by cultural diffusion? What impact does it have?

6. What factors influence readership of the print media around the world?

7. How did the global news cartel operate?

8. What problems do foreign correspondents face? How are these journalists being helped?

9. What is the nature of the Third World news controversy? What steps are being taken in response to complaints voiced by many less-developed countries?

10. What organizations and agencies are involved in seeking solutions to international mass communications problems?

11. How will the invention of Unicode speed text communication on the Internet?

## Media Questions to Think About

1. Why are American movies and TV shows so overwhelmingly popular throughout the world? Do they constitute this country's major cultural contribution to world civilization?

2. How many elements of modern communications technology can you list that make it virtually impossible for any nation to keep its citizens ignorant of developments elsewhere?

3. Can cyberspace be nationalized? Can images and messages there be censored? How? Should they be?

# APPENDIX A
## Job Opportunities in the Media

The mass media offer a stimulating variety of job opportunities. Reporting and writing, editing, speaking, managing, researching, directing, and performing are among the broad general categories.

As the individual media become increasingly intermingled through the growth of mass media conglomerates, opportunities increase for employees to move from one work area to another. A newspaper editor may switch to directing her company's cable TV news program; a television station newswriter may go on the air as weekend anchorperson; a director who has learned his craft while doing television shows may win the opportunity to direct a Hollywood movie; or a magazine editor may switch to a book publishing firm.

The following summary provides basic information about opportunities, salaries, and qualifications for work in the various media.

### Newspapers

A college degree, usually in journalism, is almost essential for anyone seeking most newsroom jobs. Employers especially seek young people with a liberal stock of knowledge, a variety of interests, and the ability to write and speak grammatical English.

Hundreds of daily newspapers have intern programs for college undergraduates in their news and advertising departments, both during summer vacation and throughout the year. In obtaining jobs, graduates who have served internships have a definite advantage over those who have not. Competition for internships is strenuous, so initial contacts should be made months before the internships will be open.

**Starting a Career.**   The usual path for a college graduate entering newspaper work is to join the staff of a small daily or weekly in order to acquire experience. On a small daily with 5000 or 10,000 circulation and a staff of only a few people, the newcomer does many things—reporting, editing, taking pictures, even helping out in other departments in emergencies. Newspapers with circulations of 100,000 or more frequently require five years of experience before they will consider hiring a candidate.

**Salaries.**   Newspaper salaries on large papers compare favorably with those in similar businesses and professions that require a good education and creative thinking. On small dailies and weeklies, where most newspaper people begin their careers, pay scales are rather low. Salaries vary widely, depending on the newspaper's size and locality. For example, while average base pay for the managing editor of a 10,000-circulation daily in 1994 was $30,160, a person holding the same position on a 100,000-circulation daily received $75,450.

Some leaders of the industry, recognizing the financial burden placed on beginning journalists, are urging newspapers to increase their starting pay level substantially. A Newspaper Association of America survey in 1994 showed the average daily reporter's entry-level base pay was $19,240.

Top minimum salaries for reporters were above the $900-per-week level in New York in the early 1990s, and directing editors received considerably more, but these levels are approached in only a few cities. The Newspaper Guild, which holds contracts covering minimum salaries and working conditions with about 150 news organizations, has played an important role in bringing up the level of newspaper salaries.

**News Services.**   The news services are among the finest training grounds in the field of mass communications for young people interested in a career of working with news. The work is challenging. It puts a premium on speed, conciseness, and judgment. These organizations have a tradition of hiring young writers of limited professional experience and training them. Since the turnover in personnel is relatively high, there are quite a few job openings each year, although the severe staff cutback at UPI has reduced the possibilities. A large increase in the number of women on news service staffs has occurred in recent years. The same is true of members of racial minorities.

A beginner is usually given routine stories to rewrite from the local newspapers, items to check by phone, and similar simple duties. The writer must learn to look outward from the local community, to weigh each story for its interest to readers in other cities. Because of the nature of the work, staff members do more editing and less original reporting than newspaper staffs do.

Those who stay with the news services for a number of years, as many do, usually become managers of small or medium-sized bureaus or are transferred into such large offices as those in Chicago and Washington. Members of the organizations' foreign staffs normally are given experience in New York or Washington before being sent abroad.

Salaries for news service work are approximately in line with those on large daily newspapers. Top salary scales for AP staff members in large cities are well above $700 per week.

**Syndicates.**   The feature syndicates do not offer very great potential for the young person seeking a job. Their editorial and sales staffs are small and mostly drawn from professional journalists with several years of editorial or business experience. Most of the artists and writers whose material is distributed by these organizations do their work outside the syndicate offices and send or bring it in for editing and approval. They work on a percentage arrangement with the syndicate, most commonly a 50-50 percentage split of the fees paid by the newspapers. Syndicate editing requires knowledge of the public taste, as well as the space problems, buying habits, and idiosyncracies of the various newspaper editors who are the customers for the syndicate products. Similarly, the odds against selling a comic strip, column, or other material to a syndicate for distribution are extremely poor. United Media receives between 5000 and 10,000 submissions per year, from which it introduces six or eight new features. King Features Syndicate annually releases approximately ten new features, from between 3000 and 3500 submissions.

## Magazines

The magazine industry provides interesting, stimulating, and generally well-paid jobs for thousands of persons. It is an especially attractive field for women, who command editorships and other key positions on many publications.

Robert E. Kenyon, Jr., former executive director of the American Society of Magazine Editors, points out that entry-level editorial jobs are hard to find unless applicants are well qualified. Says Kenyon:

> Entry-level jobs are in editing, not in writing. Too many aspirants in magazine journalism assume their first tasks will be in writing. That is not so. Your first magazine job is more likely to be in editing; that is, you will be reading proof, reviewing unsolicited manuscripts, checking facts, doing research for articles to be written by others, writing headlines, subheads, picture captions—but not cover lines. You can also expect some gofering chores. If you are lucky—and quite good—you might do an occasional column or a short by-lined piece. Writing assignments come along later, maybe.

Kenyon recommends that journalism majors take as many skill courses (reporting, writing, and editing) as possible. They should involve themselves deeply in campus journalism, having responsibilities as a senior editor of the college newspaper or magazine. In addition, internships or jobs should be spliced between course work. Liberal arts majors, Kenyon observes, should assume even greater responsibilities in campus journalism, internships, or jobs than journalism majors.

Selling a magazine some articles or stories also can open the door for jobs. The very fact that the editor buys the material indicates that he or she approves of the writer's work. Personal contacts developed in this editor–writer relationship sometimes lead to staff positions.

Much as metropolitan newspapers hire reporters and editors who have worked on small dailies, large magazines draw many staff members from company publications (see Chapter 16).

Editorial and business offices of most large national magazines are in New York and other eastern cities. Trade publication headquarters are situated throughout the United States, depending in part on the market being served. There are numerous editorial links between magazine and book publishing, and the movies as well. Some magazine material eventually finds its way into book form and even into films, one example being the article, "The Urban Cowboy." This leads to some movement of editorial workers from magazines to book publishing firms and occasionally in the other direction.

Other types of magazine jobs also can be rewarding. These include such tasks as working with the art director or editor; circulation, advertising, promotion, sales, and research; and production, including work with the printer. There are fewer applicants for these jobs than for writing and editing positions.

**Salaries.** Editorial managers of consumer and business magazines earned an average salary of $67,082 in 1995, according to the eleventh annual survey conducted by *Folio* magazine. Editors received an average salary of $49,900; senior editors, $44,500; managing editors, $41,900; and art directors, $44,600. Bonuses augmented many salaries.

Salaries were considerably higher in the Northeast, the center of magazine publishing, than elsewhere in the nation. Job experience, circulation size, and number of editorial pages were the other chief determinants of salaries. The pay offered to entry-level college graduates was in line with that offered by other media.

## Book Publishing

Many college graduates begin their careers in the trade editorial offices of book publishing firms. Often they are assigned the task of reading and making initial judgments about the merits of unsolicited manuscripts that arrive with great frequency. Some become copy and proof editors and research facts in encyclopedias and other reference works. As their judgment is corroborated by senior editors, they are assigned greater responsibilities. Editorial assistants usually start at about $14,000 per year. Successful senior editors earn $30,000 to $50,000 per year.

Young people who enjoy travel may choose to become sales representatives of the college textbook divisions of publishing houses. Their starting salaries generally range between $13,000 and $18,000 annually. All their business expenses are paid while they are on the road. With sales bonuses, experienced representatives may earn $30,000 or more in a year. Some men and women enjoy lifelong careers as sales representatives or managers. Others move into the office, where they most likely will put their road experience to work in the editorial, sales, advertising, marketing, or production departments. Eventually they may become department managers, later perhaps officers or directors of the company, with salaries in the $70,000 to $100,000 range. Hard-headed business acumen is essential for such advancement.

While some people, as noted, ascend the publishing ladder as editors, others move into marketing and publicity jobs. They write news and feature copy, help plan marketing campaigns, prepare advertising materials, compose jacket blurbs, arrange radio and television personal appearances and lecture tours, and otherwise exercise ingenuity in promoting the sale of books. For these services they may be paid from $14,000 to as high as $30,000 annually. Hundreds of persons freelance as copyeditors, indexers, and proofreaders at home, earning between $6 and $13 per hour. Most of them have had previous in-house experience.

**Qualifications.**   A good education, intelligence, talent in communicating with people, excitement about books, and an ability to keep abreast of the latest developments in many phases of life, particularly in the area of one's specialization, are prime characteristics of a good editor. One need not—and probably should not—be a creative writer. Persons with highly individual ideas and tastes are unwilling to remain anonymous and to play second fiddle to authors with quixotic personalities. The good editor has the capacity to deal in a calm, unruffled fashion with everyone, including the occasional prima donna whose genius or near-genius and ability to attract a large reading public may spell the difference between profit and loss in a publishing year. A sound grasp of the fundamentals of business practice is essential in today's financially-oriented publishing business.

Whether one wishes to become a general editor, a copyeditor, a designer, a sales representative, an advertising specialist, or a marketing and promotion person, the college graduate who aspires to a career in book publishing will profit by an education, as well as experience, in mass communications. He or she should seek to acquire a sound background in a major discipline—in literature, history, languages, the natural and social sciences, or philosophy—in fact, in any of the areas of knowledge that comprise a liberal arts education. The aim is to learn to think, find information, and acquire the ability to solve problems and make decisions. Professional education will not be overlooked, for the insights, skills, and fundamental knowledge gained in classrooms and laboratories of a school of mass communications should prove of inestimable value throughout one's career.

## Radio

Success as a performer in radio depends heavily on the kind of vocal personality the individual projects. If it is vibrant and distinctive, a voice the listener will remember, the beginning performer has a much better prospect of advancing to the large stations. A performer's physical appearance is of no importance except in occasional public appearances, but a lively, friendly personality is usually evident in a person's voice.

Voice quality, however, is not enough. Professional coaching can improve vocal technique and confidence, but it cannot create intelligence and a good command of English. Successful radio newscasters, talk-show hosts, and disc jockeys have quick minds and an ability to articulate their thoughts smoothly in ad-lib situations.

Approximately 18,000 radio news jobs exist on commercial stations, according to surveys made by Professor Vernon A. Stone of the University of Missouri for the Radio Television News Directors Association. Annual turnover in staff membership at stations is 30 percent.

The advice for a person beginning a career in radio is much the same as that for newspapers: start small. Basing his opinion on his surveys for the news directors association, Professor Stone has stated, "In summary, a college graduate who wants to start out doing air work or getting out on the scene of news stories is advised to seek a first job in a radio market of less than 1 million population or a TV market smaller than the top 50."

Most young people begin work at low-powered radio stations, then move to larger ones as they gain experience. In addition to reading and reporting news, they may fill in as disc jockeys during weekends and night hours. Not only must beginners acquire confidence and a sense of timing, they must learn production techniques and the fundamentals of radio engineering. At small stations, some announcers sell advertising during their off-air hours.

A recent survey by Professor Stone showed a wide disparity between salaries received by radio newspeople in small markets and those paid for similar work in major markets. The typical radio reporter received $30,750 in a major market and $11,740 in a small market.

Sales is an attractive, well-paying aspect of radio work. A successful salesperson needs several attributes: ability to write a commercial that attracts the listener's attention and sells the product or service, skill at preparing and explaining research material that will convince a prospective client to advertise on this particular station, and detailed knowledge of the station's programming in order to place specific commercials in the most suitable time positions. Work in sales leads to executive positions on the business staff, including that of station manager.

Announcers on small stations may function at times as station engineers. This task involves at least a rudimentary knowledge of electricity and knowing what meters to read and what switches to turn to keep the station on the air.

The ability to write radio news copy and advertising messages is important. As in television writing, the basic technique is to compose conversational English that rings true to the ear. Such writing avoids complex and inverted constructions and uses simple, declarative sentences and broken phrases in the manner in which people normally talk. Also, it uses repetition more heavily than does writing for print, especially for commercials.

Job applications for on-the-air personnel normally include demonstration tapes. A prospective employer wishes to hear the vocal styles of applicants in order to screen the candidates and select a few for personal interviews. Samples of writing style may be requested as well.

Women have a large and growing role in radio, especially in news. They comprise about one-third of the newspeople in radio, according to the Stone survey. On about one-fourth of commercial radio station staffs, they serve as news directors.

The growth of minority representation on radio news staffs has been much slower but is improving. Minority newspeople tend to be employed at stations in major markets that have large staffs.

High among the career goals of radio personnel are the positions of program director, news director, and station manager. Salaries for these posts vary widely according to the size of the station and the experience of the individual. The Stone survey showed the salary of a typical radio news director in a major market to be $37,350. Big-city disc jockey stars have incomes of $100,000 or more, depending on the agreements they have with station managements. A popular air personality attracts advertisers willing to pay higher rates in order to have their messages on the show, and the performer may earn extra fees from personal appearances. The classified advertising columns of *Broadcasting & Cable* magazine provide a guide to job opportunities and requirements in radio.

## Popular Music

Young people who wish to enter the popular music business for careers in management or writing have no clear path to follow. Some management personnel are drawn from the ranks of former performers: knowledge of electronics, sales, and marketing is more valuable than traditional training in mass communication processes. Most pop-rock songs performed by groups today are written by a member of the group or its entourage. One nontechnical, nonmusical type of job opportunity is in the promotion department of record producers and distributors, advertising new recordings and performers and urging radio and television stations to play specific new releases. The individuals best suited for such work are extroverted, personable, and aggressive, with enthusiasm for and knowledge of contemporary music.

Individuals or groups desiring to record their performances for sale submit demonstration tapes to record production companies. Chances of initial success are best with small independent producers, but competition is intense and the odds against acceptance are heavy.

## Television

Young people hoping for careers in television may find them in three areas: on-the-air performing in news and entertainment programs, production, and sales and business management.

Starting one's career at a small station is almost essential. Competition for jobs is intense, so most stations of medium and large size usually hire persons with experience. A beginner should not shun an opportunity to take what appears to be a menial job; getting a job on the "inside" is what counts. Numerous high-ranking executives of the networks started their careers in such jobs.

Approximately 20,500 jobs exist in the news departments of American commercial television stations. Constant turnover occurs as individuals advance in their careers from small stations to larger ones.

Women hold about one-third of those jobs, according to a survey by Professor Stone. They occupied the news director position at nearly 20 percent of the TV stations in the early 1990s. The survey found female representation among news directors to be greater at independent stations than at network affiliates. Approximately 40 percent of news anchors were women.

After a long period of stagnation, the percentage of minority employees at TV stations rose during the late 1980s, and by the early 1990s had passed 17 percent. With growing recognition of the diversity in television audiences, and the consequent need for multiethnic news staffs, this percentage was expected to rise.

In the news department, the entry level in a small station is that of a beat or general assignment reporter. Beginners have a few on-the-air appearances with news stories. As they develop a screen personality and prove to be accurate and dependable, the news director may allow them to sit in as weekend or vacation relief anchorpersons on a local news show. The top job in news at a station is held by the news director. When an applicant seeks a position on a larger station, the videotapes of on-the-air performances that he or she submits will play a critical part in the prospective employer's decision. A nationwide study by three University of Illinois researchers disclosed that broadcast newspeople change jobs more frequently than those in any other news occupation.

Jobs on news staffs of the networks go to people who have learned their trade at individual stations over a period of several years. The three major networks among them have approximately 200 on-air personnel.

Another major job on a TV station staff is that of the program director, who handles programming policy and scheduling. The upward route to this job is usually through the production or business staffs, rarely through the news department. The production department puts together locally produced shows and commercials, giving beginners an opportunity to work behind the cameras with cue cards, timing signals, and props, and also in the control booth.

On the business side, novices eventually may become account executives selling commercial time. To do this well, the salesperson needs technical knowledge of TV operations, understanding of the station's audience characteristics, and skill to match the time spots the station has to sell with the needs and budgets of potential advertisers. The promotion manager's role is to publicize programs that the station will present and build a friendly public image for the station.

At the top of the hierarchy is the station manager, who usually has had experience both on the air and in production.

Growth of cable television has increased job opportunities, especially in sales and management. For persons with artistic skill, the swiftly increasing application of computer graphics opens new possibilities in both broadcast and cable television.

**Salaries.**  Salaries in television vary widely, depending on the size of the station. Much attention is paid to the salaries of the star network anchors, which substantially exceed $1 million a year; however, across the whole spectrum of TV operations, average salaries are on a much more down-to-earth basis. For comparison, anchors on small stations receive less than $30,000. Salaries of news directors run at approximately $30,000 at small stations to well above $100,000 in major markets. Anchors and star reporters on metropolitan network affiliate stations often receive more than $100,000.

## Photography and Graphics

**Photography.**  Stimulating opportunities await young people who decide to enter the photographic aspect of mass communications. The work at times is exciting, and always interesting; each day brings new assignments that give the photographer room for creative expression and the use of professional techniques.

Anyone contemplating such a career should be healthy and possessed of physical stamina because the work can be dangerous on assignments such as fires and riots, and the hours frequently are irregular. The photographer must carry equipment and guard it against loss or damage. Both physical and emotional exhaustion may affect a photographer involved in a long, difficult assignment.

Career photographic communicators also should have initiative, energy, and creative motivation. A degree of aggressiveness is necessary, but it should be tempered by thoughtfulness. Visual imagination is essential—the ability to see various interpretations of a subject in a given visual form. Photographers should have an interest in design and the knack of examining pictures for each one's special qualities. They must be curious about the world around them and have an ability to mix with people. Being able to sketch scenes and individuals roughly is an important asset, but by no means a requirement.

A college graduate with photographic skills may start on a daily newspaper with a salary from $12,000 to $14,000 per year. An experienced newspaper photographer, with five years or more on the job, may earn from $18,000 to $30,000 annually in a large city. The starting salary for a college graduate photographer on a local television station will vary from $10,000 to $12,000; after five years the range is $14,000 to $22,000. A staff photographer for a general or specialized magazine can expect to earn $10,000 to $15,000 in early career years. The salary may rise rapidly, even faster than in newspaper or television work. Top professionals on *National Geographic* earn $50,000 or more.

Some photographers prefer to freelance: that is, to work for themselves and sell their pictures to clients either directly or through picture agencies. The agencies take a commission of 25 to 35 percent of the selling price of the picture. A freelancer also may work on contract, under which a magazine guarantees an agreed-upon earning in return for a commitment to be available to it on call. A freelancer usually begins as a staff photographer, then branches out after establishing a reputation and a group of clients. Freelance photographers can earn around $40,000 per year if very successful, although they start much lower in their early years. To be a successful freelancer, one must have good business sense and know how to market pictures as well as take them. The American Society of Magazine Photographers sets minimum rates for its members. The rate exceeds $350 per day plus expenses.

**Graphics.** Increased demand for computer graphics designers and artists has produced a shortage in the field. Visual imagination, of course, is important. An increasing number of computer graphics specialists are produced by schools of journalism and mass communication. Alerted by the relatively sudden demand that they master new computer graphic uses, thousands of future journalists, television and film employees, photographers, and advertising and public relations personnel are acquiring limited or substantial skills, either while in school or during their first months or years of employment. Others are entering the field from art departments or from institutions such as the School of Visual Arts in New York City.

Designers aiming for mass media employment should acquire a knowledge of journalistic practices since they will be called on to help make editorial decisions. A large number of newspaper and magazine editors acquire expert visual capabilities through years of experience in planning and laying out pages, by attending workshops and seminars and by studying design at nearby institutions. Typically, newcomers to the computer design field are tested for their news intuition by being asked to work out ideas for infographics. Other media, as well as advertising and public relations employers, have developed their own devices to screen applicants for design positions.

Opportunities have been steadily expanding for employment of graphic specialists by corporations, not-for-profit organizations, advertising agencies, and public relations firms. Computer-generated graphics enhance slide presentations, transparencies, annual reports, news releases reporting corporate sales and earnings, and other such materials.

The new breed of graphic journalist—one who has artistic talent, computer skills, and journalistic abilities—has been commanding an entry-level salary of $30,000 and up on medium-size and large newspapers. After a few years' experience, pay jumps to about $50,000 and may top out at about $70,000, according to Tony Majeri, creative director of the Chicago *Tribune*, and Newspaper Association of America surveys. Majeri predicted that these high levels likely will drop once the generation of computer-literate youth moves up in the market.

## Film

Breaking into commercial entertainment filmmaking requires technical knowledge, a creative flair, and often a stroke of good luck. Since the major studios and independent producers make roughly 400 films per year, their need for writers, directors, producers, and other innovative talent is limited. Work on production of television shows and commercials is another goal for properly trained beginners. As described earlier in this book, sponsored films offer another, broader, point of entry into the industry.

Competition for jobs is intense. Approximately 900 U.S. colleges and universities offer film or television courses: a survey by the American Film Institute reported 35,000 students enrolled in these courses. Three film schools in the Los Angeles area—University of Southern California, UCLA, and the American Film Institute—are especially popular because of their proximity to Hollywood production. Only 98 graduate students were admitted to the UCLA cinema school out of 800 applicants in a typical recent year. Total enrollment at the USC film school averages 600. An increase in the number of films being made and the emphasis on youth-oriented movies have led Hollywood producers to hire a larger number of writers directly from these and other film schools.

Older writers complain about losing work because producers are giving so many assignments to young writers who may bring new ideas and approaches.

Women have had a difficult time breaking into motion picture production, but the situation is improving slightly. A few, such as Penny Marshall, Martha Coolidge, Joan Tewksbury, Kathleen Kennedy, and Amy Heckerling, have reached the top as successful directors of feature pictures; others are earning attention as directors in television. Yet a recent survey by the Directors Guild of America showed only 5 percent of U.S. feature films were directed by women. At the craft level, women gradually are pushing through all-male union barriers to work as camera operators, lighting specialists, and assistant directors.

By working first in minor jobs in television or sponsored films, or making self-financed personal films, women can accumulate examples of their skill to use in seeking higher-level positions. Prospects are better with independent movie producers than at major studios. The organization Women in Film helps aspirants find jobs.

Both racial minorities and women have been aided by federal equal opportunity regulations regarding hiring, promotion, and pay. Nevertheless, despite the recent upsurge in African American movies, the National Association for the Advancement of Colored People contends that Hollywood still discriminates against black workers. Of the more than 7500 film and television members of the Directors Guild of America, only about 160 are black. Of these, about 145 are directors and the others are mainly assistant directors and production managers.

For those film workers who break into salaried jobs, the pay compares favorably with that in other mass communication industries and professions, and almost limitless financial returns may be achieved by highly creative, productive, and lucky individuals. In no other area of mass communications are success less predictable and the potential rewards greater.

## Advertising

Men and women with a wide variety of interests and talents qualify for careers in advertising. As the American Association of Advertising Agencies puts it:

> Whether your career interests lie in marketing or management, design or decimals, psychology or public service, fashion or finance, computers or copywriting, people or products, ideas or imagery, the medium or the message, personnel or photography, communications or commerce, sales or show business, math or music, graphics or global markets, packaging or printing, research or retail promotion, television . . . or you name it . . . the multifaceted world of advertising offers opportunities to get involved in all these areas—and more.

The advertising world is made up of people who have creative, analytical, selling, or management abilities. Successful advertising people are said to be constructive, adaptable, and eternally curious. They must be constructively optimistic because they are called on to originate ideas and to initiate action—to visualize in full operation something that has not yet been started. They must be adaptable because of the infinitely varied problems and the different types of persons they meet almost daily. And they must have an unceasing interest in people and things and the operation of business in general and the industry in particular. They must keep abreast of developments in advertising and remain keen and interested students in many fields throughout their careers.

Imagination, foresight in sensing trends, the ability to reason analytically, a sense of humor, and a sense of form are characteristics of advertising people that are frequently cited. Also emphasized is a broad general education in the liberal arts, obtained either in conjunction with the offerings of schools of communication or commerce or entirely in the humanities, social sciences, or sciences. Generally, professional preparation in advertising opens doors most quickly.

Young persons with talent and ability rise rapidly. More than one-fifth of the agencies that belong to the American Association of Advertising Agencies (4As) are run by executives who were less than 40 years of age when they stepped up to the chief executive's chair.

Women play important roles in nearly every phase of advertising. Industry reports indicate that about 50 percent of all agency employees are women, and almost one-third of the total are professionals. Most of the trainees brought into agencies from university campuses are female. Many female graduates go to work immediately as copywriters for agencies and for department stores and other companies. A number of women sell space and time for the media, with most newspapers employing virtually all women for desk jobs in their classified advertising departments.

A number of national advertising campaigns have been masterminded by women functioning as account executives. The advertising directors of some of the largest department stores are female, and women have also achieved success as media buyers for agencies. More and more women are being made vice-presidents of agencies, and a number of very successful women now head firms of their own.

Minorities are gaining increased footholds in advertising and allied industries. One survey revealed that minorities accounted for about 7 percent of professional positions and about 20 percent of nonprofessional jobs in the 4As agencies. The board of directors of the 4As, stating that "it is vital to seek out, recognize, and employ the best talents available wherever they may be found," has supported a successful summer internship program for minority professional candidates as well as basic courses for creative people and government-connected programs for nonprofessionals.

Numerous career opportunities are also available in other advertising and related areas such as *direct marketing, outdoor* (billboards), *business papers, specialty, sales promotion, trade shows, premium and incentive,* and *point-of-purchase.*

**Salaries.**   The chief executive officers of U.S. advertising agencies received an average base salary of $129,000 in 1995, according to an Advertising Age survey. Average salaries for other positions include: creative director, $90,000; art director, $51,000; chief copywriter, $56,000; media director, $58,000; senior account executive, $71,000; and account executive, $44,000.

**Direct marketing**
Exchange of goods and services resulting from direct communication with a target audience

**Specialty advertising**
Useful articles of merchandise imprinted with an advertiser's message and distributed without obligation to the recipient

**Premium and incentive**
Marketing category offering coupons and other rewards as inducement for purchase of a product or service

**Point-of-purchase advertising**
Packaging and display of products directed to a consumer in close proximity to the merchandise

Many of the 450 firms responding to the survey paid additional compensation in such forms as performance awards, stock options, use of company cars, and even child-care reimbursement and parental leaves. Salary levels were highest in the West.

As their skills and experience increase, advertising specialists generally find that they possess knowledge for which there is great demand. In moving from one agency to another, often taking accounts with them, they naturally move into higher pay brackets. A somewhat similar promotion situation is true in media and company advertising departments. The top advertising executives of newspapers, magazines, other media, and client companies generally earn about two-thirds of what their counterparts with the agencies receive. Other factors, however, such as security and fringe benefits, often more than make up for the lower salaries.

In the general magazine field, advertising directors earn from $16,000 to $200,000, depending mostly on circulation. Business paper advertising managers earn from $18,000 to $43,000. Advertising managers for newspapers are paid about the same. Commercial managers for radio and television stations earn from $13,000 to $38,000.

Beginning salaries for college graduates in both print and broadcast media and in company advertising departments range from $15,000 to $21,500. The range for those who have earned master's degrees is about $2000 higher. Once they have proven their worth, qualified advertising people generally move upward rapidly.

## Public Relations

After the 1990s recession, opportunities for employment in beginning jobs were relatively plentiful for those qualified to practice public relations; in fact, hundreds of entry-level jobs, such as those with charitable organizations, hospitals, and small business firms, have been filled each year by people with less than desirable preparation for their tasks. Many graduates still are hired directly out of school. Some, however, must be prepared to work in geographical areas or fields of public relations that are not their first choices. This is true, of course, for college graduates in many other fields; it is the time-honored path followed by many as they begin their careers.

Public relations is an attractive field for women. About 48 percent of the members of the Public Relations Society of America are female, as are three of every four members of the Public Relations Student Society of America. Women comprise 59 percent of the membership of the International Association of Business Communicators.

More than 350 colleges and universities provide some instruction in public relations. Schools of journalism and mass communications offer the greatest number of public relations degree programs, although they have been joined in recent years by an increasing number of speech communication departments. Most business schools teach public relations only as a theoretical unit within management programs but do not provide the instruction essential for specialized work in the field.

**Qualifications.**  Students who achieve undergraduate degrees in public relations are most readily employed; those who then obtain master's degrees in communications, business, or a related field such as economics, sociology, psychology, or another liberal arts area, find greater opportunities.

Many other journalism and communications majors, as well as those from traditional liberal arts programs, are being employed in beginning public relations jobs—provided they have the vital ability to write and speak well. One of the few things that experienced practitioners agree on is that the primary qualification for anyone wishing to succeed in the field is the ability to articulate: to write clearly and with facility and to express oneself well orally.

Both research ability and creative ingenuity are important. Practitioners must know how to dig out facts and then have the imagination to make the most of them by applying innovative approaches and fresh ideas to their tasks.

Practitioners also need the ability to empathize with other people, to anticipate and understand their points of view. In the managerial structure, the public relations executive bears the responsibility for estimating how a particular policy or action on the part of management will be greeted by the publics affected. More than intuitive ability is necessary here. Whatever inherent abilities practitioners may have in this area of human understanding should be supplemented by background education in the social sciences, so that their estimates of human reactions will be more than mere guesses. Of course, in many situations, when the magnitude of the problem justifies such research, practitioners will supplement their own interpretation of the situation with formal surveys of public opinion and attitudes.

A group of public relations executives listed the following, in descending order, as "very important" attributes for job seekers: ability to write, speaking skills, professionalism, maturity, poise, appearance, grade-point average, social graces, part-time work, college credit internship, recommendations, and work on campus media.

Students should not wait until graduation to acquire experience. Unless they build up a portfolio through internships, work on campus media, part-time jobs, or club or class campaigns, many likely will not find employment soon after graduation.

**Salaries.**  Readers of the *Public Relations Journal* earned a median annual salary of $56,556 in 1992, a 6.5 percent increase over 1991, according to 2019 responses to a questionnaire sent to subscribers.

The median entry-level salary for assistant account executives was $22,060 at corporations, $20,950 at government/health care/nonprofit organizations, and $18,230 at public relations firms. The highest median for all levels was $52,333 at corporations, compared with $46,863 at public relations firms, and $41,421 at government/health care/nonprofit organizations.

The highest-paying fields, in order, were industrial/manufacturing, utilities, scientific-technical, counseling firms, media/communications, and financial/insurance. Practitioners at miscellaneous nonprofits/museums and religious/charitable organizations earned substantially less. The median salary for men in all fields was 47 percent higher than for women.

## International Communications

Many students interested in international communications work will most likely find their first opportunities when, as beginning reporters and editors, they cover assignments involving international matters and, as gatekeepers, edit international news stories. As magazine and freelance writers, they may be assigned to stories with an international flavor. Those assuming advertising and public relations duties with business corporations will need to work their way into the international departments of those companies. The tourism and development divisions of state government may afford an entry point. U.S. Foreign Service examinations are the beginning requirement for those seeking federal government positions leading to international communications work. Military service often provides yet another opportunity.

For those who seek foreign assignments with newspapers, magazines, radio and television networks, and news services, the road to those assignments most likely will be long, with service first in the United States to acquire experience and establish a personnel record recommending the applicant for overseas service. The same is true for advertising and public relations people who wish to work abroad.

Students interested in international communications careers are advised to direct their programs of study toward obtaining substantive knowledge in international aspects of the social sciences, humanities, business, law, or other areas closely related to their individual talents and preferences. The choices are so numerous that career objectives should be narrowed quickly. For orientation, course work in international communications is highly desirable. Graduate study undoubtedly would be an asset.

The same necessity for early career decisions also applies to languages. Students should learn to speak and read one foreign language as well as they can. They may depend on later intensive study or living experience in another country for the language mastery that will be necessary.

# BIBLIOGRAPHY

This is a selected, annotated bibliography of books dealing with mass communications and journalism. It is organized to correspond with the six principal parts, five Issue discussions, and 17 chapters of this book.

It is the authors' aim to introduce readers to some of the basic books that, if they have the time and interest to explore them, will take them beyond the necessarily limited syntheses of an introductory survey of mass communications. A student reader who has the interest and opportunity to elect further studies in the field will encounter many of these books again in advanced courses; if the student goes no further, this bibliography will provide a personal reading list for more detailed examination of various facets of the field. It is in no sense an all-inclusive bibliography; for that purpose the reader is referred to Eleanor Blum and Frances Wilhoit, *Mass Media Bibliography: Reference, Research, and Reading* (Urbana: University of Illinois Press, 1990). Its 2100 annotated entries cover general communications, newspapers, broadcasting, film, magazines, books, advertising, and public relations. For more depth, particularly in historical areas and biographies, see the 3147 entries in Warren C. Price's *The Literature of Journalism: An Annotated Bibliography* (Minneapolis: University of Minnesota Press, 1959) and the 2172 entries in a 10-year supplement to it compiled by Price and Calder M. Pickett, *An Annotated Journalism Bibliography* (1970).

*Communication Booknotes*, edited since 1969 by Christopher H. Sterling and published bimonthly by the Center for Advanced Studies in Telecommunications, Ohio State University, offers extensive listings and annotations of books in all communication and media areas. Some currently published bibliographies include Richard A. Schwarzlose, *Newspapers: A Reference Guide* (Westport, CT: Greenwood Press, 1987), including essays and bibliographies in all areas; Wm. David Sloan, *American Journalism History: An Annotated Bibliography* (Greenwood Press, 1989); Joseph P. McKerns, *News Media and Public Policy: An Anno-*

tated *Bibliography* (New York: Garland, 1985); Donald G. Godfrey, *Reruns on File: A Guide to Electronic Media Archives* (Hillsdale, NJ: Erlbaum, 1991); Robert Armour, *Film: A Reference Guide* (Greenwood Press, 1980); George Rehrauer, *The Macmillan Film Bibliography* (New York: Macmillan, 1982); Bruce A. Austin, *The Film Audience: An International Bibliography of Research* (Metuchen, NJ: Scarecrow Press, 1983); Fred K. Paine and Nancy E. Paine, *Magazines: A Bibliography of Their Analysis with Annotations* (Scarecrow Press, 1987); Arthur F. Wertheim, *American Popular Culture: A Historical Bibliography* (New York: ABC-Clio Information Services, 1984); Benjamin F. Shearer and Marilyn Buxford, *Communications and Society: A Bibliography on Communications Technologies and Their Social Impact* (Beverly Hills, CA: Sage, 1983); Albert N. Greco, editor, *The Graphic Arts Bibliography* (New York: New York University, 1984); and Roland E. and Isabel Wolseley, *The Journalist's Bookshelf* (Indianapolis: R.J. Berg, 1986). See also the bibliographies in research journals listed below.

A remarkably useful encyclopedia, by Robert V. Hudson, is *Mass Media: A Chronological Encyclopedia of Television, Radio, Motion Pictures, Magazines, Newspapers, and Books in the United States* (New York: Garland, 1987). Its detailed entries are given by years, organized in 16 sections from 1638 to 1985. A 75-page index is vital. Equally useful is a biographical dictionary edited by Joseph P. McKerns, *Biographical Dictionary of American Journalism* (Greenwood Press, 1989), which includes 500 persons in all media fields.

*The Encyclopedia of American Journalism* (New York: Facts on File, 1983), edited by Donald Paneth, contains more than 1000 entries covering print and electronic media, documentaries and newsreels, and also bibliographies. Other valuable reference-research guides are Jo A. Cates, *Journalism: A Guide to the Reference Literature* (Englewood, CO: Libraries Unlimited, 1990); *The Aspen Handbook on the Media*, edited by William L. Rivers, Wallace Thompson, and Michael J. Nyhan (New York: Praeger, 1977); *The Mass Media: Aspen Guide to Communication Industry Trends*, edited by Christopher H. Sterling and Timothy R. Haight (Praeger, 1978); and its update, *Electronic Media: A Guide to Trends in Broadcasting and Newer Technologies, 1920–1983*, edited by Christopher H. Sterling (Praeger, 1984). *Journalism and Mass Communication Abstracts* (published by AEJMC) is an annual annotated listing of Ph.D. and M.A. theses; *Communication Abstracts* (Beverly Hills, CA: Sage) reports on research in the field.

This bibliography also lists the principal journals and trade publications with which students of mass communications should be familiar, and in a few instances makes references to articles in them. In cases where books have gone through revised editions, the date given is for the most recent revision. In subsequent listings of a book, place and date of publication are not repeated.

## Periodicals, Annual Publications, and Directories

### General Research Journals

*Journalism and Mass Communication Quarterly* Published by the Association for Education in Journalism and Mass Communication, devoted to research articles in journalism and mass communications. Contains extensive book reviews and bibliographies of articles in American and foreign journals.

*Public Opinion Quarterly* Emphasizes political and psychological phases of communication. Book reviews and summaries of public opinion polls. Published by the American Association for Public Opinion Research.

*Journal of Communication* Research Quarterly focusing on methodology; material in speech and interpersonal communication; book reviews. Published by the International Communication Association.

*Communication Research* International quarterly focusing on research methodology. Published by Sage Publications.

*Human Communication Research* Quarterly concerned with the empirical study of diverse communication subfields. Published by the International Communication Association.

*Public Opinion* Bimonthly journal; articles, reports on public opinion polls. Published by the American Enterprise Institute.

*AV Communication Review* Reports on research activities and findings in the communication area. Published quarterly by the Association for Educational Communications and Technology.

*Quarterly Journal of Speech* Research articles, book reviews. Published by the Speech Communication Association.

*Communication Monographs* Published serially by the Speech Communication Association for research findings falling between article and book lengths.

*Critical Studies in Mass Communication* Quarterly focusing on critical scholarship in the field. Published by the Speech Communication Association.

*Telematics and Informatics* International research quarterly in applied telecommunications and information sciences. Published by Pergamon Press.

*Media Studies Journal* Published quarterly by the Freedom Forum Media Studies Center, Columbia University. Scholarly discussion of media issues, research findings.

*Journalism and Mass Communication Monographs* Published serially by the Association for Education in Journalism and Mass Communication, beginning in 1966, for research findings falling between article and book lengths; approximately quarterly.

*Mass Comm Review* Quarterly publication of the Mass Communications and Society Division of the Association for Education in Journalism and Mass Communication; articles.

*Journalism History* Research quarterly; articles, notes, book reviews for mass communications history. Published by the University of Nevada, Las Vegas, with the support of the Association of Schools of Journalism and Mass Communication and the AEJMC History Division.

*American Journalism* Quarterly journal of the American Journalism Historians Association; articles, reviews.

*Media Management Review* Annual; articles that can be applied by practicing media managers. Edited by Charles Warner, University of Missouri School of Journalism.

*Journal of Popular Culture* Quarterly publication with wide interests in field; articles, book reviews. Published by Bowling Green State University in cooperation with the Popular Culture Association.

*American Quarterly* Journal of the American Studies Association; articles, reviews.

*Journal of Mass Media Ethics* Semiannual; articles, essays. Published by Lawrence Erlbaum Associates.

*Journal of Media Economics* Quarterly. Published by Lawrence Erlbaum Associates.

*Media Ethics Update* Semiannual; articles. Published by Emerson College, Boston.

*Southwestern Mass Communication Journal* Semiannual; articles. Published at Trinity University by the Southwest Education Council for Journalism and Mass Communication.

## General Professional Journals

Professional journals with general-interest articles on press problems: *Nieman Reports* (Nieman Foundation); *Columbia Journalism Review* (Columbia University Graduate School of Journalism); *Quill* (Society of Professional Journalists); *The Professional Communicator* (Women in Communications, Inc.); *Journalism and Mass Communication Educator* (Association of Schools of Journalism and Mass Communication); *Communication: Journalism Education Today* (Journalism Education Association); *Community College Journalist* (Community College Journalism Association); *American Journalism Review* (College of Journalism, University of Maryland); *News Media and the Law* (Reporters Committee for Freedom of the Press); *Communications and the Law* (Meckler Communications); *Media History Digest (Editor & Publisher); Media Report to Women* (Women's Institute for Freedom of the Press); and *nfpw* (National Federation of Press Women).

General Directories.   *Gale Directory of Publications and Broadcast Media* (formerly *Ayer Directory of Publications*). Includes newspapers, magazines, journals, radio and television stations, and cable systems.

## International Journals

Sources for those interested in international communications and media include the following publications:

Research Journals and Publications.   *Gazette* (Department of Mass Communications, University of Amsterdam); *The Nordicom Review of Nordic Mass Communication Research* (Department of Political Science, University of Göteberg); *Canadian Journal of Communications* (Ottawa); *Communication Research Trends* (Centre for the Study of Communication and Culture, London); *European Research* (European Society for Opinion and Market Research); *European Journal of Communication* (Sage Publications); *The Media Reporter* (quarterly, London); *Journal of Media Law and Practice* (quarterly, Frank Cass, London); *Media Bulletin* (European Institute for the Media, University of Manchester); *Chronicle of International Communication* (International Communication Projects, Inc.); *Intermedia* (International Institute of Communications); *Media Asia* and *Asian Journal of Communication* (Asian Mass Communication Research and Information Centre, Singapore); *The Communicator* (Indian Institute of Mass Communication); *Europa Yearbook; Media International; Television International; Space Communication and Broadcasting.*

Professional Publications.   *World Press Review* (general monthly); *IPI Report* (International Press Institute); *FIEJ Bulletin* (International Federation of Newspaper Publishers); *IFJ Information* (International Federation of Journalists);

*IAPA News* (Inter American Press Association); *International Communication Bulletin* (AEJMC); *WACC Journal* (World Association for Christian Communication); *East-West Perspectives* (East-West Center, Hawaii); *AMCB Bulletin* (Asian Mass Communication Centre, Singapore); *Indian Press* (New Delhi).

**Broadcasting.** *EBU Review* (European Broadcasting Union); *Telecommunication Journal* (International Telecommunication Union); *OIRT Information* (International Radio and Television Organization); *Combroad* (Commonwealth Broadcasting Conference).

**Directories.** George Kurian, editor, *World Press Encyclopedia* (New York: Facts on File, 1982); *World Communications Report* (Paris: UNESCO, 1989); *Ulrich's International Periodicals Directory* (New York: R. R. Bowker); *Editor & Publisher International YearBook* (daily newspapers), and the British-published *Benn's Press Directory* and *Willing's Press Guide*; *Television Factbook* (*TV Digest*, U.S.A.) and *World Radio-TV Handbook* (Denmark); *Japanese Press* (Japan Newspaper Publishers and Editors Association).

## Newspapers

**Research Journals.** *Newspaper Research Journal* (Newspaper Division, Association for Education in Journalism and Mass Communication).

**Professional Journals.** *Presstime* (Newspaper Association of America); *The American Editor* (formerly *ASNE Bulletin*, American Society of Newspaper Editors); *Masthead* (National Conference of Editorial Writers); *APME News* (Associated Press Managing Editors Association).

**Trade Journals.** *Editor & Publisher*, whose focus is on the daily newspaper and general industry problems, but which reports on advertising, marketing, and public relations areas; *News Inc.*, focused on inside news of newspaper publishing; *Publishers' Auxiliary* (National Newspaper Association), primarily covering weeklies and small dailies; *Guild Reporter* (Newspaper Guild); *Circulation Management*; *Inland Printer*, for the printing industry.

**Annual Publications.** *APME Red Book*, containing the record of the annual meeting and the reports of the continuing studies committee of the Associated Press Managing Editors Association; *Problems of Journalism*, covering the annual meeting of the American Society of Newspaper Editors; *Media Guide*, a critical review of the print media, edited by Jude Wanniski.

**Directories.** *Editor & Publisher International YearBook*, source for statistics and information about dailies; *National Directory of Weekly Newspapers* (National Newspaper Association); *News Media Yellow Book of Washington and New York*.

## Television, Radio, Cable, and Video

**Research Journals.** *Journal of Broadcasting & Electronic Media* (Broadcast Education Association); *Television Quarterly* (National Academy of Television Arts and Sciences); *Public Telecommunications Review* (National Association of Educational Broadcasters); *Historical Journal of Film, Radio, and Television*.

Professional Publications.   *RTNDA Communicator* (Radio Television News Directors Association); *Access* (National Citizens Committee on Broadcasting); *Channels of Communications; Television; World Broadcast News; Telecommunications; COMSAT Magazine; Satellite Communications; Electronic Media; Perspective on Cable Television* (National Cable Television Association); *Cable Marketing; Cable Communications* (Canada); *TV Communications* (cable); *Videocassette and CATV Newsletter; Feedback* (Broadcast Education Association).

Trade Publications.   *Broadcasting & Cable*, the voice of those industries; *TV Guide; Current*, for public telecommunications; *The Dial*, for public television; *Variety*, voice of the entertainment world; *Billboard*, music and record industry; *Cablevision, Satellite Orbit, Media Mix, Video, Video Review, Videography, Video Trade News, Video International*.

Directories.   *Broadcasting & Cable Yearbook*, source for statistics about radio and television, station listings; *Television & Cable Factbook; Broadcasting Cable Sourcebook; The Video Handbook; The Video Register; Les Brown's Encyclopedia of Television* (Gale Research).

## Film, Photographic and Graphic Communications

Research Journals.   *Cinema Journal* (Society for Cinema Studies); *Film Comment* (Film Society of Lincoln Center); *Film & History* (Historians Film Committee); *Journal of Popular Film and Television* (Bowling Green University); *Literature Film Quarterly* (Salisbury State University); *Journal of Typographic Research* (Cleveland Museum of Modern Art); *Printing History; Publishing History*.

Professional Publications.   *Film Critic* (American Federation of Film Societies); *Film Quarterly* (University of California Press); *American Cinematographer; News Photographer* (National Press Photographers Association); *Infinity* (American Society of Magazine Photographers); *Aperture* (fine photography); *Portfolio* (graphic arts); *Print & Graphics* (fine graphic arts); *Communication Arts* (graphic); *Typeworld*.

Trade Publications.   *Variety*, motion pictures; *Popular Photography; Photo Marketing; Graphic Arts Monthly*.

Directories.   *International Film Guide* (London), to international film, TV, film, and documentary markets; *Kemps International Film & Television Year Book* (London); *500 Best American Films to Buy, Rent or Videotape*, selected by the National Board of Review of Motion Pictures (New York: Simon and Schuster, 1986); Anthony Slide, editor, *International Film, Radio and Television Journals* (Westport, CT: Greenwood Press, 1985), descriptions and evaluations of more than 200 periodicals.

## Magazines and Book Publishing

Professional and Trade Journals. *Folio*, for the magazine area; *Publishers Weekly*, for the book publishing industry, whose focus is primarily on general trade and children's books; *BP Report*, for the book trade; *The Retail Bookseller*; *Bookbinding and Book Production*; *Author and Journalist*, *Writer*, and *Writer's Digest*, for freelance magazine writers.

Directories. *Literary Market Place* (R. R. Bowker) for book publishing; *Writer's Market* and *Writer's Year Book*, guides for magazine article writers; *Magazine Industry Marketplace* (R. R. Bowker).

## Advertising and Public Relations

Research Journals. *Journal of Marketing* (American Marketing Association), articles and book reviews; *Journal of Marketing Research* and *Journal of Advertising Research* (Advertising Research Foundation); *Journal of Advertising* (American Academy of Advertising); *Public Relations Review*, annual bibliography; *Journal of Public Relations Research*.

Professional Journals. *Public Relations Strategist*, quarterly; issues and trends that affect management; and *Public Relations Tactics*, monthly; news, trends, and how-to information for public relations people, both published by Public Relations Society of America; *Communication World* (International Association of Business Communicators); *International Public Relations* (formerly *IPRA Review*, International Public Relations Association); *Public Relations Quarterly*; and newsletters: *pr reporter*, *PR News*, *IABC News*, *Jack O'Dwyer's Newsletter*, *Ragan Newsletter*, *Bulldog Reporter*.

Trade Journals. *Advertising Age and Adweek*, major organs of the advertising industry; *Advertiser* (Association of National Advertisers); *Advertising Agency*; *Advertising Requirements*; *Sponsor*, for buyers of broadcast advertising; *Industrial Marketing*; *Sales Management*; *Direct Marketing*; *Marketing & Media Decision*.

Directories. Standard Rate and Data Service, *Consumer Markets*; *Editor & Publisher Market Guide*; *Broadcasting Marketbook*.

## Part One: The Media's Crucial Role

### Chapter 1: Global Reach of the Media

Books introducing the student to the communication explosion of the 1980s and 1990s include Lynne Schaefer Gross, *Telecommunications: An Introduction to Radio, Television, and the Developing Media* (Dubuque, IA: Brown, 1992), reporting on the history and current status of cable, pay TV, low-power TV, direct broadcast satellite, videotex, teletext, compact discs, videocassettes, and videodiscs; Gross, *The New Television Technologies* (Brown, 1990); Daniel Minoli, *Telecommunications Technology Handbook* (Boston: Artech, 1991), a detailed overview; Wilson P.

Dizard, Jr., *The Coming Information Age* (New York: Longman, 1989), an overview of technology, economics, and politics; and the prophetic Anthony Smith, *Goodbye Gutenberg—The Newspaper Revolution of the 1980s* (New York: Oxford University Press, 1980).

Emerging systems are reviewed in Leonard Sussman, *Power, the Press, & the Technology of Freedom: The Coming Age of ISDN* (New York: Freedom House, 1990); in 14 research articles edited by Mark R. Levy in *The VCR Age: Home Video and Mass Communication* (Newbury Park, CA: Sage, 1989); by C. David Chaffee, *The Rewiring of America: The Fiber Optics Revolution* (New York: Academic Press, 1988); by Paul Hurly, Matthias Laucht, and Denis Hlynka in *The Videotex and Teletext Handbook* (New York: Harper & Row, 1985); by David Weaver in *Videotex Journalism: Teletext, Viewdata and the News* (Hillsdale, NJ: Erlbaum, 1983); in *The Videocassette Recorder: An American Love Affair* (Washington, DC: Television Digest, 1985), compiled from 1983–1985 files; by Stuart Crump, Jr. in *Cellular Telephones: A Layman's Guide* (Blue Ridge Summit, PA: Tab Books, 1985); and in the National Association of Broadcasters' readable summary, *New Technologies Affecting Radio and Television Broadcasting* (Washington, DC: NAB Books, 1982).

Among hundreds of other books exploring communications technology and the information superhighway are Steven C. Jones, editor, *Cybersociety: Computer-Mediated Communication and Community* (Sage, 1994); Howard Rheingold, *The Virtual Community* (New York: HarperCollins, 1995); R. A. Buchanan, *The Power of the Machine: The Impact of Technology From 1700 to the Present* (London: Viking, 1992); Richard A. Lanham, *The Electronic Word: Democracy, Technology and the Arts* (Chicago: University of Chicago Press, 1993); Steven Levy, *Insanely Great: The Life and Times of Macintosh, the Computer That Changed Everything* (New York: Viking, 1994); *Media, Democracy and the Information Highway* (New York: Freedom Forum Media Studies Center, 1993); Michael O'Neill, *Roar of the Crowd: How Television and People Power Are Changing the World* (New York: Random House, 1993); Roy Tennant, *Crossing the Internet Threshold: An Instructional Handbook* (Berkeley, CA: Library Solutions Press, 1993); and Frederick Williams and John V. Pavlik, editors, *The People's Right to Know: Media, Democracy and the Information Highway* (Hillsdale, NJ: Lawrence Erlbaum Associates, 1994).

## Chapter 2: The Media's Social Impact

Philosophical problems of press freedom and responsible performance are analyzed by John Merrill in *The Dialectic of Journalism: Toward a Responsible Use of Press Freedom* (Baton Rouge: Louisiana State University Press, 1989). Earlier discussions include those by the Commission on Freedom of the Press in *A Free and Responsible Press* (Chicago: University of Chicago Press, 1947) and by William E. Hocking in *Freedom of the Press: A Framework of Principle* (Chicago: University of Chicago Press, 1947).

Among effective criticisms of broadcasting and cable are two edited guides to popular culture, *Watching Television* by Todd Gitlin, and its companion *Reading the News* by Robert Manoff and Michael Schudson (New York: Pantheon, 1986); and David Marc, *Demographic Vistas: Television in American Culture* (Philadelphia: University of Pennsylvania Press, 1984).

Herbert L. Gans examines the media impact from a sociologist's point of view in *Popular Culture and High Culture* (New York: Basic Books, 1974) and

*Deciding What's News* (New York: Pantheon, 1979). Leo Bogart, a media analyst specializing in advertising, uses a different approach in *Commercial Culture* (New York: Oxford University Press, 1994).

Much stimulating discussion of the relationship between the media and the public appears in contemporary trade journals and academic periodicals. Two examples of this material are: "Why people distrust the press and what editors can do about it," a discussion by prominent newspaper editors in *The American Editor*, published by the American Society of Newspaper Editors (September 1995) and "Undercovered: Reaching the New U.S.A." (Columbia, MO: New Directions for News, School of Journalism, University of Missouri).

## Chapter 3: Historic Press Freedoms

Companion books trace the story of American press freedom: Leonard W. Levy, *Freedom of the Press from Zenger to Jefferson*, and Harold L. Nelson, *Freedom of the Press from Hamilton to the Warren Court* (Indianapolis: Bobbs-Merrill, 1966). They are excellent surveys.

Elizabeth Eisenstein focuses on cultural and intellectual movements accompanying *The Printing Revolution in Early Modern Europe* (Cambridge: Cambridge University Press, 1984). Lucy M. Salmon's *The Newspaper and Authority* (New York: Oxford University Press, 1923), is an extensive historical survey of restrictions placed on newspapers. Important periods of the history of press freedom struggles are covered in Fred S. Siebert, *Freedom of the Press in England, 1472–1776* (Urbana: University of Illinois Press, 1952); Jeffery Smith, *Printers and Press Freedom: Ideology of Early Journalism* (New York: Oxford University Press, 1987); Leonard W. Levy, *Emergence of a Free Press* (Oxford University Press, 1985), a revision of *Legacy of Suppression: Freedom of Speech and Press in Early American History* (Cambridge, MA: Harvard University Press, 1960); Clyde A. Duniway, *The Development of Freedom of the Press in Massachusetts* (New York: Longmans, Green, 1906); John C. Miller, *Crisis in Freedom: The Alien and Sedition Acts* (Boston: Little, Brown, 1951); Frank Luther Mott, *Jefferson and the Press* (Baton Rouge: Louisiana State University Press, 1943); and Zechariah Chaffee, Jr., *Free Speech in the United States* (Cambridge, MA: Harvard University Press, 1941), a study emphasizing the effects of modern wartime conditions. James E. Pollard, *The Presidents and the Press* (New York: Macmillan, 1947), covers presidential press relations from Washington to Truman; John Tebbel and Sarah Miles Watts cover from Washington to Reagan in *The Press and the Presidency* (New York: Oxford University Press, 1985).

## Chapter 4: Audience Research: Concepts and Applications

An excellent introduction to the study of the communication process and to research in mass communication is found in Wilbur Schramm and William E. Porter's *Men, Women, Messages and Media* (New York: Harper & Row, 1982), a readable survey of communication theory, mass communication audiences, effects, and social controls. John C. Merrill and Ralph L. Lowenstein have contributed their prize-winning *Media, Messages, and Men: New Perspectives in Communication* (New York: Longman, 1979), analyzing the changing role of the mass media, the communicators and their audiences, and media concepts and ethics.

A major effort to describe mass communications research was made in *Research Methods in Mass Communication*, edited by Guido H. Stempel III and Bruce H. Westley (Englewood Cliffs, NJ: Prentice Hall, 1981). It examines both social science and documentary research fields. Two research area studies are John D. Stevens and Hazel Dicken-Garcia, *Communication History* (Beverly Hills, CA: Sage, 1980), and Klaus Krippendorff, *Content Analysis* (Sage, 1980). An historical account is Shearon A. Lowery and Melvin L. DeFleur, *Milestones in Communication Research* (New York: Longman, 1988). The first reference guide is *Communication Research: Strategies and Sources* (Belmont, CA: Wadsworth, 1992), by Rebecca B. Rubin, Alan M. Rubin, and Linda Piele.

Books that introduce the reader to research methods include H.J. Hsia, *Mass Communication Research Methods: A Step-by-Step Approach* (Hillsdale, NJ: Erlbaum, 1988); Mary John Smith, *Contemporary Communication Research Methods* (Belmont, CA: Wadsworth, 1988); Roger D. Wimmer and Joseph R. Dominick, *Mass Media Research* (Wadsworth, 1996); Frederick Williams, *Technology and Communication Behavior* (Wadsworth, 1987); Werner Severin and James Tankard, Jr., *Communication Theories: Origins, Methods, Uses* (New York: Longman, 1992), media-oriented; and Hugh M. Beville, Jr., *Audience Ratings: Radio, Television, Cable* (Hillsdale, NJ: Erlbaum, 1988), a history of ratings.

Advertising research methods are outlined in Daniel Starch, *Measuring Advertising Readership and Results* (New York: McGraw-Hill, 1966); and in Alan D. Fletcher and Thomas J. Bowers, *Fundamentals of Advertising Research* (Belmont, CA: Wadsworth, 1988). Newspaper research methods are discussed in Gerald Stone, *Examining Newspapers: What Research Reveals About America's Newspapers* (Beverly Hills, CA: Sage, 1987); and Leo Bogart, *Press and Public: Who Reads What, When, Where, and Why in American Newspapers* (Hillsdale, NJ: Erlbaum, 1989).

The complex and specialized area of communication theory may be approached through a readable survey of contemporary theory by Melvin L. De-Fleur and Sandra Ball-Rokeach. *Theories of Mass Communication* (New York: Longman, 1989); Alexis S. Tan, *Mass Communication Theories and Research* (New York: Macmillan, 1986); Leo W. Jeffres, *Mass Media: Processes and Effects* (Prospect Heights, IL: Waveland Press, 1986), an extensive research-based overview; Michael W. Singletary and Gerald Stone, *Communication Theory and Research Applications* (Ames: Iowa State University Press, 1988); and Dennis McQuail, *Mass Communication Theory: An Introduction* (Beverly Hills, CA: Sage, 1987).

The process of media economics decision-making is explored in Alison Alexander, James Owers, and Rod Carveth, *Media Economics: Theory and Practice* (Prospect Heights, IL: Lawrence Erlbaum Associates, 1993).

Provocative discussions are found in Marshall McLuhan's *Understanding Media: The Extensions of Man* (New York: McGraw-Hill, 1964); his earlier *The Gutenberg Galaxy: The Making of Typographic Man* (University of Toronto Press, 1962); and *The Medium Is the Message* (New York: Bantam Books, 1967), Philip Marchand, *Marshall McLuhan: The Medium and the Messenger* (New York: Tickner and Fields, 1989), is an excellent biography.

The role of the mass media, particularly television, in politics has been studied by Austin Ranney in *Channels of Power: The Impact of Television on American Politics* (New York: Basic Books, 1983); by Gladys Lang and Kurt Lang in *Politics and Television Re-Viewed* (Beverly Hills, CA: Sage, 1984), an update of a 1968 study; by Elisabeth Noelle-Neumann in *The Spiral of Silence* (Chicago: University of Chicago Press, 1983), an analysis of the public opinion formation process; by Garth S. Jowett and Victoria O'Donnell in *Propaganda and Persua-*

*sion* (Beverly Hills, CA: Sage, 1986); and by Kathleen Hall Jamieson in *Packaging the Presidency: A History and Criticism of Presidential Campaign Advertising* (New York: Oxford University Press, 1984), covering 1952 to 1980. The uses of polls in politics is the subject of *Polling and the Democratic Consensus*, edited by L. John Martin for the *Annals* of the American Academy of Political and Social Science, Vol. 477 (Beverly Hills, CA: Sage, 1985).

## Issue 1: Sex and Violence: Are the Media Weakening Public Morality?

Violence and Sensationalism.    Willard D. Rowland, Jr. reviews 50 years of futile efforts to force the American media to reduce violence in *The Politics of TV Violence* (Newbury Park, CA: Sage, 1983). Linda S. Lichter and S. Robert Lichter argue that television sensationalizes and distorts in *Prime Time Crime: Criminals and Law Enforcers in TV Entertainment* (Washington: The Media Institute, 1983). Sex and violence in television programming are explored in Geoffrey Cowan, *See No Evil* (New York: Simon and Schuster, 1979). Muriel Cantor, in *Prime Time Television: Content and Control* (Beverly Hills, CA: Sage, 1980), concludes that varied forces, pressures, and prejudices determine the final form of a television show. John D. Stevens dissects newspapers in *Sensationalism and the New York Press* (New York: Columbia University Press, 1991).

    *Terrorism and the Media*, edited by David L. Paletz and Alex P. Schmid (Beverly Hills, CA: Sage, 1992) reflects perspectives of the public, press, terrorists, victims, researchers. Terrorism and hostage-taking are the subjects of two other books: Dan Nimmo and James E. Combs, *Nightly Horrors: Crisis Coverage in Television Network News* (Knoxville: University of Tennessee Press, 1985), and Sarah Midgley and Virginia Rice, editors, *Terrorism and the Media in the 1980s* (Washington: The Media Institute, 1984), proceedings of a 1983 conference of news directors, politicians, and former hostages.

    Research findings have been reported by George Gerbner, et al., annually, and summarized in *Violence Profile No. 8: Trends in Network Television Drama and Viewer Conceptions of Social Reality, 1967–1976* (Philadelphia: Annenberg School of Communication, University of Pennsylvania, 1977). The Government Printing Office issued a 1982 two-volume summary and research report, *Television and Behavior: Ten Years of Scientific Progress and Implications for the Eighties, Violence and Terror in the Mass Media: An Annotated Bibliography*, compiled by Nancy Signorielli and George Gerbner (Westport, CT: Greenwood Press, 1988), contains detailed annotations of 700 items.

Children and Television.    Widely acclaimed was *The Early Window: Effects of Television on Children and Youth*, by Robert Liebert and Joyce N. Sprafkin (New York: Pergamon Press, 1989). Included in the extensive literature are Mariann Pezzella Winick and Charles Winick, *The Television Experience: What Children See* (Beverly Hills, CA: Sage, 1979); Ellen Wartella, editor, *Children Communicating* (Sage, 1979); Scott Ward, Daniel Wackman, and Ellen Wartella, *How Children Learn to Buy* (Sage, 1977); and Jerome Johnson and James Ettema, *Positive Images: Breaking Stereotypes with Children's Television* (Sage, 1982).

Censorship.    Ruth Inglis, *Freedom of the Movies* (Chicago: University of Chicago Press, 1947), argued the case for self-regulation for the Commission on Freedom of the Press. In discussions of censorship trends, the film area is covered by Ira H. Carmen, *Movies, Censorship and the Law* (Ann Arbor: University of Michigan Press, 1966), and by Richard S. Randall, *Censorship of the Movies* (Madison: University of Wisconsin Press, 1968); and books by Richard McKeon, Robert K. Merton, and Walter Gellhorn, *The Freedom to Read: Perspective and Program* (New York: Bowker, 1957). Movie and television censorship is decried in Murray Schumach's *The Face on the Cutting Room Floor* (New York: Morrow, 1964).

Pornography.    The two-volume *Final Report of the Attorney General's Commission on Pornography* (Washington, DC: Government Printing Office, 1986) explores the subject and makes recommendations for law enforcement and citizen action. Edward Donnerstein's *The Question of Pornography* (New York: The Free Press, 1987) is a research-based response to the Meese Commission's report. Donald A. Downs, *The New Politics of Pornography* (Chicago: University of Chicago Press, 1990), analyzes the opposition of radical feminists.

## Part Two: The Print Media

The most widely ranging of the journalism histories is Michael and Edwin Emery, *The Press and America: An Interpretive History of the Mass Media* (Englewood Cliffs, NJ: Prentice Hall, 1996). It correlates the narrative of journalism history with social, political, and economic trends and is especially comprehensive in its treatment of twentieth-century media—newspapers, magazines, radio and television, news services, motion pictures, books, advertising, public relations—and the relationship of the mass media to government and society.

Two briefer histories designed as core texts appeared in 1989. Jean Folkerts and Dwight L. Teeter, Jr. were co-authors of *Voices of a Nation: A History of the Media in the United States* (New York: Macmillan, 1989), paying primary attention to the print media within a social, political, and economic framework. Wm. David Sloan, James G. Stovall, and James D. Startt are co-editors of *The Media in America: A History* (Worthington, OH: Publishing Horizons, 1989), whose 18 chapters were written by 18 different professors in a chronological arrangement. Sloan, with Julie Hedgepeth Williams, inaugurated a proposed six-volume re-examination of journalism history with *The Early American Press, 1690–1763, The History of American Journalism, No. 1* (Westport, CT: Greenwood, 1994).

Frank Luther Mott's *American Journalism: A History, 1690–1960* (New York: Macmillan, 1962) contains much rich detail in its comprehensive treatment of newspapers, but puts little emphasis on other media. Alfred McClung Lee's *The Daily Newspaper in America* (New York: Macmillan, 1937) offers a sociological approach and much valuable data in its topical treatment of subjects such as newsprint, printing presses, labor, ownership and management, news, advertising, and circulation. Willard G. Bleyer's *Main Currents in the History of American Journalism* (Boston: Houghton Mifflin, 1927) remains an excellent account of American journalism until the early twentieth century, with emphasis on leading editors.

Portraits of American newspeople in the 1970s and 1980s are found in John W. C. Johnstone, Edward J. Slawski, and William W. Bowman, *The News People: A Sociological Portrait of American Journalists and Their Work* (Urbana, University of Illinois Press, 1976), based on 1300 interviews, and in David H. Weaver and G. Cleveland Wilhoit, *The American Journalist: A Portrait of U.S. News People and Their Work* (Bloomington: Indiana University Press, 1991), a similar survey. Two biographical works about journalists are Joseph P. McKerns, *The Biographical Dictionary of American Journalism* (Westport, CT: Greenwood Press, 1989), detailing some 500 newspeople in a variety of positions; *American Newspaper Journalists*, edited by Perry J. Ashley in five volumes of the *Dictionary of Literary Biography* (Chicago: Gale Research, 1983 ff.); and *American Magazine Journalists*, edited by Sam G. Riley in five other volumes of the same dictionary. Thomas B. Connery edited *A Source Book of American Literary Journalism* (Westport, CT: Greenwood Press, 1992).

J. William Snorgrass and Gloria T. Woody compiled *Blacks and Media: A Selected, Annotated Bibliography 1962–1982* (Tallahassee: Florida A&M University Press, 1985). James P. Danky was editor and Maureen E. Hady compiler of two major listings: *Native American Periodicals and Newspapers, 1829–1982: Bibliography, Publishing Record and Holdings* (Westport, CT: Greenwood Press, 1984), and *Women's Periodicals and Newspapers from the 18th Century to 1981* (Boston: G.K. Hall, 1982).

Additional references, by chapter topic, follow.

## Chapter 5: Newspapers

**History of News.** The best historical discussion of the news function is Frank Luther Mott's *The News in America* (Cambridge, MA.: Harvard University Press, 1952), a survey of the concepts, forms, and problems of news. Jim A. Hart traces the history of the editorial, from 1500 to 1800, in *Views on the News* (Carbondale: Southern Illinois University Press, 1971), and Allan Nevins continues in the introductions for sections in his collection of editorials, *American Press Opinion: Washington to Coolidge* (New York: Heath, 1928). Michael Schudson, *Discovering the News* (New York: Basic Books, 1978), and Dan Schiller, *Objectivity and the News* (Philadelphia: University of Pennsylvania Press, 1981), deal with the rise of objectivity, and Thomas C. Leonard, *The Power of the Press* (New York: Oxford University Press, 1986) with the birth of political reporting. Mitchell Stephens, *A History of News from the Drum to the Satellite* (New York: Viking, 1988) is an impressionistic international account.

The best anthologies are *Voices of the Past*, edited by Calder M. Pickett (Columbus, OH: Grid, 1977); *A Treasury of Great Reporting*, edited by Louis L. Snyder and Richard B. Morris (New York: Simon and Schuster, 1962); Bryce W. Rucker's *Twentieth Century Reporting at Its Best* (Ames: Iowa State University Press, 1964), John Hohenberg's *The Pulitzer Prize Story* (New York: Columbia University Press, 1959), and *The Best of Pulitzer Prize News Writing*, edited by William David Sloan, Valerie McCrary, and Johanna Cleary (Columbus, OH: Publishing Horizons, 1986), an anthology of 71 articles.

Some recent histories of individual newspapers and biographies and reminiscences of newspersons include Daniel W. Pfaff, *Joseph Pulitzer II and the Post-Dispatch* (University Park: Pennsylvania State Press, 1991); Vance H. Trimble, *The Astonishing Mr. Scripps* (Ames: Iowa State University Press, 1992); William

Randolph Hearst, Jr., *The Hearsts: Father and Son* (New York: Roberts Rinehart, 1991); James Reston, *Deadline* (New York: Random House, 1991); Esmond Wright, *Franklin of Philadelphia* (Cambridge, MA: Harvard University Press, 1986); Richard Kluger, *The Paper: The Life and Death of the New York Herald Tribune* (New York: Knopf, 1986); Lloyd Wendt, *The Wall Street Journal* (Chicago: Rand McNally, 1982); Harrison Salisbury, *A Journey for Our Times* (New York: Harper & Row, 1983); William L. Shirer, *The Nightmare Years, 1930–1940* (Boston: Little, Brown, 1984); Robert V. Hudson, *The Writing Game: A Biography of Will Irwin* (Ames: Iowa State University Press, 1982); Charles Whited, *Knight: Publisher in the Tumultuous Century* (New York: Dutton, 1988); and Lindsay Chaney and Michael Cleply, *The Hearsts: Family and Empire—The Later Years* (New York: Simon and Schuster, 1981).

**Women Journalists.**   Maurine Beasley and Sheila Gibbons offer excerpts from work of U.S. women journalists in *Taking Their Place: A Documentary History of Women and Journalism* (Washington: American University Press, 1993). A pioneer synthesis is Marion Marzolf, *Up From the Footnote: A History of Women Journalists* (New York: Hastings House, 1977). Kay Mills, *A Place in the News: From the Women's Pages to the Front Page* (New York: Dodd, Mead, 1988), surveys progress of many newswomen. A selected few are found in Julia Edwards, *Women of the World: The Great Foreign Correspondents* (Boston: Houghton Mifflin, 1988). Eighteen women's careers are told in *Great Women of the Press* by Madelon Golden Schlipp and Sharon M. Murphy (Carbondale: Southern Illinois University Press, 1983). Barbara Bedford deals with 24 in her biographical anthology, *Brilliant Bylines* (New York: Columbia University Press, 1986). Helen Thomas in *Dateline: White House* (New York: Macmillan, 1975) tells one story, and Sarah McClendon another in *My Eight Presidents* (New York: Wyden Books, 1978).

**Minority Press.**   Two basic historical studies of the black press are Frederick G. Detweiler, *The Negro Press in the United States* (Chicago: University of Chicago Press, 1922), and Vishnu V. Oak, *The Negro Press* (Yellow Springs, OH: Antioch Press, 1948). A comprehensive survey is *The Black Press, U.S.A.*, by Roland E. Wolseley (Ames: Iowa State University Press, 1990). *Perspective of the Black Press, 1974* (Kennebunkport, ME: Mercer House, 1974) is an extensive anthology edited by Henry G. La Brie III, whose *A Survey of Black Newspapers in America* appeared from the same press in 1979. Henry Lewis Suggs edited *The Black Press in the South 1865–1979* (Westport, CT: Greenwood Press, 1983). James and Sharon Murphy did a comprehensive synthesis in *Let My People Know: American Indian Journalism 1828–1978* (Norman: University of Oklahoma Press, 1981). A comprehensive overview is found in *The Ethnic Press in the United States*, edited by Sally M. Miller (Westport, CT: Greenwood Press, 1987).

**Alternative Press.**   Among books on the alternative and protest press are a good survey across 200 years by Lauren Kessler, *Against the Grain: The Dissident Press in America* (Beverly Hills, CA: Sage, 1984), dealing with feminists, immigrants, blacks, utopians, radicals, and pacifists; Everette E. Dennis and William

L. Rivers, *Other Voices: The New Journalism in America* (San Francisco: Canfield, 1974); an anthology edited by Tom Wolfe, *The New Journalism* (New York: Harper & Row, 1973); David Armstrong, *A Trumpet to Arms, The Alternative Press in America* (Los Angeles: Torcher, 1981); Nancy L. Roberts, *Dorothy Day and the Catholic Worker* (Albany: State University of New York Press, 1984), a longtime voice of consistent liberal protest; and Elliot Shore, *Talkin' Socialism: J.A. Wayland and the Role of the Press in American Radicalism* (Lawrence: University Press of Kansas, 1988).

**Textbooks on Reporting and Newswriting.** George A. Hough, 3rd, *Newswriting* (Boston: Houghton Mifflin, 1995); Brian Brooks, George Kennedy, Daryl Moen, and Don Ranly, *News Reporting and Writing* (New York: St. Martin's Press, 1996); Melvin Mencher, *News Reporting and Writing* (Dubuque, IA: Brown, 1994); William Metz, *Newswriting* (Englewood Cliffs, NJ: Prentice Hall, 1991); Conrad C. Fink, *Introduction to Professional Newswriting* (New York: Longman, 1992); Ken Metzler, *Newsgathering* (Englewood Cliffs, NJ: Prentice Hall, 1989); Fred Fedler, *Reporting for the Print Media* (New York: Harcourt Brace Jovanovich, 1993); Ralph S. Izard, Hugh Culbertson, and Donald A. Lambert, *Fundamentals of News Reporting* (Dubuque, IA: Kendall/Hunt, 1994); Julian Harriss, Kelly Leiter, and Stanley Johnson, *The Complete Reporter* (New York: Macmillan, 1992); and John Hohenberg, *Concise Newswriting* (New York: Hastings House, 1987).

Valuable adjuncts to the reporting texts are E. L. Callihan, *Grammar for Journalists* (Radnor, PA: Chilton, 1979); R. Thomas Berner, *Language Skills for Journalists* (Boston: Houghton Mifflin, 1984); Terry Murphy, *Classroom to Newsroom* (New York: Harper & Row, 1983); and Lauren Kessler and Duncan McDonald, *When Words Collide* (Belmont, Ca: Wadsworth, 1992).

Information gathering, ranging from library resources to data bases, is the subject of two books: Jean Ward and Kathleen A. Hansen, *Search Strategies in Mass Communication* (New York: Longman, 1993), and Lauren Kessler and Duncan McDonald, *The Search* (Belmont, CA: Wadsworth, 1995).

**Special Fields of Reporting.** Bruce Garrison, *Computer-Assisted Reporting* (Prospect Heights, IL: Lawrence Erlbaum Associates, 1995); Philip Meyer, *The New Precision Journalism* (Bloomington: Indiana University Press, 1991), a reporter's introduction to social science methods; Henry H. Schulte, *Reporting Public Affairs* (New York: Macmillan, 1981); George S. Hage, Everette E. Dennis, Arnold H. Ismach, and Stephen Hartgen, *New Strategies for Public Affairs Reporting: Investigation, Interpretation, Research* (Englewood Cliffs, NJ: Prentice Hall, 1983); Ronald P. Lovell, *Reporting Public Affairs* (Prospect Heights, IL: Waveland, 1993); Gerry Keir, Maxwell E. McCombs and Donald L. Shaw, *Advanced Reporting: Beyond News Events* (Prospect Heights, IL: Waveland Press, 1995); Bruce Garrison, *Advanced Reporting: Skills for the Professional* 1995 (Hillsdale, NJ: Erlbaum, 1992); Investigative Reporters and Editors, *The Reporter's Handbook* (New York: St. Martin's Press, 1996); Shirley Biagi, *Interviews that Work* (Belmont, CA: Wadsworth, 1992); Sharon M. Friedman, editor, *Scientists and Journalists: Reporting Science News* (New York: The Free Press, 1986); Warren Burkett, *News Reporting: Science, Medicine and High Technology* (Ames: Iowa

State University Press, 1986); Bruce Garrison, *Professional Feature Writing* (Hillsdale, NJ: Erlbaum, 1994); Edward J. Friedlander and John Lee, *Feature Writing for Newspapers and Magazines* (New York: HarperCollins, 1993); Thomas Fensch, *The Sportswriting Handbook* (Hillsdale, NJ: Erlbaum, 1995); Douglas A. Anderson, *Contemporary Sports Reporting* (Chicago: Nelson-Hall, 1994); Bruce Garrison and Mark Sabljak, *Sports Reporting* (Ames: Iowa State University Press, 1993); and Campbell B. Titchenor, *Reviewing the Arts* (Hillsdale, NJ: Erlbaum, 1988).

**Editorial Page and Opinion Writing.**　Harry W. Stonecipher, *Editorial and Persuasive Writing* (New York: Hastings House, 1979); Kenneth Rystrom, *The Why, Who and How of the Editorial Page* (New York: Random House, 1983); A. Gayle Waldrop, *Editor and Editorial Writer* (Dubuque, IA: Brown, 1967); Curtis D. MacDougall, *Principles of Editorial Writing* (Brown, 1973); John L. Hulteng, *The Opinion Function* (New York: Harper & Row, 1973).

**News Editing and Design.**　Carl Sessions Stepp, *Editing for Today's Newsroom* (Hillsdale, NJ: Erlbaum, 1990); Howard Finberg and Bruce Itule, *Visual Editing* (Belmont, CA: Wadsworth, 1990), newspaper editing, layout, design; Daryl Moen, *Newspaper Layout and Design* (Ames: Iowa State University Press, 1989); Martin L. Gibson, *Editing in the Electronic Era* (Ames: Iowa State University Press, 1991); and Robert E. Garst and Theodore M. Bernstein, *Headlines and Deadlines* (New York: Columbia University Press, 1982), a New York *Times* classic.

**Community Journalism.**　John Cameron Sim, *The Grass Roots Press: America's Community Newspapers* (Ames: Iowa State University Press, 1969); Morris Janowitz, *The Community Press in an Urban Setting* (New York: The Free Press, 1967); and Bruce M. Kennedy, *Community Journalism: How to Run a Country Weekly* (Ames: Iowa State University Press, 1974); D. Earl Newsom, editor, *The Newspaper* (Englewood Cliffs, NJ: Prentice Hall, 1981), 28 articles focusing on small dailies and weeklies.

**Management.**　Jim Willis, *Surviving in the Newspaper Business: Newspaper Management in Turbulent Times* (New York: Praeger, 1988); Conrad C. Fink, *Strategic Newspaper Management* (New York: Random House, 1996); Herbert Lee Williams, *Newspaper Organization and Management* (Ames: Iowa State University Press, 1979); and Ardyth B. Sohn, Christine L. Ogan and John E. Polich, *Newspaper Leadership* (Prentice Hall, 1986), describing the "total" approach.

## News Services and Syndicates

The best picture of the major Western news services is in Jonathan Fenby, *The International News Services* (New York: Schocken Books, 1986), which covers the histories and roles of AP, UPI, Reuters, and Agence France-Presse. Gregory Gordon and Ronald E. Cohen in *Down to the Wire: UPI's Fight for Survival* (New York: McGraw-Hill, 1989), by two UPI editors, recount the agency's historic great moments and analyze recent management upheavals. Oliver Gramling,

*AP: The Story of News* (New York: Farrar and Rinehart, 1940), and Joe Alex Morris, *Deadline Every Minute: The Story of the United Press* (New York: Doubleday, 1957), capture a good deal of the reportorial excitement of the news services.

The story of collective newsgathering and forming of news services in the United States from the 1830s to 1920 is told in Richard A. Schwarzlose, *The Nation's Newsbrokers:* Vol. 1, *The Formative Years: From Pretelegraph to 1865;* Vol. 2, *The Rush to Institution: From 1865 to 1920* (Evanston, IL: Northwestern University Press, 1989, 1990). This definitive account, based on a 25-year study of primary sources, ends with the establishment of AP, UP, and INS as institutional rivals by 1920. It supersedes for its time period Gramling's book and Victor Rosewater, *History of Cooperative News-Gathering in the United States* (New York: Appleton, 1930).

Hugh Baillie, *High Tension* (New York: Harper & Row, 1959), is the readable autobiography of a former president of UP. *Kent Cooper and the Associated Press* (New York: Random House, 1959) is the second personal account by the most famous general manager of the AP; the first, *Barriers Down* (New York: Farrar and Rinehart, 1942), is Cooper's story of his efforts to break up international news monopolies. Melville E. Stone, *Fifty Years a Journalist*, is the autobiography of the first AP general manager.

The annual *Syndicate Directory* issued by *Editor & Publisher* updates Elmo Scott Watson, *A History of Newspaper Syndicates, 1865–1935* (Chicago: Publishers' Auxiliary, 1936).

## Chapter 6: Magazines

John Tebbel and Mary Ellen Zuckerman admirably survey *The Magazine in America, 1741–1990* (New York: Oxford, 1991). A factual supplement to the magazine field texts is Leonard Mogel's *The Magazine: Everything You Need to Know to Make It in the Magazine Business* (Englewood Cliffs, NJ: Prentice Hall, 1979). William H. Taft's *American Magazines for the 1980s* (New York: Hastings House, 1982) is a state-of-the-art summary. So is *The Handbook of Magazine Publishing*, compiled by the editors of *Folio* magazine in 1983.

An overview of the field is provided by Roland E. Wolseley's *Understanding Magazines* (Ames: Iowa State University Press, 1969), which treats editorial and business operations of consumer, business, and specialized publications. Wolseley's *The Changing Magazine* (New York: Hastings House, 1973) traces trends in readership and management. *Magazine Profiles* (Evanston, IL: Medill School of Journalism, 1974) presents studies by 12 graduate students of nearly 50 magazines. John Tebbel's *The American Magazine: A Compact History* (New York: Hawthorn, 1969) emphasizes an industry-wide survey. James L. C. Ford, *Magazines for Millions* (Carbondale: Southern Illinois University Press, 1970), tells the story of specialized publications in fields such as business, religion, labor, and homemaking.

Views of specialized magazine work can be obtained from Jan V. White, *Designing for Magazines* (New York: Bowker, 1982); Ruori McLean, *Magazine Design* (London: Oxford University Press, 1969); Rowena Ferguson, *Editing the Small Magazine* (New York: Columbia University Press, 1976); Don Gussow, *The New Business Journalism* (San Diego: Harcourt Brace Jovanovich, 1984); Albert N. Greco, *Business Journalism* (New York: New York University Press, 1988), a casebook; and Edgar A. Grunwald, *The Business Press Editor* (New York University Press, 1988).

Textbooks on writing and editing include Terri Brooks, *Words' Worth: A Handbook on Writing and Selling Nonfiction* (New York: St. Martin's Press, 1989); Marcia Yudkin, *Freelance Writing for Magazines and Newspapers* (New York: Harper & Row, 1988); Edward Jay Friedlander and John Lee, *Feature Writing for Newspapers and Magazines* (HarperCollins, 1993); Conrad C. Fink and Donald E. Fink, *Introduction to Magazine Writing* (New York: Macmillan, 1994); Betsy P. Graham, *Writing Magazine Articles With Style* (New York: Holt, Rinehart and Winston, 1992); William L. Rivers and Alison R. Work, *Freelancer and Staff Writer* (Belmont, CA: Wadsworth, 1992); J. W. Click and Russell N. Baird, *Magazine Editing and Production* (Dubuque, IA: Brown, 1990); William L. Rivers, *Magazine Editing in the '80s* (Belmont, CA: Wadsworth, 1983); and Myrick E. Land, *Writing for Magazines* (Prentice Hall, 1993).

Magazine editors and writers are the subjects of books by Oswald Garrison Villard, *Fighting Years* (New York: Harcourt, Brace, 1939), the memoirs of the editor of the *Nation;* Peter Lyon, *Success Story: The Life and Times of S. S. McClure* (New York: Scribner's, 1963); S. S. McClure, *My Autobiography* (New York: Stokes, 1914); Kathleen Brady, *Ida Tarbell: Portrait of a Muckraker* (New York: Seaview Putnam, 1984); Jan Cohn, *Creating America: George Horace Lorimer and the Saturday Evening Post* (Pittsburgh: University of Pittsburgh Press, 1989); George Britt, *Forty Years—Forty Millions: The Career of Frank A. Munsey* (New York: Farrar and Rinehart, 1935); James Thurber, *The Years with Ross* (Boston: Little, Brown, 1957), the story of editor Harold Ross and the *New Yorker;* Raymond Sokolov, *Wayward Reporter: The Life of A. J. Liebling* (New York: Harper & Row, 1980), longtime *New Yorker* writer; Brendan Gill, *Here at the New Yorker* (New York: Random House, 1975); Norman Cousins, *Present Tense* (New York: McGraw-Hill, 1967), by the *Saturday Review's* editor; W. A. Swanberg, *Luce and His Empire* (New York: Scribner's, 1972); Robert T. Elson, *Time Inc.* (New York: Atheneum, 1968) and *The World of Time Inc.* (New York: Atheneum, 1973 and 1986), a three-volume history covering 1923–1941, 1941–1960, and 1960–1980; and James L. Baughman, *Henry R. Luce and the Rise of the American News Media* (Boston: Twayne, 1987).

## Chapter 7: Book Publishing

Charles G. Madison's *Book Publishing in America* (New York: McGraw-Hill, 1967) is the definitive survey of the book publishing industry by a former editor and publisher. There are many useful insights into the art of publishing and the history of the major companies. A well-rounded picture of the trade or general side of the book publishing industry is given by a score of specialists in *What Happens in Book Publishing*, edited by Chandler B. Grannis (New York: Columbia University Press, 1967). The *Media Studies Journal* offers a series of essays in its Summer 1992 issue, *Publishing Books.*

Some of the economic factors behind publishing house mergers and sales are presented in Benjamin M. Compaine, *The Book Industry in Transition: An Economic Analysis of Book Distribution and Marketing* (White Plains, NY: Knowledge Industry Publications, 1978). The impact of new technologies is presented in Oldrich Standera, *The Electronic Era of Publishing* (New York: Elsevier, 1987).

Sir Stanley Unwin, *The Truth About Publishing* (New York: Bowker, 1960), is highly readable. John P. Dessauer, *Book Publishing: What It Is, What It Does* (New York: Bowker, 1981), gives an excellent overview. William Jovanovich,

*Now, Barabbas* (New York: Harper & Row, 1964) presents thoughtful essays on his field by a publishing executive.

Elizabeth A. Geiser has edited papers from the University of Denver Publishing Institute in *The Business of Book Publishing: Papers by Practitioners* (Boulder, CO: Westview Press, 1985). Roger Smith, editor, *The American Reading Public: A Symposium* (New York: Bowker, 1964), is a particularly succinct and useful collection of authoritative essays by a number of publishing executives.

John Tebbel has completed his four-volume *A History of Book Publishing in the United States* (New York: Bowker). The first three volumes appeared in 1972, 1975, and 1978. They cover the years 1630 to 1865, 1865 to 1919, and 1920 to 1940. The last appeared in 1981. A single volume summary, *Between Covers*, was issued in 1986.

The most complete history of paperbacks is Kenneth C. Davis, *Two-Bit Culture: The Paperbacking of America* (Boston: Houghton Miflin, 1984). Thomas L. Bonn wrote *Under Cover: An Illustrated History of American Mass Market Paperbacks* (New York: Penguin, 1982). Roy Walters presents a collection of his trade journal columns for the 1970s and early 1980s in *Paperback Talk* (Chicago: Academy Chicago, 1985).

The story of a famous book editor is told by A. Scott Berg in *Max Perkins, Editor of Genius* (New York: E. P. Dutton, 1978).

### Issue 2: Ethics: Do the Media Maintain Satisfactory Standards of Social Responsibility?

William L. Rivers, Wilbur Schramm, and Clifford G. Christians, *Responsibility in Mass Communication* (New York: Harper & Row, 1980), is an excellent treatment of communications ethics. It discusses the role of the mass communicator in developing the political, social, and economic fabrics of a democratic society, and the development of modern mass communications. In a similar vein are John L. Hulteng, *The Messenger's Motives: Ethical Theory in the Mass Media* (Englewood Cliffs, NJ: Prentice Hall, 1984); Edmund B. Lambeth, *Committed Journalism: An Ethic for the Profession* (Bloomington: Indiana University Press, 1992), a framework of principles for ethical journalism; Clifford G. Christians, Kim B. Rotzoll, and Mark Fackler, *Media Ethics: Cases and Moral Reasoning* (New York: Longman, 1991); Conrad C. Fink, *Media Ethics* (New York: Allyn & Bacon, 1995); and *Communication Ethics and Global Change*, edited by Thomas W. Cooper, et al. (New York: Longman, 1989). Cooper and others also published *Television and Ethics: A Bibliography* (Boston: G. K. Hall, 1988).

Case studies from the professional press help readers understand the reasoning behind ethical decisions in Jay Black, Bob Steele, and Ralph Barney, *Doing Ethics in Journalism* (New York: Allyn and Bacon, 1995), published under the aegis of the Society of Professional Journalists. Fourteen issues are debated in A. David Gordon, John M. Kittross, and Carol Reuss, *Controversies in Media Ethics* (White Plains, NY: Longman, 1996), with commentary by John C. Merrill.

The American Society of Newspaper Editors sponsored Philip Meyer's *Editors, Publishers and Newspaper Ethics* (Reston, VA: ASNE, 1983), and *Drawing the Line: How 31 Editors Solved Their Toughest Ethical Dilemmas*, edited by Frank McCulloch (ASNE, 1984). Meyer later published *Ethical Journalism* (New York: Longman, 1987), based on his surveys. On the critical side are Tom Goldstein, *The News at Any Cost: How Journalists Compromise Their Ethics to Shape the News* (New York: Simon and Schuster, 1985), and Patrick Brogan's *Spiked: The Short*

*Life and Death of the National Press Council* (New York: Priority Press, 1985), a 20th Century Fund study of a largely ignored effort.

Criticisms of the mass media are summarized in John L. Hulteng's *The Messenger's Motives* (Englewood Cliffs, NJ: Prentice Hall, 1984), by analyzing cases involving ethical problems. In a similar vein are *Groping for Ethics in Journalism* by H. Eugene Goodwin (Ames: Iowa State University Press, 1987); James B. Lemert, *Criticizing the Media: An Empirical Approach* (Beverly Hills, CA: Sage, 1989); *Media Freedom and Responsibility*, edited by Everette E. Dennis, Donald M. Gillmor, and Theodore L. Glasser (Westport, CT: Greenwood 1989); and *Unreliable Sources: A Guide to Detecting Bias in News Media*, by Martin A. Lee and Norman Solomon (New York: Lyle, Stuart, 1991).

Criticism of press managers is the theme of Ben H. Bagdikian in *The Effete Conspiracy and Other Crimes by the Press* (New York: Harper & Row, 1972). Daniel J. Czitrom traced developing years of the telegraph, movies, and radio, then discussed media theory to 1960 in *Media and the American Mind: From Morse to McLuhan* (Chapel Hill: University of North Carolina Press, 1982). Everette Dennis and John C. Merrill took opposing sides in *Media Debates: Issues in Mass Communication* (New York: Longman, 1991). Bryce W. Rucker presents a comprehensive survey of media dilemmas while updating Morris Ernst's 1946 study by the same title, *The First Freedom* (Carbondale: Southern Illinois University Press, 1968).

## Part Three: Radio and Popular Music

### Chapter 8: Radio

Broadcast History.    An eight-year editing project by Lawrence H. Lichty and Malachi C. Topping resulted in more than 700 pages of *American Broadcasting: A Sourcebook on the History of Radio and Television* (New York: Hastings House, 1975). Two one-volume distillations are Christopher H. Sterling and John M. Kittross, *Stay Tuned: A Concise History of American Broadcasting* (Belmont, CA: Wadsworth, 1990), and F. Leslie Smith, *Perspectives on Radio and Television* (New York: Harper & Row, 1984). The story of PBS is told in John Witherspoon and Rosalie Kovitz, *History of Public Broadcasting* (Washington: Current, 1987).

Other historical accounts include Susan Smulyen, *Selling Radio: The Commercialization of American Broadcasting, 1920–1934* (Washington, DC: Smithsonian Institution Press, 1994); Robert McChesney, *Telecommunications, Mass Media, and Democracy, The Battle for Control of U.S. Broadcasting, 1928–1935* (New York: Oxford University Press, 1993); Erik Barnouw's three-volume history of American broadcasting, *A Tower in Babel*, *The Golden Web*, and *The Image Empire* (New York: Oxford University Press, 1966, 1968, 1970); Sydney W. Head and Christopher Sterling, *Broadcasting in America* (Boston: Houghton Mifflin, 1987); Susan J. Douglas, *Inventing American Broadcasting: 1899–1922* (Baltimore: Johns Hopkins University Press, 1987), best account of the rise of radio; Hugh G. J. Aitken, *The Continuous Wave: Technology and American Radio 1900–1932* (Princeton, NJ: Princeton University Press, 1985); Gleason L. Archer's classics, *History of Radio to 1926* (New York: American Historical Society, 1938) and *Big Business and Radio* (1939); and Llewellyn White's *The American Radio* (Chicago: University of Chicago Press, 1947). *Broadcasting* magazine issued a volume compiled from its files on its fiftieth anniversary in 1981, *The First 50 Years of Broadcasting*, an informal history.

Biographies include Raymond A. Schroth, *The American Journey of Eric Sevareid* (South Royalton, VT.: Steerforth Press, 1995); Kenneth Bilby, *The General: David Sarnoff and the Rise of the Communications Industry* (New York: Harper & Row, 1987); Lewis J. Paper, *Empire; William S. Paley and the Making of CBS* (New York: St. Martin's Press, 1987); Joseph E. Persico, *Edward R. Murrow: An American Original* (New York: McGraw-Hill, 1988); Ann M. Sperber, *Murrow: His Life and Times* (New York: Freundlich, 1986); Alexander Kendrick, *Prime Time: The Life of Edward R. Murrow* (Boston: Little, Brown, 1969); Roger Burlingame, *Don't Let Them Scare You: The Life and Times of Elmer Davis* (Philadelphia: Lippincott, 1961); and Irving E. Fang, *Those Radio Commentators!* (Ames: Iowa State University Press, 1977).

Autobiographies are William S. Paley, *As It Happened: A Memoir* (Garden City, NY: Doubleday, 1979); Lowell Thomas, *Good Evening Everybody* (New York: Morrow, 1976); *Father of Radio: The Autobiography of Lee De Forest* (Chicago: Wilcox & Follett, 1950); and H. V. Kaltenborn, *Fifty Fabulous Years, 1900–1950: A Personal Review* (New York: Putnam's, 1950). Two collections of writings are *In Search of Light: The Broadcasts of Edward R. Murrow 1938–1961* (New York: Knopf, 1967) and *Looking Ahead: The Papers of David Sarnoff* (New York: McGraw-Hill, 1968).

Historical accounts of networks are found in Sterling Quinlan, *Inside ABC: American Broadcasting Company's Rise to Power* (New York: Hastings House, 1979), and for CBS in David Halberstam's *The Powers That Be* (New York: Knopf, 1979). Ken Aulette in *Three Blind Mice: How the TV Networks Lost Their Way* (New York: Random House, 1991) analyzes the 1986 takeovers. The history of network news was told in Edward Bliss, Jr., *And Now the News* (New York: Columbia University Press, 1991).

Relationships with government are analyzed in Walter B. Emery, *Broadcasting and Government* (East Lansing: Michigan State University Press, 1971); and in John R. Bittner, *Broadcast Law and Regulation* (Englewood Cliffs, NJ: Prentice Hall, 1982). For sources, see Frank J. Kahn, *Documents of American Broadcasting* (Prentice Hall, 1984). Donald G. Godfrey compiled *A Directory of Broadcast Archives* (Washington: Broadcast Education Association, 1983) and Thomas A. Greenfield, *Radio: A Reference Guide* (Westport, CT: Greenwood Press, 1989).

## Radio

Introductory books for radio include Michael Keith and Joseph Krause, *The Radio Station* (Stoneham, MA: Focal Press, 1989); Robert L. Hilliard, *Radio Broadcasting* (New York: Longman, 1985); and Peter Fornatele and Joshua Mills, *Radio in the Television Age* (Woodstock, NY: Overlook Press, 1980). A specialized history is J. Fred MacDonald, *Don't Touch That Dial! Radio Programming in American Life 1920–1960* (Chicago: Nelson Hall, 1979). Two books about radio's comedy programs are Jim Harmon, *The Great Radio Comedians* (New York: Doubleday, 1970), and Arthur Wertheim, *Radio Comedy* (New York: Oxford University Press, 1979).

All electronic media are covered in Joseph Dominick, Barry J. Sherman, and Gary Copeland, *Broadcasting/Cablecasting and Beyond: An Introduction to Modern Electronic Media* (New York: McGraw-Hill, 1993).

Books dealing with radio news include Roy Gibson, *Radio and Television Reporting* (New York: Allyn & Bacon, 1990); John and Denise Bittner, *Radio Journalism* (Englewood Cliffs, NJ: Prentice Hall, 1977), including documentaries; F.

Gifford, *Tape: A Radio News Handbook* (New York: Hastings House, 1977); G. Paul Smeyak, *Broadcast News Writing* (Columbus, OH Grid, 1977); Mitchell Stephens, *Broadcast News* (New York: Holt, Rinehart and Winston, 1992); and Mervin Block, *Broadcast Newswriting; The PTNDA Reference Guide* (Chicago: Bonus Books, 1995), co-published with the Radio Television News Directors Association.

Lewis B. O'Donnell, Carl Hausman and Philip Benoit collaborated on *Radio Station Operation* (Belmont, CA: Wadsworth, 1989) and *Announcing: Broadcast Communicating Today* (Wadsworth, 1987). In radio management and production, two key books are Edd Routt, *The Business of Radio Broadcasting* (Blue Ridge Summit, PA: TAB Books, 1972), one of a series issued by that publisher, and Robert Oringel's *Audio Control Handbook* (Stoneham, MA: Focal Press, 1989). Jonne Murphy offers *Handbook of Radio Advertising* (Radnor, PA: Chilton, 1980). An excellent book about announcing is Stuart W. Hyde, *Television and Radio Announcing* (Boston: Houghton Mifflin, 1992); another is William L. Hagerman, *Broadcast Announcing* (Englewood Cliffs, NJ: Prentice Hall, 1993).

## Chapter 9: Popular Music

Celebrating the centennial of the phonograph with its third edition was Roland Gelatt's *The Fabulous Phonograph: 1877–1977* (New York: Macmillan, 1977). A popular history is C. A. Schicke, *Revolution in Sound: A Biography of the Recording Industry* (Boston: Little, Brown, 1974). Another is R. Serge Denisoff, *Solid Gold: The Popular Record Industry* (New Brunswick, NJ: Transaction Books, 1975). Denisoff wrote a sequel, *Tarnished Gold: The Record Industry Revised* (Transaction Books, 1986), and also *Inside MTV* (Transaction Books, 1988), reviewing cable's challenge to records.

## Issue 3: Who Owns the Media?

Ben Bagdikian's answer to this question is an exposé of corporate influence on publishing, in *The Media Monopoly* (Boston: Beacon Press, 1987). Loren Ghiglione presents ten case studies in *The Buying and Selling of American Newspapers* (Indianapolis, IN: R. J. Berg, 1984). Representing more than three years of work by 30 members of AEJMC's Mass Communication and Society Division is *Press Concentration and Monopoly: New Perspectives on Newspaper Ownership and Operation* (Norwood, NJ: Ablex, 1988). Edited by Robert G. Picard, James P. Winter, Well E. McCombs and Stephen Lacy, the 256-page book deals with the results of concentration and monopoly and their impact on such diverse problems as employee relations, news diversity, advertising rates, and public policy. Other studies include Robert Picard, *Media Economics: Concepts and Issues* (Beverly Hills, CA: Sage, 1989) and John Lavine and Daniel Wackman, *Managing Media Organizations* (New York: Longman, 1988).

Among biographical studies of media empire builders are the best-selling *Confessions of an S.O.B.* by Al Neuharth (New York: Doubleday, 1989); Michael Leapman, *Arrogant Aussie: The Rupert Murdoch Story* (New York: Lyle Stuart, 1985); and Christian Williams, *Lead, Follow or Get Out of the Way: The Story of Ted Turner* (New York: Times Books, 1982). Articles about the same three men are found in Agee, Ault, and Emery, *Maincurrents in Mass Communications* (New York: Harper & Row, 1989). Richard M. Clurman's *To the End of Time* (New

York: Simon and Schuster, 1992), describes "the seduction and conquest of a media empire" by Warner's Steve Ross.

*The Mass Media: Aspen Institute Guide to Communication Industry Trends*, by Christopher H. Sterling and Timothy R. Haight, is a primary source. For data and trends analysis, see Benjamin N. Compaine, editor, *Who Owns the Media? Concentration of Ownership in the Mass Communications Industry* (White Plains, NY: Knowledge Industry Publications, 1979), and Compaine's *The Newspaper Industry in the 1980s* (Knowledge Industry, 1980).

Minorities and Media.    A major discussion of the evolving relationship between the American mass media and non-European minorities is contributed by Clint C. Wilson II and Félix Gutiérrez in *Minorities and Media* (Beverly Hills, CA: Sage, 1985). They discuss media reporting about blacks, Asians, Hispanics, and Native Americans, and the rise of a segmented media. Problems of employment of minorities by the mass media are analyzed. Ana Veciana-Suarez, a Miami *Herald* journalist, has produced a narrative guide and directory, *Hispanic Media, USA* (Washington, DC: Media Institute, 1987), based on research and interviews. Another perspective is provided by Jannette Dates and William Bartow, editors, *Split Image: African-Americans in the Mass Media* (Washington, DC: Howard University Press, 1990).

## Part Four: The Visual Electronic and Film Media

### Chapter 10: Television

For major accounts of broadcast history that include both television and radio, see the bibliography for Chapter 8: Radio. Other citations, for television, include: Eric Barnouw, *Tube of Plenty: The Evolution of American Television* (New York: Oxford, 1990), updated and revised; Michael Winship, *Television* (New York: Random House, 1988), companion volume to an eight-part PBS historical series; Barbara Matusow, *The Evening Stars* (Boston: Houghton Mifflin, 1983), portraits of news anchors; Dan Rather, *The Camera Never Blinks* (New York: Morrow, 1977); Sig Mickelson, *From Whistle Stop to Sound Bite: Four Decades of Politics and Television* (New York: Praeger, 1989); Marlene Sanders and Marcia Rock, *Waiting for Prime Time: The Women of Television News* (Urbana: University of Illinois Press, 1988), interviews; David Hosely and Gayle K. Yamada, *Hard News: Women in Broadcast Journalism* (Westport, CT: Greenwood Press, 1987), showing progress since 1920.

James W. Carey edited *Media, Myths and Narratives: Television and the Press* (Newbury Park, CA: Sage, 1988). Shanto Iyengar and Donald E. Kinder wrote *News that Matters: Television and American Opinion* (Chicago: University of Chicago Press, 1987).

Introductory books for television include John R. Bittner, *Broadcasting and Telecommunication: Introduction* (Englewood Cliffs, NJ: Prentice Hall, 1991); Edgar Willis and Henry B. Aldridge, *Television, Cable, and Radio* (Prentice Hall, 1992); and Horace Newcomb, *TV: The Most Popular Art* (Garden City, NY: Doubleday Anchor, 1974), an analysis of popular TV programming.

Books that deal with television news are Irving E. Fang, *Television News, Radio News* (Minneapolis, MN: Rada Press, 1985); Richard Yoakam and Charles F.

Cremer, *ENG: Television News and the New Technology* (New York: Random House, 1989): David K. Cohler, *Broadcast Newswriting* (Englewood Cliffs, NJ: Prentice Hall, 1990); Carolyn D. Lewis, *Reporting for Television* (New York: Columbia University Press, 1984); Ted White, Adrian J. Meppen, and Stephen B. Young, *Broadcast News Writing, Reporting and Production* (New York: Macmillan, 1984); and Edward Bliss, Jr. and John M. Patterson, *Writing News for Broadcast* (New York: Columbia University Press, 1994).

Books treating various types of writing are Martin Maloney and Paul Max Rubenstein, *Writing for the Media* (Englewood Cliffs, NJ: Prentice Hall, 1980); Daniel E. Garvey and William L. Rivers, *Broadcast Writing* (New York: Longman, 1982); Peter B. Orlik, *Broadcast Cable Copywriting* (New York: Allyn & Bacon, 1990); and Milan D. Meeske and R. C. Norris, *Copywriting for the Electronic Media* (Belmont, CA: Wadsworth, 1992).

Management and Production.   Robert L. Hilliard, editor, *Television Station Operations and Management* (Stoneham, MA: Focal Press, 1989); Norman Marcus, *Broadcast and Cable Management* (Englewood Cliffs, NJ: Prentice Hall, 1986); Charles Warner, *Broadcast and Cable Selling* (Belmont, CA: Wadsworth, 1986); Thomas D. Burrows, Donald N. Wood, and Lynne S. Gross, *Television Production: Disciplines and Techniques* (Dubuque, LA: Brown, 1989); Ronald J. Compesi and Ronald E. Sherriffs, *Small Format Television* (New York: Allyn & Bacon, 1990), focusing on ENG and EFP techniques; Alan Wurtzel and Stephen R. Acker, *Television Production* (New York: McGraw-Hill, 1989); Stanley R. Alten, *Audio in Media* (Belmont, CA: Wadsworth, 1990); Alan A. Armer, *Directing Television and Film* (Wadsworth, 1986); Susan Tyler Eastman, Sydney Head, and Lewis Klein, *Broadcast Cable Programming* (Wadsworth, 1989); Richard Breyer and Peter Moller, *Making Television Programs* (New York: Longman, 1984); Herbert Zettl, *Television Production Handbook* (Belmont, CA: Wadsworth, 1984), a classic text; and Elizabeth J. Heighton and Don R. Cunningham, *Advertising in the Broadcast Media* (Wadsworth, 1984).

Methods of displaying textual information on a video display screen are described in *Videotext*, edited by Efrem Sigel (White Plains, NY: Knowledge Industry Publications, 1980).

## Chapter 11: Cable Television

Many of the bibliographical references for the preceding chapter, Television, apply to Cable Television. Some specific references follow.

Cable is the focus of Thomas Baldwin and D. Stevens McVoy in *Cable Communication* (Englewood Cliffs, NJ: Prentice Hall, 1988). Ronald Garay used narrative form in producing *Cable Television: A Reference Guide to Information* (Westport, CT.: Greenwood Press, 1988). Both books will yield bibliographical references.

Marvin Smith, *Radio, TV, and Cable* (New York: Holt, Rinehart and Winston, 1985), is an introductory book, Peter B. Orlik is author of *Broadcast/Cable Copywriting* (New York: Allyn & Bacon, 1990). *Broadcast/Cable Programming* (Belmont, Ca.: Wadsworth, 1989) is coauthored by Susan Tyler Eastman, Sydney Head, and Lewis Klein. Other specific references include Norman Marcus, *Broadcast and Cable Management* (Englewood Cliffs, NJ: Prentice Hall, 1986);

Charles Warner, *Broadcast and Cable Selling* (Wadsworth, 1986); and Hank Whittemore, *CNN: The Inside Story* (Boston: Little, Brown, 1990).

## Chapter 12: Video

*Video Economics*, by Bruce M. Owen and Steven S. Wildman (Cambridge: Harvard University Press, 1992), is a highly recommended update of Owen's 1974 *Television Economics*. Roy Armes in *On Video* (New York: Routledge, 1988), covers video's history, social context, and aesthetics. Gladys and Oswald Ganley provide a scholarly analysis in *Global Political Fallout: The First Decade of the VCR, 1976–1985* (Norwood, NJ: Ablex, 1987). James Lardner provides a lively narrative of the ups and downs of VCR competition in *Fast Forward: Hollywood, the Japanese, and the Onslaught of the VCR* (New York: Norton, 1987). New in production are James P. Walker and Robert W. Bellamy, Jr., editors, *The Remote Control in the New Age of Television* (Westport, CT: Praeger, 1993); Carl Hausman and Philip Palombo, *Modern Video Production* (New York: HarperCollins, 1993) and Henry B. Aldridge and Lucy A. Liggett, *Audio/Video Production: Theory and Practice* (Englewood Cliffs, NJ: Prentice Hall, 1990).

See the bibliography for Chapter 1, particularly Gross, *Telecommunications*, and *Television Digest*'s anthology, *The Videocassette Recorder: An American Love Affair*. Other references include Eli M. Noam, editor, *Video Media Competition* (New York: Columbia University Press, 1985), covering research and statistics, including VCRs; Fiona Richardson, editor, *Video in the UK and US* (London: Financial Times Business Information, 1984), an historical and current overview of the videocassette, videodisc, and marketing; Mark Nadel and Eli M. Noam, editors; *The Supply and Demand for Video Programming: An Anthology* (New York: Columbia University Graduate School of Business, 1983).

In the "how-to-do-it" category, but also explaining the medium are Peter Utz, *Today's Video: Equipment, Setup, and Production* (Englewood Cliffs, NJ: Prentice Hall, 1992); Pamela Levine, et al., *Complete Guide to Home Video Production* (New York: Holt, Rinehart and Winston, 1984); Ingrid Wiegand, *Professional Video Production* (White Plains, NY: Knowledge Industry Publications, 1985); and Frank Leslie Moore, *The Video Moviemaker's Handbook* (New York: New American Library, 1984).

Shemus Culhene offers an anecdotal discussion of animation on film in *Talking Animals and Other People* (New York: St. Martin's Press, 1986).

## Chapter 13: Photographic and Graphic Communications

**Photographic History and Development.** Beaumont Newhall, *The History of Photography from 1839 to the Present* (New York: Museum of Modern Art, 1982); Alma Davenport, *The History of Photography: An Overview* (Stoneham, MA: Focal Press, 1991), a good, concise account; Helmut and Alison Gernsheim, *History of Photography* (London: Oxford University Press, 1970); Peter Pollack, *Picture History of Photography* (New York: Abrams, 1969); Nathan Lyons, *Photographers on Photography* (Englewood Cliffs, NJ: Prentice Hall, 1966); R. Smith Schuneman, *Photographic Communication: Principles, Problems and Challenges of Photojournalism* (New York: Hastings House, 1972); A. William Bluem, *Documentary in American Television* (New York: Hastings House, 1965); and Paul Rotha, Sinclair Road, and Richard Griffith, *Documentary Film* (London: Faber and Faber, 1966).

Photographic Techniques. Robert Jay Hirsch, *Exploring Color Photography* (Dubuque, IA: Brown, 1989); Arnold Gassan, *Exploring Black and White Photography* (Brown, 1989); Frederick Shook, *Television Field Production and Reporting* (New York: Longman, 1989); Harold Evans, *Pictures on a Page* (Belmont, CA: Wadsworth, 1979), by the former editor of the *Sunday Times*, London; Kenneth Kobre, *Photojournalism: The Professionals' Approach* (Stoneham, MA: Focal Press, 1991); Robert B. Rhode and Floyd H. McCall, *Introduction to Photography* (New York: Macmillan, 1981); Philip C. Geraci, *Photojournalism: The Visual Approach* (Englewood Cliffs, NJ: Prentice Hall, 1993).

Biographical. James Horan, *Mathew Brady: Historian with a Camera* (New York: Crown, 1955), and *Timothy O'Sullivan: America's Forgotten Photographer* (New York: Crown, 1966); Judith Gutman, *Lewis W. Hine and the American Social Conscience* (New York: Walker, 1967); Richard Griffith, *The World of Robert Flaherty* (New York: Duell, Sloan and Pearce, 1953); Karin Becker Ohrn, *Dorothea Lange and the Documentary Tradition* (Baton Rouge: Louisiana State Press, 1980); Pare Lorentz, *F.D.R.'s Moviemaker: Memoirs and Scripts* (Reno: University of Nevada Press, 1992); Margaret Bourke-White, *Portrait of Myself* (New York: Simon and Schuster, 1963); Vickie Goldberg, *Margaret Bourke-White* (New York: Harper & Row, 1986); Ansel Adams, *An Autobiography* (Boston: Little, Brown, 1985); Richard Whelan, *Robert Capa* (New York: Knopf, 1986); David Douglas Duncan, *Yankee Nomad* (New York: Holt, Rinehart and Winston, 1966); Carl Mydans, *More Than Meets the Eye* (New York: Harper & Row, 1959); Gordon Parks, *A Choice of Weapons* (New York: Harper & Row, 1966); Edward Steichen, *A Life in Photography* (Garden City, NY: Doubleday, 1963); Cornell Capa, *Robert Capa* (New York: Grossman, 1974); Dora Jane Hamblin, *That Was the Life* (New York: W. W. Norton, 1977).

Picture Books. Alfred Eisenstaedt, *Witness to Our Times* (New York: Viking, 1966); David Douglas Duncan, *War Without Heroes* (New York: Harper & Row, 1970); William S. Johnson, editor, *W. Eugene Smith: Master of the Photographic Essay* (Millerton, NY: Aperture, 1982); Carl Mydans, *Photojournalist* (New York: Abrams, 1985); Robert Capa, *Photographs* (New York: Knopf, 1986); *Life, the First Fifty Years* (Boston: Little, Brown, 1986); John Phillips, *It Happened in Our LIFETIME* (Little, Brown, 1985); John Szarkowski, *The Photographer's Eye* (New York: Museum of Modern Art, 1966); Leonard Freed, *Black in White America* (New York: Grossman, n.d.); Cornell Capa, editor, *The Concerned Photographer* (Grossman, 1969), 200 photos of protest by six leading photographers; Charles Harbutt and Lee Jones, *America in Crisis* (New York: Holt, Rinehart and Winston, 1969); Associated Press, *The Instant It Happened* (New York: Associated Press, 1974), great news photos from the Civil War to Watergate. The University of Missouri Press began issuing an annual, *The Best of Photojournalism*, in 1975.

Graphics and Production. Edmund C. Arnold, *Designing the Total Newspaper* (New York: Harper & Row, 1981), and *Ink on Paper 2* (Harper & Row,

1972); Russell N. Baird, Duncan McDonald, Ronald K. P. Himan, and Arthur T. Turnbull, *The Graphics of Communication: Typography, Layout and Design* (New York: Harcourt Brace Jovanovich, 1992); Anthony Smith, *Goodbye Gutenberg—The Newspaper Revolution of the 1980s* (London: Oxford University Press, 1980); Mario R. Garcia, *Contemporary Newspaper Design* (Englewood Cliffs, NJ: Prentice Hall, 1993); Roy Paul Nelson, *Publication Design* (Dubuque, IA: Brown, 1991); Sean Morrison, *A Guide to Type Design* (Englewood Cliffs, NJ: Prentice Hall, 1986); Daryl R. Moen, *Newspaper Layout and Design* (Ames: Iowa State University Press, 1989); Wendell C. Crow, *Communication Graphics* (Englewood Cliffs, NJ: Prentice Hall, 1986); Roy Paul Nelson, *Design of Advertising* (Dubuque, IA: Brown, 1989); Ralph Ayers, *Graphics for Television* (Englewood Cliffs, NJ: Prentice Hall, 1984); Steven E. Ames, *Elements of Newspaper Design* (New York: Praeger, 1989); and Robert Bohle, *Publications Design for Editors* (Englewood Cliffs, NJ: Prentice Hall, 1990).

An overview of all types of art direction and design in the 1980s was offered by the editors of *Studio Magazine* in *Graphic Excellence.* The Society of Newspaper Design publishes an annual series entitled *The Best of Newspaper Design.*

## Chapter 14: The Film

Leading historical surveys of motion pictures are Paul Rotha and Richard Griffith, *The Film Till Now* (London: Spring Books, 1967), a world cinema survey; and Richard Griffith and Arthur Mayer, *The Movies* (New York: Simon and Schuster, 1970), American film history. Gerald Mast's *A Short History of the Movies* (New York: Bobbs-Merrill, 1981), offers detailed, highly readable descriptions and analyses, primarily of American and European films. A competitor is David A. Cook, *A History of Narrative Film* (New York: W. W. Norton, 1981), as are Jack C. Ellis, *A History of Film* (Englewood Cliffs, NJ: Prentice Hall, 1990), and Douglas Gomery, *Movie History: A Survey* (Belmont, CA: Wadsworth, 1991).

Other important film histories include Arthur Knight, *The Liveliest Art* (New York: Hastings House, 1978), particularly good for the years 1895 to 1930; D. J. Wenden, *The Birth of the Movies* (New York: Dutton, 1975), covering 1895 to 1927; William K. Everson, *American Silent Film* (New York: Oxford University Press, 1978), copiously illustrated; Harry Geduld, *The Birth of the Talkies: From Edison to Jolson* (Bloomington: Indiana University Press, 1975); David Bordwell, Janet Staiger, and Kristin Thompson, *The Classical Hollywood Cinema: Film Style and Mode of Production* (New York: Columbia University Press, 1985), a first-rate new version of film history, 1895 to 1960; and John Fell, editor, *Film Before Griffith* (Berkeley, CA: University of California Press, 1984).

The best social history is Garth Jowett, *Film: The Democratic Art* (Boston: Little, Brown, 1976), updating Lewis Jacobs' *The Rise of the American Film* (1939). Another is Robert Sklar, *Movie-Made America* (New York: Random House, 1975). Gerald Mast edited an anthology tracing the cultural importance of movies, *The Movies in Our Midst* (Chicago: University of Chicago Press, 1981).

The standard work on the history, principles, and technique of the documentary motion picture is Paul Rotha, Sinclair Road, and Richard Griffith, *The Documentary Film* (London: Faber and Faber, 1966). Others include Jack C. Ellis, *The Documentary Idea: A Critical History of English Language Documentary Film and Video* (Englewood Cliffs, NJ: Prentice Hall, 1989); Lewis Jacobs, *The*

*Documentary Tradition* (New York: W. W. Norton, 1979); Alan Rosenthal, *The New Documentary in Action: A Casebook in Film Making* (Berkeley: University of California Press, 1971); Richard M. Barsam, *Nonfiction Film: A Critical History* (New York: Dutton, 1973); Richard D. MacCann, *The People's Films* (New York: Hastings House, 1973), a history of United States government documentaries; Erik Barnouw, *Documentary: A History of the Non-Fiction Film* (London: Oxford University Press, 1974), a well-integrated analysis; Paul Swann, *The British Documentary Film Movement, 1926–1946* (Cambridge: Cambridge University Press, 1989); and Charles Montgomery Hammond, Jr., *The Image Decade: Television Documentary 1965–1975* (New York: Hastings House, 1981). Newsreels are covered in Raymond Fielding's *The American Newsreel, 1911–1967* (Norman: University of Oklahoma Press, 1972).

Film genres—Westerns, musicals, detectives, horror, and so on—are described by Stuart M. Kaminsky and Jeffrey H. Mahon in *American Film Genres* (Chicago: Nelson-Hall, 1985). Brian G. Rose edited *TV Genres: A Handbook and Reference Guide* (Westport, CT: Greenwood Press, 1985).

A pathbreaking reworking of contemporary film theory is offered by Edward Branigan in *Point of View in the Cinema: A Theory of Narration and Subjectivity in Classical Film* (Berlin: Mouton Books, 1984). Also in the field of theory and criticism are Gerald Mast and Marshall Cohen, editors, *Film Theory and Criticism* (New York: Oxford University Press, 1985); J. Dudley Andrew, *The Major Film Theories* (Oxford University Press, 1976); Garth Jowett and James M. Linton, *Movies as Mass Communication* (Beverly Hills, CA: Sage, 1989); and Tim Bywater and Thomas Sobchack, *An Introduction to Film Criticism* (New York: Longman, 1989), discussing major critical approaches to narrative film.

The audience was the subject of Bruce A. Austin's *Immediate Seating: A Look at Movie Audiences* (Belmont, CA: Wadsworth, 1989).

## Issue 4: Credibility: Can We Trust the Media?

An excellent basis for any discussion of the duties and the performance record of the mass media is the summary report of the Commission on Freedom of the Press, *A Free and Responsible Press* (Chicago: University of Chicago Press, 1947). The commission printed four studies, Chafee's *Government and Mass Communications*, Hocking's *Freedom of the Press*, White's *The American Radio*, and Ruth Inglis' *Freedom of the Movies*, as well as *Peoples Speaking to Peoples*, by Llewellyn White and Robert D. Leigh (Chicago: University of Chicago Press, 1946), an analysis of international news channels.

Four major research studies of press credibility and public support for the media were published in 1985 and 1986. The most elaborate, *The People & the Press*, was carried out by the Gallup Organization for the Times Mirror newspaper group (Los Angeles: Times Mirror, 1986). Two other national studies were done by MORI Research, Minneapolis: *Newspaper Credibility: Building Reader Trust* (Reston, VA: American Society of Newspaper Editors, 1986), and *Journalists and Readers: Bridging the Credibility Gap* (Reston, VA: Associated Press Managing Editors Association, 1985). A 50-year review of the literature, *The Media and the People*, summarizes the studies described above (New York: Gannett Center for Media Studies, Columbia University, 1986).

An in-depth study of four major media institutions and their principal operating heads is found in David Halberstam, *The Powers That Be* (New York: Viking, 1978). The four institutions are CBS, Time Inc., the Washington *Post*, and the Los Angeles *Times*, with the New York *Times* hovering in the background. The reportorial process is examined in Gaye Tuchman, *Making News* (New York: Free Press, 1978), and the editing process in Herbert Gans, *Deciding What's News: A Study of CBS Evening News, NBC Nightly News, Newsweek & Time* (New York: Pantheon, 1979). Tom Wicker is reflective in *On Press* (New York: Viking, 1978). Ben Wattenberg attacks conventional wisdoms of the press in *The Good News Is the Bad News Is Wrong* (New York: Simon and Schuster, 1984). Also pertinent are Rodney A. Smolla, *Suing the Press* (New York: Oxford University Press, 1986); Norman E. Isaacs, *Untended Gates: The Mismanaged Press* (New York: Columbia University Press, 1986); and J. Edward Gerald, *News of Crime* (Westport, CT: Greenwood Press, 1983). The *Aspen Notebook on Government and the Media*, edited by William L. Rivers and Michael J. Nyhan (New York: Praeger, 1973), offers a spirited debate of government-media relations and regulatory issues.

The Reagan years brought controversy and criticism of both the presidency and the press. Among the books for the turbulent 1980s are Robert E. Denton, Jr., *The Primetime Presidency of Ronald Reagan* (New York: Praeger, 1988); Mark Hertsgaard, *On Bended Knee: The Press and the Reagan Presidency* (New York: Farrar, Straus, Giroux, 1989); Doris A. Graber, *News Media and American Politics* (Washington: Congressional Quarterly Press, 1988), and also *Processing the News* (New York: Longman, 1988); and Montague Kern, *30-Second Politics: Political Advertising in the Eighties* (New York: Praeger, 1989). Presenting left- and right-wing views of the media are Edward S. Herman and Noah Chomsky, *Manufacturing Consent: The Political Economy of the Mass Media* (New York: Pantheon, 1988), arguing the media reinforce the economic, social, and political agenda of the elite; and William Rusher, *The Coming Battle for the Media: Curbing the Power of the Media Elite* (New York: Morrow, 1988), by the publisher of the right-wing *National Review*.

**Readings.**   Two books edited by Warren K. Agee provide extensive criticisms of the media: *The Press and the Public Interest* (Washington: Public Affairs Press, 1968) contains the annual William Allen White Lectures delivered by 18 of America's leading reporters, editors, and publishers; in *Mass Media in a Free Society* (Lawrence: University Press of Kansas, 1969) six media spokesmen discuss challenges and problems confronting newspapers, television, motion pictures, and magazines. Other criticisms of press performance are found in *The Press in Perspective*, edited by Ralph D. Casey (Baton Rouge: Louisiana State University Press, 1963), 17 lectures at the University of Minnesota.

Selected readings on both media issues and the mass communications industries and professions are presented in *Maincurrents in Mass Communications*, edited by Warren K. Agee, Phillip H. Ault, and Edwin Emery (New York: Harper & Row, 1989). A comprehensive collection of articles focusing on major media issues and criticisms is found in Michael C. Emery and Ted Curtis Smythe, *Readings in Mass Communication: Concepts and Issues in the Mass Media* (Dubuque, IA: Brown, 1996). Other books of readings include Shirley Biagi, *Media/Reader* (Belmont, CA: Wadsworth, 1993), and Glen O. Robinson, *Communication for Tomorrow: Policy Perspectives for the 1980s* (New York: Praeger, 1978), an Aspen-sponsored publication.

Riots.    For details on studies of violence in riots, see Robert K. Baker and Sandra J. Ball, *Violence and the Media* (Washington: Government Printing Office, 1969), a staff report to the National Commission on the Causes and Prevention of Violence giving a historical treatment and a review of research. Two major citations in commission reports are *Report of the National Advisory Commission on Civil Disorders* (Kerner Report, 1968), Chapter 15, "The News Media and the Disorders," and *Rights in Conflict*, the Walker Report to the National Commission on the Causes and Prevention of Violence, 1968, pages 287–327, "The Police and the Press."

Politics.    Two studies of political reporting are Michael B. Grossman and Martha J. Kumar, *Portraying the President* (Baltimore: Johns Hopkins University Press, 1981), and Stephen Hess, *The Washington Reporters* (Washington: Brookings Institution, 1981). A more general study is William L. Rivers, *The Other Government: Power and the Washington Media* (New York: Universe, 1982). James Deakin, White House correspondent from 1955 to 1980 for the St. Louis *Post-Dispatch*, wrote *Straight Stuff: The Reporters, the White House and the Truth* (New York: Morrow, 1984). Sam Donaldson of ABC contributed *Hold On, Mr. President!* (New York: Random House, 1987). One of the best reports on the 1972 campaign press corps was Timothy Crouse, *The Boys on the Bus* (Random House, 1973). The Kennedy years are analyzed by Montague Kern, Patricia W. Levering, and Ralph B. Levering in *The Kennedy Crises: The Press, the Presidency, and Foreign Policy* (Chapel Hill: University of North Carolina Press, 1983).

An exhaustive, well-balanced account of the Vietnam years is found in William M. Hammond's *The United States Army in Vietnam: Public Affairs, the Military and the Press*, Vol. 1, 1962–68, Vol. 2, 1968–73 (Washington: Center of Military History, 1989, 1993). The author had access to previously restricted Nixon files and presents a scholarly synthesis of military and press accounts.

A 1000-page study of the Watergate years of 1972 to 1974, objectively presented with detailed documentary support, is *Watergate: Chronology of a Crisis* (Washington: Congressional Quarterly Press, 1975), edited by Mercer Cross and Elder Witt with a staff of 30 from that research organization and contributors. Gladys Engel Lang and Kurt Lang approached Watergate from a social science perspective in *The Battle for Public Opinion: The President, the Press, and the Polls During Watergate* (New York: Columbia University Press, 1983). An excellent updated summation with insight and historical depth is Stanley I. Kutler, *The Wars of Watergate: The Last Crisis of Richard Nixon* (New York: Alfred A. Knopf, 1990).

Broadcasting and Cable.    Effective criticisms include Todd Gitlin, *Inside Prime Time* (New York: Pantheon, 1985); Jerry Jacobs, *Changing Channels* (Mountain View, CA: Mayfield, 1990), on issues in broadcast news; Robert T. Bower, *The Changing Television Audience in America* (New York: Columbia University Press, 1985), research-oriented; Philip Drummond and Richard Paterson, editors, *Television in Transition* (London: British Film Institute, 1986), papers from the 1984 International Television Studies Conference; George Comstock, *Television in America* (Beverly Hills, CA: Sage, 1980); Horace Newcomb, editor, *Television: The Critical View* (New York: Oxford University Press, 1982); Muriel Cantor, *Prime Time Television: Content and Control* (Beverly Hills, CA: Sage, 1980); and Edward Jay Epstein, *News from Nowhere: Television and the News* (New York: Random House, 1973), an evaluation of 1968 to 1969 network news. Critical appraisals by the Alfred I. DuPont-Columbia University Awards committee were begun in 1969 and published variously.

Television news crises are covered admirably in William Small, *To Kill a Messenger* (New York: Hastings House, 1970), covering the 1960s with its crises of war, violence, rioting, and political polarization. Small was then CBS Washington bureau chief. A first-hand criticism of network policy affecting CBS News appears in Fred W. Friendly, *Due to Circumstances Beyond Our Control . . .* (New York: Random House, 1967). The 1969 speeches of Vice President Spiro T. Agnew attacking the fairness of television commentators and other media news are collected in Spiro T. Agnew, *Frankly Speaking* (Washington: Public Affairs Press, 1970). Even stronger attacks were made by Edith Efron in *The News Twisters* and *How CBS Tried to Kill a Book* (Los Angeles: Nash, 1971, 1972).

## Part Five: The Persuasive Professions

### Chapter 15: Advertising

Three books, complementing each other in presenting the history of American advertising, are noteworthy additions to media literature. Daniel Pope's *The Making of Modern Advertising* (New York: Basic Books, 1983), is a thoughtful, analytic account of advertising's growth to 1920, using theoretical perspectives grounded in economics. The major contribution is Roland Marchand's *Advertising the American Dream* (Berkeley: University of California Press, 1985), which uses a cultural approach to the formative period of advertising, 1920 to 1940, describing it as both promoting technological modernity and offering relief from self-image anxiety. Stephen Fox, in *The Mirror Makers: A History of American Advertising and Its Creators* (New York: Morrow, 1984), carries the story through the 1970s, concentrating on the impact of creative people. Nineteenth century advertising and its transformation in the early years of the twentieth century are chronicled in Jackson Lears, *Fables of Abundance: A Cultural History of Advertising in America* (New York: Basic Books, 1994).

Among other histories, the standard account is Frank Presbrey, *The History and Development of Advertising* (New York: Doubleday, Doran, 1930). James Playsted Wood, *The Story of Advertising* (New York: Ronald, 1958), is very readable. E. S. Turner, *The Shocking History of Advertising* (New York: Dutton, 1953), is constructively critical. Michael Schudson, *Advertising: The Uneasy Profession* (New York: Basic Books, 1984), is a critical historical analysis.

The role of advertising in society is discussed in John W. Wright, editor, *The Commercial Connection: Advertising and the American Mass Media* (New York: Dell/Delta, 1979); in Kim B. Rotzoll, James E. Haefner, and Charles H. Sandage, editors, *Advertising in Contemporary Society* (Columbus, OH: Grid, 1976); in John S. Wright and John Mertes, *Advertising's Role in Society* (St. Paul, MN: West, 1976) and in Marilyn Kern-Foxworth, *Aunt Jemima, Uncle Sam, and Rastus: Blacks in Advertising, Yesterday, Today, and Tomorrow* (Westport, CT: Greenwood, 1994).

Research areas are outlined in Alan D. Fletcher and Thomas A. Bowers, *Fundamentals of Advertising Research* (New York: Longman, 1991). Two books on marketing strategy are Leo Bogart, *Strategy in Advertising: Matching Media and Messages to Markets and Motivation* (Lincolnwood, IL: NTC Business Books, 1995); and David J. Luck and O. C. Farrell, *Marketing Strategy and Plans* (Englewood Cliffs, NJ: Prentice Hall, 1985), using numerous case histories.

Among the general text and reference books on advertising are Charles H. Sandage, Vernon Fryburger, and Kim Rotzoll, *Advertising Theory and Practice* (New York: Longman, 1989); Jack Engel, *Advertising: The Process and Practice* (New York: McGraw-Hill, 1980); S. Watson Dunn and Arnold Barban, *Advertising: Its Role in Modern Marketing* (New York: Dryden, 1986); John S. Wright, Daniel S. Warner, and Willis L. Winter, Jr., *Advertising* (New York: McGraw-Hill, 1981); Philip Ward Burton and William Ryan, *Advertising Fundamentals* (Columbus, OH: Grid, 1980); J. Thomas Russell and W. Ronald Lane, *Kleppner's Advertising Procedure* (Englewood Cliffs, NJ: Prentice Hall, 1996), published since 1925; and Keith Adler, *Advertising Resource Handbook* (East Lansing, MI: Advertising Resources, Inc., 1989).

Media is the topic of discussion in Arnold Barban, Donald W. Jugenheimer, and Peter B. Turk, *Advertising Media Sourcebook* (Chicago: NTC Publishing, 1989); in Jack Z. Sissors and Lincoln Bumba, *Advertising Media Planning* (NTC Publishing, 1989) and in Anthony F. McGann and J. Thomas Russell, *Advertising Media: A Managerial Approach* (Homewood, IL: Irwin, 1988). Management is covered in David A. Baker and John G. Myers, *Advertising Management* (Englewood Cliffs, NJ: Prentice Hall, 1987), and in John D. Leckenby and Nugent Wedding, *Advertising Management* (Columbus, OH: Grid, 1982).

Copywriting techniques are described by David L. Malickson and John W. Nason in *Advertising—How to Write the Kind That Works* (New York: Scribner's 1977) and by Philip Ward Burton in *Advertising Copywriting* (Columbus, OH: Grid, 1979). Copy, design, and production are covered by A. Jerome Jewler in *Creative Strategy in Advertising* (Belmont, CA: Wadsworth, 1992), while Sandra E. Moriarty emphasizes theory in *Creative Advertising: Theory and Practice* (Englewood Cliffs, NJ: Prentice Hall, 1986). Others are James L. Marra, *Advertising Copywriting* (Prentice Hall, 1993) and Howard W. Berkman and Christopher Gibson, *Advertising Concepts and Strategies* (New York: Random House, 1987). Two classic writers on copy were Aesop Glim (George Laflin Miller) in *Copy—The Core of Advertising* (New York: Dover, 1963) and *How Advertising Is Written—and Why* (1961); and Clyde Bedell, *How to Write Advertising That Sells* (New York: McGraw-Hill, 1952).

Advertising Agencies.    Herbert S. Gardner, Jr., *The Advertising Agency Business* (Chicago: Crain, 1983), is a practical guide. Martin Mayer, *Madison Avenue, U.S.A.* (New York: Harper, 1958), provides a good picture of advertising agencies; Ralph M. Hower, *The History of an Advertising Agency: N. W. Ayer & Son at Work, 1869–1939* (Cambridge, MA: Harvard University Press, 1939) is a documented history of one agency. David Ogilvy tells a fascinating story about work in an agency in *Confessions of an Advertising Man* (New York: Atheneum, 1963; Dell paperback, 1964). The story of the pioneering Albert Lasker is told by John Gunther in *Taken at the Flood* (New York: Harper & Row, 1960). A look at a major agency's history is provided in Stewart Alter, *Truth Well Told: McCann-Erickson and the Pioneering of Global Advertising* (New York: McCann-Erickson

Worldwide, 1995). Forces for agency change are chronicled in Randall Rothenberg, *Where the Suckers Moon: An Advertising Story* (New York: Knopf, 1994).

## Chapter 16: Public Relations

New to the public relations field in the 1980s was *Public Relations: Strategies and Tactics*, by Dennis L. Wilcox, Phillip H. Ault, and Warren K. Agee (New York: HarperCollins, 1986, revised 1989, 1992, 1995), combining breadth and depth with coverage of "hot" topics and extended case studies. A third author was added for the sixth edition of *Effective Public Relations* by Scott Cutlip, Allen H. Center, and Glen M. Broom (Englewood Cliffs, NJ: Prentice Hall, 1985, revised 1994). H. Frazier Moore and Frank B. Kalupa brought out the ninth edition of *Public Relations: Principles, Cases and Problems* (Homewood, IL: Irwin, 1985), a text begun by Bertrand R. Canfield. Doug Newsom and Alan Scott were joined by Judy Van Slyke Turk in writing *This Is PR: The Realities of Public Relations* (Belmont, CA: Wadsworth, 1992). HarperCollins added Robert Kendall's *Public Relations Campaign Strategies* in 1992.

Entering the field were Otis Baskin and Craig Aronoff, *Public Relations: The Profession and the Practice* (Dubuque, IA: Brown, 1992); Dean Kruckeberg and Kenneth Starck, *Public Relations and Community* (New York: Praeger, 1988); David A. Haberman and Harry A. Dolphin, *Public Relations: The Necessary Art* (Ames: Iowa State University Press, 1988); Ray E. Hiebert, editor, *Precision Public Relations* (New York: Longman, 1988); Jerry A. Hendrix, *Public Relations Cases* (Belmont, CA: Wadsworth, 1992); Carl H. Botan and Vincent Hazelton, Jr., editors, *Public Relations Theory* (Hillsdale, NJ: Erlbaum, 1989); John V. Pavlik, *Public Relations: What Research Tells Us* (Beverly Hills, CA: Sage, 1987); the *Public Relations Research Annual*, Vols. 1–3, edited by James E. Grunig and Larissa A. Grunig (Hillsdale, NJ: Erlbaum, 1989, now the *Journal of Public Relations Research*); Glen Broom and David Dozier, *Using Research in Public Relations* (Englewood Cliffs, NJ: Prentice Hall, 1990); James E. Grunig, David Dozier, D. M. Ehling, Larissa A. Grunig, F. C. Repper, and J. White, editors, *Excellence in Public Relations and Communication Management* (Hillsdale, NJ: Erlbaum, 1992); Robert L. Heath, *Management of Corporate Communication* (Erlbaum, 1994); and E. W. Brody, editor, *New Technology and Public Relations* (Sarasota, FL: Institute for Public Relations Research and Education, 1991).

Other general books include Fraser P. Seitel, *The Practice of Public Relations* (New York: Macmillan, 1995); James E. Grunig and Todd Hunt, *Managing Public Relations* (New York: Holt, Rinehart and Winston, 1984); Raymond Simon, *Public Relations: Principles and Practices* (New York: John Wiley, 1984); and Allen H. Center and Frank E. Walsh, *Public Relations Practices: Managerial Case Studies* (Englewood Cliffs, NJ: Prentice Hall, 1985). Scott Cutlip profiles practitioners who shaped the development of public relations in his 807-page *The Unseen Power: Public Relations. A History* (Hillsdale, IL: Lawrence Erlbaum Associates, 1994). Erlbaum also published Cutlip's *Public Relations: Its Early History* that same year.

A leading counselor, John W. Hill, tells his story in *The Making of a Public Relations Man* (New York: McKay, 1963). Edward L. Bernays, in *Public Relations* (Norman: University of Oklahoma Press, 1979), presents a case history type of discussion by a longtime practitioner. His memoirs are in *Biography of an Idea*

(New York: Simon and Schuster, 1965). Ray E. Hiebert contributed the biography of another pioneer in his *Courtier to the Crowd: The Life Story of Ivy Lee* (Ames: Iowa State University Press, 1966). Alan R. Raucher traced early PR history in *Public Relations and Business 1900–1929* (Baltimore: The Johns Hopkins Press, 1968).

Writing techniques are analyzed in Dennis L. Wilcox and Lawrence W. Nolte, *Public Relations Writing and Media Techniques* (New York: Harper & Row, 1996); Doug Newsom and Bob Carrell, *Public Relations Writing: Form & Style* (Belmont, CA: Wadsworth, 1994); and Frank E. Walsh, *Public Relations Writer in a Computer Age* (Englewood Cliffs, NJ: Prentice Hall, 1986).

Books on fund-raising and development include Kathleen S. Kelly, *Fund-Raising and Public Relations: A Critical Analysis* (Hillsdale, NJ: Lawrence Erlbaum and Associates, 1991) and Wesley E. Lindahl, *Strategic Planning for Fund-Raising* (San Francisco: Jossey-Bass, 1992).

Bibliographies are Scott M. Cutlip, *A Public Relations Bibliography* (Madison: University of Wisconsin Press, 1965), and its extension, Robert L. Bishop, *Public Relations: A Comprehensive Bibliography* (Ann Arbor: University of Michigan Press, 1974).

## Issue 5: Legal Environment: Are the Media Restricted by Too Many Laws?

Two extensive casebooks on press law are Donald M. Gillmor, Jerome A. Barron, Todd F. Simon, and Herbert A. Terry, *Mass Communication Law: Cases and Comment* (St. Paul, MN: West, 1990), and Marc A. Franklin and David A. Anderson, *Cases and Materials on Mass Media Law* (Mineola, NY: Foundation Press, 1990). Two major case-oriented accounts are Dwight Teeter, Jr., and Don R. LaDue, *Law of Mass Communications* (Foundation Press, 1992), and William E. Francois, *Mass Media Law and Regulation* (New York: Wiley, 1986). Steering a middle course between casebook and narrative are Kent Middleton and Bill F. Chamberlin, *The Law of Public Communication* (New York: Longman, 1994), with annual update supplements; Ralph Holsinger, *Media Law* (New York: Random House, 1987); Don R. Pember, *Mass Media Law* (Dubuque, IA: Brown, 1990); and Wayne Overbeck and Rick D. Pullen, *Major Principles of Media Law* (New York: Holt, Rinehart and Winston, 1985). Accompanying Franklin's casebook is yet another major work, *The First Amendment and the Fourth Estate: The Law of Mass Media* by T. Barton Carter, Mare A. Franklin, and Jay B. Wright (Mineola, NY: Foundation Press, 1991). The same trio and publishing house produced *The First Amendment and the Fifth Estate: Regulation of Electronic Mass Media* in 1989. New in 1996 was Robert Trager, editor, *Communication Law and Policy* (Lawrence Erlbaum Associates), sponsored by the Law Division of the Association for Education in Journalism and Mass Communication.

Donald M. Gillmor argues in *Power, Publicity, and the Use of Libel Law* (New York: Oxford, 1992) that public figures should not be allowed to sue for libel, only have right of reply.

Supreme Court trends are traced in William A. Hachten's *The Supreme Court on Freedom of the Press* (Ames: Iowa State University Press, 1968) and later in Kenneth S. Devol's *Mass Media and the Supreme Court* (New York: Hastings House, 1990). J. Edward Gerald's *The Press and the Constitution* (Minneapolis:

University of Minnesota Press, 1948) analyzes constitutional law cases involving press freedom from 1931 to 1947. Law scholar Rodney A. Smolla comments on recent decisions in *Free Speech in an Open Society* (New York: Knopf, 1992).

# Part Six: Communications Worldwide

## Chapter 17: International Mass Communications

Of merit as texts for international communications classes are two 1983 Longman entries. Twenty scholars wrote chapters about six major aspects of mass media, from Western, communist, and Third World viewpoints, in *Comparative Mass Media Systems*, edited by L. John Martin and Anju Grover Chaudhary. John C. Merrill and six coauthors surveyed the world's mass media in *Global Journalism* (updated 1995). Another general text is Heinz-Dietrich Fischer and John C. Merrill, editors, *International and Intercultural Communication* (New York: Hastings House, 1976), with 45 articles by scholars in many countries. George Kurian's two-volume *World Press Encyclopedia* (New York: Facts on File, 1982) and a UNESCO publication, *World Communication Report* (Paris: UNESCO, 1989), are basic reference works for international media study. Another survey is John C. Merrill, Carter R. Bryan, and Marvin Alisky, *The Foreign Press* (Baton Rouge: Louisiana State University Press, 1970).

More detailed studies of the world's leading newspapers were made for John C. Merrill's *The Elite Press* (New York: Pitman, 1969) and its update by Merrill and Harold A. Fisher, *The World's Great Dailies: Profiles of 50 Newspapers* (New York: Hastings House, 1980). Anthony Smith's brief *The Newspaper: An International History* (London: Thames and Hudson, 1979) offers a worldwide account and 111 illustrations.

Some regional accounts include Kenneth E. Olson, *The History Makers* (Baton Rouge: Louisiana State University Press, 1966), a survey of European press history; Won Ho Chang, *Mass Media in China* (Ames: Iowa State University Press, 1989), a description of changes since 1978 by a University of Missouri journalism professor; Mark W. Hopkins, *Mass Media in the Soviet Union* (New York: Pegasus, 1970); John A. Lent, editor, *The Asian Newspapers' Reluctant Revolution* (Ames: Iowa State University Press, 1971); William A. Hachten, *Muffled Drums: The News Media in Africa* (Iowa State University Press, 1971); Elizabeth Fox, editor, *Media and Politics in Latin America* (Beverly Hills, CA: Sage, 1989), essays about eight nations by Latin-Americans; Crispin Maslog, editor, *Philippine Communication: An Introduction* (Laguna: University of the Philippines, 1987), media history and current status; G.A. Cranfield, *The Press and Society: From Caxton to Northcliffe* (London: Longman, 1978), a British overview; Anthony Smith, compiler, *The British Press Since the War* (Totowa, NJ: Rowman and Littlefield, 1974); Joel H. Wiener, editor, *Papers for the Millions: The New Journalism in Britain, 1850s to 1914* (Westport, CT: Greenwood Press, 1988); and Rowland Lorimer and Jean McNulty, *Mass Communication in Canada* (Toronto: McClelland and Stewart 1989).

Three books by Burton Paulu, all published by the University of Minnesota Press in Minneapolis, offer detailed studies of European broadcasting: *Radio and Television Broadcasting on the European Continent* (1967), *Radio and Television Broadcasting in Eastern Europe* (1974), and *Television and Radio in the United Kingdom* (1981). Asa Briggs has produced four volumes of his *History of Broadcasting in the United Kingdom* (New York: Oxford University Press, 1961–1979).

Worldwide broadcasting surveys were published by Sydney W. Head in *World Broadcasting Systems: A Comparative Analysis* (Belmont, CA: Wadsworth, 1985), and by W.J. Howell, Jr. in *World Broadcasting in the Age of the Satellite* (Norwood, NJ: Ablex, 1986). Other broadcast books: Robert L. Hillard and Michael C. Keith, *Global Broadcasting Systems* (Boston: Focal Press, 1996); Donald R. Browne, *Comparing Broadcast Systems: The Experiences of Six Industrialized Nations* (Ames: Iowa State University Press, 1989); Walter B. Emery, *National and International Systems of Broadcasting* (East Lansing: Michigan State University Press, 1969); John A. Lent, editor, *Broadcasting in Asia and the Pacific* (Philadelphia: Temple University Press, 1978), with many chapters by nationals of the countries described; Elihu Katz and George Wedell, *Broadcasting in the Third World: Promise and Performance* (Cambridge, MA: Harvard University Press, 1978); and Philip Schlesinger, *Putting 'Reality' Together: BBC News* (New York: Methuen, 1987).

Michael Emery critically analyzes coverage of major twentieth century crises in *America's Foreign Correspondents* (Lanham, MD: American University Press, 1995). Among other studies of international news flow and press associations, the scholarly synthesis is Robert W. Desmond's *The Information Process: World News Reporting to the Twentieth Century* (Iowa City: University of Iowa Press, 1978). *Windows on the World 1900–1920* (1981), *Crisis and Conflict: World News Reporting Between Two Wars 1920–1940* (1982), and *Tides of War: World News Reporting 1940–1945* (1984), continued a project interrupted by death. The best history and current description of the four Western transnationals (AP, UPI, Reuters, AFP) is Jonathan Fenby, *The International News Services* (New York: Schocken Books, 1986). Robert L. Stevenson and Donald L. Shaw analyze news reports of the four Western news agencies and the mass media of 17 countries in *Foreign News and the New World Information Order* (Ames: Iowa State University Press, 1984). Oliver Boyd-Barrett, *The International News Agencies* (Beverly Hills, CA: Sage, 1980), examines the five transnational news agencies and two Third World ones. Soon Jin Kim tells the 50-year history of *EFE: Spain's World News Agency* (Westport, CT: Greenwood Press, 1989), the world's fifth-ranking agency. John Hohenberg covered foreign correspondents in his *Foreign Correspondence—The Great Reporters and Their Times* (New York: Columbia University Press, 1964). UNESCO surveyed press associations in *News Agencies: Their Structure and Operation* (New York: Columbia University Press, 1953). Two news service histories are Graham Storey, *Reuters* (New York: Crown, 1951), and Theodore E. Kruglak, *The Two Faces of Tass* (Minneapolis: University of Minnesota Press, 1962) (see bibliography for Chapter 5, for other news service citations). Francis Williams briefly analyzed news transmission in *Transmitting World News: A Study of Telecommunications and the Press* (New York: Arno, 1972).

The dominant name in international communications research and writing has been that of Wilbur Schramm, beginning with his *Mass Media and National Development* (Stanford, CA: Stanford University Press, 1964). Two conferences at the East-West Communication Institute in Hawaii produced two books: Daniel Lerner and Wilbur Schramm, editors, *Communication and Change in the Developing Countries* (Honolulu: East-West Center, 1967) and Schramm and Lerner, editors, *Communication and Change: The Last Ten Years—and the Next* (Honolulu: University of Hawaii Press, 1976).

Hamid Mowlana provides a research-oriented overview in *Global Information and World Communication: New Frontiers in International Relations*

(New York: Longman, 1986). Other research studies: Alex S. Edelstein, et al., *Communication and Culture* (New York: Longman, 1989); and L. John Martin and Ray Eldon Hiebert, editors, *Current Issues in International Communication* (Longman, 1990); Howard H. Frederick, *Global Communications and International Relations* (Belmont, CA: Wadsworth, 1993); and Mark D. Alleyne, *International Power and International Communication* (New York: St. Martin's, 1995).

Basic documents of UNESCO's International Commission for the Study of Communication Problems (the MacBride Commission) include "The New World Information Order," a document presented by Mustapha Masmoudi of Tunisia as a spokesman for the Third World, in July 1978; the Commission's "Interim Report on Communications Problems in Modern Society," published by UNESCO in September 1978; and the Commission's "Final Report" submitted in December 1979 and published as *Many Voices, One World* (New York: Unipub, 1980).

The Third World campaign for a New World Information Order is analyzed in Robert L. Stevenson, *Communication Development and the Third World* (New York: Longman, 1988), addressing the UNESCO debate and mass media developments; in C. Anthony Giffard, *UNESCO and the Media* (Longman, 1989), a comprehensive analysis; in a superbly written book by William A. Hachten with Harva Hachten, *The World News Prism: Changing Media of International Communication* (Ames: Iowa State University Press, 1992); in a balanced compilation of major scholarly articles edited by Jim Richstad and Michael H. Anderson, *Crisis in International News: Policies and Prospects* (New York: Columbia University Press, 1981), and by Rosemary Righter in *Whose News? Politics, the Press, and the Third World* (London: Times Books, 1978).

*Videocassette Recorders in the Third World* was edited by Douglas A. Boyd, Joseph D. Straubhaar, and John A. Lent (New York: Longman, 1989). Television's impact is analyzed in Chin-Chuan Lee's *Media Imperialism Reconsidered* (Sage, 1980). Donald Shanor and Donald H. Johnston edited the proceedings of a 1982 conference in Columbia Journalism Monograph No. 4, *Third World News in American Media* (New York: Columbia University, 1983). Geoffrey Reeves, *Communications and the "Third World"* (New York: Routledge) was a 1993 entry. Michael H. Anderson used case studies from China, Singapore, Malaysia, and Indonesia in *Madison Avenue in Asia: Politics and Transnational Advertising* (Rutherford, NJ: Fairleigh Dickinson University Press, 1984). Thomas L. McPhail forecasts the future of International broadcasting and communication in *Electronic Colonialism* (Sage, 1987).

Criticisms of the American mass media abroad, giving substance to Third World arguments, were voiced by Herbert I. Schiller in *Mass Communications and American Empire* (Boston: Beacon Press, 1969) and in *Communication and Cultural Domination* (White Plains, NY: International Arts and Sciences Press, 1976). William H. Read's *America's Mass Media Merchants* (Baltimore: Johns Hopkins University Press, 1977), focuses on press agencies, news magazines, the *Reader's Digest*, television, and the movies. Thomas H. Guback described *The International Film Industry: Western Europe and America Since 1945* (Bloomington: Indiana University Press, 1969). And Jeremy Tunstall wrote *The Media Are American: Anglo-American Media in the World* (New York: Columbia University Press, 1977).

# ACKNOWLEDGMENTS

*Unless otherwise acknowledged, all photographs are the property of Scott, Foresman and Company. Page abbreviations are as follow: (t) top, (c) center, (b) bottom, (r) right.*

Page 7: George Wilson/AP/Wide World; p. 8: AP/Wide World; p. 10: © 1956, The Arizona Republic, Christine Ketih. All Rights reserved; p. 13: Copyright 1995 America Online. Used by Permission; p. 16: Courtesy AT&T Bell Laboratories; p. 25: Copyright 1995 Religion News Service, Washington, D.C.; p. 29: Courtesy of Siskel & Ebert. Photo by Bill Staimetz; p. 32: Courtesy of Star Magazine; p. 35: Beth A. Keiser/AP/Wide World; p. 37: AP/Wide World; p. 38: Sam Mircovich/Corbis-Bettmann/Reuter; p. 48: Culver Pictures; p. 53: Culver Pictures; p. 58: Clay Bennett/North America Syndicate; p. 70: © New York Daily News, L.P., used with permission; p. 72: Randy Taylor/Sygma; p. 76: Pamela Price/Picture Cube; p. 82: Shooting Star; p. 86: Jacques Pavlovsky/Sygma; p. 88: Photofest; p. 90: AP/Wide World; p. 91: New York Daily News; p. 102: Aloma/Shooting Star; p. 113: Library of Congress; p. 116: Los Angeles Times. Reprinted by permission; p. 117: Corbis-Bettmann/UPI; p. 121: Library of Congress; p. 125: Courtesy of LA OPINION; p. 126: Library of Congress; p. 127: Steve Ringman/San Francisco Chronicle; p. 129: ©1995 Newsday; p. 130: Rex Curry/AP/Wide World; p. 132: Paul Conklin/Monkmeyer Press; p. 136: Reprinted by Permission of PRESSTIME, The Journal of the American Newspaper Association; p. 149: Public Domain; p. 155: Public Domain; p. 158: Historical Pictures Service, Chicago; p. 163: © 1995 Newsday; p. 166: Grunnitus Studios; p. 169: Photograph by Mark Seliger from Rolling Stone, May 13, 1993, by Straight Arrow Publishers, Inc. 1993. All Rights Reserved, Reprinted by Permission; p. 188: Photofest; p. 191: Hugh Rogers/Monkmeyer Press; p. 211: Corbis-Bettmann/Reuters; p. 217: Library of Congress; p. 218: Library of Congress; p. 220: Corbis-Bettmann Newsphotos; p. 227: Kevin Larkin/AP/Wide World; p. 228: Eric Draper/Los Angeles Times Photo; p. 239(b): Mr. Bonzai, Courtesy of Mix Magazine; p. 239(t): AP/Wide World; p. 242: Courtesy of David Born; p. 243: Joe Traver/Reuter/Corbis-Bettmann; p. 244: AP/Wide World; p. 267: Taylor/Fabricius/Gamma Liaison; p. 269: Kobal Collection; p. 271: Kathleen Beall/AP/Wide World; p. 280: Library of Congress; p. 290: AP/Wide World; p. 293: Michelle Wise/Knight Ridder Tribune News; p. 301: Corbis-Bettmann/UPI; p. 303: Laurel Luth; p. 305 © 1995 Cable News Network, Inc. All Rights Reserved; p. 307: John Trotter/Sygma; p. 310: AP/Wide World; p. 320: Photo courtesy CNN; p. 325: National Digital Television Center; p. 332: David Strickler/Monkmeyer Press; p. 333: Photofest; p. 335: Photofest; p. 345: Charles H. Porter 4th/Sygma; p. 359: Photofest; p. 365: Shooting Star; p. 367: Culver; p. 371: Corbis-Bettmann Archive; p. 372: Library of Congress; p. 376: Photofest; p. 393: Halstead Dirck/Gamma Liaison; p. 401: AP/Wide World; p. 403: Eveready Battery Company, Inc.; p. 407: Kristi Yamaguchi © 1995 National Fluid Milk Processor Promotion Board; p. 416: Courtesy Duracell USA; p. 440: Courtesy Peanut Advisory Board; p. 443: Brown Brothers; p. 449: Courtesy Household Hazardous Materials, San Diego County; p. 460: Reprinted by Permission from PRESSTIME, The Journal of the Newspaper Association of America; p. 471: Brad Markel/Gamma Liaison; p. 489: Michelle E. Ryan; p. 492: Greg Gibson/AP/Wide World; p. 496: Readers Digest; p. 500: Courtesy Quill.

# INDEX